American Philosophies

BLACKWELL PHILOSOPHY ANTHOLOGIES

Each volume in this outstanding series provides an authoritative and comprehensive collection of the essential primary readings from philosophy's main fields of study. Designed to complement the *Blackwell Companions to Philosophy* series, each volume represents an unparalleled resource in its own right, and will provide the ideal platform for course use.

American Philosophies

An Anthology

Edited by

Leonard Harris, Scott L. Pratt, and Anne S. Waters

BLACKWELL
Publishers

Copyright © Blackwell Publishers Ltd 2002
Editorial matter and organization copyright © Leonard Harris, Scott L. Pratt, Anne S. Waters 2002

First published 2002

2 4 6 8 10 9 7 5 3 1

Blackwell Publishers Inc.
350 Main Street
Malden, Massachusetts 02148
USA

Blackwell Publishers Ltd
108 Cowley Road
Oxford OX4 1JF
UK

Library of Congress Cataloging-in-Publication Data

American philosophies: an anthology/edited by Leonard Harris, Scott L. Pratt, and Anne Waters.
    p. cm. — (Blackwell philosophy anthologies; 16)
  Includes bibliographical references and index.
  ISBN 0-631-21001-6 (alk. paper)—ISBN 0-631-21002-4 (pb.: alk. paper)
    1. Philosophy, American. I. Harris, Leonard, 1948- II. Pratt, Scott L. III. Waters, Anne. IV. Series.

B851 .A44 2001
191—dc21

                         2001035009

British Library Cataloguing in Publication Data

A CIP catalogue record for this book is available from the British Library.

Typeset in 9/11 pt Ehrhardt
by Kolam Information Services Pvt Ltd, Pondicherry, India

This book is printed on acid-free paper.

Contents

Contents

Acknowledgments

The editors and publishers would like to thank the following for permission to use copyright material:

Dover Publications Inc., for "Anarchism," in *Anarchism And Other Essays*. Published by Dover Books, 1969.

Holt Rinehart and Winston, for Susanne K. Langer and Alfred N. Whitehead, *The Practice of Philosophy*. Copyright © 1930 by Holt Rinehart and Winston. Reprinted by permission of the publisher.

The Permissions Company, for David Graham Du Bois, "Does Race Antipathy Serve Any Good Purpose?," published as "Scientific Reasons Against Race Antagonism", in *The Boston Globe*, July 19, 1914 and "The Concept of Race", in *Dusk of Dawn*. Published by Harcourt, 1940.

Southern Illinois University Press, for John Dewey, "The Supremacy of Method," in *The Collected Works of John Dewey: Later Works*, Volume 4, 1929. Copyright © by the Board of Trustees, Southern Illinois University. Reprinted by permission.

University Press Of America, for Robert Bunge, "Sioux Epistemology" (Plains Native American), in *An American Urphilosophie: An American Philosophy BP*. Published by University Press of America, 1984.

University of Nebraska, for Arthur C. Parker, "How the World Began," in *Seneca Myths and Folk Tales*. Published by University of Nebraska Press, 1989; and Zitkala-Sa, "Impressions of an Indian Childhood," in *American Indian Stories*. Published by University of Nebraska Press, 1921.

Every effort has been made to trace the copyright holders, but if any has been inadvertently overlooked, the publishers will be pleased to make the necessary arrangements at the first opportunity.

Introduction

We offer readings from widely diverse philosophies, rooted in competing traditions, forming a chorus of voices – sometimes in unison, sometimes creating a discordant wail. In offering readings from different traditions, we use a method intended to help a new generation of philosophers engage and reconstruct philosophic conversations in a way that compels them to rethink the philosophies under consideration and the living realities out of which they arise. The progressive intellectual heritage that we join and help foster is not like the tradition of American philosophic conservatism that portrays American philosophers as a staid set of peaceful reflectors and philosophies as rather benign texts in dusty libraries. Rather, in an attempt self-consciously to shape tradition, we present it as a living creation.

This Anthology is the result of joint efforts by editors with different, although often conjoined, conceptions of American philosophy. Leonard Harris, for example, rejects nationalism and believes that no new nations anywhere should be formed. Thus, for Harris, indigenous communities have entitlements as peoples – a "weak" nationalism – but not entitlements to form new nations with political borders, militaries, and currencies – a "strong" nationalism. Universal human liberation is tied, for Harris, to open communities. Thus, he defines "American philosophy" in ways that include ethno-philosophies (philosophies that are created by a people and defined by their values and practices), but focuses on philosophies created by individuals who develop unique arguments and methods. Harris favors the use of empirical evidence and the application of logic or systematic analytic tools as ways of determining whether any given philosophy should be believed. He recommends a strong skepticism toward all traditions as sources of norms that should be used to direct social life, but thinks that African American philosophic traditions can make a special contribution. Harris rejects all forms of religious expression that claim to be special, preferring a Bahá'i integration of faith, Buddhist mysticism, and agnostic attitudes.

As an American Indian, Anne Waters favors indigenous entitlements, including the possible formation of nations in the strong sense. Important to understanding nationalism in this sense is the interpretive role of the historical, social, and political context in which these national philosophies emerge. Waters's criteria for a distinct culture that justifies giving rise to a sovereign status of nationhood include having a unique group of people with a distinct language, a moral and/or religious-spiritual base, a specific geographic area where they have held power, and an authoritative organizing leadership that is acknowledged and maintained by the people. Waters views American Indian philosophy as playing a contemporary role in drawing attention to a different way of being and a different notion of sovereignty indigenous to the American continent. Ethno-philosophies of indigenous populations are highly regarded, although such philosophies about the world may not be of equal worth in maintaining harmonious relations. In this cultural context, stories, fables, reports, and expressions of faith nest philosophical reflection upon cultural knowledge and belief systems, just as empirical or systematic argument analysis in other traditions can articulate what one does or ought to believe. Waters believes that Native American philosophies offer a special contribution.

She places special value on Native American traditions as forming a pre-conquest history of philosophy on the American continent. She favors decolonizing Christianity in indigenous communities, a return to traditional notions of harmony and balance, and the philosophical acknowledgement of the interdependency that exists in all relations.

Scott Pratt sees American philosophy as a process of reflecting on and responding to the interactions of cultural, racial, gendered, and economic differences in the geographical context of North America. While some American philosophies focus on the elimination of such differences in favor of one or another form of a "melting pot," Pratt is particularly interested in the varieties of American philosophy that seek to sustain and foster differences and ongoing cultural exchange. From this perspective, Pratt holds that some forms of national formation in the strong sense may be warranted in light of particular histories of displacement. He holds that the peoples of North America – indigenous, immigrant, and enslaved – have individually and collectively made substantive contributions to the intellectual, spiritual, and moral life of what Alain Locke called the "composite" civilization of America. Ethno-philosophy for Pratt is also warranted without the need for the Eurocentric emphasis on empirical verification of systematic argumentation. He rejects the claim that any particular religious expression has a special claim to truth, but recognizes the importance of Christianity in shaping the history and philosophical context of North America. Pratt rejects the idea that any single philosophical perspective can stand as final, but believes that, taken together, the corpus of voices in America, even if some are infected with imperialist impulses, can nevertheless provide crucial insights, critical tools, and constructive alternatives to help foster the growth of human communities.

There are radical differences among African American, indigenous American, and European American philosophies about what "America" means, how one should do philosophy from the standpoint of any tradition (as well as whether one should acknowledge any particular standpoint, or assume an imperfect impartiality), and whether philosophies are epiphenomena of culturally determined values. In addition, Americans are not all neatly classified as White, Black, European, or Indigenous. Individuals are not treated as if their philosophy necessarily represents the views of a whole population, because they are not given due regard when treated as if they hold their views because they were simply caused to do so by a singular cultural standpoint. Yet, philosophical reflection always occurs amongst individuals and groups within a given location, and is necessarily influenced to some degree by such locations. Given the constantly changing demographics of America, the ethnic and religious compositions will definitely be different from the past; Latino/Chicano, Muslim, Buddhist, and Hindu-informed philosophies are increasingly likely to shape the contours of American philosophy. The reality of America as a nation-state, including forced contact between people, rape and intermarriage, annihilation of populations, and the survival of philosophies grounded in the experience of American actors, requires the bringing together of different voices under one roof, in one text. They already exist under the same sky on the same ground and share material circumstances conditioned by capitalism, a militarized state, environmental destruction, and the gulf between rich and poor. These voices, at times, have spoken to one another and, at other times, have gone unheard. In this Anthology, they speak again to new generations and a changing America.

Tensions are evident in this Anthology. While the editors each represent their own position, they retain respect for each other's different approach, and they do not consider themselves to be the sole legitimate representatives of a people's voice – all Americans or otherwise. Tension is what efforts to capture a collective reality that is itself variegated should accomplish.

The editors mutually reject the terrible history of American philosophy that has presented it as a project created, sustained, and voiced by whites, particularly by privileged white males. The entitlement to speak the truth, receive status, and acquire income from faculty positions and book contracts has been historically controlled by a narrow group of intellectuals and schools falsely parading as the only existing or legitimate voices able to address substantive issues about the nature of knowledge, existence, and the universe. This Anthology is fundamentally at odds with the history and traditions of truncated American nationalism and the white supremacy that has often defined American philosophy. It promotes a new vision: American philosophy as a complex reality, enlivened by historically marginalized, but never silent, voices.

American philosophy is like a jazz improvization, not a solo melody. It is a changing plurality of values and valuations. Nationalist white supremacists encrusted in institutions of higher education have characteristically supported the genocide of indigenous populations, the enslavement of non-whites, the subjugation of women, the exclusion of lesbigay communities, and the silencing of discourse about the needs of the least well-off. We hope to encourage readers to take seriously the individual and group voices historically excluded from the academy. In this fashion, future conversations and debates may be far more open and enriched than has been the case up till now. The future of American philosophy, thus, will look and sound very different from the past.

Given our own situations, the pressing questions considered in this Anthology are as follows. What should be the future of all persons, particularly Americans? What does it mean to be Native, African, or of European background in relation to the teleology of humanity? Why should a meaningful life involve anyone in having to live as if they were a representative of a racial or ethnic kind? What does it mean to be self-conscious? What sort of epistemological method is appealing? What type of community is warranted, given the reality of a vast array of competing interests, cultures, and ideals? What, if anything, counts as the right and the good for communities? What moral commitments and duties should we have to strangers, in light of the abominable institution of slavery and the history of ethnocide? And what form of democracy should be promoted? These are questions foregrounded by the advent of America. This Anthology attempts to provide a sense of history, a depiction of community values, and at the same time to present sophisticated philosophical arguments addressing the above questions such that the arguments have a value that is relatively independent of context. Each author, however, represents him- or herself and a particular school of thought.

The "Prolegomenon to a Tradition: What is American Philosophy?" provides an overview of a progressive view of American philosophy intended to provide the reader with a sense of the pressing issues in the field as well as setting a tone for considering competing philosophies.

Each part that follows presents works on a major theme. Primarily, but not exclusively, works are ordered by the date of their publication. From the nascent beginning of America to the well-established industrial world, readings span from 1493 to 1944. The intention is to provide a sense of history and context. Each work represents a school of thought, religious orientation, or community sentiment.

Part I, "Origin and Teleology," introduces the historical reality of competing civilizations and intentions, forming the real beginnings, in infamy and glory. It also introduces conceptions of origins and teleology – where we came from and where we are going – within a given cultural context. Conceptions of deities, whether polytheist, monotheist, pantheist, or agnostic, can interphase with views of national identity, nature, and lived experience. The belief in God, gods, and spirits is integral to the works of early Americans. Authors promote their faith and therefore hold conflicting views of origin/s and teleology.

Part II, "Minds and Selves," considers traditional epistemological issues of self-consciousness, particularly what it means to be self-aware and aware of others. Concepts of self-worth provide a way of thinking about the interlink between consciousness and self-worth. Whether self-worth is associated with recalling tradition or avoiding tradition, whether we should destroy differences between race/ethnicity, and the role of stereotypical gender/sex roles are all issues that are taken as substantive and controversial.

In Part III, "Knowledge and Inquiry," conceptions are offered about what it is to know and how it is one can proceed to acquire knowledge. This section primarily considers early American efforts to address epistemological issues inherited from Europe. The readings offer pragmatist conceptions, and conceptions that differ from pragmatism yet sustain some of its insights. An activist epistemology – one that considers knowledge as a function of experience – takes many forms. The dominant American orientation has been pragmatist, yet there are radical differences within that tradition, and authors offer alternative approaches.

"Community and Power," Part IV, offers readings that present concepts of community during America's nascent historical development. Conceptions of community are concerned with ideals of appropriate relationships between persons and notions of commitment. Appropriate forms of group rights and entitlements are considered in this section. Of particular note are background assumptions about how likely it is that power will be abused, how likely it is that persons will remain loyal to a constituency, and whether universal human interest is best promoted through small ethnic, racial, geographic groups or through compulsory unions across differences.

In Part V, "Slavery and Freedom," authors query the character of both conditions in the context of, or with particular appreciation for, a given population and circumstance. What counts as social knowledge is thereby addressed through concrete experiences. Resistance traditions present controversial views of what counts as misery and what counts as appropriate responses. There are different conceptions of harm: some rely heavily on the importance of a particular social location as the locus for discourse on the universal; others rely heavily on a religious teleology or a conception of universal good that is then capable of telling us what is unjust for each condition.

Finally, "Democracy and Utopia," Part VI, offers readings that present conceptions of the right and the good in terms of an author's view of social equity. Ideals of the right and the good society significantly differ between absolute, or nearly absolute, egalitarian utopianists, social democrats, anarchists, and national socialists. General conceptions of democracy, intended to provide guiding principles for all persons, have always been promoted in a world divided by ethnicity, race, and national commitments. This section considers notions of social equity concerned with melding diverse and competing communities: forms of association where persons have few bonds of family, religion, or culture, yet have strong reasons by dint of at least geographic proximity, if not common citizenship, to live in harmony.

Prolegomenon to a Tradition: What is American Philosophy?

American philosophy comes into existence with the exegesis of America as a nation. Defined either as an array of beliefs reflecting daily ways of living (ethno–philosophy) unique to America, or as an array of texts that address metaphysical questions by appealing to arguments rather than, or in addition to, authoritative texts rooted in American history, it is in either case contingent on the existence of "America." A native or indigenous people is always thus defined after a date or event. Prior to that date or event, the very same population was defined as a people, nation, tribe, inhabitant, invader, explorer, immigrant, or a migrant community. Everyone arrived from somewhere else; no human populations were ever owners, users, or agents communing with nature in a static location and in isolation from others from the beginning of time – unless one believes in something like spontaneous generation, such that a group is a non-humanly evolved population. Every native or indigenous population is itself a consequence of earlier population growth, migration, or invasion. American philosophy begins in a post-Columbus world, a world that slowly came into existence after the 1492 voyage of Christopher Columbus, a world named after Amerigo Vespucci. Philosophies that existed prior to Columbus are "American" in the sense that their existence occurred or originated on the continent now known as America. Pre-Columbian populations are "American" for geographical, historical, and anthropological classificatory reasons; philosophies pre-dating Columbus necessarily had a different cultural, military, ethnic, racial, religious, material, and political context within which ideas and arguments were formed. This also holds true when we define

America as the continents of both North and South America. If, however, we consider philosophies that come into existence within the context of a social world fully aware of the presence of new European and African invaders, explorers, migrants, and immigrants, with their own daily ways of living and individual philosophies, as well as that of indigenous populations in a new context, then American philosophy has its genesis after 1598. The American philosophical tradition is, from this point of view, an ongoing creation, and the pressing questions shaping American philosophy to date include conceptions of origin, teleology, theories of knowledge, and ideals of community.

One way to think about American philosophy is in terms of competing schools of thought, for example, polygenetic (separate origins) versus monogenetic (one origin) explanations for the beginning of humanity and different races. There are competing ideals of the universe, such as transcendentalism (the existence of a universe beyond appearances) in opposition to naturalism (the view that the world is explainable in natural terms); millennialism (the belief that life will reach its final goal within a given millennium) in tandem with a pessimism about the belief that human life is inclined toward any particular teleology. However, philosophers are rarely engaged in simple competing, as if they were debating the finer points of opposing beliefs in a closed room.

What marks the distinctive feature of this approach to tradition is a normative dedication to a picture of philosophy as progressive. Canonical figures are thus constantly being added, historical conversations reformed, previously ignored conversations revisited, and claims to absolute truth questioned in light of competing philosophies. A progressive tradition includes criteria for its own self-reformation; it is a self-conscious invention where well-researched discoveries and narratives are open to revaluations. Valorizing historical figures is as misleading as leaving important historical figures silent. In this tradition, to deny that our decisions are normative choices is as misleading as contending that the voices we select provide a true picture of all the relevant conversations of the past.

Progressive traditions are like jazz sessions because we select from past compositions, reliving them in the selection, even as we create a new picture that captures our own modernity, sense of mission, and portrayal of a living past. Rather than offering a linear history – a history where each author communicates with the next generation, making it appear that there is an unbroken line of reflections passing from one agent to the next – we offer a complex, rugged, incongruous, and winding history of reflections. The resulting "field" of American philosophy can be understood as a process of complex cultural exchanges, not always successful and sometimes disastrous. Alain Locke characterizes this sort of process well in *When Peoples Meet*:

> [C]ultural exchange passes in reciprocal streams from the conquerors to the conquered and from the conquered to the dominant groups. It is not always the dominant stock or the upper classes that are the carriers or importers of culture. Societies have just as frequently received infiltrations of alien culture from the bottom through the absorption of conquered and subject groups.

Progress or growth, in this sense, "seems proportional to the degree to which society has a many-sided cultural exposure." American philosophy understood this way should be seen not as a geographically isolated process of a few academicians engaged in a historically linear and unbroken line of dialogue, but as a crossroads within a North America of constantly changing population and intellectual demographics. In this setting, "all peoples and nations have contributed importantly, though often without due credit, to the sum of human civilization, which itself, most broadly viewed, is the product of an extensive collaboration of cultural forces and an age-old interchange of cultures."[1]

It is inevitable that preserving the past will be a continual project. This Anthology preserves a feature of the past and speaks to the desires of the present. If the future bears any resemblance to the past, much of what any civilization holds sacred, including all that is held sacred in America no matter what its origin, will find its way into museums – artifacts of a given era – helping to shape both the contours of museums and the people who visit them. It is hoped that among the competing traditions of philosophy and orientations to life that we offer readers will find, or weave, one of useful guidance prior to its joining either a museum collection or merging into the intellectual train that becomes a better future.

Leonard Harris

Note

1 Alain Locke, *When Peoples Meet: A Study In Race and Culture Contacts* (New York: Hinds, Hayden and Eldredge, 1946), pp. 10–11.

PART I

Origin and Teleology

American philosophy begins in a context of diverse origins. Part I presents a range of discussions on the origins of peoples and ideas in North America. Long before the arrival of Europeans, indigenous Americans offered religious accounts of origins, often presented as a polygenetic world-view. Whether viewed as historical accounts of diverse beginnings or as expressions of a logic of cultural difference, these stories provide a unique starting point for the history of contact among American European and African peoples.

Conceptions of deities, whether polytheist, monotheist, pantheist, or agnostic, interphase with lived experience. We begin with a letter from King Ferdinand of Aragon (1452–1516), which sets the tone and context of civilizations in conflict. King Ferdinand demonstrates a sense of self-confidence, deep religious faith, and moral mission. His vision of America introduces a preview of America's future.

We present two distinct American origin stories, which, taken together, affirm the value of human diversity within a given context. These stories also present distinctly non-European ways of organizing human experience, including alternative conceptions of causality, agency, and good and evil.

The Europeans who began to establish permanent settlements in the seventeenth century brought their own stories of origin, which stood in tension with the indigenous stories that greeted them. By the beginning of the nineteenth century, the conflict between such stories began to provide a starting point for a critical perspective on the philosophical legacies.

Olaudah Equiano (his African name), or Gustavus Vassa (his European name), provides a sense of the moral indignation of slavery, especially from the standpoint of the educated and well-traveled yet racialized abolitionist.

Washington Irving expresses the ambivalence of the nascent early American national identity and a critique of totalizing philosophical perspectives.

Ralph Waldo Emerson's *Nature* can be read in part as an attempt to provide a framework for understanding an American experience that included slavery, Native American removal and genocide, and the inadequacy of traditional European philosophy for responding to new circumstances. In addition, his view of nature, relying less on the religious traditions approved of by his contemporaries, continues to be controversial.

1

Letter to the Taino/Arawak Indians, 1493

King Ferdinand of Aragon

Introduction

On August 3, 1492, Columbus sailed from Palos, Spain, on his first voyage of discovery to the Indies (which became the Americas). When he set out from Cádiz in October 1493 on his second voyage, with a fleet of 17 ships and 1,500 colonists on board, King Ferdinand of Aragon (1452–1516) entrusted him with a letter to be offered to the indigenous populations of the new lands (primarily, Taino/Arawak Indians of the Leeward Islands and Lesser Antilles). The King wanted the Indians to acknowledge the Christian religion, its God, and to accept the authority of the King of Spain. The letter promises future benefits and dire threats if they do not consent. King Ferdinand's intentions are very clear and uncompromising. In many ways, his letter can be read as an opening to what became America – a monogenetic origin and a monolithic future. King Ferdinand set the context within which philosophies occur and simultaneously expresses a philosophic vision of a new world.

In the name of King Ferdinand and Juana, his daughter, Queen of Castile and Leon, etc., conquerors of barbarian nations, we notify you as best we can that our Lord God Eternal created Heaven and earth and a man and woman from whom we all descend for all times and all over the world. In the 5,000 years since creation the multitude of these generations caused men to divide and establish kingdoms in various parts of the world, among

King Ferdinand's Letter to the Taino/Arawak Indians, 1493.

whom God chose St. Peter as leader of mankind, regardless of their law, sect or belief. He seated St. Peter in Rome as the best place from which to rule the world but he allowed him to establish his seat in all parts of the world and rule all people, whether Christians, Moors, Jews, Gentiles or any other sect. He was named Pope, which means admirable and greatest father, governor of all men. Those who lived at that time obeyed St. Peter as Lord and superior King of the universe, and so did their descendants obey his successors and so on to the end of time.

The late Pope gave these islands and mainland of the ocean and the contents hereof to the above-mentioned King and Queen, as is certified in writing and you may see the documents if you should so desire. Therefore, Their Highnesses are lords and masters of this land; they were acknowledged as such when this notice was posted, and were and are being served willingly and without resistance; then, their religious envoys were acknowledged and obeyed without delay, and all subjects unconditionally and of their own free will became Christians and thus they remain. Their Highnesses received their allegiance with joy and benignity and decreed that they be treated in this spirit like good and loyal vassals and you are under the obligation to do the same.

Therefore, we request that you understand this text, deliberate on its contents within a reasonable time, and recognize the Church and its highest priest, the Pope, as rulers of the universe, and in their name the King and Queen of Spain as rulers of this land, allowing the religious fathers to preach our holy Faith to you. You own compliance as a duty to the King and we in his name will receive you with love and charity, respecting your freedom and that of your wives and sons and your rights of possession and we shall not compel you to baptism unless you, informed of the Truth, wish to convert to our holy Catholic Faith as almost all your neighbors have done in other islands, in exchange for which Their Highnesses bestow many privileges and exemptions upon you. Should you fail to comply, or delay maliciously in so doing, we assure you that with the help of God we shall use force against you, declaring war upon you from all sides and with all possible means, and we shall bind you to the yoke of the Church and of Their Highnesses; we shall enslave your persons, wives and sons, sell you or dispose of you as the King sees fit; we shall seize your possessions and harm you as much as we can as disobedient and resisting vassals. And we declare you guilty of resulting deaths and injuries, exempting Their Highnesses of such guilt as well as ourselves and the gentlemen who accompany us. We hereby request that legal signatures be affixed to this text and pray those present to bear witness for us, etc.

2

Speeches

Sa-Go-Ye-Wat-Ha

Introduction

Sa-Go-Ye-Wat-Ha (1756?–1830), or Red Jacket as he was known by European Americans of the time, was born near the present city of Geneva, New York, and was a member of the Seneca Nation. Sa-Go-Ye-Wat-Ha, whose name means "He-Who-Keeps-Them-Awake," rose to prominence in the years after the Revolution through his skills as an orator and his ability to represent the views of his community. In the years between the Revolution and the War of 1812, Sa-Go-Ye-Wat-Ha was an important spokesperson for those native people who favored the coexistence of the United States with the confederated Native American nations of the northeast. During the War of 1812, many Haudenosaunee and native people throughout central and eastern North America joined the Shawnee leader, Tecumseh, and his brother, Tens-kawatawa, or the Prophet, in an armed revolt against the United States. Sa-Go-Ye-Wat-Ha worked to keep most of the Haudenosaunee out of the conflict, asking, in part, that his people remember "the calamities which have befallen our nations in the wars of the [whites]" when native people responded to calls for help by the warring white nations. In the aftermath of Tecumseh's defeat and the aggressive reprisals by the United States against nearly all Native American nations, Sa-Go-Ye-Wat-Ha spoke out less often for the Haudenosaunee. He died on January 20, 1830, just four months before the United States Congress

Taken from "Council at Buffalo Creek in the Summer, 1805," in The Life and Times of Sa-Go-Ye-Wat-Ha, or Red Jacket, ed. William L. Stone (Albany, NY: J. Munsell, 1866).

passed the "Removal Act," which decisively changed US policy from one of potential coexistence with Native American nations to one demanding their elimination or removal.

Council at Buffalo Creek in the Summer, 1805

In the summer of 1805 the Evangelical Missionary Society of Massachusetts sent a missionary, Mr. Cram, to the Senecas to establish a mission. The missionary presented his request at a council attended by the council of chiefs and the Indian Affairs agent. The agent opened the proceedings. His brief address was followed by an address by the missionary. After several hours of deliberation, Sagoyewatha replied on behalf of the Six Nations.

[The Indian Affairs agent began as follows:] BROTHERS OF THE SIX NATIONS: I rejoice to meet you at this time, and thank the Great Spirit that he has preserved you in health, and given me another opportunity of taking you by the hand.

BROTHERS: the person who sits by me is a friend who has come a great distance to hold a talk with you. He will inform you what his business is, and it is my request that you would listen with attention to his words.

[The missionary spoke:] MY FRIENDS: I am thankful for the opportunity afforded us of uniting together at this time. I had a great desire to see you, and inquire into your state and welfare. For this purpose I have traveled a great distance, being sent by your old friends, the Boston Missionary Society. You will recollect they formerly sent missionaries among you, to instruct you in religion, and labor for your good. Although they have not heard from you for a long time, yet they have not forgotten their brothers, the Six Nations, and are still anxious to do you good.

BROTHERS: I have not come to get your lands or your money, but to enlighten your minds, and to instruct you how to worship the Great spirit agreeably to his mind and will, and to preach to you the gospel of his son Jesus Christ. There is but one religion, and but one way to serve God, and if you do not embrace the right way you cannot be happy hereafter. You have never worshipped the Great Spirit in a manner acceptable to him; but have all your lives been in great errors and darkness. To endeavor to remove these errors, and open your eyes, so that you might see clearly, is my business with you.

BROTHERS: I wish to talk with you as one friend talks with another; and if you have any objections, to receive the religion which I preach, I wish you to state them; and I will endeavor to satisfy your minds and remove the objections.

BROTHERS: I want you to speak your minds freely: for I wish to reason with you on the subject, and, if possible, remove all doubts, if there be any on your minds. The subject is an important one, and it is of consequence that you give it an early attention while the offer is made you. Your friends the Boston Missionary Society will continue to send you good and faithful ministers, to instruct and strengthen you in religion, if, on your part, you are willing to receive them.

BROTHERS: Since I have been in this part of the country, I have visited some of your small villages, and talked with your people. They appear willing to receive instruction, but as they look up to you as their older brothers in council, they want first to know your opinion on the subject. You have now heard what I have to propose at present. I hope you will take it into consideration, and give me an answer before we part.

[After deliberation, Sagoyewatha responded:] FRIEND AND BROTHER: It was the will of the Great Spirit that we should meet together this day. He orders all things, and has given us a fine day for our council. He has taken his garment from before the sun, and caused it to shine with brightness upon us. Our eyes are opened, that we see clearly; our ears are unstopped, that we have been able to hear distinctly the words you have spoken. For all these favors we thank the Great Spirit; and him *only*.

BROTHER: This council fire was kindled by you. It was at your request that we came together at this time. We have listened with attention to what you have said. You requested us to speak our minds freely. This gives us great joy; for we now consider that we stand upright before you, and can speak what we think. All have heard your voice, and all speak to you now as one man. Our minds are agreed.

BROTHER: You say you want an answer to your talk before you leave this place. It is right you should have one, as you are a great distance from home, and we do not wish to detain you. But we will first look back a little, and tell you what our fathers have told us, and what we have heard from the white people.

BROTHER: Listen to what we say. There was a time when our forefathers owned this great island. Their seats extended from the rising to the setting sun. The Great Spirit had made it for the use of Indians. He had created the buffalo, the deer, and other animals for food. He had made the bear and the beaver. Their skins served us for clothing. He had scattered them over the country, and taught us how to take them. He had caused the earth to produce corn for bread. All this he had done for his red children, because he loved them. If we had some disputes about our hunting ground, they were generally settled without the shedding of much blood. But an evil day came upon us. Your forefathers crossed the great water and landed on this island. Their numbers were small. They found friends and not enemies. They told us they had fled from their own country for fear of wicked men, and had come here to enjoy their religion. They asked for a small seat. We took pity on them, granted their request; and they sat down amongst us. We gave them corn and meat; they gave us poison . . . in return.

The white people, BROTHER, had now found our country. Tidings were carried back, and more came amongst us. Yet we did not fear them. We took them to be friends. They called us brothers. We believed them, and gave them a larger seat. At length their numbers had greatly increased. They wanted more land; they wanted our country. Our eyes were opened, and our minds became uneasy. Wars took place. Indians were hired to fight against Indians, and many of our people were destroyed. They also brought strong liquor amongst us. It was strong and powerful, and has slain thousands.

BROTHER: Our seats were once large and yours were small. You have now become a great people, and we have scarcely a place left to spread our blankets. You have got our country, but are not satisfied; you want to force your religion upon us.

BROTHER: Continue to listen. You say that you are sent to instruct us how to worship the Great spirit agreeably to his mind, and, if we do not take hold of the religion which you white people teach, we shall be unhappy hereafter. You say that you are right and we are lost. How do we know this to be true? We understand that your religion is written in a book. If it was intended for us as well as you, why has not the Great spirit given to us, and not only to us, but why did he not give to our forefathers, the knowledge of that book, with the means of understanding it rightly? We only know what you tell us about it. How shall we know when to believe, being so often deceived by the white people?

BROTHER: You say there is but one way to worship and serve the Great Spirit. If there is but one religion, why do you white people differ so much about it? Why not all agreed, as you can all read the book?

BROTHER: We do not understand these things. We are told that your religion was given to your forefathers, and has been handed down from father to son. We also have a religion, which was given to our forefathers, and has been handed down to us their children. We worship in that way. It teaches us to be thankful for all the favors we receive; to love each other, and to be united. We never quarrel about religion.

BROTHER: The Great Spirit has made us all, but he has made a great difference between his white and red children. He has given us different complexions and different customs. To you he has given the arts. To these he has not opened our eyes. We know these things to be true. Since he has made so great a difference between us in other things, why may we not conclude that he has given us a different religion according to our understanding? The Great spirit does right. He knows what is best for his children; we are satisfied.

BROTHER: We do not wish to destroy your religion, or take it from you. We only want to enjoy our own.

BROTHER: You say you have not come to get our land or our money, but to enlighten our minds. I will now tell you that I have been at your meetings, and saw you collect money from the meeting.

I cannot tell what this money was intended for, but suppose that it was for your minister, and if we should conform to your way of thinking, perhaps you may want some from us.

BROTHER: We are told that you have been preaching to the white people in this place. These people are our neighbors. We are acquainted with them. We will wait a little while, and see what effect your preaching has upon them. If we find it does them good, makes them honest and less disposed to cheat Indians, we will then consider again of what you have said.

BROTHER: You have now heard our answer to your talk, and this is all we have to say at present. As we are going to part, we will come and take you by the hand, and hope the Great Spirit will protect you on your journey, and return you safe to your friends.

[William Stone reports the end of the council this way: "Agreeably to the suggestion at the close of [Sagoyewatha's] speech, as the council was breaking up the Indians moved toward the missionary for the purpose of extending the parting hand of friendship; but Mr. Cram rose hastily from his seat, and replied that he could not take them by the hand, 'there being,' he added, 'no fellowship between the religion of God and the devil.' These words were interpreted to the Indians, but they nevertheless smiled, and retired in a peaceable manner."]

An Address to a Missionary

[Stone reports that this speech, from a manuscript obtained by one Captain Parish, is from the same period as the speeches to Mr. Cram and Mr. Alexander above.]

BROTHER: I rise to return you the thanks of this nation, and to return them back to our ancient friends – if any such we have – for their good wishes toward us in attempting to teach us your religion. Inform them we will look into this matter. We have well weighed your exertions, and find your success not to answer our expectations. But instead of producing that happy effect which you so long promised us, its introduction so far rendered us uncomfortable and miserable. You have taken a number of our young men to your schools. You have educated them and taught them your religion. They have returned to their kindred and color, neither white men nor Indians. The arts they have learned are incompatible with the chase, and ill adapted to our customs. They have been taught that which is useless to us. They have been made to feel artificial wants, which never entered the minds of their brothers. They have imbibed, in your great towns, the seeds of vices which were unknown in the forest. They become discouraged and dissipated – despised by the Indians, neglected by the whites, and without value to either – less honest than the former, and *perhaps* more knavish than the latter.

BROTHER: We were told that the failure of these first attempts was attributable to miscalculation, and we were invited to try again, by sending others of our young men to different schools, to be taught by different instructors. Brother, the result has been invariably the same. We believe it wrong for you to attempt further to promote your religion among us, or to introduce your arts, manners, habits and feelings. We believe that it is wrong for us to encourage you in so doing. We believe that the Great Spirit made the whites and the Indians, but for different purposes.

BROTHER: In attempting to pattern your example, the Great Spirit is angry – for you see he does not bless or crown your exertions.

[Stone continues: "Here according to the manuscript, [Sagoyewatha] painted in the most glowing and descriptive colors the curse that seemed to have descended upon all those Indians who had been made the objects of pious but mistaken missions...without one solitary exception where the Indian had been bettered. He then proceeded:"]

But, BROTHER, on the other hand we know that the Great Spirit is pleased that we follow the traditions and customs of our forefathers – for in so doing we receive this blessing – we have received strength and vigor for the chase. The Great Spirit has provided abundance – when we are hungry we find the forest filled with game – when thirsty, we slake our thirst at the pure streams and springs that spread around us. When weary, the leaves of the trees are our bed – we retire with contentment to rest – we rise with gratitude to the Great Preserver. Renovated strength in our limbs, and bounding joy in our hearts, we feel blessed and happy. No luxuries, no vices, no disputed titles, no avaricious desires, shake the foundations of our society, or disturb our peace and happiness. We know the Great Spirit is better pleased with his red children, than with his white, when he bestows upon us a hundred fold more blessings than upon you.

Perhaps, BROTHER, you are right in your religion: it may be peculiarly adapted to your condition. You say that you destroyed the Son of the Great Spirit. Perhaps this is the merited cause of all your troubles and misfortunes. But, brother, bear in mind that we had no participation in this murder. We disclaim it – we love the Great Spirit – and as we never had any agency in so unjust, so merciless an outrage, he therefore continues to smile upon us, and to give us peace, joy, and plenty.

BROTHER: We pity you – we wish you to bear to our good friends our best wishes. Inform them that in compassion towards them, we are willing to send them missionaries to teach them our religion, habits and customs. We would be willing they should be as happy as we are, and assure them that if they should follow our example, they would be more, far more happy than they are now. We cannot embrace your religion. It renders us divided and unhappy – but by your embracing ours, we believe that you would be more happy and more acceptable to the Great Spirit. Here (pointing his finger to several whites present who had been captured when children, and been brought up among them), here brother (with an animation and exulting triumph which cannot be described), here is the living evidence before you. Those young men have been brought up with us. They are contented and happy. Nothing would be an inducement with them to abandon their enjoyments and adopt yours – for they are too well aware of the blessings of our society, and the evils of yours. But as you have our good will, we would gladly know that you have relinquished your religion, productive of so much disagreement and inquietude among yourselves, and instead thereof that you should follow ours.

Accept of this advice, BROTHER, and take it back to your friends, as the best pledge of our wishes for your welfare. Perhaps you think we are ignorant and uninformed. Go, then, and teach the whites. Select, for example, the people of Buffalo. We will be spectators, and remain silent. Improve their morals and refine their habits – make them less disposed to cheat Indians. Make the whites generally less inclined to make Indians drunk, and to take from them their lands. Let us know the tree by the blossoms, and the blossoms by the fruit. When this shall be made clear to our minds we may be more willing to listen to you. Until then we must be allowed to follow the religion of our ancestors.

BROTHER: Farewell!

3

How the World Began

Arthur C. Parker

Introduction

Arthur C. Parker (1881–1955) was born on the Cattaraugus Indian Reservation near Buffalo, New York, the son of a white mother and Seneca father. Since the Seneca people are matrilineal, Parker was not an enrolled member of the Seneca nation. He saw himself as a product of the Seneca tradition as much as a product of European American culture. He became an ethnologist committed to "collecting" the traditional stories of the Seneca and the other peoples who were part of the Haudenosaunee Confederacy, the Onondaga, Mohawk, Oneida, Cayuga, and Tuscarora. The story here was communicated to him by Delos Big Kittle, a leading chief of the Wolf Clan of the Cattaraugus Seneca. Parker's principal works include *Seneca Myths and Folk Tales* (ed. William N. Fenton, 1989) and *Parker on the Iroquois* (ed. William N. Fenton, 1968).

Beyond the dome we call the sky there is another world. There in the most ancient of times was a fair country where lived the great chief of the up-above-world and his people, the celestial beings. This chief had a wife who was very aged in body, having survived many seasons.

In that upper world there were many things of which men of today know nothing. This world floated like a great cloud and journeyed where the great chief wished it to go. The crust of that

Taken from *Seneca Myths and Folk Tales*, ed. William N. Fenton (Lincoln and London: University of Nebraska Press, 1989), pp. 59–73. Reprinted with permission from the University of Nebraska Press.

world was not thick, but none of these men beings knew what was under the crust.

In the center of that world there grew a great tree which bore flowers and fruits and all the people lived from the fruits of the tree and were satisfied. Now, moreover, the tree bore a great blossom at its top, and it was luminous and lighted the world above, and wonderful perfume filled the air which the people breathed. The rarest perfume of all was that which resembled the smoke of sacred tobacco and this was the incense greatly loved by the great chief. It grew from the leaves that sprouted from the roots of the tree.

The roots of the tree were white and ran in four directions. Far through the earth they ran, giving firm support to the tree. Around this tree the people gathered daily, for here the Great Chief had his lodge where he dwelt. Now, in a dream he was given a desire to take as his wife a certain maiden who was very fair to look upon.[1] So, he took her as his wife for when he had embraced her he found her most pleasing. When he had eaten the marriage bread he took her to his lodge, and to his surprise found that she was with child. This caused him great anger and he felt himself deceived, but the woman loved the child, which had been conceived by the potent breath of her lover when he had embraced her. He was greatly distressed, for this fair Awĕ^{n}hā'i^{c} was of the noblest family. It is she who is customarily called Iagĕ$^{n\prime}$tci^{c}.

He, the Ancient One, fell into a troubled sleep and a dream commanded him to have the celestial tree uprooted as a punishment to his wife, and as a relief of his troubled spirit. So on the morrow he announced to his wife that he had a dream and could not be satisfied until it had been divined. Thereupon she "discovered his word," and it was that the tree should be uprooted.

"Truly you have spoken," said Ancient One, "and now my mind shall be satisfied." And the woman, his wife, saw that there was trouble ahead for the sky world, but she too found pleasure in the uprooting of the tree, wishing to know what was beneath it. Yet did she know that to uproot the tree meant disaster for her, through the anger of Ancient One against her.

It so happened that the chief called all his people together and they endeavored to uproot the tree, it being deep-rooted and firm. Then did the chief grow even more angry for Iagĕ^{nⁿ}tci had cried out that calamity threatened and nobody would avert it. Then did the chief, himself embrace the tree and with a mighty effort uprooted it, throwing it far away. His effort was tremendous, and in uprooting the tree he shook down fruits and leaves. Thereafter he went into his lodge and entered into the apartment where his wife, Iagĕ^{nⁿ}tci, lay moaning that she too must be satisfied by a look into the hole. So the chief led her to the hole made by uprooting the tree.

He caused her to seat herself on the edge of the hole and peer downward. Again his anger returned against her, for she said nothing to indicate that she had been satisfied. Long she sat looking into the hole until the chief in rage drew her blanket over her head and pushed her with his foot, seeking to thrust her into the hole, and be rid of her. As he did this she grasped the earth at her side and gathered in her fingers all manner of seeds that had fallen from the shaken tree. In her right hand she held the leaves of the plant that smelled like burning tobacco, for it grew from a root that had been broken off. Again the chief pushed the woman, whose curiosity had caused the destruction of the greatest blessing of the up-above-world. It was a mighty push, and despite her hold upon the plant and upon the ground, she fell into the hole.

Now, this hole had penetrated the crust of the upper world and when Iagĕ^{nⁿ}tci fell she went far down out of sight and the chief could not see her in the depths of the darkness below. As she fell she beheld a beast that emitted fire from its head whom she called Gaäs^{ꞌ}ioñdie^{ꞌ}t^{ꞌ}hä^ꞌ (Gahashondie-toh). It is said that as she passed by him he took out a small pot, a corn mortar, a pestle, a marrow

bone and an ear of corn and presented them to her, saying, "Because thou has thus done, thou shalt eat by these things, for there is nothing below, and all who eat shall see me once and it will be the last."

Now it is difficult to know how this Fire Beast can be seen for he is of the color of the wind and is of the color of anything that surrounds it, though some say he is pure white.

Hovering over the troubled waters below were other creatures, some like and some unlike those that were created afterward. It is said by the old people that in those times lived the spirit of Gä^{ꞌ}ha^ꞌ and of S^{ꞌ}hagodiiowe^{nⁿ}gōwä, of H^{ꞌ}no^ⁿ and of Deiodasondaiko (The Wind, the Defending Face, the Thunder and the Heavy Night.) There were also what seemed to be ducks upon the water and these also saw the descending figure.

The creature-beings knew that a new body was coming to them and that here below there was no abiding place for her. They took council together and sought to devise a way to provide for her.

It was agreed that the duck-creatures should receive her on their interknit wings and lower her gently to the surface below. The great turtle from the under-world was to arise and make his broad back a resting-place. It was as has been agreed and the woman came down upon the floating island.

Then did the creatures seek to make a world for the woman and one by one they dove to the bottom of the water seeking to find earth to plant upon the turtle's back. A duck dived but went so far that it breathed the water and came up dead. A pickerel went down and came back dead. Many creatures sought to find the bottom of the water but could not. At last the creature called Muskrat made the attempt and only succeeded in touching the bottom with his nose but this was sufficient for he was enabled to smear it upon the shell and the earth immediately grew, and as the earth-substance increased so did the size of the turtle.

After a time the woman, who lay prone, aroused herself and released what was in her hands, dropping many seeds into the folds of her garment. Likewise she spread out the earth from the heaven world which she had grasped and thus caused the seeds to spring into germination as they dropped from her dress.

The root of the tree which she had grasped she sunk into the soil where she had fallen and this too began to grow until it formed a tree with all manner of fruits and flowers and bore a luminous orb at its top by which the new world became illuminated.

Now in due season the Sky-Woman[2] lay beneath the tree and to her a daughter was born. She was then happy for she had a companion. Rapidly the girl child grew until very soon she could run about. It was then the custom of Ancient One to say: "My daughter, run about the island and return telling me what you have seen."

Day by day the girl ran around the island and each time it became larger, making her trips longer and longer. She observed that the earth was carpeted with grass and that shrubs and trees were springing up everywhere. This she reported to her mother, who sat beneath the centrally situated great tree.

In one part of the island there was a tree on which grew a long vine and upon this vine the girl was accustomed to swing for amusement and her body moved to and fro giving her great delight. Then did her mother say, "My daughter, you laugh as if being embraced by a lover. Have you seen a man?"

"I have seen no one but you, my mother," answered the girl, "but when I swing I know someone is close to me and I feel my body embraced as if with strong arms. I feel thrilled and I tingle, which causes me to laugh."

Then did the Sky-Woman look sad, and she said, "My daughter, I know not now what will befall us. You are married to Gä'ha', and he will be the father of your children. There will be two boys."

In due season the voices of two boys were heard speaking, eiä'da'goñ', and the words of one were kind and he gave no trouble, but the words of the other were harsh and he desired to kill his mother. His skin was covered with warts and boils and he was inclined to cause great pain.

When the two boys were born, Elder One made his mother happy but when Warty One was born he pierced her through the arm pit and stood upon her dead body. So did the mother perish, and because of this the Sky Woman wept.

The boys required little care but instantly became able to care for themselves. After the mother's body had been arranged for burial, the Sky Woman saw the Elder One whom she called Good Mind, approach, and he said, "Grandmother, I wish to help you prepare the grave." So he helped his grandmother who continually wept, and deposited the body of his mother in a grave. Thereupon did the grandmother speak to her daughter:

"Oh, my daughter," she said, "You have departed and made the first path to the world

from which I came bringing your life. When you reach that homeland make ready to receive many beings from this place below, for I think the path will be trodden by many."

Good Mind watched at the grave of his mother and watered the earth above it until the grass grew. He continued to watch until he saw strange buds coming out of the ground.

Where the feet were the earth sprouted with a plant that became the stringed-potato (onĕñno[n] '/dä'o[n/]wĕ') where her fingers lay sprang the beans, where her abdomen lay sprang the squash, where her breasts lay sprang the corn plant, and from the spot above her forehead sprang the tobacco plant.

Now the warty one was named Evil Mind, and he neglected his mother's grave and spent his time tearing up the land and seeking to do evil.

When the grandmother saw the plants springing from the grave of her daughter and cared for by Good Mind she was thankful and said, "By these things we shall hereafter live, and they shall be cooked in pots with fire, and the corn shall be your milk and sustain you. You shall make the corn grow in hills like breasts, for from the corn shall flow our living."

Then the Grandmother, the Sky Woman, took Good Mind about the island and instructed him how to produce plants and trees. So he spoke to the earth and said, "Let a willow here come forth," and it came. In a like manner he made the oak, the chestnut, the beech, the hemlock, the spruce, the pine, the maple, the button–ball, the tulip, the elm and many other trees that should become useful.

With a jealous stomach the Evil Mind followed behind and sought to destroy the good things but could not, so he spoke to the earth and said: "Briars come forth," and they came forth. Likewise he created poisonous plants and thorns upon bushes.

Upon a certain occasion Good Mind made inquiries of his Grandmother, asking where his father dwelt. Then did the Sky Woman say: "You shall now seek your father. He lives to the uttermost east and you shall go to the far eastern end of the island and go over the water until you behold a mountain rising from the sea. You shall walk up the mountain and there you will find your father seated upon the top."

Good Mind made the pilgrimage and came to the mountain. At the foot of the mountain he looked upward and called, "My father, where art thou?" And a great voice sounded the word: "A son of mine shall cast the cliff from the mountain's edge to the summit of this peak." Good Mind grasped the cliff and with a mighty effort flung it to the mountain top. Again he cried, "My father, where art thou?" The answer came, "A son of mine shall swim the cataract from the pool below to the top." Good Mind leaped into the falls and swam upward to the top where the water poured over. He stood there and cried again, "My father, where art thou?" The voice answered, "A son of mine shall wrestle with the wind." So, there at the edge of a terrifying precipice Good Mind grappled with Wind and the two wrestled, each endeavoring to throw the other over. It was a terrible battle and Wind tore great rocks from the mountain side and lashed the water below, but Good Mind overcame Wind, and he departed moaning in defeat. Once more Good Mind called, "My father, where art thou?" In awesome tones the voice replied, "A son of mine shall endure the flame," and immediately a flame sprang out of the mountain side and enveloped Good Mind. It blinded him and tortured him with its cruel heat, but he threw aside its entwining arms and ran to the mountain top where he beheld a being sitting in the midst of a blaze of light.

"I am thy father," said the voice. "Thou art my son."

"I have come to receive power," said the son. "I wish to rule all things on the earth."

"You have power," answered the father. "You have conquered. I give to you the bags of life, the containers of living creatures that will bless the earth."

Thus did the father and son counsel together and the son learned many things that he should do. He learned how to avoid the attractive path that descended to the place of the cave where Hanishe'ono^m dwells.

Now the father said, "How did you come to find me, seeing I am secluded by many elements?"

The Good Mind answered, "When I was about to start my journey Sky Woman, my grandmother, gave me a flute and I blew upon it, making music. Now, when the music ceased the flute spoke to me, saying, 'This way shalt thou go,' and I continued to make music and the voice of the flute spoke to me."

Then did the father say, "Make music by the flute and listen, then shalt thou continue to know the right direction."

In course of time Good Mind went down the mountain and he waded the sea, taking with him the bags with which he had been presented. As he drew near the shore he became curious to know what was within, and he pinched one bag hoping to feel its contents. He felt a movement inside which increased until it became violent. The bag began to roll about on his back until he could scarcely hold it and a portion of the mouth of the bag slipped from his hand. Immediately the things inside began to jump out and fall into the water with a great splash, and they were water animals of different kinds. The other bag began to roll around on his back but he held on tightly until he could do so no more, when a portion of the mouth slipped and out flew many kinds of birds, some flying seaward and others inland toward the trees. Then as before the third bag began to roll about but he held on very tight, but it slipped and fell into the water and many kinds of swimming creatures rushed forth, fishes, crabs and eels. The fourth bag then began to roll about, but he held on until he reached the land when he threw it down, and out rushed all the good land animals, of kinds he did not know. From the bird bag had come good insects, and from the fish bag had also come little turtles and clams.

When Good Mind came to his grandmother beneath the tree she asked what he had brought, for she heard music in the trees and saw creatures scampering about. Thereupon Good Mind related what had happened, and Sky Woman said, "We must now call all the animals and discover their names, and moreover we must so treat them that they will have fat."

So then she spoke, "Cavity be in the ground and be filled with oil." The pool of oil came, for Sky Woman had the power of creating what she desired.

Good Mind then caught the animals one by one and brought them to his grandmother. She took a large furry animal and cast it into the pool and it swam very slowly across, licking up much oil. "This animal shall hereafter be known as niagwaih (bear), and you shall be very fat." Next came another animal with much fur and it swam across and licked up the oil, and it was named degiiä$^{''}$go^n (buffalo). So in turn were named the elk, the moose, the badger, the woodchuck, and the raccoon, and all received much fat. Then came the beaver (na^{n}ga^{n}niä'go^n), the porcupine and the skunk. Now Good Mind wished the deer to enter but it was shy and bounded away, whereupon he took a small arrow and pierced its front leg, his aim being good. Then the deer came and swam across the pool and oil entered the wound and healed it.

This oil of the deer's leg is a medicine for wounds to this day and if the eyes are anointed with it one may shoot straight.

Again other animals came and one by one they were named weasel, mink, otter, fisher, panther, lynx, wild cat, fox, wolf, big wolf, squirrel, chipmunk, mole, and many others.

And many animals that were not desired plunged into the pool of oil, and these Good Mind seized as they came out and he stripped them of their fat and pulled out their bodies long. So he did to the otter, fisher, weasel and mink. So he did to the panther, wolf, big wolf, and fox, the lynx and the wildcat. Of these the fat to this day is not good tasting. But after a time Evil Mind secured a bag of creatures from the road to the Cave and unloosed it, and evil things crawled into the pool and grew fat. So did the rattlesnake and great bugs and loathly worms.

Thus did Evil Mind secure many evil monsters and insects, and he enticed good animals into his traps and perverted them and gave them appetites for men-beings. He was delighted to see how fierce he could make the animals, and set them to quarreling.

He roamed about visiting the streams of pure water made by Good Mind and filling them with mud and slime, and he kicked rocks in the rivers and creeks to make passage difficult, and he planted nettles and thorns in the paths. Thus did he do to cause annoyance.

Now Good Mind sat with his grandmother beneath the tree of light and he spoke to her of the world and how he might improve it. "Alas," said she, "I believe that only one more task awaits me and then I shall go upon my path and follow your mother back to the world beyond the sky. It remains for me to call into being certain lights in the blackness above where Heavy Night presides."

So saying she threw the contents of a bag into the sky and it quickly became sprinkled with stars. And thus there came into being constellations (haditgwä^{n}dä'), and of these we see the bear chase, the dancing brothers, the seated woman, the beaver skin, the belt, and many others.

Now it seems that Good Mind knew that there should be a luminous orb and, so it is said, he took his mother's face and flung it skyward and made the sun, and took his mother's breast and flinging it into the sky made the moon. So it is said, but there are other accounts of the creation of these lights. It is said that the first beings made them by going into the sky.

Shortly after the creation of the stars (gadji^{c}so^{n}dä'), the grandmother said unto Good Mind, "I believe that the time has come when I should depart, for nearly all is finished here. There is a road from my feet and I have a song which I shall sing by which I shall know the path. There is one more matter that troubles me for I see that your brother is jealous and will seek to kill you. Use great care that you overcome him and when you have done so confine him in the cave and send with him the evil spirit beasts, lest they injure men."

When morning came the Sky Woman had departed and her journey was toward the sky world.

Good Mind felt lonely and believed that his own mission was about at end. He had been in conflict with his brother, Evil Mind, and had sought, moreover, to overcome and to teach the Whirlwind and Wind, and the Fire Beast.

Soon Evil Mind came proposing a hunting trip and Good Mind went with him on the journey. When they had gone a certain distance the Evil Mind said, "My elder brother, I perceive that you are about to call forth men-beings who shall live on the island that we here have inhabited. I propose to afflict them with disease and to make life difficult, for this is not their world but mine, and I shall do as I please to spoil it."

Then did Good Mind answer and say, "Verily, I am about to make man-beings who shall live here when I depart, for I am going to follow the road skyward made first by my mother."

"This is good news," answered Evil Mind. "I propose that you then reveal unto me the word that has power over your life, that I may possess it and have power when you are gone."

Good Mind now saw that his brother wished to destroy him, and so he said, "It may happen that you will employ the cat-tail flag, whose sharp leaves will pierce me."

Good Mind then lay down and slumbered, but soon was awakened by Evil Mind who was lashing him with cat-tail flags, and yelling loudly, "Thou shalt die." Good Mind arose and asked his brother what he meant by lashing him and he answered, "I was seeking to awaken you from a dream, for you were speaking."

So, soon again the brother, Evil Mind, asked, "My brother, I wish to know the word that has power over you." And Good Mind perceiving his intention answered, "It may be that deer-horns will have power over me; they are sharp and hard."

Soon Good Mind slept again and was awakened by Evil Mind beating him with deer-horns, seeking to destroy him. They rushed inland to the foot of the tree and fought each other about it. Evil Mind was very fierce and rushed at his brother thrusting the horns at him and trying to pierce his chest, his face or tear his abdomen. Finally, Good Mind disarmed him, saying, "Look what you have done to the tree where Ancient One was wont to care for us, and whose branches have supplied us with food. See how you have torn this tree and stripped it of its valuable products. This tree was designed to support the life of men-beings and now you have injured it. I must banish you to the region of the great cave and you shall have the name of Destroyer."

So saying he used his good power to overcome Evil Mind's otgont (evil power) and thrust him into the mouth of the cave, and with him all manner of enchanted beasts. There he placed the white buffalo, the poison beaver, the poison otter, snakes and many bewitched things that were otgont. So there to this day abides Evil Mind seeking to emerge, and his voice is heard giving orders.

Then Good Mind went back to the tree and soon saw a being walking about. He walked over to the place where the being was pacing to and fro. He saw that it was S'hagodiiwe$^{n\prime}$gōwā, who was a giant with a grotesque face. "I am master of the earth," roared this being (called also Great Defender), for he was the whirlwind. "If you are master," said Good Mind, "prove your power."

Defender said, "What shall be our test?"

"Let this be the test," said Good Mind, "that the mountain yonder shall approach us at your bidding."

So Defender spoke saying, "Mountain, come hither." And they turned their backs that they might not see it coming until it stood at their backs. Soon they turned about again and the mountain had not moved.

"So now, I shall command," said Good Mind, and he spoke saying, "Mountain, come hither," and they turned their backs. There was a rushing of air and Defender turned to see what was behind him and fell against the onrushing mountain, and it bent his nose and twisted his mouth, and from this he never recovered.

Then did Defender say, "I do now acknowledge you to be master. Command me and I will obey."

"Since you love to wander," said Good Mind, "it shall be your duty to move about over the earth and stir up things. You shall abandon your evil intentions and seek to overcome your otgont nature, changing it to be of benefit to man-beings, whom I am about to create."

"Then," said Defender, "shall man-beings offer incense tobacco to me and make a song that is pleasing to me, and they shall carve my likeness from the substance of trees, and my orenda will enter the likeness of my face and it shall be a help to men-beings and they shall use the face as I shall direct. Then shall all the diseases that I may cause depart and I shall be satisfied."

Again Good Mind wandered, being melancholy. Looking up he saw another being approaching.

"I am Thunder," said the being.

"What can you do to be a help to me?" asked Good Mind.

"I can wash the earth and make drink for the trees and grass," said Thunder.

"What can you do to be a benefit to the men-beings I am about to create?" asked Good Mind.

"I shall slay evil monsters when they escape from the under-world," said Thunder. "I shall have scouts who will notify me and I shall shoot all otgont beings."

Then was Good Mind satisfied, and he pulled up a tree and saw the water fill the cavity where the roots had been. Long he gazed into the water until he saw a reflection of his own image. "Like unto that will I make men-beings," he thought. So then he took clay and molded it into small images of men and women. These he placed on the ground and when they were dry he spoke to them and they sprang up and lived.

When he saw them he said unto them, "All this world I give unto you. It is from me that you shall say you are descended and you are the children of the first-born of earth, and you shall say that you are the flesh of Iagĕ$^{n\prime}$tci, she the Ancient Bodied One."

When he had acquainted them with the other first beings, and shown them how to hunt and fish and to eat of the fruits of the land, he told them that they should seek to live together as friends and brothers and that they should treat each other well.

He told them how to give incense of tobacco, for Awĕ^{n}hā'i$^\prime$, Ancient Bodied One, had stripped the heaven world of tobacco when she fell, and thus its incense should be a pleasing one into which men-beings might speak their words when addressing him hereafter. These and many other things did he tell them.

Soon he vanished from the sight of created men-beings, and he took all the first beings with him upon the sky road.

Soon men-beings began to increase and they covered the earth, and from them we are descended. Many things have happened since those days, so much that all can never be told.

Notes

1   In another version this chief was killed and his body hidden in the trunk of the celestial tree. Another chief, a rival, desired to marry the daughter of the deceased one and indeed took her in the manner here related. In this version it was the bride who desired to have the tree uprooted in order that she might hunt for her father's body. The concealing of the body of the celestial father in the body of a tree reminds one of the legend of Osiris.

2   We use this name for convenience only.

4

The Interesting Narrative

Olaudah Equiano

Introduction

Olaudah Equiano (Gustavus Vassa) (1745–97) was kidnapped from his African village at the age of 11, shipped through the arduous "Middle Passage" of the Atlantic Ocean, seasoned in the West Indies, and sold to a Virginia planter. He was later bought by a British naval officer, Captain Pascal, as a present for his cousins in London. After ten years of American enslavement, where he assisted his merchant slave master and worked as a seaman, Equiano bought his freedom. In *The Interesting Narrative*, Equiano recalls his childhood in Essaka (an Igbo village in northeast Nigeria), where he was raised in the tradition of the "greatest warriors." Equally significant is Equiano's life on the high seas, which included not only travels throughout the Americas, Turkey, and the Mediterranean, but also participation in major naval battles during the French and Indian War (Seven Years War, 1756–63), as well as in the search for a northwest passage led by the Phipps expedition of 1772–3. Equiano also records his central role, along with Granville Sharpe, in the British Abolitionist Movement. As a major voice in this movement, Equiano petitioned the King of England in 1788. He was appointed to the expedition to settle London's poor blacks in Sierra Leone, a British colony on the west coast of Africa. God, according to Equiano, will create a bright future for the downtrodden.

Taken from *The Interesting Narrative of the Life of Olaudah Equiano, Written by Himself* (1789), ed. Robert J. Allison (Boston, New York: St. Martin's Press, 1995), pp. 33–46, 60–1.

I

The author's account of his country, and their manners and customs – Administration of justice – Embrenche – Marriage ceremony, and public entertainments – Mode of living – Dress – Manufactures – Buildings – Commerce – Agriculture – War and religion – Superstition of the natives – Funeral ceremonies of the priests or magicians – Curious mode of discovering poison – Some hints concerning the origin of the author's countrymen, with the opinions of different writers on that subject.

I believe it is difficult for those who publish their own memoirs to escape the imputation of vanity; nor is this the only disadvantage under which they labor: it is also their misfortune that what is uncommon is rarely, if ever, believed, and what is obvious we are apt to turn from with disgust, and to charge the writer with impertinence. People generally think those memoirs only worthy to be read or remembered which abound in great or striking events, those, in short, which in a high degree excite either admiration or pity; all others they consign to contempt and oblivion. It is therefore, I confess, not a little hazardous in a private and obscure individual, and a stranger too, thus to solicit the indulgent attention of the public, especially when I own I offer here the history of neither a saint, a hero, nor a tyrant. I believe there are few events in my life which have not happened to many; it is true the incidents of it are numerous, and, did I consider myself an European, I might say my sufferings were great; but when I compare my lot with that of most of my countrymen, I regard myself as a *particular favorite of heaven*, and acknowledge the mercies of Providence in every occurrence of my life. If, then, the following narrative does not appear sufficiently interesting to engage general attention, let my motive be some excuse for its publication. I am not so foolishly vain as to expect from it either immortality or literary reputation. If it affords any satisfaction to my numerous friends, at whose request it has been written, or in the smallest degree promotes the interests of humanity, the ends for which it was undertaken will be fully attained, and every wish of my heart gratified. Let it therefore be remembered, that, in wishing to avoid censure, I do not aspire to praise.

That part of Africa, known by the name of Guinea, to which the trade for slaves is carried on, extends along the coast above 3400 miles, from Senegal to Angola, and includes a variety of kingdoms. Of these the most considerable is the kingdom of Benin,[1] both as to extent and wealth, the richness and cultivation of the soil, the power of its king, and the number and warlike disposition of the inhabitants. It is situated nearly under the line,[2] and extends along the coast about 170 miles, but runs back into the interior part of Africa to a distance hitherto, I believe, unexplored by any traveller, and seems only terminated at length by the empire of Abyssinia, near 1500 miles from its beginning. This kingdom is divided into many provinces or districts, in one of the most remote and fertile of which, I was born, in the year 1745, situated in a charming fruitful vale, named Essaka. The distance of this province from the capital of Benin and the sea coast must be very considerable, for I had never heard of white men or Europeans, nor of the sea; and our subjection to the king of Benin was little more than nominal, for every transaction of the government, as far as my slender observation extended, was conducted by the chief or elders of the place. The manners and government of a people who have little commerce with other countries are generally very simple, and the history of what passes in one family or village may serve as a specimen of the whole nation.

My father was one of those elders or chiefs I have spoken of, and was styled Embrenche, a term, as I remember, importing the highest distinction, and signifying in our language a *mark* of grandeur. This mark is conferred on the person entitled to it, by cutting the skin across at the top of the forehead, and drawing it down to the eyebrows; and while it is in this situation applying a warm hand, and rubbing it until it shrinks up into a thick *weal* across the lower part of the forehead.[3] Most of the judges and senators were thus marked; my father had long borne it; I had seen it conferred on one of my brothers, and I also was *destined* to receive it by my parents. Those Embrenche, or chief men, decided disputes and punished crimes, for which purpose they always assembled together. The proceedings were generally short, and in most cases the law of retaliation prevailed.

I remember a man was brought before my father, and the other judges, for kidnapping a boy; and, although he was the son of a chief or senator, he was condemned to make recompense by a man or woman slave. Adultery, however, was sometimes punished with slavery or death, a punishment which I believe is inflicted on it throughout most of the nations of Africa,[4] so sacred among them is the honor of the marriage bed, and so jealous are they of the fidelity of their wives. Of this I recollect an instance – a woman was convicted before the judges of adultery, and delivered over, as the custom was, to her husband, to be punished. Accordingly he determined to put her to death; but it being found, just before her execution, that she had an infant at her breast, and no woman being prevailed on to perform the part of a nurse, she was spared on account of the child. The men, however, do not preserve the same constancy to their wives which they expect from them; for they indulge in a plurality, though seldom in more than two.

Their mode of marriage is thus – both parties are usually betrothed when young by their parents (though I have known the males to betroth themselves). On this occasion a feast is prepared, and the bride and bridegroom stand up in the midst of all their friends, who are assembled for the purpose, while he declares she is henceforth to be looked upon as his wife, and that no other person is to pay any addresses to her. This is also immediately proclaimed in the vicinity, on which the bride retires from the assembly. Some time after, she is brought home to her husband, and then another feast is made, to which the relations of both parties are invited; her parents then deliver her to the bridegroom, accompanied with a number of blessings, and at the same time they tie round her waist a cotton string of the thickness of a goose-quill, which none but married women are permitted to wear; she is now considered as completely his wife; and at this time the dowry is given to the new married pair, which generally consists of portions of land, slaves, and cattle, household goods, and implements of husbandry. These are offered by the friends of both parties; besides which the parents of the bridegroom present gifts to those of the bride, whose property she is looked upon before marriage; but after it she is esteemed the sole property of her husband. The ceremony being now ended, the festival begins, which is celebrated with bonfires and loud acclamations of joy, accompanied with music and dancing.

We are almost a nation of dancers, musicians, and poets. Thus every great event, such as a triumphant return from battle or other cause of public rejoicing, is celebrated in public dances, which are accompanied with songs and music suited to the occasion. The assembly is separated into four divisions, which dance either apart or in succession, and each with a character peculiar to itself. The first division contains the married men, who in their dances frequently exhibit feats of arms and the representation of a battle. To these succeed the married women, who dance in the second division. The young men occupy the third, and the maidens the fourth. Each represents some interesting scene of real life, such as a great achievement, domestic employment, a pathetic story, or some rural sport; and as the subject is generally founded on some recent event, it is therefore ever new. This gives our dances a spirit and variety which I have scarcely seen elsewhere.[5] We have many musical instruments, particularly drums of different kinds, a piece of music which resembles a guitar, and another much like a stickado. These last are chiefly used by betrothed virgins, who play on them on all grand festivals.

As our manners are simple, our luxuries are few. The dress of both sexes is nearly the same. It generally consists of a long piece of calico, or muslin, wrapped loosely round the body, somewhat in the form of a highland plaid. This is usually dyed blue, which is our favorite color. It is extracted from a berry, and is brighter and richer than any I have seen in Europe. Besides this, our women of distinction wear golden ornaments, which they dispose with some profusion on their arms and legs. When our women are not employed with the men in tillage, their usual occupation is spinning and weaving cotton, which they afterwards dye, and make into garments. They also manufacture earthen vessels, of which we have many kinds. Among the rest, tobacco pipes, made after the same fashion, and used in the same manner, as those in Turkey.[6]

Our manner of living is entirely plain; for as yet the natives are unacquainted with those refinements in cookery which debauch the taste: bullocks, goats, and poultry supply the greatest part of their food. These constitute likewise the principal wealth of the country, and the chief articles of its commerce. The flesh is usually stewed in a pan; to make it savory we sometimes use pepper, and other spices, and we have salt made of wood ashes. Our vegetables are mostly plantains, eadas,[7] yams, beans, and Indian corn. The head of the family usually eats alone; his wives and slaves have also their separate tables. Before we taste food we always wash our hands; indeed, our cleanliness on all occasions is extreme, but on this it is an indispensable ceremony. After washing, libation is made, by pouring out a small portion of the drink on the floor, and tossing a small quantity of the food in a certain place, for the spirits of departed relations, which the natives suppose to preside over their conduct and guard them from evil. They are totally unacquainted with strong or spirituous liquors; and their principal beverage is palm wine. This is got from a tree of that name, by tapping it at the top and fastening a large gourd to it; and sometimes one tree will yield three or four gallons in a night. When just drawn it is of a most delicious sweetness; but in a few days it acquires a tartish and more spirituous flavor, though I never saw anyone intoxicated by it. The same tree also produces nuts and oil. Our principal luxury is in perfumes: one sort of these is an odoriferous wood of delicious fragrance, the other a kind of earth, a small portion of which thrown into the fire diffuses a most powerful odor.[8] We beat this wood into powder, and mix it with palm oil, with which both men and women perfume themselves.[9]

In our buildings we study convenience rather than ornament. Each master of a family has a large square piece of ground, surrounded with a moat or fence, or enclosed with a wall made of red earth tempered, which, when dry, is as hard as brick. Within this, are his houses to accommodate his family and slaves, which, if numerous, frequently present the appearance of a village. In the middle, stands the principal building, appropriated to the sole use of the master and consisting of two apartments; in one of which he sits in the day with his family, the other is left apart for the reception of his friends. He has besides these a distinct apartment in which he sleeps, together with his male children. On each side are the apartments of his wives, who have also their separate day and night houses. The habitations of the slaves and their families are distributed throughout the rest of the enclosure. These houses never exceed one story in height; they are always built of wood, or stakes driven into the ground, crossed with wattles, and neatly plastered within and without. The roof is thatched with reeds. Our day houses are left open at the sides; but those in which we sleep are always covered, and plastered in the inside, with a composition mixed with cow-dung, to keep off the different insects which annoy us during the night. The walls and floors also of these are generally covered with mats. Our beds consist of a platform, raised three or four feet from the ground, on which are laid skins, and different parts of a spongy tree, called plantain. Our covering is calico or muslin, the same as our dress. The usual seats are a few logs of wood; but we have benches, which are generally perfumed to accommodate strangers: these compose the greater part of our household furniture. Houses so constructed and furnished require but little skill to erect them. Every man is a sufficient architect for the purpose. The whole neighborhood afford their unanimous assistance in building them, and in return receive and expect no other recompense than a feast.

As we live in a country where nature is prodigal of her favors, our wants are few and easily supplied; of course we have few manufactures. They consist for the most part of calicoes, earthen ware, ornaments, and instruments of war and husbandry.[10] But these make no part of our commerce, the principal articles of which, as I have observed, are provisions. In such a state, money is of little use; however, we have some small pieces of coin, if I may call them such. They are made something like an anchor, but I do not remember either their value or denomination. We have also markets, at which I have been frequently with my mother. These are sometimes visited by stout mahogany-colored men from the south-west of us: we call them *Oye-Eboe*, which term signifies red men living at a distance.[11] They generally bring us fire-arms, gun-powder, hats, beads, and dried fish. The last we esteemed a great rarity, as our waters were only brooks and springs. These articles they barter with us for odoriferous woods and earth, and our salt of wood ashes. They always carry slaves through our land; but the strictest account is exacted of their manner of procuring them before they are suffered to pass. Sometimes, indeed, we sold slaves to them, but they were only prisoners of war, or such among us as had been convicted of kidnapping, or adultery, and some other crimes, which we esteemed heinous. This practice of kidnapping induces me to think, that, notwithstanding all our strictness, their principal business among us was to trepan[12] our people. I remember too, they carried great sacks along with them, which not long after, I had an opportunity of fatally seeing applied to that infamous purpose.

Our land is uncommonly rich and fruitful, and produces all kinds of vegetables in great abundance. We have plenty of Indian corn, and vast quantities of cotton and tobacco. Our pineapples grow without culture; they are about the size of the largest sugar-loaf, and finely flavored. We have also spices of different kinds, particularly pepper, and a variety of delicious fruits which I have never seen in Europe, together with gums of various kinds, and honey in abundance. All our industry is exerted to improve these blessings of nature. Agriculture is our chief employment; and everyone, even the children and women, are engaged in it. Thus we are all habituated to labor from our earliest years. Everyone contributes something to the common stock; and, as we are unacquainted with idleness, we have no beggars. The benefits of such a mode of living are obvious. The West India planters prefer the slaves of Benin or Eboe[13] to those of any other part of Guinea, for their hardiness, intelligence, integrity, and zeal. Those benefits are felt by us in the general healthiness of the people, and in their vigor and activity; I might have added, too, in their comeliness. Deformity is indeed unknown amongst us, I mean that of shape. Numbers of the natives of Eboe now in London might be brought in support of this assertion: for, in regard to complexion, ideas of beauty are wholly relative. I remember while in Africa to have seen three Negro children who were tawny, and another quite white, who were universally regarded by myself, and the natives in general, as far as related to their complexions, as deformed. Our women, too, were, in my eye at least, uncommonly graceful, alert, and modest to a degree of bashfulness; nor do I remember to have heard of an instance of incontinence[14] amongst them before marriage. They are also remarkably cheerful. Indeed, cheerfulness and affability are two of the leading characteristics of our nation.

Our tillage is exercised in a large plain or common, some hour's walk from our dwellings, and all the neighbors resort thither in a body. They use no beasts of husbandry; and their only instruments are hoes, axes, shovels, and beaks, or pointed iron, to dig with. Sometimes we are visited by locusts, which come in large clouds, so as to darken the air, and destroy our harvest. This, however, happens rarely, but when it does, a famine is produced by it. I remember an instance or two wherein this happened. This common is often the theatre of war; and therefore when our people go out to till their land, they not only go in a body, but generally take their arms with them for fear of a surprise; and when they apprehend an invasion, they guard the avenues to their dwellings, by driving sticks into the ground, which are so sharp at one end as to pierce the foot, and are generally dipt in poison. From what I can recollect of these battles, they appear to have been irruptions of one little state or district on the other, to obtain prisoners or booty. Perhaps they were incited to this by those traders who brought the European goods I mentioned, amongst us. Such a mode of obtaining slaves in Africa is common; and I believe more are procured this way, and by kidnapping, than any other.[15] When a trader wants slaves, he applies to a chief for them, and tempts him with his wares. It is not extraordinary, if on this occasion he yields to the temptation with as little firmness, and accepts the price of his fellow creature's liberty, with as little reluctance as the enlightened merchant. Accordingly he falls on his neighbors, and a desperate battle ensues. If he prevails and takes prisoners, he gratifies his avarice by selling them; but, if his party be vanquished, and he falls into the hands of the enemy, he is put to death; for, as he has been known to foment their quarrels, it is thought dangerous to let him survive, and no ransom can save him, though all other prisoners may be redeemed. We have fire-arms, bows and arrows, broad two-edged swords and javelins; we have shields also which cover a man from head to foot. All are taught the use of these weapons; even our women are warriors, and march boldly out to fight along with the men. Our whole district is a kind of militia: on a certain signal given, such as the firing of a gun at night, they all rise in arms and rush upon their enemy. It is perhaps something remarkable, that when our people march to the field a red flag or banner is borne before them.

I was once a witness to a battle in our common. We had been all at work in it one day as usual, when our people were suddenly attacked. I climbed a tree at some distance, from which I beheld the fight. There were many women as well as men on both sides; among others my mother was there, and armed with a broad sword. After fighting for a considerable time with great fury, and many had been killed, our people obtained the victory, and took their enemy's Chief a prisoner. He was carried off in great triumph, and, though he offered a large ransom for his life, he was put to death. A virgin of note among our enemies had been slain in the battle, and her arm was exposed in our marketplace, where our trophies were always exhibited. The spoils were divided according to the merit of the warriors. Those prisoners which were not sold or redeemed, we kept as slaves; but how different was their condition from that of the slaves in the West Indies! With us, they do no more work than other members of the community, even their master; their food, clothing, and lodging were nearly the same as theirs (except that they were not permitted to eat with those who were free-born); and there was scarce any other difference between them, than a superior degree of importance which the head of a family possesses in our state, and that authority which, as such, he exercises over every part of his household. Some of these slaves have even slaves under them as their own property, and for their own use.

As to religion, the natives believe that there is one Creator of all things, and that he lives in the sun, and is girted round with a belt; that he may never eat or drink, but, according to some, he smokes a pipe, which is our own favorite luxury. They believe he governs events, especially our deaths or captivity; but, as for the doctrine of eternity, I do not remember to have ever heard of it; some, however, believe in the transmigration of souls in a certain degree. Those spirits which were not transmigrated, such as their dear friends or relations, they believe always attend them, and guard them from the bad spirits or their foes. For this reason they always, before eating, as I have observed, put some small portion of the meat, and pour some of their drink, on the ground for them; and they often make oblations of the blood of beasts or fowls at their graves. I was very fond of my mother, and almost constantly with her. When she went to make these oblations at her mother's tomb, which was a kind of small solitary thatched house, I sometimes attended her. There she made her libations, and spent most of the night in cries and lamentations. I have been often extremely terrified on these occasions. The loneliness of the place, the darkness of the night, and the ceremony of libation, naturally awful and gloomy, were heightened by my mother's lamentations; and these concurring with the doleful cries of birds, by which these places were frequented, gave an inexpressible terror to the scene.

We compute the year from the day on which the sun crosses the line, and on its setting that evening, there is a general shout throughout the land; at least, I can speak from my own knowledge, throughout our vicinity. The people at the same time make a great noise with rattles, not unlike the basket rattles used by children here, though much larger, and hold up their hands to heaven for a blessing. It is then the greatest offerings are made; and those children whom our wise men foretell will be fortunate are then presented to different people. I remember many used to come to see me, and I was carried about to others for that purpose. They have many offerings, particularly at full moons; generally two, at harvest, before the fruits are taken out of the ground; and when any young animals are killed, sometimes they offer up part of them as a sacrifice. These offerings, when made by one of the heads of a family, serve for the whole. I remember we often had them at my father's and my uncle's, and their families have been present. Some of our offerings are eaten with bitter herbs. We had a saying among us to anyone of a cross temper, "That if they were to be eaten, they should be eaten with bitter herbs."

We practised circumcision like the Jews, and made offerings and feasts on that occasion, in the same manner as they did. Like them also, our children were named from some event, some circumstance, or fancied foreboding, at the time of their birth. I was named *Olaudah*, which in our language signifies vicissitude, or fortunate; also, one favored, and having a loud voice and well spoken.[16] I remember we never polluted the name of the object of our adoration; on the contrary, it was always mentioned with the greatest reverence; and we were totally unacquainted with swearing, and all those terms of abuse and reproach which find their way so readily and copiously into the language of more civilized people. The only expressions of that kind I remember were, "May you rot, or may you swell, or may a beast take you."

I have before remarked that the natives of this part of Africa are extremely cleanly. This necessary habit of decency was with us a part of religion, and therefore we had many purifications and washings; indeed almost as many, and used on the same occasions, if my recollection does not fail me, as the Jews. Those that touched the dead at any time were obliged to wash and purify themselves before they could enter a dwelling-house. Every woman, too, at certain times was forbidden to come into a dwelling-house, or touch any person, or anything we eat. I was so fond of my mother I could not keep from her, or avoid touching her at some of those periods, in consequence of which I was obliged to be kept out with her, in a little house made for that purpose, till offering was made, and then we were purified.

Though we had no places of public worship, we had priests and magicians, or wise men. I do not remember whether they had different offices, or whether they were united in the same persons, but they were held in great reverence by the people. They calculated our time, and foretold events, as their name imported, for we called them *Ah-affoe-way-cah*, which signifies calculators or yearly men, our year being called *Ah-affoe*.[17] They wore their beards, and when they died, they were succeeded by their sons. Most of their implements and things of value were interred along with them. Pipes and tobacco were also put into the grave with the corpse, which was always perfumed and ornamented, and animals were offered in sacrifice to them. None accompanied their funerals, but those of the same profession or tribe. They buried them after sunset, and always returned from the grave by a different way from that which they went.

These magicians were also our doctors or physicians. They practised bleeding by cupping, and were very successful in healing wounds and expelling poisons. They had likewise some extraordinary method of discovering jealousy, theft, poisoning, the success of which, no doubt, they derived from the unbounded influence over the credulity and superstition of the people. I do not remember what those methods were, except that as to poisoning; I recollect an instance or two, which I hope it will not be deemed impertinent here to insert, as it may serve as a kind of specimen of the rest, as is still used by the Negroes in the West Indies. A young woman had been poisoned, but it was not known by whom; the doctors ordered the corpse to be taken up by some persons, and carried to the grave. As soon as the bearers had raised it on their shoulders, they seemed seized with some[18] sudden impulse, and ran to and fro, unable to stop themselves. At last, after having passed through a number of thorns and prickly bushes unhurt, the corpse fell from them close to a house, and defaced it in the fall; and the owner being taken up, he immediately confessed the poisoning.[19]

The natives are extremely cautious about poison. When they buy any eatables, the seller kisses it all round before the buyer, to shew him it is not poisoned; and the same is done when any meat or drink is presented, particularly to a stranger. We have serpents of different kinds, some of which are esteemed ominous when they appear in our houses, and these we never molest. I remember two of those ominous snakes, each of which was as thick as the calf of a man's leg, and in color resembling a dolphin in the water, crept at different times into my mother's night house, where I always lay with her, and coiled themselves into folds, and each time they crowed like a cock. I was desired by some of our wise men to touch these, that I might be interested in the good omens, which I did, for they were quite harmless, and would tamely suffer themselves to be handled; and then they were put into a large earthen pan, and set on one side of the highway. Some of our snakes, however, were poisonous; one of them crossed the road one day as I was standing on it, and passed between my feet without offering to touch me, to the great surprise of many who saw it; and these incidents were accounted by the wise men, and likewise by my mother and the rest of the people, as remarkable omens in my favor.

Such is the imperfect sketch my memory has furnished me with, of the manners and customs of a people among whom I first drew my breath. And here I cannot forbear suggesting what has long struck me very forcibly, namely, the strong analogy which even by this sketch, imperfect as it is, appears to prevail in the manners and customs of my countrymen and those of the Jews, before they reached the land of promise, and particularly the patriarchs while they were yet in that pastoral state which is described in Genesis – an analogy, which alone would induce me to think that the one people had sprung from the other. Indeed, this is the opinion of Dr. Gill, who, in his commentary on Genesis, very ably deduces the pedigree of the Africans from Afer and Afra, the descendents of Abraham by Keturah his wife and concubine (for both these titles are applied to her). It is also conformable to the sentiments of Dr. John Clarke,

formerly Dean of Sarum, in his truth of the Christian religion; both these authors concur in ascribing to us this original.[20] The reasonings of those gentlemen are still further confirmed by the scripture chronology; and if any further corroboration were required, this resemblance in so many respects, is a strong evidence in support of the opinion. Like the Israelites in their primitive state, our government was conducted by our chiefs or judges, our wise men and elders; and the head of a family with us enjoyed a similar authority over his household, with that which is ascribed to Abraham and the other patriarchs. The law of retaliation obtained almost universally with us as with them: and even their religion appeared to have shed upon us a ray of its glory, though broken and spent in its passage, or eclipsed by the cloud with which time, tradition, and ignorance might have enveloped it; for we had our circumcision (a rule, I believe, peculiar to that people), we had also our sacrifices and burnt-offerings, our washings and purifications, and on the same occasions as they did.

As to the difference of color between the Eboan Africans and the modern Jews, I shall not presume to account for it. It is a subject which has engaged the pens of men of both genius and learning, and is far above my strength. The most able and Reverend Mr. T. Clarkson, however, in his much admired *Essay on the Slavery and Commerce of the Human Species*,[21] has ascertained the cause in a manner that at once solves every objection on that account, and, on my mind at least, has produced the fullest conviction. I shall therefore refer to that performance for the theory,[22] contenting myself with extracting a fact as related by Dr. Mitchel.[23] "The Spaniards, who have inhabited America, under the torrid zone, for any time, are become as dark colored as our native Indians of Virginia; of which *I myself have been a witness*." There is also another instance[24] of a Portuguese settlement at Mitomba, a river in Sierra Leone, where the inhabitants are bred from a mixture of the first Portuguese discoverers with the natives, and are now become in their complexion, and in the woolly quality of their hair, *perfect Negroes*, retaining however a smattering of the Portuguese language.[25]

These instances, and a great many more which might be adduced, while they show how the complexions of the same persons vary in different climates, it is hoped may tend also to remove the prejudice that some conceive against the natives of

Africa on account of their color. Surely the minds of the Spaniards did not change with their complexions! Are there not causes enough to which the apparent inferiority of an African may be ascribed, without limiting the goodness of God, and supposing he forebore to stamp understanding on certainly his own image, because "carved in ebony." Might it not naturally be ascribed to their situation? When they come among Europeans, they are ignorant of their language, religion, manners, and customs. Are any pains taken to teach them these? Are they treated as men? Does not slavery itself depress the mind, and extinguish all its fire and every noble sentiment? But, above all, what advantages do not a refined people possess, over those who are rude and uncultivated? Let the polished and haughty European recollect that his ancestors were once, like the Africans, uncivilized, and even barbarous. Did Nature make *them* inferior to their sons? and should *they too* have been made slaves? Every rational mind answers, No. Let such reflections as these melt the pride of their superiority into sympathy for the wants and miseries of their sable brethren, and compel them to acknowledge that understanding is not confined to feature or color. If, when they look round the world, they feel exultation, let it be tempered with benevolence to others, and gratitude to God, "who hath made of one blood all nations of men for to dwell on all the face of the earth";[26] "and whose wisdom is not our wisdom, neither are our ways his ways."

[. . .]

II

The author is carried to Virginia – His distress – Surprise at seeing a picture and a watch – Is bought by Captain Pascal, and sets out for England – His terror during the voyage.

I now totally lost the small remains of comfort I had enjoyed in conversing with my countrymen; the women too, who used to wash and take care of me were all gone different ways, and I never saw one of them afterwards.

I stayed in this island for a few days, I believe it could not be above a fortnight, when I, and some few more slaves that were not saleable amongst the rest, from very much fretting, were shipped off in a sloop for North America. On the passage we were better treated than when we were coming from Africa, and we had plenty of rice and fat pork. We were landed up a river a good way from the sea, about Virginia county, where we saw few or none of our native Africans, and not one soul who could talk to me. I was a few weeks weeding grass and gathering stones in a plantation; and at last all my companions were distributed different ways, and only myself was left. I was now exceedingly miserable, and thought myself worse off than any of the rest of my companions, for they could talk to each other, but I had no person to speak to that I could understand. In this state, I was constantly grieving and pining, and wishing for death rather than anything else.

While I was in this plantation, the gentleman, to whom I suppose the estate belonged, being unwell, I was one day sent for to his dwelling-house to fan him; when I came into the room where he was I was very much affrighted at some things I saw, and the more so as I had seen a black woman slave as I came through the house, who was cooking the dinner, and the poor creature was cruelly loaded with various kinds of iron machines; she had one particularly on her head, which locked her mouth so fast that she could scarcely speak; and could not eat nor drink. I was much astonished and shocked at this contrivance, which I afterwards learned was called the iron muzzle. Soon after I had a fan put in my hand, to fan the gentleman while he slept; and so I did indeed with great fear. While he was fast asleep I indulged myself a great deal in looking about the room, which to me appeared very fine and curious.

The first object that engaged my attention was a watch which hung on the chimney, and was going. I was quite surprised at the noise it made, and was afraid it would tell the gentleman anything I might do amiss; and when I immediately after observed a picture hanging in the room, which appeared constantly to look at me, I was still more affrighted, having never seen such things as these before. At one time I thought it was something relative to magic; and not seeing it move, I thought it might be some way the whites had to keep their great men when they died, and offer them libations as we used to do our friendly spirits. In this state of anxiety I remained till my master awoke, when I was dismissed out of the room, to my no small satisfaction and relief; for I thought that these people were all made up of wonders.

In this place I was called Jacob; but on board the *African Snow*, I was called Michael. I had been some time in this miserable, forlorn, and much dejected state, without having anyone to talk to, which made my life a burden, when the kind and unknown hand of the Creator (who in every deed leads the blind in a way they know not) now began to appear, to my comfort; for one day the captain of a merchant ship, called the *Industrious Bee*, came on some business to my master's house. This gentleman, whose name was Michael Henry Pascal, was a lieutenant in the Royal Navy, but now commanded this trading ship, which was somewhere in the confines of the county many miles off. While he was at my master's house, it happened that he saw me, and liked me so well that he made a purchase of me. I think I have often heard him say he gave thirty or forty pounds sterling for me; but I do not remember which. However, he meant me for a present to some of his friends in England: and as I was sent accordingly from the house of my then master (one Mr. Campbell) to the place where the ship lay; I was conducted on horseback by an elderly black man (a mode of travelling which appeared very odd to me). When I arrived I was carried on board a fine large ship, loaded with tobacco, &c., and just ready to sail for England.

I now thought my condition much mended; I had sails to lie on, and plenty of good victuals to eat; and everybody on board used me very kindly, quite contrary to what I had seen of any white people before; I therefore began to think that they were not all of the same disposition. A few days after I was on board we sailed for England. I was still at a loss to conjecture my destiny. By this time, however, I could smatter a little imperfect English; and I wanted to know as well as I could where we were going. Some of the people of the ship used to tell me they were going to carry me back to my own country, and this made me very happy. I was quite rejoiced at the idea of going back, and thought if I could get home what wonders I should have to tell. But I was reserved for another fate, and was soon undeceived when we came within sight of the English coast.

While I was on board this ship, my captain and master named me *Gustavus Vassa*.[27] I at that time began to understand him a little, and refused to be called so, and told him as well as I could that I would be called Jacob; but he said I should not, and still called me Gustavus: and when I refused to answer to my new name, which I at first did, it gained me many a cuff; so at length I submitted, and by which I have been known ever since.

The ship had a very long passage; and on that account we had very short allowance of provisions. Towards the last, we had only one pound and a half of bread per week, and about the same quantity of meat, and one quart of water a day. We spoke with only one vessel the whole time we were at sea, and but once we caught a few fishes. In our extremities the captain and people told me in jest they would kill and eat me; but I thought them in earnest, and was depressed beyond measure, expecting every moment to be my last. While I was in this situation, one evening they caught, with a good deal of trouble, a large shark, and got it on board. This gladdened my poor heart exceedingly, as I thought it would serve the people to eat instead of their eating me; but very soon, to my astonishment, they cut off a small part of the tail, and tossed the rest over the side. This renewed my consternation; and I did not know what to think of these white people, though I very much feared they would kill and eat me.

Notes

1 The kingdom of Benin, with its capital in the city of Benin, extended from the Niger delta to the city of Lagos.

2 The equator.

3 The Ibo phrase *igbu ichi* refers to this scarring of the face, and *mgburichi*, which Equiano renders as *Embrenche*, means "men who bear such scars." Both derive from *ichi*, "to crown" (Catherine Obianuju Acholonu, *The Igbo Roots of Olaudah Equiano: An Anthropological Research* (Owerri, Nigeria: Afa Publications, 1989), 10–12, 29–30).

4 See Benezet's "Account of Guinea," throughout. [Equiano's note.] Anthony Benezet (1713–1784), a Philadelphia Quaker, wrote *Some Historical Account of Guinea: Its situation, produce, and the general disposition of its inhabitants with an inquiry into the rise and progress of the Slave Trade its nature and lamentable effects* (1771) and other antislavery tracts.

5 When I was in Smyrna I have frequently seen the Greeks dance after this manner. [Equiano's note.]

6 The bowl is earthen, curiously figured, to which a long reed is fixed as a tube. This tube is sometimes so long as to be borne by one, and frequently out of grandeur, two boys. [Equiano's note.]

7 Probably eddo, or cocoa yam.

8   When I was in Smyrna I saw the same kind of earth, and brought some of it with me to England; it resembles musk in strength, but is more delicious in scent, and is not unlike the smell of a rose. [Equiano's note.]

9   Camwood, or *uhie*, was ground to a powder, mixed with oil, then spread on the skin; the *uhiguihi* is a fruit resembling a piece of wood that produces a fragrance when burned (Acholonu, *Igbo Roots*, 21).

10 Farming.

11 *Oyibo* is "light-colored person." Acholonu suggests that these may have been Aro people, a mahogany-colored people from south of Isseke. Those from Arochukwu were involved in the slave trade, exchanging their captives for guns, gunpowder, and other European goods (Acholonu, *Igbo Roots*, 14).

12 To trick or trap.

13 Ibo or Igbo.

14 Lack of self-restraint, especially related to sexual appetites.

15 See Benezet's "Account of Guinea," throughout. [Equiano's note.]

16 *Ola*, or ring, is a symbol of good fortune to the Ibo. *Ude* means "pleasing sound" (Acholonu, *Igbo Roots*, 42–3).

17 *Ofo-nwanchi* were traveling men who calculated the years. Often dwarfs, they were sometimes called *afo-nwa-ika*, or "funny monkeys," by children in the villages they visited. Local priests were *nze nzu* (Acholonu, *Igbo Roots*, 18–19).

18 See also Lieutenant Matthew's Voyage, p. 123. [Equiano's note.] John Matthews, *A Voyage to the River Sierra Leone . . . with a Letter on the . . . African Slave Trade* (London, 1788).

19 An instance of this kind happened at Montserrat, in the West Indies, in the year 1763. I then belonged to the *Charming Sally*, Capt. Doran. The chief mate, Mr. Mansfield, and some of the crew being one day on shore, were present at the burying of a poisoned Negro girl. Though they had often heard of the circumstance of the running in such cases, and had even seen it, they imagined it to be a trick of the corpse bearers. The mate therefore desired two of the sailors to take up the coffin, and carry it to the grave. The sailors, who were all of the same opinion, readily obeyed, but they had scarcely raised it to their shoulders before they began to run furiously about, quite unable to direct themselves, till at last, without intention, they came to the hut of him who had poisoned the girl. The coffin then immediately fell from their shoulders against the hut, and damaged part of the wall. The owner of the hut was taken into custody on this, and confessed the poisoning. I give this story as it was related by the mate and crew on their return to the ship. The credit which is due to it, I leave with the reader. [Equiano's note.]

20 Dr. John Gill (1697–1771), a Baptist divine, published his multivolume *Exposition of the Holy Scriptures* in 1766. John Clarke's *Truth of the Christian Religion, in Six Books* (1711) is a translation of Hugo Grotius (1583–1645), *De veritatus religionis christianae* (1627).

21 Thomas Clarkson, *Essay on the Slavery and Commerce of the Human Species, Particularly the African* (London, 1786). Clarkson (1760–1846) wrote this essay for an academic competition at Cambridge in 1785. He won the contest and became a lifelong abolitionist. His documentation of the horrors of the slave trade became a foundation for antislavery activity. His brother John, a Royal Navy officer, helped to found the Sierra Leone colony.

22 Pages 178 to 216. [Equiano's note.]

23 Philos. Trans. No. 476, Sec. 4, cited by Mr. Clarkson, p. 205. [Equiano's note.] John Mitchell, "An Essay upon the Causes of the Different Colours of People in Different Climates," *Philosophical Transactions of the Royal Society* 43 (1746).

24 Same page. [Equiano's note.]

25 The Portuguese established a trading post at Mitombe, Sierra Leone, in the 1460s.

26 Acts 17: 26. [Equiano's note.]

27 Gustavus Ericksson Vasa, a Swedish nobleman, led a successful revolt against Danish rule in the 1520s; as Gustavus I he ruled Sweden from 1523 to 1560. At the time of Equiano's capture Henry Brooke's *Gustavus Vasa, the Deliverer of His Country* was a popular English play.

5

A History of New York

Washington Irving

Introduction

Washington Irving (1783–1859) is best known for his collection of short stories, *The Sketch-Book of Geoffrey Crayon, Gent.* (1820). *The History of New York*, published in 1809, is a satiric work grounded in historical research but written to challenge the nationalism of the early United States. In this selection, the criticism of nationalism combines with a critique of totalizing philosophical perspectives.

I

Description of the world.

According to the best authorities, the world in which we dwell is a huge, opaque, reflecting, inanimate mass, floating in the vast ethereal ocean of infinite space. It has the form of an orange, being an oblate spheroid, curiously flattened at opposite parts, for the insertion of two imaginary poles, which are supposed to penetrate and unite at the centre; thus forming an axis on which the mighty orange turns with a regular diurnal revolution.

The transitions of light and darkness, whence proceed the alternations of day and night, are produced by this diurnal revolution successively

Taken from *A History of the World* (1809), bk I, chs 1–4; republished in *The Complete Works of Washington Irving*, vol. VII (Boston: Twayne Publishers, 1984), pp. 21–40.

presenting the different parts of the earth to the rays of the sun. The latter is, according to the best, that is to say, the latest accounts, a luminous or fiery body, of a prodigious magnitude, from which this world is driven by a centrifugal or repelling power, and to which it is drawn by a centripetal or attractive force; otherwise called the attraction of gravitation; the combination, or rather the counteraction of these two opposing impulses producing a circular and annual revolution. Hence result the different seasons of the year, viz., spring, summer, autumn and winter.

This I believe to be the most approved modern theory on the subject – though there be many philosophers who have entertained very different opinions; some, too, of them entitled to much deference from their great antiquity and illustrious characters. Thus it was advanced by some of the ancient sages, that the earth was an extended plain, supported by vast pillars; and by others, that it rested on the head of a snake, or the back of a huge tortoise – but as they did not provide a resting place for either the pillars or the tortoise, the whole theory fell to the ground, for want of proper foundation.

The Brahmins assert, that the heavens rest upon the earth, and the sun and moon swim therein like fishes in the water, moving from east to west by day, and gliding along the edge of the horizon to their original stations during the night; while, according to the Pauranicas of India, it is a vast plain, encircled by seven oceans of milk, nectar and other delicious liquids; that it is studded with seven mountains, and ornamented in the centre by a mountainous rock of burnished gold; and that a great dragon occasionally swallows up the moon, which accounts for the phenomena of lunar eclipses.

Beside these, and many other equally sage opinions, we have the profound conjectures of ABOUL-HASSAN-ALY, son of Al Khan, son of Aly, son of Abderrahman, son of Abdallah, son of Masoudel-Hadheli, who is commonly called MASOUDI, and surnamed Cothbeddin, but who takes the humble title of Laheb-ar-rasoul, which means the companion of the ambassador of God. He has written a universal history, entitled "Mouroudge-ed-dharab, or the Golden Meadows, and the Mines of Precious Stones." In this valuable work he has related the history of the world, from the creation down to the moment of writing; which was under the Khaliphat of Mothi Billah, in the month Dgioumadi-el-aoual of the 336th year of the Hegira or flight of the Prophet. He informs us that the earth is a huge bird, Mecca and Medina constituting the head, Persia and India the right wing, the land of Gog the left wing, and Africa the tail. He informs us, moreover, that an earth has existed before the present (which he considers as a mere chicken of 7,000 years), that it has undergone divers deluges, and that, according to the opinion of some well-informed Brahmins of his acquaintance, it will be renovated every seventy thousandth hazarouam; each hazarouam consisting of 12,000 years.

These are a few of the many contradictory opinions of philosophers concerning the earth, and we find that the learned have had equal perplexity as to the nature of the sun. Some of the ancient philosophers have affirmed that it is a vast wheel of brilliant fire; others that it is merely a mirror or sphere of transparent crystal; and a third class, at the head of whom stands Anaxagoras, maintained that it was nothing but a huge ignited mass of iron or stone – indeed, he declared the heavens to be merely a vault of stone – and that the stars were stones whirled upward from the earth, and set on fire by the velocity of its revolutions. But I give little attention to the doctrines of this philosopher, the people of Athens having fully refuted them, by banishing him from their city; a concise mode of answering unwelcome doctrines, much resorted to in former days. Another sect of philosophers do declare, that certain fiery particles exhale constantly from the earth, which, concentrating in a single point of the firmament by day, constitute the sun, but being scattered and rambling about in the dark at night, collect in various points, and

form stars. These are regularly burnt out and extinguished, not unlike to the lamps in our streets, and require a fresh supply of exhalations for the next occasion.

It is even recorded, that at certain remote and obscure periods, in consequence of a great scarcity of fuel, the sun has been completely burnt out, and sometimes not rekindled for a month at a time. A most melancholy circumstance, the very idea of which gave vast concern to Heraclitus, that worthy weeping philosopher of antiquity. In addition to these various speculations, it was the opinion of Herschel, that the sun is a magnificent, habitable abode; the light it furnishes arising from certain empyreal, luminous or phosphoric clouds, swimming in its transparent atmosphere.

But we will not enter farther at present into the nature of the sun, that being an inquiry not immediately necessary to the development of this history; neither will we embroil ourselves in any more of the endless disputes of philosophers touching the form of this globe, but content ourselves with the theory advanced in the beginning of this chapter, and will proceed to illustrate, by experiment, the complexity of motion therein ascribed to this our rotatory planet.

Professor Von Poddingcoft (or Puddinghead, as the name may be rendered into English) was long celebrated in the university of Leyden, for profound gravity of deportment, and a talent at going to sleep in the midst of examinations, to the infinite relief of his hopeful students, who thereby worked their way through college with great ease and little study. In the course of one of his lectures, the learned professor, seizing a bucket of water, swung it around his head at arm's length. The impulse with which he threw the vessel from him, being a centrifugal force, the retention of his arm operating as a centripetal power, and the bucket, which was a substitute for the earth, describing a circular orbit round about the globular head and ruby visage of Professor Von Poddingcoft, which formed no bad representation of the sun. All of these particulars were duly explained to the class of gaping students around him. He apprised them, moreover, that the same principle of gravitation, which retained the water in the bucket, restrains the ocean from flying from the earth in its rapid revolutions; and he farther informed them that should the motion of the earth be suddenly checked, it would incontinently fall into the sun, through the centripetal force of gravitation; a most ruinous event to this planet, and one which would also obscure, though it most probably would not extinguish, the solar luminary. An unlucky stripling, one of those vagrant geniuses, who seem sent into the world merely to annoy worthy men of the puddinghead order, desirous of ascertaining the correctness of the experiment, suddenly arrested the arm of the professor, just at the moment that the bucket was in its zenith, which immediately descended with astonishing precision upon the philosophic head of the instructor of youth. A hollow sound, and a red-hot hiss, attended the contact; but the theory was in the amplest manner illustrated, for the unfortunate bucket perished in the conflict; but the blazing countenance of Professor Von Poddingcoft emerged from amidst the waters, glowing fiercer than ever with unutterable indignation, whereby the students were marvellously edified, and departed considerably wiser than before.

It is a mortifying circumstance, which greatly perplexes many a painstaking philosopher, that nature often refuses to second his most profound and elaborate efforts; so that after having invented one of the most ingenious and natural theories imaginable, she will have the perverseness to act directly in the teeth of his system, and flatly contradict his most favorite positions. This is a manifest and unmerited grievance, since it throws the censure of the vulgar and unlearned entirely upon the philosopher; whereas the fault is not to be ascribed to his theory, which is unquestionably correct, but to the waywardness of dame Nature, who, with the proverbial fickleness of her sex, is continually indulging in coquetries and caprices, and seems really to take pleasure in violating all philosophic rules, and jilting the most learned and indefatigable of her adorers. Thus it happened with respect to the foregoing satisfactory explanation of the motion of our planet; it appears that the centrifugal force has long since ceased to operate, while its antagonist remains in undiminished potency: the world, therefore, according to the theory as it originally stood, ought in strict propriety to tumble into the sun; philosophers were convinced that it would do so, and awaited in anxious impatience the fulfillment of their prognostics. But the untoward planet pertinaciously continued her course, notwithstanding that she had reason, philosophy and a whole university of learned professors opposed to her conduct. The philosophers took this in very ill part, and it is thought they would never have pardoned the slight and affront which they conceived put upon them by the world, had not a good-natured professor kindly officiated as a mediator between the parties, and effected a reconciliation.

Finding the world would not accommodate itself to the theory, he wisely determined to accommodate the theory to the world: he therefore informed his brother philosophers, that the circular motion of the earth round the sun was no sooner engendered by the conflicting impulses above described, than it became a regular revolution, independent of the causes which gave it origin. His learned brethren readily joined in the opinion, being heartily glad of any explanation that would decently extricate them from their embarrassment – and ever since that memorable era the world has been left to take her own course, and to revolve around the sun in such orbit as she thinks proper.

II

Cosmogony, or creation of the world; with a multitude of excellent theories, by which the creation of a world is shown to be no such difficult matter as common folk would imagine.

Having thus briefly introduced my reader to the world, and given him some idea of its form and situation, he will naturally be curious to know from whence it came, and how it was created. And, indeed, the clearing up of these points is absolutely essential to my history, inasmuch as if this world had not been formed, it is more than probable, that this renowned island on which is situated the city of New York, would never have had an existence. The regular course of my history, therefore, requires that I should proceed to notice the cosmogony or formation of this our globe.

And now I give my readers fair warning, that I am about to plunge, for a chapter or two, into as complete a labyrinth as ever historian was perplexed withal: therefore, I advise them to take fast hold of my skirts, and keep close at my heels, venturing neither to the right hand nor to the left, lest they get bemired in a slough of unintelligible learning, or have their brains knocked out by some of those hard Greek names which will be flying about in all directions. But should any of them be too indolent or chicken-hearted to accompany me in this perilous undertaking, they had better take a short cut round, and wait for me at the beginning of some smoother chapter.

Of the creation of the world, we have a thousand contradictory accounts; and though a very satisfactory one is furnished us by divine revelation, yet every philosopher feels himself in honor bound to furnish us with a better. As an impartial historian, I consider it my duty to notice their several theories, by which mankind have been so exceedingly edified and instructed.

Thus it was the opinion of certain ancient sages, that the earth and the whole system of the universe was the Deity himself; a doctrine most strenuously maintained by Xenophanes and the whole tribe of Eleatics, as also by Strato and the sect of peripatetic philosophers. Pythagoras likewise inculcated the famous numerical system of the monad, dyad and triad, and by means of his sacred quaternary elucidated the formation of the world, the arcana of nature and the principles both of music and morals. Other sages adhered to the mathematical system of squares and triangles; the cube, the pyramid and the sphere; the tetrahedron, the octahedron, the icosahedron and dodecahedron. While others advocated the great elementary theory, which refers the construction of our globe and all that it contains, to the combinations of four material elements, air, earth, fire and water; with the assistance of a fifth, an immaterial and vivifying principle.

Nor must I omit to mention the great atomic system taught by old Moschus, before the siege of Troy; revived by Democritus of laughing memory; improved by Epicurus, that king of good fellows, and modernized by the fanciful Descartes. But I decline inquiring, whether the atoms, of which the earth is said to be composed, are eternal or recent; whether they are animate or inanimate; whether, agreeably to the opinion of the atheists, they were fortuitously aggregated, or, as the theists maintain, were arranged by a supreme intelligence. Whether, in fact, the earth be an insensate clod, or whether it be animated by a soul; which opinion was strenuously maintained by a host of philosophers, at the head of whom stands the great Plato, that temperate sage, who threw the cold water of philosophy on the form of sexual intercourse, and inculcated the doctrine of Platonic love – an exquisitely refined intercourse, but much better adapted to the ideal inhabitants of his imaginary island of Atlantis than to the sturdy race, composed of rebellious flesh and blood, which populates the little matter of fact island we inhabit.

Beside these systems, we have, moreover, the poetical theogony of old Hesiod, who generated the whole universe in the regular mode of procreation, and the plausible opinion of others, that the earth was hatched from the great egg of night, which floated in chaos, and was cracked by the horns of the celestial bull. To illustrate this last doctrine, Burnet in his theory of the earth, has favored us with an accurate drawing and description, both of the form and texture of this mundane egg; which is found to bear a marvellous resemblance to that of a goose. Such of my readers as take a proper interest in the origin of this our planet, will be pleased to learn, that the most profound sages of antiquity, among the Egyptians, Chaldeans, Persians, Greeks and Latins, have alternately assisted at the hatching of this strange bird, and that their cacklings have been caught, and continued in different tones and inflections, from philosopher to philosopher, unto the present day.

But while briefly noticing long-celebrated systems of ancient sages, let me not pass over with neglect those of other philosophers; which, though less universal and renowned, have equal claims to attention, and equal chance for correctness. Thus it is recorded by the Brahmins, in the pages of their inspired Shastah, that the angel Bistnoo, transforming himself into a great boar, plunged into the watery abyss, and brought up the earth on his tusks. Then issued from him a mighty tortoise, and a mighty snake; and Bistnoo placed the snake erect upon the back of the tortoise, and he placed the earth upon the head of the snake.

The negro philosophers of Congo affirm that the world was made by the hands of angels, excepting their own country, which the Supreme Being constructed himself, that it might be supremely excellent. And he took great pains with the inhabitants, and made them very black, and beautiful; and when he had finished the first man, he was well pleased with him, and smoothed him over the face, and hence his nose, and the nose of all his descendants, became flat.

The Mohawk philosophers tell us, that a pregnant woman fell down from heaven, and that a tortoise took her upon its back, because every place was covered with water; and that the woman, sitting upon the tortoise, paddled with her hands in the water, and raked up the earth, whence it finally happened that the earth became higher than the water.

But I forbear to quote a number more of these ancient and outlandish philosophers, whose deplorable ignorance, in despite of all their erudition, compelled them to write in languages which but few of my readers can understand; and I shall proceed briefly to notice a few more intelligible and fashionable theories of their modern successors.

And, first, I shall mention the great Buffon, who conjectures that this globe was originally a globe of liquid fire, scintillated from the body of the sun, by the percussion of a comet, as a spark is generated by the collision of flint and steel. That at first it was surrounded by gross vapors, which, cooling and condensing in process of time, constituted, according to their densities, earth, water and air; which gradually arranged themselves, according to their respective gravities, round the burning or vitrified mass that formed their centre.

Hutton, on the contrary, supposes that the waters at first were universally paramount; and he terrifies himself with the idea that the earth must be eventually washed away by the force of rain, rivers and mountain torrents, until it is confounded with the ocean, or, in other words, absolutely dissolves into itself. – Sublime idea! far surpassing that of the tender-hearted damsel of antiquity, who wept herself into a fountain; or the good dame of Narbonne in France, who, for a volubility of tongue unusual in her sex, was doomed to peel five hundred thousand and thirty-nine ropes of onions, and actually run out at her eyes before half the hideous task was accomplished.

Whiston, the same ingenious philosopher who rivaled Ditton in his researches after the longitude (for which the mischief-loving Swift discharged on their heads a most savory stanza), has distinguished himself by a very admirable theory respecting the earth. He conjectures that it was originally a *chaotic comet*, which being selected for the abode of man, was removed from its eccentric orbit, and whirled round the sun in its present regular motion; by which change of direction, order succeeded to confusion in the arrangement of its component parts. The philosopher adds, that the deluge was produced by an uncourteous salute from the watery tail of another comet; doubtless through sheer envy of its improved condition: thus furnishing a melancholy proof that jealousy may prevail, even among the heavenly bodies, and discord interrupt that celestial harmony of the spheres, so melodiously sung by the poets.

But I pass over a variety of excellent theories, among which are those of Burnet, and Woodward,

and Whitehurst; regretting extremely that my time will not suffer me to give them the notice they deserve – and shall conclude with that of the renowned Dr. Darwin. This learned Theban, who is as much distinguished for rhyme as reason, and for good-natured credulity as serious research, and who has recommended himself wonderfully to the good graces of the ladies, by letting them into all the gallantries, amours, debaucheries and other topics of scandal of the court of Flora, has fallen upon a theory worthy of his combustible imagination. According to his opinion, the huge mass of chaos took a sudden occasion to explode, like a barrel of gunpowder, and in that act exploded the sun – which in its flight, by a similar convulsion, exploded the earth – which in like guise exploded the moon – and thus by a concatenation of explosions, the whole solar system was produced, and set most systematically in motion!

By the great variety of theories here alluded to, every one of which, if thoroughly examined, will be found surprisingly consistent in all its parts, my unlearned readers will perhaps be led to conclude, that the creation of a world is not so difficult a task as they at first imagined. I have shown at least a score of ingenious methods in which a world could be constructed; and I have no doubt, that had any of the philosophers above quoted the use of a good manageable comet, and the philosophical warehouse *chaos* at his command, he would engage to manufacture a planet as good, or, if you would take his word for it, better than this we inhabit.

And here I cannot help noticing the kindness of Providence, in creating comets for the great relief of bewildered philosophers. By their assistance more sudden evolutions and transitions are effected in the system of nature than are wrought in a pantomimic exhibition, by the wonder-working sword of Harlequin. Should one of our modern sages, in his theoretical flights among the stars, ever find himself lost in the clouds, and in danger of tumbling into the abyss of nonsense and absurdity, he has but to seize a comet by the beard, mount astride of its tail and away he gallops in triumph, like an enchanter on his hyppogriff, or a Connecticut witch on her broomstick, "to sweep the cobwebs out of the sky."

It is an old and vulgar saying about a "beggar on horseback," which I would not for the world have applied to these reverend philosophers: but I must confess, that some of them, when they are mounted on one of those fiery steeds, are as wild in their curvetings as was Phaeton of yore, when he aspired to manage the chariot of Phœbus. One drives his comet at full speed against the sun, and knocks the world out of him with the mighty concussion; another, more moderate, makes his comet a kind of beast of burthen, carrying the sun a regular supply of food and fagots – a third, of more combustible disposition, threatens to throw his comet, like a bombshell, into the world, and blow it up like a powder magazine; while a fourth, with no great delicacy to this planet, and its inhabitants, insinuates that some day or other, his comet – my modest pen blushes while I write it – shall absolutely turn tail upon our world, and deluge it with water! – Surely, as I have already observed, comets were bountifully provided by Providence for the benefit of philosophers, to assist them in manufacturing theories.

And now, having adduced several of the most prominent theories that occur to my recollection, I leave my judicious readers at full liberty to choose among them. They are all serious speculations of learned men – all differ essentially from each other – and all have the same title to belief. It has ever been the task of one race of philosophers to demolish the works of their predecessors, and elevate more splendid fantasies in their stead, which in their turn are demolished and replaced by the air castles of a succeeding generation. Thus it would seem that knowledge and genius, of which we make such great parade, consist but in detecting the errors and absurdities of those who have gone before, and devising new errors and absurdities, to be detected by those who are to come after us. Theories are the mighty soap bubbles with which the grown up children of science amuse themselves – while the honest vulgar stand gazing in stupid admiration, and dignify these learned vagaries with the name of wisdom! – Surely Socrates was right in his opinion, that philosophers are but a soberer sort of madmen, busying themselves in things totally incomprehensible, or which, if they could be comprehended, would be found not worthy the trouble of discovery.

For my own part, until the learned have come to an agreement among themselves, I shall content myself with the account handed down to us by Moses; in which I do but follow the example of our ingenious neighbors of Connecticut; who at their first settlement proclaimed, that the colony should be governed by the laws of God – until they had time to make better.

One thing, however, appears certain – from the unanimous authority of the before-quoted philosophers, supported by the evidence of our own senses (which, though very apt to deceive us, may be cautiously admitted as additional testimony), it appears, I say, and I make the assertion deliberately, without fear of contradiction, that this globe really *was created*, and that it is composed of *land and water*. It farther appears that it is curiously divided and parceled out into continents and islands, among which I boldly declare the renowned ISLAND OF NEW YORK will be found by any one who seeks for it in its proper place.

III

How that famous navigator, Noah, was shamefully nicknamed; and how he committed an unpardonable oversight in not having four sons; with the great trouble of philosophers caused thereby, and the discovery of America.

Noah, who is the first sea-faring man we read of, begat three sons, Shem, Ham and Japhet. Authors, it is true, are not wanting, who affirm that the patriarch had a number of other children. Thus Berosus makes him father of the gigantic Titans, Methodius gives him a son called Jonithus, or Jonicus, and others have mentioned a son, named Thuiscon, from whom descended the Teutons or Teutonic, or in other words, the Dutch nation.

I regret exceedingly that the nature of my plan will not permit me to gratify the laudable curiosity of my readers, by investigating minutely the history of the great Noah. Indeed, such an undertaking would be attended with more trouble than many people would imagine; for the good old patriarch seems to have been a great traveler in his day, and to have passed under a different name in every country that he visited. The Chaldeans, for instance, give us his story, merely altering his name into Xisuthrus – a trivial alteration, which, to an historian skilled in etymologies, will appear wholly unimportant. It appears, likewise, that he had exchanged his tarpawling and quadrant among the Chaldeans, for the gorgeous insignia of royalty, and appears as a monarch in their annals. The Egyptians celebrate him under the name of Osiris; the Indians as Menu; the Greek and Roman writers confound him with Ogyges, and the Theban with Deucalion and Saturn. But the Chinese, who deservedly rank among the most extensive and authentic historians, inasmuch as they have known the world much longer than any one else, declare that Noah was no other than Fohi; and what gives this assertion some air of credibility is, that it is a fact, admitted by the most enlightened literati, that Noah traveled into China, at the time of the building of the tower of Babel (probably to improve himself in the study of languages), and the learned Dr. Shackford gives us the additional information, that the ark rested on a mountain on the frontiers of China.

From this mass of rational conjectures and sage hypotheses, many satisfactory deductions might be drawn; but I shall content myself with the simple fact stated in the Bible, viz., that Noah begat three sons, Shem, Ham and Japhet. It is astonishing on what remote and obscure contingencies the great affairs of this world depend, and how events the most distant, and to the common observer unconnected, are inevitably consequent the one to the other. It remains to the philosopher to discover these mysterious affinities, and it is the proudest triumph of his skill, to detect and drag forth some latent chain of causation, which at first sight appears a paradox to the inexperienced observer. Thus many of my readers will doubtless wonder what connection the family of Noah can possibly have with this history – and many will stare when informed, that the whole history of this quarter of the world has taken its character and course from the simple circumstance of the patriarch's having but three sons – but to explain:

Noah, we are told by sundry very credible historians, becoming sole surviving heir and proprietor of the earth, in fee simple, after the deluge, like a good father, portioned out his estate among his children. To Shem he gave Asia; to Ham, Africa; and to Japhet, Europe. Now it is a thousand times to be lamented that he had but three sons, for had there been a fourth, he would doubtless have inherited America; which, of course, would have been dragged forth from its obscurity on the occasion; and thus many a hard-working historian and philosopher would have been spared a prodigious mass of weary conjecture respecting the first discovery and population of this country. Noah, however, having provided for his three sons, looked in all probability upon our country as mere wild unsettled land, and said nothing about it; and to this unpardonable taciturnity of the patriarch may we ascribe the misfortune, that America did not come into the world as early as the other quarters of the globe.

It is true, some writers have vindicated him from this misconduct towards posterity, and asserted that he really did discover America. Thus it was the opinion of Mark Lescarbot, a French writer, possessed of that ponderosity of thought, and profoundness of reflection, so peculiar to his nation, that the immediate descendants of Noah peopled this quarter of the globe, and that the old patriarch himself, who still retained a passion for the sea-faring life, superintended the transmigration. The pious and enlightened father, Charlevoix, a French Jesuit, remarkable for his aversion to the marvellous, common to all great travelers, is conclusively of the same opinion; nay, he goes still farther, and decides upon the manner in which the discovery was effected, which was by sea, and under the immediate direction of the great Noah. "I have already observed," exclaims the good father, in a tone of becoming indignation, "that it is an arbitrary supposition that the grandchildren of Noah were not able to penetrate into the new world, or that they never thought of it. In effect, I can see no reason that can justify such a notion. Who can seriously believe, that Noah and his immediate descendants knew less than we do, and that the builder and pilot of the greatest ship that ever was, a ship which was formed to traverse an unbounded ocean, and had so many shoals and quicksands to guard against, should be ignorant of, or should not have communicated to his descendants the art of sailing on the ocean?" Therefore, they did sail on the ocean – therefore, they sailed to America – therefore, America was discovered by Noah!

Now all this exquisite chain of reasoning, which is so strikingly characteristic of the good father, being addressed to the faith, rather than the understanding, is flatly opposed by Hans de Laet, who declares it a real and most ridiculous paradox, to suppose that Noah ever entertained the thought of discovering America; and as Hans is a Dutch writer, I am inclined to believe he must have been much better acquainted with the worthy crew of the ark than his competitors, and of course possessed of more accurate sources of information. It is astonishing how intimate historians do daily become with the patriarchs and other great men of antiquity. As intimacy improves with time, and as the learned are particularly inquisitive and familiar in their acquaintance with the ancients, I should not be surprised if some future writers should gravely give us a picture of men and manners as they existed before the flood, far more copious and accurate than the Bible; and that, in the course of another century, the log-book of the good Noah should be as current among historians, as the voyages of Captain Cook, or the renowned history of Robinson Crusoe.

I shall not occupy my time by discussing the huge mass of additional suppositions, conjectures and probabilities respecting the first discovery of this country, with which unhappy historians overload themselves, in their endeavors to satisfy the doubts of an incredulous world. It is painful to see these laborious wights panting, and toiling, and sweating under an enormous burthen, at the very outset of their works, which, on being opened, turns out to be nothing but a mighty bundle of straw. As, however, by unwearied assiduity, they seem to have established the fact, to the satisfaction of all the world, that this country *has been discovered*, I shall avail myself of their useful labors to be extremely brief upon this point.

I shall not, therefore, stop to inquire, whether America was first discovered by a wandering vessel of that celebrated Phœnician fleet, which, according to Herodotus, circumnavigated Africa; or by that Carthaginian expedition, which Pliny, the naturalist, informs us, discovered the Canary Islands; or whether it was settled by a temporary colony from Tyre, as hinted by Aristotle and Seneca. I shall neither inquire whether it was first discovered by the Chinese, as Vossius with great shrewdness advances; nor by the Norwegians in 1002, under Biorn; nor by Behem, the German navigator, as Mr. Otto has endeavored to prove to the savans of the learned city of Philadelphia.

Nor shall I investigate the more modern claims of the Welsh, founded on the voyage of Prince Madoc in the eleventh century, who having never returned, it has since been wisely concluded that he must have gone to America, and that for a plain reason – if he did not go there, where else could he have gone? – a question which most socratically shuts out all farther dispute.

Laying aside, therefore, all the conjectures above mentioned, with a multitude of others, equally satisfactory, I shall take for granted the vulgar opinion, that America was discovered on the 12th of October, 1492, by Christovallo Colon, a Genoese, who has been clumsily nicknamed Columbus, but for what reason I cannot discern. Of the voyages and adventures of this Colon, I shall say nothing, seeing that they are already sufficiently known. Nor shall I undertake to prove that this country should have been called Colonia, after his name, that being notoriously self-evident.

Having thus happily got my readers on this side of the Atlantic, I picture them to myself, all impatience to enter upon the enjoyment of the land of promise, and in full expectation that I will immediately deliver it into their possession. But if I do, may I ever forfeit the reputation of a regular bred historian! No – no – most curious and thrice learned readers (for thrice learned ye are if ye have read all that has gone before, and nine times learned shall ye be, if ye read that which comes after), we have yet a world of work before us. Think you the first discoverers of this fair quarter of the globe had nothing to do but go on shore and find a country ready laid out and cultivated like a garden, wherein they might revel at their ease? No such thing – they had forests to cut down, underwood to grub up, marshes to drain and savages to exterminate.

In like manner, I have sundry doubts to clear away, questions to resolve and paradoxes to explain, before I permit you to range at random; but these difficulties once overcome, we shall be enabled to jog on right merrily through the rest of our history. Thus my work shall, in a manner, echo the nature of the subject, in the same manner as the sound of poetry has been found by certain shrewd critics to echo the sense – this being an improvement in history, which I claim the merit of having invented.

IV

Showing the great difficulty philosophers have had in peopling America – And how the aborigines came to be begotten by accident – To the great relief and satisfaction of the author.

The next inquiry at which we arrive in the regular course of our history is to ascertain, if possible, how this country was originally peopled – a point fruitful of incredible embarrassments; for unless we prove that the Aborigines did absolutely come from somewhere, it will be immediately asserted in this age of skepticism that they did not come at all; and if they did not come at all, then was this country never populated – a conclusion perfectly agreeable to the rules of logic, but wholly irreconcilable to every feeling of humanity, inasmuch as it must syllogistically prove fatal to the innumerable Aborigines of this populous region.

To avert so dire a sophism, and to rescue from logical annihilation so many millions of fellow creatures, how many wings of geese have been plundered! what oceans of ink have been benevolently drained! and how many capacious heads of learned historians have been addled, and for ever confounded! I pause with reverential awe, when I contemplate the ponderous tomes, in different languages, with which they have endeavored to solve this question, so important to the happiness of society, but so involved in clouds of impenetrable obscurity. Historian after historian has engaged in the endless circle of hypothetical argument, and after leading us a weary chase through octavos, quartos and folios, has let us out at the end of his work just as wise as we were at the beginning. It was doubtless some philosophical wild-goose chase of the kind that made the old poet Macrobius rail in such a passion at curiosity, which he anathematizes most heartily, as "an irksome agonizing care, a superstitious industry about unprofitable things, an itching humour to see what is not to be seen, and to be doing what signifies nothing when it is done." But to proceed:

Of the claims of the children of Noah to the original population of this country I shall say nothing, as they have already been touched upon in my last chapter. The claimants next in celebrity, are the descendants of Abraham. Thus Christovallo Colon (vulgarly called Columbus) when he first discovered the gold mines of Hispaniola, immediately concluded, with a shrewdness that would have done honor to a philosopher, that he had found the ancient Ophir, from whence Solomon procured the gold for embellishing the temple at Jerusalem; nay, Colon even imagined that he saw the remains of furnaces of veritable Hebraic construction, employed in refining the precious ore.

So golden a conjecture, tinctured with such fascinating extravagance, was too tempting not to be immediately snapped at by the gudgeons of learning; and accordingly, there were divers profound writers, ready to swear to its correctness, and to bring in their usual load of authorities, and wise surmises, wherewithal to prop it up. Vetablus and Robertus Stephens declared nothing could be more clear – Arius Montanus, without the least hesitation, asserts that Mexico was the true Ophir, and the Jews the early settlers of the country. While Possevin, Becan and several other sagacious writers, lug in a *supposed* prophecy of the fourth book of Esdras, which being inserted in the mighty hypothesis, like the keystone of an arch, gives it, in their opinion, perpetual durability.

Scarce, however, have they completed their goodly superstructure, than in trudges a phalanx of opposite authors, with Hans de Laet, the great Dutchman, at their head, and at one blow tumbles the whole fabric about their ears. Hans, in fact, contradicts outright all the Israelitish claims to the first settlement of this country, attributing all those equivocal symptoms, and traces of Christianity and Judaism, which have been said to be found in divers provinces of the new world, to the *Devil*, who has always affected to counterfeit the worship of the true Deity. "A remark," says the knowing old Padre d'Acosta, "made by all good authors who have spoken of the religion of nations newly discovered, and founded besides on the authority of the *fathers of the church*."

Some writers again, among whom it is with much regret I am compelled to mention Lopez de Gomara, and Juan de Leri, insinuate that the Canaanites, being driven from the land of promise by the Jews, were seized with such a panic that they fled without looking behind them, until stopping to take breath, they found themselves safe in America. As they brought neither their national language, manners nor features with them, it is supposed they left them behind in the hurry of their flight – I cannot give my faith to this opinion.

I pass over the supposition of the learned Grotius, who being both an ambassador and a Dutchman to boot, is entitled to great respect; that North America was peopled by a strolling company of Norwegians, and that Peru was founded by a colony from China – Manco or Mango Capac, the first Incas, being himself a Chinese. Nor shall I more than barely mention, that father Kircher ascribes the settlement of America to the Egyptians, Rudbeck to the Scandinavians, Charron to the Gauls, Juffredus Petri to a skating party from Friesland, Milius to the Celtæ, Marinocus the Sicilian to the Romans, Le Compte to the Phœnicians, Postel to the Moors, Martyn d'Angleria to the Abyssinians, together with the sage surmise of De Laet, that England, Ireland and the Orcades may contend for that honor.

Nor will I bestow any more attention or credit to the idea that America is the fairy region of Zipangri, described by that dreaming traveler, Marco Polo, the Venetian; or that it comprises the visionary island of Atlantis, described by Plato. Neither will I stop to investigate the heathenish assertion of Paracelsus, that each hemisphere of the globe was originally furnished with an Adam and Eve. Or the more flattering opinion of Dr. Romayne, supported by many nameless authorities, that Adam was of the Indian race – or the startling conjecture of Buffon, Helvetius and Darwin, so highly honorable to mankind, that the whole human species is accidentally descended from a remarkable family of monkeys!

This last conjecture, I must own, came upon me very suddenly and very ungraciously. I have often beheld the clown in a pantomime, while gazing in stupid wonder at the extravagant gambols of a harlequin, all at once electrified by a sudden stroke of the wooden sword across his shoulders. Little did I think at such times, that it would ever fall to my lot to be treated with equal discourtesy, and that while I was quietly beholding these grave philosophers, emulating the eccentric transformations of the hero of pantomime, they would on a sudden turn upon me and my readers, and with one hypothetical flourish metamorphose us into beasts! I determined from that moment not to burn my fingers with any more of their theories, but content myself with detailing the different methods by which they transported the descendants of these ancient and respectable monkeys to this great field of theoretical warfare.

This was done either by migrations by land or transmigrations by water. Thus Padre Joseph D'Acosta enumerates three passages by land – first by the north of Europe, secondly by the north of Asia and thirdly by regions southward of the Straits of Magellan. The learned Grotius marches his Norwegians by a pleasant route across frozen rivers and arms of the sea, through Iceland, Greenland, Estotiland and Naremberga: and various writers, among whom are Angleria, De Hornn and Buffon, anxious for the accommodation of these travelers, have fastened the two continents together by a strong chain of deductions – by which means they could pass over dry-shod. But should even this fail, Pinkerton, that industrious old gentleman, who compiles books, and manufactures geographies, has constructed a natural bridge of ice, from continent to continent, at the distance of four or five miles from Behring's Straits – for which he is entitled to the grateful thanks of all the wandering aborigines who ever did or ever will pass over it.

It is an evil much to be lamented, that none of the worthy writers above quoted could ever commence his work, without immediately declaring hostilities against every writer who had treated of the same subject. In this particular, authors may be compared to a certain sagacious bird, which in building its nest, is sure to pull to pieces the nests of all the birds in its neighborhood. This unhappy propensity tends grievously to impede the progress of sound knowledge. Theories are at best but brittle productions, and when once committed to the stream, they should take care that like the notable pots which were fellow-voyagers, they do not crack each other.

My chief surprise is, that among the many writers I have noticed, no one has attempted to prove that this country was peopled from the moon – or that the first inhabitants floated hither on islands of ice, as white bears cruise about the northern oceans – or that they were conveyed hither by balloons, as modern aeronauts pass from Dover to Calais – or by witchcraft, as Simon Magus posted among the stars – or after the manner of the renowned Scythian Abaris, who, like the New England witches on full-blooded broomsticks, made most unheard-of journeys on the back of a golden arrow, given him by the Hyperborean Apollo.

But there is still one mode left by which this country could have been peopled, which I have reserved for the last, because I consider it worth all the rest: it is – *by accident!* Speaking of the islands of Solomon, New Guinea and New Holland, the profound father Charlevoix observes, "in fine, all these countries are peopled, and *it is possible,* some have been so *by accident.* Now if it could have happened in that manner, why might it not have been at the *same time,* and by the *same means,* with *the other* parts of the globe?" This ingenious mode of deducing certain conclusions from possible premises, is an improvement in syllogistic skill, and proves the good father superior even to Archimedes, for he can turn the world without any thing to rest his lever upon. It is only surpassed by the dexterity with which the sturdy old Jesuit, in another place, cuts the gordian knot – "Nothing," says he, "is more easy. The inhabitants of both hemispheres are certainly the descendants of the same father. The common father of mankind received an express order from Heaven to people the world, and *accordingly it has been peopled.* To bring this about, it was necessary to overcome all difficulties in the way, *and they have also been overcome!*" Pious logician! How does he put all the herd of laborious theorists to the blush, by explaining, in five words, what it has cost them volumes to prove they knew nothing about!

From all the authorities here quoted, and a variety of others which I have consulted, but which are omitted through fear of fatiguing the unlearned reader, I can only draw the following conclusions, which luckily, however, are sufficient for my purpose. First, that this part of the world has actually *been peopled* (Q.E.D.), to support which we have living proofs in the numerous tribes of Indians that inhabit it. Secondly, that it has been peopled in five hundred different ways, as proved by a cloud of authors who, from the positiveness of their assertions, seem to have been eye-witnesses to the fact. Thirdly, that the people of this country had a *variety of fathers*, which, as it may not be thought much to their credit by the common run of readers, the less we say on the subject the better. The question, therefore, I trust, is for ever at rest.

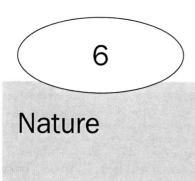

Nature

Ralph Waldo Emerson

Introduction

Ralph Waldo Emerson (1803–82) was born in Boston, Massachusetts. He was a founder of the Transcendental Movement and also of a distinctly American philosophy emphasizing optimism, individuality, and mysticism. Raised to be a minister in Puritan New England, Emerson sought to "create all things new" with a philosophy stressing the recognition of God Immanent, the presence of ongoing creation and revelation by a god apparent in all things and who exists within everyone. Also crucial to Emerson's thought is the related Eastern concept of the essential unity of all thoughts, persons, and things in the divine whole. Traditional values of right and wrong, good and evil appear in his work as necessary opposites, evidencing the effect of German philosopher G. W. F. Hegel's system of dialectical metaphysics. Emerson's works also emphasize individualism and each person's quest to break free from the trappings of the illusory world (*maya*) in order to discover the godliness of the inner self. Emerson became identified with the Transcendental Movement in the 1840s, serving as its spokesperson, and as founder and guiding force of that group's quarterly periodical, the *Dial*. Introducing the public to the works of Amos Bronson Alcott, Margaret Fuller, and Henry David Thoreau, a group of writers who shared Emerson's philosophy, the journal also published Emerson's first poems.

Taken from *Writings* (New York: Library of America, 1983), pp. 5–49.

A subtle chain of countless rings
The next unto the farthest brings;
The eye reads omens where it goes,
And speaks all languages the rose;
And, striving to be man, the worm
Mounts through all the spires of form.

Introduction

Our age is retrospective. It builds the sepulchres of the fathers. It writes biographies, histories, and criticism. The foregoing generations beheld God and nature face to face; we, through their eyes. Why should not we also enjoy an original relation to the universe? Why should not we have a poetry and philosophy of insight and not of tradition, and a religion by revelation to us, and not the history of theirs? Embosomed for a season in nature, whose floods of life stream around and through us, and invite us by the powers they supply, to action proportioned to nature, why should we grope among the dry bones of the past, or put the living generation into masquerade out of its faded wardrobe? The sun shines to-day also. There is more wool and flax in the fields. There are new lands, new men, new thoughts. Let us demand our own works and laws and worship.

Undoubtedly we have no questions to ask which are unanswerable. We must trust the perfection of the creation so far, as to believe that whatever curiosity the order of things has awakened in our minds, the order of things can satisfy. Every man's condition is a solution in hieroglyphic to those inquiries he would put. He acts it as life, before he apprehends it as truth. In like manner, nature is already, in its forms and tendencies, describing its own design. Let us interrogate the great apparition, that shines so peacefully around us. Let us inquire, to what end is nature?

All science has one aim, namely, to find a theory of nature. We have theories of races and of functions, but scarcely yet a remote approach to an idea of creation. We are now so far from the road to truth, that religious teachers dispute and hate each other, and speculative men are esteemed unsound and frivolous. But to a sound judgment, the most abstract truth is the most practical. Whenever a true theory appears, it will be its own evidence. Its test is, that it will explain all phenomena. Now many are thought not only unexplained but inexplicable; as language, sleep, madness, dreams, beasts, sex.

Philosophically considered, the universe is composed of Nature and the Soul. Strictly speaking, therefore, all that is separate from us, all which Philosophy distinguishes as the NOT ME, that is, both nature and art, all other men and my own body, must be ranked under this name, NATURE. In enumerating the values of nature and casting up their sum, I shall use the word in both senses – in its common and in its philosophical import. In inquiries so general as our present one, the inaccuracy is not material; no confusion of thought will occur. *Nature*, in the common sense, refers to essences unchanged by man; space, the air, the river, the leaf. *Art* is applied to the mixture of his will with the same things, as in a house, a canal, a statue, a picture. But his operations taken together are so insignificant, a little chipping, baking, patching, and washing, that in an impression so grand as that of the world on the human mind, they do not vary the result.

Nature

To go into solitude, a man needs to retire as much from his chamber as from society. I am not solitary whilst I read and write, though nobody is with me. But if a man would be alone, let him look at the stars. The rays that come from those heavenly worlds, will separate between him and what he touches. One might think the atmosphere was made transparent with this design, to give man, in the heavenly bodies, the perpetual presence of the sublime. Seen in the streets of cities, how great they are! If the stars should appear one night in a thousand years, how would men believe and adore; and preserve for many generations the remembrance of the city of God which had been shown! But every night come out these envoys of beauty, and light the universe with their admonishing smile.

The stars awaken a certain reverence, because though always present, they are inaccessible; but all natural objects make a kindred impression, when the mind is open to their influence. Nature never wears a mean appearance. Neither does the wisest man extort her secret, and lose his curiosity by finding out all her perfection. Nature never became a toy to a wise spirit. The flowers, the animals, the mountains, reflected the wisdom of his best hour, as much as they had delighted the simplicity of his childhood.

When we speak of nature in this manner, we have a distinct but most poetical sense in the mind. We mean the integrity of impression made by manifold natural objects. It is this which distinguishes the stick of timber of the wood-cutter, from the tree of the poet. The charming landscape which I saw this morning, is indubitably made up of some twenty or thirty farms. Miller owns this field, Locke that, and Manning the woodland beyond. But none of them owns the landscape. There is a property in the horizon which no man has but he whose eye can integrate all the parts, that is, the poet. This is the best part of these men's farms, yet to this their warranty-deeds give no title.

To speak truly, few adult persons can see nature. Most persons do not see the sun. At least they have a very superficial seeing. The sun illuminates only the eye of the man, but shines into the eye and the heart of the child. The lover of nature is he whose inward and outward senses are still truly adjusted to each other; who has retained the spirit of infancy even into the era of manhood. His intercourse with heaven and earth, becomes part of his daily food. In the presence of nature, a wild delight runs through the man, in spite of real sorrows. Nature says – he is my creature, and maugre all his impertinent griefs, he shall be glad with me. Not the sun or the summer alone, but every hour and season yields its tribute of delight; for every hour and change corresponds to and authorizes a different state of the mind, from breathless noon to grimmest midnight. Nature is a setting that fits equally well a comic or a mourning piece. In good health, the air is a cordial of incredible virtue. Crossing a bare common, in snow puddles, at twilight, under a clouded sky, without having in my thoughts any occurrence of special good fortune, I have enjoyed a perfect exhilaration. I am glad to the brink of fear. In the woods too, a man casts off his years, as the snake his slough, and at what period soever of life, is always a child. In the woods, is perpetual youth. Within these plantations of God, a decorum and sanctity reign, a perennial festival is dressed, and the guest sees not how he should tire of them in a thousand years. In the woods, we return to reason and faith. There I feel that nothing can befall me in life – no disgrace, no calamity (leaving me my eyes) which nature cannot repair. Standing on the bare ground – my head bathed by the blithe air, and uplifted into infinite space – all mean egotism vanishes. I become a transparent eyeball; I am nothing; I see all; the currents of the Universal Being circulate through me; I am part or particle of God. The name of the nearest friend sounds then foreign and accidental: to be brothers, to be acquaintances – master or servant, is then a trifle and a disturbance. I am the lover of uncontained and immortal beauty. In the wilderness, I find something more dear and connate than in streets or villages. In the tranquil landscape, and especially in the distant line of the horizon, man beholds somewhat as beautiful as his own nature.

The greatest delight which the fields and woods minister, is the suggestion of an occult relation between man and the vegetable. I am not alone and unacknowledged. They nod to me, and I to them. The waving of the boughs in the storm, is new to me and old. It takes me by surprise, and yet is not unknown. Its effect is like that of a higher thought or a better emotion coming over me, when I deemed I was thinking justly or doing right.

Yet it is certain that the power to produce this delight, does not reside in nature, but in man, or in a harmony of both. It is necessary to use these pleasures with great temperance. For, nature is not always tricked in holiday attire, but the same scene which yesterday breathed perfume and glittered as for the frolic of the nymphs, is overspread with melancholy today. Nature always wears the colors of the spirit. To a man laboring under calamity, the heat of his own fire hath sadness in it. Then, there is a kind of contempt of the landscape felt by him who has just lost by death a dear friend. The sky is less grand as it shuts down over less worth in the population.

Commodity

Whoever considers the final cause of the world, will discern a multitude of uses that enter as parts into that result. They all admit of being thrown into one of the following classes; Commodity; Beauty; Language; and Discipline.

Under the general name of Commodity, I rank all those advantages which our senses owe to nature. This, of course, is a benefit which is temporary and mediate, not ultimate, like its service to the soul. Yet although low, it is perfect in its kind, and is the only use of nature which all men apprehend. The misery of man appears like childish petulance, when we explore the steady and prodigal provision that has been made for his support and delight on this green ball which floats him through the heavens. What angels invented these splendid ornaments, these rich conveniences, this ocean of air above, this ocean of water beneath, this firmament of earth between? this zodiac of lights, this tent of dropping clouds, this striped coat of climates, this fourfold year? Beasts, fire, water, stones, and corn serve him. The field is at once his floor, his work-yard, his play-ground, his garden, and his bed.

> More servants wait on man
> Than he'll take notice of.—

Nature, in its ministry to man, is not only the material, but is also the process and the result. All the parts incessantly work into each other's hands for the profit of man. The wind sows the seed; the sun evaporates the sea; the wind blows the vapor to the field; the ice, on the other side of the planet, condenses rain on this; the rain feeds the plant; the plant feeds the animal; and thus the endless circulations of the divine charity nourish man.

The useful arts are reproductions or new combinations by the wit of man, of the same natural benefactors. He no longer waits for favoring gales, but by means of steam, he realizes the fable of Æolus's bag, and carries the two and thirty winds in the boiler of his boat. To diminish friction, he paves the road with iron bars, and, mounting a coach with a ship-load of men, animals, and merchandise behind him, he darts through the country, from town to town, like an eagle or a swallow through the air. By the aggregate of these aids, how is the face of the world changed, from the era of Noah to that of Napoleon! The private poor man hath cities, ships, canals, bridges, built for him. He goes to the post-office, and the human race run on his errands; to the book-shop, and the human race read and write of all that happens, for him; to the court-house, and nations repair his wrongs. He sets his house upon the road, and the human race go forth every morning, and shovel out the snow, and cut a path for him.

But there is no need of specifying particulars in this class of uses. The catalogue is endless, and the examples so obvious, that I shall leave them to the reader's reflection, with the general remark, that this mercenary benefit is one which has respect to a farther good. A man is fed, not that he may be fed, but that he may work.

Beauty

A nobler want of man is served by nature, namely, the love of Beauty.

The ancient Greeks called the world κόσμος, beauty. Such is the constitution of all things, or such the plastic power of the human eye, that the primary forms, as the sky, the mountain, the tree, the animal, give us a delight *in and for themselves*; a pleasure arising from outline, color, motion, and grouping. This seems partly owing to the eye itself. The eye is the best of artists. By the mutual action of its structure and of the laws of light, perspective is produced, which integrates every mass of objects, of what character soever, into a well colored and shaded globe, so that where the particular objects are mean and unaffecting, the landscape which they compose, is round and symmetrical. And as the eye is the best composer, so light is the first of painters. There is no object so foul that intense light will not make beautiful. And the stimulus it affords to the sense, and a sort of infinitude which it hath, like space and time, make all matter gay. Even the corpse has its own beauty. But besides this general grace diffused over nature, almost all the individual forms are agreeable to the eye, as is proved by our endless imitations of some of them, as the acorn, the grape, the pine-cone, the wheat-ear, the egg, the wings and forms of most birds, the lion's claw, the serpent, the butterfly, sea-shells, flames, clouds, buds, leaves, and the forms of many trees, as the palm.

For better consideration, we may distribute the aspects of Beauty in a threefold manner.

1 First, the simple perception of natural forms is a delight. The influence of the forms and actions in nature, is so needful to man, that, in its lowest functions, it seems to lie on the confines of commodity and beauty. To the body and mind which have been cramped by noxious work or company, nature is medicinal and restores their tone. The tradesman, the attorney comes out of the din and craft of the street, and sees the sky and the woods, and is a man again. In their eternal calm, he finds himself. The health of the eye seems to demand a horizon. We are never tired, so long as we can see far enough.

But in other hours, Nature satisfies by its loveliness, and without any mixture of corporeal benefit. I see the spectacle of morning from the hill-top over against my house, from day-break to sun-rise, with emotions which an angel might share. The long slender bars of cloud float like fishes in the sea of crimson light. From the earth, as a shore, I look out into that silent sea. I seem to partake its rapid transformations: the active enchantment reaches my dust, and I dilate and conspire with the morning wind. How does Nature deify us with a few and cheap elements! Give me health and a day, and I will make the pomp of emperors ridiculous. The dawn is my Assyria; the sun-set and moon-rise my Paphos, and unimaginable realms of faerie; broad noon shall be my England of the senses and the understanding; the night shall be my Germany of mystic philosophy and dreams.

Not less excellent, except for our less susceptibility in the afternoon, was the charm, last evening, of a January sunset. The western clouds divided and subdivided themselves into pink flakes modulated with tints of unspeakable softness; and the air had so much life and sweetness, that it was a pain to come within doors. What was it that nature would say? Was there no meaning in the live repose of the valley behind the mill, and which Homer or Shakespeare could not re-form for me in words? The leafless trees become spires of flame in the sunset, with the blue east for their background, and the stars of the dead calices of flowers, and every withered stem and stubble rimed with frost, contribute something to the mute music.

The inhabitants of cities suppose that the country landscape is pleasant only half the year. I please myself with the graces of the winter scenery, and believe that we are as much touched by it as by the genial influences of summer. To the attentive eye, each moment of the year has its own beauty, and in the same field, it beholds, every hour, a picture which was never seen before, and which shall never be seen again. The heavens change every moment, and reflect their glory or gloom on the plains beneath. The state of the crop in the surrounding farms alters the expression of the earth from week to week. The succession of native plants in the pastures and roadsides, which makes the silent clock by which time tells the summer hours, will make even the divisions of the day sensible to a keen observer. The tribes of birds and insects, like the plants punctual to their time, follow each other, and the year has room for all. By water-courses, the variety is greater. In July, the blue pontederia or pickerel-weed blooms in large beds in the shallow parts of our pleasant river, and swarms with yellow butterflies in continual motion. Art cannot rival this pomp of purple and gold. Indeed the river is a perpetual gala, and boasts each month a new ornament.

But this beauty of Nature which is seen and felt as beauty, is the least part. The shows of day, the dewy morning, the rainbow, mountains, orchards in blossom, stars, moonlight, shadows in still water, and the like, if too eagerly hunted, become shows merely, and mock us with their unreality. Go out of the house to see the moon, and 't is mere tinsel; it will not please as when its light shines upon your necessary journey. The beauty that shimmers in the yellow afternoons of October, who ever could clutch it? Go forth to find it, and it is gone: 't is only a mirage as you look from the windows of diligence.

2 The presence of a higher, namely, of the spiritual element is essential to its perfection. The high and divine beauty which can be loved without effeminacy, is that which is found in combination with the human will. Beauty is the mark God sets upon virtue. Every natural action is graceful. Every heroic act is also decent, and causes the place and the bystanders to shine. We are taught by great actions that the universe is the property of every individual in it. Every rational creature has all nature for his dowry and estate. It is his, if he will. He may divest himself of it; he may creep into a corner, and abdicate his kingdom, as most men do, but he is entitled to the world by his constitution. In proportion to the energy of his thought and will, he takes up the world into himself. "All those things for which men plough, build, or sail, obey virtue;" said Sallust. "The winds and waves," said Gibbon, "are always on

the side of the ablest navigators." So are the sun and moon and all the stars of heaven. When a noble act is done – perchance in a scene of great natural beauty; when Leonidas and his three hundred martyrs consume one day in dying, and the sun and moon come each and look at them once in the steep defile of Thermopylæ; when Arnold Winkelried, in the high Alps, under the shadow of the avalanche, gathers in his side a sheaf of Austrian spears to break the line for his comrades; are not these heroes entitled to add the beauty of the scene to the beauty of the deed? When the bark of Columbus nears the shore of America – before it, the beach lined with savages, fleeing out of all their huts of cane; the sea behind; and the purple mountains of the Indian Archipelago around, can we separate the man from the living picture? Does not the New World clothe his form with her palm-groves and savannahs as fit drapery? Ever does natural beauty steal in like air, and envelope great actions. When Sir Harry Vane was dragged up the Tower-hill, sitting on a sled, to suffer death, as the champion of the English laws, one of the multitude cried out to him, "You never sate on so glorious a seat." Charles II, to intimidate the citizens of London, caused the patriot Lord Russel to be drawn in an open coach, through the principal streets of the city, on his way to the scaffold. "But," his biographer says, "the multitude imagined they saw liberty and virtue sitting by his side." In private places, among sordid objects, an act of truth or heroism seems at once to draw to itself the sky as its temple, the sun as its candle. Nature stretcheth out her arms to embrace man, only let his thoughts be of equal greatness. Willingly does she follow his steps with the rose and the violet, and bend her lines of grandeur and grace to the decoration of her darling child. Only let his thoughts be of equal scope, and the frame will suit the picture. A virtuous man is in unison with her works, and makes the central figure of the visible sphere. Homer, Pindar, Socrates, Phocion, associate themselves fitly in our memory with the geography and climate of Greece. The visible heavens and earth sympathize with Jesus. And in common life, whosoever has seen a person of powerful character and happy genius, will have remarked how easily he took all things along with him – the persons, the opinions, and the day, and nature became ancillary to a man.

3 There is still another aspect under which the beauty of the world may be viewed, namely, as it becomes an object of the intellect. Beside the

relation of things to virtue, they have a relation to thought. The intellect searches out the absolute order of things as they stand in the mind of God, and without the colors of affection. The intellectual and the active powers seem to succeed each other, and the exclusive activity of the one, generates the exclusive activity of the other. There is something unfriendly in each to the other, but they are like the alternate periods of feeding and working in animals; each prepares and will be followed by the other. Therefore does beauty, which, in relation to actions, as we have seen, comes unsought, and comes because it is unsought, remain for the apprehension and pursuit of the intellect; and then again, in its turn, of the active power. Nothing divine dies. All good is eternally reproductive. The beauty of nature reforms itself in the mind, and not for barren contemplation, but for new creation.

All men are in some degree impressed by the face of the world; some men even to delight. This love of beauty is Taste. Others have the same love in such excess, that, not content with admiring, they seek to embody it in new forms. The creation of beauty is Art.

The production of a work of art throws a light upon the mystery of humanity. A work of art is an abstract or epitome of the world. It is the result or expression of nature, in miniature. For, although the works of nature are innumerable and all different, the result or the expression of them all is similar and single. Nature is a sea of forms radically alike and even unique. A leaf, a sun-beam, a landscape, the ocean, make an analogous impression on the mind. What is common to them all – that perfectness and harmony, is beauty. The standard of beauty is the entire circuit of natural forms – the totality of nature; which the Italians expressed by defining beauty "il piu nell' uno." Nothing is quite beautiful alone: nothing but is beautiful in the whole. A single object is only so far beautiful as it suggests this universal grace. The poet, the painter, the sculptor, the musician, the architect, seek each to concentrate this radiance of the world on one point, and each in his several work to satisfy the love of beauty which stimulates him to produce. Thus is Art, a nature passed through the alembic of man. Thus in art, does nature work through the will of a man filled with the beauty of her first works.

The world thus exists to the soul to satisfy the desire of beauty. This element I call an ultimate end. No reason can be asked or given why the soul seeks beauty. Beauty, in its largest and profoundest sense, is one expression for the universe. God is the all-fair. Truth, and goodness, and beauty, are but different faces of the same All. But beauty in nature is not ultimate. It is the herald of inward and eternal beauty, and is not alone a solid and satisfactory good. It must stand as a part, and not as yet the last or highest expression of the final cause of Nature.

Language

Language is a third use which Nature subserves to man. Nature is the vehicle of thought, and in a simple, double, and threefold degree.

1 Words are signs of natural facts.
2 Particular natural facts are symbols of particular spiritual facts.
3 Nature is the symbol of spirit.

1 Words are signs of natural facts. The use of natural history is to give us aid in supernatural history: the use of the outer creation, to give us language for the beings and changes of the inward creation. Every word which is used to express a moral or intellectual fact, if traced to its root, is found to be borrowed from some material appearance. *Right* means *straight*; *wrong* means *twisted*. *Spirit* primarily means *wind*; *transgression*, the crossing of a *line*; *supercilious*, the *raising of the eyebrow*. We say the *heart* to express emotion, the *head* to denote thought; and *thought* and *emotion* are words borrowed from sensible things, and now appropriated to spiritual nature. Most of the process by which this transformation is made, is hidden from us in the remote time when language was framed; but the same tendency may be daily observed in children. Children and savages use only nouns or names of things, which they convert into verbs, and apply to analogous mental acts.

2 But this origin of all words that convey a spiritual import – so conspicuous a fact in the history of language – is our least debt to nature. It is not words only that are emblematic; it is things which are emblematic. Every natural fact is a symbol of some spiritual fact. Every appearance in nature corresponds to some state of the mind, and that state of the mind can only be described by presenting that natural appearance as its picture. An enraged man is a lion, a cunning man is a fox, a firm man is a rock, a learned man is

a torch. A lamb is innocence; a snake is subtle spite; flowers express to us the delicate affections. Light and darkness are our familiar expression for knowledge and ignorance; and heat for love. Visible distance behind and before us, is respectively our image of memory and hope.

Who looks upon a river in a meditative hour, and is not reminded of the flux of all things? Throw a stone into the stream, and the circles that propagate themselves are the beautiful type of all influence. Man is conscious of a universal soul within or behind his individual life, wherein, as in a firmament, the natures of Justice, Truth, Love, Freedom, arise and shine. This universal soul, he calls Reason: it is not mine, or thine, or his, but we are its; we are its property and men. And the blue sky in which the private earth is buried, the sky with its eternal calm, and full of everlasting orbs, is the type of Reason. That which, intellectually considered, we call Reason, considered in relation to nature, we call Spirit. Spirit is the Creator. Spirit hath life in itself. And man in all ages and countries, embodies it in his language, as the FATHER.

It is easily seen that there is nothing lucky or capricious in these analogies, but that they are constant, and pervade nature. These are not the dreams of a few poets, here and there, but man is an analogist, and studies relations in all objects. He is placed in the centre of beings, and a ray of relation passes from every other being to him. And neither can man be understood without these objects, nor these objects without man. All the facts in natural history taken by themselves, have no value, but are barren, like a single sex. But marry it to human history, and it is full of life. Whole Floras, all Linnæus' and Buffon's volumes, are dry catalogues of facts; but the most trivial of these facts, the habit of a plant, the organs, or work, or noise of an insect, applied to the illustration of a fact in intellectual philosophy, or, in any way associated to human nature, affects us in the most lively and agreeable manner. The seed of a plant – to what affecting analogies in the nature of man, is that little fruit made use of, in all discourse, up to the voice of Paul, who calls the human corpse a seed – "It is sown a natural body; it is raised a spiritual body." The motion of the earth round its axis, and round the sun, makes the day, and the year. These are certain amounts of brute light and heat. But is there no intent of an analogy between man's life and the seasons? And do the seasons gain no grandeur or

pathos from that analogy? The instincts of the ant are very unimportant, considered as the ant's; but the moment a ray of relation is seen to extend from it to man, and the little drudge is seen to be a monitor, a little body with a mighty heart, then all its habits, even that said to be recently observed, that it never sleeps, become sublime.

Because of this radical correspondence between visible things and human thoughts, savages, who have only what is necessary, converse in figures. As we go back in history, language becomes more picturesque, until its infancy, when it is all poetry; or all spiritual facts are represented by natural symbols. The same symbols are found to make the original elements of all languages. It has moreover been observed, that the idioms of all languages approach each other in passages of the greatest eloquence and power. And as this is the first language, so is it the last. This immediate dependence of language upon nature, this conversion of an outward phenomenon into a type of somewhat in human life, never loses its power to affect us. It is this which gives that piquancy to the conversation of a strong-natured farmer or backwoodsman, which all men relish.

A man's power to connect his thought with its proper symbol, and so to utter it, depends on the simplicity of his character, that is, upon his love of truth, and his desire to communicate it without loss. The corruption of man is followed by the corruption of language. When simplicity of character and the sovereignty of ideas is broken up by the prevalence of secondary desires, the desire of riches, of pleasure, of power, and of praise – and duplicity and falsehood take place of simplicity and truth, the power over nature as an interpreter of the will, is in a degree lost; new imagery ceases to be created, and old words are perverted to stand for things which are not; a paper currency is employed, when there is no bullion in the vaults. In due time, the fraud is manifest, and words lose all power to stimulate the understanding or the affections. Hundreds of writers may be found in every long-civilized nation, who for a short time believe, and make others believe, that they see and utter truths, who do not of themselves clothe one thought in its natural garment, but who feed unconsciously on the language created by the primary writers of the country, those, namely, who hold primarily on nature.

But wise men pierce this rotten diction and fasten words again to visible things; so that picturesque language is at once a commanding certificate that he who employs it, is a man in alliance with truth and God. The moment our discourse rises above the ground line of familiar facts, and is inflamed with passion or exalted by thought, it clothes itself in images. A man conversing in earnest, if he watch his intellectual processes, will find that a material image, more or less luminous, arises in his mind, contemporaneous with every thought, which furnishes the vestment of the thought. Hence, good writing and brilliant discourse are perpetual allegories. This imagery is spontaneous. It is the blending of experience with the present action of the mind. It is proper creation. It is the working of the Original Cause through the instruments he has already made.

These facts may suggest the advantage which the country-life possesses for a powerful mind, over the artificial and curtailed life of cities. We know more from nature than we can at will communicate. Its light flows into the mind evermore, and we forget its presence. The poet, the orator, bred in the woods, whose senses have been nourished by their fair and appeasing changes, year after year, without design and without heed – shall not lose their lesson altogether, in the roar of cities or the broil of politics. Long hereafter, amidst agitation and terror in national councils – in the hour of revolution – these solemn images shall reappear in their morning lustre, as fit symbols and words of the thoughts which the passing events shall awaken. At the call of a noble sentiment, again the woods wave, the pines murmur, the river rolls and shines, and the cattle low upon the mountains, as he saw and heard them in his infancy. And with these forms, the spells of persuasion, the keys of power are put into his hands.

3 We are thus assisted by natural objects in the expression of particular meanings. But how great a language to convey such pepper-corn informations! Did it need such noble races of creatures, this profusion of forms, this host of orbs in heaven, to furnish man with the dictionary and grammar of his municipal speech? Whilst we use this grand cipher to expedite the affairs of our pot and kettle, we feel that we have not yet put it to its use, neither are able. We are like travellers using the cinders of a volcano to roast their eggs. Whilst we see that it always stands ready to clothe what we would say, we cannot avoid the question, whether the characters are not significant of themselves. Have mountains, and waves, and skies, no significance but what we consciously give them, when we employ them as emblems of our thoughts? The

world is emblematic. Parts of speech are metaphors, because the whole of nature is a metaphor of the human mind. The laws of moral nature answer to those of matter as face to face in a glass. "The visible world and the relation of its parts, is the dial plate of the invisible." The axioms of physics translate the laws of ethics. Thus, "the whole is greater than its part;" "reaction is equal to action;" "the smallest weight may be made to lift the greatest, the difference of weight being compensated by time;" and many the like propositions, which have an ethical as well as physical sense. These propositions have a much more extensive and universal sense when applied to human life, than when confined to technical use.

In like manner, the memorable words of history, and the proverbs of nations, consist usually of a natural fact, selected as a picture or parable of a moral truth. Thus; A rolling stone gathers no moss; A bird in the hand is worth two in the bush; A cripple in the right way, will beat a racer in the wrong; Make hay while the sun shines; 'Tis hard to carry a full cup even; Vinegar is the son of wine; The last ounce broke the camel's back; Long-lived trees make roots first – and the like. In their primary sense these are trivial facts, but we repeat them for the value of their analogical import. What is true of proverbs, is true of all fables, parables, and allegories.

This relation between the mind and matter is not fancied by some poet, but stands in the will of God, and so is free to be known by all men. It appears to men, or it does not appear. When in fortunate hours we ponder this miracle, the wise man doubts, if, at all other times, he is not blind and deaf:

 — Can these things be,
 And overcome us like a summer's cloud,
 Without our special wonder?

for the universe becomes transparent, and the light of higher laws than its own, shines through it. It is the standing problem which has exercised the wonder and the study of every fine genius since the world began; from the era of the Egyptians and the Brahmins, to that of Pythagoras, of Plato, of Bacon, of Leibnitz, of Swedenborg. There sits the Sphinx at the road-side, and from age to age, as each prophet comes by, he tries his fortune at reading her riddle. There seems to be a necessity in spirit to manifest itself in material forms; and day and night, river and storm, beast and bird, acid and alkali, preëxist in necessary Ideas in the mind of God, and are what they are by virtue of preceding affections, in the world of spirit. A Fact is the end or last issue of spirit. The visible creation is the terminus or the circumference of the invisible world. "Material objects," said a French philosopher, "are necessarily kinds of *scoriæ* of the substantial thoughts of the Creator, which must always preserve an exact relation to their first origin; in other words, visible nature must have a spiritual and moral side."

This doctrine is abstruse, and though the images of "garment," "scoriæ," "mirror," &c., may stimulate the fancy, we must summon the aid of subtler and more vital expositors to make it plain. "Every scripture is to be interpreted by the same spirit which gave it forth" – is the fundamental law of criticism. A life in harmony with nature, the love of truth and of virtue, will purge the eyes to understand her text. By degrees we may come to know the primitive sense of the permanent objects of nature, so that the world shall be to us an open book, and every form significant of its hidden life and final cause.

A new interest surprises us, whilst, under the view now suggested, we contemplate the fearful extent and multitude of objects; since "every object rightly seen, unlocks a new faculty of the soul." That which was unconscious truth, becomes, when interpreted and defined in an object, a part of the domain of knowledge – a new weapon in the magazine of power.

Discipline

In view of the significance of nature, we arrive at once at a new fact, that nature is a discipline. This use of the world includes the preceding uses, as parts of itself.

Space, time, society, labor, climate, food, locomotion, the animals, the mechanical forces, give us sincerest lessons, day by day, whose meaning is unlimited. They educate both the Understanding and the Reason. Every property of matter is a school for the understanding – its solidity or resistance, its inertia, its extension, its figure, its divisibility. The understanding adds, divides, combines, measures, and finds nutriment and room for its activity in this worthy scene. Meantime, Reason transfers all these lessons into its own world of thought, by perceiving the analogy that marries Matter and Mind.

1 Nature is a discipline of the understanding in intellectual truths. Our dealing with sensible objects is a constant exercise in the necessary lessons of difference, of likeness, of order, of being and seeming, of progressive arrangement; of ascent from particular to general; of combination to one end of manifold forces. Proportioned to the importance of the organ to be formed, is the extreme care with which its tuition is provided – a care pretermitted in no single case. What tedious training, day after day, year after year, never ending, to form the common sense; what continual reproduction of annoyances, inconveniences, dilemmas; what rejoicing over us of little men; what disputing of prices, what reckonings of interest – and all to form the Hand of the mind – to instruct us that "good thoughts are no better than good dreams, unless they be executed!"

The same good office is performed by Property and its filial systems of debt and credit. Debt, grinding debt, whose iron face the widow, the orphan, and the sons of genius fear and hate – debt, which consumes so much time, which so cripples and disheartens a great spirit with cares that seem so base, is a preceptor whose lessons cannot be forgone, and is needed most by those who suffer from it most. Moreover, property, which has been well compared to snow – "if it fall level to-day, it will be blown into drifts tomorrow" – is the surface action of internal machinery, like the index on the face of a clock. Whilst now it is the gymnastics of the understanding, it is hiving in the foresight of the spirit, experience in profounder laws.

The whole character and fortune of the individual are affected by the least inequalities in the culture of the understanding; for example, in the perception of differences. Therefore is Space, and therefore Time, that man may know that things are not huddled and lumped, but sundered and individual. A bell and a plough have each their use, and neither can do the office of the other. Water is good to drink, coal to burn, wool to wear; but wool cannot be drunk, nor water spun, nor coal eaten. The wise man shows his wisdom in separation, in gradation, and his scale of creatures and of merits is as wide as nature. The foolish have no range in their scale, but suppose every man is as every other man. What is not good they call the worst, and what is not hateful, they call the best.

In like manner, what good heed, nature forms in us! She pardons no mistakes. Her yea is yea, and her nay, nay.

The first steps in Agriculture, Astronomy, Zoology (those first steps which the farmer, the hunter, and the sailor take) teach that nature's dice are always loaded; that in her heaps and rubbish are concealed sure and useful results.

How calmly and genially the mind apprehends one after another the laws of physics! What noble emotions dilate the mortal as he enters into the counsels of the creation, and feels by knowledge the privilege to Be! His insight refines him. The beauty of nature shines in his own breast. Man is greater that he can see this, and the universe less, because Time and Space relations vanish as laws are known.

Here again we are impressed and even daunted by the immense Universe to be explored. "What we know, is a point to what we do not know." Open any recent journal of science, and weigh the problems suggested concerning Light, Heat, Electricity, Magnetism, Physiology, Geology, and judge whether the interest of natural science is likely to be soon exhausted.

Passing by many particulars of the discipline of nature, we must not omit to specify two.

The exercise of the Will or the lesson of power is taught in every event. From the child's successive possession of his several senses up to the hour when he saith, "Thy will be done!" he is learning the secret, that he can reduce under his will, not only particular events, but great classes, nay the whole series of events, and so conform all facts to his character. Nature is thoroughly mediate. It is made to serve. It receives the dominion of man as meekly as the ass on which the Saviour rode. It offers all its kingdoms to man as the raw material which he may mould into what is useful. Man is never weary of working it up. He forges the subtile and delicate air into wise and melodious words, and gives them wing as angels of persuasion and command. One after another, his victorious thought comes up with and reduces all things, until the world becomes, at last, only a realized will – the double of the man.

2 Sensible objects conform to the premonitions of Reason and reflect the conscience. All things are moral; and in their boundless changes have an unceasing reference to spiritual nature. Therefore is nature glorious with form, color, and motion, that every globe in the remotest heaven; every chemical change from the rudest crystal up to the laws of life; every change of vegetation from the first principle of growth in the eye of a leaf, to the tropical forest and antediluvian coal-mine;

every animal function from the sponge up to Hercules, shall hint or thunder to man the laws of right and wrong, and echo the Ten Commandments. Therefore is nature ever the ally of Religion: lends all her pomp and riches to the religious sentiment. Prophet and priest, David, Isaiah, Jesus, have drawn deeply from this source. This ethical character so penetrates the bone and marrow of nature, as to seem the end for which it was made. Whatever private purpose is answered by any member or part, this is its public and universal function, and is never omitted. Nothing in nature is exhausted in its first use. When a thing has served an end to the uttermost, it is wholly new for an ulterior service. In God, every end is converted into a new means. Thus the use of commodity, regarded by itself, is mean and squalid. But it is to the mind an education in the doctrine of Use, namely, that a thing is good only so far as it serves; that a conspiring of parts and efforts to the production of an end, is essential to any being. The first and gross manifestation of this truth, is our inevitable and hated training in values and wants, in corn and meat.

It has already been illustrated, that every natural process is a version of a moral sentence. The moral law lies at the centre of nature and radiates to the circumference. It is the pith and marrow of every substance, every relation, and every process. All things with which we deal, preach to us. What is a farm but a mute gospel? The chaff and the wheat, weeds and plants, blight, rain, insects, sun – it is a sacred emblem from the first furrow of spring to the last stack which the snow of winter overtakes in the fields. But the sailor, the shepherd, the miner, the merchant, in their several resorts, have each an experience precisely parallel, and leading to the same conclusion: because all organizations are radically alike. Nor can it be doubted that this moral sentiment which thus scents the air, grows in the grain, and impregnates the waters of the world, is caught by man and sinks into his soul. The moral influence of nature upon every individual is that amount of truth which it illustrates to him. Who can estimate this? Who can guess how much firmness the sea-beaten rock has taught the fisherman? how much tranquillity has been reflected to man from the azure sky, over whose unspotted deeps the winds forevermore drive flocks of stormy clouds, and leave no wrinkle or stain? how much industry and providence and affection we have caught from the pantomime of brutes? What a searching preacher of self-command is the varying phenomenon of Health!

Herein is especially apprehended the unity of Nature – *the unity in variety* – which meets us everywhere. All the endless variety of things make an identical impression. Xenophanes complained in his old age, that, look where he would, all things hastened back to Unity. He was weary of seeing the same entity in the tedious variety of forms. The fable of Proteus has a cordial truth. A leaf, a drop, a crystal, a moment of time is related to the whole, and partakes of the perfection of the whole. Each particle is a microcosm, and faithfully renders the likeness of the world.

Not only resemblances exist in things whose analogy is obvious, as when we detect the type of the human hand in the flipper of the fossil saurus, but also in objects wherein there is great superficial unlikeness. Thus architecture is called "frozen music," by De Stael and Goethe. Vitruvius thought an architect should be a musician. "A Gothic church," said Coleridge, "is a petrified religion." Michael Angelo maintained, that, to an architect, a knowledge of anatomy is essential. In Haydn's oratorios, the notes present to the imagination not only motions, as, of the snake, the stag, and the elephant, but colors also; as the green grass. The law of harmonic sounds reappears in the harmonic colors. The granite is differenced in its laws only by the more or less of heat, from the river that wears it away. The river, as it flows, resembles the air that flows over it; the air resembles the light which traverses it with more subtle currents; the light resembles the heat which rides with it through Space. Each creature is only a modification of the other; the likeness in them is more than the difference, and their radical law is one and the same. A rule of one art, or a law of one organization, holds true throughout nature. So intimate is this Unity, that, it is easily seen, it lies under the undermost garment of nature, and betrays its source in Universal Spirit. For, it pervades Thought also. Every universal truth which we express in words, implies or supposes every other truth. *Omne verum vero consonat.* It is like a great circle on a sphere, comprising all possible circles; which, however, may be drawn, and comprise it, in like manner. Every such truth is the absolute Ens seen from one side. But it has innumerable sides.

The central Unity is still more conspicuous in actions. Words are finite organs of the infinite mind. They cannot cover the dimensions of what is in truth. They break, chop, and impoverish it.

An action is the perfection and publication of thought. A right action seems to fill the eye, and to be related to all nature. "The wise man, in doing one thing, does all; or, in the one thing he does rightly, he sees the likeness of all which is done rightly."

Words and actions are not the attributes of brute nature. They introduce us to the human form, of which all other organizations appear to be degradations. When this appears among so many that surround it, the spirit prefers it to all others. It says, "From such as this, have I drawn joy and knowledge; in such as this, have I found and beheld myself; I will speak to it; it can speak again; it can yield me thought already formed and alive." In fact, the eye – the mind – is always accompanied by these forms, male and female; and these are incomparably the richest informations of the power and order that lie at the heart of things. Unfortunately, every one of them bears the marks as of some injury; is marred and superficially defective. Nevertheless, far different from the deaf and dumb nature around them, these all rest like fountain-pipes on the unfathomed sea of thought and virtue where to they alone, of all organizations, are the entrances.

It were a pleasant inquiry to follow into detail their ministry to our education, but where would it stop? We are associated in adolescent and adult life with some friends, who, like skies and waters, are coextensive with our idea; who, answering each to a certain affection of the soul, satisfy our desire on that side; whom we lack power to put at such focal distance from us, that we can mend or even analyze them. We cannot choose but love them. When much intercourse with a friend has supplied us with a standard of excellence, and has increased our respect for the resources of God who thus sends a real person to outgo our ideal; when he has, moreover, become an object of thought, and, whilst his character retains all its unconscious effect, is converted in the mind into solid and sweet wisdom – it is a sign to us that his office is closing, and he is commonly withdrawn from our sight in a short time.

Idealism

Thus is the unspeakable but intelligible and practicable meaning of the world conveyed to man, the immortal pupil, in every object of sense. To this one end of Discipline, all parts of nature conspire.

A noble doubt perpetually suggests itself, whether this end be not the Final Cause of the Universe; and whether nature outwardly exists. It is a sufficient account of that Appearance we call the World, that God will teach a human mind, and so makes it the receiver of a certain number of congruent sensations, which we call sun and moon, man and woman, house and trade. In my utter impotence to test the authenticity of the report of my senses, to know whether the impressions they make on me correspond with outlying objects, what difference does it make, whether Orion is up there in heaven, or some god paints the image in the firmament of the soul? The relations of parts and the end of the whole remaining the same, what is the difference, whether land and sea interact, and worlds revolve and intermingle without number or end – deep yawning under deep, and galaxy balancing galaxy, throughout absolute space – or, whether, without relations of time and space, the same appearances are inscribed in the constant faith of man? Whether nature enjoy a substantial existence without, or is only in the apocalypse of the mind, it is alike useful and alike venerable to me. Be it what it may, it is ideal to me, so long as I cannot try the accuracy of my senses.

The frivolous make themselves merry with the Ideal theory, as if its consequences were burlesque; as if it affected the stability of nature. It surely does not. God never jests with us, and will not compromise the end of nature, by permitting any inconsequence in its procession. Any distrust of the permanence of laws, would paralyze the faculties of man. Their permanence is sacredly respected, and his faith therein is perfect. The wheels and springs of man are all set to the hypothesis of the permanence of nature. We are not built like a ship to be tossed, but like a house to stand. It is a natural consequence of this structure, that, so long as the active powers predominate over the reflective, we resist with indignation any hint that nature is more short-lived or mutable than spirit. The broker, the wheelwright, the carpenter, the tollman, are much displeased at the intimation.

But whilst we acquiesce entirely in the permanence of natural laws, the question of the absolute existence of nature still remains open. It is the uniform effect of culture on the human mind, not to shake our faith in the stability of particular phenomena, as of heat, water, azote; but to lead us to regard nature as a phenomenon, not a substance; to attribute necessary existence to spirit; to esteem nature as an accident and an effect.

To the senses and the unrenewed understanding, belongs a sort of instinctive belief in the absolute existence of nature. In their view, man and nature are indissolubly joined. Things are ultimates, and they never look beyond their sphere. The presence of Reason mars this faith. The first effort of thought tends to relax this despotism of the senses, which binds us to nature as if we were a part of it, and shows us nature aloof, and, as it were, afloat. Until this higher agency intervened, the animal eye sees, with wonderful accuracy, sharp outlines and colored surfaces. When the eye of Reason opens, to outline and surface are at once added, grace and expression. These proceed from imagination and affection, and abate somewhat of the angular distinctness of objects. If the Reason be stimulated to more earnest vision, outlines and surfaces become transparent, and are no longer seen; causes and spirits are seen through them. The best moments of life are these delicious awakenings of the higher powers, and the reverential withdrawing of nature before its God.

Let us proceed to indicate the effects of culture.

1 Our first institution in the Ideal philosophy is a hint from nature herself.

Nature is made to conspire with spirit to emancipate us. Certain mechanical changes, a small alteration in our local position apprizes us of a dualism. We are strangely affected by seeing the shore from a moving ship, from a balloon, or through the tints of an unusual sky. The least change in our point of view, gives the whole world a pictorial air. A man who seldom rides, needs only to get into a coach and traverse his own town, to turn the street into a puppet-show. The men, the women – talking, running, bartering, fighting – the earnest mechanic, the lounger, the beggar, the boys, the dogs, are unrealized at once, or, at least, wholly detached from all relation to the observer, and seen as apparent, not substantial beings. What new thoughts are suggested by seeing a face of country quite familiar, in the rapid movement of the rail-road car! Nay, the most wonted objects (make a very slight change in the point of vision) please us most. In a camera obscura, the butcher's cart, and the figure of one of our own family amuse us. So a portrait of a well-known face gratifies us. Turn the eyes upside down, by looking at the landscape through your legs, and how agreeable is the picture, though you have seen it any time these twenty years!

In these cases, by mechanical means, is suggested the difference between the observer and the spectacle – between man and nature. Hence arises a pleasure mixed with awe; I may say, a low degree of the sublime is felt from the fact, probably, that man is hereby apprized, that, whilst the world is a spectacle, something in himself is stable.

2 In a higher manner, the poet communicates the same pleasure. By a few strokes he delineates, as on air, the sun, the mountain, the camp, the city, the hero, the maiden, not different from what we know them, but only lifted from the ground and afloat before the eye. He unfixes the land and the sea, makes them revolve around the axis of his primary thought, and disposes them anew. Possessed himself by a heroic passion, he uses matter as symbols of it. The sensual man conforms thoughts to things; the poet conforms things to his thoughts. The one esteems nature as rooted and fast; the other, as fluid, and impresses his being thereon. To him, the refractory world is ductile and flexible; he invests dust and stones with humanity, and makes them the words of the Reason. The Imagination may be defined to be, the use which the Reason makes of the material world. Shakespeare possesses the power of subordinating nature for the purposes of expression, beyond all poets. His imperial muse tosses the creation like a bauble from hand to hand, and uses it to embody any caprice of thought that is uppermost in his mind. The remotest spaces of nature are visited, and the farthest sundered things are brought together, by a subtle spiritual connection. We are made aware that magnitude of material things is relative, and all objects shrink and expand to serve the passion of the poet. Thus, in his sonnets, the lays of birds, the scents and dyes of flowers, he finds to be the *shadow* of his beloved; time, which keeps her from him, is his *chest*; the suspicion she has awakened, is her *ornament*:

> The ornament of beauty is Suspect,
> A crow which flies in heaven's sweetest air.

His passion is not the fruit of chance; it swells, as he speaks, to a city, or a state:

> No, it was builded far from accident;
> It suffers not in smiling pomp, nor falls
> Under the brow of thralling discontent;
> It fears not policy, that heretic,
> That works on leases of short numbered hours,
> But all alone stands hugely politic.

In the strength of his constancy, the Pyramids seem to him recent and transitory. The freshness of youth and love dazzles him with its resemblance to morning:

> Take those lips away
> Which so sweetly were forsworn;
> And those eyes – the break of day,
> Lights that do mislead the morn.

The wild beauty of this hyperbole, I may say, in passing, it would not be easy to match in literature.

This transfiguration which all material objects undergo through the passion of the poet – this power which he exerts to dwarf the great, to magnify the small – might be illustrated by a thousand examples from his Plays. I have before me the Tempest, and will cite only these few lines:

> ARIEL. The strong based promontory
> Have I made shake, and by the spurs plucked up
> The pine and cedar.

Prospero calls for music to soothe the frantic Alonzo, and his companions:

> A solemn air, and the best comforter
> To an unsettled fancy, cure thy brains
> Now useless, boiled within thy skull.

Again:

> The charm dissolves apace,
> And, as the morning steals upon the night,
> Melting the darkness, so their rising senses
> Begin to chase the ignorant fumes that mantle
> Their clearer reason.
> Their understanding
> Begins to swell: and the approaching tide
> Will shortly fill the reasonable shores
> That now lie foul and muddy.

The perception of real affinities between events (that is to say, of *ideal* affinities, for those only are real) enables the poet thus to make free with the most imposing forms and phenomena of the world, and to assert the predominance of the soul.

3 Whilst thus the poet animates nature with his own thoughts, he differs from the philosopher only herein, that the one proposes Beauty as his main end; the other Truth. But the philosopher, not less than the poet, postpones the apparent order and

relations of things to the empire of thought. "The problem of philosophy," according to Plato, "is, for all that exists conditionally, to find a ground unconditioned and absolute." It proceeds on the faith that a law determines all phenomena, which being known, the phenomena can be predicted. That law, when in the mind, is an idea. Its beauty is infinite. The true philosopher and the true poet are one, and a beauty, which is truth, and a truth, which is beauty, is the aim of both. Is not the charm of one of Plato's or Aristotle's definitions, strictly like that of the Antigone of Sophocles? It is, in both cases, that a spiritual life has been imparted to nature; that the solid seeming block of matter has been pervaded and dissolved by a thought; that this feeble human being has penetrated the vast masses of nature with an informing soul, and recognised itself in their harmony, that is, seized their law. In physics, when this is attained, the memory disburthens itself of its cumbrous catalogues of particulars, and carries centuries of observation in a single formula.

Thus even in physics, the material is degraded before the spiritual. The astronomer, the geometer, rely on their irrefragable analysis, and disdain the results of observation. The sublime remark of Euler on his law of arches, "This will be found contrary to all experience, yet is true;" had already transferred nature into the mind, and left matter like an outcast corpse.

4 Intellectual science has been observed to beget invariably a doubt of the existence of matter. Turgot said, "He that has never doubted the existence of matter, may be assured he has no aptitude for metaphysical inquiries." It fastens the attention upon immortal necessary uncreated natures, that is, upon Ideas; and in their presence, we feel that the outward circumstance is a dream and a shade. Whilst we wait in this Olympus of gods, we think of nature as an appendix to the soul. We ascend into their region, and know that these are the thoughts of the Supreme Being. "These are they who were set up from everlasting, from the beginning, or ever the earth was. When he prepared the heavens, they were there; when he established the clouds above, when he strengthened the fountains of the deep. Then they were by him, as one brought up with him. Of them took he counsel."

Their influence is proportionate. As objects of science, they are accessible to few men. Yet all men are capable of being raised by piety or by passion, into their region. And no man touches these divine natures, without becoming, in some degree, himself divine. Like a new soul, they renew the body. We become physically nimble and lightsome; we tread on air; life is no longer irksome, and we think it will never be so. No man fears age or misfortune or death, in their serene company, for he is transported out of the district of change. Whilst we behold unveiled the nature of Justice and Truth, we learn the difference between the absolute and the conditional or relative. We apprehend the absolute. As it were, for the first time, *we exist*. We become immortal, for we learn that time and space are relations of matter; that, with a perception of truth, or a virtuous will, they have no affinity.

5 Finally, religion and ethics, which may be fitly called – the practice of ideas, or the introduction of ideas into life – have an analogous effect with all lower culture, in degrading nature and suggesting its dependence on spirit. Ethics and religion differ herein; that the one is the system of human duties commencing from man; the other, from God. Religion includes the personality of God; ethics does not. They are one to our present design. They both put nature under foot. The first and last lesson of religion is, "The things that are seen, are temporal; the things that are unseen, are eternal." It puts an affront upon nature. It does that for the unschooled, which philosophy does for Berkeley and Viasa. The uniform language that may be heard in the churches of the most ignorant sects, is – "Contemn the unsubstantial shows of the world; they are vanities, dreams, shadows, unrealities; seek the realities of religion." The devotee flouts nature. Some theosophists have arrived at a certain hostility and indignation towards matter, as the Manichean and Plotinus. They distrusted in themselves any looking back to these flesh-pots of Egypt. Plotinus was ashamed of his body. In short, they might all say of matter, what Michael Angelo said of external beauty, "it is the frail and weary weed, in which God dresses the soul, which he has called into time."

It appears that motion, poetry, physical and intellectual science, and religion, all tend to affect our convictions of the reality of the external world. But I own there is something ungrateful in expanding too curiously the particulars of the general proposition, that all culture tends to imbue us with idealism. I have no hostility to nature, but a child's love to it. I expand and live in the warm day like corn and melons. Let us speak her fair. I do not wish to fling stones at my beautiful mother, nor soil my gentle nest. I only wish to indicate the true position of nature in regard to man, wherein to establish man, all right education tends; as the ground which to attain is the object of human life, that is, of man's connection with nature. Culture inverts the vulgar views of nature, and brings the mind to call that apparent, which it uses to call real, and that real, which it uses to call visionary. Children, it is true, believe in the external world. The belief that it appears only, is an afterthought, but with culture, this faith will as surely arise on the mind as did the first.

The advantage of the ideal theory over the popular faith, is this, that it presents the world in precisely that view which is most desirable to the mind. It is, in fact, the view which Reason, both speculative and practical, that is, philosophy and virtue, take. For, seen in the light of thought, the world always is phenomenal; and virtue subordinates it to the mind. Idealism sees the world in God. It beholds the whole circle of persons and things, of actions and events, of country and religion, not as painfully accumulated, atom after atom, act after act, in an aged creeping Past, but as one vast picture, which God paints on the instant eternity, for the contemplation of the soul. Therefore the soul holds itself off from a too trivial and microscopic study of the universal tablet. It respects the end too much, to immerse itself in the means. It sees something more important in Christianity, than the scandals of ecclesiastical history, or the niceties of criticism; and, very incurious concerning persons or miracles, and not at all disturbed by chasms of historical evidence, it accepts from God the phenomenon, as it finds it, as the pure and awful form of religion in the world. It is not hot and passionate at the appearance of what it calls its own good or bad fortune, at the union or opposition of other persons. No man is its enemy. It accepts whatsoever befalls, as part of its lesson. It is a watcher more than a doer, and it is a doer, only that it may the better watch.

Spirit

It is essential to a true theory of nature and of man, that it should contain somewhat progressive. Uses that are exhausted or that may be, and facts that end in the statement, cannot be all that is true of this brave lodging wherein man is harbored, and wherein all his faculties find appropriate and endless exercise. And all the uses of nature admit of being summed in one, which yields the activity of man an infinite scope. Through all its kingdoms, to the suburbs and outskirts of things, it is faithful to the cause whence it had its origin. It always speaks of Spirit. It suggests the absolute. It is a perpetual effect. It is a great shadow pointing always to the sun behind us.

The aspect of nature is devout. Like the figure of Jesus, she stands with bended head, and hands folded upon the breast. The happiest man is he who learns from nature the lesson of worship.

Of that ineffable essence which we call Spirit, he that thinks most, will say least. We can foresee God in the coarse, and, as it were, distant phenomena of matter; but when we try to define and describe himself, both language and thought desert us, and we are as helpless as fools and savages. That essence refuses to be recorded in propositions, but when man has worshipped him intellectually, the noblest ministry of nature is to stand as the apparition of God. It is the organ through which the universal spirit speaks to the individual, and strives to lead back the individual to it.

When we consider Spirit, we see that the views already presented do not include the whole circumference of man. We must add some related thoughts.

Three problems are put by nature to the mind; What is matter? Whence is it? and Whereto? The first of these questions only, the ideal theory answers. Idealism saith: matter is a phenomenon, not a substance. Idealism acquaints us with the total disparity between the evidence of our own being, and the evidence of the world's being. The one is perfect; the other, incapable of any assurance; the mind is a part of the nature of things; the world is a divine dream, from which we may presently awake to the glories and certainties of day. Idealism is a hypothesis to account for nature by other principles than those of carpentry and chemistry. Yet, if it only deny the existence of matter, it does not satisfy the demands of the spirit. It leaves God out of me. It leaves me in the splendid labyrinth of my perceptions, to wander without end. Then the heart resists it, because it balks the affections in denying substantive being to men and women. Nature is so pervaded with human life, that there is something of humanity in all, and in every particular. But this theory makes nature foreign to me, and does not account for that consanguinity which we acknowledge to it.

Let it stand, then, in the present state of our knowledge, merely as a useful introductory hypothesis, serving to apprize us of the eternal distinction between the soul and the world.

But when, following the invisible steps of thought, we come to inquire, Whence is matter? and Whereto? many truths arise to us out of the recesses of consciousness. We learn that the highest is present to the soul of man, that the dread universal essence, which is not wisdom, or love, or beauty, or power, but all in one, and each entirely, is that for which all things exist, and that by which they are; that spirit creates; that behind nature, throughout nature, spirit is present; one and not compound, it does not act upon us from without, that is, in space and time, but spiritually, or through ourselves: therefore, that spirit, that is, the Supreme Being, does not build up nature around us, but puts it forth through us, as the life of the tree puts forth new branches and leaves through the pores of the old. As a plant upon the earth, so a man rests upon the bosom of God; he is nourished by unfailing fountains, and draws, at his need, inexhaustible power. Who can set bounds to the possibilities of man? Once inhale the upper air, being admitted to behold the absolute natures of justice and truth, and we learn that man has access to the entire mind of the Creator, is himself the creator in the finite. This view, which admonishes me where the sources of wisdom and power lie, and points to virtue as to

The golden key
Which opes the palace of eternity,

carries upon its face the highest certificate of truth, because it animates me to create my own world through the purification of my soul.

The world proceeds from the same spirit as the body of man. It is a remoter and inferior incarnation of God, a projection of God in the unconscious. But it differs from the body in one important respect. It is not, like that, now subjected to the human will. Its serene order is inviolable by us. It is, therefore, to us, the present expositor of the divine mind. It is a fixed point whereby we may measure our departure. As we degenerate, the contrast between us and our house is more evident. We are as much strangers in nature, as we are aliens from God. We do not understand the notes of birds. The fox and the deer run away from us; the bear and tiger rend us. We do not know the uses of more than a few plants, as corn and the apple, the potato and the vine. Is not the landscape, every glimpse of which

hath a grandeur, a face of him? Yet this may show us what discord is between man and nature, for you cannot freely admire a noble landscape, if laborers are digging in the field hard by. The poet finds something ridiculous in his delight, until he is out of the sight of men.

Prospects

In inquiries respecting the laws of the world and the frame of things, the highest reason is always the truest. That which seems faintly possible – it is so refined, is often faint and dim because it is deepest seated in the mind among the eternal verities. Empirical science is apt to cloud the sight, and, by the very knowledge of functions and processes, to bereave the student of the manly contemplation of the whole. The savant becomes unpoetic. But the best read naturalist who lends an entire and devout attention to truth, will see that there remains much to learn of his relation to the world, and that it is not to be learned by any addition or subtraction or other comparison of known quantities, but is arrived at by untaught sallies of the spirit, by a continual self-recovery, and by entire humility. He will perceive that there are far more excellent qualities in the student than preciseness and infallibility; that a guess is often more fruitful than an indisputable affirmation, and that a dream may let us deeper into the secret of nature than a hundred concerted experiments.

For, the problems to be solved are precisely those which the physiologist and the naturalist omit to state. It is not so pertinent to man to know all the individuals of the animal kingdom, as it is to know whence and whereto is this tyrannizing unity in his constitution, which evermore separates and classifies things, endeavoring to reduce the most diverse to one form. When I behold a rich landscape, it is less to my purpose to recite correctly the order and superposition of the strata, than to know why all thought of multitude is lost in a tranquil sense of unity. I cannot greatly honor minuteness in details, so long as there is no hint to explain the relation between things and thoughts; no ray upon the *metaphysics* of conchology, of botany, of the arts, to show the relation of the forms of flowers, shells, animals, architecture, to the mind, and build science upon ideas. In a cabinet of natural history, we become sensible of a certain occult recognition and sympathy in regard to the most unwieldy and eccentric forms of beast, fish, and insect. The American who has been confined, in his own country, to the sight of buildings designed after foreign models, is surprised on entering York Minster or St. Peter's at Rome, by the feeling that these structures are imitations also – faint copies of an invisible archetype. Nor has science sufficient humanity, so long as the naturalist overlooks that wonderful congruity which subsists between man and the world; of which he is lord, not because he is the most subtile inhabitant, but because he is its head and heart, and finds something of himself in every great and small thing, in every mountain stratum, in every new law of color, fact of astronomy, or atmospheric influence which observation or analysis lay open. A perception of this mystery inspires the muse of George Herbert, the beautiful psalmist of the seventeenth century. The following lines are part of his little poem on Man.

Man is all symmetry,
Full of proportions, one limb to another,
And to all the world besides.
Each part may call the farthest, brother;
For head with foot hath private amity,
And both with moons and tides.

Nothing hath got so far
But man hath caught and kept it as his prey;
His eyes dismount the highest star;
He is in little all the sphere.
Herbs gladly cure our flesh, because that they
Find their acquaintance there.

For us, the winds do blow,
The earth doth rest, heaven move, and
    fountains flow;
Nothing we see, but means our good,
As our delight, or as our treasure;
The whole is either our cupboard of food,
Or cabinet of pleasure.

The stars have us to bed:
Night draws the curtain; which the sun
    withdraws.
Music and light attend our head.
All things unto our flesh are kind,
In their descent and being; to our mind,
In their ascent and cause.

More servants wait on man
Than he'll take notice of. In every path,
He treads down that which doth befriend him

When sickness makes him pale and wan.
Oh mighty love! Man is one world, and hath
    Another to attend him.

The perception of this class of truths makes the attraction which draws men to science, but the end is lost sight of in attention to the means. In view of this half-sight of science, we accept the sentence of Plato, that, "poetry comes nearer to vital truth than history." Every surmise and vaticination of the mind is entitled to a certain respect, and we learn to prefer imperfect theories, and sentences, which contain glimpses of truth, to digested systems which have no one valuable suggestion. A wise writer will feel that the ends of study and composition are best answered by announcing undiscovered regions of thought, and so communicating, through hope, new activity to the torpid spirit.

I shall therefore conclude this essay with some traditions of man and nature, which a certain poet sang to me; and which, as they have always been in the world, and perhaps reappear to every bard, may be both history and prophecy.

"The foundations of man are not in matter, but in spirit. But the element of spirit is eternity. To it, therefore, the longest series of events, the oldest chronologies are young and recent. In the cycle of the universal man, from whom the known individuals proceed, centuries are points, and all history is but the epoch of one degradation.

"We distrust and deny inwardly our sympathy with nature. We own and disown our relation to it, by turns. We are, like Nebuchadnezzar, dethroned, bereft of reason, and eating grass like an ox. But who can set limits to the remedial force of spirit?

"A man is a god in ruins. When men are innocent, life shall be longer, and shall pass into the immortal, as gently as we awake from dreams. Now, the world would be insane and rabid, if these disorganizations should last for hundreds of years. It is kept in check by death and infancy. Infancy is the perpetual Messiah, which comes into the arms of fallen men, and pleads with them to return to paradise.

"Man is the dwarf of himself. Once he was permeated and dissolved by spirit. He filled nature with his overflowing currents. Out from him sprang the sun and moon; from man, the sun; from woman, the moon. The laws of his mind, the periods of his actions externized themselves into day and night, into the year and the seasons.

But, having made for himself this huge shell, his waters retired; he no longer fills the veins and veinlets; he is shrunk to a drop. He sees, that the structure still fits him, but fits him colossally. Say, rather, once it fitted him, now it corresponds to him from far and on high. He adores timidly his own work. Now is man the follower of the sun, and woman the follower of the moon. Yet sometimes he starts in his slumber, and wonders at himself and his house, and muses strangely at the resemblance betwixt him and it. He perceives that if his law is still paramount, if still he have elemental power, if his word is sterling yet in nature, it is not conscious power, it is not inferior but superior to his will. It is Instinct." Thus my Orphic poet sang.

At present, man applies to nature but half his force. He works on the world with his understanding alone. He lives in it, and masters it by a penny-wisdom; and he that works most in it, is but a half-man, and whilst his arms are strong and his digestion good, his mind is imbruted, and he is a selfish savage. His relation to nature, his power over it, is through the understanding; as by manure; the economic use of fire, wind, water, and the mariner's needle; steam, coal, chemical agriculture; the repairs of the human body by the dentist and the surgeon. This is such a resumption of power, as if a banished king should buy his territories inch by inch, instead of vaulting at once into his throne. Meantime, in the thick darkness, there are not wanting gleams of a better light – occasional examples of the action of man upon nature with his entire force – with reason as well as understanding. Such examples are; the traditions of miracles in the earliest antiquity of all nations; the history of Jesus Christ; the achievements of a principle, as in religious and political revolutions, and in the abolition of the Slave-trade; the miracles of enthusiasm, as those reported of Swedenborg, Hohenlohe, and the Shakers; many obscure and yet contested facts, now arranged under the name of Animal Magnetism; prayer; eloquence; self-healing; and the wisdom of children. These are examples of Reason's momentary grasp of the sceptre; the exertions of a power which exists not in time or space, but an instantaneous in-streaming causing power. The difference between the actual and the ideal force of man is happily figured by the schoolmen, in saying, that the knowledge of man is an evening knowledge, *vespertina cognitio*, but that of God is a morning knowledge, *matutina cognitio*.

The problem of restoring to the world original and eternal beauty, is solved by the redemption of the soul. The ruin or the blank, that we see when we look at nature, is in our own eye. The axis of vision is not coincident with the axis of things, and so they appear not transparent but opake. The reason why the world lacks unity, and lies broken and in heaps, is, because man is disunited with himself. He cannot be a naturalist, until he satisfies all the demands of the spirit. Love is as much its demand, as perception. Indeed, neither can be perfect without the other. In the uttermost meaning of the words, thought is devout, and devotion is thought. Deep calls unto deep. But in actual life, the marriage is not celebrated. There are innocent men who worship God after the tradition of their fathers, but their sense of duty has not yet extended to the use of all their faculties. And there are patient naturalists, but they freeze their subject under the wintry light of the understanding. Is not prayer also a study of truth – a sally of the soul into the unfound infinite? No man ever prayed heartily, without learning something. But when a faithful thinker, resolute to detach every object from personal relations, and see it in the light of thought, shall, at the same time, kindle science with the fire of the holiest affections, then will God go forth anew into the creation.

It will not need, when the mind is prepared for study, to search for objects. The invariable mark of wisdom is to see the miraculous in the common. What is a day? What is a year? What is summer? What is woman? What is a child? What is sleep? To our blindness, these things seem unaffecting. We make fables to hide the baldness of the fact and conform it, as we say, to the higher law of the mind. But when the fact is seen under the light of an idea, the gaudy fable fades and shrivels. We behold the real higher law. To the wise, therefore, a fact is true poetry, and the most beautiful of fables. These wonders are brought to our own door. You also are a man. Man and woman, and their social life, poverty, labor, sleep, fear, fortune, are known to you. Learn that none of these things is superficial, but that each phenomenon has its roots in the faculties and affections of the mind. Whilst the abstract question occupies your intellect, nature brings it in the concrete to be solved by your hands. It were a wise inquiry for the closet, to compare, point by point, especially at remarkable crises in life, our daily history, with the rise and progress of ideas in the mind.

So shall we come to look at the world with new eyes. It shall answer the endless inquiry of the intellect – What is truth? and of the affections –

What is good? by yielding itself passive to the educated Will. Then shall come to pass what my poet said: "Nature is not fixed but fluid. Spirit alters, moulds, makes it. The immobility or bruteness of nature, is the absence of spirit; to pure spirit, it is fluid, it is volatile, it is obedient. Every spirit builds itself a house; and beyond its house a world; and beyond its world, a heaven. Know then, that the world exists for you. For you is the phenomenon perfect. What we are, that only can we see. All that Adam had, all that Cæsar could, you have and can do. Adam called his house, heaven and earth; Cæsar called his house, Rome; you perhaps call yours, a cobler's trade; a hundred acres of ploughed land; or a scholar's garret. Yet line for line and point for point, your dominion is as great as theirs, though without fine names. Build, therefore, your own world. As fast as you conform your life to the pure idea in your mind, that will unfold its great proportions. A correspondent revolution in things will attend the influx of the spirit. So fast will disagreeable appearances, swine, spiders, snakes, pests, mad-houses, prisons, enemies, vanish; they are temporary and shall be no more seen. The sordor and filths of nature, the sun shall dry up, and the wind exhale. As when the summer comes from the south; the snow-banks melt, and the face of the earth becomes green before it, so shall the advancing spirit create its ornaments along its path, and carry with it the beauty it visits, and the song which enchants it; it shall draw beautiful faces, warm hearts, wise discourse, and heroic acts, around its way, until evil is no more seen. The kingdom of man over nature, which cometh not with observation – a dominion such as now is beyond his dream of God – he shall enter without more wonder than the blind man feels who is gradually restored to perfect sight."

PART II

Minds and Selves

The plurality of origins that demand attention in the history of American philosophy lead to a concurrent demand to consider the origins of selves and souls, both as individuals and as selves bound to their communities, histories, and places.

Zit Kala Sa provides notions of fate and ways of relying on religious faith as a source of self-formation. That self-formation offers a way of thinking that begins in childhood and is a source of reflection and argument.

Jonathan Edwards, who was a Puritan minister, a missionary to the Native people of Western Massachusetts, and President of Princeton University, is often recognized as America's first philosopher in the European tradition. He argues for perfectionism-consciousness as, at best, a perfect reflection of God's desire. In an important way, his earliest works, written when he was a teenager, present a range of fundamental conflicts that provide a starting point for debating alternative conceptions of self and mind. On the one hand, he advocates a philosophical idealism that tends to reduce the experience of differences, human and otherwise, to the common mind of a Christian god. On the other, he recognizes the fundamental role of pluralism in establishing self-consciousness and the relationship between human beings and their communities. The remaining excerpts in this section take up a range of closely related questions and offer alternative conceptions of self and mind.

Josiah Royce, working from a version of European idealism and his own life along the border of

European American, Native American, and Latin American culture, argues for the intrinsic connections between human individuals, each other, other beings within nature, and nature itself. He offers an evolutionist view of consciousness.

William James tries to affirm Royce's commitment to connections, but transforms it in ways that affirm the value of experience and the irreducible pluralism of human selves. It is a stream of consciousness that he favors.

Charlotte Perkins Gilman takes up the question of selves as embodied in a way that can affirm differences between the experiences of men and women and their ways of understanding and acting. She directly addresses the idea of consciousness embedded in brains, patriarchy, and sex.

W. E. B. Du Bois carries James's commitment to experience toward a conception of racialized selves that can comprehend both a common ground of experience and fundamental differences based on differences of material conditions, history, and community. Du Bois makes problematic any conception of self-worth and consciousness grounded on romantic ideals of an ethnic/racial kind or one denying the obvious reality of ethnicity/race.

George Herbert Mead returns to the importance of community in understanding the nature of selves, focusing on the constructive function of what he calls the "generalized other." His interactionalism is foregrounded.

7

Impressions of an Indian Childhood

Zit Kala Sa

Introduction

Zit Kala Sa (Gertie S. Bonnin) (1876–1938) was a Sioux of Yankton, Plains Indian, South Dakota. She published her autobiographical essays in *Atlantic Monthly*, in 1900, and her first book, *Old Indian Legends*, in 1901. After her early home education, she attended White's Manual Institute in Wabash, Indiana, and the Earlham College in Richmond, Indiana. She promoted pan-Indian identity and in 1926 founded the National Council of American Indians and promoted a form of progressivism (conjoining tradition and modernity).

An Indian Childhood

The big red apples

The first turning away from the easy, natural flow of my life occurred in an early spring. It was in my eighth year; in the month of March, I afterward learned. At this age I knew but one language, and that was my mother's native tongue.

From some of my playmates I heard that two paleface missionaries were in our village. They were from that class of white men who wore big hats and carried large hearts, they said. Running direct to my mother, I began to question her why these two strangers were among us. She told me, after I had teased much, that they had come to take

Taken from *American Indian Stories* (Lincoln: University of Nebraska Press, 1921). Reprinted with permission from University of Nebraska Press.

away Indian boys and girls to the East. My mother did not seem to want me to talk about them. But in a day or two, I gleaned many wonderful stories from my playfellows concerning the strangers.

"Mother, my friend Judéwin is going home with the missionaries. She is going to a more beautiful country than ours; the palefaces told her so!" I said wistfully, wishing in my heart that I too might go.

Mother sat in a chair, and I was hanging on her knee. Within the last two seasons my big brother Dawée had returned from a three years' education in the East, and his coming back influenced my mother to take a farther step from her native way of living. First it was a change from the buffalo skin to the white man's canvas that covered our wigwam. Now she had given up her wigwam of slender poles, to live, a foreigner, in a home of clumsy logs.

"Yes, my child, several others besides Judéwin are going away with the palefaces. Your brother said the missionaries had inquired about his little sister," she said, watching my face very closely.

My heart thumped so hard against my breast, I wondered if she could hear it.

"Did he tell them to take me, mother?" I asked, fearing lest Dawée had forbidden the palefaces to see me, and that my hope of going to the Wonderland would be entirely blighted.

With a sad, slow smile, she answered: "There! I knew you were wishing to go, because Judéwin has filled your ears with the white man's lies. Don't believe a word they say! Their words are sweet, but, my child, their deeds are bitter. You will cry for me, but they will not even soothe you. Stay with me, my little one! Your brother Dawée says that going East, away from your mother, is too hard an experience for his baby sister."

Thus my mother discouraged my curiosity about the lands beyond our eastern horizon; for it was not yet an ambition for Letters that was stirring me. But on the following day the missionaries did come to our very house. I spied them coming up the footpath leading to our cottage. A third man was with them, but he was not my brother Dawée. It was another, a young interpreter, a paleface who had a smattering of the Indian language. I was ready to run out to meet them, but I did not dare to displease my mother. With great glee, I jumped up and down on our ground floor. I begged my mother to open the door, that they would be sure to come to us. Alas! They came, they saw, and they conquered!

Judéwin had told me of the great tree where grew red, red apples; and how we could reach out our hands and pick all the red apples we could eat. I had never seen apple trees. I had never tasted more than a dozen red apples in my life; and when I heard of the orchards of the East, I was eager to roam among them. The missionaries smiled into my eyes and patted my head. I wondered how mother could say such hard words against him.

"Mother, ask them if little girls may have all the red apples they want, when they go East," I whispered aloud, in my excitement.

The interpreter heard me, and answered: "Yes, little girl, the nice red apples are for those who pick them; and you will have a ride on the iron horse if you go with these good people."

I had never seen a train, and he knew it.

"Mother, I am going East! I like big red apples, and I want to ride on the iron horse! Mother, say yes!" I pleaded.

My mother said nothing. The missionaries waited in silence; and my eyes began to blur with tears, though I struggled to choke them back. The corners of my mouth twitched, and my mother saw me.

"I am not ready to give you any word," she said to them. "Tomorrow I shall send you my answer by my son."

With this they left us. Alone with my mother, I yielded to my tears, and cried aloud, shaking my head so as not to hear what she was saying to me. This was the first time I had ever been so unwilling to give up my own desire that I refused to hearken to my mother's voice.

There was a solemn silence in our home that night. Before I went to bed I begged the Great Spirit to make my mother willing I should go with the missionaries.

The next morning came, and my mother called me to her side. "My daughter, do you still persist in wishing to leave your mother?" she asked.

"Oh, mother, it is not that I wish to leave you, but I want to see the wonderful Eastern land," I answered.

My dear old aunt came to our house that morning, and I heard her say, "Let her try it."

I hoped that, as usual, my aunt was pleading on my side. My brother Dawée came for mother's decision. I dropped my play, and crept close to my aunt.

"Yes, Dawée, my daughter, though she does not understand what it all means, is anxious to go. She will need an education when she is grown, for then there will be fewer real Dakotas, and many more palefaces. This tearing her away, so young, from her mother is necessary, if I would have her an educated woman. The palefaces, who owe us a large debt for stolen lands, have begun to pay a tardy justice in offering some education to our children. But I know my daughter must suffer keenly in this experiment. For her sake, I dread to tell you my reply to the missionaries. Go, tell them that they may take my little daughter, and that the Great Spirit shall not fail to reward them according to their hearts."

Wrapped in my heavy blanket, I walked with my mother to the carriage that was soon to take us to the iron horse. I was happy. I met my playmates, who were also wearing their best thick blankets. We showed one another our new beaded moccasins, and the width of the belts that girdled our new dresses. Soon we were being drawn rapidly away by the white man's horses. When I saw the lonely figure of my mother vanish in the distance, a sense of regret settled heavily upon me. I felt suddenly weak, as if I might fall limp to the ground. I was in the hands of strangers whom my mother did not fully trust. I no longer felt free to be myself, or to voice my own feelings. The tears trickled down my cheeks, and I buried my face in the folds of my blanket. Now the first step, parting me from my mother, was taken, and all my belated tears availed nothing.

Having driven thirty miles to the ferryboat, we crossed the Missouri in the evening. Then riding again a few miles eastward, we stopped before a massive brick building. I looked at it in amazement, and with a vague misgiving, for in our village I had never seen so large a house. Trembling with fear and distrust of the palefaces, my teeth chattering from the chilly ride, I crept noiselessly in my soft moccasins along the narrow hall, keeping very close to the bare wall. I was as frightened and bewildered as the captured young of a wild creature.

The School Days of an Indian Girl

The land of red apples

There were eight in our party of bronzed children who were going East with the missionaries. Among us were three young braves, two tall girls, and we three little ones, Judéwin, Thowin, and I.

We had been very impatient to start on our journey to the Red Apple Country, which, we were told, lay a little beyond the great circular horizon of the Western prairie. Under a sky of rosy apples we dreamt of roaming as freely and happily as we had chased the cloud shadows on the Dakota plains. We had anticipated much pleasure from a ride on the iron horse, but the throngs of staring palefaces disturbed and troubled us.

On the train, fair women, with tottering babies on each arm, stopped their haste and scrutinized the children of absent mothers. Large men, with heavy bundles in their hands, halted near by, and riveted their glassy blue eyes upon us.

I sank deep into the corner of my seat, for I resented being watched. Directly in front of me, children who were no larger than I hung themselves upon the backs of their seats, with their bold white faces toward me. Sometimes they took their forefingers out of their mouths and pointed at my moccasined feet. Their mothers, instead of reproving such rude curiosity, looked closely at me, and attracted their children's further notice to my blanket. This embarrassed me, and kept me constantly on the verge of tears.

I sat perfectly still, with my eyes downcast, daring only now and then to shoot long glances around me. Chancing to turn to the window at my side, I was quite breathless upon seeing one familiar object. It was the telegraph pole which strode by at short paces. Very near my mother's dwelling, along the edge of a road thickly bordered with wild sunflowers, some poles like these had been planted by white men. Often I had stopped, on my way down the road, to hold my ear against the pole, and, hearing its low moaning, I used to wonder what the paleface had done to hurt it. Now I sat watching for each pole that glided by to be the last one.

In this way I had forgotten my uncomfortable surroundings, when I heard one of my comrades call out my name. I saw the missionary standing very near, tossing candies and gums into our midst. This amused us all, and we tried to see who could catch the most of the sweetmeats.

Though we rode several days inside of the iron horse, I do not recall a single thing about our luncheons.

It was night when we reached the school grounds. The lights from the windows of the large buildings fell upon some of the icicled trees that stood beneath them. We were led toward an open door, where the brightness of the lights within flooded out over the heads of the excited palefaces who blocked our way. My body trembled more from fear than from the snow I trod upon.

Entering the house, I stood close against the wall. The strong glaring light in the large whitewashed room dazzled my eyes. The noisy hurrying of hard shoes upon a bare wooden floor increased the whirring in my ears. My only safety seemed to be in keeping next to the wall. As I was wondering in which direction to escape from all this confusion, two warm hands grasped me firmly, and in the same moment I was tossed high in midair. A rosy-cheeked paleface woman caught me in her arms. I was both frightened and insulted by such trifling. I stared into her eyes, wishing her to let me stand on my own feet, but she jumped me up and down with increasing enthusiasm. My mother had never made a play-thing of her wee daughter. Remembering this I began to cry aloud.

They misunderstood the cause of my tears, and placed me at a white table loaded with food. There our party were united again. As I did not hush my crying, one of the older ones whispered to me, "Wait until you are alone in the night."

It was very little I could swallow besides my sobs, that evening.

"Oh, I want my mother and my brother Dawée! I want to go to my aunt!" I pleaded; but the ears of the palefaces could not hear me.

From the table we were taken along an upward incline of wooden boxes, which I learned afterward to call a stairway. At the top was a quiet hall, dimly lighted. Many narrow beds were in one straight line down the entire length of the wall. In them lay sleeping brown faces, which peeped just out of the coverings. I was tucked into bed with one of the tall girls, because she talked to me in my mother tongue and seemed to soothe me.

I had arrived in the wonderful land of rosy skies, but I was not happy, as I had thought I should be. My long travel and the bewildering sights had exhausted me. I fell asleep, heaving deep, tired sobs. My tears were left to dry themselves in streaks, because neither my aunt nor my mother was near to wipe them away.

The cutting of my long hair

The first day in the land of apples was a bitter-cold one; for the snow still covered the ground, and the trees were bare. A large bell rang for breakfast, its loud metallic voice crashing through the belfry overhead and into our sensitive ears. The annoying clatter of shoes on bare floors gave us no peace. The constant clash of harsh noises, with an under-current of many voices murmuring an unknown tongue, made a bedlam within which I was securely tied. And though my spirit tore itself in struggling for its lost freedom, all was useless.

A paleface woman, with white hair, came up after us. We were placed in a line of girls who were marching into the dining room. These were Indian girls, in stiff shoes and closely clinging dresses. The small girls wore sleeved aprons and shingled hair. As I walked noiselessly in my soft moccasins, I felt like sinking to the floor, for my blanket had been stripped from my shoulders. I looked hard at the Indian girls, who seemed not to care that they were even more immodestly dressed than I, in their tightly fitting clothes. While we marched in, the boys entered at an opposite door. I watched for the three young braves who came in our party. I spied them in the rear ranks, looking as uncomfortable as I felt.

A small bell was tapped, and each of the pupils drew a chair from under the table. Supposing this act meant they were to be seated, I pulled out mine and at once slipped into it from one side. But when I turned my head, I saw that I was the only one seated, and all the rest at our table remained stand-ing. Just as I began to rise, looking shyly around to see how chairs were to be used, a second bell was sounded. All were seated at last, and I had to crawl back into my chair again. I heard a man's voice at one end of the hall, and I looked around to see him. But all the others hung their heads over their plates. As I glanced at the long chain of tables, I caught the eyes of a paleface woman upon me.

Immediately I dropped my eyes, wondering why I was so keenly watched by the strange woman. The man ceased his mutterings, and then a third bell was tapped. Every one picked up his knife and fork and began eating. I began crying instead, for by this time I was afraid to venture anything more.

But this eating by formula was not the hardest trial in that first day. Late in the morning, my friend Judéwin gave me a terrible warning. Judé-win knew a few words of English; and she had overheard the paleface woman talk about cutting our long, heavy hair. Our mothers had taught us that only unskilled warriors who were captured had their hair shingled by the enemy. Among our people, short hair was worn by mourners, and shingled hair by cowards!

We discussed our fate some moments, and when Judéwin said, "We have to submit, because they are strong," I rebelled.

"No, I will not submit! I will struggle first!" I answered.

I watched my chance, and when no one noticed I disappeared. I crept up the stairs as quietly as I could in my squeaking shoes – my moccasins had been exchanged for shoes. Along the hall I passed, without knowing whither I was going. Turning aside to an open door, I found a large room with three white beds in it. The windows were covered with dark green curtains, which made the room very dim. Thankful that no one was there, I direc-ted my steps toward the corner farthest from the door. On my hands and knees I crawled under the bed, and cuddled myself in the dark corner.

From my hiding place I peered out, shuddering with fear whenever I heard footsteps near by. Though in the hall loud voices were calling my name, and I knew that even Judéwin was searching for me, I did not open my mouth to answer. Then the steps were quickened and the voices became excited. The sounds came nearer and nearer. Women and girls entered the room. I held my breath and watched them open closet doors and peep behind large trunks. Some one threw up the curtains, and the room was filled with sudden light. What caused them to stoop and look under the bed I do not know. I remember being dragged out, though I resisted by kicking and scratching wildly. In spite of myself, I was carried downstairs and tied fast in a chair.

I cried aloud, shaking my head all the while until I felt the cold blades of the scissors against my neck, and heard them gnaw off one of my thick braids. Then I lost my spirit. Since the day I was taken from my mother I had suffered extreme indignities. People had stared at me. I had been tossed about in the air like a wooden puppet. And now my long hair was shingled like a coward's! In my anguish I moaned for my mother, but no one came to comfort me. Not a soul reasoned quietly with me, as my own mother used to do; for now I was only one of many little animals driven by a herder.

The snow episode

A short time after our arrival we three Dakotas were playing in the snowdrift. We were all still deaf to the English language, excepting Judéwin, who always heard such puzzling things. One morning we learned through her ears that we were forbidden to fall lengthwise in the snow, as we had been doing, to see our own impressions. However, before many hours we had forgotten the order, and were having great sport in the snow, when a shrill voice called us. Looking up, we saw an imperative hand beckoning us into the house. We shook the snow off ourselves, and started toward the woman as slowly as we dared.

Judéwin said: "Now the paleface is angry with us. She is going to punish us for falling into the snow. If she looks straight into your eyes and talks loudly, you must wait until she stops. Then, after a tiny pause, say, 'No.'" The rest of the way we practiced upon the little word "no."

As it happened, Thowin was summoned to judgment first. The door shut behind her with a click.

Judéwin and I stood silently listening at the keyhole. The paleface woman talked in very severe tones. Her words fell from her lips like crackling embers, and her inflection ran up like the small end of a switch. I understood her voice better than the things she was saying. I was certain we had made her very impatient with us. Judéwin heard enough of the words to realize all too late that she had taught us the wrong reply.

"Oh, poor Thowin!" she gasped, as she put both hands over her ears.

Just then I heard Thowin's tremulous answer, "No."

With an angry exclamation, the woman gave her a hard spanking. Then she stopped to say something. Judéwin said it was this: "Are you going to obey my word the next time?"

Thowin answered again with the only word at her command, "No."

This time the woman meant her blows to smart, for the poor frightened girl shrieked at the top of her voice. In the midst of the whipping the blows ceased abruptly, and the woman asked another question: "Are you going to fall in the snow again?"

Thowin gave her bad password another trial. We heard her say feebly, "No! No!"

With this the woman hid away her half-worn slipper, and led the child out, stroking her black shorn head. Perhaps it occurred to her that brute force is not the solution for such a problem. She did nothing to Judéwin nor to me. She only returned to us our unhappy comrade, and left us alone in the room.

During the first two or three seasons misunderstandings as ridiculous as this one of the snow episode frequently took place, bringing unjustifiable frights and punishments into our little lives.

Within a year I was able to express myself somewhat in broken English. As soon as I comprehended a part of what was said and done, a mischievous spirit of revenge possessed me. One day I was called in from my play for some misconduct. I had disregarded a rule which seemed to me very needlessly binding. I was sent into the kitchen to mash the turnips for dinner. It was noon, and steaming dishes were hastily carried into the dining-room. I hated turnips, and their odor which came from the brown jar was offensive to me. With fire in my heart, I took the wooden tool that the paleface woman held out to me. I stood upon a step, and, grasping the handle with both hands, I bent in hot rage over the turnips. I worked my vengeance upon them. All were so busily occupied that no one noticed me. I saw that the turnips were in a pulp, and that further beating could not improve them; but the order was, "Mash these turnips," and mash them I would! I renewed my energy; and as I sent the masher into the bottom of the jar, I felt a satisfying sensation that the weight of my body had gone into it.

Just here a paleface woman came up to my table. As she looked into the jar, she shoved my hands roughly aside. I stood fearless and angry. She placed her red hands upon the rim of the jar. Then she gave one lift and strode away from the table. But lo! the pulpy contents fell through the crumbled bottom to the floor! She spared me no scolding phrases that I had earned. I did not heed them. I felt triumphant in my revenge, though deep within me I was a wee bit sorry to have broken the jar.

As I sat eating my dinner, and saw that no turnips were served, I whooped in my heart for having once asserted the rebellion within me.

The devil

Among the legends the old warriors used to tell me were many stories of evil spirits. But I was taught to fear them no more than those who stalked about in material guise. I never knew there was an insolent chieftain among the bad spirits, who dared to array his forces against the Great Spirit, until I heard this white man's legend from a paleface woman.

Out of a large book she showed me a picture of the white man's devil. I looked in horror upon the strong claws that grew out of his fur-covered fingers. His feet were like his hands. Trailing at his heels was a scaly tail tipped with a serpent's open jaws. His face was a patchwork: he had bearded cheeks, like some I had seen palefaces wear; his nose was an eagle's bill, and his sharp-pointed ears were pricked up like those of a sly fox. Above them a pair of cow's horns curved upward. I trembled with awe, and my heart throbbed in my throat, as I looked at the king of evil spirits. Then I heard the paleface woman say that this terrible creature roamed loose in the world, and that little girls who disobeyed school regulations were to be tortured by him.

That night I dreamt about this evil divinity. Once again I seemed to be in my mother's cottage. An Indian woman had come to visit my mother. On opposite sides of the kitchen stove, which stood in the center of the small house, my mother and her guest were seated in straight-backed chairs. I played with a train of empty spools hitched together on a string. It was night, and the wick burned feebly. Suddenly I heard some one turn our door-knob from without.

My mother and the woman hushed their talk, and both looked toward the door. It opened gradually. I waited behind the stove. The hinges squeaked as the door was slowly, very slowly pushed inward.

Then in rushed the devil! He was tall! He looked exactly like the picture I had seen of him in the white man's papers. He did not speak to my mother, because he did not know the Indian language, but his glittering yellow eyes were fastened upon me. He took long strides around the stove,

passing behind the woman's chair. I threw down my spools, and ran to my mother. He did not fear her, but followed closely after me. Then I ran round and round the stove, crying aloud for help. But my mother and the woman seemed not to know my danger. They sat still, looking quietly upon the devil's chase after me. At last I grew dizzy. My head revolved as on a hidden pivot. My knees became numb, and doubled under my weight like a pair of knife blades without a spring. Beside my mother's chair I fell in a heap. Just as the devil stooped over me with outstretched claws my mother awoke from her quiet indifference, and lifted me on her lap. Whereupon the devil vanished, and I was awake.

On the following morning I took my revenge upon the devil. Stealing into the room where a wall of shelves was filled with books, I drew forth The Stories of the Bible. With a broken slate pencil I carried in my apron pocket, I began by scratching out his wicked eyes. A few moments later, when I was ready to leave the room, there was a ragged hole in the page where the picture of the devil had once been.

Iron routine

A loud-clamoring bell awakened us at half-past six in the cold winter mornings. From happy dreams of Western rolling lands and unlassoed freedom we tumbled out upon chilly bare floors back again into a paleface day. We had short time to jump into our shoes and clothes, and wet our eyes with icy water, before a small hand bell was vigorously rung for roll call.

There were too many drowsy children and too numerous orders for the day to waste a moment in any apology to nature for giving her children such a shock in the early morning. We rushed downstairs, bounding over two high steps at a time, to land in the assembly room.

A paleface woman, with a yellow-covered roll book open on her arm and a gnawed pencil in her hand, appeared at the door. Her small, tired face was coldly lighted with a pair of large gray eyes.

She stood still in a halo of authority, while over the rim of her spectacles her eyes pried nervously about the room. Having glanced at her long list of names and called out the first one, she tossed up her chin and peered through the crystals of her spectacles to make sure of the answer "Here."

Relentlessly her pencil black-marked our daily records if we were not present to respond to our names, and no chum of ours had done it successfully for us. No matter if a dull headache or the painful cough of slow consumption had delayed the absentee, there was only time enough to mark the tardiness. It was next to impossible to leave the iron routine after the civilizing machine had once begun its day's buzzing; and as it was inbred in me to suffer in silence rather than to appeal to the ears of one whose open eyes could not see my pain, I have many times trudged in the day's harness heavy-footed, like a dumb sick brute.

Once I lost a dear classmate. I remember well how she used to mope along at my side, until one morning she could not raise her head from her pillow. At her deathbed I stood weeping, as the paleface woman sat near her moistening the dry lips. Among the folds of the bedclothes I saw the open pages of the white man's Bible. The dying Indian girl talked disconnectedly of Jesus the Christ and the paleface who was cooling her swollen hands and feet.

I grew bitter, and censured the woman for cruel neglect of our physical ills. I despised the pencils that moved automatically, and the one teaspoon which dealt out, from a large bottle, healing to a row of variously ailing Indian children. I blamed the hard-working, well-meaning, ignorant woman who was inculcating in our hearts her superstitious ideas. Though I was sullen in all my little troubles, as soon as I felt better I was ready again to smile upon the cruel woman. Within a week I was again actively testing the chains which tightly bound my individuality like a mummy for burial.

The melancholy of those black days has left so long a shadow that it darkens the path of years that have since gone by. These sad memories rise above those of smoothly grinding school days. Perhaps my Indian nature is the moaning wind which stirs them now for their present record. But, however tempestuous this is within me, it comes out as the low voice of a curiously colored seashell, which is only for those ears that are bent with compassion to hear it.

Four strange summers

After my first three years of school, I roamed again in the Western country through four strange summers.

During this time I seemed to hang in the heart of chaos, beyond the touch or voice of human aid. My brother, being almost ten years my senior, did not quite understand my feelings. My mother had

never gone inside of a schoolhouse, and so she was not capable of comforting her daughter who could read and write. Even nature seemed to have no place for me. I was neither a wee girl nor a tall one; neither a wild Indian nor a tame one. This deplorable situation was the effect of my brief course in the East, and the unsatisfactory "teenth" in a girl's years.

It was under these trying conditions that, one bright afternoon, as I sat restless and unhappy in my mother's cabin, I caught the sound of the spirited step of my brother's pony on the road which passed by our dwelling. Soon I heard the wheels of a light buckboard, and Dawée's familiar "Ho!" to his pony. He alighted upon the bare ground in front of our house. Tying his pony to one of the projecting corner logs of the low-roofed cottage, he stepped upon the wooden doorstep.

I met him there with a hurried greeting, and, as I passed by, he looked a quiet "What?" into my eyes.

When he began talking with my mother, I slipped the rope from the pony's bridle. Seizing the reins and bracing my feet against the dashboard, I wheeled around in an instant. The pony was ever ready to try his speed. Looking backward, I saw Dawée waving his hand to me. I turned with the curve in the road and disappeared. I followed the winding road which crawled upward between the bases of little hillocks. Deep water-worn ditches ran parallel on either side. A strong wind blew against my cheeks and fluttered my sleeves. The pony reached the top of the highest hill, and began an even race on the level lands. There was nothing moving within that great circular horizon of the Dakota prairies save the tall grasses, over which the wind blew and rolled off in long, shadowy waves.

Within this vast wigwam of blue and green I rode reckless and insignificant. It satisfied my small consciousness to see the white foam fly from the pony's mouth.

Suddenly, out of the earth a coyote came forth at a swinging trot that was taking the cunning thief toward the hills and the village beyond. Upon the moment's impulse, I gave him a long chase and a wholesome fright. As I turned away to go back to the village, the wolf sank down upon his haunches for rest, for it was a hot summer day; and as I drove slowly homeward, I saw his sharp nose still pointed at me, until I vanished below the margin of the hilltops.

In a little while I came in sight of my mother's house. Dawée stood in the yard, laughing at an old warrier who was pointing his forefinger, and again waving his whole hand, toward the hills. With his blanket drawn over one shoulder, he talked and motioned excitedly. Dawée turned the old man by the shoulder and pointed me out to him.

"Oh, han!" (Oh, yes) the warrior muttered, and went his way. He had climbed the top of his favorite barren hill to survey the surrounding prairies, when he spied my chase after the coyote. His keen eyes recognized the pony and driver. At once uneasy for my safety, he had come running to my mother's cabin to give her warning. I did not appreciate his kindly interest, for there was an unrest gnawing at my heart.

As soon as he went away, I asked Dawée about something else.

"No, my baby sister, I cannot take you with me to the party tonight," he replied. Though I was not far from fifteen, and I felt that before long I should enjoy all the priviliges of my tall cousin, Dawée persisted in calling me his baby sister.

That moonlight night, I cried in my mother's presence when I heard the jolly young people pass by our cottage. They were no more young braves in blankets and eagle plumes, nor Indian maids with prettily painted cheeks. They had gone three years to school in the East, and had become civilized. The young men wore the white man's coat and trousers, with bright neckties. The girls wore tight muslin dresses, with ribbons at neck and waist. At these gatherings they talked English. I could speak English almost as well as my brother, but I was not properly dressed to be taken along. I had no hat, no ribbons, and no close-fitting gown. Since my return from school I had thrown away my shoes, and wore again the soft moccasins.

While Dawée was busily preparing to go I controlled my tears. But when I heard him bounding away on his pony, I buried my face in my arms and cried hot tears.

My mother was troubled by my unhappiness. Coming to my side, she offered me the only printed matter we had in our home. It was an Indian Bible, given her some years ago by a missionary. She tried to console me. "Here, my child, are the white man's papers. Read a little from them," she said most piously.

I took it from her hand, for her sake; but my enraged spirit felt more like burning the book, which afforded me no help, and was a perfect delusion to my mother. I did not read it, but laid it unopened on the floor, where I sat on my feet. The dim yellow light of the braided muslin burning in a small vessel of oil flickered and sizzled in the awful silent storm which followed my rejection of the Bible.

Now my wrath against the fates consumed my tears before they reached my eyes. I sat stony, with a bowed head. My mother threw a shawl over her head and shoulders, and stepped out into the night.

After an uncertain solitude, I was suddenly aroused by a loud cry piercing the night. It was my mother's voice wailing among the barren hills which held the bones of buried warriors. She called aloud for her brothers' spirits to support her in her helpless misery. My fingers grew icy cold, as I realized that my unrestrained tears had betrayed my suffering to her, and she was grieving for me.

Before she returned, though I knew she was on her way, for she had ceased her weeping, I extinguished the light, and leaned my head on the window sill.

Many schemes of running away from my surroundings hovered about in my mind. A few more moons of such a turmoil drove me away to the eastern school. I rode on the white man's iron steed, thinking it would bring me back to my mother in a few winters, when I should be grown tall, and there would be congenial friends awaiting me.

8

Of Being and Original Sin

Jonathan Edwards

Introduction

Jonathan Edwards (1703–58), third president of
Princeton University for a brief period in 1758,
was born in East Windsor, Connecticut and became
a noted Colonial Congregational preacher and
theologian. He was especially noted for requiring
evidence of conversion beyond verbal public assent
and, later, for encouraging individual interpretation
of sacred texts. Edwards entered Yale when he was
not yet 13 years old. He studied theology, preached
in a Presbyterian pulpit in New York, and in 1724
returned to Yale as tutor for two years. In 1728 he succeeded his maternal grandfather as pastor at North-
ampton, Massachusetts. He moved to Stockbridge,
Massachusetts, then a frontier settlement, where
he ministered to a tiny congregation and served as
missionary to the Housatonic Indians. He completed
*A Careful and Strict Enquiry...of the Freedom of the
Will* in 1754 and two dissertations in 1765: "The
Nature of True Virtue" and "Concerning the End for
which God Created the World." Edwards led the religious revival movement known as the Great Awakening. The selections presented here illustrate a
complex attempt to adapt English empiricism and
Puritan theology to the American context. Here,
Edwards recognizes the importance of experience

for knowledge, even as he recognizes the inherent
fallibilism and pluralism of experience.

Of Being

That there should absolutely be nothing at all is
utterly impossible. The mind can never, let it
stretch its conceptions ever so much, bring itself
to conceive of a state of perfect nothing. It puts the
mind into mere convulsion and confusion to
endeavor to think of such a state, and it contradicts
the very nature of the soul to think that it should
be; and it is the greatest contradiction, and the
aggregate of all contradictions, to say that there
should not be. 'Tis true we can't so distinctly shew
the contradiction by words, because we cannot talk
about it without speaking horrid nonsense and
contradicting ourselves at every word, and because
"nothing" is that whereby we distinctly shew
other particular contradictions. But here we are
run up to our first principle, and have no other
to explain the nothingness or not being of nothing
by. Indeed, we can mean nothing else by "nothing" but a state of absolute contradiction. And if
any man thinks that he can think well enough how
there should be nothing, I'll engage that what he
means by "nothing" is as much something as anything that ever he thought of in his life; and I
believe that if he knew what nothing was it
would be intuitively evident to him that it could
not be. So that we see it is necessary some being
should eternally be. And 'tis a more palpable contradiction still to say that there must be being

"Of Being" is taken from *Scientific and Philosophical
Writings*, ed. Wallace E. Anderson (New Haven and
London: Yale University Press, 1980); "Original Sin"
is taken from *Original Sin*, ed. Clyde A. Holbrook
(New Haven and London: Yale University Press,
1970).

somewhere, and not otherwhere; for the words "absolute nothing" and "where" contradict each other. And besides, it gives as great a shock to the mind to think of pure nothing in any one place, as it does to think of it in all; and it is self-evident that there can be nothing in one place as well as in another, and so if there can be in one, there can be in all. So that we see this necessary, eternal being must be infinite and omnipresent.

This infinite and omnipresent being cannot be solid. Let us see how contradictory it is to say that an infinite being is solid; for solidity surely is nothing but resistance to other solidities.

Space is this necessary, eternal, infinite and omnipresent being. We find that we can with ease conceive how all other beings should not be. We can remove them out of our minds, and place some other in the room of them; but space is the very thing that we can never remove and conceive of its not being. If a man would imagine space anywhere to be divided, so as there should be nothing between the divided parts, there remains space between notwithstanding, and so the man contradicts himself. And it is self-evident, I believe, to every man, that space is necessary, eternal, infinite and omnipresent. But I had as good speak plain: I have already said as much as that space is God. And it is indeed clear to me, that all the space there is not proper to body, all the space there is without the bounds of the creation, all the space there was before the creation, is God himself. And nobody would in the least stick at it, if it were not because of the gross conceptions that we have of space.

And how doth it grate upon the mind, to think that something should be from all eternity, and nothing all the while be conscious of it. Let us suppose, to illustrate it, that the world had a being from all eternity, and had many great changes and wonderful revolutions, and all the while nothing knew; there was no knowledge in the universe of any such thing. How is it possible to bring the mind to imagine? Yea, it is really impossible it should be, that anything should be, and nothing know it. Then you'll say, if it be so, it is because nothing has any existence anywhere else but in consciousness. No, certainly nowhere else, but either in created or uncreated consciousness.

Supposing there were another universe only of bodies, created at a great distance from this, created in excellent order and harmonious motions, and a beautiful variety; and there was no created

intelligence in it, nothing but senseless bodies. Nothing but God knew anything of it. I demand in what respect this world has a being, but only in the divine consciousness. Certainly in no respect. There would be figures and magnitudes, and motions and proportions – but where? Where else, but in the Almighty's knowledge. How is it possible there should? Then you'll say: For the same reason, in a room close shut up, that nobody sees nor hears nothing in it, there is nothing any other way than in God's knowledge. I answer: Created beings are conscious of the effects of what is in the room; for perhaps there is not one leaf of a tree, nor spire of grass, but what has effects all over the universe, and will have to the end of eternity. But any otherwise, there is nothing in a room shut up, but only in God's consciousness. How can anything be there any other way? This will appear to be truly so to anyone that thinks of it with the whole united strength of his mind. Let us suppose for illustration this impossibility, that all the spirits in the universe to be for a time deprived of their consciousness, and God's consciousness at the same time to be intermitted. I say, the universe for that time would cease to be, of itself; and not only, as we speak, because the Almighty could not attend to uphold the world, but because God knew nothing of it. 'Tis our foolish imagination that will not suffer us to see. We fancy there may be figures and magnitudes, relations and properties, without anyone's knowing of it. But it is our imagination hurts us. We don't know what figures and properties are.

Our imagination makes us fancy we see shapes and colors and magnitudes though nobody is there to behold it. But to help our imagination let us thus state the case: Let us suppose the world deprived of every ray of light, so that there should not be the least glimmering of light in the universe. Now all will own that in such a case, the universe would be immediately really deprived of all its colors. One part of the universe is no more red, or blue, or green, or yellow, or black, or white, or light, or dark, or transparent or opaque than another. There would be no visible distinction between the world and the rest of the incomprehensible void – yea, there would be no difference in these respects between the world and the infinite void. That is, any part of that void would really be as light and as dark, as white and as black, as red and green, as blue and as brown, as transparent and as opaque as any part of the universe. Or, as there would be in such case no difference between the world and nothing in these respects, so there would be no difference between one part of the world and another. All, in these respects, is alike confounded with and indistinguishable from infinite emptiness.

At the same time, also let us suppose the universe to be altogether deprived of motion, and all parts of it to be at perfect rest (the former supposition is indeed included in this, but we distinguish them for better clearness). Then the universe would not differ from the void in this respect; there will be no more motion in one than the other. Then also solidity would cease. All that we mean or can be meant by solidity is resistance – resistance to touch, the resistance of some parts of space. This is all the knowledge we get of solidity by our senses, and, I am sure, all that we can get any other way. But solidity shall be shewn to be nothing else more fully hereafter. But there can be no resistance if there is no motion. One body cannot resist another when there is perfect rest amongst them. But you'll say, though there is not actually resistance, yet there is potential existence, that is such and such parts of space would resist upon occasion. But this is all I would have: that there is no solidity now; not but that God would cause there to be on occasion. And if there is no solidity, there is no extension, for extension is the extendedness of the solidity. Then all figure and magnitude and proportion immediately ceases.

Put both these suppositions together, that is, deprive the world of light and motion, and the case would stand thus with the world: There would be neither white nor black, neither blue nor brown, bright nor shaded, pellucid nor opaque; no noise or sound, neither heat nor cold, neither fluid nor wet nor dry, hard nor soft, nor solidity, nor extension, nor figure, nor magnitude, nor proportion; nor body, nor spirit. What then is become of the universe? Certainly, it exists nowhere but in the divine mind. This will be abundantly clearer to one after having read what I have further to say of solidity, etc. So that we see that a world without motion can exist nowhere else but in the mind, either infinite or finite.

Corollary 1. It follows from hence, that those beings which have knowledge and consciousness are the only proper and real and substantial beings, inasmuch as the being of other things is only by these. From hence we may see the gross mistake of those who think material things the most substan-

tial beings, and spirits more like a shadow; whereas spirits only are properly substance.

[...]

Original Sin

That great objection against the imputation of Adam's sin to his posterity considered, that such imputation is unjust and unreasonable, inasmuch as Adam and his posterity are not one and the same. With a brief reflection subjoined, on what some have supposed, of God's imputing the guilt of Adam's sin to his posterity, but in an infinitely less degree, than to Adam himself.

That we may proceed with the greater clearness in considering the main objections against supposing the guilt of Adam's sin to be imputed to his posterity, I would premise some observations with a view to the right stating of the doctrine of the imputation of Adam's first sin; and then shew the *reasonableness* of this doctrine, in opposition to the great clamor raised against it on this head.

I think, it would go far towards directing us to the more clear and distinct conceiving and right stating of this affair, if we steadily bear this in mind; that God, in each step of his proceeding with Adam, in relation to the covenant or constitution established with him, looked on his posterity as being one with him. (The propriety of his looking upon them so, I shall speak to afterwards.) And though he dealt more immediately with Adam, yet it was as the head of the whole body, and the root of the whole tree; and in his proceedings with him, he dealt with all the branches, as if they had been then existing in their root.

From which it will follow, that both guilt, or exposedness to punishment, and also depravity of heart, came upon Adam's posterity just as they came upon him, as much as if he and they had all coexisted, like a tree with many branches; allowing only for the difference necessarily resulting from the place Adam stood in, as head or root of the whole, and being first and most immediately dealt with, and most immediately acting and suffering. Otherwise, it is as if, in every step of proceeding, every alteration in the root had been attended, at the same instant, with the same steps and alterations throughout the whole tree, in each individual branch. I think, this will naturally follow on the supposition of there being a constituted *oneness* or *identity* of Adam and his posterity in this affair.

Therefore I am humbly of opinion, that if any have supposed the children of Adam to come into the world with a *double guilt*, one the guilt of Adam's sin, another the guilt arising from their having a corrupt heart, they have not so well conceived of the matter. The guilt a man has upon his soul at his first existence, is one and simple: viz. the guilt of the original apostacy, the guilt of the sin by which the species first rebelled against God. This, and the guilt arising from the first corruption or depraved disposition of the heart, are not to be looked upon as two things, distinctly imputed and charged upon men in the sight of God. Indeed the guilt, that arises from the corruption of the heart, as it remains a confirmed principle, and appears in its consequent operations, is a distinct and additional guilt: but the guilt arising from the first existing of a depraved disposition in Adam's posterity, I apprehend, is not distinct from their guilt of Adam's first sin. For so it was not in Adam himself. The first evil disposition or inclination of the heart of Adam to sin, was not properly distinct from his first act of sin, but was included in it. The external act he committed was no otherwise his, than as his heart was in it, or as that action proceeded from the wicked inclination of his heart. Nor was the guilt he had, double, as for two distinct sins: one, the wickedness of his heart and will in that affair; another, the wickedness of the external act, caused by his heart. His guilt was all truly from the act of his inward man; exclusive of which the motions of his body were no more than the motions of any lifeless instrument. His sin consisted in wickedness of heart, fully sufficient *for*, and entirely amounting *to*, all that appeared in the act he committed.

The depraved disposition of Adam's heart is to be considered two ways. (1) As the first rising of an evil inclination in his heart, exerted in his first act of sin, and the ground of the complete transgression. (2) An evil disposition of heart continuing afterwards, as a confirmed principle, that came by God's forsaking him; which was a *punishment* of his first transgression. This confirmed corruption, by its remaining and continued operation, brought additional guilt on his soul.

And in like manner, depravity of heart is to be considered two ways in Adam's posterity. The first existing of a corrupt disposition in their hearts is not to be looked upon as sin belonging to them, distinct from their participation of Adam's first sin: it is as it were the *extended pollution* of that sin, through the whole tree, by virtue of the con-

stituted union of the branches with the root; or the inherence of the sin of that head of the species in the members, in the consent and concurrence of the hearts of the members with the head in that first act. (Which may be, without God's being the author of sin; about which I have spoken in a former chapter.) But the depravity of nature, remaining an *established principle* in the heart of a child of Adam, and as exhibited in after-operations, is a consequence and punishment of the first apostacy thus participated, and brings new guilt. The first being of an evil disposition in the heart of a child of Adam, whereby he is disposed to *approve* of the sin of his first father, as fully as he himself approved of it when he committed it, or so far as to imply a full and perfect consent of heart to it, I think, is not to be looked upon as a consequence of the imputation of that first sin, any more than the full consent of Adam's own heart in the act of sinning; which was not consequent on the imputation of his sin to himself, but rather *prior* to it in the order of nature. Indeed the derivation of the evil disposition to the hearts of Adam's posterity, or rather the *coexistence* of the evil disposition, implied in Adam's first rebellion, in the root and branches, is a consequence of the union, that the wise Author of the world has established between Adam and his posterity: but not properly a consequence of the imputation of his sin; nay, rather *antecedent* to it, as it was in Adam himself. The first depravity of heart, and the imputation of that sin, are both the consequences of that established union: but yet in such order, that the evil disposition is *first*, and the charge of guilt *consequent*; as it was in the case of Adam himself.[1]

The first existence of an evil disposition of heart, amounting to a full consent to Adam's sin, no more infers God's being the author of that evil disposition in the child, than in the father. The first arising or existing of that evil disposition in the heart of Adam, was by God's *permission*; who could have prevented it, if he had pleased, by giving such influences of his spirit, as would have been absolutely effectual to hinder it; which, it is plain in fact, he did withhold: and whatever mystery may be supposed in the affair, yet no Christian will presume to say, it was not in perfect consistence with God's holiness and righteousness, notwithstanding Adam had been guilty of no offense before. So root and branches being one, according to God's wise constitution, the case in fact is, that by virtue of this oneness, answerable changes of effects through all the branches coexist with the changes in the root: consequently an evil disposition exists in the hearts of Adam's posterity, equivalent to that which was exerted in his own heart, when he eat the forbidden fruit. Which God has no hand in, any otherwise, than in *not* exerting such an influence, as might be effectual to prevent it; as appears by what was observed in the former chapter.

But now the grand objection is against the *reasonableness*, of such a constitution, by which Adam and his posterity should be looked upon as one, and dealt with accordingly, in an affair of such infinite consequence; so that if Adam sinned, they must necessarily be made sinners by his disobedience, and come into existence with the same depravity of disposition, and be looked upon and treated as though they were partakers with Adam in his act of sin. I have not room here to rehearse all Dr. Taylor's vehement exclamations against the reasonableness and justice of this. The reader may at his leisure consult his book, and see them in places referred to in the margin. Whatever black colors and frightful representations are employed on this occasion, all may be summed up in this, that Adam and his posterity are *not one*, but entirely *distinct agents*. But with respect to this mighty outcry made against the reasonableness of any such constitution, by which God is supposed to treat Adam and his posterity as one, I would make the following observations.

I. It signifies nothing, to exclaim against plain fact. Such is the fact, most evident and acknowledged fact, with respect to the state of all mankind, without exception of one individual among all the natural descendants of Adam, as makes it apparent, that God actually deals with Adam and his posterity as one, in the affair of his apostacy, and its infinitely terrible consequences. It has been demonstrated, and shewn to be in effect plainly acknowledged, that every individual of mankind comes into the world in such circumstances, as that there is no hope or possibility of any other than their violating God's holy law (if they ever live to act at all, as moral agents), and being thereby justly exposed to eternal ruin. And it is thus by God's ordering and disposing of things. And God either thus deals with mankind, because he looks upon them as one with their first father, and so treats them as sinful and guilty by his apostacy; or (which won't mend the matter) he, without viewing them as at all concerned in that affair, but as in every respect perfectly innocent, does nevertheless subject them to this infinitely

dreadful calamity. Adam by his sin was exposed to the calamities and sorrows of this life, to temporal death, and eternal ruin; as is confessed. And 'tis also in effect confessed, that all his posterity come into the world in such a state, as that the certain consequence is their being exposed, and justly so, to the sorrows of this life, to temporal death, and eternal ruin, unless saved by grace. So that we see, God in fact deals with them together, or as one. If God orders the consequences of Adam's sin, with regard to his posterity's welfare, even in those things which are most important, and which do in the highest degree concern their eternal interest, to be the same with the consequences to Adam himself, then he treats Adam and his posterity as in that affair one. Hence, however the matter be attended with difficulty, fact obliges us to get over the difficulty, either by finding out some solution, or by shutting our mouths, and acknowledging the weakness and scantiness of our understandings; as we must in innumerable other cases, where apparent and undeniable fact, in God's works of creation and providence, is attended with events and circumstances, the manner and reason of which are difficult to our understandings. But to proceed,

II. We will consider the difficulties themselves, insisted on in the objections of our opposers. They may be reduced to these two: first, that such a constitution is *injurious* to Adam's posterity. Secondly, that it is altogether *improper*, as it implies *falsehood*; viewing and treating those as one, which indeed are not one, but entirely distinct.

First difficulty, that the appointing Adam to stand in this great affair, as the moral head of his posterity, and so treating them as one with him, as standing or falling with him, is *injurious* to them, and tends to their hurt. To which I answer, it is demonstrably otherwise; that such a constitution was so far from being injurious and hurtful to Adam's posterity, or tending to their calamity, any more than if every one had been appointed to stand for himself personally, that it was, in itself considered, very much of a contrary tendency, and was attended with a more eligible probability of an happy issue, than the latter would have been: and so is a constitution truly expressing the goodness of its author. For here the following things are to be considered.

1 'Tis reasonable to suppose, that Adam was *as likely*, on account of his capacity and natural talents, to *persevere* in obedience, as his posterity

(taking one with another), if they had all been put on the trial singly for themselves. And supposing, that there was a constituted union or oneness of him and his posterity, and that he stood as a public person, or common head, all by this constitution would have been as sure to partake of the benefit of his obedience, as of the ill consequence of his disobedience, in case of his fall.

2 There was a *greater tendency* to a happy issue, in such an appointment, than if every one had been appointed to stand for himself; especially on two accounts. (1) That Adam had *stronger motives* to watchfulness, than his posterity would have had; in that not only his own eternal welfare lay at stake, but also that of all his posterity. (2) Adam was in a state of complete *manhood*, when his trial began. It was a constitution very agreeable to the goodness of God, considering the state of mankind, which was to be propagated in the way of generation, that their first father should be appointed to stand for all. For by reason of the manner of their coming into existence in a state of infancy, and their coming so gradually to mature state, and so remaining for a great while in a state of childhood and comparative imperfection, after they were become moral agents, they would be less fit to stand for themselves, than their first father to stand for them.

If any man, notwithstanding these things, shall say, that for his own part, if the affair had been proposed to him, he should have chosen to have his eternal interest trusted in *his own hands*: 'tis sufficient to answer, that no man's vain opinion of himself, as more fit to be trusted than others, alters the true nature and tendency of things, as they demonstrably are in themselves. Nor is it a just objection, that this constitution has in event proved for the hurt of mankind. For it don't follow, that no advantage was given for a happy event, in such an establishment, because it was not such as to make it utterly impossible there should be any other event.

3 The goodness of God in such a constitution with Adam appears in this: that if there had been no *sovereign gracious* establishment at all, but God had proceeded only on the foot of mere justice, and had gone no further than this required, he might have demanded of Adam and all his posterity, that they should perform *perfect perpetual* obedience, without ever failing in the least instance, on pain of eternal death; and might have made this demand without the promise of any positive reward for their obedience. For perfect obedience is a debt,

that every one owes to his Creator; and therefore is what his Creator was not obliged to pay him for. None is obliged to pay his debtor, only for discharging his just debt. But such was evidently the constitution with Adam, that an eternal happy life was to be the consequence of his persevering fidelity, to all such as were included within that constitution (of which the Tree of Life was a sign), as well as eternal death to be the consequence of his disobedience. I come now to consider the

Second difficulty. It being thus manifest, that this constitution, by which Adam and his posterity are dealt with as one, is not unreasonable upon account of its being injurious and hurtful to the interest of mankind, the only thing remaining in the objection against such a constitution, is the *impropriety* of it, as implying *falsehood*, and contradiction to the true nature of things; as hereby they are viewed and treated as one, who are not one, but wholly distinct; and no arbitrary constitution can ever make that to be true, which in itself considered is not true.

The objection, however specious, is really founded on a false hypothesis, and wrong notion of what we call *sameness* or *oneness*, among created things; and the seeming force of the objection arises from ignorance or inconsideration of the degree, in which created identity or oneness with past existence, in general, depends on the sovereign constitution and law of the Supreme Author and Disposer of the universe.

Some things, being most simply considered, are entirely distinct, and very diverse; which yet are so united by the established law of the Creator, in some respects and with regard to some purposes and effects, that by virtue of that establishment it is with them as if they were one. Thus a tree, grown great, and an hundred years old, is one plant with the little sprout, that first came out of the ground, from whence it grew, and has been continued in constant succession; though it's now so exceeding diverse, many thousand times bigger, and of a very different form, and perhaps not one atom the very same: yet God, according to an established law of nature, has in a constant succession communicated to it many of the same qualities, and most important properties, as if it were one. It has been his pleasure, to constitute an union in these respects, and for these purposes, naturally leading us to look upon all as one. So the body of man at forty years of age, is one with the infant body which first came into the world, from whence it grew; though now constituted of different substance, and the greater part of the substance probably changed scores (if not hundreds) of times; and though it be now in so many respects exceeding diverse, yet God, according to the course of nature, which he has been pleased to establish, has caused, that in a certain method it should communicate with that infantile body, in the same life, the same senses, the same features, and many the same qualities, and in union with the same soul; and so, with regard to these purposes, 'tis dealt with by him as one body. Again, the body and soul of a man are one, in a very different manner, and for different purposes. Considered in themselves, they are exceeding different beings, of a nature as diverse as can be conceived; and yet, by a very peculiar divine constitution or law of nature, which God has been pleased to establish, they are strongly united, and become one, in most important respects; a wonderful mutual communication is established; so that both become different parts of the same man. But the union and mutual communication they have, has existence, and is entirely regulated and limited, according to the sovereign pleasure of God, and the constitution he has been pleased to establish.

And if we come even to the *personal identity* of created intelligent beings, though this be not allowed to consist wholly in that which Mr. Locke places it in, i.e. *same consciousness*; yet I think it can't be denied, that this is one thing essential to it. But 'tis evident, that the communication or continuance of the same consciousness and memory to any subject, through successive parts of duration, depends wholly on a divine establishment. There would be no necessity, that the remembrance and ideas of what is past should continue to exist, but by an arbitrary constitution of the Creator. If any should here insist, that there is no need of having recourse to any such constitution, in order to account for the continuance of the *same consciousness*; and should say, that the very nature of the soul is such as will sufficiently account for it; and that the soul will retain the ideas and consciousness it once had, according to the course of nature: then let it be remembered, who it is, gives the soul this nature; and let that be remembered, which Dr. Taylor says of the course of nature, before observed; denying, that "the course of nature is a proper active cause, which will work and go on by itself without God, if he lets and permits it"; saying, that "the course of nature, separate from the agency of God, is no

cause, or nothing," and affirming, that "it's absolutely impossible, the course of nature should continue itself, or go on to operate by itself, any more than produce itself" and that "God, the original of all being, is the *only cause* of all natural effects." Here is worthy also to be observed, what Dr. Turnbull says of the laws of nature, in words which he cites from Sir Isaac Newton. "It is the will of the mind that is the first cause, that gives a subsistence and efficacy to all those laws, who is the efficient cause that produces the phenomena, which appear in analogy, harmony and agreement, according to these laws." And he says, "The same principles must take place in things pertaining to moral, as well as natural philosophy."

From these things it will clearly follow, that identity of consciousness depends wholly on a law of nature; and so, on the sovereign will and agency of God; and therefore, that personal identity, and so the derivation of the pollution and guilt of past sins in the same person, depends on an arbitrary divine constitution: and this, even though we should allow the same consciousness not to be the only thing which constitutes oneness of person, but should, besides that, suppose sameness of substance requisite. For if same consciousness be one thing necessary to personal identity, and this depends on God's sovereign constitution, it will still follow, that personal identity depends on God's sovereign constitution.

And with respect to the identity of created substance itself, in the different moments of its duration, I think, we shall greatly mistake, if we imagine it to be like that absolute independent identity of the first being, whereby "he is the same yesterday, today, and forever." Nay, on the contrary, it may be demonstrated, that even this oneness of created substance, existing at different times, is a merely *dependent* identity; dependent on the pleasure and sovereign constitution of him who worketh all in all. This will follow from what is generally allowed, and is certainly true, that God not only created all things, and gave them being at first, but continually preserves them, and upholds them in being. This being a matter of considerable importance, it may be worthy here to be considered with a little attention. Let us inquire therefore, in the first place, whether it ben't evident, that God does continually, by his immediate power, uphold every created substance in being; and then let us see the consequence.

That God does, by his immediate power, *uphold* every created substance in being, will be manifest, if we consider, that their present existence is a *dependent* existence, and therefore is an *effect*, and must have some *cause*: and the cause must be one of these two: either the *antecedent existence* of the same substance, or else the *power of the Creator.* But it can't be the antecedent existence of the same substance. For instance, the existence of the body of the moon at this present moment, can't be the effect of its existence at the last foregoing moment. For not only was what existed the last moment, no active cause, but wholly a passive thing; but this also is to be considered, that no cause can produce effects in a *time* and *place* on which itself is *not*. 'Tis plain, nothing can exert itself, or operate, when and where it is not existing. But the moon's past existence was neither *where* nor *when* its present existence is. In point of time, what is *past* entirely ceases, when *present* existence begins; otherwise it would not be *past*. The past moment is ceased and gone, when the present moment takes place; and does no more coexist with it, than does any other moment that had ceased twenty years ago. Nor could the past existence of the particles of this moving body produce effects in any other place, than where it then was. But its existence at the present moment, in every point of it, is in a different place, from where its existence was at the last preceding moment. From these things, I suppose, it will certainly follow, that the present existence, either of this, or any other created substance, cannot be an effect of its past existence. The existences (so to speak) of an effect, or thing dependent, in different parts of space or duration, though ever so *near* one to another, don't at all coexist one with the other; and therefore are as truly different effects, as if those parts of space and duration were ever so far asunder: and the prior existence can no more be the proper cause of the new existence, in the next moment, or next part of space, than if it had been in an age before, or at a thousand miles distance, without any existence to fill up the intermediate time or space. Therefore the existence of created substances, in each successive moment, must be the effect of the *immediate* agency, will, and power of God.

If any shall say, this reasoning is not good, and shall insist upon it, that there is no need of any immediate divine power, to produce the present existence of created substances, but that their present existence is the effect or consequence of past existence, according to the nature of things; that the established course of nature is sufficient to continue existence, where existence is once given;

I allow it: but then it should be remembered, what nature is, in created things: and what the established course of nature is; that, as has been observed already, it is nothing, separate from the agency of God; and that, as Dr. Taylor says, "God, the Original of all being, is the only cause of all natural effects." A father, according to the course of nature, begets a child; an oak, according to the course of nature, produces an acorn, or a bud; so according to the course of nature, the former existence of the trunk of the tree is followed by its new or present existence. In the one case, and the other, the new effect is consequent on the former, only by the established laws, and settled course of nature; which is allowed to be nothing but the continued immediate efficiency of God, according to a constitution that he has been pleased to establish. Therefore, as our author greatly urges, that the child and the acorn, which come into existence according to the course of nature, in consequence of the prior existence and state of the parent and the oak, are truly *immediately* created or made by God; so must the existence of each created person and thing, at each moment of it, be from the immediate *continued* creation of God. It will certainly follow from these things, that God's *preserving* created things in being is perfectly equivalent to a *continued creation*, or to his creating those things out of nothing at *each moment* of their existence. If the continued existence of created things be wholly dependent on God's preservation, then those things would drop into nothing, upon the ceasing of the present moment, without a new exertion of the divine power to cause them to exist in the following moment. If there be any who own, that God preserves things in being, and yet hold that they would continue in being without any further help from him, after they once have existence; I think, it is hard to know what they mean. To what purpose can it be, to talk of God's preserving things in being, when there is no need of his preserving them? Or to talk of their being dependent on God for continued existence, when they would of themselves continue to exist, without his help; nay, though he should wholly withdraw his sustaining power and influence?

It will follow from what has been observed, that God's upholding created substance, or causing its existence in each successive moment, is altogether equivalent to an *immediate production out of nothing*, at each moment, because its existence at this moment is not merely in part from God, but wholly from him; and not in any part, or degree, from its antecedent existence. For the supposing, that its antecedent existence *concurs* with God in *efficiency*, to produce some part of the effect, is attended with all the very same absurdities, which have been shown to attend the supposition of its producing it wholly. Therefore the antecedent existence is nothing, as to any proper influence or assistance in the affair: and consequently God produces the effect as much from *nothing*, as if there had been nothing *before*. So that this effect differs not at all from the first creation, but only *circumstantially*; as in first creation there had been no such act and effect of God's power before; whereas, his giving existence afterwards, *follows* preceding acts and effects of the same kind, in an established order.

Now, in the next place, let us see how the consequence of these things is to my present purpose. If the existence of created substance, in each successive moment, be wholly the effect of God's immediate power, in that moment, without any dependence on prior existence, as much as the first creation out of nothing, then what exists at this moment, by this power, is a *new effect*; and simply and absolutely considered, not the same with any past existence, though it be like it, and follows it according to a certain established method.[2] And there is no identity or oneness in the case, but what depends on the *arbitrary* constitution of the Creator; who by his wise sovereign establishment so unites these successive new effects, that he *treats them as one*, by communicating to them like properties, relations, and circumstances; and so, leads us to regard and treat them as one. When I call this an arbitrary constitution, I mean, that it is a constitution which depends on nothing but the divine will; which *divine will* depends on nothing but the *divine wisdom*. In this sense, the whole course of nature, with all that belongs to it, all its laws and methods, and constancy and regularity, continuance and proceeding, is an *arbitrary constitution*. In this sense, the continuance of the very being of the world and all its parts, as well as the manner of continued being, depends entirely on an arbitrary constitution: for it don't all *necessarily* follow, that because there was sound, or light, or color, or resistance, or gravity, or thought, or consciousness, or any other dependent thing the last moment, that therefore there shall be the like at the next. All dependent existence whatsoever is in a constant flux, ever passing and returning; renewed every moment, as

the colors of bodies are every moment renewed by the light that shines upon them; and all is constantly proceeding from God, as light from the sun. "In him we live, and move, and have our being."

Thus it appears, if we consider matters strictly, there is no such thing as any identity or oneness in created objects, existing at different times, but what depends on *God's sovereign constitution*. And so it appears, that the objection we are upon, made against a supposed divine constitution, whereby Adam and his posterity are viewed and treated as one, in the manner and for the purposes supposed, as if it were not consistent with truth, because no constitution can make those to be one, which are not one; I say, it appears that this objection is built on a false hypothesis: for it appears, that a *divine constitution* is the thing which *makes truth*, in affairs of this nature. The objection supposes, there is a oneness in created beings, whence qualities and relations are derived down from past existence, distinct from, and prior to any oneness that can be supposed to be founded on divine constitution. Which is demonstrably false; and sufficiently appears so from things conceded by the adversaries themselves: and therefore the objection wholly falls to the ground.

There are *various kinds* of identity and oneness, found among created things, by which they become one in different manners, respects and degrees, and to various purposes; several of which differences have been observed; and every kind is ordered, regulated and limited, in every respect, by divine constitution. Some things, existing in different times and places, are treated by their Creator as one in *one respect*, and other in *another*; some are united for this communication, and others for that; but all according to the sovereign pleasure of the Fountain of all being and operation.

It appears, particularly, from what has been said, that all oneness, by virtue whereof pollution and guilt from past wickedness are derived, depends entirely on a divine establishment. 'Tis this, and this only, that must account for guilt and an evil taint on any individual soul, in consequence of a crime committed twenty or forty years ago, remaining still, and even to the end of the world and forever. 'Tis this, that must account for the continuance of any such thing, anywhere, as *consciousness* of acts that are past; and for the continuance of all *habits*, either good or bad: and on this depends everything that can belong to *personal identity*. And all communications, derivations, or continuation of qualities, properties, or relations, natural or moral, from what is past, as if the subject were one, depends on no other foundation.

And I am persuaded, no solid reason can be given, why God, who constitutes all other created union or oneness, according to his pleasure, and for what purposes, communications, and effects he pleases, may not establish a constitution whereby the natural posterity of Adam, proceeding from him, much as the buds and branches from the stock or root of a tree, should be treated as one with him, for the derivation, either of righteousness and communion in rewards, or of the loss of righteousness and consequent corruption and guilt.[3]

As I said before, all oneness in created things, whence qualities and relations are derived, depends on a divine constitution that is arbitrary, in every other respect, excepting that it is regulated by divine wisdom. The wisdom, which is exercised in these constitutions, appears in these two things, First, in a beautiful *analogy* and *harmony* with *other* laws or constitutions, especially relating to the same subject: and secondly, in the good *ends* obtained, or useful *consequences* of such a constitution. If therefore there be any objection still lying against this constitution with Adam and his posterity, it must be, that it is not sufficiently wise in these respects. But what extreme arrogance would it be in us, to take upon us to act as judges of the beauty and wisdom of the laws and established constitutions of the supreme Lord and Creator of the universe? And not only so, but if this constitution, in particular, be well considered, its wisdom, in the two forementioned respects, may easily be made evident. There is an apparent manifold analogy to other constitutions and laws, established and maintained through the whole system of vital nature in this lower world; all parts of which, in all successions, are derived from the *first of the kind*, as from their root, or fountain; each deriving from thence all properties and qualities, that are proper to the nature and capacity of the kind, or species: no derivative having any one perfection (unless it be what is merely circumstantial) but what was in its primitive. And that Adam's posterity should be without that original righteousness, which Adam had lost, is also analogous to other laws and establishments, relating to the nature of mankind; according to which, Adam's posterity have no one perfection of nature, in any kind, superior to what was in him, when the human race began to be propagated from him.

And as such a constitution was *fit* and *wise* in other respects, so it was in this that follows. Seeing the divine constitution concerning the manner of mankind's coming into existence in their propagation, was such as did so naturally unite them, and made 'em in so many respects one, naturally leading them to a close union in society, and manifold intercourse, and mutual dependence, things were wisely so established, that all should naturally be in one and the same *moral state*; and not in such exceeding different states, as that some should be perfectly innocent and holy, but others corrupt and wicked; some needing a saviour, but others needing none; some in a confirmed state of perfect *happiness*, but others in a state of public condemnation to perfect and eternal *misery*; some justly exposed to great calamities in this world, but others by their innocence raised above all suffering. Such a vast diversity of state would by no means have agreed with the natural and necessary constitution and unavoidable situation and circumstances of the world of mankind; "all made of one blood, to dwell on all the face of the earth," to be united and blended in society, and to partake together in the natural and common goods and evils of this lower world.

Dr. Taylor urges, that *sorrow* and *shame* are only for *personal* sin: and it has often been urged, that *repentance* can be for no other sin. To which I would say, that the use of words is very arbitrary: but that men's hearts should be deeply affected with grief and humiliation before God, for the pollution and guilt which they bring into the world with them, I think, is not in the least *unreasonable*. Nor is it a thing strange and unheard of, that men should be ashamed of things done by others, whom they are nearly concerned in. I am sure, it is not unscriptural; especially when they are justly looked upon in the sight of God, who sees the disposition of their hearts, as fully consenting and concurring.

From what has been observed it may appear, there is no sure ground to conclude, that it must be an absurd and impossible thing, for the race of mankind truly to partake of the sin of the first apostasy, so as that this, in reality and propriety, shall become *their* sin; by virtue of a real union between the root and branches of the world of mankind (truly and properly availing to such a consequence) established by the Author of the whole system of the universe; to whose establishment is owing all propriety and reality of union, in any part of that system; and by virtue of the full consent of the hearts of Adam's posterity to that first apostacy. And therefore the sin of the apostacy is not theirs, merely because God *imputes* it to them; but it is *truly* and *properly* theirs, and on that ground, God imputes it to them.

By reason of the established union between Adam and his posterity, the case is far otherwise between him and them, than it is between distinct parts or individuals of Adam's race; betwixt whom is no such constituted union: as between children and other ancestors. Concerning whom is apparently to be understood that place (Ezek. 18: 1–20), where God reproves the Jews for the use they made of that proverb, "The fathers have eaten sour grapes, and the children's teeth are set on edge"; and tells them, that hereafter they shall no more have occasion to use this proverb; and that if a son sees the wickedness of his father, and sincerely disapproves it and avoids it, and he himself is righteous, "he shall not die for the iniquity of his father; that all souls, both the soul of the father and the son, are his; and that therefore the son shall not bear the iniquity of his father, nor the father bear the iniquity of the son; but the soul that sinneth, it shall die; that the righteousness of the righteous shall be upon him, and the wickedness of the wicked shall be upon him." The thing denied, is communion in the guilt and punishment of the sins of others, that are distinct parts of Adam's race; and expressly, in that case, where there is no consent and concurrence, but a sincere disapprobation of the wickedness of ancestors. It is declared, that children who are adult and come to act for themselves, who are righteous, and don't approve of, but sincerely condemn the wickedness of their fathers, shall not be punished for their disapproved and avoided iniquities. The occasion of what is here said, as well as the design and plain sense, shews, that nothing is here intended in the least degree inconsistent with what has been supposed concerning Adam's posterity's sinning and falling in his apostacy. The occasion is, the people's murmuring at God's methods under the Mosaic dispensation; agreeable to that in Lev. 26: 29, "And they that are left of you, shall pine away in their iniquity in their enemies' land, and also in the iniquities of their fathers shall they pine away with them." And other parallel places, respecting external judgments, which were the punishments most plainly threatened, and chiefly insisted on, under that dispensation (which was, as it were, an *external* and *carnal* covenant) and particularly the people's suffering such terrible judgments at that day, even in Ezekiel's time, for the sins of Manasseh; according to what God says by Jeremiah (Jer. 15: 4), and agreeable to what is said in that confession (Lam. 5: 7), "Our fathers have sinned and are not, and we have borne their iniquities."

In what is said here, there is a special respect to the introducing the gospel-dispensation; as is greatly confirmed by comparing this place with Jer. 31: 29, 30, 31. Under which dispensation, the righteousness of God's dealings with mankind would be more fully manifested, in the clear revelation then to be made of the method of the judgment of God, by which the final state of wicked men is determined; which is not according to the behavior of their particular ancestors; but every one is dealt with according to the sin of his own wicked heart, or sinful nature and practice. The affair of derivation of the natural corruption of mankind in general and of their consent to, and participation of, the primitive and common apostacy, is not in the least intermeddled with, or touched, by anything meant or aimed at in the true scope and design of this place in Ezekiel.

On the whole, if any don't like the philosophy, or the metaphysics (as some perhaps may choose to call it) made use of in the foregoing reasonings; yet I cannot doubt, but that a proper consideration of what is apparent and undeniable in fact, with respect to the dependence of the state and course of things in this universe on the sovereign constitutions of the supreme Author and Lord of all, "who gives none account of any of his matters, and whose ways are past finding out," will be sufficient, with persons of common modesty and sobriety, to stop their mouths from making peremptory decisions against the justice of God, respecting what is so plainly and fully taught in his Holy Word, concerning the derivation of a depravity and guilt from Adam to his posterity; a thing so abundantly confirmed by what is found in the experience of all mankind in all ages.

This is enough, one would think, forever to silence such bold expressions as these – "If this be just," "if the Scriptures teach such doctrine etc., then the Scriptures are of no use," "understanding is no understanding," and "what a God must he be, that can thus curse innocent creatures!" "Is this thy God, O Christian?" etc. etc.

It may not be improper here to add something (by way of supplement to this chapter, in which we have had occasion to say so much about the imputation of Adam's sin), concerning the opinions of two divines, of no inconsiderable note among the dissenters in England, relating to a partial imputation of Adam's first sin.

One of them supposes, that this sin, though truly imputed to infants, so that thereby they are exposed to a proper punishment, yet is not imputed to them in such a degree, as that upon this account they should be liable to eternal punishment, as Adam himself was, but only to temporal death, or annihilation; Adam himself, the immediate actor, being made infinitely more guilty by it, than his posterity. On which I would observe: that to suppose, God imputes not *all* the guilt of Adam's sin, but only some *little* part of it, this relieves nothing but one's *imagination*. To think of poor little infants bearing such torments for Adam's sin, as they sometimes do in this world, and these torments ending in death and annihilation, may sit easier on the imagination, than to conceive of their suffering eternal misery for it. But it does not at all relieve one's *reason*. There is no rule of reason, that can be supposed to lie against imputing a sin in the whole of it, which was committed by one, to another who did not personally commit it, but what will also lie against its being so imputed and punished in part. For all the reasons (if there are any) lie against the imputation; not the *quantity* or *degree of what is imputed*. If there be any rule of reason, that is strong and good, lying against a proper derivation or communication of guilt, from one that acted, to another that did not act; then it lies against *all* that is of this nature. The force of the reasons brought against imputing Adam's sin to his posterity (if there be any force in them) lies in this, that Adam and his posterity are not one. But this lies as properly against charging a part of the guilt, as the whole. For Adam's posterity, by not being the same with him, had no more hand in a *little* of what was done, than in the whole. They were as absolutely free from being concerned in that act partly, as they were wholly. And there is no reason can be brought, why one man's sin can't be justly reckoned to another's account, who was not then in being, in the whole of it; but what will as properly lie against its being reckoned to him in any part, so as that he should be subject to any condemnation or punishment on that account. If those reasons are good, all the *difference* there can be, is this; that to bring a great punishment on infants for Adam's sin, is a great act of injustice, and to bring a comparatively *small* punishment, is a *smaller* act of injustice; but not, that this is not as

truly and *demonstrably* an act of injustice, as the other.

To illustrate this by an instance something parallel. 'Tis used as an argument why I may not exact from one of my neighbors, what was due to me from another, that he and my debtor are not the same; and that their concerns, interests and properties are entirely distinct. Now if this argument be good, it lies as truly against my demanding from him a part of the debt, as the whole. Indeed it is a *greater* act of injustice, for me to take from him the whole of it, than a part; but not more truly and certainly an act of injustice.

The other divine thinks, there is truly an imputation of Adam's sin, so that infants can't be looked upon as *innocent* creatures; yet seems to think it not agreeable to the perfections of God, to make the state of infants in another world *worse* than a state of *nonexistence*. But this to me appears plainly a *giving up* that grand point of the imputation of Adam's sin, both in whole and in part. For it supposes it to be not right, for God to bring any evil on a child of Adam, which is innocent as to personal sin, without *paying for it*, or balancing it with good; so that still the state of the child shall be as good, as could be demanded in justice, in case of mere innocence. Which plainly supposes, that the child is not exposed to any proper punishment at all, or is not at all in debt to divine justice, on the account of Adam's sin. For if the child were truly in *debt*; then surely *justice* might *take* something from him, *without paying for it*, or without giving that which makes its state as good, as mere innocence could in justice require. If he owes the suffering of some punishment, then there is no need that justice should requite the infant for suffering that punishment; or make up for it, by conferring some good, that shall countervail it, and in effect remove and disannul it; so that, on the whole, good and evil shall be at an even balance, yea, so that the scale of good shall *preponderate*. If it is unjust in a judge, to order any quantity of money to be taken from another, without paying him again, and fully making it up to him, it must be because he had justly *forfeited none* at all.

It seems to me pretty manifest, that none can, in good consistence with themselves, own a real imputation of the guilt of Adam's first sin to his posterity, without owning that they are justly viewed and treated as sinners, truly guilty, and children of wrath, on that account; nor unless they allow a just imputation of the whole of the evil of that transgression; at least, all that pertains to the essence of that act, as a full and complete violation of the covenant, which God had established; even as much as if each one of mankind had the like covenant established with him singly, and had by the like direct and full act of rebellion, violated it for himself.

Notes

1 My meaning, in the whole of what has been here said, may be illustrated thus: let us suppose, that Adam and all his posterity had *coexisted*, and that his posterity had been, through a law of nature established by the Creator, *united* to him, something as the branches of a tree are united to the root, or the members of the body to the head; so as to constitute as it were *one* complex person, or *one* moral whole: so that by the law of union there should have been a *communion* and *coexistence* in acts and affections; all jointly participating, and all concurring, as *one whole*, in the disposition and action of the head: as we see in the body natural, the whole body is affected as the head is affected; and the whole body concurs when the head acts. Now, in this case, the hearts of all the branches of mankind, by the constitution of nature and the law of union, would have been affected just as the heart of Adam, their common root, was affected. When the heart of the root, by a full disposition committed the first sin, the hearts of all the branches would have concurred; and when the root, in consequence of this, became guilty, so would all the branches; and when the heart of the root, as a punishment of the sin committed, was forsaken of God, in like manner would it have fared with all the branches; and when the heart of the root, in consequence of this, was confirmed in permanent depravity, the case would have been the same with all the branches; and as new guilt on the soul of Adam would have been consequent on this, so also would it have been with his moral branches. And thus all things, with relation to evil disposition, guilt, pollution and depravity, would exist, in the same order and dependence, in each branch, as in the root. Now, difference of the *time* of existence don't at all hinder things succeeding in the same order, any more than difference of *place* in a coexistence of time.

Here may be worthy to be observed, as in several respects to the present purpose, some things that are said by Stapferus, an eminent divine of Zurich in Switzerland, in his *Theologia Polemica*, published about fourteen years ago; in English as follows. "Seeing all Adam's posterity are derived from their first parent, as their root, the whole of the human kind, with its root, may be considered as constituting but one whole, or one mass; so as not to be properly a thing distinct from its root; the posterity not differing from it, any otherwise than the branches from the tree. From which it easily appears, how that when the root sinned, all that which is derived from it, and with it constitutes but one whole, may be looked upon as also sinning; seeing it is not distinct from the root, but is one with it." Tome I, ch. 3, nos. 856–7.

"'Tis objected, against the imputation of Adam's sin, that we never committed the same sin with Adam, neither in number nor in kind. I answer, we should distinguish here between the *physical* act itself, which Adam committed, and the *morality* of the action, and *consent* to it. If we have respect only to the external act, to be sure it must be confessed, that Adam's posterity did not put forth their hands to the forbidden fruit: in which sense, that act of transgression, and that fall of Adam cannot be *physically* one with the sin of his posterity. But if we consider the *morality* of the action, and what *consent* there is to it, it is altogether to be maintained, that his posterity committed the *same* sin, both in number and in kind, inasmuch as they are to be looked upon as consenting to it. For where there is consent to a sin, there the same sin is committed. Seeing therefore that Adam with all his posterity constitute but *one moral person*, and are united in the same Covenant, and are transgressors of the same law, they are also to be looked upon as having, in a moral estimation, committed the same transgression of the law, both in number and in kind. Therefore this reasoning avails nothing against the righteous imputation of the sin of Adam to all mankind, or to the whole moral person that is consenting to it. And for the reason mentioned, we may rather argue thus; the sin of the posterity, on account of their consent, and the moral view in which they are to be taken, is the same with the sin of Adam, not only in kind, but in number; therefore the sin of Adam is rightfully imputed to his posterity." Ibid. Tome IV, ch. 16, nos. 60, 61.

"The imputation of Adam's first sin consists in nothing else than this, that his posterity are viewed as in the same place with their father, and are like him. But seeing, agreeable to what we have already proved, God might, according to his own righteous judgment, which was founded on his most righteous law, give Adam a posterity that were *like himself*; and indeed it could not be otherwise, according to the very laws of nature: therefore he might also in righteous judgment impute Adam's sin to them: inasmuch as to give Adam a posterity like himself, and to impute his sin to them, is one and the same thing. And therefore if the former be not contrary to the divine perfections, so neither is the latter. Our adversaries contend with us chiefly on this account, that according to our doctrine of original sin, such an imputation of the first sin is maintained, whereby God, without any regard to universal native corruption, esteems all Adam's posterity as guilty, and holds them as liable to condemnation, purely on account of that sinful act of their first parent; so that they, without any respect had to their own sin, and so, as innocent in themselves, are destined to eternal punishment ... I have therefore ever been careful to shew, that they do *injuriously suppose* those things to be *separated*, in our doctrine, which are by no means to be separated. The whole of the controversy they have with us about this matter, evidently arises from this, that they suppose the *mediate* and the *immediate* imputation are distinguished one from the other, not only in the manner of conception, but in reality. And so indeed they consider imputation only as *immediate*, and abstractly from the *mediate*; when yet our divines suppose, that neither ought to be considered *separately* from the other. Therefore I chose not to use any such distinction, or to suppose any such thing, in what I've said on the subject; but only have endeavored to explain the thing itself, and to reconcile it with the divine attributes. And therefore I have everywhere conjoined both these conceptions concerning the imputation of the first sin, as inseparable; and judged, that one ought never to be considered without the other ... While I have been writing this note, I consulted all the systems of divinity, which I have by me, that I might see what was the true and genuine opinion of our chief divines in this affair; and I found that they were of the same mind with me; namely, that these two kinds of imputation are by no means to be separated, or to be considered abstractly one from the other, but that one does involve the other." He there particularly cites those two famous reformed divines, Vitringa and Lampius. Tome IV, ch. 17, no. 78.

2   When I suppose, that an effect which is produced, every moment, by a new action or exertion of power, must be a *new* effect in each moment, and not absolutely and numerically the same with that which existed in preceding moments, the thing that I intend, may be illustrated by this example. The lucid color or brightness of the moon, as we look steadfastly upon it, seems to be a *permanent* thing, as though it were perfectly the same brightness continued. But indeed it is an effect produced every moment. It ceases, and is renewed, in each successive point of time; and so becomes altogether a new effect at each instant; and no one thing that belongs to it, is numerically the same that existed in the preceding moment. The rays of the sun, impressed on that body, and reflected from it, which cause the effect, are none of them the same: the impression, made in each moment on our sensory, is by the stroke of new rays: and the sensation, excited by the stroke, is a new effect, an effect of a new impulse. Therefore the

brightness or lucid whiteness of this body is no more numerically the same thing with that which existed in the preceding moment, than the sound of the wind that blows now, is individually the same with the sound of the wind that blew just before, which, though it be like it, is not the same, any more than the agitated air, that makes the sound, is the same; or than the water, flowing in a river, that now passes by, is individually the same with that which passed a little before. And if it be thus with the brightness or color of the moon, so it must be with its solidity, and everything else belonging to its substance, if all be, each moment, as much the immediate effect of a new exertion or application of power.

The matter may perhaps be in some respects still more clearly illustrated by this. The images of things in a glass, as we keep our eye upon them, seem to remain precisely the same, with a continuing perfect identity. But it is known to be otherwise. Philosophers well know, that these images are constantly renewed, by the impression and reflection of new rays of light; so that the image impressed by the former rays is constantly vanishing, and a new image impressed by new rays every moment, both on the glass and on the eye. The image constantly renewed, by new successive rays, is no more numerically the same, than if it were by some artist put on anew with a pencil, and the colors constantly vanishing as fast as put on. And the new images being put on *immediately* or instantly, don't make 'em the same, any more than if it were done with the intermission of an hour or a day. The image that exists this moment, is not at all derived from the image which existed the last preceding moment: as may be seen, because, if the succession of new rays be intercepted, by something interposed between the object and the glass, the image immediately ceases; the *past existence* of the image has no influence to uphold it, so much as for one moment. Which shews, that the image is altogether new-made every moment; and strictly speaking, is in no part numerically the same with that which existed the moment preceding. And truly so the matter must be with the bodies themselves, as well as their images: they also cannot be the same, with an absolute identity, but must be wholly renewed every moment, if the case be as has been proved, that their present existence is not, strictly speaking, at all the effect of their past existence; but is wholly, every instant, the effect of a new agency, or exertion of the power, of the cause of their existence. If so, the existence caused is every instant a new effect, whether the cause be light, or immediate divine power, or whatever it be.

3   I appeal to such as are not wont to content themselves with judging by a superficial appearance and view of things, but are habituated to examine things strictly and closely, that they may judge righteous judgment,

whether on supposition that all mankind had *coex-isted*, in the manner mentioned before, any good reason can be given, why their Creator might not, if he had pleased, have established such an union between Adam and the rest of mankind, as was in that case supposed. Particularly, if it had been the case, that Adam's posterity had actually, according to a law of nature, somehow grown out of him, and yet remained continuous and literally united to him, as the branches to a tree, or the members of the body to the head; and had all, before the fall, existed together at the same time, though in different places, as the head and members are in different places; in this case, who can determine, that the Author of nature might not, if it had pleased him, have established such an union between the root and branches of this complex being, as that all should constitute one moral whole; so that by the law of union, there should be a communion in each moral alteration, and that the heart of every branch should at the same moment participate with the heart of the root, be conformed to it and concurring with it in all its affections and acts, and so jointly partaking in its state, as a part of the same thing? Why might not God, if he had pleased, have fixed such a kind of union as this, an union of the various parts of such a moral whole, as well as many other unions, which he has actually fixed, according to his sovereign pleasure? And if he might, by his sovereign constitution, have established such an union of the various branches of mankind, when existing in different places, I don't see why he might not also do the same, though they exist in different times. I know not why succession, or diversity of time, should make any such constituted union more unreasonable, than diversity of place. The only reason, why diversity of time can seem to make it unreasonable, is, that difference of time shews, there is no absolute identity of the things existing in those different times: but it shews this, I think, not at all more than the difference of the place of existence.

9

Principles of Psychology

William James

Introduction

William James (1842–1910) was born in Boston. He
was trained as a physician at Harvard, where, later,
he taught psychology and philosophy. The selection
here is drawn from a shorter version of his major
work, *The Principles of Psychology*, published in
1890, which served as a foundation for the philosophical work of the next generation of American
academic philosophers, including Royce and Dewey.
His best-known works include the collections of
essays, *The Will to Believe* and *Essays in Radical Empiricism*, and his book, *Pragmatism*.

The Stream of Consciousness

The order of our study must be analytic. We are
now prepared to begin the introspective study of
the adult consciousness itself. Most books adopt
the so-called synthetic method. Starting with
"simple ideas of sensation," and regarding these
as so many atoms, they proceed to build up the
higher states of mind out of their "association,"
"integration," or "fusion," as houses are built by
the agglutination of bricks. This has the didactic
advantages which the synthetic method usually
has. But it commits one beforehand to the very
questionable theory that our higher states of consciousness are compounds of units; and instead of

Taken from *Psychology: Briefer Course* (New York:
Henry Holt and Co., 1900).

starting with what the reader directly knows,
namely his total concrete states of mind, it starts
with a set of supposed "simple ideas" with which
he has no immediate acquaintance at all, and concerning whose alleged interactions he is much at
the mercy of any plausible phrase. On every
ground, then, the method of advancing from the
simple to the compound exposes us to illusion. All
pedants and abstractionists will naturally hate to
abandon it. But a student who loves the fulness of
human nature will prefer to follow the "analytic"
method, and to begin with the most concrete facts,
those with which he has a daily acquaintance in his
own inner life. The analytic method will discover
in due time the elementary parts, if such exist,
without danger of precipitate assumption. [. . .]

The fundamental fact. The first and foremost
concrete fact which every one will affirm to belong
to his inner experience is the fact that *consciousness
of some sort goes on*. "States of mind" *succeed each
other in him*. If we could say in English "it thinks,"
as we say "it rains" or "it blows," we should be
stating the fact most simply and with the minimum of assumption. As we cannot, we must
simply say that *thought goes on*.

Four characters in consciousness. How does it go
on? We notice immediately four important characters in the process, of which it shall be the duty of
the present chapter to treat in a general way:

1   Every "state" tends to be part of a personal
    consciousness.

2 Within each personal consciousness states are always changing.

3 Each personal consciousness is sensibly continuous.

4 It is interested in some parts of its object to the exclusion of others, and welcomes or rejects – *chooses* from among them, in a word – all the while.

In considering these four points successively, we shall have to plunge *in medias res* as regards our nomenclature and use psychological terms which can only be adequately defined in later chapters of the book. But every one knows what the terms mean in a rough way; and it is only in a rough way that we are now to take them. This chapter is like a painter's first charcoal sketch upon his canvas, in which no niceties appear.

When I say every *"state"* or *"thought"* is part of a *personal consciousness*, "personal consciousness" is one of the terms in question. Its meaning we know so long as no one asks us to define it, but to give an accurate account of it is the most difficult of philosophic tasks. This task we must confront in the next chapter; here a preliminary word will suffice.

In this room – this lecture-room, say – there are a multitude of thoughts, yours and mine, some of which cohere mutually, and some not. They are as little each-for-itself and reciprocally independent as they are all-belonging-together. They are neither: no one of them is separate, but each belongs with certain others and with none beside. My thought belongs with *my* other thoughts, and your thought with *your* other thoughts. Whether anywhere in the room there be a *mere* thought, which is nobody's thought, we have no means of ascertaining, for we have no experience of its like. The only states of consciousness that we naturally deal with are found in personal consciousnesses, minds, selves, concrete particular I's and you's.

Each of these minds keeps its own thoughts to itself. There is no giving or bartering between them. No thought even comes into direct *sight* of a thought in another personal consciousness than its own. Absolute insulation, irreducible pluralism, is the law. It seems as if the elementary psychic fact were not *thought* or *this thought* or *that thought*, but *my thought*, every thought being *owned*. Neither contemporaneity, nor proximity in space, nor similarity of quality and content are able to fuse thoughts together which are sundered by this barrier of belonging to different personal minds. The breaches between such thoughts are the most absolute breaches in nature. Every one will recognize this to be true, so long as the existence of *something* corresponding to the term "personal mind" is all that is insisted on, without any particular view of its nature being implied. On these terms the personal self rather than the thought might be treated as the immediate datum in psychology. The universal conscious fact is not "feelings and thoughts exist," but "I think" and "I feel." No psychology, at any rate, can question the *existence* of personal selves. Thoughts connected as we feel them to be connected are *what we mean* by personal selves. The worst a psychology can do is so to interpret the nature of these selves as to rob them of their *worth*.

Consciousness is in constant change. I do not mean by this to say that no one state of mind has any duration – even if true, that would be hard to establish. What I wish to lay stress on is this, that *no state once gone can recur and be identical with what it was before*. Now we are seeing, now hearing; now reasoning, now willing; now recollecting, now expecting; now loving, now hating; and in a hundred other ways we know our minds to be alternately engaged. But all these are complex states, it may be said, produced by combination of simpler ones; do not the simpler ones follow a different law? Are not the *sensations* which we get from the same object, for example, always the same? Does not the same piano-key, struck with the same force, make us hear in the same way? Does not the same grass give us the same feeling of green, the same sky the same feeling of blue, and do we not get the same olfactory sensation no matter how many times we put our nose to the same flask of cologne? It seems a piece of metaphysical sophistry to suggest that we do not; and yet a close attention to the matter shows that *there is no proof that an incoming current ever gives us just the same bodily sensation twice*.

What is got twice is the same *object*. We hear the same *note* over and over again; we see the same *quality* of green, or smell the same objective perfume, or experience the same *species* of pain. The realities, concrete and abstract, physical and ideal, whose permanent existence we believe in, seem to be constantly coming up again before our thought, and lead us, in our carelessness, to suppose that our "ideas" of them are the same ideas. When we come, some time later, to the chapter on Perception, we shall see how inveterate is our habit of simply using our sensible impressions as stepping-stones to pass over to the recognition of the realities whose presence they reveal. The grass out of the window now looks to me of the same green in the sun as in the shade, and yet a painter would have to paint one part of it dark brown, another part bright yellow, to give its real sensational effect. We take no heed, as a rule, of the different way in which the same things look and sound and smell at different distances and under different circumstances. The sameness of the *things* is what we are concerned to ascertain; and any sensations that assure us of that will probably be considered in a rough way to be the same with each other. This is what makes off-hand testimony about the subjective identity of different sensations well-nigh worthless as a proof of the fact. The entire history of what is called Sensation is a commentary on our inability to tell whether two sensible qualities received apart are exactly alike. What appeals to our attention far more than the absolute quality of an impression is its *ratio* to whatever other impressions we may have at the same time. When everything is dark a somewhat less dark sensation makes us see an object white. Helmholtz calculates that the white marble painted in a picture representing an architectural view by moonlight is, when seen by daylight, from ten to twenty thousand times brighter than the real moonlit marble would be.

Such a difference as this could never have been *sensibly* learned; it had to be inferred from a series of indirect considerations. These make us believe that our sensibility is altering all the time, so that the same object cannot easily give us the same sensation over again. We feel things differently accordingly as we are sleepy or awake, hungry or full, fresh or tired; differently at night and in the morning, differently in summer and in winter; and above all, differently in childhood, manhood, and old age. And yet we never doubt that our feelings reveal the same world, with the same sensible qualities and the same sensible things occupying it. The difference of the sensibility is shown best by the difference of our emotion about the things from one age to another, or when we are in different organic moods. What was bright and exciting becomes weary, flat, and unprofitable. The bird's song is tedious, the breeze is mournful, the sky is sad.

To these indirect presumptions that our sensations, following the mutations of our capacity for feeling, are always undergoing an essential change, must be added another presumption, based on what must happen in the brain. Every sensation corresponds to some cerebral action. For an identical sensation to recur it would have to occur the second time *in an unmodified brain*. But as this, strictly speaking, is a physiological impossibility, so is an unmodified feeling an impossibility; for to every brain-modification, however small, we suppose that there must correspond a change of equal amount in the consciousness which the brain subserves.

But if the assumption of "simple sensations" recurring in immutable shape is so easily shown to be baseless, how much more baseless is the assumption of immutability in the larger masses of our thought!

For there it is obvious and palpable that our state of mind is never precisely the same. Every thought we have of a given fact is, strictly speaking, unique, and only bears a resemblance of kind with our other thoughts of the same fact. When the identical fact recurs, we *must* think of it in a fresh manner, see it under a somewhat different angle, apprehend it in different relations from those in which it last appeared. And the thought by which we cognize it is the thought of it-in-those-relations, a thought suffused with the consciousness of all that dim context. Often we are ourselves struck at the strange differences in our successive views of the same thing. We wonder how we ever could have opined as we did last month about a certain matter. We have outgrown the possibility of that state of mind, we know not how. From one year to another we see things in new lights. What was unreal has grown real, and what was exciting is insipid. The friends we used to care the world for are shrunken to shadows; the women once so divine, the stars, the woods, and the waters, how now so dull and common! – the young girls that brought an aura of infinity, at present hardly distinguishable existences; the pictures so empty; and as for the books, what *was* there to find so mysteriously significant in Goethe, or in John Mill so full of weight? Instead of all this, more zestful than ever is the work, the work; and fuller and deeper the import of common duties and of common goods.

I am sure that this concrete and total manner of regarding the mind's changes is the only true manner, difficult as it may be to carry it out in detail. If anything seems obscure about it, it will grow clearer as we advance. Meanwhile, if it be true, it is certainly also true that no two "ideas" are ever exactly the same, which is the proposition we started to prove. The proposition is more important theoretically than it at first sight seems. For it makes it already impossible for us to follow obediently in the footprints of either the Lockian or the Herbartian school, schools which have had almost unlimited influence in Germany and among ourselves. No doubt it is often *convenient* to formulate the mental facts in an atomistic sort of way, and to treat the higher states of consciousness as if they were all built out of unchanging simple ideas which "pass and turn again." It is convenient often to treat curves as if they were composed of small straight lines, and electricity and nerve-force as if they were fluids. But in the one case as in the other we must never forget that we are talking symbolically, and that there is nothing in nature to answer to our words. A permanently existing "Idea" which makes its appearance before the footlights of consciousness at periodical intervals is as mythological an entity as the Jack of Spades.

Within each personal consciousness, thought is sensibly continuous. I can only define "continuous" as that which is without breach, crack, or division. The only breaches that can well be conceived to occur within the limits of a single mind would either be *interruptions*, *time*-gaps during which the consciousness went out; or they would be breaks in the content of the thought, so abrupt that what followed had no connection whatever with what went before. The proposition that consciousness feels continuous, means two things:

a That even where there is a time-gap the consciousness after it feels as if it belonged together with the consciousness before it, as another part of the same self;
b That the changes from one moment to another in the quality of the consciousness are never absolutely abrupt.

The case of the time-gaps, as the simplest, shall be taken first.

a When Paul and Peter wake up in the same bed, and recognize that they have been asleep, each one of them mentally reaches back and makes connection with but *one* of the two streams of thought which were broken by the sleeping hours. As the current of an electrode buried in the ground unerringly finds its way to its own similarly buried mate, across no matter how much intervening earth; so Peter's present instantly finds out Peter's past, and never by mistake knits itself on to that of Paul. Paul's thought in turn is as little liable to go astray. The past thought of Peter is appropriated by the present Peter alone. He may have a *knowledge*, and a correct one too, of what Paul's last drowsy states of mind were as he sank into sleep, but it is an entirely different sort of knowledge from that which he has of his own last states. He *remembers* his own states, whilst he only *conceives* Paul's. Remembrance is like direct feeling; its object is suffused with a warmth and intimacy to which no object of mere conception ever attains. This quality of warmth and intimacy and immediacy is what Peter's *present* thought also possesses for itself. So sure as this present is me, is mine, it says, so sure is anything else that comes with the same warmth and intimacy and immediacy, me and mine. What the qualities called warmth and intimacy may in themselves be will have to be matter for future consideration. But whatever past states appear with those qualities must be admitted to receive the greeting of the present mental state, to be owned by it, and accepted as belonging together with it in a common self. This community of self is what the time-gap cannot break in twain, and is why a present thought, although not ignorant of the time-gap, can still regard itself as continuous with certain chosen portions of the past.

Consciousness, then, does not appear to itself chopped up in bits. Such words as "chain" or "train" do not describe it fitly as it presents itself in the first instance. It is nothing jointed; it flows. A "river" or a "stream" are the metaphors by which it is most naturally described. In talking of it hereafter, let us call it the stream of thought, of consciousness, or of subjective life.

b But now there appears, even within the limits of the same self, and between thoughts all of which alike have this same sense of belonging together, a kind of jointing and separateness among the parts, of which this statement seems to take no account. I refer to the breaks that are produced by sudden *contrasts in the quality* of the successive segments of the stream of thought. If the words "chain" and "train" had no natural fitness in them, how came such words to be used at all? Does not a loud explosion rend the consciousness upon which it abruptly breaks, in twain? No; for even into our awareness of the thunder the awareness of the previous silence creeps and continues; for what we hear when the thunder crashes is not thunder *pure*, but thunder-breaking-upon-silence-and-contrasting-with-it. Our feeling of the same objective thunder, coming in this way, is quite different from what it would be were the thunder a continuation of previous thunder. The thunder itself we believe to abolish and exclude the silence; but the *feeling* of the thunder is also a feeling of the silence as just gone; and it would be difficult to find in the actual concrete consciousness of man a feeling so limited to the present as not to have an inkling of anything that went before.

"Substantive" and "transitive" states of mind.
When we take a general view of the wonderful stream of our consciousness, what strikes us first is the different pace of its parts. Like a bird's life, it seems to be an alternation of flights and perchings. The rhythm of language expresses this, where every thought is expressed in a sentence, and every sentence closed by a period. The resting-places are usually occupied by sensorial imaginations of some sort, whose peculiarity is that they can be held before the mind for an indefinite time, and contemplated without changing; the places of flight are filled with thoughts of relations, static or dynamic, that for the most part obtain between the matters contemplated in the periods of comparative rest.

Let us call the resting-places the "substantive parts," and the places of flight the "transitive parts," of the stream of thought. It then appears that our thinking tends at all times towards some other substantive part than the one from which it has just been dislodged. And we may say that the main use of the transitive parts is to lead us from one substantive conclusion to another.

Now it is very difficult, introspectively, to see the transitive parts for what they really are. If they are but flights to a conclusion, stopping them to look at them before the conclusion is reached is really annihilating them. Whilst if we wait till the conclusion *be* reached, it so exceeds them in vigor and stability that it quite eclipses and swallows them up in its glare. Let anyone try to cut a thought across in the middle and get a look at its section, and he will see how difficult the introspective observation of the transitive tracts is. The rush of the thought is so headlong that it almost always brings us up at the conclusion before we can arrest it. Or if our purpose is nimble enough and we do arrest it, it ceases forthwith to be itself. As a snowflake crystal caught in the warm hand is no longer a crystal but a drop, so, instead of

catching the feeling of relation moving to its term, we find we have caught some substantive thing, usually the last word we were pronouncing, statically taken, and with its function, tendency, and particular meaning in the sentence quite evaporated. The attempt at introspective analysis in these cases is in fact like seizing a spinning top to catch its motion, or trying to turn up the gas quickly enough to see how the darkness looks. And the challenge to *produce* these transitive states of consciousness, which is sure to be thrown by doubting psychologists at anyone who contends for their existence, is as unfair as Zeno's treatment of the advocates of motion, when, asking them to point out in what place an arrow *is* when it moves, he argues the falsity of their thesis from their inability to make to so preposterous a question an immediate reply.

The results of this introspective difficulty are baleful. If to hold fast and observe the transitive parts of thought's stream be so hard, then the great blunder to which all schools are liable must be the failure to register them, and the undue emphasizing of the more substantive parts of the stream. Now the blunder has historically worked in two ways. One set of thinkers have been led by it to *Sensationalism*. Unable to lay their hands on any substantive feelings corresponding to the innumerable relations and forms of connection between the sensible things of the world, finding no *named* mental states mirroring such relations, they have for the most part denied that any such states exist; and many of them, like Hume, have gone on to deny the reality of most relations *out of* the mind as well as in it. Simple substantive "ideas," sensations and their copies, juxtaposed like dominoes in a game, but really separate, everything else verbal illusion – such is the upshot of this view. The *Intellectualists*, on the other hand, unable to give up the reality of relations *extra mentem*, but equally unable to point to any distinct substantive feelings in which they were known, have made the same admission that such feelings do not exist. But they have drawn an opposite conclusion. The relations must be known, they say, in something that is no feeling, no mental "state," continuous and consubstantial with the subjective tissue out of which sensations and other substantive conditions of consciousness are made. They must be known by something that lies on an entirely different plane, by an *actus purus* of Thought, Intellect, or Reason, all written with capitals and considered to mean something unutterably superior to any passing perishing fact of sensibility whatever.

But from our point of view both Intellectualists and Sensationalists are wrong. If there be such things as feelings at all, then so surely as relations between objects exist *in rerum natura*, so surely, and more surely, do feelings exist to which these relations are known. There is not a conjunction or a preposition, and hardly an adverbial phrase, syntactic form, or inflection of voice, in human speech, that does not express some shading or other of relation which we at some moment actually feel to exist between the larger objects of our thought. If we speak objectively, it is the real relations that appear revealed; if we speak subjectively, it is the stream of consciousness that matches each of them by an inward coloring of its own. In either case the relations are numberless, and no existing language is capable of doing justice to all their shades.

We ought to say a feeling of *and*, a feeling of *if*, a feeling of *but*, and a feeling of *by*, quite as readily as we say a feeling of *blue* or a feeling of *cold*. Yet we do not: so inveterate has our habit become of recognizing the existence of the substantive parts alone, that language almost refuses to lend itself to any other use. Consider once again the analogy of the brain. We believe the brain to be an organ whose internal equilibrium is always in a state of change – the change affecting every part. The pulses of change are doubtless more violent in one place than in another, their rhythm more rapid at this time than at that. As in a kaleidoscope revolving at a uniform rate, although the figures are always rearranging themselves, there are instants during which the transformation seems minute and interstitial and almost absent, followed by others when it shoots with magical rapidity, relatively stable forms thus alternating with forms we should not distinguish if seen again; so in the brain the perpetual rearrangement must result in some forms of tension lingering relatively long, whilst others simply come and pass. But if consciousness corresponds to the fact of rearrangement itself, why, if the rearrangement stop not, should the consciousness ever cease? And if a lingering rearrangement brings with it one kind of consciousness, why should not a swift rearrangement bring another kind of consciousness as peculiar as the rearrangement itself?

[. . .]

Consciousness is always interested more in one part of its object than in another, and welcomes and rejects, or chooses, all the while it thinks. The phenomena of selective attention and of deliberative will are of course patent examples of this choosing activity. But few of us are aware how incessantly it is at work in operations not ordinarily called by these names. Accentuation and Emphasis are present in every perception we have. We find it quite impossible to disperse our attention impartially over a number of impressions. A monotonous succession of sonorous strokes is broken up into rhythms, now of one sort, now of another, by the different accent which we place on different strokes. The simplest of these rhythms is the double one, ticktock, tick-tock, tick-tock. Dots dispersed on a surface are perceived in rows and groups. Lines separate into diverse figures. The ubiquity of the distinctions, *this* and *that*, *here* and *there*, *now* and *then*, in our minds is the result of our laying the same selective emphasis on parts of place and time.

But we do far more than emphasize things, and unite some, and keep others apart. We actually *ignore* most of the things before us. Let me briefly show how this goes on.

To begin at the bottom, what are our very senses themselves but organs of selection? Out of the infinite chaos of movements, of which physics teaches us that the outer world consists, each sense-organ picks out those which fall within certain limits of velocity. To these it responds, but ignores the rest as completely as if they did not exist. Out of what is in itself an undistinguishable, swarming *continuum*, devoid of distinction or emphasis, our senses make for us, by attending to this motion and ignoring that, a world full of contrasts, of sharp accents, of abrupt changes, of picturesque light and shade.

If the sensations we receive from a given organ have their causes thus picked out for us by the conformation of the organ's termination, Attention, on the other hand, out of all the sensations yielded, picks out certain ones as worthy of its notice and suppresses all the rest. We notice only those sensations which are signs to us of *things* which happen practically or aesthetically to interest us, to which we therefore give substantive names, and which we exalt to this exclusive status of independence and dignity. But in itself, apart from my interest, a particular dust-wreath on a windy day is just as much of an individual *thing*, and just as much or as little deserves an individual name, as my own body does.

And then, among the sensations we get from each separate thing, what happens? The mind selects again. It chooses certain of the sensations to represent the thing most *truly*, and considers the rest as its appearances, modified by the conditions of the moment. Thus my table-top is named *square*, after but one of an infinite number of retinal sensations which it yields, the rest of them being sensations of two acute and two obtuse angles; but I call the latter *perspective* views, and the four right angles the *true* form of the table, and erect the attribute squareness into the table's essence, for æsthetic reasons of my own. In like manner, the real form of the circle is deemed to be the sensation it gives when the line of vision is perpendicular to its centre – all its other sensations are *signs* of this sensation. The real sound of the cannon is the sensation it makes when the ear is close by. The real color of the brick is the sensation it gives when the eye looks squarely at it from a near point, out of the sunshine and yet not in the gloom; under other circumstances it gives us other color-sensations which are but signs of this – we then see it looks pinker or bluer than it really is. The reader knows no object which he does not represent to himself by preference as in some typical attitude, of some normal size, at some characteristic distance, of some standard tint, etc., etc. But all these essential characteristics, which together form for us the genuine objectivity of the thing and are contrasted with what we call the subjective sensations it may yield us at a given moment, are mere sensations like the latter. The mind chooses to suit itself, and decides what particular sensation shall be held more real and valid than all the rest.

Next, in a world of objects thus individualized by our mind's selective industry, what is called our "experience" is almost entirely determined by our habits of attention. A thing may be present to a man a hundred times, but if he persistently fails to notice it, it cannot be said to enter into his experience. We are all seeing flies, moths, and beetles by the thousand, but to whom, save an entomologist, do they say anything distinct? On the other hand, a thing met only once in a lifetime may leave an indelible experience in the memory. Let four men make a tour in Europe. One will bring home only picturesque impressions – costumes and colors, parks and views and works of architecture, pictures and statues. To another all this will be non-existent; and distances and prices, populations and drainage-arrangements, door- and window-fastenings, and other useful statistics will take their place. A third will give a rich account of the theatres, restaurants, and public halls, and naught beside; whilst the fourth will perhaps have been so wrapped in his own subjective broodings as to be able to tell little more than a few names of places through which he passed. Each has selected, out of the same mass of presented objects, those which suited his private interest and has made his experience thereby.

If now, leaving the empirical combination of objects, we ask how the mind proceeds *rationally* to connect them, we find selection again to be omnipotent. In a future chapter we shall see that all Reasoning depends on the ability of the mind to break up the totality of the phenomenon reasoned about, into parts, and to pick out from among these the particular one which, in the given emergency, may lead to the proper conclusion. The man of genius is he who will always stick in his bill at the right point, and bring it out with the right element – "reason" if the emergency be theoretical, "means" if it be practical – transfixed upon it.

If now we pass to the aesthetic department, our law is still more obvious. The artist notoriously selects his items, rejecting all tones, colors, shapes, which do not harmonize with each other and with the main purpose of his work. That unity, harmony, "convergence of characters," as M. Taine calls it, which gives to works of art their superiority over works of nature, is wholly due to *elimination*. Any natural subject will do, if the artist has wit enough to pounce upon some one feature of it as characteristic, and suppress all merely accidental items which do not harmonize with this.

Ascending still higher, we reach the plane of Ethics, where choice reigns notoriously supreme. An act has no ethical quality whatever unless it be chosen out of several all equally possible. To sustain the arguments for the good course and keep them ever before us, to stifle our longing for more flowery ways, to keep the foot unflinchingly on the arduous path, these are characteristic ethical energies. But more than these; for these but deal with the means of compassing interests already felt by the man to be supreme. The ethical energy *par excellence* has to go farther and choose which *interest* out of several, equally coercive, shall become supreme. The issue here is of the utmost pregnancy, for it decides a man's entire career. When he debates, Shall I commit this crime? choose that profession? accept that office, or marry this fortune? – his choice really lies between one of several equally possible future Characters. What he shall *become* is fixed by the conduct of this moment.

Schopenhauer, who enforces his determinism by the argument that with a given fixed character only one reaction is possible under given circumstances, forgets that, in these critical ethical moments, what consciously *seems* to be in question is the complexion of the character itself. The problem with the man is less what act he shall now resolve to do than what being he shall now choose to become.

Taking human experience in a general way, the choosings of different men are to a great extent the same. The race as a whole largely agrees as to what it shall notice and name; and among the noticed parts we select in much the same way for accentuation and preference, or subordination and dislike. There is, however, one entirely extraordinary case in which no two men ever are known to choose alike. One great splitting of the whole universe into two halves is made by each of us; and for each of us almost all of the interest attaches to one of the halves; but we all draw the line of division between them in a different place. When I say that we all call the two halves by the same names, and that those names are "*me*" and "*not-me*" respectively, it will at once be seen what I mean. The altogether unique kind of interest which each human mind feels in those parts of creation which it can call *me* or *mine* may be a moral riddle, but it is a fundamental psychological fact. No mind can take the same interest in his neighbor's *me* as in his own. The neighbor's me falls together with all the rest of things in one foreign mass against which his own *me* stands out in startling relief. Even the trodden worm, as Lotze somewhere says, contrasts his own suffering self with the whole remaining universe, though he have no clear conception either of himself or of what the universe may be. He is for me a mere part of the world; for him it is I who am the mere part. Each of us dichotomizes the Kosmos in a different place.

Descending now to finer work than this first general sketch, let us in the next chapter try to trace the psychology of this fact of self-consciousness to which we have thus once more been led.

The Self

The Me and the I. Whatever I may be thinking of, I am always at the same time more or less aware of *myself*, of my *personal existence*. At the same time it is *I* who am aware; so that the total self of me, being as it were duplex, partly known and partly knower, partly object and partly subject, must have two aspects discriminated in it, of which for shortness we may call one the *Me* and the other the *I*. I call these "discriminated aspects," and not separate things, because the identity of *I* with *Me*, even in the very act of their discrimination, is perhaps the most ineradicable dictum of common-sense, and must not be undermined by our terminology here at the outset, whatever we may come to think of its validity at our inquiry's end.

I shall therefore treat successively of (A) the self as known, or the *Me*, the "empirical ego" as it is sometimes called; and of (B) the self as knower, or the *I*, the "pure ego" of certain authors.

(A) The self as known

The empirical self or Me. Between what a man calls *me* and what he simply calls *mine* the line is difficult to draw. We feel and act about certain things that are ours very much as we feel and act about ourselves. Our fame, our children, the work of our hands, may be as dear to us as our bodies are, and arouse the same feelings and the same acts of reprisal if attacked. And our bodies themselves, are they simply ours, or are they *us?* Certainly men have been ready to disown their very bodies and to regard them as mere vestures, or even as prisons of clay from which they should some day be glad to escape.

We see then that we are dealing with a fluctuating material; the same object being sometimes treated as a part of me, at other times as simply mine, and then again as if I had nothing to do with it at all. In its widest possible sense, however, a man's Me is the sum total of all that he *can* call his, not only his body and his psychic powers, but his clothes and his house, his wife and children, his ancestors and friends, his reputation and works, his lands and horses, and yacht and bank-account. All these things give him the same emotions. If they wax and prosper, he feels triumphant; if they dwindle and die away, he feels cast down – not necessarily in the same degree for each thing, but in much the same way for all. Understanding the Me in this widest sense, we may begin by dividing the history of it into three parts, relating respectively to:

a   its constituents;
b   the feelings and emotions they arouse – *self-appreciation*;

c the act to which they prompt – *self-seeking and self-preservation.*

a The constituents of the Me may be divided into two classes, those which make up, respectively, the material Me; the social Me; and the spiritual Me.

The material Me. The *body* is the innermost part of the material Me in each of us; and certain parts of the body seem more intimately ours than the rest. The clothes come next. The old saying that the human person is composed of three parts – soul, body and clothes – is more than a joke. We so appropriate our clothes and identify our selves with them that there are few of us who, if asked to choose between having a beautiful body clad in raiment perpetually shabby and unclean, and having an ugly and blemished form always spotlessly attired, would not hesitate a moment before making a decisive reply. Next, our immediate family is a part of ourselves. Our father and mother, our wife and babes, are bone of our bone and flesh of our flesh. When they die, a part of our very selves is gone. If they do anything wrong, it is our shame. If they are insulted, our anger flashes forth as readily as if we stood in their place. Our home comes next. Its scenes are part of our life; its aspects awaken the tenderest feelings of affection; and we do not easily forgive the stranger who, in visiting it, finds fault with its arrangements or treats it with contempt. All these different things are the objects of instinctive preferences coupled with the most important practical interests of life. We all have a blind impulse to watch over our body, to deck it with clothing of an ornamental sort, to cherish parents, wife, and babes, and to find for ourselves a house of our own which we may live in and "improve."

An equally instinctive impulse drives us to collect property; and the collections thus made become, with different degrees of intimacy, parts of our empirical selves. The parts of our wealth most intimately ours are those which are saturated with our labor. There are few men who would not feel personally annihilated if a life-long construction of their hands or brains – say an entomological collection or an extensive work in manuscript – were suddenly swept away. The miser feels similarly towards his gold; and although it is true that a part of our depression at the loss of possessions is due to our feeling that we must now go without certain goods that we expected the possessions to bring in their train, yet in every case there remains, over and above this, a sense of the shrinkage of our personality, a partial conversion of ourselves to nothingness, which is a psychological phenomenon by itself. We are all at once assimilated to the tramps and poor devils whom we so despise, and at the same time removed farther than ever away from the happy sons of earth who lord it over land and sea and men in the full-blown lustihood that wealth and power can give, and before whom, stiffen ourselves as we will by appealing to anti-snobbish first principles, we cannot escape an emotion, open or sneaking, of respect and dread.

The social Me. A man's social Me is the recognition which he gets from his mates. We are not only gregarious animals, liking to be in sight of our fellows, but we have an innate propensity to get ourselves noticed, and noticed favorably, by our kind. No more fiendish punishment could be devised, were such a thing physically possible, than that one should be turned loose in society and remain absolutely unnoticed by all the members thereof. If no one turned round when we entered, answered when we spoke, or minded what we did, but if every person we met "cut us dead," and acted as if we were non-existing things, a kind of rage and impotent despair would ere long well up in us, from which the cruellest bodily tortures would be a relief; for these would make us feel that, however bad might be our plight, we had not sunk to such a depth as to be unworthy of attention at all.

Properly speaking, a man has as many social selves as there are individuals who recognize him and carry an image of him in their mind. To wound any one of these his images is to wound him. But as the individuals who carry the images fall naturally into classes, we may practically say that he has as many different social selves as there are distinct *groups* of persons about whose opinion he cares. He generally shows a different side of himself to each of these different groups. Many a youth who is demure enough before his parents and teachers, swears and swaggers like a pirate among his "tough" young friends. We do not show ourselves to our children as to our club-companions, to our customers as to the laborers we employ, to our own masters and employers as to our intimate friends. From this there results what practically is a division of the man into several selves; and this may be a discordant splitting, as where one is afraid to let one set of his acquaintances know him as he is elsewhere; or it may be a perfectly harmonious division of labor, as where one tender to his children is stern to the soldiers or prisoners under his command.

The most peculiar social self which one is apt to have is in the mind of the person one is in love with. The good or bad fortunes of this self cause the most intense elation and dejection – unreasonable enough as measured by every other standard than that of the organic feeling of the individual. To his own consciousness he *is* not, so long as this particular social self fails to get recognition, and when it is recognized his contentment passes all bounds.

A man's *fame*, good or bad, and his *honor* or dishonor, are names for one of his social selves. The particular social self of a man called his honor is usually the result of one of those splittings of which we have spoken. It is his image in the eyes of his own "set," which exalts or condemns him as he conforms or not to certain requirements that may not be made of one in another walk of life. Thus a layman may abandon a city infected with cholera; but a priest or a doctor would think such an act incompatible with his honor. A soldier's honor requires him to fight or to die under circumstances where another man can apologize or run away with no stain upon his social self. A judge, a statesman, are in like manner debarred by the honor of their cloth from entering into pecuniary relations perfectly honorable to persons in private life. Nothing is commoner than to hear people discriminate between their different selves of this sort: "As a man I pity you, but as an official I must show you no mercy"; "As a politician I regard him as an ally, but as a moralist I loathe him"; etc., etc. What may be called "club-opinion" is one of the very strongest forces in life. The thief must not steal from other thieves; the gambler must pay his gambling-debts, though he pay no other debts in the world. The code of honor of fashionable society has throughout history been full of permissions as well as of vetoes, the only reason for following either of which is that so we best serve one of our social selves. You must not lie in general, but you may lie as much as you please if asked about your relations with a lady; you must accept a challenge from an equal, but if challenged by an inferior you may laugh him to scorn: these are examples of what is meant.

The spiritual Me. By the "spiritual Me," so far as it belongs to the empirical self, I mean no one of my passing states of consciousness. I mean rather the entire collection of my states of consciousness, my psychic faculties and dispositions taken concretely. This collection can at any moment become an object to my thought at that moment and awaken emotions like those awakened by any of the other portions of the Me. When we think of ourselves as thinkers, all the other ingredients of our Me seem relatively external possessions. Even within the spiritual Me some ingredients seem more external than others. Our capacities for sensation, for example, are less intimate possessions, so to speak, than our emotions and desires; our intellectual processes are less intimate than our volitional decisions. The more *active-feeling* states of consciousness are thus the more central portions of the spiritual Me. The very core and nucleus of our self, as we know it, the very sanctuary of our life, is the sense of activity which certain inner states possess. This sense of activity is often held to be a direct revelation of the living substance of our Soul. Whether this be so or not is an ulterior question. I wish now only to lay down the peculiar *internality* of whatever states possess this quality of seeming to be active. It is as if they *went out to meet* all the other elements of our experience. In thus feeling about them probably all men agree.

b   The feelings and emotions of self come after the constituents.

Self-appreciation. This is of two sorts, *self-complacency* and *self-dissatisfaction.* "Self-love" more properly belongs under the division *C*, of *acts*, since what men mean by that name is rather a set of motor tendencies than a kind of feeling properly so called.

Language has synonyms enough for both kinds of self-appreciation. Thus pride, conceit, vanity, self-esteem, arrogance, vainglory, on the one hand; and on the other modesty, humility, confusion, diffidence, shame, mortification, contrition, the sense of obloquy, and personal despair. These two opposite classes of affection seem to be direct and elementary endowments of our nature. Associationists would have it that they are, on the other hand, secondary phenomena arising from a rapid computation of the sensible pleasures or pains to which our prosperous or debased personal predicament is likely to lead, the sum of the represented pleasures forming the self-satisfaction, and the sum of the represented pains forming the opposite feeling of shame. No doubt, when we are self-satisfied, we do fondly rehearse all possible rewards for our desert, and when in a fit of self-despair we forebode evil. But the mere expectation of reward *is* not the self-satisfaction, and the mere apprehension of the evil *is* not the self-despair; for there is a certain average tone of self-feeling which each one of us carries about with him, and which is independent of the objective reasons we may have for satisfaction or discontent. That is, a very meanly-conditioned man may abound in unfaltering conceit, and one whose success in life is secure, and who is esteemed by all, may remain diffident of his powers to the end.

One may say, however, that the normal *provocative* of self-feeling is one's actual success or failure, and the good or bad actual position one holds in the world. "He put in his thumb and pulled out a plum, and said, 'What a good boy am I!'" A man with a broadly extended empirical Ego, with powers that have uniformly brought him success, with place and wealth and friends and fame, is not likely to be visited by the morbid diffidences and doubts about himself which he had when he was a boy. "Is not this great Babylon, which I have planted?" Whereas he who has made one blunder after another, and still lies in middle life among the failures at the foot of the hill, is liable to grow all sicklied o'er with self-distrust, and to shrink from trials with which his powers can really cope.

The emotions themselves of self-satisfaction and abasement are of a unique sort, each as worthy to be classed as a primitive emotional species as are, for example, rage or pain. Each has its own peculiar physiognomical expression. In self-satisfaction the extensor muscles are innervated, the eye is strong and glorious, the gait rolling and elastic, the nostril dilated, and a peculiar smile plays upon the lips. This whole complex of symptoms is seen in an exquisite way in lunatic asylums, which always contain some patients who are literally mad with conceit, and whose fatuous expression and absurdly strutting or swaggering gait is in tragic contrast with their lack of any valuable personal quality. It is in these same castles of despair that we find the strongest examples of the opposite physiognomy, in good people who think they have committed "the unpardonable sin" and are lost forever, who crouch and cringe and slink from notice, and are unable to speak aloud or look us in the eye. Like fear and like anger, in similar morbid conditions, these opposite feelings of Self may be aroused with no adequate exciting cause. And in fact we ourselves know how the barometer of our self-esteem and confidence rises and falls from one day to another through causes that seem to be visceral and organic rather than rational, and which certainly answer to no corresponding variations in the esteem in which we are held by our friends.

c Self-seeking and self-preservation come next. These words cover a large number of our fundamental instinctive impulses. We have those of *bodily self-seeking*, those of *social self-seeking*, and those of *spiritual self-seeking*.

Bodily self-seeking. All the ordinary useful reflex actions and movements of alimentation and defence are acts of bodily self-preservation. Fear and anger prompt to acts that are useful in the same way. Whilst if by self-seeking we mean the providing for the future as distinguished from maintaining the present, we must class both anger and fear, together with the hunting, the acquisitive, the home-constructing and the tool-constructing instincts, as impulses to self-seeking of the bodily kind. Really, however, these latter instincts, with amativeness, parental fondness, curiosity and emulation, seek not only the development of the bodily Me, but that of the material Me in the widest possible sense of the word.

Our *social self-seeking*, in turn, is carried on directly through our amativeness and friendliness, our desire to please and attract notice and admiration, our emulation and jealousy, our love of glory, influence, and power, and indirectly through whichever of the material self-seeking impulses prove serviceable as means to social ends. That the direct social self-seeking impulses are probably pure instincts is easily seen. The noteworthy thing about the desire to be "recognized" by others is that its strength has so little to do with the worth of the recognition computed in sensational or rational terms. We are crazy to get a visiting-list which shall be large, to be able to say when any one is mentioned, "Oh! I know him well," and to be bowed to in the street by half the people we meet. Of course distinguished friends and admiring recognition are the most desirable – Thackeray somewhere asks his readers to confess whether it would not give each of *them* an exquisite pleasure to be met walking down Pall Mall with a duke on either arm. But in default of dukes and envious salutions almost anything will do for some of us; and there is a whole race of beings to-day whose passion is to keep their names in the newspapers, no matter under what heading, "arrivals and departures," "personal paragraphs," "interviews" – gossip, even scandal, will suit them if nothing better is to be had. Guiteau, Garfield's assassin, is an example of the extremity to which this sort of craving for the notoriety of print may go in a pathological case. The newspapers bounded his mental horizon; and in the poor wretch's prayer on the scaffold, one of the most heart-felt expressions was: "The newspaper press of this land has a big bill to settle with thee, O Lord!"

Not only the people but the places and things I know enlarge my Self in a sort of metaphoric social way. "*Ça me connaît*," as the French workman says of the implement he can use well. So that it comes about that persons for whose *opinion* we care nothing are nevertheless persons whose notice we woo; and that many a man truly great, many a woman truly fastidious in most respects, will take a deal of trouble to dazzle some insignificant cad whose whole personality they heartily despise.

Under the head of *spiritual self-seeking* ought to be included every impulse towards psychic progress, whether intellectual, moral, or spiritual in the narrow sense of the term. It must be admitted, however, that much that commonly passes for spiritual self-seeking in this narrow sense is only material and social self-seeking beyond the grave. In the Mohammedan desire for paradise and the Christian aspiration not to be damned in hell, the materiality of the goods sought is undisguised. In the more positive and refined view of heaven, many of its goods, the fellowship of the saints and of our dead ones, and the presence of God, are but social goods of the most exalted kind. It is only the search of the redeemed inward nature, the spotlessness from sin, whether here or hereafter, that can count as spiritual self-seeking pure and undefiled.

But this broad external review of the facts of the life of the Me will be incomplete without some account of the rivalry and conflict of the different mes.

With most objects of desire, physical nature restricts our choice to but one of many represented goods, and even so it is here. I am often confronted by the necessity of standing by one of my empirical selves and relinquishing the rest. Not that I would not, if I could, be both handsome and fat and well dressed, and a great athlete, and make a million a year, be a wit, a *bon-vivant*, and a lady-killer, as well as a philosopher; a philanthropist, statesman, warrior, and African explorer, as well as a "tone-poet" and saint. But the thing is simply impossible. The millionaire's work would run counter to the saint's; the *bon-vivant* and the philanthropist would trip each other up; the philosopher and the lady-killer could not well keep house in the same tenement of clay. Such different characters may conceivably at the outset of life be alike *possible* to a man. But to make any one of them actual, the rest must more or less be suppressed. So the seeker of his truest, strongest, deepest self must review the list carefully, and pick out the one on which to stake his salvation. All other selves thereupon become unreal, but the fortunes of this self are real. Its failures are real failures, its triumphs real triumphs, carrying shame and gladness with them. This is as strong an example as there is of that selective industry of the mind on which I insisted some pages back (pp. 94 ff.). Our thought, incessantly deciding, among many things of a kind, which ones for it shall be realities, here chooses one of many possible selves or characters, and forthwith reckons it no shame to fail in any of those not adopted expressly as its own.

So we have the paradox of a man shamed to death because he is only the second pugilist or the second oarsman in the world. That he is able to beat the whole population of the globe minus one is nothing; he has "pitted" himself to beat that one; and as long as he doesn't do that nothing else counts. He is to his own regard as if he were not, indeed he *is* not. Yonder puny fellow, however, whom every one can beat, suffers no chagrin about it, for he has long ago abandoned the attempt to "carry that line," as the merchants say, of self at all. With no attempt there can be no failure; with no failure, no humiliation. So our self-feeling in this world depends entirely on what we *back* ourselves to be and do. It is determined by the ratio of our actualities to our supposed potentialities; a fraction of which our pretensions are the denominator and the numerator our success: thus,

$$\text{self-esteem} = \frac{\text{success}}{\text{pretensions}}$$

Such a fraction may be increased as well by diminishing the denominator as by increasing the numerator. To give up pretensions is as blessed a relief as to get them gratified; and where disappointment is incessant and the struggle unending, this is what men will always do. The history of evangelical theology, with its conviction of sin, its self-despair, and its abandonment of salvation by works, is the deepest of possible examples, but we meet others in every walk of life. There is the strangest lightness about the heart when one's nothingness in a particular line is once accepted in good faith. *All* is not bitterness in the lot of the lover sent away by the final inexorable "No." Many Bostonians, *crede experto* (and inhabitants of other cities, too, I fear), would be happier women and men to-day, if they could once for all abandon the notion of keeping up a Musical Self, and without shame let people hear them call a symphony a nuisance. How pleasant is the day when we give up striving to be young – or slender! Thank God! we say, *those* illusions are gone. Everything added to the Self is a burden as well as a pride. A certain man who lost every penny during our civil war went and actually rolled in the dust, saying he had not felt so free and happy since he was born.

Once more, then, our self-feeling is in our power. As Carlyle says: "Make thy claim of wages a zero, then hast thou the world under thy feet. Well did the wisest of our time write, it is only with *renunciation* that life, properly speaking, can be said to begin."

Neither threats nor pleadings can move a man unless they touch some one of his potential or actual selves. Only thus can we, as a rule, get a "purchase" on another's will. The first care of diplomatists and monarchs and all who wish to rule or influence is, accordingly, to find out their victim's strongest principle of self-regard, so as to make that the fulcrum of all appeals. But if a man has given up those things which are subject to foreign fate, and ceased to regard them as parts of himself at all, we are well-nigh powerless over him. The Stoic receipt for contentment was to dispossess yourself in advance of all that was out of your own power – then fortune's shocks might rain down unfelt. Epictetus exhorts us, by thus narrowing and at the same time solidifying our Self to make it invulnerable: "I must die; well, but must I die groaning too? I will speak what appears to be right, and if the despot says, 'Then I will put you to death,' I will reply, 'When did I ever tell you that I was immortal? You will do your part, and I mine; it is yours to kill, and mine to die intrepid; yours to banish, mine to depart untroubled.' How do we act in a voyage? We choose the pilot, the sailors, the hour. Afterwards comes a storm. What have I to care for? My part is performed. This matter belongs to the pilot. But the ship is sinking; what then have I to do? That which alone I can do – submit to being drowned without fear, without clamor or accusing of God, but as one who knows that what is born must likewise die."

This Stoic fashion, though efficacious and heroic enough in its place and time, is, it must be confessed, only possible as an habitual mood of the soul to narrow and unsympathetic characters. It proceeds altogether by exclusion. If I am a Stoic, the goods I cannot appropriate cease to be *my* goods, and the temptation lies very near to deny that they are goods at all. We find this mode of protecting the Self by exclusion and denial very common among people who are in other respects not Stoics. All narrow people *intrench* their Me, they *retract* it – from the region of what they cannot securely possess. People who don't resemble them, or who treat them with indifference, people over whom they gain no influence, are people on whose existence, however meritorious it may intrinsically be, they look with chill negation, if not with positive hate. Who will not be mine I will exclude from existence altogether; that is, as far as I can make it so, such people shall be as if they were not. Thus may a certain absoluteness and definiteness in the outline of my Me console me for the smallness of its content.

Sympathetic people, on the contrary, proceed by the entirely opposite way of expansion and inclusion. The outline of their self often gets uncertain enough, but for this the spread of its content more than atones. *Nil humani a me alienum.* Let them despise this little person of mine, and treat me like a dog, *I* shall not negate *them* so long as I have a soul in my body. They are realities as much as I am. What positive good is in them shall be mine too, etc., etc. The magnanimity of these expansive natures is often touching indeed. Such persons can feel a sort of delicate rapture in thinking that, however sick, ill-favored, mean-conditioned, and generally forsaken they may be, they yet are integral parts of the whole of this brave world, have a fellow's share in the strength of the dray-horses, the happiness of the young people, the wisdom of the wise ones, and are not altogether without part or lot in the good fortunes of the Vanderbilts and the Hohenzollerns themselves. Thus either by negating or by embracing, the Ego may seek to establish itself in reality. He who, with Marcus Aurelius, can truly say, "O Universe, I wish all that thou wishest," has a self from which every trace of negativeness and obstructiveness has been removed – no wind can blow except to fill its sails.

The hierarchy of the Mes. A tolerably unanimous opinion ranges the different selves of which a man may be "seized and possessed," and the consequent different orders of his self-regard, in an hierarchical scale, with the bodily Me at the bottom, the spiritual Me at the top, and the extra-corporeal material selves and the various social selves between. Our merely natural self-seeking would lead us to aggrandize all these selves; we give up deliberately only those among them which we find we cannot keep. Our unselfishness is thus apt to be a "virtue of necessity"; and it is not without all show of reason that cynics quote the fable of the fox and the grapes in describing our progress therein. But this is the moral education of the race; and if we agree in the result that on the whole the selves we can keep are the intrinsically best, we need not complain of being led to the knowledge of their superior worth in such a tortuous way.

Of course this is not the only way in which we learn to subordinate our lower selves to our higher. A direct ethical judgment unquestionably also plays its part, and last, not least, we apply to our own persons judgments originally called forth by the acts of others. It is one of the strangest laws of our nature that many things which we are well satisfied with in ourselves disgust us when seen in others. With another man's bodily "hoggishness" hardly anyone has any sympathy; almost as little with his cupidity, his social vanity and eagerness, his jealousy, his despotism, and his pride. Left absolutely to myself I should probably allow all these spontaneous tendencies to luxuriate in me unchecked, and it would be long before I formed a distinct notion of the order of their subordination. But having constantly to pass judgment on my associates, I come ere long to see, as Herr Horwicz says, my own lusts in the mirror of the lusts of others, and to *think* about them in a very different way from that in which I simply *feel*. Of course, the moral generalities which from childhood have been instilled into me accelerate enormously the advent of this reflective judgment on myself.

So it comes to pass that, as aforesaid, men have arranged the various selves which they may seek in an hierarchical scale according to their worth. A certain amount of bodily selfishness is required as a basis for all the other selves. But too much sensuality is despised, or at best condoned on account of the other qualities of the individual. The wider material selves are regarded as higher than the immediate body. He is esteemed a poor creature who is unable to forego a little meat and drink and warmth and sleep for the sake of getting on in the world. The social self as a whole, again, ranks higher than the material self as a whole. We must care more for our honor, our friends, our human ties, than for a sound skin or wealth. And the spiritual self is so supremely precious that, rather than lose it, a man ought to be willing to give up friends and good fame, and property, and life itself.

In each kind of Me, material, social, and spiritual, men distinguish between the immediate and actual, and the remote and potential, between the narrower and the wider view, to the detriment of the former and the advantage of the latter. One must forego a present bodily enjoyment for the sake of one's general health; one must abandon the dollar in the hand for the sake of the hundred dollars to come; one must make an enemy of his present interlocutor if thereby one makes friends of a more valued circle; one must go without learning and grace and wit, the better to compass one's soul's salvation.

Of all these wider, more potential selves, *the potential social Me* is the most interesting, by reason of certain apparent paradoxes to which it leads in conduct, and by reason of its connection with our moral and religious life. When for motives of honor and conscience I brave the condemnation of my own family, club, and "set"; when, as a Protestant, I turn Catholic; as a Catholic, freethinker; as a "regular practitioner," homœopath, or what not, I am always inwardly strengthened in my course and steeled against the loss of my actual social self by the thought of other and better *possible* social judges than those whose verdict goes against me now. The ideal social self which I thus seek in appealing to their decision may be very remote: it may be represented as barely possible. I may not hope for its realization during my lifetime; I may even expect the future generations, which would approve me if they knew me, to know nothing about me when I am dead and gone. Yet still the emotion that beckons me on is indubitably the pursuit of an ideal social self, of a self that is at least *worthy* of approving recognition by the highest *possible* judging companion, if such companion there be. This self is the true, the intimate, the ultimate, the permanent Me which I seek. This judge is God, the Absolute Mind, the "Great Companion." We hear, in these days of scientific enlightenment, a great deal of discussion about the efficacy of prayer; and many reasons are given us why we should not pray, whilst others are given us why we should. But in all this very little is said of the reason why we *do* pray, which is simply that we cannot help praying. It seems probable that, in spite of all that "science" may do to the contrary, men will continue to pray to the end of time, unless their mental nature changes in a manner which nothing we know should lead us to expect. The impulse to pray is a necessary consequence of the fact that whilst the innermost of the empirical selves of a man is a Self of the *social* sort, it yet can find its only adequate *Socius* in an ideal world.

All progress in the social Self is the substitution of higher tribunals for lower; this ideal tribunal is the highest; and most men, either continually or occasionally, carry a reference to it in their breast. The humblest outcast on this earth can feel himself to be real and valid by means of this higher recognition. And, on the other hand, for most of us, a world with no such inner refuge when the outer social self failed and dropped from us would be the abyss of horror. I say "for most of us," because it is probable that individuals differ a good deal in the degree in which they are haunted by this sense of an ideal spectator. It is a much more essential part of the consciousness of some men than of others. Those who have the most of it are possibly the most *religious* men. But I am sure that even those who say they are altogether without it deceive themselves, and really have it in some degree. Only a non-gregarious animal could be completely without it. Probably no one can make sacrifices for "right," without to some degree personifying the principle of right for which the sacrifice is made, and expecting thanks from it. *Complete* social unselfishness, in other words, can hardly exist; *complete* social suicide hardly occur to a man's mind. Even such texts as Job's, "Though He slay me, yet will I trust Him," or Marcus Aurelius's, "If gods hate me and my children, there is a reason for it," can least of all be cited to prove the contrary. For beyond all doubt Job revelled in the thought of Jehovah's recognition of the worship after the slaying should have been done; and the Roman emperor felt sure the Absolute Reason would not be all indifferent to his acquiescence in the gods' dislike. The old test of piety, "Are you willing to be damned for the glory of God?" was probably never answered in the affirmative except by those who felt sure in their heart of hearts that God would "credit" them with their willingness, and set more store by them thus than if in His unfathomable scheme He had not damned them at all.

Teleological uses of self-interest. On zoological principles it is easy to see why we have been endowed with impulses of self-seeking and with emotions of self-satisfaction and the reverse. Unless our consciousness were something more than cognitive, unless it experienced a partiality for certain of the objects, which, in succession, occupy its ken, it could not long maintain itself in existence; for, by an inscrutable necessity, each human mind's appearance on this earth is conditioned upon the integrity of the body with which it belongs, upon the treatment which that body gets from others, and upon the spiritual dispositions which use it as their tool, and lead it either towards longevity or to destruction. Its own body, then, first of all, its friends next, and finally its spiritual dispositions, *must* be the supremely interesting objects for each human mind. Each mind, to begin with, must have a certain minimum of selfishness in the shape of instincts of bodily self-seeking in order to exist. This minimum must be there as a basis for all farther conscious acts, whether of self-negation or of a selfishness more subtle still. All minds must have come, by the way of the survival of the fittest, if by no directer path, to take an intense interest in the bodies to which they are yoked, altogether apart from any interest in the pure Ego which they also possess.

And similarly with the images of their person in the minds of others. I should not be extant now had I not become sensitive to looks of approval or disapproval on the faces among which my life is cast. Looks of contempt cast on other persons need affect me in no such peculiar way. My spiritual powers, again, must interest me more than those of other people, and for the same reason. I should not be here at all unless I had cultivated them and kept them from decay. And the same law which made me once care for them makes me care for them still.

All these three things form the *natural Me.* But all these things are *objects*, properly so called, to the thought which at any time may be doing the thinking; and if the zoological and evolutionary point of view is the true one, there is no reason why one object *might* not arouse passion and interest as primitively and instinctively as any other. The phenomenon of passion is in origin and essence the same, whatever be the target upon which it is discharged; and what the target actually happens to be is solely a question of fact. I might conceivably be as much fascinated, and as primitively so, by the care of my neighbor's body as by the care of my own. I *am* thus fascinated by the care of my child's body. The only check to such exuberant non-egoistic interests is natural selection, which would weed out such as were very harmful to the individual or to his tribe. Many such interests, however, remain unweeded out – the interest in the opposite sex, for example, which seems in mankind stronger than is called for by its utilitarian need; and alongside of them remain interests, like that in alcoholic intoxication, or in musical sounds, which, for aught we can see, are without any utility whatever. The sympathetic instincts and the egoistic ones are thus coördinate. They arise, so far as we can tell, on the same psychologic level. The only difference between them is that the instincts called egoistic form much the larger mass.

Summary. Table 9.1, showing how the empirical life of Self is divided, may serve for a summary of what has been said thus far.

(B)   The self as knower

The I, or "pure ego," is a very much more difficult subject of inquiry than the Me. It is that which at any given moment *is* conscious, whereas the Me is only one of the things which it is conscious *of*. In other words, it is the *Thinker*; and the question immediately comes up, *what* is the thinker? Is it the passing state of consciousness itself, or is it something deeper and less mutable? Yet each of us spontaneously considers that by "I," he means something always the same. This has led most

philosophers to postulate behind the passing state of consciousness a permanent Substance or Agent whose modification or act it is. This Agent is the thinker; the "state" is only its instrument or means. "Soul," "transcendental Ego," "Spirit," are so many names for this more permanent sort of Thinker. Not discriminating them just yet, let us proceed to define our idea of the passing state of consciousness more clearly.

The unity of the passing thought.   Already, in speaking of "sensations," from the point of view of Fechner's idea of measuring them, we saw that there was no ground for calling them compounds. But what is true of sensations cognizing simple qualities is also true of thoughts with complex objects composed of many parts. This proposition unfortunately runs counter to a widespread prejudice, and will have to be defended at some length. Common-sense, and psychologists of almost every school, have agreed that whenever an object of thought contains many elements, the thought itself must be made up of just as many ideas, one idea for each element, all fused together in appearance, but really separate.

"There can be no difficulty in admitting that association *does* form the ideas of an indefinite number of individuals into one complex idea," says James Mill, "because it is an acknowledged fact. Have we not the idea of an army? And is not that precisely the ideas of an indefinite number of men formed into one idea?"

Similar quotations might be multiplied, and the reader's own first impressions probably would rally to their support. Suppose, for example, he thinks that "the pack of cards is on the table." If he begins to reflect, he is as likely as not to say: "Well, isn't that a thought of the pack of cards? Isn't it of the cards as included in the pack? Isn't it of the

Table 9.1

	Material	Social	Spiritual
Self-seeking	Bodily appetites and instincts	Desire to please, be noticed, admired, etc.	Intellectual, moral and religious aspirations, conscientiousness
	Love of adornment, foppery, acquisitiveness, constructiveness	Sociability, emulation, envy, love, pursuit of honor, ambition, etc.	
	Love of home, etc.		
Self-estimation	Personal vanity, modesty, etc. Pride of wealth, fear of poverty	Social and family pride, vain-glory, snobbery, humility, shame, etc.	Sense of moral or mental superiority, purity, etc. Sense of inferiority or of guilt

table? And of the legs of the table as well? Hasn't my thought, then, all these parts – one part for the pack and another for the table? And within the pack-part a part for each card, as within the table-part a part for each leg? And isn't each of these parts an idea? And can thought, then, be anything but an assemblage or pack of ideas, each answering to some element of what it knows?"

Plausible as such considerations may seem, it is astonishing how little force they have. In assuming a pack of ideas, each cognizant of some one element of the fact one has assumed, nothing has been assumed which knows the whole fact *at once*. The idea which, on the hypothesis of the pack of ideas, knows, e.g., the ace of spades must be ignorant of the leg of the table, since to account for that knowledge another special idea is by the same hypothesis invoked; and so on with the rest of the ideas, all equally ignorant of each other's objects. And yet in the actual living human mind what knows the cards also knows the table, its legs, etc., for all these things are known in relation to each other and at once. Our notion of the abstract numbers eight, four, two is as truly one feeling of the mind as our notion of simple unity. Our idea of a couple is not a couple of ideas. "But," the reader may say, "is not the taste of lemonade composed of that of lemon *plus* that of sugar?" No! I reply, this is taking the combining of objects for that of feelings. The physical lemonade contains both the lemon and the sugar, but its taste does not contain their tastes; for if there are any two things which are certainly *not* present in the taste of lemonade, those are the pure lemon-sour on the one hand and the pure sugar-sweet on the other. These tastes are absent utterly. A taste somewhat *like* both of them is there, but that is a distinct state of mind altogether.

Distinct mental states cannot "fuse." But not only is the notion that our ideas are combinations of smaller ideas improbable, it is logically unintelligible; it leaves out the essential features of all the "combinations" which we actually know.

All the "combinations" which we actually know are *effects*, wrought by the units said to be "combined," *upon some entity other than themselves*. Without this feature of a medium or vehicle, the notion of combination has no sense.

In other words, no possible number of entities (call them as you like, whether forces, material particles, or mental elements) can sum *themselves* together. Each remains, in the sum, what it always was; and the sum itself exists only *for a bystander*

who happens to overlook the units and to apprehend the sum as such; or else it exists in the shape of some other effect on an entity external to the sum itself. When H_2 and O are said to combine into "water," and thenceforward to exhibit new properties, the "water" is just the old atoms in the new position, H–O–H; the "new properties" are just their combined *effects*, when in this position, upon external media, such as our sense-organs and the various reagents on which water may exert its properties and be known. Just so, the strength of many men may combine when they pull upon one rope, of many muscular fibres when they pull upon one tendon.

In the parallelogram of forces, the "forces" do not combine *themselves* into the diagonal resultant; a *body* is needed on which they may impinge, to exhibit their resultant effect. No more do musical sounds combine *per se* into concords or discords. Concord and discord are names for their combined effects on that external medium, the *ear*.

Where the elemental units are supposed to be feelings, the case is in no wise altered. Take a hundred of them, shuffle them and pack them as close together as you can (whatever that may mean); still each remains the same feeling it always was, shut in its own skin, windowless, ignorant of what the other feelings are and mean. There would be a hundred-and-first feeling there, if, when a group or series of such feelings were set up, a consciousness *belonging to the group as such* should emerge, and this one hundred and first feeling would be a totally new fact; the one hundred original feelings might, by a curious physical law, be a signal for its *creation*, when they came together – we often have to learn things separately before we know them as a sum – but they would have no substantial identity with the new feeling, nor it with them; and one could never deduce the one from the others, or (in any intelligible sense) say that they *evolved* it out of themselves.

Take a sentence of a dozen words, and take twelve men and tell to each one word. Then stand the men in a row or jam them in a bunch, and let each think of his word as intently as he will: nowhere will there be a consciousness of the whole sentence. We talk, it is true, of the "spirit of the age," and the "sentiment of the people," and in various ways we hypostatize "public opinion." But we know this to be symbolic speech, and never dream that the spirit, opinion, or sentiment constitutes a consciousness other than, and additional to, that of the several individuals whom the words "age," "people," or "public" denote. The private minds do not agglomerate into a higher compound mind. This has always been the invincible contention of the spiritualists against the associationists in Psychology. The associationists say the mind is constituted by a multiplicity of distinct "ideas" *associated* into a unity. There is, they say, an idea of *a*, and also an idea of *b*. *Therefore*, they say, there is an idea of *a* + *b*, or of *a* and *b* together. Which is like saying that the mathematical square of *a* plus that of *b* is equal to the square of *a* + *b*, a palpable untruth. Idea of *a* + idea of *b* is *not* identical with idea of (*a* + *b*). It is one, they are two; in it, what knows *a* also knows *b*; in them, what knows *a* is expressly posited as not knowing *b*; etc. In short, the two separate ideas can never by any logic be made to figure as one idea. If one idea (of *a* + *b*, for example) come as a matter of fact after the two separate ideas (of *a* and of *b*), then we must hold it to be as direct a product of the later conditions as the two separate ideas were of the earlier conditions.

The simplest thing, therefore, if we are to assume the existence of a stream of consciousness at all, would be to suppose that things that are known together are known in single pulses of that stream. The things may be many, and may occasion many currents in the brain. But the psychic phenomenon correlative to these many currents is one integral "state," transitive or substantive (see p. 92), to which the many things appear.

The soul as a combining medium. The spiritualists in philosophy have been prompt to see that things which are known together are known by one *something*, but that something, they say, is no mere passing thought, but a simple and permanent spiritual being on which many ideas combine their effects. It makes no difference in this connection whether this being be called Soul, Ego, or Spirit, in either case its chief function is that of a combining medium. This is a different vehicle of knowledge from that in which we just said that the mystery of knowing things together might be most simply lodged. Which is the real knower, this permanent being, or our passing state? If we had other grounds, not yet considered, for admitting the Soul into our psychology, then getting there on those grounds, she might turn out to be the knower too. But if there be no *other* grounds for admitting the Soul, we had better cling to our passing "states" as the exclusive agents of knowledge; for we have to assume their existence anyhow in psychology, and the knowing of many things together is just as well accounted for when we call it one of their functions as when we call it a reaction of the Soul. *Explained* it is not by either conception, and has to figure in psychology as a datum that is ultimate.

But there are other alleged grounds for admitting the Soul into psychology, and the chief of them is:

The sense of personal identity. It was stated (see p. 89) that the thoughts which we actually know to exist do not fly about loose, but seem each to belong to some one thinker and not to another. Each thought, out of a multitude of other thoughts of which it may think, is able to distinguish those which belong to it from those which do not. The former have a warmth and intimacy about them of which the latter are completely devoid, and the result is a Me of yesterday, judged to be in some peculiarly subtle sense the *same* with the I who now make the judgment. As a mere subjective phenomenon the judgment presents no special mystery. It belongs to the great class of judgments of sameness; and there is nothing more remarkable in making a judgment of sameness in the first person than in the second or the third. The intellectual operations seem essentially alike, whether I say "I am the same as I was," or whether I say "the pen is the same as it was, yesterday." It is as easy to think this as to think the opposite and say "neither of us is the same." The only question which we have to consider is whether it be a right judgment. *Is the sameness predicated really there?*

Sameness in the Self as known. If in the sentence "I am the same that I was yesterday," we take the "I" broadly, it is evident that in many ways I am *not* the same. As a concrete Me, I am somewhat different from what I was: then hungry, now full; then walking, now at rest; then poorer, now richer; then younger, now older; etc. And yet in other ways I *am* the same, and we may call these the essential ways. My name and profession and relations to the world are identical, my face, my faculties and store of memories, are practically indistinguishable, now and then. Moreover the Me of now and the Me of then are *continuous*: the alterations were gradual and never affected the whole of me at once. So far, then, my personal identity is just like the sameness predicated of any other aggregate thing. It is a conclusion grounded either on the resemblance in essential respects, or on the continuity of the phenomena compared. And it must not be taken to mean more than these grounds warrant, or treated as a sort of metaphysical or absolute Unity in which all differences are overwhelmed. The past and present selves compared are the same just so far as they *are* the same, and no farther. They are the same in *kind*. But this generic sameness coexists with generic differences just as real; and if from the one point of view I am one self, from another I am quite as truly many. Similarly of the attribute of continuity: it gives to the self the unity of mere connectedness, or unbrokenness, a perfectly definite phenomenal thing – but it gives not a jot or tittle more.

Sameness in the Self as knower.   But all this is said only of the Me, or Self as known. In the judgment "I am the same," etc., the "I" was taken broadly as the concrete person. Suppose, however, that we take it narrowly, as the *Thinker*, as "*that to which*" all the concrete determinations of the Me belong and are known: does there not then appear an absolute identity at different times? That something which at every moment goes out and knowingly appropriates the *Me* of the past, and discards the non-Me as foreign, is it not a permanent abiding principle of spiritual activity identical with itself wherever found?

That it is such a principle is the reigning doctrine both of philosophy and common–sense, and yet reflection finds it difficult to justify the idea. *If there were no passing states of consciousness*, then indeed we might suppose an abiding principle, absolutely one with itself, to be the ceaseless thinker in each one of us. But if the states of consciousness be accorded as realities, no such "substantial" identity in the thinker need be supposed. Yesterday's and to–day's states of consciousnesses have no *substantial* identity, for when one is here the other is irrevocably dead and gone. But they have a *functional* identity, for both know the same objects, and so far as the by-gone Me is one of those objects, they react upon it in an identical way, greeting it and calling it *mine*, and opposing it to all the other things they know. This functional identity seems really the only sort of identity in the thinker which the facts require us to suppose. Successive thinkers, numerically distinct, but all aware of the same past in the same way, form an adequate vehicle for all the experience of personal unity and sameness which we

actually have. And just such a train of successive thinkers is the stream of mental states (each with its complex object cognized and emotional and selective reaction thereupon) which psychology treated as a natural science has to assume.

The logical conclusion seems then to be that the states of consciousness are all that psychology needs to do her work with. Metaphysics or theology may prove the Soul to exist; but for psychology the hypothesis of such a substantial principle of unity is superfluous.

How the I appropriates the Me.   But *why* should each successive mental state appropriate the same past Me? I spoke a while ago of my own past experiences appearing to me with a "warmth and intimacy" which the experiences thought of by me as having occurred to other people lack. This leads us to the answer sought. My present Me is felt with warmth and intimacy. The heavy warm mass of my body is there, and the nucleus of the "spiritual me," the sense of intimate activity (p. 98), is there. We cannot realize our present self without simultaneously feeling one or other of these two things. Any other object of thought which brings these two things with it into consciousness will be thought with a warmth and an intimacy like those which cling to the present Me.

Any *distant* object which fulfils this condition will be thought with such warmth and intimacy. But which distant objects *do* fulfil the condition, when represented?

Obviously those, and only those, which fulfilled it when they were alive. *Them* we shall still represent with the animal warmth upon them; to them may possibly still cling the flavor of the inner activity taken in the act. And by a natural consequence, we shall assimilate them to each other and to the warm and intimate self we now feel within us as we think, and separate them as a collection from whatever objects have not this mark, much as out of a herd of cattle let loose for the winter on some wide Western prairie the owner picks out and sorts together, when the round–up comes in the spring, all the beasts on which he finds his own particular brand. Well, just such objects are the past experiences which I now call mine. Other men's experiences, no matter how much I may know about them, never bear this vivid, this peculiar brand. This is why Peter, awakening in the same bed with Paul, and recalling what both had in mind before they went to sleep, reidentifies and appropriates the "warm" ideas as his, and is never tempted to confuse them with those cold and pale-appearing ones which he ascribes to Paul. As well might he confound Paul's body, which he only sees, with his own body, which he sees but also feels. Each of us when he awakens says, Here's the same old Me again, just as he says, Here's the same old bed, the same old room, the same old world.

And similarly in our waking hours, though each pulse of consciousness dies away and is replaced by another, yet that other, among the things it knows, knows its own predecessor, and finding it "warm," in the way we have described, greets it, saying: "Thou art *mine*, and part of the same self with me." Each later thought, knowing and including thus the thoughts that went before, is the final receptacle – and appropriating them is the final owner – of all that they contain and own. As Kant says, it is as if elastic balls were to have not only motion but knowledge of it, and a first ball were to transmit both its motion and its consciousness to a second, which took both up into *its* consciousness and passed them to a third, until the last ball held all that the other balls had held, and realized it as its own. It is this trick which the nascent thought has of immediately taking up the expiring thought and "adopting" it, which leads to the appropriation of most of the remoter constituents of the self. Who owns the last self owns the self before the last, for what possesses the possessor possesses the possessed. It is impossible to discover any *verifiable* features in personal identity which this sketch does not contain, impossible to imagine how any transcendent principle of Unity (were such a principle there) could shape matters to any other result, or be known by any other fruit, than just this production of a stream of consciousness each successive part of which should know, and knowing, hug to itself and adopt, all those that went before – thus standing as the *representative* of an entire past stream with which it is in no wise to be identified.

10

Self-Consciousness, Social Consciousness and Nature

Josiah Royce

Introduction

Josiah Royce (1855–1916) was born in Grass Valley, California, and was educated at the new University of California and Johns Hopkins University in Baltimore. He joined the philosophy faculty at Harvard University where he advocated a philosophy he described as "absolute pragmatism." He was one of the few academic philosophers of the time to consider issues of race and racism, in his volume, *Race Questions, Provincialism, and Other American Problems.* His principal works include *The Religious Aspect of Philosophy, The World and the Individual, The Philosophy of Loyalty,* and *The Problem of Christianity.*

The ultimate purpose of the present paper is to reach, and, in closing, to sketch some views as to the relation of Man to Nature. By way of introduction, I must first define the place of my inquiry in the general catalogue of philosophical questions, and must then state the theses that I mean to defend.

There are two great divisions of philosophy – theoretical and practical. The present paper concerns itself with a matter belonging to theoretical philosophy. Within the range of theoretical philosophy, however, one may distinguish between the discussion of the ultimate problems of knowledge and of truth, and the treatment of the more special theoretical problems suggested by our human experience. General Epistemology and general Meta-

Taken from *Studies of Good and Evil: A Series of Essays upon Problems of Philosophy and of Life* (New York: D. Appleton and Co., 1906).

physics have to do with what can be made out about the deepest nature of our knowledge and the final constitution of the universe. But there are, within the scope of theoretical philosophy, other problems relating to the constitution of our finite world – problems which are often grouped together as the questions of special metaphysics, or of the Philosophy of Nature – a doctrine to which has also sometimes been given the name Cosmology. The problems of Cosmology are such as the questions: What is the truth behind what we mortals call Nature, or the physical world? What are finite minds, and how are they related to physical reality? What, if any, is the philosophical interpretation to be given to the doctrine of Evolution?

Now the present paper, as I just said, is an inquiry within the region of theoretical philosophy. Within that region my investigation, however, here concerns itself only secondarily with the ultimate problems of general metaphysics. I shall chiefly aim to reach, before I close, light as to a certain problem of philosophical cosmology. Here about us, as we all admit, whatever our ultimate metaphysical views, is the natural world, the world that appears to our senses – a world manifesting some sort of finite, and obviously, as we mortals see it, some sort of highly fragmentary truth. Now man, as we phenomenally know him, appears as a part of nature, a product of nature, a being whose destinies seem to be the sport of purely physical laws. The problem that this paper aims in the end to approach is: What is the meaning of this phenomenal relation of man to nature?

Now, as I need not say, a real answer to this question must lead us past, if not through, the realms of the most ultimate and general sort of metaphysical inquiry. Nor will this paper wholly escape the responsibility of considering to some extent, as we proceed, such ultimate matters. But on the other hand, all philosophical students are used to the fragmentary, and I shall not here attempt completeness. Such general metaphysical views as come in sight in this paper will remain, after all, of rather secondary importance. I shall attempt only to clear some of the way that leads from the study of man as we ordinarily know him towards the regions where general philosophy attempts to grapple with the ultimate issues of life, and with the rational constitution of the universe.

The relation of man to nature – this, then, is our immediate topic. But why, you may ask, if such is the purpose of this paper, have I chosen my actual title? Why does a study of the relations of Self-consciousness and Social Consciousness seem adapted to throw light on the cosmological problem of the relation of human beings to natural processes? To this preliminary question let us at once address ourselves.

I

The philosophical examination of man's social consciousness has been left, rather too exclusively, in the hands of the students of ethics. Even the psychologists, until very recently, have paid a very inadequate attention to the distinctively social aspects of their science. It is far too customary, in consequence, for the ethical philosophers themselves to begin their study of the duties of man with a very abstract view of the nature of the social consciousness, and of its original relations to our self-consciousness. We hear nowadays, for instance, in popular philosophy, a great deal about the supposed primal and natural conflict between Egoism and Altruism. Egoism, so we are told, is the original human tendency – the natural and innate bias of any one of us mortals. And it is so because, as soon as one becomes self-conscious, i.e., aware of one's Ego, one finds one's self, as an animal, instinctively selfish. The practical tendency of the self-preserving animal organism, translated into the terms of self-consciousness, becomes deliberate Egoism. Hence the moral problem is to make a man altruistic. The philosophical problem of ethics, on the other hand, is to

show a man why he ought to be altruistic, i.e., why Egoism, which is naturally prior and apparently self-evident, ought rationally to be subordinated, upon reflection, to its derived and slowly acquired natural opponent, Altruism.

But now, I insist that, as a fact, this far too customary notion of a natural and fatal opposition between self-consciousness, Egoism, and our socially determined and derived Altruism, is also far too falsely abstract a notion. There are evil tendencies in plenty in human nature, and common sense has a very wholesome meaning in mind when it condemns our natural selfishness. But when one defines in philosophical terms our evil tendencies, or undertakes to analyse in an ultimate sense what common sense knows as our selfishness, one does ill if one merely substitutes abstract distinctions for our concrete and passionate life-conflicts. As a fact, the abstract opposition, Ego and Alter, or Egoism and Altruism, ill suggests the meaning of the opposed ethical aims that struggle in us. This whole customary popular and philosophical opposition between a man's self-consciousness, as if it were something primitive and lonely, and his social consciousness, as if that were something acquired, apart from his self-consciousness, through intercourse with his fellows, is false to human nature. As a fact, a man becomes self-conscious only in the most intimate connection with the growth of his social consciousness. These two forms of consciousness are not separable and opposed regions of a man's life; they are thoroughly interdependent. I am dependent on my fellows, not only physically, but to the very core of my conscious self-hood, not only for what, physically speaking, I am, but for what I take myself to be. Take away the Alter from consciousness, and the conscious Ego, so far as in this world we know it, languishes, and languishing dies, whatever may become of the organism in whose fortunes this Ego, while it is known to persist, seems to be involved. Hence, I am not first self-conscious, and then secondarily conscious of my fellow. On the contrary, I am conscious of myself, on the whole, as in relation to some real or ideal fellow, and apart from my consciousness of my fellows I have only secondary and derived states and habits of self-consciousness. I cannot really will to preserve the Ego, then – this derived conscious creature of the habits of my social consciousness; I cannot really will to preserve the Ego, without also willing to preserve and to defend some sort of Alter, and some sort of relation to my fellow who is this Alter, and upon whom my conscious Ego depends for its very life. It is only in abstraction that I can be merely egoistic. In the concrete case I can only be egoistic by being also voluntarily altruistic, however base may be the sort of Altruism that I chance to prefer. I can aim, for instance, to be a political "boss." That appears to be a very egoistic aim. But the political "boss" exists by the suffrages of interested people, and must aim at their conscious, even if illusory, sense of advantage in so far as he wills them to be sincerely interested. I can will to be a flattering demagogue, admired for vain show by a crowd of fools. The end is selfish; but it also involves wishing to be agreeable in the eyes of many people; and even a saint might on occasion wisely include so much of the demagogue's aim in his own vastly different context of voluntary life. The tyrant wills the lives and even the limited good fortune of his subjects, for without powerful and numerous and even devoted subjects he would be no tyrant. The master wills his slave's preservation, even in willing to preserve his own mastery. Even the thief or the defaulter wills that the hoarding of valuable property should be on the average sufficiently advantageous to others to make them willing and careful to provide him with the wherewithal to win his thief's livelihood. Even the murderer, although he directly aims to destroy his fellow, does so, in general, and whenever the act is deliberate and intelligent, for a social end – honor, property, power – all of them ends which involve willing the preservation, and even the prosperity, of many social relations involving others than the murderer himself. There is, then, much bad Altruism in the world, much base, wishing of social relations which do involve the preservation, and even the relative private advantage of others besides the evil-doer. But bad Altruism is not mere Egoism, nor is it identical with a lower animal's unconsciously naïve selfishness. The mere instincts of the self-preservation of this organism have to be far transcended before one can become consciously egoistic. Vanity, pride, love of social power, the greed of mastery, covetousness, oppression – all these are tendencies that, just in so far as they are conscious and deliberate, involve not only Egoism, i.e., the love of the advantage of this individual, but also some more or less evil form of Altruism – the love of the preservation, and often of a certain limited advantage, of those of one's fellows who form the necessary other term of the social relation which satisfies one's vanity, one's greed, or one's love of power. In brief, speaking ethically, you cannot consciously be merely egoistic. For you, as

a man, exist only in human relations. Your aims have to be more or less social, just so far as you clearly define them. The ethical problem is not: Shall I aim to preserve social relations? but: What social relations shall I aim to preserve?

But to return from these illustrations to the general topic: my first point on this occasion is that, just as there is no conscious Egoism without some distinctly social reference, so there is, on the whole, in us men, no self-consciousness apart from some more or less derived form of the social consciousness. I am I in relation to some sort of a non-Ego. And, as a fact, the non-Ego that I am accustomed to deal with when I think and act, is primarily some real or ideal finite fellow-being, in actual or possible social relations with me, and this social non-Ego, real or ideal, is only secondarily to be turned into anything else, as, for example, into a natural object that I regard as a mere dead thing. And I have dwelt upon these facts here for the sake of first introducing a matter towards whose final definition the whole of the following argument is to tend, viz., the assertion that what you and I mean by Nature is, as a finite reality, something whose very conception we have actually derived from our social relations with one another; so that, as we shall see, to believe that there really exists a finite reality called Nature, is of necessity, when you rightly analyze the facts, to believe that there is, in the real universe, an extra-human, but finite conscious life, manifesting its presence to us by means substantially similar to those whereby we have become assured of the presence of the inner life of our human fellows. As it is not true that we are primarily and in unsocial abstraction merely egoistic, just so it is not true that we primarily know merely our own inner life as individuals, apart from an essentially social contrast with other minds. While it is true, as all idealistic analysis has affirmed, that the object of knowledge is precisely what it is known as being, it is not true that you and I ever know our own individual inner world of objects, without contrasting these objects with others that we regard as present to some sort of conscious life beyond our own. But primarily we learn to contrast our own inner life with what we regard as the inner life of our fellows in human society. It is by virtue of this very contrast of our own inner life with a finite conscious life beyond our own, viz., that of our human fellows, that we become self-conscious. When later, for reasons that I shall soon define, we learn to oppose to ourselves as finite knowers, a world of relatively independent natural objects, which we conceive as existent apart from any human insight, all the categories in terms of which we can learn to think of these nature-objects are categories derived from our social experience, and modified, but not really transformed, to suit the peculiar behavior of the relatively unsocial beings whose existence our experience seems to indicate to us in nature. Our relations with nature are thus such as involve a more or less social contrast between our life and the life of nature. And upon this principle every philosophy of nature must rest.

II

I have begun our research, as you see, by some decidedly general and positive assertions. I must next try to show you more precisely and more in detail what these assertions mean, and why I find myself obliged to hold them.

The theses of the present paper, set forth in particular, run as follows:

1 A man is conscious of himself, as this finite being, only in so far as he contrasts himself, in a more or less definitely social way, with what he takes to be the life, and, in fact, the conscious life, of some other finite being – unless, indeed, he modifies his natural self-consciousness by contrasting his own life with the conceived fullness of the life of God. But except by virtue of some such contrast one cannot become self-conscious, and the result is that, as a matter of simple and necessary meaning, if any metaphysical argument is to prove that I am I, viz., this finite being, then at the same time this argument will prove that there is other conscious life besides mine. For otherwise my own finite life as this Ego cannot be defined or conceived.

2 The other conscious life that I must contrast with mine, in order to become self-conscious, is primarily, in our human relations, the life of my fellow in the social order. The original, as Hume would say, of the conception of a non-Ego is given to me in my social experiences. The real other being that I, as this finite Ego, can know is, at first, the human being. A man who had no social relations could form no clear conception of the reality of any finite non-Ego, and so could get no clear notion of the reality of the non-Ego now called Nature. Our conception of physical reality as such is secondary to our conception of our social fellow-beings, and is actually derived therefrom.

3 In consequence, any metaphysical proof that what we human beings mean by physical nature exists at all, must also be a proof that behind the phenomena of nature, just in so far as nature has finite reality, there is other conscious life, finite like our own, but unlike human life in so far as it, the nature-life, does not enter into closer social relations with us human beings. Yet all that manifests to us the external existence of nature, does so by virtue of a more or less definite appeal to the categories of our social consciousness.

4 But, as a fact, a probable proof, not amounting to philosophical demonstration, but capable of an indefinite degree of extension and illustration, does exist for the existence of a real finite world called the Realm of Nature. Hence, this very proof indicates that there is behind the phenomena of nature a world of finite life in more or less remote, but socially disposed relations to us human beings.

5 This proof of the finite reality of a conscious life behind the phenomena of nature is furnished by the whole mass of facts that in modern times have come to be conceived together as the basis of the doctrine of Evolution. And the doctrine of Evolution must in the end be interpreted in terms of this notion. In other words, the doctrine of Evolution seems to me the beginning of what promises to become a sort of universal Sociology, tending towards a definition of the social relations of the finite beings that together must make up the whole natural world, both human and extra-human.

6 Yet, on the other hand, the view of nature thus indicated ought to be very sharply distinguished, both from most traditional forms of Animism and of Hylozoism, and from the modern doctrine of Mind-Stuff. The view that I have in mind is not Schopenhauer's doctrine of the Will in Nature, nor Schelling's *Naturphilosophie* nor von Hartmann's theory of the Unconscious as manifested in physical phenomena. From such theories mine is to be distinguished by its genesis. It tries to avoid all premature dogmatism as to the inner aspect of the life of nature. But it conceives the possibility of a gradual and, as one may hope, a very significant enlargement, through the slow growth of human experience, of our insight into the inner meaning of nature's life, and into the essentially social constitution of the finite world. Meanwhile this conception of the natural order as a vast social organism, of which human society is only a part, is founded upon no merely animistic analogies between the physical phenomena and the phenomena of our organisms, but upon a

decidedly deeper analysis of the very nature of our conception of other finite beings besides ourselves. And further, if my conception is true, it quite transforms certain important aspects of our whole notion of the meaning of Evolution. For the process of Evolution, as I now view it, becomes, not the history of the growth of life from the lifeless, but the history of the differentiation of one colony, as it were, of the universal society from the parent social order of the finite world in its wholeness.

Such, in some detail, are my theses. They need, of course, both analysis and defense. I will take them up in their order, dwelling perhaps too long upon the first thesis, upon which all the rest depends.

III

First, then, as to the thesis that one is conscious of one's Ego only by virtue of the contrast between this Ego and some consciousness which one regards as external to one's finite self.

Speaking in psychological terms, one can say that our finite self-consciousness is no primitive possession at all, but is the hard-earned outcome of the contact between the being capable of becoming rational and the rationally-disposed world in which he slowly learns to move. A child becomes self-conscious only by degrees. When, as infant, he cries for his food, or even, when more intelligent, shows lively disappointment if his expectations are not met, he is not yet self-conscious. When later, as older child, he struts about, playing soldier, or shyly hides from strangers, or asks endless questions merely to see what you will say, or quarrels with his fellows at play, or shrinks from reproof, or uses his little arts to win praise and caresses, he is self-conscious. These latter conditions are all of them such as involve a contrast between his own deeds and meanings and the deeds and meanings that he takes to be those of other conscious beings, whom, just *as* his conscious fellows, he loves or hates, fears or imitates, regards with social curiosity, or influences by devices adapted to what he thinks to be their states of mind. In brief, then, I should assert here, as a matter of psychology, what I have elsewhere worked out more at length, that a child is taught to be self-conscious just as he is taught everything else, by the social order that brings him up. Could he grow up alone with lifeless nature, there is nothing to indicate that he would become as self-conscious as is now a fairly educated cat.

But in the present paper I am dealing, not with psychology, but with certain aspects of the constitution of our knowledge. Let us consider briefly our self-consciousness, now that it has developed. It is a familiar paradox of idealistic analysis that we can have true knowledge of ideas or other objects of consciousness only in so far as they have first been presented to ourselves in our own inner life. Whatever I know must be really known to me, one says, only in so far as it is in me. I know, or can conceivably come to know, my own states, my own presentations, my own thoughts, my own experiences. Things external to me can be known only in so far as they first appear inside my conscious world. When I pretend to know something about a far-off star, that something which I know proves, upon analysis, to be my own state, my experience, or my thought – nothing else. I cannot transcend consciousness. And consciousness is for me *my* consciousness, or, at least, can always come to be regarded as mine. "Das 'Ich denke,'" says Kant, "muss alle meine Vorstellungen begleiten können."

Now all this is, in one sense, quite true. There is an aspect of knowledge which is always dependent upon my presentations, my direct acquaintance with mental contents. Without such direct acquaintance, I have no knowledge. But, on the other hand, if one asks a little more closely about the implications of our inner consciousness, one comes upon another, a strongly contrasted, and a highly momentous aspect of our human knowledge. And this aspect is indicated by the well-known fact that if I can only really know my own inner states in so far as they are inner, still, on the other hand, I can never really define to myself just how much is actually presented at any one moment to my inner life. One can know the far-off star only by virtue of ideas and experiences that get presented in the inner life; but, on the other hand, this presentation, merely as such, is not enough. For if anything present in the inner life were, as such, at once and altogether known to me, I should always be able to know just what it is, just how much it is, that now constitutes the whole filling and meaning of my inner life. But alas, I never can find out in all my life, precisely the whole of what it is that gets presented to me in any one moment. Are you now conscious of all that is in your field of vision, e.g., of the head of every person who sits in this audience within this instant's range of your vision? Obviously you are not, or at least are not equally conscious of all the possible objects of your momentary visual attention. You are now clearly aware only of what you are now attending to, and not of all the contents that are present but that you merely *might* attend to if you chose. But once more, what is precisely the whole of what you are now attending to – words, thoughts, sights, faces? It is impossible just now exhaustively to tell yourself, unless – unless you first attend to your own process of attention, capriciously fixate its normal fluctuating attitudes, and so give an artificially prepared account of a deliberately falsified situation. The inner life, as we get it, is conscious, but normally very unequally self-conscious – possesses contents, but cannot precisely define to itself what they are; seeks not to hold the present, but to fly to the next; scorns the immediate, the presented, and looks endlessly for the oncoming, the sought, the wished-for, the absent, so that the inner eye gazes on a flowing stream of events, but beholds rather what they hint at than what they present.

Now it is this other, this curiously contrasted aspect, of our finite knowledge, that constitutes one of the deepest problems of the life of human reason. I can know only what can get presented to me. But, on the other hand, most of what gets presented to me always escapes my knowledge. I know not the merely presented, as such, but only that which in the presented facts I can hold, apperceive, contrast with other contents, and define as to the real meaning of this object which I am to know. But alas, the moment flits. What I now know turns into what I just now knew, even while I reflect upon it. The direct gets lost in the indirect, the instant in the imperfectly known series of states; and my best approach to finite knowledge appears as only a sort of substituting of expectations and of memories for the desired presentations. If, then, on the one hand, I can know only my own ideas, states, thoughts, presentations, our present unhappy result seems to be that, as a fact, owing to the ceaseless flux of consciousness, I cannot fully know even these. For, once more, I can know only what I can examine with steadily fixated attention; but while I fixate my attention upon the inner object, it changes even while I observe it. *Only the presented can be known*: this idealistic proposition seems to be mockingly answered by the fairly tragic counter-assertion: *Not even the presented is, as such, known.*

In view of these paradoxes of our finitude, in view of the fact that only the presented can, as such, be known, while the presented never stays long enough in one moment of consciousness to allow us fully to know what it is, the actual situation of our human knowledge is simply this: What is always most clearly present to our consciously inquiring intelligence is the conceived relation between some content now immediately apprehended but very imperfectly comprehended, and that which, as we hope, believe, or expect, *will be* or *would be* apprehended, when we come more fully to know, or if we now more fully knew the meaning of this immediate datum. What I now experience leads me to expect another experience. My conscious knowledge is, then, mainly of this relation of transition from the immediate fact to the expected outcome. Or again, what I now experience leads me to believe that, were I otherwise situated, I should apprehend such and such other facts. My knowledge is here again consciously concerned with the relation between my actual and my conceived possible experience. Or, once more, I now have passing through my mind an assertion, a belief, an opinion. And I am thinking just what it is that I mean by this opinion. In this case, my meaning is partly presented to me, partly conceived as a more fully developed meaning, which I should get presented, or shall find presented, upon a further consideration of what I am aiming to do.

Thus, you see, the original paradox of our idealistic analysis gets corrected by this other paradox. To the unknowableness of whatever cannot get presented is now opposed the equal unknowableness of whatever merely gets immediately presented, without being held through a constant inner appeal from what *is* presented to what in future will be presented, or to what conceivably *would be* presented, were consciousness otherwise determined. I know only my own states and ideas; but those I know only by virtue of their conceived relation to states and ideas that will be, or that would be, under other conditions, or in other moments, the contents of my experience.

But, from this point of view, the nature of the world of our knowledge gets transformed. Our only approach to that ideal of knowledge which complete and fixated presentation would involve if we *had* it, is afforded us by the imperfectly presented relation between fleeting actual presentations and conceived possible presentations. And therefore you will observe at once that my notion of my own Ego and of its contents depends upon a certain contrast between these contents and a conceived world of actual or possible experience beyond this Ego. For what I come nearest to knowing at any moment is the relation between imperfectly grasped immediate contents and the conceived experience beyond the moment. It is indeed true, as idealism is accustomed to say, that of a *Ding-an-sich*, out of relation to possible knowledge, I have and can have no sort of knowledge or conception. For, as soon as I try to tell what such a *Ding-an-sich* is, I turn it into actual or conceived possible experience, and conceive it only as in such experience. But, on the other hand, my whole knowledge of my inner finite Self and of its meaning is dependent upon the contrast between the immediate experiences of this self and a world of abstractly possible or of genuine experiences not presented to any moment of my inner self as such. Thus, all my finite knowledge involves as much mediation as it contains immediacy – assures me of fact only by sending me elsewhere for truth; lets me know something, never the whole, of my actual experience, but through its contrast with possible experience; verifies merely by presupposing experiences now unverified; instructs me by suggesting further problems; tells me who I am by indicating whither I am to go to look for my true self; suggests fulfillment of insight, yet all the while sending me out to wander for more insight; arouses the question, What do I mean? at the very moment when I am attempting to answer the question, What is the experienced datum?

Now this realm of contrasts, of the light of present experience and of the shadow of possible or of distant other experience, of presentation and of thought; this dwelling in hope rather than in fulfillment, in search for a lost self rather than in enjoyment of a present self; this realm, I say, and this dwelling constitute the inner finite life of every one of us, in so far as he lives rationally at all. My actual inner life is, then, always contrasted with experience other than is now mine; and the problem of my intellectual life, whatever my worldly calling, is this: Where is the rest of my experience? or, What is the content of the other experience with which mine is even now contrasted?

But it is, of course, vain to regard my inner view of myself as constituted solely by the contrast between my individual presentation and a possible inner experience that I view as merely my own private, but still *individually* possible experience. My possible experience and the world of other experience than is now mine – these terms, in a wide but an essentially human sense, constantly include not merely the conceived experiences that I alone in my individual capacity am likely ever to have, or to find individually accessible, but also the whole world of experiences that other human

beings either have had, or will have, or may have. The upper Nile valley is, in the general and abstract sense, a possible experience of mine; but I individually shall doubtless never come to get that experience. Yet the upper Nile valley is, and has been, a system of actual and of accessibly possible experiences for very many of my fellow-men. When I conceive the upper Nile valley, there are presented to my inner life words, images, map-experiences, and the like; and these I know as meaning something to me, in so far as I contrast these relatively immediate data with the conceived contents of the experience of other men who more directly verify what I only conceive as to that region. And, in fact, the whole contents of my individual experience get regarded as one conscious system of remembered and expected contents, in so far as, in conception, I contrast my own private inner life with the experiences which I attribute to my actual or conceived fellows. I often say that my own inner life, as a whole, past and future, actual and accessibly possible, is better known to me, is more immediate, is more accessible to me, than is your inner life. But what do I mean by saying this? Surely both my past and my future are now as truly and literally unpresentable to me as are your inner states. I have now only my memories of my past, as I have only my beliefs as to your inner states. Directly I can now verify neither set of ideas. What I mean by the relative intimacy and accessibility of my own individual past is, then, only the fact that my notion of my past has a "warmth," a definiteness, a sort of inner assurance, which contrasts with the notion that I form of the past of any other man.

You see, whatever way I turn, I am definable to myself only in terms of a contrast with other experience which might, abstractly speaking, be conceived as mine, but which, as a fact, is viewed either as now inaccessible in comparison with my present experience, or else as the actual or possible experience of my fellow, and so as now more remote than even my own relatively warm and quasi-accessible, although actually unpresentable past experience appears to me to be. But to define any sphere whatever as the sphere of my own finite life, i.e., to define my life either as the sphere of my momentary finite life, or as the sphere of my whole human individuality, involves in each case a contrast between what is within my defined Ego, in the way of relatively realized, or warm, or accessible contents of experience, and what is beyond my defined Ego, as a sphere of experiences that, abstractly speaking, I regard as possibly mine, while, as a fact, I contrast them with mine, as being really somehow beyond me, and relatively inaccessible to me. These other experiences, which are not mine in precisely the degree in which what I call mine is viewed as belonging to me – these other experiences are, primarily, the actual experiences of other men. *My* opinion means, in general, my opinion as contrasted with opinions which I attribute to other men. *My* private experience means, primarily, whatever nobody else but myself has experienced, and is therefore defined by contrast with the conception of what everybody else has experienced. In brief, take away the concept of that world of abstractly possible other experience, which might be mine, or which would be mine, if I were you, or Cæsar, or any one else, or which would now be mine if I were once more my past self – take all this other experience out of my conception, and forthwith I lose all means of becoming conscious of my experience as mine, or of knowing what I mean either by my whole individuality, or by my present Ego.

IV

So far, then, for our first thesis. To myself, I am I, not merely in so far as my inner contents get presented to me, but in so far as I contrast my experience present, or the sum total of my conceived individual experience, with an experience which is, in some sense, not mine, but which is conceived as other than mine.

But now what warrant have I, philosophically speaking, for assuming that there is any other experience than mine at all – any experience past or future, remote or warm, like my present experience, or unlike it? Is this merely a practically warranted assertion of common-sense, or has it a deeper philosophical basis?

The general answer to this question is simply that I know the presented experience as such, and in so far as, in passing it is imperfectly grasped at all, *only* by virtue of its contrast to the conceived other experience. Without knowledge that the other experience is, there can be then no meaning in saying that the presented experience itself exists. That the present is, he alone can say who regards the past and future as real. That I as this individual am, I can say only if I contrast myself with some conceived other experience. The judgment: "There is experience," can have meaning only if one defines some experi-

ence that is to be thus real. But the only way to define any finite experience is by its contrast with other experience. The total object of true knowledge is therefore never the immediate experience of my own state as such and alone, although there never is any knowledge without some immediate experience as one of its elements. The judgment: "There is experience" means, then, for any finite being, "There is my finite experience, known as somehow contrasted with other experience than what is here presented as mine." Thus, then, the conviction that there is other experience than what is presented to me here, has not only a common-sense value but a philosophical warrant. But if one says: "No, but the contrast is itself something given, and so is not the contrast between my experience and any experience that is really known to be other than mine, but is only a contrast between my presented experience and one that is not presented as other than mine, but that is merely conceived as other than mine" – then to this objection, once more, the answer is, that the very conception of other experience than what is now presented as mine either actually relates to such other experience, or else is a meaningless conception. But if it is to be meaningless, even while it takes itself, as it does, to have a meaning, then this conception that always shadows my presentations, this conception of other experience than mine, is itself an experience that is in fact other than it takes itself to be. For it always takes itself to mean something; although, unless it actually does refer to other experience than mine, it is meaningless. But to say that a conception, or any other presented content of consciousness, is other than it seems, and is, for example, really meaningless when it seems to mean something, this is already to distinguish between my erroneous experience of its nature, and another, a fuller experience of its nature which, if I knew it better, I should have. But thus to distinguish between what my experience really is and what it seems to be, is simply to distinguish between a presented and a not presented aspect of the very experience in question. For what can one say of an experience which is not what it seems to be, and which is yet only a presentation after all – a mere matter of the instant in which it happens to live? If an experience, viz., here the conception of other experience than mine, presents itself as meaning something beyond the moment when it really means nothing beyond the moment, then this very experience itself is really other than the experience as it is presented, and once more one gets a real contrast between my experience as presented, and related experience which is not presented. The conception of other experience than mine must, therefore, in any case, have relation to a real experience which is other than my presentation.

Thus, then, that there is some experience not individually mine, is an assertion precisely as sure as the assertion that my own experience is. For neither assertion has meaning apart from the other. On the other hand, it is impossible to contrast my experience with any *Ding-an-sich*, existent apart from all experience, because the instant that I tell what I mean by a *Ding-an-sich*, I have converted it into an experience, actual or possible, and other than mine.

But finally, in this connection, one must still further insist that our now frequently illustrated contrast cannot ultimately be one between my presented experience and an experience other than mine which is *barely* a possible experience, and not an actual experience at all. A possible experience, not now mine, is a notion that has a very sound meaning in case it has some direct or indirect relation to a real experience not now mine. But bare possibilities, to which no actualities correspond, are indeed meaningless. Are there real facts or aspects of experience not now presented to me, then I can easily define these in terms of logical possibilities. But possibilities need realities to give them meaning. There must then be other experience than mine, not merely as possible experience, but as actual experience. Given such actual experience, there is not only convenience, but rational necessity in the attempt to define its nature in terms of all sorts of conceived possibilities; but unless you have some actual experience upon which to base your possibilities, then the possibilities themselves become mere contradictions. A barely possible experience is, as Mr. Bradley has well said, the same as an impossible experience.

V

There is, then, an universe of other actual experience than my own finite experience, presented or remembered. Were this central truth not known to me, I should have no means of being conscious of myself as this finite Ego. The general constitution of this world of other experience, in its wholeness, I must here leave to metaphysics. We are now concerned with the finite aspects of the complex of experiences with which, as human beings, we have to do.

Concretely, we get information about the contents of experience not our own, when we communicate socially with our fellows. And the essence of social communication is this: My fellow does something in a certain situation – deals with his environment so or so. He uses tools, utters words, makes gestures. If these deeds of his are new to me, they do not convey to me his inner experience. These deeds are so far, for me, phenomena in my own experience. I cannot directly view my fellow's experience at all. How, then, is a word, or gesture, or other deed, which as yet conveys no meaning to me, to acquire a meaning, or to become expressive to me of my fellow's inner life as such? The answer is, that, from infancy on, my fellow's expressive acts get a meaning to me as the suggestion of his concrete inner life, just in so far as I am able to imitate these deeds of his by bodily acts of my own, brought to pass under conditions like those in which he, my fellow, acts. For when I definitely repeat a bodily act that expresses any human meaning, the act, as I repeat it, under definite conditions, gets for me an inner meaning which I could never grasp so long as I merely observed such an act from without, as an event in my perceived phenomenal world. But this inner meaning which the act gets when I repeat it, becomes for me the objective meaning of the act as my fellow performs it; and thus the meaning of the imitated act, interpreted for me at the moment of my imitation, gets conceived as the real meaning, the inner experience of my fellow, at the moment when he performs the act which is my model. If you laugh, I know what you mean just in so far as, under similar conditions, I can join with you and laugh heartily also, and can thus, by fully imitating your deed, get a sense of your meaning. But if I see you laughing under circumstances that absolutely forbid me even to conceive myself as imitating your expression of mirth, then I have frankly to say that I do not in the least know what you mean by laughing at just this situation, and so cannot conceive in so far what your inner experience is. If I see you playing cards, or chess, I can only make out what your inner experience is in case I learn the cards, the pieces, the rules, or the moves of the game, and proceed to play it myself. If I want to know what the poets mean when they sing of love, I must myself become a lover. When I have imitated, in my measure, the lover's situation, and the lover's sincerely expressed devotion, then I know something of what love meant for the poet. In general, I believe in other human experience than mine in so far as I notice other people's expressive acts, and then gradually interpret them through social conformity. What I cannot interpret by imitation, I cannot definitely realize as another man's experience. Yet as my imitations always remain incomplete, and my interpretations correspondingly indefinite, I have constantly to contrast my fellow's experience, so far as I can realize it, with my fellow's experience so far as it attracts my efforts to interpret it, but also sets a limit to the success of these efforts. And thus I get a notion of a boundless world of human meanings which I can partially, but not wholly, grasp. In the effort, by social conformity, i.e., by imitation of expressive actions, to interpret such inadequately grasped human meanings, a great part of my social life consists. This effort is constantly supplemented by my efforts to convey my own meanings to others; and thus my self-consciousness and my social consciousness, each helped and each limited by the other, since each exists only in contrast with the other, get organized and developed in the endless giving and taking of social communications.

Thus far, then, we have been illustrating our first and second theses. Their application to our notion of Nature remains to be developed.

VI

So far, then, a reality, external to my finite Ego, means a world of other experience with which my experience is contrasted. This world is concretely defined, in the first place, as the world of other human experiences than my own. What these experiences actually are, I learn only by myself repeating the expressive deeds of my fellows, and by attributing to these deeds, when performed by my fellows, an inner meaning similar to the one which I more directly observe in the deeds when I myself repeat them under conditions similar to those in which my fellows have already performed them. Of course, no such interpretation of any human meaning is infallible; but I am verifiably right in saying that, at every step, this social process does really bring me into relation with experience which, until I performed the deeds of social imitativeness, *was not* mine. This concrete new experience, which was not mine until I imitated, was then before my imitation, at the very least, a possible experience other than mine. The whole social world is full of suggestions of such actually possible experiences. If every real possibility must,

logically speaking, have a basis in actuality, I am philosophically warranted in saying that all these suggestions of other human experience which social imitation interprets, and which common-sense trusts, do as a fact stand not only for a barely possible enlargement of my inner Ego, but for real experience which, however fallible my private interpretations of it may be, has an actuality contrasted with, and existent apart from, my finite individuality. The world of my fellows' experiences may not be real just as I, in my narrowness, interpret it. But this world is still, from the philosophical as from the common-sense point of view, a real world, a complex of experiences other than mine, and more or less imperfectly communicated to me. And thus it is that one in general defines the metaphysics of the social consciousness. You observe once more the essential relativity of the individual Ego and the social Alter. Neither conception has any clearness apart from the other.

But now, in our human world of experience, there are, yonder, the phenomena of physical nature. Our next question is, in what sense are we to attribute reality to them?

J. S. Mill's answer to this question is well known, and is, in one aspect, closely and instructively similar to Kant's answer, despite all the differences between the two philosophers as to other matters. The phenomena of nature, e.g., the upper Nile valley, the other side of yonder wall, or of the moon – these one conceives as systems of possible experiences, experiences which, in general, I now have not, but could have under definable conditions. Nature, as such, contains, apart from the bodies of my fellows and of the higher animals, no objects that I conceive as communicating to me any now intelligible inner intents, meanings, plans, or other socially interesting contents. Nature consists of masses of "possibilities of sensation." The problem is, in what sense have these possibilities of experience any inner or self existent sort of reality? Is nature a *Ding-an-sich*, whose reality is absolutely inscrutable, but self-possessed? The answer to this last and special question is that such a notion is simply meaningless. I can contrast my experience with other experience, and can regard myself as limited by facts of experience not now presented to me. And such a way of regarding myself is, as we have seen, absolutely essential to even my self-consciousness. But I cannot contrast experience with what is no experience at all. Even to say that there now exist certain possibilities of experience which I do not realize, is to raise the issue already several times touched upon in the foregoing. A bare possibility is a mere fiction. It cannot be real. To my true definition of a given experience as merely possible for me, there may correspond an experience which, as it is in itself, is very unlike my private definition of the real possibility. But if I am right in saying, "There is a possibility of experience not now mine," then to such a real possibility some sort of real experience, other than mine, must correspond. The question arises: Is there any such real experience behind those nature-facts which we conceive is our own possible experiences?

But there is another aspect of natural phenomena which perhaps brings us nearer to our goal. The reality of the facts of nature, when we actually confirm their presence, is always viewed as capable of being submitted to social tests. The real nature-phenomenon is not merely conceived as the object of my possible experience, but in general as the object of my fellows' actual or possible experience as well. If the star that I see is a real star, then you, if you are a normal observer, can see that star as well as I. This is the common-sense presupposition as to nature. Natural objects are viewed as phenomena that are, in some sense, public property, in so far as many different human observers could make them objects of possible inspection. The presupposition of common-sense is, that many observers could, on occasion, verify the *same* natural fact; so that the physical world will consist, for common-sense, not merely of possibilities of my individual experience, but of possibilities of common experience on the part of many observers.

Here surely is a well-known, but a paradoxical aspect of our nature-experience. I cannot observe your mind, but, as common-sense supposes, I can observe the same external natural fact that you observe. This presupposition is, in effect, a basis in terms of which we often define the facts of nature. What I alone experience, belongs to my inner life. What you can experience as well as I, is as such a physical fact, and, mind you, this means that, when we deal with nature-phenomena, common-sense supposes us, not merely to have similar inner states, but to refer to actually the *same* fact. If you as finite being count ten, and I as finite being count ten, we perform similar inner acts, but our objects are so far *not* the same; for the ten that you count is not the ten that I count. We can in this case be referring to the same truth only if there is, as a fact, some sort of extra-human reality possessed by the truths of arithmetic, and actually referred to by both of us. But just such

extra-human reality common-sense actually attributes to the facts of nature. If ten stones lie on the highway, and you and I count them, common-sense supposes that though your counting of ten is not my counting of ten, though your perception of the stones is not mine, though your inner life is in no fashion, here noteworthy, identical with mine, still the real stones that I count are identically the same as the real stones that you count. Now any natural fact, as common-sense conceives it, could, without losing its identity, be made the common object of as many observers as could come to get the right hints of its nature through their inner experience. All these possible observers, so common-sense holds, would really refer to the same natural fact.

The nature-things, then, are not merely possible experiences for me; they pretend to be possible objects of common experience for many observers.

Now when the nature-facts make such puzzling demands upon us as this, there are only two ways of viewing the situation thus created. One way is to say that in truth, all this common-sense notion of nature is illusory. As a fact, one might insist, it is impossible for two finite observers of nature to have the same external fact actually referred to by both of them at once. What one means is, that, as our social consciousness indicates, human beings have many similar experiences, and can socially convey to one another this similarity of their inner lives. When I rejoice, you may rejoice too; yet our rejoicings are not the same, but only similar. Just so, one might insist, when I point at my star, you may point at your star also. But what happens is that your experience then resembles mine; but has not the same outer object at all. Nature is the sum-total of those facts of our various experiences, concerning which our perceptual experience seems most easily to agree. But this agreement means merely a certain social communicable similarity of our experiences – not unity or sameness of natural object.

This, I say, is one possible hypothesis as to nature. But observe at once: There is *one* class of nature-objects in case of which just this negative and sceptical hypothesis simply cannot be carried out without destroying the very basis of our social consciousness itself. And this class of seeming outer objects is made up of the very bodies of our human fellows whom we observe, and with whom we socially communicate. The social consciousness, upon which, as we have seen, our very self-consciousness itself depends for its definition in finite terms, involves, as an integral part of its unity, the observation of certain natural phenomena definable as the expressive movements, the gestures, words, deeds, of our fellows. Now these phenomena are not merely to be viewed as reducible to the possible similar experiences of the various people who may observe their fellows from without. For these phenomena, on the contrary, have, whoever observes them, their identical and inner aspect; for they indicate the inner life of the social fellow-being who thus expresses himself. Many of you are now observing me. Are all of your various inner experiences of me now actually referring to the *same* fact, external to you but having for me its presented internal aspect, identically the same whoever it is that regards himself as observing my movements? The answer is here, at once: Yes. If I am I, and am communicating to you through deeds which are represented in you by systems of similar experiences, then, when you experience, in your inner lives, the observable phenomenal aspects of these my deeds, you are all at once meaning, referring to, listening to, the same genuinely real object.

Paradox though it be, the social consciousness insists that the same fellow-man can phenomenally manifest his presence to as many observers as can get some experience of his expressive deeds. All these observers can agree, with due care, as to their accounts of his deeds. These deeds, then, are so far nature-phenomena, like any others. My movements appear to any one of you in space, even as does this desk. So far, one could say, the fact is that the observers have experiences that are similar in one man's case to the experiences of his observing fellow. The observed deeds are merely such similar perceptions in the various observers. The various observers do not see the same real deeds; but they do possess similar perceptions, which they call perceptions of expressive deeds.

But no, this conclusion the social consciousness declines to accept. All your various but similar individual perceptions of my deeds really refer to the *same* genuine object, precisely in so far as I am I, and in so far as it is my inner experience that is manifested in these deeds. Thus, then, you could say that, if this desk were alone here, you could indeed so far talk sceptically of phenomenal experiences, in various observers, which only seemed to be experiences relating to the same object, but which as a fact do not demand the real sameness of their object. But it is no longer so if, in terms of the social consciousness, you consider not the desk, but me as your nature-object. For I am to you

not only nature-phenomenon, represented in you by comparable and merely similar perceptual experiences of your various private worlds; but I am, as communicating fellow-man, the same outer object for all of you.

Now a similar proposition holds true of any fellow-man. Any man you please has for you his phenomenal aspect. In this aspect he is viewed as object of possible experiences, and the real facts corresponding to this view are, so far, expressible by saying that all of his observant fellows have similar experiences whenever they come into certain definable groups of relations to their own inner worlds. But this man has another existence than the existence of certain images that his fellows form. All of these images refer to him, to the same man, to his manifested inner experience, and so to one reality. And this is what the social consciousness insists. Give up that insistence, in any general form, and you have no social consciousness, no fellow-men with similar experiences, no definable self-consciousness – yes, nothing but an inexpressible immediacy of inner presentations. But hold by that insistence, and what can you say? I answer: You can and must say that to one portion of phenomenal nature, viz., to the observed bodily movements of your fellows, there corresponds an inner life which is the same in essence, however many may be the phenomenal images that observers form of it when they refer to it as a reality.

The first view of nature, viz., that nature consists of a total of possible experiences, similar in various observers, thus fails as to all those nature-objects that present themselves as our expressively moving fellows. Our fellows are real beings, phenomenally observable from without by as many observers as you please, but self-existent as masses of inner experience, contrasted with one another, and with our own experiences.

But now how can you separate the phenomenal fellow, the originally real finite being, the original of your notion of your non-Ego, from the phenomenal nature of which he appears as a part, and with whose existence he appears to be, in all his life, absolutely continuous? For at this point there returns to help us our whole knowledge of human nature as such. A man's phenomenal expressive movements, objects of possible experience for all observers, stand for, and phenomenally accompany, his inner life. They then are real manifestations of a real interior finite life. But his movements cannot be thus regarded as real unless his limbs, his muscles, his nerves, his brain, his circulatory and nutritive processes, the food that he eats, the desk from which he speaks, the air that he breathes, the room where he speaks, the ancestors from whom he descended – yes, in the end, the whole phenomenal nature-order with which he is phenomenally continuous, unless all these things be also regarded as real in the same general sense, viz., as inner finite experience. In short, you cannot separate your phenomenal fellows from the order of phenomenal nature. The continuity between man and nature, known to us first as the absolute inseparability of the expressive movements of our fellows from the nature-processes in which these movements appear to be imbedded, and of which they are phenomenally a part, has now become, in the light of our whole experience of natural phenomena, an all-embracing continuity, extending to cerebral and to general physiological processes, and to the ancestry and evolution of the human race, so that the highest in expressive human nature is now phenomenally linked by the most intimate ties to the simplest of physical processes. If, then, one's fellow is real, the whole of the phenomenal nature from which his phenomenal presence is continuous must be real in the same general fashion.

But observe, *this* deduction of the reality of the natural objects implies something very significant as to what nature is. The only possible way to get at the existence of a finite non-Ego is through some form of the social consciousness. What a finite non-Ego is, your fellow teaches you when he communicates to you the fact that he has inner experience, and is the same object, however many observers view him. Now if his continuity with the phenomenal nature of whose processes his observed expressive movements are an inseparable and continuous part, impels you to say that if he is real his whole body, and so, in the end, the whole nature of which that body is an inseparable part and an evolutionary product, is also real, in an inner and finite sense, then the only possible way to interpret this relation is to say: "Nature, by itself, is a system of finite experience which, on occasion, and by means of perfectly continuous evolutionary processes, passes over into, or differentiates from its own organization, the communicative form of socially intelligible experience that you and I call human."

VII

The force of this proof is limited, of course, by the fact that it is precisely an argument from continuity. It is capable of endless development and illustration; and I take it to be the only possible proof that nature exists in any way beyond the actual range of our more or less similar human experiences of nature's observable facts. Yet no argument from any continuity of apparent processes has absolute force. It does not follow that every hypothetical conception which you and I now form of this or that natural process, e.g., of the atoms, or of gravitation, corresponds to any distinct form of the inner nature-experience. As a fact, I take it that our scientifically conceived laws of nature are largely phenomenal generalizations from very superficial aspects of the inner life of nature, and that very much indeed of what we now call nature has existence only for human perception and thought, as a matter of the similarities of the experiences of various human observers. But my point is here not a detailed theory, but a general conception of nature. And my general conception is this: There is a vast system of finite experience, real as our socially communicative fellows are real, and manifesting its existence to us just as they do, viz., through the phenomena which appear to our senses as material movements in space and time. What this inner experience is we know, in case of our human fellows, by social communication. What the rest of the nature-experience is, we can only make out very indirectly. But the continuity proves that the nature-experience passes over, on occasion, by unbroken although vastly complex processes, into the form of human experience. All the facts grouped together as the doctrine of Evolution, make this continuity seem the more elaborate, minute, and significant, the better we know it. In consequence we have no sort of right to speak in any way as if the inner experience behind any fact of nature were of a grade lower than ours, or less conscious, or less rational, or more atomic. Least of all have we a right, as the Mind Stuff theories do, to accept our hypothetical atoms as corresponding to real nature-entities, and then to say that inorganic nature consists of a mass of scattered sensations. Of the reality of organized experience we all know; but scattered sensory states are mere abstractions, just as the atoms of physics are. There is no evidence for the reality of nature-facts which is not defined for us by the very categories of the social consciousness. No evidence, then, can indicate nature's inner reality without also indicating that this reality is, like that of our own experience, conscious, organic, full of clear contrasts, rational, definite. We ought not to speak of dead nature. We have only a right to speak of uncommunicative nature. Natural objects, if they are real at all, are *prima facie* simply other finite beings, who are, so to speak, not in our own social set, and who communicate to us, not their minds, but their presence. For, I repeat, a real being can only mean to me other experience than mine; and other experience does not mean deadness, unconsciousness, disorganization, but presence, life, inner light.

But it is customary to say, by way of getting rid of any sort of animism, that we have no right to reason by mere analogy from our inner experience to anything resembling life in inorganic nature. To this I answer that, were the foregoing argument one from analogy, it would be open to the same objections as could be urged against any form of animism. But the whole point of the foregoing analysis has been that you do not first find nature as something real, and occult, and *then* proceed to argue from analogy that this occult reality is alive. On the contrary, I have first insisted that occult realities, things in themselves, in the abstract sense, are absurd; that the social consciousness gives us the only notion of finite reality that we can have; and that the social consciousness recognizes, as real, beings having conscious experience. After this point was reached, and only then, could we turn, in our argument, to the phenomena of nature to ask if they must be regarded as conforming to just such a concept of finite reality, since, as a fact, this is our only possible concept of what a real being is. Now a phenomenon of nature, on the face of it, is solely something suggested to us by the agreement between the series of experiences present in various men. And no purely physical experience can possibly prove that nature has other reality than this, viz., reality as a series of parallel trains of experience in various people. So far we had not to interpret nature, but only to wonder why nature gets taken to be real at all, apart from these parallel series of experiences. Then it was that there came to our aid the argument from continuity. Certain of the phenomena of nature

do stand for real inner experience, viz., the expressive movements of men. It is impossible to separate these latter phenomena, however, from the rest of the natural world, whose phenomenal unity the doctrine of Evolution is now daily making more manifest. Hence – so we reasoned – the rest of phenomenal nature must be regarded as standing for systems of finite experience, whose inner unity has to be defined in the way that human experience illustrates. And it is thus, not by analogy, but by the very process whereby nature comes to be defined as real at all, that natural facts get conceived as like other finite experience. Of the relation of this "other experience than ours" in the cosmos, to our human type of experience we can then at once say, that, in the process of evolution, our human experience has become differentiated, by long and continuous processes, from the whole, so that relatively continuous intermediate stages now probably link us to the rest of the cosmical inner life. Of "unconscious" experience in nature we have no right to speak, precisely because consciousness means the very form and fashion of the being of experience itself, as we know it. Of transformations of conscious experience, with a preservation of continuity through the whole process, our own inner life gives us numerous examples.

Meanwhile, let us lay aside, once for all, the petty human Philistinism that talks of the evolution of humanity out of so-called "dead nature," as if it were necessarily a vast progress from "lower" to "higher," or from the meaningless to the world full of meaning. What value human life may get we in a measure know. But we certainly do not know that the nature-experience whose inner sense is not now communicated to us is in the least lower or less full of meaning. Our human evolution is, as it were, simply the differentiation of one nature-dialect, whereby a group of finite beings now communicate together. We have no right to call the other tongues with which nature speaks, barbarous, because, in our evolutionary isolation from the rest of nature, we have forgotten what they mean.

Note

A paper read before the Philosophical Club of Brown University, May 23, 1895, and later considerably enlarged and supplemented.

11

Our Brains and What Ails Them

Charlotte Perkins Gilman

Introduction

Charlotte Perkins Gilman (1860–1935) was a well-known author, theorist, and feminist activist. She argued, in part, for the recognition of the embodied differences between men and women and the cultural constructed differences between feminine and masculine. Her article, "Our Brains and What Ails Them," was serialized in *The Forerunner*, a periodical that Gilman wrote, edited, and published for nearly eight years. Here she follows James in adopting a conception of human selves as embodied, culturally situated organisms who are constrained in part by the "natural" abilities of bodies and the constraints of culture. Liberation becomes a matter of transforming the culture to foster growth of the embodied self. Gilman's principal works include *Women and Economics* (1898), *The Man-made World* (1911), and a number of influential short stories, including "The Yellow Wallpaper" (1892).

> Love: To wish well to all the human race;
> To will toward happiness for every one.
> To feel, to guard, to give—
>   Love actual.
>
> Work: Not pay-earning, but the outflow wide
> Of one's best powers in special services,
> Those subtle services that build the world,
> Each for the others, organized and strong.
> This is the Human Law. So we should live,

Taken from *The Forerunner*, 3 (1912).

> Each honestly fulfilling one's own task,
> In love and courage; seeing in that work
> The smooth fulfilment of our nature's law,
>   Even though some may fail. . . .

What Education Does to Us

When cripples – unique and abhorrent cripples, were of market value, being used to solicit alms for their masters, or to amuse the idle hours of the great ones of the earth, cripples were manufactured for that market.

Ingenious means were devised to produce the desired eccentricities in physical development; just as we have devised ingenious means to produce dwarf trees and "pet animals" of unnatural appearance. We, who still do not hesitate to crop the ears of dogs, to dock the tails of horses, and to shamefully mutilate the cat we "love," in those still darker days performed similar outrages upon people, even upon children.

It seems now, to our present degree of enlightenment and cultivated human sympathy, as incredibly revolting that we should ever have had the callous cruelty to stunt and mutilate the defenseless body of a child. But we did; we, human beings, with brains, and in fact because we had brains – brains sufficiently developed to conceive of this means of making a profit, and insufficiently developed to see the horror and needlessness of such a process. Try to parallel it in the conduct of any other animal; and you get a powerful sidelight on the eccentricities of the human mind.

Suppose we choose our more immediate ancestors, apes; conceive of these creatures as having developed a system by which they could have more and better food, more safety and comfort, than ever before, by means of their combined activities; then conceive of them as making use of this improved condition to deprive the majority of their number of the advantage of these improvements, and this deprivation to be inflicted upon the very ones who performed the labor which created the advantages. Then conceive of the apes who retained the advantages as becoming sufficiently sensitive to object to the sight of the suffering of the deprived ones (though not sufficiently intelligent to see whose fault it was); and further, as developing a virtue – a specific virtue, in giving of their surplus to those who had none. Conceive then of the hungry ones also considering this to be a virtue; and consenting to spend their time in exhibiting their special limitations and begging for a livelihood. Then – being intelligent apes – conceive of them as perceiving that those who had the worst deformities and diseases obtained the most charity, and deliberately setting themselves to blind, to amputate, to stunt, cripple and deform, the little baby apes – that they might thus appeal more strongly to the sensibilities of the wealthy! This particular grade and quality of intelligence has never been attained by apes, however, and it is difficult to consider our own behavior as dispassionately as that of other creatures.

We may still obtain some perspective by looking at our conduct in other races and other ages; and therefore this instance of the artificial deforming of children's bodies is here put forward. A familiar and vivid illustration is in the years of helpless anguish and permanent crippling sustained by so many of the girl children of China. Yet the Chinese brain is a marvelous organ, clear and powerful, able to play a game as much more difficult than chess as chess is more difficult than jack-straws; and developed, through many long centuries, by an elaborate system of education.

Education is the base of all aristocracy and political advancement in China, and the main reason for its general status among nations. Their religion has for its major chord, father-worship. Ancestor-worship, so-called, is distinctly an androcentric religion, and going hand in hand with the degradation of women; in its essential nature it is the apotheosis of male pride in paternity.

Their economic condition, in which a competent human stock, occupying an originally fertile country, has been reduced to permanent poverty by overcrowding, is the result of the false ideas of this religion; and the permanence of such a condition, in defiance of economic law, of human comfort, of social progress, is due to the continual pressure upon the race mind, of an arbitrary system of education. The mind may be artificially altered as well as the body.

Of all the peculiar influences acting upon human life, accounting for the maze of paradoxes in human conduct, no single one is more powerful than the influence of education.

What is education?

I am not asking what the word means, and quoting Latin as if the ancient Romans were the final authority on pedagogy.

What is the process? What does it do to us?

Making our usual detour to get a back view, to see this phenomenon in its inception; we find education to originate as part of mother-service, and to consist, then, in fitting the young for life. To transmit to the younger the acquired knowledge and skill of the older – to show them how to live – that is the original process of education.

With animals, living in separate families, and having no functions but those of maintenance and reproduction, education was a simple process, competently fulfilled by the mother. Each mother-bear or fox or cat knew what was necessary for bears, foxes and cats to know, and taught the same to her young ones. If some individual mother was less successful herself and taught less successfully, she and her young were eliminated in favor of the better taught; so that the average kept well up to the level of necessity.

How has it been with us?

The moment we enter the field of human life we find the growing complications due to our group nature. The tendency to specialize in the social service, that organic differentiation which is the essential condition of humanity, begins at once, and is accompanied, of course, by individual inequalities. These inequalities, which would be fatal if the individual was self-supporting, are more than compensated for by the improved productivity which results from specialization – or would be if those results were normally distributed. But since our conscious apprehension of social processes has always lagged behind their real development, we observe humanity from the beginning failing to take advantage of its own new powers, and misusing them under the limitation of previous ideas – as a man might misuse a gun by handling it as a sword or spear.

As human activities developed human skill, and as that skill began to spread wide and specialize – one child inheriting more of this tendency, and another of that – education had to specialize also. The primitive mother could teach her children the common primitive tasks; but when tasks became complex she was no longer able to do so, and the child must learn his special "craft" of his father, or, later, of a skilled craftsman not his father.

Note here that with the beginning of this period the work of man and woman separates completely; he taking the whole range of the specialized industries which constitute social growth; and she being confined to those primitive industries which may be performed, up to a certain grade, by anybody. We have to consider later the effect of this division of labor upon the brain, through the mother, the original educator; but here we follow the development of education as a specialized human function, from that remote date until our own so well nigh exclusively monopolized by men.

That there are exceptions is frankly admitted. "It is hard to keep a good man down," or a good woman, and one of the keys to our social mysteries is the ceaseless pressure of man's efforts to suppress the normal development of woman. She is the natural educator, and, as a mother, must needs educate; also, whenever allowed, at whatever cost, we find our Aspasias and Hypatias, our Lady Abbesses, and fair Lady Doctors of Padua and Milan.

Nevertheless the vast bulk of education proper; i.e., specialized education, has been performed by men, not only in the act of teaching, but in *the things taught*. The women educators taught from men's books.

What things have been taught us? What ceaseless, long, uninterrupted procession of concepts, assertions, mental attitudes, proportion and relation of ideas, has been poured into the human mind since men began to do the educating?

Again we may mark a broad, general division. So far as teaching has followed the line of immediate utility, in all the trades and crafts and businesses that our lives depend on, the natural pre-social laws have had some chance to work. In carpentry or masonry, pottery or weaving, we may study the orderly results of our age-long progress. A craft is learned of people who know how, by people who have to do it – and do it. One does not learn to blow glass merely as something to

boast of; nor as something to teach over again to others; but as something to do – and then one does it.

The most marked evil in this department of education is in the comparative mental starvation of both teacher and learner; and in the injurious effects of other mental habits upon the race mind. If our teachers of trades were so educated as to know the whole history of their trades; if the master-plumber could discourse upon the sanitary system in Knossos, the Cloaca Maxima, the giant sewers of Paris; and if the young plumber, learning, learned the breadth of all modern sanitary knowledge, and gloried in his work as vitally essential to our social life; we should find an improvement not only in plumbing, but in plumbers. The man who keeps the city drains clean is precisely as valuable as the man who removes your most unclean appendix – but we are not educated to see this.

The great distinction between Education as such, and the mere learning how to keep the world going, came in large part, as Veblen has so convincingly shown, from the development of a Leisure Class; and also most directly from the development of specialized religion – with its priesthood. Mr. Veblen's book, "The Theory of the Leisure Class," a valuable, interesting, and occasionally delightful work; shows how, with the appearance of "Leisure" as an attribute of power and pride, and its accompanying contempt for all useful arts, together with the physical inability of the human mind to remain an absolute vacuum, there arose numbers of purely unnecessary and inutile forms of knowledge, the possession of which proved that the expert had had time to learn all that – and therefore stood clear of the faintest suspicion of ever having had to do anything useful. To all interested in following up this extremely valuable line of suggestion, Mr. Veblen's book will be a pleasure.

Here I will take up the second branch of this division, the establishment of a professional priesthood.

We come now to the idea of gradations in the value of knowledge; certain pieces of information, views of attitudes of mind, being essential; others vitally important; others elegant and ornamental – and all this with no relation whatever to the real necessities of life. "The necessities of life" has in fact become a vulgar phrase, applicable to pauper relief, and meaning the lowest grade of *animal* necessities, not those of human life at all.

Human life is identical with social life; human progress with social progress; one may enjoy all of what we call "the necessities of life" and yet not live at all – humanly speaking; as in the case of a warm, well-fed idiot. But education, when it cut loose from action; when it confined itself to knowing things and despised doing things; really cut itself off from Life.

The brain's ultimate use is that of a transmitter – a transmitter of power into action. Living consists of doing things; to know them is merely a preliminary. Where the brain is developed as a container, and not used as a transmitter, it becomes abnormal. In this abnormality it has developed one ultra-ridiculous perversion of function; a thing so incredibly absurd that it would be impossible to any creature but the human, with our enormous system of mutual support which allows for such a margin of usefulness – and mischief. The human brain, forcibly developed through so many ages as a container, has produced on the one hand a morbid passion for learning, in which the sufferer seeks continually to stuff himself with information and is never satisfied; and on the other, being pushed to it by its innate capacity for transmitting, develops a kind of vicious circle, or spiral, rather, in which good, useful, human brains spend their youth in acquiring a quantity of knowledge for the sole purpose of teaching it to others – that they may teach it to others – forever and ever, none of this knowledge ever touching the earth as it were. Such education never "comes out" at all; it merely flows on from mind to mind, like endless generations of unborn children.

These peculiar developments in education find their origin in the early priesthoods, based on the adventitious value attached to what they considered right belief, and on the very practical value of the knowledge of certain arts and mysteries which they for so long monopolized. This does not involve blame for any individuals or for any particular religion. Social functions have their laws of growth like any other life processes, and are as liable to eccentricity and disease. As in the physical organism health requires the normal use of every part, and neglect or misuse invites disease, exactly so in the organic life of society, unless a given social process is properly used it tends to become deformed and diseased.

Religion, for instance, is a distinctly social development, but for its normal use it must be felt and practiced by all; it cannot be followed as a profession, by a few, and its benefits extended to others, as in dentistry or architecture. Owing,

however, to the initial mistake of making religion a trade, a means of support, this universal psychic process became instead a limited economic process, with the necessary morbid results of such confusion of function. A slight study of religious history clearly shows the more conspicuous effects of this; the inevitable corruption of religion as it became economically prosperous and powerful, and the constant pushing forth of healthy sprouts of true religion, always in courageous poverty, always pressing out from the priestly cult to reach the whole people.

We are not here following these broad results, but wish merely to indicate how the professional priesthood seized upon the mental faculties as their stronghold, and strove to monopolize the brains of the world and the training of them.

If only the beginnings of mental culture, as developed by men fed on sacrifices and free to think, could have been put in circulation at once; made a social gain instead of a class gain; we should have had a very different history. But, following lines of class power and class aggrandizement, the priests and scholars remained one for many ages, and when the irresistible social demand tore education from the cloisters, it was so heavily clericalized that our few brief centuries of partial liberty have by no means freed us from its influence.

We are generally familiar with the main lines of modern growth in education – the steps toward knowledge applied in action of the manual training system; the development of powers of observation and reasoning by the laboratory system; and at last, a movement among that sub-clerical set of subjects, our teachers, for freedom and dignity in the performance of their office.

Education is perhaps the most valuable of social functions, if one can so differentiate in organic values; yet it is even among us in the United States today so heavily encumbered with vestigial rudiments, with ancient prejudices, with the slow, stiff, creaking disability of unused powers, that it leaves plenty of room for free discussion and suggestions of further improvement.

We have to consider, in a study of the results of education; first, the superficial effect of the information acquired; and second, the deep and lasting effects of the methods of acquirement upon the brain. Here we have a system of brain handling now practically universal among us – or at least we strive to make it so – in which every child is submitted to a certain process; as far as possible to the same process.

What, if we could see it, is the effect of this process on that childish brain?

There is some marked error in our process; some trouble of the gravest importance – this is widely felt; and education has almost as many healthy revolutionaries as religion.

As a perfectly natural social process this great function is accompanied by the normal organic stimulus of desire, and rewarded by the pleasure of fulfillment of function. Wherever we find it working normally we find both these phenomena: every healthy mind dearly loves both to teach and to learn. Since "teaching" and "learning" have become weighed down with many technical associations, I hasten to explain that "learning," as here used, means the receipt of new impressions, and "teaching," the transference of superior knowledge. A normal brain, from ravenous infancy to hale old age, eagerly enjoys new impressions, and as eagerly enjoys the sensation of knowing more than the other fellow and being able to "tell him how."

If education were normal we would find it a wide, free, subtly adjusted system of transference of knowledge wherein each and all could delightedly bring their minds to be fed, life-long; and wherein those most gifted as teachers: i.e., most enjoying the active side of that transference, could delightedly do the feeding.

In place of this we find a singularly complete perversion of function. Learning, that process of life-long joy, has become a prison sentence; rigid confinement of body; forcible feeding of brain; during the years which suffer most under such treatment – childhood. And teaching, noblest of human arts, exquisite pleasure of touching brain to brain and feeling the current of power pour through; pleasure as of a nursing mother; pleasure as of an artist and benefactor; personal delight in the process and glorious conviction of its immense social value – this we have made a nerve-exhausting treadmill, acting to most injure the best teachers and tending to maintain duller and less able minds in that office.

In the mechanical field of life we are continually making progress, developing newer, quicker, easier, cheaper, better ways of doing things. In religion, there has been ceaseless effort to maintain the oldest possible methods and beliefs; and in education, the after effects of religion are still painfully visible.

For instance, one of the very oldest religious concepts maintains that there is virtue in pain and difficulty. The underlying truth lies far, far back – the savage's hardening processes by which he schooled himself to bear hardship, effort and torture – the inert race mind retaining the associate sense of virtue in those processes long after they ceased to be useful. Running to unchecked excess in that fenceless field of mental activity detached from life, this became the doctrine of asceticism, an almost universal tenet of early religions. There is no extreme to which this morbid tendency has not cheerfully gone – death being nothing to it; celibacy a trifle; imprisonment for life welcome; and the bitterest tortures accepted triumphantly.

Nothing could better prove the dangerous nature of brain processes detached from their natural relation to life. This alone would have led to the prompt extinction of humanity, but for the overwhelming healthiness of the average mind, which would not accept it. But, with our social power of keeping alive the useless and injurious; and with the tremendous grip of that organized mentality which for so long found its only expression through the church, we have maintained throughout the ages a body of doctrines revered and accepted as doctrines even when mercifully withheld from expression; and of these none is more mischievous than this deep-seated racial error of the virtue of suffering.

Our present beliefs are not, for the most part, new inventions. If you look carefully at your beliefs you find them to rest on other beliefs, older, less defensible; and because the group of concepts covered by religion was not to be studied and thought about it has remained intact for a longer time than any other groups – unless it be those concerning sex.

Transmitted from the church to the school, this ancient error finds its continuing result in our common belief that it is good for the children to have a hard time there. Because some fifty thousand years ago the little savage, doomed to hunger and thirst, to cold and pain, was fitted for it by forced endurance of these evils, therefore – consider the stretch of that "therefore"! – our children must be made to undergo the "discipline" of the school that they may the better bear "the discipline of life." Now take that long-attenuated "therefore" which has stretched all down the ages without a leg to stand on and look at this end of it – for once.

Will anyone show how the arbitrary dreariness of our "system of education" fits for life – for Human Life, to-day?

Children in school must sit in fixed seats at regular distances in large groups for long hours. When, out of school, will they ever be required to do this? In church, you say. Exactly. That is where the idea came from. They must sit there in decorous silence and unnatural quiet because congregations must so sit, in order that they may be preached to. Now education is not preaching.

In school, children are required to continually use their minds in learning and remembering statements oral and written. When, out of school, is this required of people?

In school, children are continually required to regurgitate what they have learned, to "pass examinations" at stated intervals – to see if they know what they know. When, out of school, is this required of people?

"But," it will be earnestly advanced, "we have to take this period of their lives to fill their minds with knowledge they will need afterward and have not time to acquire."

Now will any man, in any business whatever, or any woman, in a business or out of it, stand up and explain how much of what they learned in school they ever use in life? Take any group of a hundred middle-aged people and put them through an examination as to what they learned when they were in school. Precious little could they recite to-day of what was so glib upon their tongues at ten or twelve. And of what they do remember, what is the use in life?

Our "therefore" does not fit.

The things we teach are selected according to standards centuries behind us and the methods we use are those of the black, forgotten past. Our study here is not so much to account for this, nor to suggest improvements, but to show its effect upon the brain.

As to matter: the child learns things necessary and unnecessary, without regard to real social values, and in so doing accustoms the mind to false perspective and relation. Still worse, he is thus arbitrarily accustomed to dissociate learning from doing, and shows the same silly pride in "knowing" this or that which distinguishes the "scholars" of the dark ages, or the suffering candidates for a mandarinship in the dynasty of Ming.

Some necessary, some valuable, some beautiful things he learns; but much that is none of these, and never to distinguish between them.

Far more important is the manner of his education. The most glaring first effect is that of forcible feeding. No words can exaggerate the outrage and injury which is thus perpetrated upon the brain as an organ. The appetite of the brain is as necessary to the healthful acquirement of knowledge as the appetite of the stomach to the healthful acquirement of food. If the brain is normal, not over-used and exhausted, it keeps that appetite for life.

Our education, seizing upon the child mind, forces it, under various penalties to "pay attention" and to receive, among its limp, reluctant cells, information for which it has no desire; in receiving which it takes no pleasure; the retention of which is as arbitrary an act as the holding of pebbles in the mouth. An enormous share of the dull indifference of the average mind to any knowledge, of its case-hardened callosity to efforts to impress it, is directly due to this abominable mishandling of the brain in childhood.

As if it were not enough to force into the mind what it does not want we then add that incredible use of the stomach pump – the examination. This is more foreign to any natural function of the brain than the similar act is to the stomach. The stomach, being poisoned or over-full, tends to relieve itself that way. The brain has no such muscles. Its only safety is in forgetting. Most mercifully we do forget most of our education, but education does all it can to prevent it. Over and over the child is required to forcibly bring out what we forcibly put in. The result on the brain as an organ is to make of it a worn and withered wallet, a mere bag, to be stuffed and turned inside out at pleasure. By so far as this process is effective do we lose our most precious mental capacities; that eager questing appetite for knowledge, that subtle and reliable arrangement and correlation of ideas, their easy retention and prompt reappearance when wanted, which distinguish the normal brain. It is common knowledge that our most useful minds are by no means identical with those best educated. Too much is lost in the process.

One other gross evil marks our educative process – the competitive system. Anything more foreign than this to real brain culture it would be hard to find. The competitive instinct is wholly androcentric, being in origin, a sex-characteristic of the male. Through his monopoly of all specialized professions he has inevitably infected them with this spirit.

As a masculine sex-instinct competition is healthy, right and proper. By means of it males compete for the favor of females, to the improvement of the species. As a social instinct it is wholly out of place, and therefore mischievous.

In economics it detracts from wealth rather than adds to it. In all trades and professions it degrades, and in the higher social functions, the arts, the sciences, in religion, in education, its evil results are most evident.

We use this sex-instinct as an incentive to spur the flagging energies of little children. We have, by making it an integral part of education, sought to develop it in girls as well as boys, though grossly foreign to their natures, and made it a common force in life. This is absolute social injury. As well might we set children to compete in eating as to compete in learning. Brains differ. *In their difference lies their social value.*

When we can muster strength enough to really let go of the worst and oldest mistakes of our ancestors, and let our brains grow; when we are strong-minded enough and clear-minded enough to see what education might be to us; then we shall enter a period of mental growth which it is good to contemplate.

Think of a magnificent body of specialists who loved teaching better than any work, and were free to teach. Think of the ceaseless effort from generation to generation, to so simplify, classify, and relate necessary knowledge as to make it absorbable with the least effort. Think of the delicate, varied arts with which such knowledge might be arranged, like a great tempting garden before the child mind. Think of the careful study to distinguish those priceless social benefits – the variations in brains; and to cultivate them. Think of every little young brain, fed and never forced, exercised and never tired, growing in freedom and eager joy, and each bringing to the problems of life its special complement of power and individual capacity.

In those days teachers will not be brow-beaten by cheapjack politicians; "feminization" will be no more dreaded than "masculinization"; and people will learn throughout life – and enjoy it.

The Effect of the Position of Woman on the Race Mind

Is the brain a secondary – or even a tertiary – sex-characteristic? Does it differ, physiologically, between men and women? Are the mental processes and capabilities of women different from those of men?

These questions are promptly answered in the affirmative by most people, even to-day; and in the past there would have been no dissenting voice. It has been universally believed that women's minds were not as men's minds; that they were, as Miss Tarbell has so emphatically phrased this general distinction – "subtly, wonderfully, bafflingly different." If this is true, it would go a long way to account for many of the paradoxes of human mentality.

That men and women differ as males and females is obvious; each sex transmitting its special capacities to its descendants without confusion. But in their lungs and livers, hearts and stomachs, there does not seem to be any law of associate sex-heredity to carry down an endless line of female lungs or male livers. These organs are not distinctive of sex, but common to the race; even, indeed, to other races; we have no race monopoly of breathing and digesting.

How about thinking? Is the brain, in its lower stages, as found in less intelligent animals, or in its higher stages, as a human distinction, modified by sex?

Let us first study it among lower types. From its inception, that growing ganglion may be traced up through the changing life forms, developing always in proportion to the widening activities of the race, until we find, in the higher animals, a considerable degree of brain power. Among those with which we are most familiar – those which we hunt, and the ones which we use or pet, there are conspicuous differences in mental capacity as between the different races. To use common instances, the fox is more intelligent than the hare; the dog than the horse; the cat than the guinea-pig. But as between dog-fox and vixen, mare and stallion, or any male and female of these common types, do we find the brain modified by sex – in favor of the male? Is there any case in nature below humanity in which the male of a given species is distinguished by a higher mentality than the female?

On the contrary, in following up the line of brain evolution, we find it, like any and all organs, developed by use, and most developed by most use. That race, sex, or individual, exercising the most varied activities, tends to develop the most brains; and as, in these lower races, the female has to perform all the activities of race and add to them the complex activities of motherhood, she tends to develop greater brain power. If, as with the guinea-pig, her maternal functions are crude and simple, being mainly physiological, she develops little brain power thereby; but if, as with the fox, maternal functions require a wide range of activity, the mother must needs put forth the required mentality – and does so. If, again, these activities are shared by both parents, the male also, through his fatherhood, develops brain power; as is seen in all those creatures where the need for the care of the two parents has led to monogamy and its ensuing mentality, much or little. If the parental functions, required of both sexes alike, are complex, so are the brain processes; but if we find monogamy with a low order of activity required, as with the ostrich, we find equality indeed, but low-grade brains.

Mental power, like all power, is acquired by use based on need; and, in the lower races, it bears no relation to sex, save that the female as a rule, has more need of it, makes more use of it, and therefore manifests more of it.

In entering the field of human inquiry, an entirely different condition appears. That degree of mental capacity which distinguishes the human race is absolutely conditioned upon social relation and the increasing complexity of social processes. What has been the position of women in regard to those processes?

We find the human animal in its pre-social state engaged in activities similar to those of other animals; the mother necessarily the more intelligent of the two sexes in that her activities were more complex. She had indeed, in her maternal relation, the base of all higher brain growth; the need and capacity to think for more than one. As mother, she must extend her consciousness to include her young; her action to minister to them as well as to herself; and, as the period of immaturity increased and thus action became continuous for many years, her mental capacity must needs increase.

So far as the father shared that continuous parental activity did his increase with hers. Under the stimulus of maternal necessity came the first stages of productive industry; the mother-brain, the mother-hand, being at the root of all the primitive arts. The constructive energy of motherhood was long the mainspring of human life.

Then came that farther process which is our major race distinction, that essentially human condition which is the base of all our higher life, and which, for the first time, opened a stage of life-processes in no way connected with either self-maintenance or with reproduction.

Life may be maintained by individuals through mere cell division for endless centuries, without sex distinction. Life may be reproduced, with sex distinction, for endless centuries without further progress. But life, for fulfillment of upward growth, evolves new processes. The entire range of human life, with its powers and joys, its hopes and dangers, lies beyond the initial processes of maintenance and reproduction.

When human life, growing naturally from its root in mother-love and mother-work, entered upon its endless field of upward expansion, it encountered its initial difficulties, inevitably, in the disabilities of its own organ – the brain. All human relation is psychic. It is possible only through brain capacities. In its development it must needs build the kind of brain it needs. But it had to begin with the kind of brain already there, and that was one wholly keyed to personal and parental uses. The pre-social brain was keen and strong as far as used; but its reactions were wholly personal and parental; the processes which had built it and were still exercising it were wholly personal and parental. The further problem of human progress was to accustom the brain to perform social processes that it might develop social faculties.

Before we look farther and are confronted with grief, shame and horror, let us clearly hold in mind the fact that social life is but of yesterday – that we are scarcely born yet, as human beings; that our first stages of blundering experiment were unavoidable, and are no more to be regretted than those million millions of Nature's trial sketches left behind in the chalk cliffs, or still patiently carrying on their cheerful but irrelevant attempts at life.

In the time before us, and coming very shortly, too, when we shall have visioned enough of our real power and happiness to appreciate the pleasure of being human, we shall be too much occupied with the unfolding centuries in our hands; with the kindling splendors of world-making, to waste any regrets or apologies on a few thousand years of bumps and bruises and dirty habits. Stirred by the glory of that resistless future, and as a wise step toward it, it is necessary now, however, that we should frankly recognize what unbelievable fools we have been.

In the very inception of our social life we left out the female of the species. Not intentionally, of course. Primitive man had no more idea of what he was doing than she had. The brains of both of them were filled with personal and parental consciousness, and to this day, most of our brains are still so dominated, to the grievous exclusion of the social consciousness.

But as a matter of historical fact, the social processes were monopolized by the male, and the female left to the personal and parental ones. To this day the primitive mind, which is still with us, maintains that this is her true position.

Consider in this light those oft-quoted illuminating sentences in which men of our own times have put themselves on record as to the place of women in the scheme of things: Grant Allen's statement that women are "not the human race, nor even half the human race, but a sub-species told off for purposes of reproduction merely"; Kipling's "for it has pleased the Lord to make her for one purpose only and him for several"; Marriot Watson's delicate reference to "those functions which alone excuse or explain her existence"; and the last apotheosis of ultra-masculine perversion, Sir Almroth Wright's statement that "the minds of women are never out of danger from the reverberations of their physiological emergencies."

When humanity began, women were engaged in sex-processes, major and minor, with their proto-social enlargement into productive industry of a maternal nature; industry in which various arts and crafts were practiced and a high degree of skill developed, but for family consumption only; and now, after all these years of social evolution, the majority of men – and women too – hold that these major and minor sex processes constitute her only duties.

To him all the mental and physical activities; personal, parental, and social. To her the personal and parental only.

How has this affected the brain, the "female mind," and the race mind? As the brain is developed only by use, this restriction has, of course, checked the development of the brain of women. As the brain is not, however, a sex-organ, but a common race-organ, it is transmitted indiscriminately by heredity. The daughter may inherit the brain of a line of scholars, as a Chinese woman may inherit the legs of a line of runners; but the "female leg" in China has been sadly modified *by its environment* – and so has "the female mind!"

Not by birth. Not as a sex-distinction. The legs of a mare are as good to run with as the legs of a horse; and so would be the legs of a girl as good as a boy's *if she used them!* The so-called "female mind," with its pathetic and ridiculous limitations, its lack of the later human faculty of reasoning, its persistent retention of the pre-social and even pre-human faculties of "instinct," "intuition" and the

like, is merely a painful and pitiful spectacle, like those withered extremities so laboriously produced by years of torture, and poetically described as "Golden Lilies." Those are not "female feet" – they are crippled feet.

By denying it social use, we have deliberately crippled, stunted, atrophied, "the female mind" – that is all! It is all there at birth; all there in the keen, eager, questioning child. But for all these ages behind us, up to our own late and partial change, it has been denied the exercise essential to human growth.

The results have been far-reaching. If the crippled women of China, besides repeating the infliction upon their daughters, had had a crippling influence upon the legs of their husbands and the legs of their sons – then indeed would the evil have been greater than it is. Stunted legs are not contagious. Stunted brains are.

The brain is the organ of humanity, the essential base of social life, the means and measure of its existence. Social life is as imperative in its instincts and appetites as any other form of life. The brain, its dominating organ, cries for use, for exercise, and suffers without it like a man in prison. If one wishes to gather a sense of pain to last throughout life, cast one shuddering look down the ages at the condition of women's brains. Each girl born with as much brain as her brother. Each woman, throughout her entire life, denied the use of it, suffering her life long the gnawing of an unappeasable appetite – a wholly natural and righteous appetite, the strongest appetite in human life – that of the soul, as we call it; the psychic demand for association, specialization and interchange.

None of these things for her. Personally she was kept alive and well or ill-treated as it happened; but kept alive at least long enough for reproduction, else the race perished. Maternally she was encouraged, yes forced, to full activity. But for the whole range of faculties and interests which distinguish the civilized man from the savage, none were for her save a few partial and perverse activities like those of what we designate with such exquisite absurdity – "Society."

As to the results of this deprivation, history is luminous and loud. The demand of a healthy brain for the information denied it we have called "feminine curiosity." The uneasiness of a brain so starved on the larger side, so over-developed on the lesser, we have called "feminine unrest." Whatever morbid results appeared from this wholly morbid condition we unhesitatingly set

down to the peculiarities of sex, and having produced a paradoxical, contradictory, sub-human,
extra-human creature, we regarded it with fond
pride and sagely remarked: "Woman is an enigma."
If we had done this to some outside creation,
producing our amusing monstrosity in tree or
flower, the results would have been less injurious.
The deadly work was done upon the human race –
and the most important half for its effect upon the
whole – the mother.

These were women. Men had to live with them
to some degree. Children were born of them; children were reared by them – the earliest years of
education were left to the uneducated. That transmission of thought and feeling from mind to mind
which is so essential to the human life was denied
to half of it.

To be human we must congregate – associate –
exchange. Women must not. They must remain in
the original pre-human relation, that of the family,
in its separate dwelling. How they have seeped and
leaked out of their isolation whenever possible.
How they have gathered together, irresistibly, at
the well, in the market place, in the ball-room, in
the church. Human beings *must* associate, must
exchange, must engage in collective activities. It
is the imperative governing condition of human
life. Women have done what they could at it –
under criticism.

And the men? Being human they had to combine. Being male they had to compete. History
becomes more luminous – and louder. Men had
to get together, specialize, produce and exchange,
and they have done so freely, splendidly; building
the world we have so long – shall we say enjoyed?

But they were males; preponderantly males; and
their maleness has been grievously in the way of
their humanness. Fight they must; the masculine
instinct to overcome and to destroy competitors;
and our smooth fruitful human progress has been
visibly jarred by this untoward complication. If the
women had been there, human too – but they were
not. The women were at home, being females.

So the human brain has grown, by normal use
and exercise, in the male; and been stunted, denied
normal use and exercise in the female; and the
more normal brain has been injured by the unavoidable contact with the less normal, and the
race-brain – the common inheritance of us all –
has been steadily robbed and weakened by the
injury to the mother-half.

This is the effect of the position of women on
the brain. Let us follow it more in detail; first

personally, upon the woman's mind; then reactively, upon the man's; and then, through inheritance, association, and direct education, upon the
child's.

The "feminine mind" to which we so feelingly
allude, in which we point out such deep-seated
ineradicable differences from the male mind, is
not a sex-mind, but a class-mind. Its mysterious
peculiarities are by no means due to the female sex,
but are due to the artificial environment with
which that sex has been surrounded. "Homekeep-
ing youths have ever homely wits." The one bald
fact that women have been kept shut up, confined
to the house, in varying degrees of imprisonment,
while men have been free to move, both locally and
abroad, is enough to explain most of that "subtle,
baffling, wonderful" difference.

If men had been arbitrarily divided into two
classes; if half of them had been given the range
of all the trades, crafts, arts and sciences, all education, all experience, and achievement, and the
other half shut up at home, never allowed out
alone, and taken under escort to only a small part
of life's attractions; confined exclusively to a few
primitive industries; denied education as well as
experience, we would find mysterious, subtle, baffling differences between the two classes.

Of later years, in some countries, education in
the technical sense has been gradually extended to
women; and they have shown a singularly human
capacity for absorbing it. Even in the ages behind
us, wherever women were given education, no
baffling difference in brains prevented their receiving it as readily as their brothers. When our
modern colleges refused admission to women, the
old objection was that their minds were incapable
of competing with those of the young men. Now
an objection to co-education is that it puts too
great a strain upon the young man to compete
with the woman.

Education, in so far as it consists in learning
from books and lectures, presents no difficulties
to the "feminine mind." The difference which
does present itself, in varying degree, and which
is now steadily diminishing, is in the *attitude
toward life*.

"The feminine mind," we say, is more submissive, less critical, less argumentative, less
experimental; it lacks initiative; and then we
proudly repeat that "no mind of the highest
order has appeared among women." A favorite
clincher, added to this, is that even in music,
where women have had every advantage

and encouragement, we have no leading feminine composer.

There is no question whatever as to the statements given, but questions many and searching as to the underlying facts, and especially as to definitions. Remember that the whole measure of merit and honor in the world is masculine; the standards are masculine; the judges are masculine; and that all our human achievements, so far, are heavily masculinized. We have made our disparaging distinctions as to "the female mind," but it has never occurred to us to consider "the male mind" and its limitations.

It is true that the brain is not a sex-distinction; either of man or woman; but it is also true that as an organ developed by use it is distinctly modified by the special activities of the user. If the lifelong activities of the individual are sharply differentiated along sex lines, then the brain is reactively affected. Men have the advantage of the whole range of human experience to develop the human brain; but they have the disadvantage of being more heavily modified to sex, by nature, than the woman.

The female of the species is more nearly the race-type; the male is more especially the sex-type. This we have never seen because of the universal assumption that the dominant masculine tastes, abilities and instincts were human. They are not in the least human; they are merely masculine, distinguishing all male creatures, human or not. The dominant masculine characteristics are Desire, Combat, and Self-Expression. These have heavily colored all human life, in every department; and in their associative reaction have modified the race-mind male-wards. This over-developed "male mind" naturally considers any divergent action shown by the other sex as "female"; whereas it may not be female at all, but merely human.

When all the honors of the world were given to Military Conquerors and the adored Climax of such Superiority was found in that megalomaniac destroyer, Napoleon – of course no female name could be rated so high. When we honor constructive industry as much as warfare we shall have more female heroes. When we honor illimitable endurance as much as combativeness; when we recognize the anti-social quality of the ultra-male belligerence, and the social value of the adaptable, persistent serviceableness we have hitherto considered "female," we shall put up other monuments than those to soldiers. After a few centuries of full human usefulness on the part of the women, we

shall have not only new achievements to measure, but new standards of measurement.

This will give a new view of "the feminine mind." It will be seen that those qualities in which it differs from "the male mind" are not necessarily female ones; that she is nearer the norm than he; that he often does the differing, branching off widely from essential human qualities in the direction of mere masculinity.

When all this is said, and appreciated, it remains true that the majority of women to date, have not succeeded in developing a degree of brain power other than that produced by their conditions; and have not succeeded in wringing from a male world any recognition or admiration for anything in particular except their feminine qualities – which were all that the male world wanted of them. It is not feminine qualities which distinguish the minds of women so sharply; it is the quality of domestic labor; they are heavily modified by kitchen service, by parlor imprisonment. The major lack in the minds of women is in experience. Beginning with childhood, when the boy is allowed to be out on the platform asking questions, and the girl is compelled to sit still, pulling her offensively short skirts over her inoffensively long legs, the boy knows more about things than the girl possibly can. He knows more streets, more places, more people, more processes, more "life." This difference increases with their growth. It is quite true, blessedly true, that this is all changing today; that our girls are rapidly losing that fine know-nothing "bloom," which gave such disproportionate and gratifying superiority to any "male mind"; that "bloom" which is brushed off so soon by exercise, which disappears so quickly in the light of knowledge. This makes us wonder if, after all, it was bloom – or perhaps mould.

But heretofore, and still to a great extent, this is the major disability of the "feminine mind" – mere lack of information and experience. It remains a heavy handicap even now. The judgement of women is narrowed because they do not know the premises. Our tardy allowance of school and college education does not give knowledge of life.

The next great lack is in responsibility. Suppose that life required an assured skill in the art of sailing. Suppose that in the first instance girls were never allowed in boats, nor taught anything about them. Suppose, secondly, they were occasionally "taken sailing," but never allowed to touch rope or tiller. Suppose, thirdly, they were really taught sailing – by the use of models, but though they could pass oral examinations, they were never allowed to sail a boat. To be human today, in a civilized country, requires the trained intelligence of big business men (not the malefactors, but the real workers) and that intelligence is not developed except by doing big business.

If Andrew Carnegie had passed his life between kitchen, bedroom, and parlor, he might have been esteemed and beloved by those who profited by his services, but would not be a planter of libraries and a promoter of world peace.

A girl may lead her brother in school and college, and then continue to amass "culture" for the rest of her life, but that does not develop the human faculties of the brain. Our humanity requires those basic conditions, Association, Specialization, Interchange. The acquisition of knowledge for private consumption is not a social function. Suppose her brother, after his valedictory address, spent the rest of his life as a private housekeeper; would his "education" suffice to occupy and exercise his mind?

We quote in blissful acquiescence Tennyson's dictum: "For woman is not undeveloped man, but diverse." If he had said "female is not undeveloped male, but diverse," which is what he meant, and what we all mean, he would have been quite correct. But if by man he meant "human," he is exactly wrong. Women are undeveloped human beings, that is what ails them; and their brains, are more severely affected than their bodies.

It is bad enough to see the bodies of women so excessively modified to sex that they almost lose the power of locomotion, but it is worse to see their minds so excessively modified by the narrow range of exercise allowed them that they live in a sort of prehistoric state of sub-social domesticity. If we could see it, if it could be expressed to us pictorially, it would be as if Mr. Horse was mated to Mrs. Eohippus – the same species, but a trifle behind the times. If we did mate our horses thus, it would have a curious effect on the strain of trotters.

It has a curious effect on humanity. Men are always being bewildered, puzzled, enraged, by the unaccountable discrepancies they discover between their minds and women's. They have explained it all by simple sweeping attribute of sex – women were that way – because they were peculiar. Why the female of genus homo should be so mysterious while the female of other species was so easily comprehensible they did not ask. And they did not concern themselves much about this abysmal difference between their minds, because it was not their minds that they married. So long as white men cheerfully, though temporarily, mate with African and Indian, Hawaiian and Filipino, we cannot expect them to be very critical about their wives' brains. The brains of women are less developed humanly, but their taste in selection is certainly higher than man's.

The brain difference remains a serious race disadvantage, however, whether men object to it or not.

If white men continually married their Semgambian transients, and reared families by them, the race-mind would be markedly affected. Even the scant association of home life, from which most men escape as far as possible, has its benumbing and belittling effect on the minds of men. "Women talk about such little things!" said one disgusted man. He thought it was because they were women. What does he talk about? He "talks shop" – his business, whatever it is; and he "talks politics" – the world business, as far as he touches it. He talks of his experience and his responsibilities. So does she. But her experience is identical with that of her million sisters for all the years, sex experience and household experience. The mental effects of the first she cannot share with him; the mental effects of the second he flees from.

The wider-experienced, more-socially developed man seeks woman as a female – and avoids her as a friend and companion.

12

Race

W. E. B. Du Bois

Introduction

W. E. B. Du Bois (1863–1963) was born in Great Barrington, Massachusetts. He attended Fisk University (1885–8) and was awarded a PhD from Harvard in 1895. His doctoral dissertation later became the noted book, *The Suppression of the African Slave Trade, 1638–1870*. From 1892 to 1894 he studied at the University of Berlin. In 1899 he wrote *The Philadelphia Negro*, a study of black life in the ghetto. He served as Professor of Sociology, History, and Economics at Atlanta University (1898–1910) and went on to put together a collection of essays on the study of the Negro problem in *The Souls of Black Folk* in 1903. In 1905 he participated in the Niagara Movement, which eventually became the National Association for the Advancement of Colored People (NAACP). Serving as the director of publications and research for the NAACP in 1910, he edited *Crisis: A Record of the Darker Races* from 1910 to 1934. He later founded *Phylon: A Review of Race and Culture* (1940–4) and completed his autobiography, *Dusk of Dawn*, in 1940. Du Bois was also a noted novelist, publishing such works as *The Quest of the Silver Fleece* (1911) and *Dark Princess* (1928). His novels normally featured dark-skinned black women as heroines, an extreme rarity for his time. He was indicted as a foreign agent in 1951 and his passport was revoked. In 1959 he

"Does Race Antipathy Serve Any Good Purpose" is taken from the *Boston Globe*, July 19, 1914; "The Concept of Race" is taken from *Dusk of Dawn* (New York: Harcourt, Brace and Co., 1975[1940]). Reprinted with permission from The Permissions Company.

received the Lenin Prize and in 1961 he joined the Communist Party. He died in 1963 in Accra, Ghana, just after becoming a naturalized Ghanaian citizen.

Does Race Antipathy Serve Any Good Purpose?

There are four classes of reasons usually given in defense of race antagonism.

1 It is an instinctive repulsion from something harmful and is, therefore, a subtle condition of ultimate survival.

The difficulty with this theory is that it does not square with the facts: race antipathy is not instinctive but a matter of careful education. Black and white children play together gladly and know no prejudice until it is implanted precept upon precept and by strong social pressure; and when it is so implanted it is just as strong in cases where there is no physical difference as it is where physical differences are striking. The racial repulsion in the Balkans among peoples of practically the same blood is today greater than it was between whites and blacks on the Virginia plantations.

2 Racial antagonism, whether instinctive or not, is a reasonable measure of self-defense against undesirable racial traits.

This second proposition is the one which usually follows careful examination of the first. After all, it is admitted "instinct" is an unimportant fact. Instincts are simply accumulated reasons in the individual or in the race. The reasons for antagonizing inferior races are clear and may be summed up as follows:

- poor health and stamina;
- low ability;
- harmful ideals of life.

We are now on surer ground because we can now appeal to facts. But no sooner do we make this appeal than we are astonished to find that there are surprising little data. Is it true that the Negro as a physical animal is inferior to the white man or is he superior? Is the high death rate of the Indian a proof of his poor physique or is it proof of wretched conditions of life which would long ago have killed off a weaker people? And, again, is spiritual superiority always in direct proportion to physical strength in races any more than in individuals? Connected with this matter of health comes the question of physical beauty, but surely, if beauty were to become a standard of survival how small our world population would be!

It is argued, however, that it may be granted that the physical stamina of all races is probably approximately the same and that physical comeliness is rather a matter of taste and selection than of absolute racial difference. However, when it comes to intellectual ability the races differ so enormously that superior races must in self-defense repel the inferior sternly, even brutally. Two things, however, must be said in answer to this: first, the prejudice against the Jews, age-long and worldwide, is surely not based on inferior ability. We have only to name Jeremiah, D'Israeli, and Jesus Christ to set our minds at rest on that point. Moreover, if we compare the intellectual ability of Teuton and Chinese, which is inferior? Or, if we take Englishman and Bantu, is the difference a difference of native ability or of training and environment? The answer to this is simple: we do not know. But arguing from all known facts and analogies we must certainly admit, in the words of the secretary of the First International Races Congress, that "an impartial investigator would be inclined to look upon the various important peoples of the world as, to all intents and purposes, essentially equals in intellect, enterprise, morality and physique."[1]

3 Racial antipathy is a method of race development.

We may admit so far as physique and native ability go that, as Ratzel says, "There is only one species of man; the variations are numerous, but do not go deep."[2] At the same time it is plain that Europe has outstripped China in civilization, and China has outstripped Africa. Here at least are plain facts. Is not racial antipathy a method of maintaining the European level of culture? But is it necessary for the runner to hate and despise the man he is outdistancing? Can we only maintain culture in one race by increasing barbarism in others? Does it enhance the "superiority" of white men to allow them to steal from yellow men and enslave black men and reduce colored women to concubinage and prostitution? Surely not. Admitting that in the world's history again and again this or that race has outstripped another in culture, it is impossible to prove that inherent racial superiority was the cause or that the level of culture has been permanently raised in one race by keeping other races down.

4 Race antipathy is a method of group specialization.

This argument admits the essential equality of races but insists on the difference in gifts and argues that antipathy between races allows each to develop its own peculiar gifts and aptitudes. Does it? That depends on the antipathy. If antipathy means the enslaving of the African, the exploitation of the Chinese, the peonage of Mexicans, and the denial of schools to American Negroes, then it is hard to see where the encouragement comes in. If it means the generous encouragement of all men according to their gifts and ability then why speak of race antipathy or encourage it? Let us call it human uplift and universal brotherhood and be done with it.

Such are the arguments. Most persons use all four at once and skillfully skip from one to the other. Each argument has in other days been applied to individuals and social classes, but we have outgrown that. We apply it today to races because race is a vague, unknown term which may be made to cover a multitude of sins. After all, what is a Race? and how many races are there? Von Luschan, one of the greatest of modern anthropologists, says, "The question of the number of human races has quite lost its raison d'etre, and has become a subject rather of philosophic speculation than of scientific research."[3] What we have on earth is men. Shall we help them or hinder them? Shall we hate and kill them or love and preserve and uplift them? Which method will do us most good? This is the real question of race antipathy.

The Concept of Race

I want now to turn aside from the personal annals of this biography to consider the conception which is after all my main subject. The concept of race lacks something in personal interest, but personal interest in my case has always depended primarily upon this race concept and I wish to examine this now. The history of the development of the race concept in the world and particularly in America, was naturally reflected in the education offered me. In the elementary school it came only in the matter of geography when the races of the world were pictured: Indians, Negroes and Chinese, by their most uncivilized and bizarre representatives; the whites by some kindly and distinguished-looking philanthropist. In the elementary and high school, the matter was touched only incidentally, due I doubt not to the thoughtfulness of the teachers; and again my racial inferiority could not be dwelt upon because the single representative of the Negro race in the school did not happen to be in any way inferior to his fellows. In fact it was not difficult for me to excel them in many ways and to regard this as quite natural.

At Fisk, the problem of race was faced openly and essential racial equality asserted and natural inferiority strenuously denied. In some cases the teachers expressed this theory; in most cases the student opinion naturally forced it. At Harvard, on the other hand, I began to face scientific race dogma: first of all, evolution and the "Survival of the Fittest." It was continually stressed in the community and in classes that there was a vast difference in the development of the whites and the "lower" races; that this could be seen in the physical development of the Negro. I remember once in a museum, coming face to face with a demonstration: a series of skeletons arranged from a little monkey to a tall well-developed white man, with a Negro barely outranking a chimpanzee. Eventually in my classes stress was quietly transferred to brain weight and brain capacity, and at last to the "cephalic index."

In the graduate school at Harvard and again in Germany, the emphasis again was altered, and race became a matter of culture and cultural history. The history of the world was paraded before the observation of students. Which was the superior race? Manifestly that which had a history, the white race; there was some mention of Asiatic culture, but no course in Chinese or Indian history or culture was offered at Harvard, and quite unanimously in America and Germany, Africa was left without culture and without history. Even when the matter of mixed races was touched upon their evident and conscious inferiority was mentioned. I can never forget that morning in the class of the great Heinrich von Treitschke in Berlin. He was a big aggressive man, with an impediment in his speech which forced him to talk rapidly lest he stutter. His classes were the only ones always on time, and an angry scraping of feet greeted a late comer. Clothed in black, big, bushy-haired, peering sharply at the class, his words rushed out in a flood: "Mulattoes," he thundered, "are inferior." I almost felt his eyes boring into me, although probably he had not noticed me. "Sie fühlen sich niedriger!" "Their actions show it," he asserted. What contradiction could there be to that authoritative dictum?

The first thing which brought me to my senses in all this racial discussion was the continuous change in the proofs and arguments advanced. I could accept evolution and the survival of the fittest, provided the interval between advanced and backward races was not made too impossible. I balked at the usual "thousand years." But no sooner had I settled into scientific security here, than the basis of race distinction was changed without explanation, without apology. I was skeptical about brain weight; surely much depended upon what brains were weighed. I was not sure about physical measurements and social inquiries. For instance, an insurance actuary published in 1890 incontrovertible statistics showing how quickly and certainly the Negro race was dying out in the United States through sheer physical inferiority. I lived to see every assumption of Hoffman's "Race Traits and Tendencies" contradicted; but even before that, I doubted the statistical method which he had used. When the matter of race became a question of comparative culture, I was in revolt. I began to see that the cultural equipment attributed to any people depended largely on who estimated it; and conviction came later in a rush as I realized what in my education had been suppressed concerning Asiatic and African culture.

It was not until I was long out of school and indeed after the World War that there came the hurried use of the new technique of psychological tests, which were quickly adjusted so as to put black folk absolutely beyond the possibility of civilization. By this time I was unimpressed. I had too often seen science made the slave of caste and race hate. And it was interesting to see Odum, McDougall and Brigham eventually turn somersaults from absolute scientific proof of Negro inferiority to repudiation of the limited and questionable application of any test which pretended to measure innate human intelligence.

So far I have spoken of "race" and race problems quite as a matter of course without explanation or definition. That was our method in the nineteenth century. Just as I was born a member of a colored family, so too I was born a member of the colored race. That was obvious and no definition was needed. Later I adopted the designation "Negro" for the race to which I belong. It seemed more definite and logical. At the same time I was of course aware that all members of the Negro race were not black and that the pictures of my race which were current were not authentic nor fair portraits. But all that was incidental. The world was divided into great primary groups of folk who belonged naturally together through heredity of physical traits and cultural affinity.

I do not know how I came first to form my theories of race. The process was probably largely unconscious. The differences of personal appearance between me and my fellows, I must have been conscious of when quite young. Whatever distinctions came because of that did not irritate me; they rather exalted me because, on the whole, while I was still a youth, they gave me exceptional position and a chance to excel rather than handicapping me.

Then of course, when I went South to Fisk, I became a member of a closed racial group with rites and loyalties, with a history and a corporate future, with an art and philosophy. I received these eagerly and expanded them so that when I came to Harvard the theory of race separation was quite in my blood. I did not seek contact with my white fellow students. On the whole I rather avoided them. I took it for granted that we were training ourselves for different careers in worlds largely different. There was not the slightest idea of the permanent subordination and inequality of my world. Nor again was there any idea of racial amalgamation. I resented the assumption that we desired it. I frankly refused the possibility while in Germany and even in America gave up courtship with one "colored" girl because she looked quite white, and I should resent the inference on the street that I had married outside my race.

All this theory, however, was disturbed by certain facts in America, and by my European experience. Despite everything, race lines were not fixed and fast. Within the Negro group especially there were people of all colors. Then too, there were plenty of my colored friends who resented my ultra "race" loyalty and ridiculed it. They pointed out that I was not a "Negro," but a mulatto; that I was not a Southerner but a Northerner, and my object was to be an American and not a Negro; that race distinctions must go. I agreed with this in part and as an ideal, but I saw it leading to inner racial distinction in the colored group. I resented the defensive mechanism of avoiding too dark companions in order to escape notice and discrimination in public. As a sheer matter of taste I wanted the color of my group to be visible. I hotly championed the inclusion of two black school mates whose names were not usually on the invitation list to our social affairs. In Europe my friendships and close contact with white folk made my own ideas waver. The eternal walls between races did not seem so stern and exclusive. I began to emphasize the cultural aspects of race.

It is probably quite natural for persons of low degree, who have reached any status, to search feverishly for distinguished ancestry, as a sort of proof of their inherent desert. This is particularly true in America and has given rise to a number of organizations whose membership depends upon ancestors who have made their mark in the world. Of course, it is clear that there must be here much fable, invention and wishful thinking, facilitated by poor vital statistics and absence of written records. For the mass of Americans, and many Americans who have had the most distinguished careers, have been descended from people who were quite ordinary and even less; America indeed has meant the breaking down of class bars which imprisoned personalities and capabilities and allowing new men and new families to emerge. This is not, as some people assume, a denial of the importance of heredity and family. It is rather its confirmation. It shows us that the few in the past who have emerged are not necessarily the best; and quite certainly are not the only ones worthy of development and distinction; that, on the contrary, only a comparatively few have, under our present economic and social organization, had a chance to show their capabilities.

I early began to take a direct interest in my own family as a group and became curious as to that physical descent which so long I had taken for granted quite unquestioningly. But I did not at first think of any but my Negro ancestors. I knew little and cared less of the white forebears of my father. But this chauvinism gradually changed. There is, of course, nothing more fascinating than the question of the various types of mankind and their intermixture. The whole question of heredity and human gift depends upon such knowledge; but ever since the African slave trade and before the rise of modern biology and sociology, we have been afraid in America that scientific study in this direction might lead to conclusions with which we were loath to agree; and this fear was in reality because the economic foundation of the modern world was based on the recognition and preservation of so-called racial distinctions. In accordance with this, not only Negro slavery could be justified, but the Asiatic coolie profitably used and the labor classes in white countries kept in their places by low wage.

It is not singular then that here in America and in the West Indies, where we have had the most astonishing modern mixture of human types, scientific study of the results and circumstances of this mixture has not only lagged but been almost non-existent. We have not only not studied race and race mixture in America, but we have tried almost by legal process to stop such study. It is for this reason that it has occurred to me just here to illustrate the way in which Africa and Europe have been united in my family. There is nothing unusual about this interracial history. It has been duplicated thousands of times; but on the one hand, the white folk have bitterly resented even a hint of the facts of this intermingling; while black folk have recoiled in natural hesitation and affected disdain in admitting what they know.

I am, therefore, relating the history of my family and centering it around my maternal great-great-grandfather, Tom Burghardt, and my paternal grandfather, Alexander Du Bois.

Absolute legal proof of facts like those here set down is naturally unobtainable. Records of birth are often non-existent, proof of paternity is exceedingly difficult and actual written record rare. In the case of my family I have relied on oral tradition in my mother's family and direct word and written statement from my paternal grandfather; and upon certain general records which I have been able to obtain. I have no doubt of the substantial accuracy of the story that I am to tell.

Of my own immediate ancestors I knew personally only four: my mother and her parents and my paternal grandfather. One other I knew at second hand – my father. I had his picture. I knew what my mother told me about him and what others who had known him, said. So that in all, five of my immediate forebears were known to me. Three others, my paternal great-grandfather and my maternal great-grandfather and great-great-grandfather, I knew about through persons who knew them and through records; and also I knew many of my collateral relatives and numbers of their descendants. My known ancestral family, therefore, consisted of eight or more persons. None of these had reached any particular distinction or were known very far beyond their own families and localities. They were divided into whites, blacks and mulattoes, most of them being mulattoes.

My paternal great-grandfather, Dr. James Du Bois, was white and descended from Chrétien Du Bois who was a French Huguenot farmer and perhaps artisan and resided at Wicres near Lille in French Flanders. It is doubtful if he had any ancestors among the nobility, although his white American descendants love to think so. He had two, possibly three, sons of whom Louis and Jacques came to America to escape religious persecution. Jacques went from France first to Leiden in the Netherlands, where he was married and had several children, including a second Jacques or James. In 1674 that family came to America and settled at Kingston, New York. James Du Bois appears in the Du Bois family genealogy as a descendant of Jacques in the fifth generation, although the exact line of descent is not clear; but my grandfather's written testimony establishes that James was a physician and a landholder along the Hudson and in the West Indies. He was born in 1750, or later. He may have been a loyalist refugee. One such refugee, Isaac Du Bois, was given a grant of five hundred acres in Eleuthera after the Revolutionary War.

The career of Dr. James Du Bois was chiefly as a plantation proprietor and slave owner in the Bahama Islands with his headquarters at Long Cay. Cousins of his named Gilbert also had plantations near. He never married, but had one of his slaves as his common-law wife, a small brown-skinned woman born on the island. Of this couple two sons were born, Alexander and John. Alexander, my grandfather, was born in 1803, and about 1810, possibly because of the death of the mother, the father brought both these boys to America and planned to give them the education of gentlemen. They were white enough in appearance to give no inkling of their African descent. They were entered in the private Episcopal school at Cheshire, Connecticut, which still exists there and has trained many famous men. Dr. James Du Bois used often to visit his sons there, but about 1812, on his return from a visit, he had a stroke of apoplexy and died. He left no will and his estate descended to a cousin.

The boys were removed from school and bound out as apprentices, my grandfather to a shoemaker. Their connection with the white Du Bois family ceased suddenly, and was never renewed. Alexander Du Bois thus started with a good common school and perhaps some high school training and with the instincts of a gentleman of his day. Naturally he passed through much inner turmoil. He became a rebel, bitter at his lot in life, resentful at being classed as a Negro and yet implacable in his attitude toward whites. Of his brother, John, I have only a picture. He may have been the John Du Bois who helped Bishop Payne to purchase Wilberforce University.

If Alexander Du Bois, following the footsteps of Alexander Hamilton, had come from the West Indies to the United States, stayed with the white group and married and begotten children among them, anyone in after years who had suggested his Negro descent would have been unable to prove it and quite possibly would have been laughed to scorn, or sued for libel. Indeed the legal advisers of the publishers of my last book could write: "We may assume as a general proposition that it is libelous to state erroneously that a white man or woman has colored blood." Lately in Congress the true story, in a WPA history, of miscegenation affecting a high historic personage raised a howl of protest.

Alexander Du Bois did differently from Hamilton. He married into the colored group and his oldest son allied himself with a Negro clan but four generations removed from Africa. He himself first married Sarah Marsh Lewis in 1823 and then apparently set out to make his way in Haiti. There my father was born in 1825, and his elder sister, Augusta, a year earlier, either there or just as the family was leaving the United States. Evidently the situation in Haiti did not please my grandfather or perhaps the death of his young wife when she was scarcely thirty turned him back to America. Within a year he married Emily Basset who seems to have been the widow of a man named Jacklyn and lived in New Milford. Leonard Bacon, a well-known Congregational clergyman, performed his second marriage.

The following year, Alexander began his career in the United States. He lived in New Haven, Springfield, Providence, and finally in New Bedford. For some time, he was steward on the New York–New Haven boat and insisted on better treatment for his colored help. Later about 1848 he ran a grocery store at 23 Washington Street, New Haven, and owned property at different times in the various cities where he lived. By his first wife, my grandmother, he had two children, and by his second wife, one daughter, Henrietta. Three or four children died in infancy. Alexander was a communicant of Trinity Parish, New Haven, and was enrolled there as late as 1845; then something happened, because in 1847 he was among that group of Negroes who formed the new colored Episcopal Parish of St. Luke, where he was for years their senior warden. Probably this indicates one of his bitter fights and rebellions, for nothing but intolerable insult would have led him into a segregated church movement. Alexander Crummell was his first rector here.

As I knew my grandfather, he was a short, stern, upstanding man, sparing but precise in his speech and stiff in manner, evidently long used to repressing his feelings. I remember as a boy of twelve, watching his ceremonious reception of a black visitor, John Freedom; his stately bow, the way in which the red wine was served and the careful almost stilted conversation. I had seen no such social ceremony in my simple western Massachusetts home. The darkened parlor with its horsehair furniture became a very special and important place. I was deeply impressed. My grandfather evidently looked upon me with a certain misgiving if not actual distaste. I was brown, the son of his oldest son, Alfred, and Alfred and his father had never gotten on together.

The boy Alfred was a throwback to his white grandfather. He was small, olive-skinned and handsome and just visibly colored, with curly hair; and he was naturally a play-boy. My only picture of him shows him clothed in the uniform of the Union Army; but he never actually went to the front. In fact, Alfred never actually did much of anything. He was gay and carefree, refusing to settle long at any one place or job. He had a good elementary school training but nothing higher. I think that my father ran away from home several times. Whether he got into any very serious scrapes or not, I do not know, nor do I know whether he was married early in life; I imagine not. I think he was probably a free lance, gallant and lover, yielding only to marital bonds when he found himself in the rather strict clannishness of my mother's family. He was barber, merchant and preacher, but always irresponsible and charming. He had wandered out from eastern New England where his father lived and come to the Berkshire valley in 1867 where he met and married my brown mother.

The second wife of Alexander Du Bois died in 1865. His oldest daughter, Augusta, married a light mulatto and has descendants today who do not know of their Negro blood. Much later Alexander Du Bois married his third wife, Annie Green, who was the grandmother that I knew, and who knew and liked my father Alfred, and who brought me and my grandfather together. Alexander Du Bois died December 9, 1887, at the age of eighty-four, in New Bedford, and lies buried today in Oak Grove Cemetery near the Yale campus in New Haven, in a lot which he owned and which is next to that of Jehudi Ashmun of Liberian fame.

My father, by some queer chance, came into western Massachusetts and into the Housatonic Valley at the age of forty-two and there met and quickly married my brown mother who was then thirty-six and belonged to the Burghardt clan. This brings us to the history of the black Burghardts.

In 1694, Rev. Benjamin Wadsworth, afterwards president of Harvard College, made a journey through western Massachusetts, and says in regard to the present site of the town of Great Barrington, "Ye greatest part of our road this day was a hideous, howling wilderness." Here it was that a committee of the Massachusetts General Court confirmed a number of land titles in 1733–4, which had previously been in dispute between the English, Dutch, and Indians. In the "fifth division" of this land appears the name of a Dutchman, who signed himself as "Coenraet Borghghardt." This Borghghardt, Bogoert or Burghardt family has been prominent in Dutch colonial history and its descendants have been particularly identified with the annals of the little town of about five thousand inhabitants which today still lies among the hills of middle Berkshire.

Coenrod Burghardt seems to have been a shrewd pushing Dutchman and is early heard of in Kinderhook, together with his son John. This family came into possession of an African Negro named Tom, who had formerly belonged to the family of Etsons (Ettens?) and had come to the Burghardts by purchase or possibly by marriage. This African has had between one hundred and fifty and two hundred descendants, a number of whom are now living and reach to the eighth generation.

Tom was probably born about 1730. His granddaughter writes me that her father told her that Tom was born in Africa and was brought to this country when he was a boy. For many years my youthful imagination painted him as certainly the son of a tribal chief, but there is no warrant for this even in family tradition. Tom was probably just a stolen black boy from the West African Coast, nameless and lost, either a war captive or a tribal pawn. He was probably sent overseas on a Dutch ship at the time when their slave trade was beginning to decline and the vast English expansion to begin. He was in the service of the Burghardts and was a soldier in the Revolutionary War, going to the front probably several times; of only one of these is there official record when he appeared with the rank of private on the muster and payroll of Colonel John Ashley's Berkshire County regiment and Captain John Spoor's company in 1780. The company marched northward by order of Brigadier-General Fellows on an alarm when Fort Anne and Fort George were taken by the enemy. It is recorded that Tom was "reported a Negro." (Record Index of the Military Archives of Massachusetts, Vol. 23, p. 2.)

Tom appears to have been held as a servant and possibly a legal slave first by the family of Etsons or Ettens and then to have come into the possession of the Burghardts who settled at Great Barrington. Eventually, probably after the Revolutionary War, he was regarded as a freeman. There is record of only one son, Jacob Burghardt, who continued in the employ of the Burghardt family, and was born apparently about 1760. He is listed in the census of 1790 as "free" with two in his family. He married a wife named Violet who was apparently newly arrived from Africa and brought with her an African song which became traditional in the family. After her death, Jacob married Mom Bett, a rather celebrated figure in western Massachusetts history. She had been freed under the Bill of Rights of 1780 and the son of the judge who freed her wrote, "Even in her humble station, she had, when occasion required it, an air of command which conferred a degree of dignity and gave her an ascendancy over those of her rank, or color. Her determined and resolute character, which enabled her to limit the ravages of Shays's mob, was manifested in her conduct and deportment during her whole life. She claimed no distinction, but it was yielded to her from her superior experience, energy, skill and sagacity. Having known this woman as familiarly as I knew either of my parents, I cannot believe in the moral or physical inferiority of the race to which she belonged. The degradation of the African must have been otherwise caused than by natural inferiority."

Family tradition has it that her husband, Jacob, took part in suppressing this Shays's Rebellion. Jacob Burghardt had nine children, five sons of whom one was my grandfather, and four daughters. My grandfather's brothers and sisters had many children: Harlow had ten and Ira also ten; Maria had two. Descendants of Harlow and Ira still survive. Three of these sons, Othello, Ira, Harlow, and one daughter Lucinda settled on South Egremont plain near Great Barrington, where they owned small adjoining farms. A small part of one of these farms I continue to own.

Othello was my grandfather (see figure 12.1). He was born November 18, 1791, and married Sarah Lampman in 1811. Sarah was born in Hillsdale, New York, in 1793, of a mother named Lampman. There is no record of her father. She was probably the child of a Dutchman perhaps with Indian blood. This couple had ten children, three sons and seven daughters. Othello died in 1872 at the age of eighty-one and Sarah or Sally in 1877 at the age of eighty-six. Their sons and daughters married and drifted to town as laborers and servants. I thus had innumerable cousins up and down the valley. I was brought up with the Burghardt clan and this fact determined largely my life and "race." The white relationship and connections were quite lost and indeed unknown until long years after. The black Burghardts were ordinary farmers, laborers and servants. The children usually learned to read and write. I never heard or knew of any of them of my mother's generation or later who were illiterate. I was, however, the first one of the family who finished in the local high school. Afterward, one or two others did. Most of the members of the family left Great Barrington. Parts of the family are living and are fairly prosperous in the Middle West and on the Pacific Coast. I have heard of one or two high school graduates in the Middle West branch of the family.

This, then, was my racial history and as such it was curiously complicated. With Africa I had only one direct cultural connection and that was the African melody which my great-grandmother Violet used to sing. Where she learned it, I do not know. Perhaps she herself was born in Africa or had it of a mother or father stolen and transported. But at any rate, as I wrote years ago in the "Souls of Black Folk," "coming to the valleys of the Hudson and Housatonic, black, little, and lithe, she shivered and shrank in the harsh north winds, looked longingly at the hills, and often crooned a heathen melody to the child between her knees, thus:

Do bana coba, gene me, gene me!
Do bana coba, gene me, gene me!
Ben d' nuli, nuli, nuli, nuli, ben d' le.

The child sang it to his children and they to their children's children, and so two hundred years it has traveled down to us and we sing it to our children, knowing as little as our fathers what its words may mean, but knowing well the meaning of its music."

Living with my mother's people I absorbed their culture patterns and these were not African so much as Dutch and New England. The speech was an idiomatic New England tongue with no African dialect; the family customs were New England, and the sex mores. My African racial feeling was then purely a matter of my own later learning and reaction; my recoil from the assumptions of the whites; my experience in the South at Fisk. But it was none the less real and a large determinant of my life and character. I felt myself African by "race" and by that token was African and an integral member of the group of dark Americans who were called Negroes.

At the same time I was firm in asserting that these Negroes were Americans. For that reason and on the basis of my great-great-grandfather's Revolutionary record I was accepted as a member of the Massachusetts Society of the Sons of the American Revolution, in 1908. When, however, the notice of this election reached the headquarters in Washington and was emphasized by my requesting a national certificate, the secretary, A. Howard Clark of the Smithsonian Institution, wrote to Massachusetts and demanded "proof of

1600

(W) Chrétien Du Bois

(W) Louis

(W) Jacques

(W) Jacques — (W) S. Legge

1700

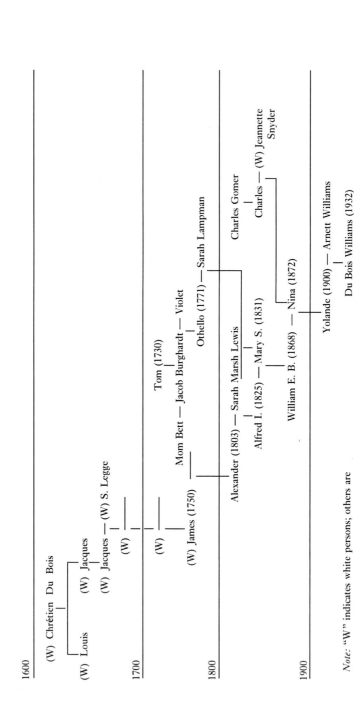

(W)

(W)

(W) James (1750)

Mom Bett — Jacob Burghardt — Violet

Tom (1730)

Othello (1771) — Sarah Lampman

1800

Charles Gomer

Alexander (1803) — Sarah Marsh Lewis

Alfred I. (1825) — Mary S. (1831)

Charles — (W) Jeannette Snyder

William E. B. (1868) — Nina (1872)

1900

Yolande (1900) — Arnett Williams

Du Bois Williams (1932)

Note: "W" indicates white persons; others are Negroes or Mulattoes

Figure 12.1

marriage of the ancestor of Tom Burghardt and record of birth of the son." He knew, of course, that the birth record of a stolen African slave could not possibly be produced. My membership was, therefore, suspended.

Countee Cullen sings:

What is Africa to me:
Copper sun or scarlet sea,
Jungle star or jungle track,
Strong bronzed men, or regal black
Women from whose loins I sprang
When the birds of Eden sang?
One three centuries removed
From the scenes his fathers loved,
Spicy grove, cinnamon tree,
What is Africa to me?

What is Africa to me? Once I should have answered the question simply: I should have said "fatherland" or perhaps better "motherland" because I was born in the century when the walls of race were clear and straight; when the world consisted of mutually exclusive races; and even though the edges might be blurred, there was no question of exact definition and understanding of the meaning of the word. One of the first pamphlets that I wrote in 1897 was on "The Conservation of Races" wherein I set down as the first article of a proposed racial creed: "We believe that the Negro people as a race have a contribution to make to civilization and humanity which no other race can make."

Since then the concept of race has so changed and presented so much of contradiction that as I face Africa I ask myself: what is it between us that constitutes a tie which I can feel better than I can explain? Africa is, of course, my fatherland. Yet neither my father nor my father's father ever saw Africa or knew its meaning or cared overmuch for it. My mother's folk were closer and yet their direct connection, in culture and race, became tenuous; still, my tie to Africa is strong. On this vast continent were born and lived a large portion of my direct ancestors going back a thousand years or more. The mark of their heritage is upon me in color and hair. These are obvious things, but of little meaning in themselves; only important as they stand for real and more subtle differences from other men. Whether they do or not, I do not know nor does science know today.

But one thing is sure and that is the fact that since the fifteenth century these ancestors of mine and their other descendants have had a common history; have suffered a common disaster and have one long memory. The actual ties of heritage between the individuals of this group, vary with the ancestors that they have in common and many others: Europeans and Semites, perhaps Mongolians, certainly American Indians. But the physical bond is least and the badge of color relatively unimportant save as a badge; the real essence of this kinship is its social heritage of slavery; the discrimination and insult; and this heritage binds together not simply the children of Africa, but extends through yellow Asia and into the South Seas. It is this unity that draws me to Africa.

When shall I forget the night I first set foot on African soil? I am the sixth generation in descent from forefathers who left this land. The moon was at the full and the waters of the Atlantic lay like a lake. All the long slow afternoon as the sun robed herself in her western scarlet with veils of misty cloud, I had seen Africa afar. Cape Mount – that mighty headland with its twin curves, northern sentinel of the realm of Liberia – gathered itself out of the cloud at half past three and then darkened and grew clear. On beyond flowed the dark low undulating land quaint with palm and breaking sea. The world grew black. Africa faded away, the stars stood forth curiously twisted – Orion in the zenith – the Little Bear asleep and the Southern Cross rising behind the horizon. Then afar, ahead, a lone light shone, straight at the ship's fore. Twinkling lights appeared below, around, and rising shadows. "Monrovia," said the Captain.

Suddenly we swerved to our left. The long arms of the bay enveloped us and then to the right rose the twinkling hill of Monrovia, with its crowning star. Lights flashed on the shore – here, there. Then we sensed a darker shading in the shadows; it lay very still. "It's a boat," one said. "It's two boats!" Then the shadow drifted in pieces and as the anchor roared into the deep, five boats outlined themselves on the waters – great ten-oared barges with men swung into line and glided toward us.

It was nine at night – above, the shadows, there the town, here the sweeping boats. One forged ahead with the flag – stripes and a lone star flaming behind, the ensign of the customs floating wide; and bending to the long oars, the white caps of ten black sailors. Up the stairway clambered a soldier in khaki, aide-de-camp of the President of the Republic, a customhouse official, the clerk of the American legation – and after them sixty-five lithe, lean black stevedores with whom the steamer would work down to Portuguese Angola and back. A few moments of formalities, greetings and good-bys and I was in the great long boat with the President's aide – a brown major in brown khaki. On the other side, the young clerk and at the back, the black barelegged pilot. Before us on the high thwarts were the rowers: men, boys, black, thin, trained in muscle and sinew, little larger than the oars in thickness, they bent their strength to them and swung upon them.

One in the center gave curious little cackling cries to keep up the rhythm, and for the spurts and the stroke, a call a bit thicker and sturdier; he gave a low guttural command now and then; the boat, alive, quivering, danced beneath the moon, swept a great curve to the bar to breast its narrow teeth of foam – "t'chick-a-tickity, t'chick-a-tick-ity," sang the boys, and we glided and raced, now between boats, now near the landing – now cast aloft at the dock. And lo! I was in Africa.

Christmas Eve, and Africa is singing in Monrovia. They are Krus and Fanti – men, women and children, and all the night they march and sing. The music was once the music of mission revival hymns. But it is that music now transformed and the silly words hidden in an unknown tongue – liquid and sonorous. It is tricked out and ex-pounded with cadence and turn. And this is that same rhythm I heard first in Tennessee forty years ago: the air is raised and carried by men's strong voices, while floating above in obbligato, come the high mellow voices of women – it is the ancient African art of part singing, so curiously and insist-ently different.

So they come, gay appareled, lit by transpar-ency. They enter the gate and flow over the high steps and sing and sing and sing. They saunter round the house, pick flowers, drink water and sing and sing and sing. The warm dark heat of the night steams up to meet the moon. And the night is song.

On Christmas Day, 1923, we walk down to the narrow, crooked wharves of Monrovia, by houses old and gray and step-like streets of stone. Before is the wide St. Paul River, double-mouthed, and beyond, the sea, white, curling on the sand. Before us is the isle – the tiny isle, hut-covered and guarded by a cotton tree, where the pioneers lived in 1821. We board the boat, then circle round – then up the river. Great bowing trees, festoons of flowers, golden blossoms, star-faced palms and thatched huts; tall spreading trees

lifting themselves like vast umbrellas, low shrub-bery with gray and laced and knotted roots – the broad, black, murmuring river. Here a tree holds wide fingers out and stretches them over the water in vast incantation; bananas throw their wide green fingers to the sun. Iron villages, scarred clearings with gray, sheet-iron homes staring, grim and bare, at the ancient tropical flood of green.

The river sweeps wide and the shrubs bow low. Behind, Monrovia rises in clear, calm beauty. Gone are the wharves, the low and clustered houses of the port, the tight-throated business village, and up sweep the villas and the low wall, brown and cream and white, with great mango and cotton trees, with lighthouse and spire, with porch and pillar and the color of shrubbery and blossom.

We climbed the upright shore to a senator's home and received his wide and kindly hospitality – curious blend of feudal lord and modern farmer – sandwiches, cake, and champagne. Again we glided up the drowsy river – five, ten, twenty miles and came to our hostess, a mansion of five generations with a compound of endless native servants and cows under the palm thatches. The daughters of the family wore, on the beautiful black skin of their necks, the exquisite pale gold chains of the Liberian artisan and the slim, black little granddaughter of the house had a wide pink ribbon on the thick curls of her dark hair, that lay like sudden sunlight on the shadows. Double porches, one above the other, welcomed us to ease. A native man, gay with Christmas and a dash of gin, sang and danced in the road. Children ran and played in the blazing sun. We sat at a long broad table and ate duck, chicken, beef, rice, plan-tain, collards, cake, tea, water and Madeira wine. Then we went and looked at the heavens, the uptwisted sky – Orion and Cassiopeia at zenith; the Little Bear beneath the horizon, now unfamil-iar sights in the Milky Way – all awry, a-living – sun for snow at Christmas, and happiness and cheer.

The shores were lined with old sugar planta-tions, the buildings rotting and falling. I looked upon the desolation with a certain pain. What had happened, I asked? The owners and planters had deserted these homes and come down to Monro-via, but why? After all, Monrovia had not much to offer in the way of income and occupation. Was this African laziness and inefficiency? No, it was a specimen of the way in which the waves of modern industry broke over the shores of far-off Africa. Here during our Civil War, men hastened to raise sugar and supply New York. They built their own boats and filled the river and sailed the sea. But afterwards, Louisiana came back into the Union, colored Rillieux invented the vacuum pan; the sugar plantations began to spread in Cuba and the Sugar Trust monopoly of refining machinery, together with the new beet sugar industry, drove Liberia quickly from the market. What all this did not do, the freight rates finished. So sugar did not pay in Liberia and other crops rose and fell in the same way.

As I look back and recall the days, which I have called great – the occasions in which I have taken part and which have had for me and others the widest significance, I can remember none like the first of January, 1924. Once I took my bachelor's degree before a governor, a great college president, and a bishop of New England. But that was rather personal in its memory than in any way epochal. Once before the assembled races of the world I was called to speak in London in place of the suddenly sick Sir Harry Johnston. It was a great hour. But it was not greater than the day when I was presented to the President of the Negro Republic of Liberia.

Liberia had been resting under the shock of world war into which the Allies forced her. She had asked and been promised a loan by the United States to bolster and replace her stricken trade. She had conformed to every preliminary requirement and waited when waiting was almost fatal. It was not simply money, it was world prestige and protection at a time when the little republic was sorely beset by creditors and greedy imperial powers. At the last moment, an insurgent Senate peremptorily and finally refused the request and strong recommendation of President Wilson and his advisers, and the loan was refused. The Department of State made no statement to the world, and Liberia stood naked, not only well-nigh bankrupt, but peculiarly defenseless amid scowling and unbelieving powers.

It was then that the United States made a gesture of courtesy; a little thing, and merely a gesture, but one so unusual that it was epochal. President Coolidge, at the suggestion of William H. Lewis, a leading colored lawyer of Boston, named me, an American Negro traveler, Envoy Extraordinary and Minister Plenipotentiary to Liberia – the highest rank ever given by any country to a diplomatic agent in black Africa. And it named this Envoy the special representative of the President of the United States to the President of Liberia, on the occasion of his inauguration;

charging the Envoy with a personal word of encouragement and moral support. It was a significant action. It had in it nothing personal. Another appointee would have been equally significant. But Liberia recognized the meaning. She showered upon the Envoy every mark of appreciation and thanks. The Commander of the Liberian Frontier Force was made his special aide, and a sergeant, his orderly. At ten a.m. New Year's morning, 1924, a company of the Frontier Force, in red fez and khaki, presented arms before the American Legation and escorted Solomon Porter Hood, the American Minister Resident, and myself as Envoy Extraordinary and my aide to the Presidential Mansion – a beautiful white, verandaed house, waving with palms and fronting a grassy street.

Ceremonials are old and to some antiquated and yet this was done with such simplicity, grace and seriousness that none could escape its spell. The Secretary of State met us at the door, as the band played the impressive Liberian National hymn, and soldiers saluted:

> All hail! Liberia, hail!
> In union strong, success is sure.
> We cannot fail.
> With God above,
> Our rights to prove,
> We will the world assail.

We mounted a broad stairway and into a great room that stretched across the house. Here in semi-circle were ranged the foreign consuls and the cabinet – the former in white, gilt with orders and swords; the latter in solemn black. Present were England, France, Germany, Spain, Belgium, Holland, and Panama, to be presented to me in order of seniority by the small brown Secretary of State with his perfect poise and ease. The President entered – frock-coated with the star and ribbon of a Spanish order on his breast. The American Minister introduced me, and I said:

"The President of the United States has done me the great honor of designating me as his personal representative on the occasion of your inauguration. In so doing, he has had, I am sure, two things in mind. First, he wished publicly and unmistakably to express before the world the interest and solicitude which the hundred million inhabitants of the United States of America have for Liberia. Liberia is a child of the United States, and a sister Republic. Its progress and success is the progress and success of democracy everywhere and for all men; and the United States would view with sorrow and alarm any misfortune which might happen to this Republic and any obstacle that was placed in her path.

"But special and peculiar bonds draw these two lands together. In America live eleven million persons of African descent; they are citizens, legally invested with every right that inheres in American citizenship. And I am sure that in this special mark of the President's favor, he has had in mind the wishes and hopes of Negro Americans. He knows how proud they are of the hundred years of independence which you have maintained by force of arms and by brawn and brain upon the edge of this mighty continent; he knows that in the great battle against color caste in America, the ability of Negroes to rule in Africa has been and ever will be a great and encouraging reenforcement. He knows that the unswerving loyalty of Negro Americans to their country is fitly accompanied by a pride in their race and lineage, a belief in the potency and promise of Negro blood which makes them eager listeners to every whisper of success from Liberia, and eager helpers in every movement for your aid and comfort. In a special sense, the moral burden of Liberia and the advancement and integrity of Liberia is the sincere prayer of America."

And now a word about the African himself – about this primitive black man: I began to notice a truth as I entered southern France. I formulated it in Portugal. I knew it as a great truth one Sunday in Liberia. And the Great Truth was this: efficiency and happiness do not go together in modern culture. Going south from London, as the world darkens it gets happier. Portugal is deliciously dark. Many leading citizens would have difficulty keeping off a Georgia "Jim Crow" car. But, oh, how lovely a land and how happy a people! And so leisurely. Little use of trying to shop seriously in Lisbon before eleven. It isn't done. Nor at noon; the world is lunching or lolling in the sun. Even after four p.m. one takes chances, for the world is in the Rocio. And the banks are so careless and the hotels so leisurely. How delightfully angry Englishmen get at the "damned, lazy" Portuguese!

But if this of Portugal, what of Africa? Here darkness descends and rests on lovely skins until brown seems luscious and natural. There is sunlight in great gold globules and soft, heavy-scented heat that wraps you like a garment. And laziness; divine, eternal, languor is right and good and true. I remember the morning; it was Sunday, and the night before we heard the leopards crying down

there. Today beneath the streaming sun we went down into the gold-green forest. It was silence – silence the more mysterious because life abundant and palpitating pulsed all about us and held us drowsy captives to the day. Ahead the gaunt missionary strode, alert, afire, with his gun. He apologized for the gun, but he did not need to, for I saw the print of a leopard's hind foot. A monkey sentinel screamed, and I heard the whir of the horde as they ran.

Then we came to the village; how can I describe it? Neither London, nor Paris, nor New York has anything of its delicate, precious beauty. It was a town of the Veys and done in cream and pale purple – still, clean, restrained, tiny, complete. It was no selfish place, but the central abode of fire and hospitality, clean-swept for wayfarers, and best seats were bare. They quite expected visitors, morning, noon, and night; and they gave our hands a quick, soft grasp and talked easily. Their manners were better than those of Park Lane or Park Avenue. Oh, much better and more natural. They showed breeding. The chief's son – tall and slight and speaking good English – had served under the late Colonel Young. He made a little speech of welcome. Long is the history of the Veys and comes down from the Eastern Roman Empire, the great struggle of Islam and the black empires of the Sudan.

We went on to other villages – dun-colored, not so beautiful, but neat and hospitable. In one sat a visiting chief of perhaps fifty years in a derby hat and a robe, and beside him stood a shy young wife done in ebony and soft brown, whose liquid eyes would not meet ours. The chief was taciturn until we spoke of schools. Then he woke suddenly – he had children to "give" to a school. I see the last village fading away; they are plastering the wall of a home, leisurely and carefully. They smiled a good-by – not effusively, with no eagerness, with a simple friendship, as we glided under the cocoa trees and into the silent forest, the gold and silent forest.

And there and elsewhere in two long months I began to learn: primitive men are not following us afar, frantically waving and seeking our goals; primitive men are not behind us in some swift foot-race. Primitive men have already arrived. They are abreast, and in places ahead of us; in others behind. But all their curving advance line is contemporary, not prehistoric. They have used other paths and these paths have led them by scenes sometimes fairer, sometimes uglier than ours, but always toward the Pools of Happiness. Or, to put it otherwise, these folk have the leisure of true aristocracy – leisure for thought and courtesy, leisure for sleep and laughter. They have time for their children – such well-trained, beautiful children with perfect, unhidden bodies. Have you ever met a crowd of children in the east of London or New York, or even on the Avenue at Forty-second or One Hundred and Forty-second Street, and fled to avoid their impudence and utter ignorance of courtesy? Come to Africa, and see well-bred and courteous children, playing happily and never sniffling and whining.

I have read everywhere that Africa means sexual license. Perhaps it does. Most folk who talk sex frantically have all too seldom revealed their source material. I was in West Africa only two months, but with both eyes wide. I saw children quite naked and women usually naked to the waist – with bare bosom and limbs. And in those sixty days I saw less of sex dalliance and appeal than I see daily on Fifth Avenue. This does not mean much, but it is an interesting fact.

The primitive black man is courteous and dignified. If the platforms of Western cities had swarmed with humanity as I have seen the platforms swarm in Senegal, the police would have a busy time. I did not see one respectable quarrel. Wherefore shall we all take to the Big Bush? No. I prefer New York. But my point is that New York and London and Paris must learn of West Africa and may learn.

The one great lack in Africa is communication – communication as represented by human contact, movement of goods, dissemination of knowledge. All these things we have – we have in such crushing abundance that they have mastered us and defeated their real good. We meet human beings in such throngs that we cannot know or even understand them – they become to us inhuman, mechanical, hateful. We are choked and suffocated, tempted and killed by goods accumulated from the ends of the earth; our newspapers and magazines so overwhelm us with knowledge – knowledge of all sorts and kinds from particulars as to our neighbors' underwear to Einstein's mathematics – that one of the great and glorious joys of the African bush is to escape from "news."

On the other hand, African life with its isolation has deeper knowledge of human souls. The village life, the forest ways, the teeming markets, bring in intimate human knowledge that the West misses, sinking the individual in the social. Africans know

fewer folk, but know them infinitely better. Their intertwined communal souls, therefore, brook no poverty nor prostitution – these things are to them un-understandable. On the other hand, they are vastly ignorant of what the world is doing and thinking, and of what is known of its physical forces. They suffer terribly from preventable disease, from unnecessary hunger, from the freaks of the weather.

Here, then, is something for Africa and Europe both to learn; and Africa is eager, breathless, to learn – while Europe? Europe laughs with loud guffaws. Learn of Africa? Nonsense. Poverty cannot be abolished. Democracy and firm government are incompatible. Prostitution is world old and inevitable. And Europe proceeds to use Africa as a means and not as an end; as a hired tool and welter of raw materials and not as a land of human beings.

I think it was in Africa that I came more clearly to see the close connection between race and wealth. The fact that even in the minds of the most dogmatic supporters of race theories and believers in the inferiority of colored folk to white, there was a conscious or unconscious determination to increase their incomes by taking full advantage of this belief. And then gradually this thought was metamorphosed into a realization that the income-bearing value of race prejudice was the cause and not the result of theories of race inferiority; that particularly in the United States the income of the Cotton Kingdom based on black slavery caused the passionate belief in Negro inferiority and the determination to enforce it even by arms.

I have wandered afield from miscegenation in the West Indies to race blending and segregation in America and to a glimpse of present Africa. Now to return to the American concept of race. It was in my boyhood, as I have intimated, an adventure. In my youth, it became the vision of a glorious crusade where I and my fellows were to match our mettle against white folk and show them what black folk could do. But as I grew older the matter became more serious and less capable of jaunty settlement. I not only met plenty of persons equal in ability to myself but often with greater ability and nearly always with greater opportunity. Racial identity presented itself as a matter of trammels and impediments as "tightening bonds about my feet." As I looked out into my racial world the whole thing verged on tragedy. My "way was cloudy" and the approach to its high goals by no means straight and clear. I saw the race problem was not as I conceived, a matter of clear, fair competition, for which I was ready and eager. It was rather a matter of segregation, of hindrance and inhibitions, and my struggles against this and resentment at it began to have serious repercussions upon my inner life.

It is difficult to let others see the full psychological meaning of caste segregation. It is as though one, looking out from a dark cave in a side of an impending mountain, sees the world passing and speaks to it; speaks courteously and persuasively, showing them how these entombed souls are hindered in their natural movement, expression, and development; and how their loosening from prison would be a matter not simply of courtesy, sympathy, and help to them, but aid to all the world. One talks on evenly and logically in this way, but notices that the passing throng does not even turn its head, or if it does, glances curiously and walks on. It gradually penetrates the minds of the prisoners that the people passing do not hear; that some thick sheet of invisible but horribly tangible plate glass is between them and the world. They get excited; they talk louder; they gesticulate. Some of the passing world stop in curiosity; these gesticulations seem so pointless; they laugh and pass on. They still either do not hear at all, or hear but dimly, and even what they hear, they do not understand. Then the people within may become hysterical. They may scream and hurl themselves against the barriers, hardly realizing in their bewilderment that they are screaming in a vacuum unheard and that their antics may actually seem funny to those outside looking in. They may even, here and there, break through in blood and disfigurement, and find themselves faced by a horrified, implacable, and quite overwhelming mob of people frightened for their own very existence.

It is hard under such circumstances to be philosophical and calm, and to think through a method of approach and accommodation between castes. The entombed find themselves not simply trying to make the outer world understand their essential and common humanity but even more, as they become inured to their experience, they have to keep reminding themselves that the great and oppressing world outside is also real and human and in its essence honest. All my life I have had continually to haul my soul back and say, "All white folk are not scoundrels nor murderers. They are, even as I am, painfully human."

One development continually recurs: any person outside of this wall of glass can speak to his own fellows, can assume a facile championship of the entombed, and gain the enthusiastic and even gushing thanks of the victims. But this method is subject to two difficulties: first of all, not being possibly among the entombed or capable of sharing their inner thought and experience, this outside leadership will continually misinterpret and compromise and complicate matters, even with the best of will. And secondly, of course, no matter how successful the outside advocacy is, it remains impotent and unsuccessful until it actually succeeds in freeing and making articulate the submerged caste.

Practically, this group imprisonment within a group has various effects upon the prisoner. He becomes provincial and centered upon the problems of his particular group. He tends to neglect the wider aspects of national life and human existence. On the one hand he is unselfish so far as his inner group is concerned. He thinks of himself not as an individual but as a group man, a "race" man. His loyalty to this group idea tends to be almost unending and balks at almost no sacrifice. On the other hand, his attitude toward the environing race congeals into a matter of unreasoning resentment and even hatred, deep disbelief in them and refusal to conceive honesty and rational thought on their part. This attitude adds to the difficulties of conversation, intercourse, understanding between groups.

This was the race concept which has dominated my life, and the history of which I have attempted to make the leading theme of this book. It had as I have tried to show all sorts of illogical trends and irreconcilable tendencies. Perhaps it is wrong to speak of it at all as "a concept" rather than as a group of contradictory forces, facts and tendencies. At any rate I hope I have made its meaning to me clear. It was for me as I have written first a matter of dawning realization, then of study and science; then a matter of inquiry into the diverse strands of my own family; and finally consideration of my connection, physical and spiritual, with Africa and the Negro race in its homeland. All this led to an attempt to rationalize the racial concept and its place in the modern world.

Notes

1 See Du Bois's account of Gustav Spiller's remarks in W. E. B. Du Bois, "The First Universal Races Congress," in Herbert Aptheker, ed., *Writings by W. E. B. Du Bois in Periodicals Edited by Others*, 4 vols. (Millwood, NY: Kraus-Thomson, 1982), 2: 50.

2 Friedrich Ratzel, *The History of Mankind*, trans. from 2nd German edn by A. J. Butler, introduction by E. B. Tylor, 3 vols. (New York: Macmillan, 1896), 1: 9.

3 Felix von Luschan, quoted in Du Bois, "The First Universal Races Congress," 2: 49.

13

The Genesis of the Self and Social Control

George Herbert Mead

Introduction

George Herbert Mead (1863–1931) was both an academic philosopher and a social psychologist. As a close friend and colleague of John Dewey, Mead focused on developing a pragmatist understanding of human selves in society. As with the other pragmatists, Mead agreed that minds and selves emerge from social interaction. In this selection, he argues that the process turns on the development, in interaction, of a "generalized other," whose perspective serves to ground shared meaning.

It is my desire to present an account of the appearance of the self in social behavior, and then to advert to some implications of such an account in their bearings upon social control.

The term "behavior" indicates the standpoint of what follows, that of a behavioristic psychology. There is an aspect of this psychology that calls for an emphasis which I think has not been sufficiently given it. It is not simply the objectivity of this psychology which has commended it. All recent psychology, in so far as it lays claim to a scientific approach, considers itself objective. But behavioristic psychology, coming in by the door of the study of animals lower than man, has perforce shifted its interest from psychical states to external conduct. Even when this conduct is followed into the central nervous system, it is not to find the correlate of the neurosis in a psychosis, but to

Taken from *International Journal of Ethics*, 36 (1925): 251–77.

complete the act, however distant this may be in space and time. This doctrine finds itself in sympathetic accord with recent realism and pragmatism, which places the so-called sensa and the significances of things in the object. While psychology has been turning to the act as a process, philosophic thought has been transferring contents that had been the subject-matter of earlier psychology from the field of states of consciousness to the objective world. Prebehavioristic psychology had a foot in two worlds. Its material was found in consciousness and in the world of physiology and physics. As long, however, as psychology was occupied with states of consciousness which constituted objects, there was an inevitable duplication. The whole physiological and physical apparatus could be stated in terms of states of consciousness, and solipsism hovered in the background. A psychology that is called upon to analyze the object into the states of consciousness which it is studying may conceivably be an empirical science, but in so far its world is not the world of the other sciences. A behavioristic psychology, on the other hand, that is not responsible for the content of the object, becomes a science that is cognate with physiology and dynamics, and escapes the trail of the epistemological serpent.

I am not concerned with the philosophical justification of this attitude of behavioristic psychology; I merely wish to emphasize its inevitable tendency to deal with processes, that is, with acts, and to find its objects given in the world with which all science deals. From Descartes' time on, it has been a border state, lying between philosophy and the natural sciences, and has suffered the inconveniences which attend buffer states. Descartes' unambiguous and uncompromising division between an extended physical world, and an unextended world of thought, when it reached the pineal gland found itself in ambiguous territory, and only avoided compromise by leaving the relations of mind and body to the infinite power of his *deus ex machina*. The difficulties which have attended psychology's regulation of these relations have been only in part metaphysical. More fundamentally they have been logical. The natural sciences start pragmatically with a world that is there, within which a problem has arisen, and introduce hypothetical reconstructions only in so far as its solution demands them. They always have their feet upon the solid ground of unquestioned objects of observation and experiment, where Samuel Johnson placed his in his summary refutation of Berkeley's idealism. Speculative philosophy, beset with the problem of epistemology, found its problem in the nature and very existence of the world inside which the problems of the natural sciences appeared, and which furnished the test of its hypotheses. Thus psychology as a philosophic discipline carried the epistemological problem into the experience of the individual, but as a science located the problem in a given world which its epistemological problem could not accept as given. Between the two, its sympathies have always been with the presuppositions and method of the natural sciences. On the one hand, as empirical science it has sought to regard the so-called consciousness of the individual as merely given in the sense of the objects of the natural sciences, but as states of consciousness were still regarded as cognitive, they had inevitably inherited the epistemological diathesis. On the other hand, as experimental science it was forced to place states of consciousness within or without the processes it was studying. Placing them in interactionism within the natural processes ran counter to the presuppositions of its scientific procedure, so that the prevailing attitude has been that of epiphenomenalism, an adaptation of Leibnitz's pre-established harmony and Spinoza's parallel attributes. They ran as harmless conscious shadows beside the physical and physiological processes with which science could come to immediate terms. But this proved but an unstable compromise. The conscious streak that accompanied the neuroses could answer only to sensing and thinking as processes; as qualities and significance

of things, states of consciousness became hardly tolerable reduplications of things, except in the case of the secondary qualities. The molecular structure of things seemed to remove these from the hypothetical objects of physical science, and consciousness proved a welcome dumping-ground for them. This bifurcation of nature proves equally unsatisfactory. The horns and the hoofs go with the hide. States of contact experience have no better right to objective existence than those of distance experience. Psychology, however, has not been interested in these epistemological and metaphysical riddles, it has been simply irritated by them. It has shifted its interest to the processes, where phenomenalism is most harmless, appearing as physiological psychology, as functional psychology, as dynamic psychology, and has ignored the problems for which it had no care. The effect of this has been to give to the central nervous system a logical pre-eminence in the procedure and textbooks of psychology which is utterly unwarranted in the analysis of the experience of the individual. The central nervous system has been unwittingly assimilated to the logical position of consciousness. It occupies only an important stage in the act, but we find ourselves locating the whole environment of the individual in its convolutions. It is small wonder, then, that behaviorism has been welcomed with unmistakable relief, for it has studied the conduct of animals in necessary ignoration of consciousness, and it has been occupied with the act as a whole, not as a nervous arc.

But the relief with which one turns to conduct and away from states of consciousness has not disposed of the problems involved in the ambiguous term "consciousness," even for the psychologist. Bergson's theory of perception was at least a step toward the clarification of this ambiguity. It recognizes that in so far as the content of the percept can be termed consciousness, it indicates a diminution of the reality of the object rather than an addition, and this diminution answers to the active interests of the organism, which are represented in the central nervous system by paths of possible response. These co-ordinated paths in some sense cut out the object of perception. The percept is relative to the perceiving individual, but relative to his active interest, not relative in the sense that its content is a state of his consciousness. It is at least meaningless to lodge the so-called sensuous characters of things in the cortex. When, however, Bergson suggests that certain of these qualities may be the condensation of vibrations, we seem again to be in the presence of qualities that are states of consciousness. Presumably the condensations, e.g., the actual quality of color, do not exist in the object, but in the condensing mind. However, Bergson's statement at least placed the central nervous system in the world of things, of percepts, on the one hand, and on the other placed the characters of things in pure perception in the things themselves; but the divorce of duration, as psychical, from a static intellectualized spatial world left a dichotomy which was functional only from the standpoint of a Bergsonian metaphysics. Neo-realism undertook to return all the qualities of things to the things, over against a mind which was simply aware of the sensa. This simple, radical procedure left problems of a perception which was still cognitive in its nature, which a Critical Realism sought to solve by retreating to representative perception again. It remained for pragmatism to take the still more radical position that in immediate experience the percept stands over against the individual, not in a relation of awareness, but simply in that of conduct. Cognition is a process of finding out something that is problematical, not of entering into relation with a world that is there.

There is an ambiguity in the word "consciousness." We use it in the sense of "awareness," "consciousness of," and are apt to assume that in this sense it is coextensive with experience, that it covers the relation of the sentient organism to its environment in so far as the environment exists for the organism. We thus predicate of this existence of the environment for the organism the attitude of cognition on the part of the organism. The other use of consciousness to which I refer is in the sense of certain contents, to wit, the sense qualities of things, more especially the so-called secondary qualities, the affections of the body of the sentient organism, especially those that are pleasurable and painful, the contents of the images of memory and imagination, and of the activities of the organism, so far as they appear in its experience. There is another field, that of self-consciousness, to which I am not as yet referring. There is a common character which in varying degree belongs to all of these contents, that is, that these contents could not appear at all, or exactly as they do appear, in the experience of any other organism. They are in this sense private, though this privacy does not imply necessarily anything more than difference of access or of perspective on the part of the different organisms. If we take the pragmatic attitude, referred to above, consciousness in the first

sense, that of awareness, would disappear from immediate experience, while the world that is there for the organism would still be there. A particular organism would become conscious from this standpoint, that is, there would be a world that would exist for the organism, when the organism marked or plotted or, to use Bergson's term, canalized its environment in terms of its future conduct. For Bergson, a percept is an object of possible action for an organism, and it is the active relationship of the organism to the distant object that constitutes it an object. Bergson meets the difficulty that the organism can exercise no physical influence upon the distant object by his assumption that consciousness in this sense is in reality not an addition to the object, but an abstraction from all in the relation of the organism to the object which does not bear upon this action. There arises, then, a selected series of objects, determined by the active interests of the organism.

An environment thus arises for an organism through the selective power of an attention that is determined by its impulses that are seeking expression. This peculiar environment does not exist in the consciousness of the form as a separate milieu, but the consciousness of the organism consists in the fact that its future conduct outlines and defines its objects. In so far as the organization of one individual differs from that of others, it will have a private environment, though these differences may be called those of standpoint. They are objective differences. They exist in nature. The most fundamental phase of these differences is found in the determination of what the relativist calls a "consentient set," i.e., the selection of those objects which may all be considered as "here" with reference to the individual. It is this set, which is co-gredient with the individual, that constitutes an environment within which motion may take place. These perspectives of nature exist in nature, not in the consciousness of the organism as a stuff. In this relation of a peculiar environment for an individual, there is no implication of an awareness. All that is implied is that the ongoing activity of the individual form marks and defines its world for the form, which thus exists for it as it does not for any other form. If this is called consciousness, a behavioristic psychology can state it in terms of conduct.

Consciousness in the second sense, that of a peculiar content or contents, implies relativity in another sense, in the sense of emergence, as this has been defined by Alexander, in *Space Time and the Deity*, and accepted by Lloyd Morgan, in

Emergent Evolution. In evolution not only have new forms appeared, but new qualities or contents in experience. It is the sensitivities of forms that are the occasions for the appearance, in the worlds of these forms, of new characters of things, answering to all the senses, and new meanings answering to their new capacities for conduct. And these new characters and new meanings exist in nature as do the forms of physical objects, though they are relative to the sensitivities and capacities of the individual forms. If we drop awareness from immediate experience, Alexander's distinction between perception and enjoyment may be also dropped. This distinction lies between the awareness of perception of external objects and that of the experience of the individual in perception and his other processes. Pleased palates and irritated or suffering members are there in the same sense as other percepts or objects. And this is true also of straining muscles, of fearful objects, or a turned stomach, or an attractive thing, nor can we deny this sort of objectivity to imagery, because access to it is confined to the individual in whose world it appears. Part of this imagery fits into the world that is there, and is with great difficulty analyzed out. That which will not fit in becomes located in our pasts or in futures of varying degrees of definiteness.

If my friend enters the room, and I catch a glimpse of his face, the imagery of his face fills out the countenance, and I see him with his whole complement of features. The same imagery might have figured in my memory of last meeting him. Or it might have figured in the plan I entertained of calling, on the following evening. It belongs either to the passing present, or to the irrevocable past, or to the contingent future. This imagery is for the percipient as objective as the so-called sense object. It may enter that object and be indistinguishable from it. Where it can be distinguished, however, it is recognized as having this private character; that is, while we assume that the color of the object perceived, even if it vary from eye to eye, is in some respects identical for all eyes in so far as the organs are alike, it is not assumed that the image which one has is there for other eyes, or imaginations. While this sole accessibility of imagery to the individual does not in itself render it less objective, it places it at the disposal of the individual, when he attains to a mind which it can furnish. The same is true of the other class of objects which in his experience is accessible only to him. I refer to the objects which the individual possesses from the inside, so to speak, the parts of his organism, especially as they are painful or pleasurable. In the so-called lower animals, there is no evidence that this private field is organized and used as the possession of a self. The passing present is neither extended into a memory series, nor into an anticipated future.

Imagery is but one phase of the presence of the past in the passing present. In the living form it appears as facility in the response, and in the selection of the stimulus, in selective discrimination, in the stimulus. Imagery emerges, in the sense of Alexander, as the content of the past in the stimulus, and as meaning in the response. Imagery and meaning are there in the objects as contents, before they become material for the mind, before the mind appears in conduct.

I have referred to the doctrine of relativity. More specifically, my reference was to formulation of the doctrine given in Professor Whitehead's three books, *The Principles of Natural Knowledge, The Concept of Nature,* and *The Principle of Relativity.* What I have had particularly in mind is Whitehead's recognition, as over against current Einsteinian doctrine, that if motion is to be accepted as an objective fact, we must also accept the existence in nature of so-called consentient sets at rest, determined by their relation to so-called percipient events. The same events in nature appear in different consentient sets, as these events are ordered in different time systems, and this ordering in different time systems is dependent upon their relations to different percipient events. Motion in nature implies rest in nature. Rest in nature implies co-gredience, i.e., a persistent relation of here and there with reference to some individual, and it is this that determines the time system in accordance with which events are ordered. If rest is a fact in nature, we must conceive of it as stratified, to use Whitehead's term, by the different temporal perspectives of different individuals, though a group of individuals may have the same perspective; we must, however, remember that this is a stratification of nature not in a static space, but a nature whose extension is affected with a time dimension.

It is this conception of the existence in nature of consentient sets determined by their relations to percipient events that I wish to generalize so that it will cover the environment in relation to the living form, and the experienced world with reference to the experiencing individual. This is evidently only possible if we conceive life as a process and not a series of static physico-chemical situations, and if we regard experience as conduct or behavior, not as a series of conscious states. This I take to be the essence of Bergson's philosophy of change, in accordance with which our perceptual world is determined by the actions that are taking place. Conduct does cut out and fashion the objects upon which action is directed. It is only with reference to life as an ongoing process that the animal determines his habitat. The most convincing illustration can be found in the different presentation of the life of a community, in terms of a social statics, the statistical data of population and occupations and the like, or in terms of the actual lives of the different individuals who make up the community. In the latter case we realize that each individual has a world that differs in some degree from that of any other member of the same community, that he slices the events of the community life that are common to all from a different angle from that of any other individual. In Whitehead's phrase, each individual stratifies the common life in a different manner, and the life of the community is the sum of all these stratifications, and all of these stratifications exist in nature. It is this recognition that takes psychology out of its isolation, as a science that deals with what is found in the mind of an individual, and makes of it the standpoint from which to approach reality as it is going on.

It is evident that a statement of the life of each individual in terms of the results of an analysis of that which is immediately experienced would offer a common plane of events, in which the experience of each would differ from the experiences of others only in their extent, and the completeness or incompleteness of their connections. These differences disappear in the generalized formulations of the social sciences. The experiences of the same individuals, in so far as each faces a world in which objects are plans of action, would implicate in each a different succession of events. In the simplest illustration, two persons approach a passing automobile. To one it is a moving object that he will pass before it reaches the portion of the street that is the meeting-place of their two paths. The other sees an object that will pass this meeting-point before he reaches it. Each slices the world from the standpoint of a different time system. Objects which in a thousand ways are identical for the two individuals, are yet fundamentally different through their location in one spatio-temporal plane, involving a certain succession of events, or in another. Eliminate the temporal dimension, and

bring all events back to an instant that is timeless, and the individuality of these objects which belongs to them in behavior is lost, except in so far as they can represent the results of past conduct. But taking time seriously, we realize that the seemingly timeless character of our spatial world and its permanent objects is due to the consentient set which each one of us selects. We abstract time from this space for the purposes of our conduct. Certain objects cease to be events, cease to pass as they are in reality passing and in their permanence become the conditions of our action, and events take place with reference to them. Because a whole community selects the same consentient set does not make the selection less the attitude of each one of them. The life-process takes place in individual organisms, so that the psychology which studies that process in its creative determining function becomes a science of the objective world.

Looked at from the standpoint of an evolutionary history, not only have new forms with their different spatio-temporal environments and their objects arisen, but new characters have arisen answering to the sensitivities and capacities for response. In the terms of Alexander, they have become differently qualitied. It is as impossible to transfer these characters of the habitats to the consciousness of the forms as it is to transfer the spatio-temporal structure of the things to such a so-called consciousness. If we introduce a fictitious instantaneousness into a passing universe, things fall to pieces. Things that are spatio-temporally distant from us can be brought into this instant only in terms of our immediate contact experience. They are what they would be if we were there and had our hands upon them. They take on the character of tangible matter. This is the price of their being located at the moment of our bodies' existence. But this instantaneous view has the great advantage of giving to us a picture of what the contact experience will be when we reach the distant object, and of determining conditions under which the distance characters arise. If the world existed at an instant in experience, we should be forced to find some realm such as consciousness into which to transport the distance or so-called secondary qualities of things. If consciousness in evolutionary history, then, has an unambiguous significance, it refers to that stage in the development of life in which the conduct of the individual marks out and defines the future field and objects which make up its environment, and in which emerge characters in the objects and sensitivities in the individuals that answer to each other. There is a relativity of the living individual and its environment, both as to form and content.

What I wish to trace is the fashion in which self and the mind has arisen within this conduct.

It is the implication of this undertaking that only selves have minds, that is, that cognition only belongs to selves, even in the simplest expression of awareness. This, of course, does not imply that below the stage of self-consciousness sense characters and sensitivity do not exist. This obtains in our own immediate experience in so far as we are not self-conscious. It is further implied that this development has taken place only in a social group, for selves exist only in relation to other selves, as the organism as a physical object exists only in its relation to other physical objects. There have been two fields within which social groups have arisen which have determined their environment together with that of their members, and the individuality of its members. These lie in the realm of the invertebrates and in that of the vertebrates. Among the Hymenoptera and termites there are societies whose interests determine for the individuals their stimuli and habitats, and so differentiate the individuals themselves, mainly through the sexual and alimentary processes, that the individual is what he is because of his membership within those societies. In the complex life of the group, the acts of the individuals are completed only through the acts of other individuals, but the mediation of this complex conduct is found in the physiological differentiation of the different members of the society. As Bergson has remarked of the instincts, the implements by which a complex act is carried out are found in the differentiated structure of the form. There is no convincing evidence that an ant or a bee is obliged to anticipate the act of another ant or bee, by tending to respond in the fashion of the other, in order that it may integrate its activity into the common act. And by the same mark there is no evidence of the existence of any language in their societies. Nor do we need to go to the invertebrates to discover this type of social conduct. If one picks up a little child who has fallen, he adapts his arms and attitude to the attitude of the child, and the child adapts himself to the attitude of the other; or in boxing or fencing one responds to stimulus of the other, by acquired physiological adjustment.

Among the vertebrates, apart from the differentiation of the sexes and the nurture and care of infant forms, there is little or no inherited physio-logical differentiation to mediate the complexities of social conduct. If we are to co-operate successfully with others, we must in some manner get their ongoing acts into ourselves to make the common act come off. As I have just indicated, there is a small range of social activity in which this is not necessary. The suckling of an infant form, or a dog fight, if this may be called a social activity, does not call for more than inherited physiological adjustment. Perhaps the so-called herding instinct should be added, but it hardly comes to more than the tendency of the herd to stick together in their various activities. The wooing and mating of forms, the care of the infant form, the bunching of animals in migrations, and fighting, about exhaust vertebrate social conduct, and beyond these seasonal processes vertebrate societies hardly exist till we reach man. They exhaust the possibilities in vertebrate structure of the mediation of social conduct, for the vertebrate organism has shown no such astonishing plasticity in physiological differentiation as that which we can trace among the insects, from isolated forms to members of the societies of the termites, the ants, and the bees.

A social act may be defined as one in which the occasion or stimulus which sets free an impulse is found in the character or conduct of a living form that belongs to the proper environment of the living form whose impulse it is. I wish, however, to restrict the social act to the class of acts which involve the co-operation of more than one individual, and whose object as defined by the act, in the sense of Bergson, is a social object. I mean by a social object one that answers to all the parts of the complex act, though these parts are found in the conduct of different individuals. The objective of the act is then found in the life-process of the group, not in those of the separate individuals alone. The full social object would not exist in the environments of the separate individuals of the societies of the Hymenoptera and termites, nor in the restricted societies of the vertebrates whose basis is found alone in physiological adjustment. A cow that licks the skin of a calf stuffed with hay, until the skin is worn away, and then eats the hay, or a woman who expends her parental impulse upon a poodle, cannot be said to have the full social object involved in the entire act in their environments. It would be necessary to piece together the environments of the different individuals or superimpose them upon each other to reach the environment and objects of the societies in question.

Where forms such as those of the Hymenoptera and the termites exhibit great plasticity in development, social acts based on physiological adjustment, and corresponding societies, have reached astonishing complexity. But when the limit of that plasticity is reached, the limit of the social act and the society is reached also. Where, as among the vertebrates, that physiological adjustment which mediates a social act is limited and fixed, the societies of this type are correspondingly insignificant. But another type of social act, and its corresponding society and object, has been at least suggested by the description of the social act based upon physiological adjustment. Such an act would be one in which the different parts of the act which belong to different individuals should appear in the act of each individual. This cannot mean, however, that the single individual could carry out the entire act, for then, even if it were possible, it would cease to be a social act, nor could the stimulus which calls out his own part of the complex act be that which calls out the other parts of the act in so far as they appear in his conduct. If the social object is to appear in his experience, it must be that the stimuli which set free the responses of the others involved in the act should be present in his experience, not as stimuli to his response, but as stimuli for the responses of others; and this implies that the social situation which arises after the completion of one phase of the act, which serves as the stimulus for the next participant in the complex procedure, shall in some sense be in the experience of the first actor, tending to call out, not his own response, but that of the succeeding actor. Let us make the impossible assumption that the wasp, in stinging a spider which it stores with its egg, finds in the spider a social object in the sense which I have specified. The spider would have to exist in the experience of the wasp as live but quiescent food for the larva when it emerges from the egg. In order that the paralyzed spider should so appear to the wasp, the wasp would need to be subject to the same stimulus as that which sets free the response of the larva; in other words, the wasp would need to be able to respond in some degree as the larva. And of course the wasp would have to view the spider under the time dimension, grafting a hypothetical future onto its passing present, but the occasion for this would have to lie in the wasp's tending to respond in rôle of larva to the appropriate food which it is placing in storage. This, then, presents another possible principle of social organization, as distinguished from that of physiological differentiation. If the objects that answer to the complex social act can exist spatio-temporally in the experience of the different members of the society, as stimuli that set free not only their own responses, but also as stimuli to the responses of those who share in the composite act, a principle of co-ordination might be found which would not depend upon physiological differentiation. And one necessary psychological condition for this would be that the individual should have in some fashion present in his organism the tendencies to respond as the other participants in the act will respond. Much more than this would be involved, but this at least would be a necessary precondition. A social object answering to the responses of different individuals in a society could be conceived of as existing in the experiences of individuals in that society, if the different responses of these individuals in the complex acts could be found in sufficient degree in the natures of separate individuals to render them sensitive to the different values of the object answering to the parts of the act.

The cortex of the vertebrate central nervous system provides at least a part of the mechanism which might make this possible. The nervous currents from the column and the stem of the brain to the cortex can there bring the acts that go out from these lower centers into relation with each other so that more complex processes and adjustments can arise. The centers and paths of the cortex represent an indefinite number of possible actions; particularly they represent acts which, being in competition with each other, inhibit each other, and present the problem of organization and adjustment so that overt conduct may proceed. In the currents and cross-currents in the gray matter and its association fibers, there exist the tendencies to an indefinite number of responses. Answering to these adjustments are the objects organized into a field of action, not only spatially but temporally; for the tendency to grasp the distant object, while already excited, is so linked with the processes of approach that it does not get its overt expression till the intervening stretch is passed. In this vertebrate apparatus of conduct, then, the already excited predispositions to thousands of acts, that far transcend the outward accomplishments, furnish the inner attitudes implicating objects that are not immediate objectives of the individual's act.

But the cortex is not simply a mechanism. It is an organ that exists in fulfilling its function. If these tendencies to action which do not get immediate expression appear and persist, it is because they belong to the act that is going on. If, for example, property is a social object in the experience of men, as distinguished from the nut which the squirrel stores, it is because features of the food that one buys innervate the whole complex of responses by which property is not only acquired, but respected and protected, and this complex so innervated is an essential part of the act by which the man buys and stores his food. The point is not that buying food is a more complicated affair than picking it up from the ground, but that exchange is an act in which a man excites himself to give by making an offer. An offer is what it is because the presentation is a stimulus to give. One cannot exchange otherwise than by putting one's self in the attitude of the other party to the bargain. Property becomes a tangible object, because all essential phases of property appear in the actions of all those involved in exchange, and appear as essential features of the individual's action.

The individual in such an act is a self. If the cortex has become an organ of social conduct, and has made possible the appearance of social objects, it is because the individual has become a self, that is, an individual who organizes his own response by the tendencies on the part of others to respond to his act. He can do this because the mechanism of the vertebrate brain enables the individual to take these different attitudes in the formation of the act. But selves have appeared late in vertebrate evolution. The structure of the central nervous system is too minute to enable us to show the corresponding structural changes in the paths of the brain. It is only in the behavior of the human animal that we can trace this evolution. It has been customary to mark this stage in development by endowing man with a mind, or at least with a certain sort of mind. As long as consciousness is regarded as a sort of spiritual stuff out of which are fashioned sensations and affections and images and ideas or significances, a mind as a locus of these entities is an almost necessary assumption, but when these contents have been returned to things, the necessity of quarters for this furniture has disappeared also.

It lies beyond the bounds of this paper to follow out the implications of this shift for logic and epistemology, but there is one phase of all so-called mental processes which is central to this discussion, and that is self-consciousness. If the suggestions which I have made above should prove tenable, the self that is central to all so-called mental experience has appeared only in the social conduct of human vertebrates. It is just because the individual finds himself taking the attitudes of the others who are involved in his conduct that he becomes an object for himself. It is only by taking the roles of others that we have been able to come back to ourselves. We have seen above that the social object can exist for the individual only if the various parts of the whole social act carried out by other members of the society are in some fashion present in the conduct of the individual. It is further true that the self can exist for the individual only if he assumes the roles of the others. The presence in the conduct of the individual of the tendencies to act as others act may be, then, responsible for the appearance in the experience of the individual of a social object, i.e., an object answering to complex reactions of a number of individuals, and also for the appearance of the self. Indeed, these two appearances are correlative. Property can appear as an object only in so far as the individual stimulates himself to buy by a prospective offer to sell. Buying and selling are involved in each other. Something that can be exchanged can exist in the experience of the individual only in so far as he has in his own make-up the tendency to sell when he has also the tendency to buy. And he becomes a self in his experience only in so far as one attitude on his own part calls out the corresponding attitude in the social undertaking.

This is just what we imply in "self-consciousness." We appear as selves in our conduct in so far as we ourselves take the attitude that others take toward us, in these correlative activities. Perhaps as good an illustration of this as can be found is in a "right." Over against the protection of our lives or property, we assume the attitude of assent of all members in the community. We take the role of what may be called the "generalized other." And in doing this we appear as social objects, as selves. It is interesting to note that in the development of the individual child, there are two stages which present the two essential steps in attaining self-consciousness. The first stage is that of play, and the second that of the game, where these two are distinguished from each other. In play in this sense, the child is continually acting as a parent, a teacher, a preacher, a grocery man, a policeman, a pirate, or an Indian. It is the period of childish existence which Wordsworth has described as that of "endless imitation." It is the period of Froebel's kindergarten plays. In it, as Froebel recognized, the child is acquiring the rôles of those who belong to his society. This takes place because the child is continually exciting in himself the responses to his own social acts. In his infant dependence upon the responses of others to his own social stimuli, he is peculiarly sensitive to this relation. Having in his own nature the beginning of the parental response, he calls it out by his own appeals. The doll is the universal type of this, but before he plays with a doll, he responds in tone of voice and in attitude as his parents respond to his own cries and chortles. This has been denominated imitation, but the psychologist now recognizes that one imitates only in so far as the so-called imitated act can be called out in the individual by his appropriate stimulation. That is, one calls or tends to call out in himself the same response that he calls out in the other.

The play antedates the game. For in a game there is a regulated procedure, and rules. The child must not only take the role of the other, as he does in the play, but he must assume the various roles of all the participants in the game, and govern his action accordingly. If he plays first base, it is as the one to whom the ball will be thrown from the field or from the catcher. Their organized reactions to him he has imbedded in his own playing of the different positions, and this organized reaction becomes what I have called the "generalized other" that accompanies and controls his conduct. And it is this generalized other in his experience which provides him with a self. I can only refer to the bearing of this childish play attitude upon so-called sympathetic magic. Primitive men call out in their own activity some simulacrum of the response which they are seeking from the world about. They are children crying in the night.

The mechanism of this implies that the individual who is stimulating others to response is at the same time arousing in himself the tendencies to the same reactions. Now, that in a complex social act which serves as the stimulus to another individual to his response is not as a rule fitted to call out the tendency to the same response in the individual himself. The hostile demeanor of one animal does not frighten the animal himself, presumably. Especially in the complex social reactions of the ants or termites or the bees, the part of the act of one form which does call out the appropriate reaction of another can hardly be conceived of as arousing a like reaction in the form in question, for here the complex social act is dependent upon physiological differentiation, such an unlikeness in structure exists that the same stimulus could not call out like responses. For such a mechanism as has been suggested, it is necessary to find first of all some stimulus in the social conduct of the members of an authentic group that can call out in the individual, that is responsible for it, the same response that it calls out in the other; and in the second place, the individuals in the group must be of such like structure that the stimulus will have the same value for one form that it has for the other. Such a type of social stimulus is found in the vocal gesture in a human society. The term gesture I am using to refer to that part of the act or attitude of one individual engaged in a social act which serves as the stimulus to another individual to carry out his part of the whole act. Illustrations of gestures, so defined, may be found in the attitudes and movements of others to which we respond in passing them in a crowd, in the turning of the head toward the glance of another's eye, in the hostile attitude assumed over against a threatening gesture, in the thousand and one different attitudes which we assume toward different modulations of the human voice, or in the attitudes and suggestions of movements in boxers or fencers, to which responses are so nicely adjusted. It is to be noted that the attitudes to which I have referred are but stages in the act as they appear to others, and include expressions of countenance, positions of the body, changes in breathing rhythm, outward evidence of circulatory changes, and vocal sounds. In general these so-called gestures belong to the beginning of the overt act, for the adjustments of others to the social process are best made early in the act. Gestures are, then, the early stages in the overt social act to which other forms involved in the same act respond. Our interest is in finding gestures which can affect the individual that is responsible for them in the same manner as that in which they affect other individuals. The vocal gesture is at least one that assails our ears who make it in the same physiological fashion as that in which it affects others. We hear our own vocal gestures as others hear them. We may see or feel movements of our hands as others see or feel them, and these sights and feels have served in the place of the vocal gestures in the case of those who are congenitally deaf or deaf and blind. But it has been the vocal gesture that has pre-eminently provided the medium of social organization in human society. It belongs historically to the beginning of the act, for it arises out of the change in breathing rhythm that accompanies the preparation for sudden action, those actions to which other forms must be nicely adjusted.

If, then, a vocal gesture arouses in the individual who makes it a tendency to the same response that it arouses in another, and this beginning of an act of the other in himself enters into his experience, he will find himself tending to act toward himself as the other acts toward him. In our self-conscious experience we understand what he does or says. The possibility of this entering into his experience we have found in the cortex of the human brain. There the co-ordinations answering to an indefinite number of acts may be excited, and while holding each other in check enter into the neural process of adjustment which leads to the final overt conduct. If one pronounces and hears himself pronounce the word "table," he has aroused in himself the organized attitudes of his response to that object, in the same fashion as that in which he has aroused it in another. We commonly call such an aroused organized attitude an idea, and the ideas of what we are saying accompany all of our significant speech. If we may trust to the statement in one of St. Paul's epistles, some of the saints spoke with tongues which had no significance to them. They made sounds which called out no response in those that made them. The sounds were without meaning. Where a vocal gesture uttered by one individual leads to a certain response in another, we may call it a symbol of that act; where it arouses in the man who makes it the tendency to the same response, we may call it a significant symbol. These organized attitudes which we arouse in ourselves when we talk to others are, then, the ideas which we say are in our minds, and in so far as they arouse the same attitudes in others, they are in their minds, in so far as they are self-conscious in the sense in which I have used that term. But it is not necessary that we should talk to another to have these ideas. We can talk to ourselves, and this we do in the inner forum of what we call thought. We are in possession of selves just in so far as we can and do take the attitudes of others toward ourselves and respond to those attitudes. We approve of ourselves and condemn ourselves. We pat ourselves upon the back and in blind fury attack ourselves. We assume the generalized attitude of the group, in the censor that stands at the door of our imagery and inner conversations, and in the affirmation of the laws and axioms of the universe of discourse.

Quod semper, quod ubique. Our thinking is an inner conversation in which we may be taking the roles of specific acquaintances over against ourselves, but usually it is with what I have termed the "generalized other" that we converse, and so attain to the levels of abstract thinking, and that impersonality, that so-called objectivity that we cherish. In this fashion, I conceive, have selves arisen in human behavior and with the selves their minds. It is an interesting study, that of the manner in which the self and its mind arises in every child, and the indications of the corresponding manner in which it arose in primitive man. I cannot enter into a discussion of this. I do wish, however, to refer to some of the implications of this conception of the self for the theory of social control.

I wish to recur to the position, taken earlier in this paper, that, if we recognize that experience is a process continually passing into the future, objects exist in nature as the patterns of our actions. If we reduce the world to a fictitious instantaneous present, all objects fall to pieces. There is no reason to be found, except in an equally fictitious mind, why any lines should be drawn about any group of physical particles, constituting them objects. However, no such knife-edge present exists. Even in the so-called specious present there is a passage, in which there is succession, and both past and future are there, and the present is only that section in which, from the standpoint of action, both are involved. When we take this passage of nature seriously, we see that the object of perception is the existent future of the act. The food is what the animal will eat, and his refuge is the burrow where he will escape from his pursuer. Of course the future is, as future, contingent. He may not escape, but in nature it exists there as the counterpart of his act. So far as there are fixed relations there, they are of the past, and the object involves both, but the form that it has arises from the ongoing act. Evolutionary biology, in so far as it is not mere physics and chemistry, proceeds perhaps unwittingly upon this assumption, and so does social science in so far as it is not static. Its objects are in terms of the habitat, the environment. They are fashioned by reactions. I am merely affirming the existence of these objects, affirming them as existent in a passing universe answering to acts.

In so far as there are social acts, there are social objects, and I take it that social control is bringing the act of the individual into relation with this social object. With the control of the object over the act, we are abundantly familiar. Just because the object is the form of the act, in this character it controls the expression of the act. The vision of the distant object is not only the stimulus to movement toward it. It is also, in its changing distance values, a continual control of the act of approach. The contours of the object determine the organization of the act of its seizure, but in this case the whole act is in the individual and the object is in his field of experience. Barring a breakdown in the structure or function, the very existence of the object insures its control of the act. In the social act, however, the act is distributed among a number of individuals. While there is or may be an object answering to each part of the act, existing in the experience of each individual, in the case of societies dependent upon physiological differentiation the whole object does not exist in the experience of any individual. The control may be exercised through the survival of those physiological differentiations that still carry out the life-process involved in the complex act. No complication of the act which did not mediate this could survive. Or we may take refuge in a controlling factor in the act, as does Bergson, but this is not the situation that interests us. The human societies in which we are interested are societies of selves. The human individual is a self only in so far as he takes the attitude of another toward himself. In so far as this attitude is that of a number of others, and in so far as he can assume the organized attitudes of a number that are co-operating in a common activity, he takes the attitudes of the group toward himself, and in taking this or these attitudes he is defining the object of the group, that which defines and controls the response. Social control, then, will depend upon the degree to which the individual does assume the attitudes of those in the group who are involved with him in his social activities. In the illustration already used, the man who buys controls his purchase from the standpoint of a value in the object that exists for him only in so far as he takes the attitude of a seller as well as a buyer. Value exists as an object only for individuals within whose acts in exchange are present those attitudes which belong to the acts of the others who are essential to the exchange.

The act of exchange becomes very complicated; the degree to which all the essential acts involved in it enter into the acts of all those engaged therein varies enormously, and the control which the object, i.e., the value, exercises over the acts varies proportionately. The Marxian theory of state ownership of capital, i.e., of exclusive state production, is a striking illustration of the breakdown of such control. The social object, successful economic production, as presented in this theory, fails to assume the attitudes of individual initiative which successful economic production implies. Democratic government, on the theory of action through universal interest in the issues of a campaign, breaks down as a control, and surrenders the government largely to the political machine, whose object more nearly answers to the attitudes of the voters and the non-voters.

Social control depends, then, upon the degree to which the individuals in society are able to assume the attitudes of the others who are involved with them in common endeavor. For the social object will always answer to the act developing itself in self-consciousness. Besides property, all of the institutions are such objects, and serve to control individuals who find in them the organization of their own social responses.

The individual does not, of course, assume the attitudes of the numberless others who are in one way or another implicated in his social conduct, except in so far as the attitudes of others are uniform under like circumstances. One assumes, as I have said, the attitudes of generalized others. But even with this advantage of the universal over the multiplicity of its numberless instances, the number of different responses that enter into our social conduct seems to defy any capacity of any individual to assume the rôles which would be essential to define our social objects. And yet, though modern life has become indefinitely more complex than it was in earlier periods of human history, it is far easier for the modern man than for his predecessor to put himself in the place of those who contribute to his necessities, who share with him the functions of government, or join with him in determining prices. It is not the number of participants, or even the number of different functions, that is of primary importance. The important question is whether these various forms of activities belong so naturally to the member of a human society that, in taking the role of another, his activities are found to belong to one's own nature. As long as the complexities of human society do not exceed those of the central nervous system, the problem of an adequate social object, which is identical with that of an adequate self-consciousness, is not that of becoming acquainted with the indefinite number of acts that are involved in social behavior, but that of so overcoming the distances in space and time, and the barriers of language and convention and social status, that we can converse with ourselves in the roles of those who are involved with us in the common undertaking of life. A journalism that is insatiably curious about the human attitudes of all of us is the sign of the times. The other curiosities as to the conditions under which other people live, and work, and fight each other, and love each other, follow from the fundamental curiosity which is the passion of self-consciousness. We must be others if we are to be ourselves. The modern realistic novel has done more than technical education in fashioning the social object that spells social control. If we can bring people together so that they can enter into each other's lives, they will inevitably have a common object, which will control their common conduct.

The task, however, is enormous enough, for it involves not simply breaking down passive barriers such as those of distance in space and time and vernacular, but those fixed attitudes of custom and status in which our selves are imbedded. Any self is a social self, but it is restricted to the group whose roles it assumes, and it will never abandon

this self until it finds itself entering into the larger society and maintaining itself there. The whole history of warfare between societies and within societies shows how much more readily and with how much greater emotional thrill we realize our selves in opposition to common enemies than in collaboration with them. All over Europe, and more specifically at Geneva, we see nationals with great distrust and constant rebounds trying to put themselves in each other's places and still preserve the selves that have existed upon enmities, that they may reach the common ground where they may avoid the horror of war, and meliorate unendurable economic conditions. A Dawes Plan is such a social object, coming painfully into existence, that may control the conflicting interests of hostile communities, but only if each can in some degree put himself in the other's place in operating it. The World Court and the League of Nations are other such social objects that sketch out common plans of action if there are national selves that can realize themselves in the collaborating attitudes of others.

161

PART III

Knowledge and Inquiry

An activist epistemology – one that considers knowledge as a function of experience – takes many forms. The dominant American orientation has been pragmatist, yet there are radical differences within that tradition and the authors represented here offer competing approaches.

By the 1830s few women were better known and better loved and hated than Frances Wright. A popular lecturer, Wright spoke for women and workers at a time when these two groups were largely excluded from leadership, prosperity, and individual rights, on the grounds that they were unable to understand the issues at hand. Wright called for a dramatic reformation of how Americans understood knowledge and the process of inquiry. For Wright, knowledge is power and if oppressed women and workers hoped to become free it would be by means of generating a new epistemology, a new conception of knowing in a democracy. Wright's call for a new conception of knowledge and inquiry echoes the call of Cadwallader Colden, former Lieutenant Governor of the British province of New York, an adopted Mohawk and author of the first English language history of the Iroquois Confederacy. Writing in the middle of the eighteenth century, Colden offered a critique of the dominant epistemologies of European philosophy and proposed an alternative grounded in the idea that what is known is the product of interaction. To know what a thing is, in effect, is to know what it does in interaction. This general commitment of Colden, and the idea of an activist epistemology advocated by Wright, help to set the stage for the emergence of American pragmatism, here presented in the work of Charles Sanders Peirce and John Dewey.

For Peirce and Dewey, knowledge is an interactive process that demands both a contextual approach to knowing and a recognition of fallibilism. Pragmatists challenge the central distinction inherited from British empiricism and continental rationalism that facts and values are fundamentally separate. Instead, they argue, knowing is a value-charged practice, grounded in situations and demanding the recognition of pluralism, both epistemological and ontological.

Susanne Langer, trained in the American pragmatist tradition, proposes to connect the pragmatist conception of knowledge to the methods and concerns of the positivist empiricism that came to dominate academic philosophy by the middle of the twentieth century. The conception of knowledge as the product of interaction provides a central commitment with which to engage the response by American thinkers to the lived problems of American society, which both affirms the necessity of pluralism and the need, at times, to resolve situations in collective action.

Robert Bunge's "Sioux Epistemology" draws from the pragmatist tradition yet creates a way of seeing within modernity, reforming notions of polygraphic knowing, and offering his own philosophy of BP – beyond pragmatism.

14

Knowledge

Frances Wright

Introduction

Frances Wright (1795–1852) was born in Scotland, raised in London, and emigrated to the United States in the 1820s. She became known in America for her book *Views of Society and Manners in America* (1821), a report of an 1818 trip to North America. When she returned to America in 1824, she helped to found a utopian community, Nashoba, in Tennessee. Later, working with Robert Dale Owen, son of the founder of the utopian community New Harmony, she edited the *New Harmony Gazette* and the *Free Enquirer* and was a vocal advocate for the abolition of slavery and for equal rights for women. The selection here is one of Wright's lectures, delivered to an audience of working-class people in Philadelphia.

Introductory Address to the Second Course

[As delivered for the second time in New York]

The circumstances under which I now meet this assemblage of the people of New York, are, I believe, unparalleled in the history of the world. All nations have had their revolutions – all cities, in the hitherto unfortunate annals of the human race, their disturbances, and their disturbers; but truly, the sight and the sound is alike novel, of

Taken from *Course of Popular Lectures*, republished in *Life, Letters, and Lectures, 1834/1844* (New York: Arno Press, 1972).

privilege and pretension arraying all the forces of a *would-be* hierarchy and a *would-be* aristocracy, to assassinate the liberties of a free state in the person of a single individual, and to outrage public order and public decency, by ribald slanders and incendiary threats, against the reputation and person of a woman. Truly the signs are novel which mark this hour, and truly the place assigned to myself by the clamour and artifice of a body of men, trembling for privileges and profits, and eager to drown with noisy words that which they cannot confute by argument might cower the strength of one less confident in her cause or less ardent for its success. But, so surely as I know the strength of the ground which I have assumed, and the weakness of that which *they* have to defend, will I stand fast, and stand firm. And did I need, in this hour, ought beyond or without my own bosom to sustain me, I should find it in my conviction of the destined triumph of the cause I serve, and in the pure decision of wiser and happier generations to come, who (be what it may, the momentary issue of this hour, and its momentary consequences, to me) shall write my name and preserve my memory among those of the champions of human liberty and heralds of human improvement.

I know of none, from the modest Socrates and gentle Jesus, down to the least or the greatest reformers of our own time, who have remembered the poor, the ignorant, or the oppressed, raised their voice in favour of more equal distributions of knowledge and liberty, or dared to investigate the causes of vice and wretchedness, with a view to their remedy; I know of none, I say, who have not been the mark of persecution, drunk the poison of calumny, or borne the cross of martyrdom. What better and wiser have endured, I shall not lack courage to meet. Having put my hand to the plough, I will not draw back, nor, having met the challenge so long cast at human nature and human reason, alike by privilege and superstition, will I refuse to meet all hazards in their cause.

I have already pledged myself to show evidence for all my opinions; I pledge myself farther, to *show all my opinions*, for, so truly as I have taken man for my study, and his happiness for my object, do I believe that all my opinions can bring facts to their support, and will, sooner or later, find an echo in every thinking mind and feeling heart.

It hath been asked again and again, amid all the confusion of reports and assertions, threats and declamations, conjured up to fright the timidity of woman, and alarm the protecting tenderness of man, why I do not reply to the slander of enemies, and supply arguments to friends?

If among the present assemblage there be any who have followed all or some of my previous discourses, I would put it to their memory and their reason, if I, on those occasions, presented arguments and evidence for the opinions advanced; and if any one of those arguments has been by a single individual refuted, or that evidence, in whole or in part, by one single individual impugned. And I will here call upon you to observe, that my opponents have had the command of the whole press and all the pulpits of this city. To what account have these been turned? To heap on my name and person, outrage and abuse. To libel my audience, intimidate women, attack the interests of men, invoke the interference of the magistracy of the city, and threaten the lessees of this house with "riot, fire, and bloodshed."

My friends, I appeal to your reason, if, by resorting to such measures, my opponents have not substantiated their own weakness, and supplied an acknowledgment, that so far as I have spoken they cannot gainsay me?

And now, then, I will ask, and that rather for the sake of good order and common sense, than for any personal interest of mine, if on the topics I *have* spoken, I have neither outraged your reason nor your feelings, and remain unanswered by my enemies – if it be not at the least probable that on the topics I have *not* spoken, I may be rational also. I have nothing in my head or my heart to hold back from such my fellow creatures, as may desire to read either, with a view to the eliciting of truth. I

have already sketched out to you the subject matter of many future investigations, embracing all our weightiest duties and responsibilities, as reasoning and sentient beings.

But, as I have opened our discussions in order, so *in order* must I pursue them, if pursued at all. We cannot speak to all things at once, nor demonstrate the last problem in Euclid, ere we have substantiated the first.

In compliance with the wishes of a mass of the citizens, as conveyed to me by individuals, and attested by my own observations of the many disappointed of entrance in our former places of meeting, I have consented to redeliver my elementary course on the nature of all knowledge, physical and moral.

Without a thorough understanding of the primary truths which it has been my attempt, in this elementary course, familiarly to elucidate, the public mind must be unfit for any discussion; therefore it is, that I commence with these primary truths; and therefore it is, that I shall decline the discussion of all other topics, until our first premises being laid, we are supplied with a standard by which to test all existing opinions and existing practice.

Whenever hereafter I may be called, in peace and with seriousness, to deliver my views on any subject of general interest to my fellow beings, I will meet their wishes. My opinions, whatever they may be, I am not accustomed to *defend*, but I will willingly *explain*; and explain with that simplicity, which befits inquiry after truth, and that tenderness to the feelings of others, which I think I am not apt to forget.

Before we open our discussions of the evening, I would suggest to the audience, the propriety of bearing in mind the circumstances under which we meet, the former futile attempts to disturb our meetings in the Masonic Hall, and the possible presence of some mistaken and misguided individuals, ready to excite false alarm, and to take advantage of any the least disturbance, with a view to the injury of the cause of human improvement, which we are met to promote, and to the injury of the lessees of the building which we now occupy.

In case of any attempt to disturb our meeting, by cries of alarm, I beg the audience to bear in mind, that the house is under vigilant and double police.

I shall now, then, present you with the opening discourse, formerly delivered in the Masonic Hall. And, as it will be in matter and words the same, you will judge of the accuracy of the reports presented in your daily papers.

Lecture I: On the Nature of Knowledge

Who among us, that hath cast even an occasional and slightly observant glance on the face of society, but must have remarked the differing opinions, which distract the human mind; the opposing creeds and systems, each asserting its claim to infallibility, and rallying around its standard pertinacious disciples, enthusiastic proselytes, ardent apologists, fiery combatants, obsequious worshippers, conscientious followers, and devoted martyrs? If we extend our observation over the surface of our globe, and consider its diversified population, however varied in hue and feature, we find it yet more varied in opinions, in one opinion only invariably agreed, viz. that of its infallibility. The worshipper of sculptured idols bows before the image of his hand, and shrinks with unfeigned terror, if a sacrilegious intruder profane the sanctuary of his superstition. The adorer of the bright luminary which marks our days and seasons, sees in the resplendent orb, not a link in the vast chain of material existence, but the source of all existence; and so from the most unpretending savage, to the most lettered nation of a lettered age, we find *all* shaping their superstitions, according to the measure of their ignorance or their knowledge, and each devoutly believing his faith and practice to be the true and the just. Or let us confine our observation within the limits of the country we inhabit – how varying the creeds arising out of one system of faith! How contradictory the assertions and expectations of sects, all equally positive, and equally, we may presume, conscientious! How conflicting the opinions and feelings of men upon all subjects, trivial or important! until we are tempted to exclaim, "Where, then, is right or wrong but in human imagination, and what is truth more than blind opinion?" Few of us prone to study or observation, yet educated after existing methods, but must have asked these questions, and halted for a reply.

Should the problem here started be, I say not impossible, but even difficult of solution, lamentable must be the human condition to the end of time! Had truth no test – no standard – no positive, no tangible existence, behold us, then, sold to error, and, while to error, to misery, through all the generations of our race! But, fortunately, the answer is simple; only too simple, it would appear, for mystery-loving, mystery-seeking man, to perceive and acknowledge.

Let not the present audience imagine, that I am about to add one more to the already uncountable, unnameable systems, which distract the understandings of men, or to draw yet new doctrines and precepts from the fertile alembic of the human brain. I request you to behold in me an inquirer, not a teacher; one who conceives of truth as a jewel to be found, not to be coined; a treasure to be discovered by observation, and accumulated by careful, persevering industry, not invented and manufactured by learned art or aspiring quackery, like the once fashionable elixer of immortality and philosopher's stone. My object will be simply to take with you a survey of the field of human inquiry; to ascertain its nature, its extent, its boundaries, its limits; to discover, in the first place, what there is for us to know; secondly, the means we possess for acquiring such knowledge as is of possible attainment, and, thirdly, having satisfied ourselves as to what can be known, and as to what we know, to seek in our knowledge the test of our opinions.

It must be admitted, that, as all our opinions must rest upon some evidence, real or imagined, so upon the truth or falsehood of the evidence admitted, must rest the truth or falsehood of the opinions based thereupon. It is evident, therefore, that before we can apply any safe or certain test to our opinions, we must well understand the nature of true evidence; before we can reflect, we must have something to reflect upon; before we can think accurately respecting any thing, we must know accurately all relating to it; and wheresoever our knowledge be complete, will our opinion be just.

Seeing, then, that just opinions are the result of just knowledge, and perceiving, as we must all perceive, how much confusion arises to society out of the conflicting opinions, which divide alike nations and families into sects and parties, it is equally our interest and our duty, to aim at the acquisition of just knowledge, with a view to the formation of just opinions. And, as we shall hereafter have occasion to observe, just practice being the result of past opinions, and human happiness being the certain result of just practice, it is equally our interest and our duty to aim at the formation of just opinions, with a view to the attainment of happiness.

We shall, therefore, open our investigations by an inquiry into the nature and object of just knowledge; and if we succeed in ascertaining these, we will farther examine the causes which at present impede our progress, and the means best calculated at once to remove such impediments, and to advance us in the course which it is our interest to pursue.

If we consider man in comparison with other animals, we find him distinguished by one principle. This principle, which is shared by no other existence within the range of our observation, gives him all his pre-eminence. It constitutes, indeed, all his existence. By its neglect or cultivation he remains ignorant and degraded, or becomes intelligent and happy; and, as he owes to it all that has elevated him above the brute in past time or at the present, so in it may he find rich hope and promise for the future.

Much does it behove us, then, earnestly to consider this distinguishing principle of our nature. Much does it behove us to understand the fulness of its importance and its power, and to know that, as without it we should be as the beasts of the field, so with it we may rise in the scale of being, until every vice which now degrades, every fear which unnerves, and every prejudice which enchains us, shall disappear beneath its influence.

I advert to the simple but all-important principle of improvement. Weak as we are, compared to the healthy strength we are conscious would be desirable; ignorant as we are, compared to the height, and breadth, and depth of knowledge which extends around us as far as the universal range of matter itself; miserable as we are, compared to the happiness of which we feel ourselves capable, yet in this living principle we see nothing beyond or above us, nothing to which we or our descendants may not attain, of great, of beautiful, of excellent. But to *feel* the power of this mighty principle, to urge it forward in its course, and accelerate the change in our condition which it promises, we must awaken to its observation.

Are we yet awake to this? Do we know what we are, or have we ever asked ourselves what we might be? Are we even desirous of becoming wiser, and better, and happier? and, if desirous, are we earnestly applied to effect the change?

It is probable that some vague desire of advancing in knowledge pervades every bosom. We find every where some deference paid to the great principle of our nature in the growing demand for schools and colleges. We seem to have discovered that the faculties of man demand care for

their development; and that, like the marble of the quarry, he must be shaped and polished ere he will present the line of beauty.

But, alas! here is the difficulty. If agreed that something must be done, we see but darkly what that something is. While eager to be doing, we are still in doubt both as to the end to be attained and the means to be employed. While anxious to learn, we are but too often ignorant of the very nature of knowledge. We are unacquainted with her haunts and her habitation, and seek her where she is not to be found. It may be useful, then, before we engage in the labyrinth of learning, that we examine carefully what knowledge is.

If we ask this in our schools, we shall be told, that knowledge is an acquaintance with the structure of our own language; a familiarity with foreign, especially with dead languages. We shall, moreover, hear of history, geography, astronomy, &c. Do we ask the same in our colleges, we shall hear farther of law, medicine, surgery, theology, mathematics, chemistry, and philosophy, natural and mental: and we shall be farther told, that when a youth has mastered all these sounding names, and puzzled through all the learning, useful or useless, attached to them – he is well taught and thoroughly educated. It may be so. And yet may he be also very ignorant of what it most imports him to know. Nay, more! in despite of an intimate acquaintance with all the most esteemed branches of knowledge, he may be utterly unacquainted with the object and nature of knowledge itself. Let us, then, enquire again, *what knowledge is.*

It is not, in the first place, acquaintance with ourselves? and secondly, with all things to which we stand in relation?

How are we to obtain this acquaintance? By observation and patient inquiry.

What are the means we possess from this observation and inquiry? Our senses; and our faculties, as awakened and improved in and by the exercise of our senses.

Let us now examine what are the objects really submitted to the investigation of our senses.

These may be all embraced under the generic term matter, implying the whole of existence within the range of our inspection.

Were we to proceed minutely in our analysis, we should observe that matter, as existing around us, appears under three forms, the gaseous, the liquid, and the solid; and that under one or other of these forms may be accurately classed all that is submitted to our observation – all, in short, that we can see, hear, feel, taste, or smell. But to enter at present into such details would be foreign to our purpose.

I shall, therefore, pass on to observe that the accurate and patient investigation of matter, in all its subdivisions, together with all its qualities and changes, constitutes a just education. And that in proportion as we ascertain, in the course of investigation, the real qualities and actual changes of matter, together with the judicious application of all things to the use of man, and influence of all occurrences on the happiness of man, so do we acquire knowledge. In other words, knowledge is an accumulation of facts, and signifies *things known*. In proportion, therefore, as the sphere of our observation is large, and our investigation of all within that sphere careful, in proportion is our knowledge.

The view of knowledge we have here taken is simple; and it may be observed, that not in this case only, but in all others, accuracy and simplicity go hand in hand. All truth is simple, for truth is only fact. The means of attaining truth are equally simple. We have but to seek and we shall find; to open our eyes and our ears; without prejudice to observe; without fear to listen, and dispassionately to examine, compare, and draw conclusions.

The field of knowledge is around, and about, and within us. Let us not be alarmed by sounding words, and let us not be *deceived* by them. Let us look to things. It is things which we have to consider. Words are, or, more correctly, should be, only the signs of things. I say they *should be*; for it is a most lamentable truth, that they are now very generally conceived to constitute the very substance of knowledge. Words, indeed, should seem at present contrived rather for the purpose of confusing our ideas, than administering to their distinctness and arrangement. Instead of viewing them as the shadows, we mistake them for the substance; and conceive that in proportion as we enlarge our vocabulary, we multiply our acquirements.

Vain, then, will be the attempt to increase our knowledge, until we understand where we are to look for it, and in what it consists. Here is the first stepping stone. Let our foot but firmly strike it, and our after progress is easy.

And in what lies the importance of this first step in human knowledge? In the accuracy which it brings to all our ideas. It places us at once on firm ground, introduces us into the field of real inquiry, and lays the rein of the imagination in the hand of the judgment. Difficult were it to exaggerate the importance of the step which involves such consequences. Until we bring accuracy to our thoughts, and, we may add, accuracy to the words employed for their expression – we can make no progress. We may wander, indeed, and most certainly shall wander, in various paths; but they will be paths of error. The straight broad road of improvement it will not be ours to tread, until we take heed unto our feet, and know always whither we are going.

Imagine – and how easy is it to imagine, when we have but to look around us or within ourselves – imagine the confusion of hopes, desires, ambitions, and expectations, with which the scholar enters, and but too often leaves the halls of science. On entering them, he conceives that some mysterious veil, like the screen of the holy of holies, is about to be withdrawn, and that he is to look at things far removed from real life, and raised far above the vulgar apprehension. On leaving them, he has his memory surcharged with a confusion of ideas, and a yet more confusion of words. He knows, perhaps, the properties of ciphers and of angels; the names and classification of birds, fishes, quadrupeds, insects, and minerals; the chemical affinities of bodies; can measure star from star; analyze invisible substances; detail in chronological order the rise and fall of nations, with their arts, sciences, and sects of philosophy. He can do all this, and more; and yet, perhaps, is there neither arrangement in his knowledge, distinctness in his ideas, nor accuracy in his language. And, while possessed of many valuable facts, there is blended with all and with each, a thousand illusions. Thus it is that so many wordy pedants, and hair-brained or shallow disputants, are sent forth from the schools of all countries, while those who do honour to their species, by rendering service in their generation, are, most generally, what is called self-taught. And the reason of this is evident. Our existing modes of education, being equally false and deficient, and the instruction of our schools full of fallacies, theories, and hypotheses, the more regularly a youth is trained in fashionable learning, the more confused is usually his perception of things, and the more prostrated his reason by the dogmatism of teachers, the sophism of words, and the false principles engrafted by means of pretended science, ostentatiously inculcated, or real science, erroneously imparted. While, on the other hand, a vigorous intellect, if stimulated by fortunate circumstances to inquiry, and left to accumulate information by the efforts of its own industry, though its early progress may be slow, and its aberrations numerous, yet in the free exercise of its powers, is more likely to collect accurate knowledge, than those who are methodically fed with learned error and learnedly disguised truth.

I shall have occasion, in a more advanced stage of our inquiries, to examine minutely the errors in the existing mode of instruction, and which are of a nature to perplex the human mind from infancy to age, and to make even learning an additional stumbling block in the way of knowledge. For the present, I would confine myself to establishing the simple position, that *all real knowledge is derived from positive sensations.*

In proportion to the number of senses we bring to bear upon an object, is the degree of our acquaintance with that object. Whatever we see, and feel, and attentively examine with *all* our senses, we *know*; and respecting the things thus investigated, we can afterwards form a correct opinion. Wherever, respecting such things, our opinions are erroneous, it is where our investigation of them has been insufficient, or our recollection of them imperfect; and the only certain way of rectifying the error, is to refer again to the object itself.

Things which we have not ourselves examined, and occurrences which we have not ourselves witnessed, but which we receive on the attested sensations of others, we may *believe*, but we do not *know*. Now, as these two modes of intellectual assent are generally, if not universally, confounded; and, as their accurate distinction is, in its consequences, of immense importance, I shall risk the straining of your attention for a few minutes, while I attempt its elucidation.

To select a familiar, and at the moment a pertinent example. The present audience *know* that an individual is now addressing them, because they see her person, and hear her voice. They may *believe* that some other speaker occupies the pulpit of a church in this town, if assured to that effect by a person of ordinary veracity; but, let the testimony of that person be as well substantiated in their opinion as possible, the fact received through his reported sensations, they would *believe*; the fact of my presence, admitted upon their own sensations, they will *know*.

My hearers will understand that my object in presenting these definitions, is not to draw a mere verbal distinction, but a distinction between different states of the human mind; the distinction in words only being important, in that it is necessary to a clear understanding of the mental phenomena it is desirable to illustrate.

Did the limits of our present discourse permit such a development, or did I not apprehend to weary the attention, it would not be difficult to draw the line between knowledge and belief, and again between the different grades of belief, through all the varieties of intellectual assent from the matter-of-fact certainty supplied by knowledge, down to the lowest stage of probability supplied by belief. But having suggested the distinction, I must leave you to draw it for yourselves; requesting you only to observe – that, as your own positive sensations can alone give you knowledge of a thing, so is your belief of any thing stronger, in proportion as you can more accurately establish, or approach nearer to, the sensations of those whose testimony you receive.

Thus: if a friend, or, more particularly, if several friends of tried veracity and approved judgment, relate to us a circumstance of which they declare themselves to have been attentive spectators – our belief is of the highest kind. If they relate a circumstance which they shall have received from another, or from other individuals, for whose veracity and judgment they also vouch, our belief, though in a measure accorded, is very considerably weakened; and so on, until, after a few more removes from the original sensations of the reported spectators, our belief is reduced to zero.

But farther, it is here of importance to observe that belief – that is, the belief of a well trained mind – can never be accorded to the attested sensations of others, should those attested sensations be contradicted by our own well established experience, or by the unvarying and agreeing experience of mankind. Thus: should one, or twenty, or a thousand individuals, swear to the fact of having seen a man, by effort of his unaided volition, raise himself through the air to the top of the steeple in this city, we should believe – what? Not the eccentric occurrence, however attested, but one of two very common occurrences – either that the individuals were seeking to impose upon us, or that their own ignorant credulity had been deceived by false appearances.

But now let us suppose a case, very likely to be presented in form of an objection, although in reality capable of furnishing a forcible elucidation of the simple truth we are now attempting to illustrate. Let us suppose that some of our organs should become diseased – those of sight, for instance; and that we should, in consequence, imagine the appearance of an object not perceptible to more healthy individuals. If the phantasy presented nothing uncommon in any of its parts, or inconsistent with the course of previous sensations, we should at first, undoubtedly, yield credence to our eyes; until, in consequence, perhaps, of some incongruity, we should be led to appeal to our other senses, when, if they did not concur with the testimony of our vision, we should distinguish the appearance, immediately, for the effect of disease, and apply ourselves, on the instant, to its investigation and remedy.

But again, let us suppose (a case by no means uncommon in the history of the human pathology) that two of our senses should be diseased – our sight and our hearing; and that we should in consequence see the spectral illusion of a human being; and, farther, imagine such illusion to discourse with us. Our belief would be now strongly accorded to this two–fold evidence; but we should still have a resource in our sense of touch. Should this last not confirm the evidence supplied by our vision and our hearing, we should suspect as in the former case, the health of our organs, and consult on the subject with an able physician.

But let us now suppose that *all* the organs of sense, in some individual, should become suddenly diseased, and sight, hearing, feeling, taste, and smell, should *combine* to cheat him into the belief of existences not perceptible to the more healthy sensations of his fellow creatures. I do not conceive that such an individual, however naturally strong or highly cultivated his judgment, and even supposing his judgment to retain its activity in the midst of the general disorder, could for any length of time struggle with the delusion, but must gradually yield intellectual assent to his diseased sensations, however incongruous these might be, or however at variance with past experience. I conceive that an individual thus diseased in all his organs of sense, must rapidly lose all control over his reasoning faculties, and present, consequently, to his fellow creatures, the afflicting spectacle of one labouring under mental insanity.

If we look to the unfortunate maniac, or to the sufferer tossing in fever delirium, we shall perceive how implicit the credence given to his diseased sensations. The phantoms which he hears, and feels, and sees, are all realities to him, and, as realities, govern his thoughts and decide his actions. How, in such cases, does the enlightened physician proceed? He does not argue with the incongruous ideas of his patient; he examines his disordered frame, and as he can restore healthy action to all its parts, so does he hope to restore healthy sensations to the body, and accurate ideas to the mind. Here, then, we see, in sickness as in health, our sensations supplying us with all intellectual food. In fever, they supply us with dreams; in health, if accurately studied, with knowledge.

The object of these observations is to show, that as we can only *know* a thing by its immediate contact with our senses, so is *all knowledge compounded of the accurately observed, accumulated, and agreeing sensations of mankind.*

The field of knowledge, then, we have observed to be the field of nature, or of material existence around and within us. The number of objects comprised within the circle of human observation, is so multiplied, and the properties or qualities of these objects so diversified, that with a view to convenient and suitable divisions in the great work of inspecting the whole, and also with a view to the applying of more order and method in the arrangement of the facts collated in the wide field of nature, they have been classed under different heads, each of which we may call a *branch of knowledge*, or, more succinctly, *a science.*

Thus: do we consider the various living tribes which people the elements? We class our observations under the head of natural history. Do we direct our attention to the structure and mechanism of their bodies? We designate the results of our inspection under the heads anatomy and physiology. Do we trace the order of occurrences and appearances in the wide field of nature? We note them under natural philosophy. Do we analyze substances and search out their simple elements? Chemistry. Do we apply ourselves to the measurement of bodies, or calculate the heights and distances of objects? Geometry. And so on, through all the range of human observation, extending from the relative position of the heavenly bodies, and accurate calculation of their courses, to the uses, habits, structure, and physiology of the delicate plant which carpets our earth.

Now, all the sciences, properly so called, being compounded of facts, ascertained or ascertainable by the sensations of each individual, so all that is not so ascertainable is not knowledge, only belief, and can never constitute for us matter–of–fact certainty, only greater or less probability. In elucidation, we might remark that the facts we glean, in the study of chemistry, supply us with knowledge; those received upon testimony, as in the study of history, supply us with probabilities, or with improbabilities, as it may be, and constitute belief.

Now, again – as our knowledge is supplied by our own individual sensations, and our belief by the attested sensations of others, it is possible, while pretending to communicate knowledge, only to communicate belief. This we know to be the system pursued in all our schools and colleges, where the truths of the most demonstrable sciences are presented under the disguise of oral or written lessons, instead of being exposed, in practical illustrations, to the eye, and the ear, and the touch, in the simple, incontrovertible fact. This method, while it tends to hide and perpetuate the errors of teachers, so does it also inculcate credulity and blind belief in the scholar, and finally establishes the conclusion in the mind, that knowledge is compounded of words, and signs, and intellectual abstractions, instead of facts and human sensations.

Greatly, very greatly to be desired, is a just mode of instruction. It would not only shorten the road of knowledge, it would carpet it with flowers. We should then tread it in childhood with smiles of cheerfulness; and, as we followed its pleasant course, horizon after horizon would open upon us, delighting and improving our minds and feelings, through life, unto our latest hour. But if it is of the first importance to be launched aright in infancy, the moment we distinctly perceive what knowledge is, we may, at any age, start boldly for its attainment.

I have said, we may start *boldly* – ay! and there lies the surety of our success. If we bring not the good courage of minds covetous of truth, and truth only, prepared to hear all things, examine all things, and decide upon all things, according to evidence, we should do more wisely to sit down contented in ignorance, than to bestir ourselves only to reap disappointment. But let us once look around upon this fair material world, as upon the book which it behoves us to read; let us understand, that in this book there are no puzzling mysteries, but a simple train of occurrences, which it imports us to observe, with an endless variety of substances and existences, which it imports us to study – what is there, then, to frighten us? what is there not rather, to encourage our advance?

Yet how far are we from this simple perception of simple things! how far from that mental composure which can alone fit us for inquiry! How prone are we to come to the consideration of every question with heads and hearts preoccupied! how prone to shrink from any opinion, however reasonable, if it be opposed to any, however unreasonable, of our own! How disposed are we to judge, in anger, those who call upon us to think, and encourage us to inquire! To question our prejudices, seems nothing less than sacrilege; to break the chains of our ignorance nothing short of impiety!

Perhaps at this moment, she who speaks is outraging a prejudice – (shall I be forgiven the word?) Perhaps among those who hear me, there are who deem it both a presumption and an impropriety for a woman to reason with her fellow creatures.

Did I know, of a surety, this prejudice to prevail among my hearers, I should, indeed, be disposed to reason with *them*. I should be tempted to ask, whether truth had any sex; and I should venture farther to ask, whether they count for nothing, for something, or for every thing, the influence of women over the destinies of our race.

Shall I be forgiven for adverting, most unwillingly, to myself? Having assumed an unusual place, I feel, that to my audience some explanation is due.

Stimulated in my early youth, by I know not what of pitying sympathy with human suffering, and by I know not what persuasion, that our race was not of necessity born to ignorance, and its companion, vice, but that it possessed faculties and qualities which pointed to virtue and enjoyment; stimulated, at once, by this pity for the actual condition of man, and this hope of a possible melioration, I applied myself to the discovery of the causes of the one, and of the means for effecting the other.

I have as little the inclination to obtrude on you the process of investigation and course of observation I followed through the period of an eventful youth, as you would probably have to listen to them. Suffice it, that I have been led to consider the growth of knowledge, and the equal distribution of knowledge, as the best – may I say, the only means for reforming the condition of mankind. Shall I be accused of presumption for imagining that I could be instrumental in promoting this, as it appears to me, good work? Shall I appear additionally presumptuous for believing that my sex and my situation tend rather to qualify than to incapacitate me for the undertaking.

So long as the mental and moral instruction of man is left solely in the hands of hired servants of the public – let them be teachers of religion, professors of colleges, authors of books, or editors of journals or periodical publications, dependent upon their literary labours for their daily bread, so long shall we hear but half the truth; and well if we hear so much. Our teachers, political, scientific, moral, or religious; our writers, grave or gay, are *compelled* to administer to our prejudices, and to perpetuate our ignorance. They dare not speak that which, by endangering their popularity, would endanger their fortunes. They have to discover not what is true, but what is palatable: not what will search into the hearts and minds of their hearers, but what will open their purse strings. They have to weigh every sentiment before they hazard it, every word before they pronounce it, lest they wound some cherished vanity, or aim at some favourite vice. A familiar instance will bring this home to an American audience.

I have been led to inspect, far and wide, the extensive and beautiful section of this country which is afflicted with slavery. I have heard in the cities, villages, and forests of this afflicted region, religious shepherds of all persuasions haranguing their flocks; and I have never heard *one* bold enough to comment on the evil which saps the industry, vitiates the morals, and threatens the tranquility of the country. The reason of this forbearance is evident. The master of the slave is he who pays the preacher, and the preacher must not irritate his paymaster. I would not here be understood to express the opinion, that the preaching of religious teachers against slavery would be desirable. I am convinced of the contrary – convinced that it would be of direful mischief to both parties, the oppressor and the oppressed. To judge from the tone but too generally employed by religious writers in the northern states, where (as denunciation against the vice of the south risks no patronage and wins cheap credit for humanity) negro philanthropy is not so scarce – to judge, I say, from the tone employed by northern religionists, when speaking of their southern neighbours, and their national crime and affliction, one must suppose them as little capable of counselling foreign as home offenders – as little capable of advising in wisdom as of judging in mercy, or speaking with gentleness. The harshest physician with which I am acquainted is the religious physician. Instead of soothing, he irritates; instead of convincing, he disgusts; instead of weighing circumstances, tracing causes, allowing for the bias of early example, the constraining force of implanted prejudice, the absence of every judicious stimulus, and the presence of every bad one; he arraigns,

tries, convicts, condemns – himself accuser, jury, judge, and executioner; nobly immolating interests which are not his, generously commanding sacrifices which he has not to share, indignantly anathematizing crimes which he cannot commit, and virtuously kindling the fires of hell to consume sinners, to whose sins, as he is without temptation, so *for* whose sins he is without sympathy. I would not be understood, therefore, as regretting in this matter the supineness of the southern clergy; I would only point it out to you, desirous that you should observe how well the tribe of Levi know when and where to smite, and when and where to spare.

And though I have quoted an instance more peculiarly familiar to Americans, every country teems with similar examples. The master vice, wherever or whatever it be, is never touched. In licentious aristocracies, or to look no farther than the towns and cities of these states, the rich and pampered few are ever spared, or so gently dealt with, as rather agreeably to tickle the ear, than to probe the conscience, while the crimes of the greatly-tempted, greatly-suffering poor, are visited with unrelenting vigour.

Is any discovery made in science, tending to open to us farther the book of knowledge, and to purge our minds of superstitious beliefs in occult causes and unsubstantiated creeds – where has it ever found opposers – or, might we not say, persecutors? Even among our hired preachers and licensed teachers of old doctrines and old ways. Is any inquiry instituted into the truth of received opinions and the advantage of existing practice – who are the last to encourage it? nay, the foremost to cry out "heresy!" and stop the mouth of knowledge? Who but those who live by the ignorance of the age, and the intolerance of the hour? Is any improvement suggested in our social arrangements, calculated to equalize property, labour, instruction, and enjoyment; to destroy crime by removing provocation; vice, by removing ignorance; and to build up virtue in the human breast by exchanging the spirit of self abasement for that of self respect – who are the foremost to treat the suggestions as visionary, the reform as impossible? Even they who live by the fears and the vices of their fellow creatures; and who obtain their subsistence on earth by opening and shutting the door of heaven.

Nor, as we have seen, are our licensed and pensioned teachers the only individuals interested in disguising the truth. All who write for the public market, all who plead in our courts of law, all who harangue in our halls of legislature, all who are, or who aspire to be, popular servants or popular teachers of the people, all are *compelled* to the support of existing opinions, whether right or wrong – all, more or less, do, and more or less must, pander to the weaknesses, vices, and prejudices of the public, who pays them with money or applause.

I have said not only that they do, but that they *must*; and most assuredly they must conciliate the popular feeling, or forego the popular favour. Here is intended no satire upon any individuals, professions, nor employments. The object is merely to expose a fact, but a fact highly important to be known; that as, to be popular, men must not speak truths, so, when we would hear truths, we must seek them from other mouths and other pens than those which are dependent upon popular patronage, or which are ambitious of popular admiration.

And here, then, is the cause why I have presumed to reason with my fellow creatures; why, in my earliest years, I devoted myself to the study of their condition, past and present; why I searched into their powers and their capabilities, examined their practice, and weighed their opinions; and why, when I found these both wanting, I volunteered to declare it. I believe that I see some truths important for my fellow beings to know; I feel that I have the courage and the independence to speak that which I believe; and where is the friend to his species that will not say, "*Happy, most happy shall it be for human kind, when all independent individuals, male or female, citizens or foreigners, shall feel the debt of kindness they owe to their fellow beings, and fearlessly step forth to reveal unbought truths and hazard unpopular opinions.*"

Until this be done, and done ably, fearlessly, and frequently, the reign of human error must continue; and, with human error, human vice, and human suffering. The advocates of just knowledge must be armed with courage to dare all things, and to bear all things, for the truths they revere; and to seek, as they may only find, the reward of their exertions in the impression, great or little, slow or rapid, as it may be, which their exertions may produce on public opinion, and through the public opinion, on the public practice.

We have now sufficiently considered, so far as I have found possible in a single discourse on so wide a topic, the main subject of our introductory inquiries: viz. the nature and object of just knowledge. We have examined, also, some of the errors vulgarly entertained on the subject, and many of the impediments which now obstruct our advances in the road of improvement. We have seen that just knowledge is easy of acquirement, but that few are interested in revealing its simple principles; while many are driven by circumstances to interpret or dissemble them. We have remarked that, to accelerate the progress of our race, two means present themselves; a just system of education, and a fearless spirit of inquiry; and that while the former would remove all difficulties from the path of future generations, the latter would place far in advance even the present. We have also observed on the advantage which would accrue to mankind, if all independent individuals would volunteer the task, for which appointed teachers and professional men are now but too frequently unfit, by devoting themselves to the promulgation of truth, without regard to fashionable prejudice. I have been led, also, incidentally to advert to the influence exerted over the fortunes of our race by those who are too often overlooked in our social arrangements and in our civil rights – I allude to women.

Leaving to a future opportunity the more complete development of the important subject, we have this evening approached – the nature of all knowledge – as well as the equally important subject of youthful education, I shall, at our next meeting, consider the other two enumerated means of improvement, viz. by free inquiry. And as this is for us of the present generation the *only* means, so shall I endeavour to show how much it is our interest, and how imperiously it is our duty to improve it to the uttermost.

It is with delight that I have distinguished, at each successive meeting, the increasing ranks of my own sex. Were the vital principle of human equality universally acknowledged, it would be to my fellow beings without regard to nation, class, sect, or sex, that I should delight to address myself. But until equality prevail in condition, opportunity, and instruction, it is every where to the least favoured in these advantages, that I most especially and anxiously incline.

Nor is the ignorance of our sex a matter of surprise, when efforts, as violent as unrelaxed, are every where made for its continuance.

It is not as of yore. Eve puts not forth her hand to gather the fair fruit of knowledge. The wily serpent now hath better learned his lesson; and, to secure his reign in the garden, beguileth her *not* to eat. Promises, entreaties, threats, tales of wonder, and, alas! tales of horror, are all poured in her tender ears. Above, her agitated fancy hears the voice of a god in thunders; below, she sees the yawning pit; and, before, behind, around, a thousand phantoms, conjured from the prolific brain of insatiate priestcraft, confound, alarm, and overwhelm her reason!

Oh! were that worst evil withdrawn which now weighs upon our race, how rapid were its progress in knowledge! Oh! were men – and, yet more, women, absolved from fear, how easily, and speedily, and gloriously would they hold on their course in improvement! The difficulty is not to convince, it is to *win attention*. Could truth only be heard, the conversion of the ignorant were easy. And well do the hired supporters of error understand this fact. Well do they *know*, that if the daughters of the present, and mothers of the future generation, were to drink of the living waters of knowledge, their reign would be ended – "their occupation gone." So well do they know it, that, far from obeying to the letter the command of their spiritual leader, "Be ye fishers of men," we find them every where *fishers of women*. Their own sex, old and young, they see with indifference swim by their nets; but closely and warily are their meshes laid, to entangle the female of every age.

Fathers and husbands! Do ye not also understand this fact? Do ye not see how, in the mental bondage of your wives and fair companions, ye yourselves are bound? Will ye fondly sport yourselves in your imagined liberty, and say, "it matters not if our women be mental slaves?" Will ye pleasure yourselves in the varied paths of knowledge, and imagine that women, hoodwinked and unawakened, will make the better servants and the easier playthings? They are greatly in error who so strike the account; as many a bankrupt merchant and sinking mechanic, not to say drowning capitalist, could bear witness. But setting aside dollars and cents, which men, in their present uncomfortable state of existence, are but too prone exclusively to regard, how many nobler interests of the mind and the heart cry "treason!" to this false calculation?

At our next meeting, we shall consider these interests, which will naturally present themselves during our investigations on the subject of free inquiry. In what just knowledge consists we have cursorily examined; to put ourselves in the way of attaining that knowledge, be our next object.

15

An Introduction to the Study of Phylosophy Wrote in America for the Use of a Young Gentleman

Cadwallader Colden

Introduction

Cadwallader Colden (1688–1776) was born in Ireland and trained as a physician at the University of Edinburgh. He emigrated to North America in 1716 and, after failing to establish a medical practice in Philadelphia, moved to New York, where he was appointed Surveyor General. For several years Colden traveled along the borders of New York, becoming familiar with Native American culture. The Mohawk people adopted him during this time, and in 1727 he published the first English-language history of the Haudenosaunee (Iroquois) Confederacy. He was soon appointed Lieutenant Governor of New York province and, in the 1740s, began to publish philosophical and scientific treatises. His best-known work at the time, *The Principles of Action in Matter*, explicitly establishes an epistemology and ontology grounded in a principle of interaction. The selection reproduced here was written as a letter to a nephew and introduces Colden's thought in the context of a critique of the European rationalism that was dominant at the time.

I

You are now, my ——, going to the college, in order to learn those principles, which may be of use to you in all your future inquiries; and to acquire that knowledge, by which you may be

Taken from *American Philosophic Addresses: 1700–1900*, ed. Joseph L. Blau (New York: Columbia University Press, 1946).

enabled to distinguish yourself in every part of your life, either in public employments, or in private life, or that you may become an useful member of the commonwealth and of a private family. But the common methods of teaching, hitherto generally in use in the public Schools, is so far from answering these good purposes, that it serves only to fill young people's heads with useless notions and prejudices, which unfit them for the acquiring of real and useful knowledge. The design of my present writing is to guard you against these common errors, and to instruct you how to avoid them. In doing this I have supposed that you have a general notion of the sciences, which are usually taught. I could not do otherwise, within the limits I have set to myself, and therefore be not discouraged, if at present you do not comprehend the full scope and view of what I write. When you come to read on any of the sciences I hope you will then find it of use to you.

History informs us, that the Egyptian priests, the Chald[ee] and Persian magi had acquired great knowledge in physics, before the Christian era, such as exceeds the knowledge of th[e] most learned of the moderns. It is certain that they had carr[ied] Geometry, Ast[r]onomy and Mechanics to a great perfection. The Greeks were only meer Scholars of the Egyptians. It may be questioned whether they made any discovery absolutely their own: and it is not improbable, that, like meer Scholars, they did not perfectly understand the principles of the Egyptian philosophy; and yet it is from the Greeks only that we have any knowledge of the learning of these ancients. Pythagoras was the best instructed of any of the Greeks in the Egyptian learning. It appears from the little which remains of his doctrine, that the Egyptians knew what of late times has been called the Copernican System, and that he knew the general apparent attraction between bodies, which has been rediscovered in the last century by Sir Isaac Newton. But as we have nothing remaining of the Pythagorean philosophy, except what is found in a few abstracts in much later writers, we know very little of what were the true principles of that philosophy. It may be that we are now regaining the Principles of Physics, which were known many ages before the beginning of the Christian era. Wars, and the irruption of barbarous nations into the countries where learning flourished, have been the destruction of knowledge in those countries. But nothing so much prevented the propagation of knowledge as the Craft of the pagan priests, who, in order to secure their influence over the people, confined learning to their own order, and communicated their knowledge only to the *Initiated*, to such only of whose taciturnity and fidelity, after a severe trial, they were well assured. Whoever attempted to put mankind on a free inquiry into the truth of popularly received opinions, certainly suffered under a cruel persecution of the heathen priests. Socrates was persecuted and condemned to death, as a corrupter of youth, as an enemy to the Gods, and of the orthodox religion of his country; and yet Socrates, in all after ages, has been deemed the wisest man, and the man of the greatest probity that ever appeared among the pagans.

Nothing, in later ages, so much obstructed the advancement of knowledge as the craft of the popish priests, when they, in imitation of the pagan priests, founded the power of their dominion on the ignorance and credulity of the laity: by which they established a Tyranny in the Pope and the Clergy over Kings and Princes as well as over private persons, under pretence of their being intrusted with the keys of heaven and hell, and exerted their power more absolutely than ever had been done by any potentate before that time. To serve these purposes, all books, which might propagate real and useful knowledge, and thereby detect this priestcraft, were proscribed: they were, under the severest penalties, ordered to be brought in and burnt, and it became an unpardonable sin to read them. For the same purposes, the clergy assumed the sole power of licensing books; that is, without their consent no book could be published or was permitted to be read. By these means the best books of antiquity are lost, or curtailed, while the lascivious poets are transmitted to us entire. Copernicus durst not publish his system, till he was near his death, when he thought himself out of the reach of their persecution. He lived to see only one printed copy of it. Galileo was the first who applied the telescope to astronomical observations, and thereby absolutely confirmed the Copernican system. The nobility of Italy flocked to his house to view the planets. They saw clearly that the planets are really globular bodies, similar to our earth: and they saw the satellites of Jupiter, like so many moons, moving round the body of that planet. The priests could not bear that they should be convicted of teaching errors in philosophy, or that any knowledge can be obtained otherwise than from them. Galileo was clapt into the inquisition, and to free himself from the rack and a cruel death, he was forced to recant, and to give himself the lie publicly, he was forced to deny the truth of what he and many others had seen distinctly. Had not the reformation in religion taken place about that time, and several nations thrown off the authority of the Pope, the learning and knowledge of the present age had been nipt in the bud, and we should at this day have been in barbarous ignorance.

Nothing was so effectual in establishing the dominion of the priests as the education of youth, which they assumed solely to themselves. All the professors and teachers in the public Schools and universities were priests, none others were allowed to teach, nor are any others allowed at this day in popish countries. They know well how easy it is to instill strong prejudices into young minds, and of what force these prejudices are in the whole course of life.

To divert inquisitive minds (for such there are in all ages) from applying their thoughts and inquiries after real knowledge, the priests introduced into their schools a kind of learning of things, which, like dreams, exist nowhere but in the imagination: Abstracted notions, a multiplicity of terms or hard words, which have no meaning but to cover ignorance, perplexed definitions, Distinctions without real difference, from which were introduced endless disputes about mysterious trifles, of no real use, either to the advancement of knowledge or conduct in life; but served well to divert the inquisitive mind from inquiring into any kind of knowledge, which may be prejudicial to the dominion of the priests.

This kind of learning, at first introduced into the popish schools, has of late obtained the name of *school learning*, in opposition to the real knowledge of things. The *School Logic* is the art of continuing an argument or dispute without end, and without convincing or being convinced, without design to discover truth, but to cover ignorance, and defend error: and therefore well fitted to the chicanery of the law, or for perpetuating religious controversies, for it equally serves to defend the opinions of all sects.

The school learning is now expelled from the sciences. You'll find nothing of it in the modern astronomy, or in any of the mathematical sciences: the best writers in medicine are ashamed to make use of it; but it is to be found plentifully in books of Theology and Law. It is really surprising, that wherever the clergy, even among protestants, have the direction of the schools, that the youth are obliged to waste so much time in the study of this useless learning, or rather hurtful learning: for it really unfits them for the acquiring of real and useful knowledge. It must not be supposed that the protestant clergy do this, with a view to blindfold the laity, that they may have the leading of them: I rather suppose, that the first of the protestant clergy having been educated in the popish schools, they were not able to divest themselves of the prejudices which they received there, and by continuing their successors in the same studies, the same prejudices continue. But surely that kind of learning, by which only enthusiasm and superstition can be defended and propagated, cannot be the proper method to extirpate them. I hope therefore, that either the protestant clergy will expel this kind of learning from their schools, or that they no longer shall be suffered to have the direction of the schools of learning.

As to the Law, it is not to be expected that any reformation can come from the lawyers. No number of men will act contrary to their private interest, when they are too powerful in the state to be easily reduced to order. It can only be done by such a prince as the King of Prussia. I think it appears evidently from history, that when the people become generally uneasy under any great abuse, they throw the Society into confusion; but they are never able to give proper redress, by setting things on a proper and lasting foundation. This, at all times, has been done by the uncommon abilities of some single person. Is there anything in popery, or in the grossest idolatry more absurd than this, that to know how a man is to act in the common affairs of life, without endangering his liberty, property, or life, it should be necessary to study several years in the inns of court, and to have 2 or 300 books? Such are the mischievous effects of school learning; for without it such abuses could never have prevailed among mankind. Unless the understandings of mankind had been greatly depraved, the defending of fraud and villainy, and perverting of Justice must allwise have been held in abhorrence: and yet there is no rogue or villain (if he have money) who cannot find a lawyer to defend him, and to endeavour knowingly to pervert or at least to delay Justice, in favour of the rogue, and to the prejudice of the innocent, and this lawyer still preserves among his neighbours the character of a good lawyer, tho' in all cases, even in defence of right, he be a sort of licensed pickpocket. Ought not the truly good lawyers to spurn such men from among them, as the disgrace of their profession?

It may be now proper to give you some more particular knowledge of the school learning by informing you of the principles of the Schools in Physiology.

II

The Schoolmen tell us, that everything is either a Substance, a Quality, an Accident or a Mode.

A *Substance* is defined to be, something we conceive to subsist of itself, independently of any created being, or any particular mode or accident.

A *Quality* is that affection of a thing, whence it is denominated such: or that which occasions a thing to affect our senses, in this or that manner.

A *Mode* is a manner of being: or a quality or attribute of a substance or subject, which we conceive as necessarily depending on the subject, and incapable of subsisting without it. An *Accident* is something additional, or superadded to substance: or not essentially belonging thereto, but capable indifferently either of being or not being in it, without the destruction thereof.

Definitions ought to give clear and distinct ideas or conceptions of the things defined, especially when they are introductory to everything we learn afterwards: and are the foundations of our knowledge as these definitions are designed to be. You can judge, whether you have received from them any clearer conceptions of the real differences of things, than you had before you read them: or whether your conceptions be not rather more perplexed thereby than enlightened. These, however, have been received generally in all the universities and Schools of Europe, and have been delivered out by the learned Doctors, to their Scholars, as the Foundation of all knowledge.

Let us try what we can make of them, in discovering the nature of things. For example, let us try to find out what the substance of the candle now before us, is.

It is round; but this is only a mode, it might have been channelled, or square, or triangular, and still a candle.

It is white, this is a quality; it might have been yellow, or green, and it is of no colour in the dark.

It is greasy and of a certain stiffness. These likewise are only qualities, and the substance of the candle may subsist without them.

It may be set on fire, and it will burn and give light. This is only an accident, for it is as much a candle when it does not burn, as when it does.

Now to find out the substance of the candle, or to discover what the candle really is, we must remove all these qualities, modes, and accidents, which are only outside coverings and meer appearances, that we may come at the substance. But after you have removed the shape, the colour, the greasiness and stiffness, and its being capable of burning, what idea of the candle have you remaining? Have you any kind of conception of the substance? We are told by these learned doctors, that what we know of things by our senses are only qualities, only appearances or sensations, which often deceive us, and exist nowhere but in our own brains: for they have no existence but while they are felt or perceived. To know, therefore, what things really are, we must divest them of all their qualities, and throw aside our own sensations. Try to do this, and then tell me what the candle is. If, by this kind of learning, you can neither form any notion or conception of things to yourself, nor talk intelligibly to others, of what use is it? Why must two or three years of the best time of life be thrown away in acquiring it? Truly I think it will be difficult to assign any other reason, than what has been already mentioned, viz: to divert the inquisitive mind from all real and useful knowledge.

However a popish priest may show you some use of it in a remarkable instance. All the sensible qualities of bread, its colour, taste, smell, and consistence may be removed, without destroying the substance of the bread. So all the appearances, to the senses, of Flesh may be taken away, without destroying the substance of the Flesh. Then if the Substance of Flesh be substituted under the qualities of bread, there is no absurdity in conceiving transubstantiation, with a small degree of Faith or credulity in the divine power of the priesthood, after the disciple is well instructed in school learning; but if the disciple be defective in this learning, it must require much more credulity to be able to swallow either transubstantiation or consubstantiation.

In short, the most part of the logic and metaphysics, taught not only in the popish and church of England schools, but likewise in the Schools of the dissenters is of the kind of stuff, which I have just now shewn you. They have served the purposes of Robert Barclay, as well as the purposes of Cardinal Bellarmine, and of both with equal success.

III

The Schoolmen continued dictators in the republic of literature. *The Master or the Doctor said it* was an irresistible argument, 'till about the year 1640, when René Descartes, a Frenchman, published his philosophy. He, in opposition to them, boldly asserted, that we must receive nothing in philosophy on meer authority. We must doubt the truth of every proposition, 'till we have sufficient evidence of its truth. He has the honour of asserting the liberty of philosophising, and of thereby introducing all the discoveries which have been since made in physics. He carried the humour of doubting a little too far. The only, or rather first, self evident proposition, which he allowed, was *I think, therefore I am*; but surely I can as little doubt of your existence, who sit by me, as I can of my own. His physics are founded on ingenious hypotheses by which he attempts to explain the phenomena of nature; but, as in forming these hypotheses, he had not the advantage of the accurate observations, and numerous experiments, which have been since made, and many phenomena have been discovered, of which in his time they had no knowledge, it is no wonder that he should have failed in many things, and that his system of physics is rather an amusing philosophic romance than a true natural history. However he had the honour of exciting that passion for new discoveries, which, from his time to the present, has so much advanced real and useful knowledge: and he was the first among the moderns who made use of Geometry in physical researches.

This liberty in philosophising, which Descartes assumed, alarmed all the Doctors of the Schools. They, whose assertions had passed uncontested on their single authority, could not bear such freedom of doubting and inquiring. As they could not withstand the force of Descartes' arguments, they took that course of silencing him which a Quaker, after their example, lately took with a gentleman's dog, that had been disorderly among his sheep. When the gentleman did not give the Quaker the redress which he expected, he told the gentleman, that he would give his dog an ill-name: and accordingly the next time the dog appeared in the street, the Quaker bawl'd out, a mad dog, a mad dog, on which the neighbours dispatched him with stones. The Doctors published every where that Descartes is an atheist but at that time the priests had in a great measure lost their influence in France, and their exclamations had not the effect they expected. They applied therefore to the Parliament of Paris to have Descartes' books suppressed: and, it is said, they would have succeeded, had not the parliament been diverted by a burlesque petition. Ridicule often is of more force than a serious argument. You may generally observe that when any use scurrility in argument they are sensible of the want of other force.

My present purpose does not allow me to give you a particular account of Descartes' system. I shall only mention his general distinction of Matter and Spirit. The essence of matter, he says, consists in extension, that it cannot be conceived but of some length, breadth, and thickness: and the essence of Spirit in thinking. But supposing that a spirit is not united to body, in the manner the soul is, it is difficult, if not impossible to shew, that it thinks, or that it has any kind of action similar to what we call thinking. Extension cannot distinguish any one being from another: for can any thing be conceived to exist, or to be any where, or in any part of space, and to be of no length, breadth, or thickness? I cannot conceive anything to exist, but either by an universal extension or expansion through all space, or by a limited extension in some part of space, otherwise it exists nowhere, which to me is to say that it does not exist. Extension, therefore, can make no distinction between matter and spirit, unless it be said, that Spirit is universally extended, and matter confined within limits. Again the properties of everything depends on its essence, and may be evidently deduced from it; but I think, none have attempted to deduce the properties and phenom-

ena of matter from meer extension, and it is impossible to do it: for meer extension gives no idea of any power by which any effect or phenomenon can be produced.

To avoid these difficulties and just exceptions, the present teachers in the Schools tell us, that the essential difference between matter and spirit is in *Inactivity* and *Activity*. Matter, they say, is an absolutely passive substance, which can do nothing of itself: it receives all action from the active substance or from spirit.

May I ask, what idea or conception can I have of a thing which does nothing? A definition which consists wholly of negatives is a definition of nothing. An absolute negation is a denial of existence. Something must be positively affirmed of a thing before I can receive any conception of it. We have no idea or perception of any thing external to us but in consequence of some impression on our senses, if any thing can exist, which has no kind of power, action, or force, we can by no means discover that it exists. A being absolutely inactive can produce no one phenomenon; it is absolutely useless, and no reason of the least probability can be given for its existence.

For these reasons Dr. Berkeley denied the existence of Matter, and affirmed, that everything which we call matter exists nowhere but in our own mind. That neither our thoughts, passions, nor ideas formed by Imagination exist without the mind, he says, is evident; nor is it less evident that the various ideas or sensations imprinted on the sense, however blended or combined (that is whatever objects they compose) cannot exist otherwise, than as in a mind perceiving them. What are hills and trees etc., but things perceived by sense; and what do we perceive but our own ideas and sensations: and can any one of these, or any combination of them exist unperceived? Thus your body, head, hands, etc. are only the ideas of body, head, hands, etc. which exist only in my mind; and my body is only an idea which exists in your mind and in the mind of others who perceive it. You will hardly believe, I suppose, that he was in earnest when he wrote these things. Yes he was, he wrote a large and learned treatise in proof of this doctrine: and he has obtained disciples, who have formed a sect in philosophy called *Idealists*, which has extended to America, where you will find men of sense advocates for it. In truth, if matter be really and absolutely inactive, that it does nothing, Dr. Berkeley's arguments are unanswerable; but if it be said, that all these ideas, which we have of bodies, are excited in consequence of some action of matter, they are of no force.

From what proceeds it is a necessary consequence, that matter, if there be any such thing, must have some power or force. Our next inquiry shall be what power or force this is, which distinguishes matter from all other beings.

IV

Matter or body (which is some certain quantity of matter) in some degree or other resists our touch, and thereby excites the sense of feeling. This is so general an observation that if we can feel nothing in any place we conclude there is no body there.

When a body is at rest it requires some force to move it. If it require a certain degree of force to make a body move one foot in a second, it requires double that force to make it move two feet in a second, and thrice the force to make it move three feet in the same time. Again if it require a certain force to move a certain quantity of matter one foot in a second, it requires a double force to move a double quantity of the same matter the same distance in the same time, and thrice the force to move a treble quantity of matter. From these observations, which may be made every day, it is evident, that there is some power or force in matter, by which it persists in its present state, and resists any change of its state. It cannot be by meer inactivity, or by doing nothing; because one absolute want of any thing cannot be greater or less than any other absolute want. It is nonsense to say, one thing does nothing, and another thing does twice as much nothing.

If a body swimming in water, receive any degree of motion, it from time to time loses its motion gradually, till at last it rests. If the same body receive the same degree of motion in the air, it loses its motion at last, but continues it to a greater distance and longer time. If the same body be put in motion in a place void of air it continues its motion longer than it did in air. From these observations it is concluded, that a body once put in motion, would continue to move with the same degree of velocity, if it meet with no resistance from some other body, or from the medium in which it moves. And if any quantity of matter, moving with a certain velocity, require a certain degree of force to stop it, double the quantity of matter, moving with the same velocity, requires double the force to stop it, and so on. From these

observations equally true, at all times and in all places, it is concluded, that there is a power or force in matter, by which it persists in its present state, whether it be in motion or at rest. When two bodies move with the same degree of motion, and have different force, and this difference is constantly observed to be in proportion to the quantity of matter in each, it cannot arise from the motion; for it is equal in both; and therefore can only arise from the quantity of matter, to which it is allwise in proportion.

When you take a ball in your hand, and put your hand and the ball in motion, and then suddenly withdraw your hand from the ball, the ball continues to move after your hand, which gave it motion, is withdrawn from it. So likewise when a ball receives motion, from the explosion of gunpowder within a gun barrel, the ball continues its motion with great velocity to a great distance, after the gunpowder has entirely ceased to act upon it. What is it, which continues this motion in the ball, after your hand is withdrawn and the gunpowder ceases to act? Not your hand, nor the gunpowder: for nothing can act where it is not, nor after it has ceased to act. If you attend to the proper conception of cause and effect, anything can as little act at the distance of one hair's breadth, as it can at the distance of one thousand miles, without something passing from it to the other thing on which it acts, or without some middle thing or medium, by which the action is continued from the one to the other: for nothing can act where it is not, or produce any effect after it has ceased to act, more than it can after it has ceased to be or to exist. Therefore the continuance of motion in the ball is by some power in the ball itself, that is, by that power by which matter resists all change in its present state, whether it be in motion or at rest.

You have, my ——, thrown many a stone, without imagining that there was any difficulty in conceiving how the stone moved of itself, after it was gone from your hand. You may hence learn, how the powers of things may be discovered, from the most common and trivial effects, when properly and attentively considered: and that a truly philosophic turn of mind can never want opportunities of improving in knowledge, without the expense of any apparatus for experiments.

Sir Isaac was the first who observed this power in matter, that it is essential to it and distinguishes it from all other beings. Is it not wonderful, that where the means of discovery are so easy and obvious, that the discovery was not made before his time: tho' it be a power every where to be observed, from its effects, and without which none of the phenomena of matter can be explained, and the understanding of it be of the greatest use in the arts and sciences? Can any other reason be given, than that the inquisitive mind was diverted by the vain subtilities of the schools, and the prejudices early received there?

Sir Isaac Newton called this power in matter *Vis inertia*. It is difficult to find an English word to convey a proper idea of this power. It has been commonly turned into the word *Inactivity*, and this was done, I suppose, in favour of the prevailing opinion, that matter is absolutely passive and unactive. But this can never express Sir Isaac Newton's meaning: for to talk of a power or force which does nothing, can only serve to make people laugh. It is as plain a contradiction to say force without action as to say force without force. Power without force, and force without action, or which does nothing is as unintelligible as any absurdity can be. This power is more properly called the power of resisting any change in its present state, whether it be in motion or at rest, as Sir Isaac defines it; for resistance carries the idea of force and of action with it, or of doing something.

Some cannot conceive any action without motion. This arises from a faulty connection of ideas, by joining motion to all kind of action: for which no kind of reason can be given. Thinking is certainly doing something, or is a kind of action; but we conceive no kind of motion in thinking. Some likewise expect that we shall tell them in what manner the resisting power acts. To this it is answered, that we cannot explain the manner of acting of any simple power otherwise than by its effects. Motion can no otherwise be explained than by change of place; but change of place is only the effect of motion: and the effects of the resisting power can be as clearly shewn, as the effects of motion can be.

I told you before that the school learning is really a misapplication of time, in learning of things which exist nowhere but in the imaginations of idle, monkish, useless men, and serves no good purpose in life. It is otherwise in acquiring knowledge of the powers and force of those things on which our well-being depends. Our life and health, our pleasures and pain all depend on the powers of those beings, which constitute the human system, and on the powers of other things, which are continually acting upon it. Not only the speculative sciences, the explaining of all the phenomena

which strike our senses, depend on the knowledge of these powers; but likewise all the practical arts depend on them. This knowledge is useful to us in every circumstance of life, whether as individuals and private persons, or as members of Society: as will very evidently appear to you, when you shall apply your thoughts to any particular art or science.

From the resisting power of matter we form a clear conception of its impenetrability, or that no quantity of matter can occupy the same space, which any other quantity of matter does: for if it could, we lose the idea of its resisting power, this power must be supposed to be destroyed, and with it we lose every conception we have of matter. We cannot conceive two quantities of matter in the same space, without losing any idea we have at least of one of them: all ideas which distinguish them are lost. In short, take away the idea of resistance from matter and we have no idea of matter remaining. Its essence, therefore, consists in its power of resisting all change of its present state, from which all the phenomena or properties of matter are deduced, as the effects of this power, and without it none of them can be understood.

V

Nothing so much prevents the advancement of knowledge, as false maxims, when received on the authority of great names, as the test and evidence of truth. They are, in our progress to knowledge, like shackles on our legs in walking, they are not only a continual hindrance to our advancing, but frequently throw us down in the dirt. It may be of use to discover such, and to expose them, especially when supported by venerable names, which otherwise have great respect due to them.

In consequence of the maxim, that activity is peculiar to spiritual substances, and that the material are entirely passive, it is said that God, in the beginning, created a certain quantity of motion, and distributed it, in certain proportions, through the universe: that the same quantity in the whole allwise remains; but that the distribution of it in the several parts is continually changing, some bodies are losing all or part of their motion, while others are acquiring or increasing motion. It is said, God created motion, because it is not to be imagined, that he communicates motion by impulse, or by projecting: for thereby we should reduce our conceptions of God, to that of some finite material being. So far in a proper sense is true, but then they add, that when God created motion, he did not create any being, or real thing: for then there must be some active being besides spirit. He created, they say, only a quality or an action, which he distributed through the universe. Can any thing be more ridiculous in all the exploded School learning than this? God created a certain quantity of no real thing, or he created no being, but only a certain quantity of a mode or an action. May we not with the same propriety say God in the beginning created a certain quantity of colours and sounds, of darkness and silence? or, that he created a certain quantity of round, square, triangular, and other figures or forms, and distributed them over the universe, which are continually changing from one part of the universe to another. And thus we may receive any kind of learned jargon that can enter the most disordered imagination.

On this supposition, that the same quantity of motion remains allwise, when anything acquires motion some other thing must lose as much motion, and nothing can communicate more motion than it had and loses. A single spark of fire gradually sets a large city all in fire, or a single spark sets fire to a quantity of gunpowder, which with immense force throws rocks and castles up into the air. Can it be imagined that all that motion, which appears while a whole city is in flames, was really in the little spark which began the fire, or that the whole force of motion, produced by the gunpowder, was in the little spark, which set fire to it? Is it not more reasonable to think that some active being, which has in itself the power of moving, is included in the materials of the city, or in the gunpowder, which, in the one case, was gradually set at liberty to act, and in the other case suddenly all in one instant?

It is therefore more natural, or consistent with common sense, to say: God in the beginning created a certain being, to which he gave the power of motion; and distributed this being, in certain proportions, in the several parts of the universe. The granting of this is no negative to the existence of spirits; they may, and undoubtedly both exist, without including any contradiction.

It is not difficult to discover a being evidently distinct both from matter and spirit, as I think may clearly appear from what follows. We cannot open our eyes in daylight without discovering it, and the effects produced by it. Wherever we discover light we discover motion. Take away motion from light,

and every conception we have of it ceases; that is, we cannot conceive any effect from light, without conceiving it to be in motion: and from motion alone, and from the different velocities of the several rays of light, all the phenomena of light can be explained, without supposing that it has any other power or property; and without supposing that the parts of light are of any magnitude or of any shape. By the increase of the sun's light, in the several parts of the earth, motion is everywhere increased in summer: and by the lessening the degree of light in winter, motion is lessened; as is evident in vegetables, animals, and fluids. Generally light either precedes or attends all violent motions, and our not seeing it, wherever we perceive motion, is no proof of its absence; but only that there is not sufficient light to affect our senses. Cats, owls, bats, etc., see clearly with a degree of light by which we can discover nothing. The motion of the planets seems to put it beyond dispute, that their motion proceeds from the light of the sun: for their velocities is precisely as the density or force of light at their several distances from the sun; that is in a ratio reciprocal to the squares of their distances from the sun.

However it is to be carefully observed, that tho' bodies originally receive their motion from light, yet they very generally continue that motion by their resisting power only: and by this same power communicate motion from one to another. This is very different from simple motion or light, as the effects of it likewise are. It is a compound effect or action of the moving and resisting powers united: for it is allwise in a compound ratio of the degree of motion or velocity and the quantity of matter in the body which moves. For this reason, Sir Isaac Newton has distinguished this compound force by a peculiar name; he calls it *Momentum*. None of our teachers, so far as I know, have distinguished the moving power from this compound effect of the moving and resisting powers. The whole doctrine or laws of motion, which you'll find in books, is only of bodies in motion, and of their effects on other bodies, either in motion or at rest. For this reason you'll often find strange perplexity in their writings, by distinguishing velocity from motion, as if velocity were something else than a greater or less degree of motion.

The natural simple powers can only be distinguished by their effects, or by the phenomena which they produce; some very obvious appearances, which every man may observe, lead us to such knowledge of light, as will sufficiently distinguish it from every other being. As rays of light pass from every visible point of an illuminated room, to every other point of that room, to which a straight line can be drawn: for this point can be seen by an eye placed in any of the other points. Then every ray of light, moving from any one point of the room, meets with another ray moving in a direct opposite direction; yet the motion of no one ray is stopt by their meeting in opposite directions, nor are they in the least turned aside. Again, the ray which moves from any one point, in the corner of the room, to the opposite corner of the room, is crossed in every point of that line, by rays from every point in the room: for every point of the room can be seen by eyes placed in every point of that line. And yet the motion of the ray from corner to corner is in no manner obstructed or its direction diverted, by these innumerable rays which cross it. The like is to be observed in the rays from the fixed stars; they pass through an immense distance, and everywhere in that immense space cross the rays from the sun, from other fixed stars, and from the planets, yet nowhere are they stopt or diverted from their course in a straight line.

From these and innumerable other phenomena, it is evident, that the rays of light are mutually penetrable: and that light has no power of resisting; consequently that light and resisting matter are essentially different beings or substances. Tho' this be so very obvious, how few, if any, have made this reflexion. The reason of it can only be, from a prejudice we have received from our infancy, that there are no other beings except matter and spirit: and yet I know no one reason for this assertion, if the authority of venerable names be excepted.

Since light has no power of resisting, and its parts are mutually penetrable, it follows that any quantity of light may be contained in any space: that the smallest quantity in bulk or extension may be so expanded as to fill the largest space, without leaving any vacuity between its parts: and the largest quantity may be condensed into the smallest space. No doubt, this appears to be a paradox to you; but if I can shew that in fact it is so, there can be no absurdity in asserting it. Consider how prodigiously light is expanded by the explosion of gunpowder, by the distance at which it can be seen in every direction: and consider what small space this light occupied, in the gunpowder, before explosion, after the space occupied by the resisting matter of the gunpowder is deducted. A

candle may be seen at the distance of one mile at least, in a clear serene air and a dark night. Sailors will inform you, that a ship at sea has been discovered at a much greater distance, by the light of a candle on board. Light is emitted by momentary vibrations, and the light emitted, from a candle, in every one of these momentary vibrations fills at least a spherical space of two miles diameter; because no point within that space can be assigned, which is not in that moment illuminated. Now if it be considered what a small quantity of a candle is dissolved, in that instant of one emission of light, and the resisting matter of the candle be deducted from that quantity, the light, which filled the sphere of two miles diameter, must have been contained in a less space than can be imagined. Sir Isaac Newton has shewn in his Optics that the vibrations of light are in less time than in the thirds or fourths of time, none of which can be distinguished by our senses.

Consider the vast expansion of light which is emitted from the surface of the sun, the vast expansion of the same light when reflected from the surface of the moon, and lastly its vast expansion when reflected from every point of any body on the earth, which is seen either by the naked eye or by the help of a microscope, and it must appear that this expansion exceeds anything which we can conceive by imagination; and after all this vast expansion, not the least vacuity or distance between the parts of light can, by any means, be discovered.

When what precedes is well considered, you cannot doubt of light's being a distinct substance from matter, and that they have nothing in common between them, except that they both may be considered as of some quantity, that there may be a greater and a less quantity of light, and that it may be confined within certain limits, by some other power. It is easy to conceive from what precedes that light is the moving power or the principle of motion: and you will find this confirmed by every observation you shall make of the great and small phenomena in nature.

The contemplation of the wonderful power of light, and of its universal influence in every part of the world, especially on animals and vegetables, led the ancient Persians into a kind of enthusiasm, which made them deify the sun, the source of light. Their descendants to this day continue to worship the sun and fire, as the fountains of light and life. It cannot be a doubt, that they conceived light as a real being distinct from all others.

VI

The occult qualities have been long exploded and excluded from the republic of learning, as only artful coverings of ignorance, by which pretenders to knowledge would make others believe that they know things of which they are absolutely ignorant. This they do by imposing words, which have no meaning, in place of real knowledge. When you ask one of these learned Doctors, who is unwilling to be thought ignorant of any thing, by what means amber draws a straw, or a feather to it, they gravely tell you it is by an occult quality in the amber. Why a stone falls to the earth? It is by an occult quality in the stone, by which it allwise tends to the center of the earth. Put these answers into plain English and they are no other than this. Amber attracts a feather or a straw; but I know not how. A stone allwise falls to the ground; but I know not why. Such plain and direct answers are inconsistent with the pretensions of the learned professor: and, which is worse, would not please the Scholar. Mankind in general are better pleased to be duped, with the unmeaning appearance of knowledge, than to allow that their teachers are ignorant or deceitful.

Notwithstanding that in this enlightened age, no maxims in philosophy are admitted, but what are self evident, and which the unlearned as well as the learned clearly perceive to be true: and no theorem or conclusions are received, but what are demonstratively deduced from these maxims; yet we find many, of great reputation for their knowledge in physics, asserting, that all bodies attract each other, while at a distance from each other, without supposing any thing between these bodies, or passing from the one to the other, by which any kind of action can pass from the one to the other; but by some inherent quality or power in the bodies themselves. Can anything in the occult qualities of the Schools be more absurd than this? If it be supposed, that a body can act on another at the least distance from where it is, without something passing or some medium between them, by which the action is continued, it may in the like manner act at the greatest distance with equal force: for where nothing passes and nothing is between the bodies, no reason can be given for its acting with less force at any distance. It supposes that bodies

act where they are not, and with equal reason they may be supposed to act after they have ceased to be. I can see no reason why a man who admits of this mutual attraction in bodies should be shocked at Transubstantiation, or at any other fashionable absurdity.

Innumerable phenomena shew that all bodies tend to each other, by some force or other; but no phenomenon can shew, that it is done by an attractive quality in themselves: nor can it be done by any of emission from themselves, for no motion from a body can give motion to the same body. It seems, then, necessary to conclude, that this mutual tendency and motion of bodies to each other is by the action of some medium, surrounding all bodies, or in which all bodies are placed. The knowledge of the nature or power of this medium can only be obtained, as the knowledge of all other powers is, by an accurate observation of the effects or phenomena produced by it. I suppose none will affirm, that nothing exists, but what we either feel, see, hear, smell, or taste. The existence of some things may be as evident by reflexion on the phenomena, or on the effects produced by them, or by reasoning, as the existence of others is by immediate perception. Where effects are evidently perceived, it is with the greatest certainty concluded, that something exists which has sufficient power to produce these effects. In truth we have no other method to discover the existence of anything, but by its effects either mediately, or immediately on the senses. Neither can I conceive any necessity to think that this medium consists either of resisting matter or of light, or of both united. Its effects shew it to be something different from either of them, some being which has a power peculiar to itself, the nature of which is to be discovered by its effects, as the powers of matter and light are, by an accurate observation of the effects produced by them.

From an accurate observation of the effects between bodies at a distance from each other, I conclude, that the parts of the medium in which they are placed are all, in every respect, contiguous; and therefore it cannot be conceived as consisting of particles, of any shape or dimensions. Nevertheless, it may be conceived as of different quantities, or as occupying a smaller or larger quantity of space, in the same manner as space is considered as of different quantities. From the same observation I conclude that this medium receives equally the action of resisting from any contiguous body, or of motion from light which passes through it: and that the parts or quantity of the medium contiguous to the body receives the action immediately from the body and communicates the same to the next contiguous parts or quantity and so on to a great distance. This communication to the greatest distance is done in one instant, because there is no distance between the parts of the medium, in the same manner as any motion is communicated from one end of a rod, however long it be, in the same instant to the other end. Immediately after any quantity of this medium has received the action, either of resisting or of moving, it reacts the same with the same force which it received. This alternate action and reaction is made evident in Sir Isaac Newton's Optics, by the alternate transmission and stopping of light on passing through pellucid bodies. You may imagine this reaction as something similar to what you feel, when taking one end of a rod in your hand, you push the other end against a wall, you feel the wall react or push the rod against your hand, with the same force with which you pushed the rod. In the next place it is constantly observed, that the resisting power in matter, is opposite, or a negative power to motion: it allwise either destroys, or stops, or lessens the action of motion.

These observations being premised, call this medium Ether, for it is proper to give it a name, suppose the Ether, surrounding any spherical body of resisting matter, be divided into equidistant concentric spherical surfaces, it is evident that these spherical surfaces increase the farther they are from the center of the spherical body. Geometers demonstrate that this increase is in the ratio of the squares of their diameters or of the distance of the surface from the common center. Again it is observed that if any certain force communicate a degree of force to any certain quantity, it communicates half the degree of force to double the quantity, or that the degree of action communicated is reciprocal to the quantity of the thing which receives the action. Then it follows that the quantity of the action of resisting, which is communicated to the several parts of Ether surrounding a spherical body, decreases continually from the body, in a ratio reciprocal to the square of their distance from the body. Since the action of resistance is negative to motion, if motion be communicated by light to the Ether the reaction of motion will be more lessened the nearer the parts of the Ether are to the body: consequently the reaction will be allwise stronger on the side of any small body farther distant from the other large spherical body than

on the side nearest to it and the little body will be moved toward the great body. Thus I have indeavoured to give you some conception how one body may appear to be attracted by another at a distance from it, tho' the effect be really that of a third thing acting upon it.

Since it is impossible, that anything can act where it is not, we may safely conclude that it is done in the manner and by such powers as are sufficient to produce all the phenomena of apparent mutual attraction. We have no other method of discovering the powers which produce the phenomena, and when they appear evidently sufficient, we cannot doubt of their existence. My present purpose does not allow me to go through all the phenomena of mutual apparent attraction, and of gravitation, and to shew how clearly they are deduced from a reacting medium as before described; the understanding of it requires more skill in Geometry, than you have as yet obtained. What I have now wrote may be of use to you, when you come to read what has been wrote on this subject, with the assistance of your Master of Mathematics.

After what you have read in the preceding pages, I must imagine, that you will be surprised afterwards to find that men who pretend to receive nothing but what is self-evident, or demonstratively deduced from such, at this time teach that bodies mutually attract each other at a distance by an inherent quality in themselves: and they teach this, they say, on the authority of Sir Isaac Newton. No authority is sufficient to establish an absurdity; but in the present case Sir Isaac takes care to guard against this absurdity. He tells that bodies in appearance only attract each other at a distance from each other, and that this apparent attraction is reciprocal to the squares of their distances. He says this must be done by the power of some medium, of which, he candidly confesses, he has not obtained sufficient knowledge; but he nowhere asserts that it is by any power inherent in matter: on the contrary he asserts that such a supposition is so great an absurdity, that he believes, no man, who has a competent faculty of thinking in philosophical matters, can fall into it. You will find many late writers in physics, who pretend to deduce their theorems from mathematical principles; and yet, notwithstanding of these high pretensions, and geometrical figures, and algebraical calculations, are often falling into gross errors in physics. You will find some of them assuming geometrical figures as physical causes.

It is necessary, therefore, to guard you against such high pretenders.

No doubt, the method of geometrical demonstration, and algebraical investigation is the best Logic: and may be of the greatest use, in accustoming young people to a regular method of reasoning. But to be perpetually poring [on lines] and figures, and jumbling together algebraical characters, cramps the imagination; they become like the dog in a wheel, perpetually running the same round, and is good for nothing else. You will find some of these high mathematicians as ignorant of the true principles of knowledge, as any pretenders whatsoever, and as little fitted for the most useful parts of life, or for common conversation.

The gentleman, who proposes to be generally useful in society, ought not to fix his thoughts singly on any one branch of science, but to have a competent knowledge of the principles of every branch, which he may obtain without fatiguing his imagination, by too continued an application. While he reads and thinks by turns, he should, in the intervals, cultivate his intellectual faculties by general conversation, where he may obtain more useful knowledge, than can be learned from books. The mere Scholar, the mere Physician, the mere Lawyer, Musician or painter, take them out of their own way, and they are often more insipid, than the mere plowman.

16

What Pragmatism Is

Charles Sanders Peirce

Introduction

Charles Sanders Peirce (1839–1914) was born in Cambridge, Massachusetts, the son of the renowned mathematician and Harvard professor, Benjamin Peirce. Charles was educated at Harvard and lectured occasionally at Johns Hopkins University, where he taught logic (John Dewey was one of his students), and at Harvard. William James credits him with founding pragmatism as a philosophical movement while he and James were members of a philosophy group at Harvard in the 1870s. Peirce did not, however, agree with James's conception of pragmatism, and in this selection he attempts to clarify his own position against the version advocated by James.

The writer of this article has been led by much experience to believe that every physicist, and every chemist, and, in short, every master in any department of experimental science, has had his mind moulded by his life in the laboratory to a degree that is little suspected. The experimentalist himself can hardly be fully aware of it, for the reason that the men whose intellects he really knows about are much like himself in this respect. With intellects of widely different training from his own, whose education has largely been a thing learned out of books, he will never become inwardly intimate, be he on ever so familiar terms with them; for he and they are as oil and water, and though they be shaken up together, it is remarkable how quickly they will go their several mental

Taken from The Monist, XV (April, 1905): 161–81.

ways, without having gained more than a faint flavor from the association. Were those other men only to take skilful soundings of the experimentalist's mind – which is just what they are unqualified to do, for the most part – they would soon discover that, excepting perhaps upon topics where his mind is trammelled by personal feeling or by his bringing up, his disposition is to think of everything just as everything is thought of in the laboratory, that is, as a question of experimentation. Of course, no living man possesses in their fullness all the attributes characteristic of his type: it is not the typical doctor whom you will see every day driven in buggy or coupé, nor is it the typical pedagogue that will be met with in the first schoolroom you enter. But when you have found, or ideally constructed upon a basis of observation, the typical experimentalist, you will find that whatever assertion you may make to him, he will either understand as meaning that if a given prescription for an experiment ever can be and ever is carried out in act, an experience of a given description will result, or else he will see no sense at all in what you say. If you talk to him as Mr. Balfour talked not long ago to the British Association, saying that "the physicist seeks for something deeper than the laws connecting possible objects of experience," that "his object is a physical reality" unrevealed in experiments, and that the existence of such non-experiential reality "is the unalterable faith of science," to all such ontological meaning you will find the experimentalist mind to be color-blind. What adds to that confidence in this which the writer owes to his conversations with experimentalists is that he himself may almost be said to have inhabited a laboratory from the age of six until long past maturity; and having all his life associated mostly with experimentalists, it has always been with a confident sense of understanding them and of being understood by them.

That laboratory life did not prevent the writer (who here and in what follows simply exemplifies the experimentalist type) from becoming interested in methods of thinking; and when he came to read metaphysics, although much of it seemed to him loosely reasoned and determined by accidental prepossessions, yet in the writings of some philosophers, especially Kant, Berkeley, and Spinoza, he sometimes came upon strains of thought that recalled the ways of thinking of the laboratory, so that he felt he might trust to them; all of which has been true of other laboratory-men.

Endeavoring, as a man of that type naturally would, to formulate what he so approved, he framed the theory that a *conception*, that is, the rational purport of a word or other expression, lies exclusively in its conceivable bearing upon the conduct of life: so that, since obviously nothing that might not result from experiment can have any direct bearing upon conduct, if one can define accurately all the conceivable experimental phenomena which the affirmation or denial of a concept could imply, one will have therein a complete definition of the concept, and *there is absolutely nothing more in it*. For this doctrine he invented the name *pragmatism*. Some of his friends wished him to call it *practicism* or *practicalism* (perhaps on the ground that πρακτικός is better Greek than πραγματικός). But for one who had learned philosophy out of Kant, as the writer, along with nineteen out of every twenty experimentalists who have turned to philosophy, had done, and who still thought in Kantian terms most readily, *praktisch* and *pragmatisch* were as far apart as the two poles, the former belonging in a region of thought where no mind of the experimentalist type can ever make sure of solid ground under his feet, the latter expressing relation to some definite human purpose. Now quite the most striking feature of the new theory was its recognition of an inseparable connection between rational cognition and rational purpose; and that consideration it was which determined the preference for the name *pragmatism*.

Concerning the matter of philosophical nomenclature, there are a few plain considerations, which the writer has for many years longed to submit to the deliberate judgment of those few fellow-students of philosophy, who deplore the present state of that study, and who are intent upon rescuing it therefrom and bringing it to a condition like that of the natural sciences, where investigators, instead of contemning each the work of most of the others as misdirected from beginning to end, co-operate, stand upon one another's shoulders, and multiply incontestible results; where every observation is repeated, and isolated observations go for little; where every hypothesis that merits attention is subjected to severe but fair examination, and only after the predictions to which it leads have been remarkably borne out by experience is trusted at all, and even then only provisionally; where a radically false step is rarely taken, even the most faulty of those theories which gain wide credence being true in their main experiential predictions. To those students, it is submitted that no study can become scientific in the sense described, until it provides itself with a suitable technical nomenclature, whose every term has a single definite meaning universally accepted among students of the subject, and whose vocables have no such sweetness or charms as might tempt loose writers to abuse them – which is a virtue of scientific nomenclature too little appreciated. It is submitted that the experience of those sciences which have conquered the greatest difficulties of terminology, which are unquestionably the taxonomic sciences, chemistry, mineralogy, botany, zoölogy, has conclusively shown that the one only way in which the requisite unanimity and requisite ruptures with individual habits and preferences can be brought about is so to shape the canons of terminology that they shall gain the support of *moral principle* and of every man's sense of decency; and that, in particular (under defined restrictions) the general feeling shall be that he who introduces a new conception into philosophy is under an obligation to invent acceptable terms to express it, and that when he has done so, the duty of his fellow-students is to accept those terms, and to resent any wresting of them from their original meanings, as not only a gross discourtesy to him to whom philosophy was indebted for each conception, but also as an injury to philosophy itself; and furthermore, that once a conception has been supplied with suitable and sufficient words for its expression, no other *technical* terms denoting the same things, considered in the same relations, should be countenanced.

Should this suggestion find favor, it might be deemed needful that the philosophians in congress assembled should adopt, after due deliberation, convenient canons to limit the application of the principle. Thus, just as is done in chemistry, it might be wise to assign fixed meanings to certain prefixes and suffixes. For example, it might be agreed, perhaps, that the prefix *prope-* should mark a broad and rather indefinite extension of the meaning of the term to which it was prefixed; the name of a doctrine would naturally end in *-ism*, while *-icism* might mark a more strictly defined acception of that doctrine, etc. Then again, just as in biology no account is taken of terms antedating Linnæus, so in philosophy it might be found best not to go back of the scholastic terminology. To illustrate another sort of limitation, it has probably never happened that any philosopher has attempted to give a general name to his own doctrine without that name's soon acquiring in common philosophical usage, a signification much broader than was originally intended. Thus, special systems go by the names Kantianism, Benthamism, Comtianism, Spencerianism, etc., while transcendentalism, utilitarianism, positivism, evolutionism, synthetic philosophy, etc. have irrevocably and very conveniently been elevated to broader governments.

After awaiting in vain, for a good many years, some particularly opportune conjuncture of circumstances that might serve to recommend his notions of the ethics of terminology, the writer has now, at last, dragged them in over head and shoulders, on an occasion when he has no specific proposal to offer nor any feeling but satisfaction at the course usage has run without any canons or resolutions of a congress. His word "pragmatism" has gained general recognition in a generalised sense that seems to argue power of growth and vitality. The famed psychologist, James, first took it up, seeing that his "radical empiricism" substantially answered to the writer's definition of pragmatism, albeit with a certain difference in the point of view. Next, the admirably clear and brilliant thinker, Mr. Ferdinand C. S. Schiller, casting about for a more attractive name for the "anthropomorphism" of his *Riddle of the Sphinx*, lit, in that most remarkable paper of his on *Axioms as Postulates*, upon the same designation "pragmatism," which in its original sense was in generic agreement with his own doctrine, for which he has since found the more appropriate specification

"humanism," while he still retains "pragmatism" in a somewhat wider sense. So far all went happily. But at present, the word begins to be met with occasionally in the literary journals, where it gets abused in the merciless way that words have to expect when they fall into literary clutches. Sometimes the manners of the British have effloresced in scolding at the word as ill-chosen – ill-chosen, that is, to express some meaning that it was rather designed to exclude. So then, the writer, finding his bantling "pragmatism" so promoted, feels that it is time to kiss his child good-by and relinquish it to its higher destiny; while to serve the precise purpose of expressing the original definition, he begs to announce the birth of the word "pragmaticism," which is ugly enough to be safe from kidnappers.[1]

Much as the writer has gained from the perusal of what other pragmatists have written, he still thinks there is a decisive advantage in his original conception of the doctrine. From this original form every truth that follows from any of the other forms can be deduced, while some errors can be avoided into which other pragmatists have fallen. The original view appears, too, to be a more compact and unitary conception than the others. But its capital merit, in the writer's eyes, is that it more readily connects itself with a critical proof of its truth. Quite in accord with the logical order of investigation, it usually happens that one first forms an hypothesis that seems more and more reasonable the further one examines into it, but that only a good deal later gets crowned with an adequate proof. The present writer having had the pragmatist theory under consideration for many years longer than most of its adherents, would naturally have given more attention to the proof of it. At any rate, in endeavoring to explain pragmatism, he may be excused for confining himself to that form of it that he knows best. In the present article there will be space only to explain just what this doctrine (which, in such hands as it has now fallen into, may probably play a pretty prominent part in the philosophical discussions of the next coming years) really consists in. Should the exposition be found to interest readers of *The Monist*, they would certainly be much more interested in a second article which would give some samples of the manifold applications of pragmaticism (assuming it to be true) to the solution of problems of different kinds. After that, readers might be prepared to take an interest in a proof that the doctrine is true – a proof which seems to the writer to leave no reasonable doubt on the subject, and to be the one contribution of value that he has to make to philosophy. For it would essentially involve the establishment of the truth of synechism.

The bare definition of pragmaticism could convey no satisfactory comprehension of it to the most apprehensive of minds, but requires the commentary to be given below. Moreover, this definition takes no notice of one or two other doctrines without the previous acceptance (or virtual acceptance) of which pragmaticism itself would be a nullity. They are included as a part of the pragmatism of Schiller, but the present writer prefers not to mingle different propositions. The preliminary propositions had better be stated forthwith.

The difficulty in doing this is that no formal list of them has ever been made. They might all be included under the vague maxim, "Dismiss make-believes." Philosophers of very diverse stripes propose that philosophy shall take its start from one or another state of mind in which no man, least of all a beginner in philosophy, actually is. One proposes that you shall begin by doubting everything, and says that there is only one thing that you cannot doubt, as if doubting were "as easy as lying." Another proposes that we should begin by observing "the first impressions of sense," forgetting that our very percepts are the results of cognitive elaboration. But in truth, there is but one state of mind from which you can "set out," namely, the very state of mind in which you actually find yourself at the time you do "set out" – a state in which you are laden with an immense mass of cognition already formed, of which you cannot divest yourself if you would; and who knows whether, if you could, you would not have made all knowledge impossible to yourself? Do you call it *doubting* to write down on a piece of paper that you doubt? If so, doubt has nothing to do with any serious business. But do not make believe; if pedantry has not eaten all the reality out of you, recognise, as you must, that there is much that you do not doubt, in the least. Now that which you do not at all doubt, you must and do regard as infallible, absolute truth. Here breaks in Mr. Make Believe: "What! Do you mean to say that one is to believe what is not true, or that what a man does not doubt is *ipso facto* true?" No, but unless he can make a thing white and black at once, *he* has to regard what he does not doubt as absolutely true. Now you, *per hypothesiu*, are that man. "But you tell me there are scores of things I do not doubt. I really cannot persuade myself that there is not some one of them

about which I am mistaken." You are adducing one of your make-believe facts, which, even if it were established, would only go to show that doubt has a *limen*, that is, is only called into being by a certain finite stimulus. You only puzzle yourself by talking of this metaphysical "truth" and metaphysical "falsity," that you know nothing about. All you have any dealings with are your doubts and beliefs,[2] with the course of life that forces new beliefs upon you and gives you power to doubt old beliefs. If your terms "truth" and "falsity" are taken in such senses as to be definable in terms of doubt and belief and the course of experience (as for example they would be, if you were to define the "truth" as that to a belief in which belief would tend if it were to tend indefinitely toward absolute fixity) well and good: in that case, you are only talking about doubt and belief. But if by truth and falsity you mean something not definable in terms of doubt and belief in any way, then you are talking of entities of whose existence you can know nothing, and which Ockham's razor would clean shave off. Your problems would be greatly simplified, if, instead of saying that you want to know the "Truth," you were simply to say that you want to attain a state of belief unassailable by doubt.

Belief is not a momentary mode of consciousness; it is a habit of mind essentially enduring for some time, and mostly (at least) unconscious; and like other habits, it is (until it meets with some surprise that begins its dissolution) perfectly self-satisfied. Doubt is of an altogether contrary genus. It is not a habit, but the privation of a habit. Now a privation of a habit, in order to be anything at all, must be a condition of erratic activity that in some way must get superseded by a habit.

Among the things which the reader, as a rational person, does not doubt, is that he not merely has habits, but also can exert a measure of self-control over his future actions; which means, however, *not* that he can impart to them any arbitrarily assignable character, but, on the contrary, that a process of self-preparation will tend to impart to action (when the occasion for it shall arise) one fixed character, which is indicated and perhaps roughly measured by the absence (or slightness) of the feeling of self-reproach, which subsequent reflection will induce. Now, this subsequent reflection is part of the self-preparation for action on the next occasion. Consequently, there is a tendency, as action is repeated again and again, for the action to approximate indefinitely toward the perfection of that fixed character, which would be marked by entire absence of self-reproach. The more closely this is approached, the less room for self-control there will be; and where no self-control is possible there will be no self-reproach.

These phenomena seem to be the fundamental characteristics which distinguish a rational being. Blame, in every case, appears to be a modification, often accomplished by a transference, or "projection," of the primary feeling of self-reproach. Accordingly, we never blame anybody for what had been beyond his power of previous self-control. Now, thinking is a species of conduct which is largely subject to self-control. In all their features (which there is no room to describe here) logical self-control is a perfect mirror of ethical self-control – unless it be rather a species under that genus. In accordance with this, what you cannot in the least help believing is not, justly speaking, wrong belief. In other words, for you it is the absolute truth. True, it is conceivable that what you cannot help believing to-day, you might find you thoroughly disbelieve to-morrow. But then there is a certain distinction between things you "cannot" do, merely in the sense that nothing stimulates you to the great effort and endeavors that would be required, and things you cannot do because in their own nature they are insusceptible of being put into practice. In every stage of your excogitations, there is something of which you can only say, "I cannot think otherwise," and your experientially based hypothesis is that the impossibility is of the second kind.

There is no reason why "thought," in what has just been said, should be taken in that narrow sense in which silence and darkness are favorable to thought. It should rather be understood as covering all rational life, so that an experiment shall be an operation of thought. Of course, that ultimate state of habit to which the action of self-control ultimately tends, where no room is left for further self-control, is, in the case of thought, the state of fixed belief, or perfect knowledge.

Two things here are all-important to assure oneself of and to remember. The first is that a person is not absolutely an individual. His thoughts are what he is "saying to himself," that is, is saying to that other self that is just coming into life in the flow of time. When one reasons, it is that critical self that one is trying to persuade; and all thought whatsoever is a sign, and is mostly of the nature of language. The second thing to remember is that the man's circle of society (however widely or narrowly this phrase may be understood) is a sort

of loosely compacted person, in some respects of higher rank than the person of an individual organism. It is these two things alone that render it possible for you – but only in the abstract, and in a Pickwickian sense – to distinguish between absolute truth and what you do not doubt.

Let us now hasten to the exposition of pragmaticism itself. Here it will be convenient to imagine that somebody to whom the doctrine is new, but of rather preternatural perspicacity, asks questions of a pragmaticist. Everything that might give a dramatic illusion must be stripped off, so that the result will be a sort of cross between a dialogue and a catechism, but a good deal liker the latter – something rather painfully reminiscent of *Mangnall's Historical Questions*.

Questioner: I am astounded at your definition of your pragmatism, because only last year I was assured by a person above all suspicion of warping the truth – himself a pragmatist – that your doctrine precisely was "that a conception is to be tested by its practical effects." You must surely, then, have entirely changed your definition very recently.

Pragmatist: If you will turn to Vols. VI and VII of the *Revue Philosophique*, or to the *Popular Science Monthly* for November 1877 and January 1878, you will be able to judge for yourself whether the interpretation you mention was not then clearly excluded. The exact wording of the English enunciation (changing only the first person into the second) was: "Consider what effects that might conceivably have practical bearings you conceive the object of your conception to have. Then your conception of those effects is the WHOLE of your conception of the object."

Questioner: Well, what reason have you for asserting that this is so?

Pragmatist: That is what I specially desire to tell you. But the question had better be postponed until you clearly understand what those reasons profess to prove.

Questioner: What, then, is the *raison d'être* of the doctrine? What advantage is expected from it?

Pragmatist: It will serve to show that almost every proposition of ontological metaphysics is either meaningless gibberish – one word being defined by other words, and they by still others, without any real conception ever being reached – or else is downright absurd; so that all such rubbish being swept away, what will remain of philosophy will be a series of problems capable of investigation by the observational methods of the true sciences – the truth about which can be reached without those interminable misunderstandings and disputes which have made the highest of the positive sciences a mere amusement for idle intellects, a sort of chess – idle pleasure its purpose, and reading out of a book its method. In this regard, pragmaticism is a species of prope-positivism. But what distinguishes it from other species is, first, its retention of a purified philosophy; secondly, its full acceptance of the main body of our instinctive beliefs; and thirdly, its strenuous insistence upon the truth of scholastic realism (or a close approximation to that, well-stated by the late Dr. Francis Ellingwood Abbot in the Introduction to his *Scientific Theism*). So, instead of merely jeering at metaphysics, like other prope-positivists, whether by long drawn-out parodies or otherwise, the pragmaticist extracts from it a precious essence, which will serve to give life and light to cosmology and physics. At the same time, the moral applications of the doctrine are positive and potent; and there are many other uses of it not easily classed. On another occasion, instances may be given to show that it really has these effects.

Questioner. I hardly need to be convinced that your doctrine would wipe out metaphysics. Is it not as obvious that it must wipe out every proposition of science and everything that bears on the conduct of life? For you say that the only meaning that, for you, any assertion bears is that a certain experiment has resulted in a certain way: Nothing else but an experiment enters into the meaning. Tell me, then, how can an experiment, in itself, reveal anything more than that something once happened to an individual object and that subsequently some other individual event occurred?

Pragmatist: That question is, indeed, to the purpose – the purpose being to correct any misapprehensions of pragmaticism. You speak of an experiment in itself, emphasising "*in itself.*" You evidently think of each experiment as isolated from every other. It has not, for example, occurred to you, one might venture to surmise, that every connected series of experiments constitutes a single collective experiment. What are the essential ingredients of an experiment? First, of course, an experimenter of flesh and blood. Secondly, a verifiable hypothesis. This is a proposition[3] relating to the universe environing the experimenter, or to some well-known part of it and affirming or denying of this only some experimental possibility or impossibility. The third indispensable ingredient

is a sincere doubt in the experimenter's mind as to the truth of that hypothesis. Passing over several ingredients on which we need not dwell, the purpose, the plan, and the resolve, we come to the act of choice by which the experimenter singles out certain identifiable objects to be operated upon. The next is the external (or quasi-external) ACT by which he modifies those objects. Next, comes the subsequent *reaction* of the world upon the experimenter in a perception; and finally, his recognition of the teaching of the experiment. While the two chief parts of the event itself are the action and the reaction, yet the unity of essence of the experiment lies in its purpose and plan, the ingredients passed over in the enumeration.

Another thing: in representing the pragmaticist as making rational meaning to consist in an experiment (which you speak of as an event in the past) you strikingly fail to catch his attitude of mind. Indeed, it is not in an experiment, but in *experimental phenomena*, that rational meaning is said to consist. When an experimentalist speaks of a *phenomenon*, such as "Hall's phenomenon," "Zeemann's phenomenon" and its modification, "Michelson's phenomenon," or "the chess-board phenomenon," he does not mean any particular event that did happen to somebody in the dead past, but what *surely will* happen to everybody in the living future who shall fulfil certain conditions. The phenomenon consists in the fact that when an experimentalist shall come to *act* according to a certain scheme that he has in mind, then will something else happen, and shatter the doubts of sceptics, like the celestial fire upon the altar of Elijah.

And do not overlook the fact that the pragmaticist maxim says nothing of single experiments or of single experimental phenomena (for what is conditionally true *in futuro* can hardly be singular) but only speaks of *general kinds* of experimental phenomena. Its adherent does not shrink from speaking of general objects as real, since whatever is true represents a real. Now the laws of nature are true.

The rational meaning of every proposition lies in the future. How so? The meaning of a proposition is itself a proposition. Indeed, it is no other than the very proposition of which it is the meaning: it is a translation of it. But of the myriads of forms into which a proposition may be translated, what is that one which is to be called its very meaning? It is, according to the pragmaticist, that form in which the proposition becomes applicable to human conduct, not in these or those special circumstances, nor when one entertains this or that special design, but that form which is most directly applicable to self-control under every situation, and to every purpose. This is why he locates the meaning in future time; for future conduct is the only conduct that is subject to self-control. But in order that that form of the proposition which is to be taken as its meaning should be applicable to every situation and to every purpose upon which the proposition has any bearing, it must be simply the general description of all the experimental phenomena which the assertion of the proposition virtually predicts. For an experimental phenomenon is the fact asserted by the proposition that action of a certain description will have a certain kind of experimental result; and experimental results are the only results that can affect human conduct. No doubt, some unchanging idea may come to influence a man more than it had done; but only because some experience equivalent to an experiment has brought its truth home to him more intimately than before. Whenever a man acts purposively, he acts under a belief in some experimental phenomenon. Consequently, the sum of the experimental phenomena that a proposition implies makes up its entire bearing upon human conduct. Your question, then, of how a pragmaticist can attribute any meaning to any assertion other than that of a single occurrence is substantially answered.

Questioner: I see that pragmaticism is a thorough-going phenomenalism. Only why should you limit yourself to the phenomena of experimental science rather than embrace all observational science? Experiment, after all, is an uncommunicative informant. It never expiates: it only answers "yes" or "no"; or rather it usually snaps out "No!" or, at best, only utters an inarticulate grunt for the negation of its "no." The typical experimentalist is not much of an observer. It is the student of natural history to whom nature opens the treasury of her confidence, while she treats the cross-examining experimentalist with the reserve he merits. Why should your phenomenalism sound the meagre jews-harp of experiment rather than the glorious organ of observation?

Pragmaticist: Because pragmaticism is not definable as "thorough-going phenomenalism," although the latter doctrine may be a kind of pragmatism. The *richness* of phenomena lies in their sensuous quality. Pragmaticism does not intend to define the phenomenal equivalents of words and general ideas, but, on the contrary, eliminates their sential element, and endeavors to define the rational purport, and this it finds in the purposive bearing of the word or proposition in question.

Questioner: Well, if you choose so to make Doing the Be-all and the End-all of human life, why do you not make meaning to consist simply in doing? Doing has to be done at a certain time upon a certain object. Individual objects and single events cover all reality, as everybody knows, and as a practicalist ought to be the first to insist. Yet, your meaning, as you have described it, is *general*. Thus, it is of the nature of a mere word and not a reality. You say yourself that your meaning of a proposition is only the same proposition in another dress. But a practical man's meaning is the very thing he means. What do you make to be the meaning of "George Washington"?

Pragmaticist: Forcibly put! A good half dozen of your points must certainly be admitted. It must be admitted, in the first place, that if pragmaticism really made Doing to be the Be-all and the End-all of life, that would be its death. For to say that we live for the mere sake of action, as action, regardless of the thought it carries out, would be to say that there is no such thing as rational purport. Secondly, it must be admitted that every proposition professes to be true of a certain real individual object, often the environing universe. Thirdly, it must be admitted that pragmaticism fails to furnish any translation or meaning of a proper name, or other designation of an individual object. Fourthly, the pragmaticistic meaning is undoubtedly general; and it is equally indisputable that the general is of the nature of a word or sign. Fifthly, it must be admitted that individuals alone exist; and sixthly, it may be admitted that the very meaning of a word or significant object ought to be the very essence of reality of what it signifies. But when, those admissions having been unreservedly made, you find the pragmaticist still constrained most earnestly to deny the force of your objection, you ought to infer that there is some consideration that has escaped you. Putting the admissions together, you will perceive that the pragmaticist grants that a proper name (although it is not customary to say that it has a *meaning*) has a certain denotative function peculiar, in each case, to that name and its equivalents; and that he grants that every assertion contains such a denotative or pointing-out function. In its peculiar individuality, the pragmaticist excludes this from the rational purport of the assertion, although *the like* of it, being common to all assertions, and so, being general and not individual, may enter into the pragmaticistic purport. Whatever exists, *ex-sists*, that is, really acts upon other existents, so obtains a self-identity, and is definitely individual. As to the general, it will be a help to thought to notice that there are two ways of being general. A statue of a soldier on some village monument, in his overcoat and with his musket, is for each of a hundred families the image of its uncle, its sacrifice to the union. That statue, then, though it is itself single, represents any one man of whom a certain predicate may be true. It is *objectively* general. The word "soldier," whether spoken or written, is general in the same way; while the name, "George Washington," is not so. But each of these two terms remains one and the same noun, whether it be spoken or written, and whenever and wherever it be spoken or written. This noun is not an existent thing: it is a *type*, or *form*, to which objects, both those that are externally existent and those which are imagined, may *conform*, but which none of them can exactly be. This is subjective generality. The pragmaticistic purport is general in both ways.

As to reality, one finds it defined in various ways; but if that principle of terminological ethics that was proposed be accepted, the equivocal language will soon disappear. For *realis* and *realitas* are not ancient words. They were invented to be terms of philosophy in the thirteenth century, and the meaning they were intended to express is perfectly clear. That is *real* which has such and such characters, whether anybody thinks it to have those characters or not. At any rate, that is the sense in which the pragmaticist uses the word. Now, just as conduct controlled by ethical reason tends toward fixing certain habits of conduct, the nature of which (as to illustrate the meaning, peaceable habits and not quarrelsome habits) does not depend upon any accidental circumstances, and *in that sense*, may be said to be *destined*; so, thought, controlled by a rational experimental logic, tends to the fixation of certain opinions, equally destined, the nature of which will be the same in the end, however the perversity of thought of whole generations may cause the postponement of the ultimate fixation. If this be so, as every man of us virtually assumes that it is, in regard to each matter the truth of which he seriously discusses, then, according to the adopted definition of "real," the state of things which will be believed in that ultimate opinion is real. But, for the most part, such opinions will be general. Consequently, *some* general objects are

real. (Of course, nobody ever thought that *all* generals were real; but the scholastics used to assume that generals were real when they had hardly any, or quite no, experiential evidence to support their assumption; and their fault lay just there, and not in holding that generals could be real.) One is struck with the inexactitude of thought even of analysts of power, when they touch upon modes of being. One will meet, for example, the virtual assumption that what is relative to thought cannot be real. But why not, exactly? *Red* is relative to sight, but the fact that this or that is in that relation to vision that we call being red is not *itself* relative to sight; it is a real fact.

Not only may generals be real, but they may also be *physically efficient*, not in every metaphysical sense, but in the common-sense acception in which human purposes are physically efficient. Aside from metaphysical nonsense, no sane man doubts that if I feel the air in my study to be stuffy, that thought may cause the window to be opened. My thought, be it granted, was an individual event. But what determined it to take the particular determination it did, was in part the general fact that stuffy air is unwholesome, and in part other *Forms*, concerning which Dr. Carus has caused so many men to reflect to advantage – or rather, *by* which, and the general truth concerning which Dr. Carus's mind was determined to the forcible enunciation of so much truth. For truths, on the average, have a greater tendency to get believed than falsities have. Were it otherwise, considering that there are myriads of false hypotheses to account for any given phenomenon, against one sole true one (or if you will have it so, against every true one) the first step toward genuine knowledge must have been next door to a miracle. So, then, when my window was opened, because of the truth that stuffy air is malsain, a physical effort was brought into existence by the efficiency of a general and non-existent truth. This has a droll sound because it is unfamiliar; but exact analysis is with it and not against it; and it has besides, the immense advantage of not blinding us to great facts – such as that the ideas "justice" and "truth" are, notwithstanding the iniquity of the world, the mightiest of the forces that move it. Generality is, indeed, an indispensable ingredient of reality; for mere individual existence or actuality without any regularity whatever is a nullity. Chaos is pure nothing.

That which any true proposition asserts is *real*, in the sense of being as it is regardless of what you or I may think about it. Let this proposition be a general conditional proposition as to the future, and it is a real general such as is calculated really to influence human conduct; and such the pragmaticist holds to be the rational purport of every concept.

Accordingly, the pragmaticist does not make the *summum bonum* to consist in action, but makes it to consist in that process of evolution whereby the existent comes more and more to embody those generals which were just now said to be *destined*, which is what we strive to express in calling them *reasonable*. In its higher stages, evolution takes place more and more largely through self-control, and this gives the pragmaticist a sort of justification for making the rational purport to be general.

There is much more in elucidation of pragmaticism that might be said to advantage, were it not for the dread of fatiguing the reader. It might, for example, have been well to show clearly that the pragmaticist does not attribute any different essential mode of being to an event in the future from that which he would attribute to a similar event in the past, but only that the practical attitude of the thinker toward the two is different. It would also have been well to show that the pragmaticist does not make Forms to be the *only* realities in the world, any more than he makes the reasonable purport of a word to be the only kind of meaning there is. These things are, however, implicitly involved in what has been said. There is only one remark concerning the pragmaticist's conception of the relation of his formula to the first principles of logic which need detain the reader.

Aristotle's definition of universal predication, which is usually designated (like a papal bull or writ of court, from its opening words) as the *Dictum de omni*, may be translated as follows: "We call a predication (be it affirmative or negative) *universal*, when, and only when, there is nothing among the existent individuals to which the subject affirmatively belongs, but to which the predicate will not likewise be referred (affirmatively or negatively, according as the universal predication is affirmative or negative)." The Greek is: λέγομεν τὸ κατὰ παντὸς κατηγορ εἶσθαι ὅταν μηδὲν ἤ λαβεῖν τῶν τοῦ ὑποκει μένου καθ' οἰθάτερον οὐ λεχθήσεται καὶ τὸ κατὰ μηδενὸς ὡσαύτως. The important words "existent individuals" have been introduced into the translation (which English idiom would not here permit to be literal); but it is plain that existent individuals were what Aristotle meant. The

other departures from literalness only serve to give modern English forms of expression. Now, it is well known that propositions in formal logic go in pairs, the two of one pair being convertible into another by the interchange of the ideas of antecedent and consequent, subject and predicate, etc. The parallelism extends so far that it is often assumed to be perfect; but it is not quite so. The proper mate of this sort to the *Dictum de omni* is the following definition of affirmative predication: We call a predication *affirmative* (be it universal or particular) when, and only when, there is nothing among the sensational effects that belong universally to the predicate which will not be (universally or particularly, according as the affirmative predication is universal or particular) said to belong to the subject. Now, this is substantially the essential proposition of pragmaticism. Of course, its parallelism to the *dictum de omni* will only be admitted by a person who admits the truth of pragmaticism.

Suffer me to add one word more on this point. For if one cares at all to know what the pragmaticist theory consists in, one must understand that there is no other part of it to which the pragmaticist attaches quite as much importance as he does to the recognition in his doctrine of the utter inadequacy of action or volition or even of resolve or actual purpose, as materials out of which to construct a conditional purpose or the concept of conditional purpose. Had a purposed article concerning the principle of continuity and synthetising the ideas of the other articles of a series in the early volumes of *The Monist* ever been written, it would have appeared how, with thorough consistency, that theory involved the recognition that continuity is an indispensable element of reality, and that continuity is simply what generality becomes in the logic of relatives, and thus, like generality, and more than generality, is an affair of thought, and is the essence of thought. Yet even in its truncated condition, an extra-intelligent reader might discern that the theory of those cosmological articles made reality to consist in something more than feeling and action could supply, inasmuch as the primeval chaos, where those two elements were present, was explicitly shown to be pure nothing. Now, the motive for alluding to that theory just here is, that in this way one can put in a strong light a position which the pragmaticist holds and must hold, whether that cosmological theory be ultimately sustained or exploded, namely, that the third category – the category of thought, representation, triadic relation, mediation, genuine thirdness, thirdness as such – is an essential ingredient of reality, yet does not by itself constitute reality, since this category (which in that cosmology appears as the element of habit) can have no concrete being without action, as a separate object on which to work its government, just as action cannot exist without the immediate being of feeling on which to act. The truth is that pragmaticism is closely allied to the Hegelian absolute idealism, from which, however, it is sundered by its vigorous denial that the third category (which Hegel degrades to a mere stage of thinking) suffices to make the world, or is even so much as self-sufficient. Had Hegel, instead of regarding the first two stages with his smile of contempt, held on to them as independent or distinct elements of the triune Reality, pragmaticists might have looked up to him as the great vindicator of their truth. (Of course, the external trappings of his doctrine are only here and there of much significance.) For pragmaticism belongs essentially to the triadic class of philosophical doctrines, and is much more essentially so than Hegelianism is. (Indeed, in one passage, at least, Hegel alludes to the triadic form of his exposition as to a mere fashion of dress.)

POSTSCRIPT. During the last five months, I have met with references to several objections to the above opinions, but not having been able to obtain the text of these objections, I do not think I ought to attempt to answer them. If gentlemen who attack either pragmatism in general or the variety of it which I entertain would only send me copies of what they write, more important readers they could easily find, but they could find none who would examine their arguments with a more grateful avidity for truth not yet apprehended, nor any who would be more sensible of their courtesy.

Notes

1 To show how recent the general use of the word "pragmatism" is, the writer may mention that, to the best of his belief, he never used it in copy for the press before to-day, except by particular request, in *Baldwin's Dictionary*. Toward the end of 1890, when this part of the *Century Dictionary* appeared, he did not deem that the word had sufficient status to appear in that work. But he has used it continually in philosophical conversation since, perhaps, the mid-seventies.

2 It is necessary to say that "belief" is throughout used merely as the name of the contrary to doubt, without regard to grades of certainty nor to the nature of the proposition held for true, i.e. "believed."

3 The writer, like most English logicians, invariably uses the word *proposition*, not as the Germans define their equivalent, *Satz*, as the language-expression of a judgment (*Urtheil*), but as that which is related to any assertion, whether mental and self-addressed or outwardly expressed, just as any possibility is related to its actualisation. The difficulty of the, at best, difficult problem of the essential nature of a Proposition has been increased, for the Germans, by their *Urtheil*, confounding, under one designation, the mental *assertion* with the *assertible*.

17

The Supremacy of Method

John Dewey

Introduction

John Dewey (1859–1952) was born in Burlington, Vermont, and educated at the University of Vermont and Johns Hopkins University. He advocated a form of pragmatism that brought together a theory of inquiry, a theory of valuation, and a theory of community grounded in interaction and framed by the idea of growth. Dewey's philosophical scope is broad, with significant works in philosophy of education, logic, ethics, social philosophy, aesthetics, and epistemology. The selection here is from his 1929 Gifford Lectures given at the University of Edinburgh. The lectures as a whole provide a systematic critique of European philosophy and present Dewey's pragmatic alternative, which begins by seeing knowledge as the product of a process of inquiry that binds together knowledge and value.

Uncertainty is primarily a practical matter. It signifies uncertainty of the *issue* of present experiences; these are fraught with future peril as well as inherently objectionable. Action to get rid of the objectionable has no warrant of success and is itself perilous. The intrinsic troublesome and uncertain quality of situations lies in the fact that they hold outcomes in suspense; they move to evil or to good fortune. The natural tendency of man is to do something at once; there is impatience with sus-

Taken from *The Collected Works of John Dewey: Later Works*, vol. IV (Carbondale: Southern Illinois University Press, 1929). Reprinted with permission from the Board of Trustees, Southern Illinois University.

pense, and lust for immediate action. When action lacks means for control of external conditions, it takes the form of acts which are the prototypes of rite and cult. Intelligence signifies that direct action has become indirect. It continues to be overt, but it is directed into channels of examination of conditions, and doings that are tentative and preparatory. Instead of rushing to "do something about it," action centres upon finding out something about obstacles and resources and upon projecting inchoate later modes of definite response. Thinking has been well called deferred action. But not all action is deferred; only that which is final and in so far productive of irretrievable consequences. Deferred action is present exploratory action.

The first and most obvious effect of this change in the quality of action is that the dubious or problematic situation becomes *a* problem. The risky character that pervades a situation as a whole is translated into an object of inquiry that locates what the trouble is, and hence facilitates projection of methods and means of dealing with it. Only after expertness has been gained in special fields of inquiry does the mind set out at once from problems: even then in novel cases, there is a preliminary period of groping through a situation which is characterized throughout by confusion, instead of presenting a clear-cut problem for investigation.

Many definitions of mind and thinking have been given. I know of but one that goes to the heart of the matter: response to the doubtful as such. No inanimate thing reacts to things *as* problematic. Its behavior to other things is capable of description in terms of what is determinately there. Under given conditions, it just reacts or does not react. Its reactions merely enstate a new set of conditions, in which reactions continue without regard to the nature of their outcome. It makes no difference, so to say, to a stone what are the results of its interactions with other things. It enjoys the advantage that it makes no difference how it reacts, even if the effect is its own pulverization. It requires no argument to show that the case is different with a living organism. To live signifies that a connected continuity of acts is effected in which preceding ones prepare the conditions under which later ones occur. There is a chain of cause and effects, of course, in what happens with inanimate things. But for living creatures, the chain has a particular cumulative continuity, or else death ensues.

As organisms become more complex in structure and thus related to a more complex environment, the importance of a particular act in establishing conditions favorable to subsequent acts that sustain the continuity of the life process, becomes at once more difficult and more imperative. A juncture may be so critical that the right or wrong present move signifies life or death. Conditions of the environment become more ambivalent: it is more uncertain what sort of action they call for in the interests of living. Behavior is thus compelled to become more hesitant and wary, more expectant and preparatory. In the degree that responses take place to the doubtful *as* the doubtful, they acquire *mental* quality. If they are such as to have a directed tendency to change the precarious and problematic into the secure and resolved, they are *intellectual* as well as mental. Acts are then relatively more instrumental and less consummatory or final; even the latter are haunted by a sense of what may issue from them.

This conception of the mental brings to unity various modes of response; emotional, volitional and intellectual. It is usual to say that there is no fundamental difference among these activities – that they are all different phases or aspects of a common action of mind. But I know of but one way of making this assertion good: that in which they are seen to be distinctive modes of response to the uncertain. The emotional aspect of responsive behavior is its *immediate* quality. When we are confronted with the precarious, an ebb and flow of emotion marks a disturbance of the even tenor of existence. Emotions are conditioned by the in-

determinateness of present situations with respect to their issue. Fear and hope, joy and sorrow, aversion and desire, as perturbations, are qualities of a divided response. They involve concern, solicitude, for what the present situation may *become*. "Care" signifies two quite different things: fret, worry and anxiety, and cherishing attention to that in whose potentialities we are interested. These two meanings represent different poles of reactive behavior to a present having a future which is ambiguous. Elation and depression, moreover, manifest themselves only under conditions wherein not everything from start to finish is completely determined and certain. They may occur at a final moment of triumph or defeat, but this moment is one of victory or frustration in connection with a previous course of affairs whose issue was in suspense. Love for a Being so perfect and complete that our regard for it can make no difference to it is not so much affection as (a fact which the scholastics saw) it is concern for the destiny of our own souls. Hate that is sheer antagonism without any element of uncertainty is not an emotion, but is an energy devoted to ruthless destruction. Aversion is a state of affectivity only in connection with an obstruction offered by the disliked object or person to an end made uncertain by it.

The volitional phase of mental life is notoriously connected with the emotional. The only difference is that the latter is the immediate, the cross-sectional, aspect of response to the uncertain and precarious, while the volitional phase is the tendency of the reaction to modify indeterminate, ambiguous conditions in the direction of a preferred and favored outcome; to actualize one of its possibilities rather than another. Emotion is a hindrance or an aid to resolute will according as it is overwhelming in its immediacy or as it marks a gathering together of energy to deal with the situation whose issue is in doubt. Desire, purpose, planning, choice, have no meaning save in conditions where something is at stake, and where action in one direction rather than another may eventuate in bringing into existence a new situation which fulfills a need.

The intellectual phase of mental action is identical with an *indirect* mode of response, one whose purpose is to locate the nature of the trouble and form an idea of how it may be dealt with – so that operations may be directed in view of an intended solution. Take any incident of experience you choose, seeing a color, reading a book, listening to conversation, manipulating apparatus, studying a lesson, and it has or has not intellectual, cognitive, quality according as there is deliberate endeavor to deal with the indeterminate so as to dispose of it, to settle it. Anything that may be called knowledge, or a known object, marks a question answered, a difficulty disposed of, a confusion cleared up, an inconsistency reduced to coherence, a perplexity mastered. Without reference to this mediating element, what is called knowledge is but direct and unswerving action or else a possessive enjoyment. Similarly, thinking is the actual transition from the problematic to the secure, as far as that is intentionally guided. There is no separate "mind" gifted in and of itself with a faculty of thought; such a conception of thought ends in postulating the mystery of a power outside of nature and yet able to intervene within it. Thinking is objectively discoverable as that mode of serial responsive behavior to a problematic situation in which transition to the relatively settled and clear is effected.

The concrete pathologies of belief, its failures and perversions, whether of defect or excess, spring from failure to observe and adhere to the principle that knowledge is the completed resolution of the inherently indeterminate or doubtful. The commonest fallacy is to suppose that since the state of doubt is accompanied by a feeling of uncertainty, knowledge arises when this feeling gives way to one of assurance. Thinking then ceases to be an effort to effect change in the objective situation and is replaced by various devices which generate a change in feeling or "consciousness." Tendency to premature judgment, jumping at conclusions, excessive love of simplicity, making over of evidence to suit desire, taking the familiar for the clear, etc., all spring from confusing the feeling of certitude with a certified situation. Thought hastens toward the settled and is only too likely to force the pace. The natural man dislikes the dis-ease which accompanies the doubtful and is ready to take almost any means to end it. Uncertainty is got rid of by fair means or foul. Long exposure to danger breeds an overpowering love of security. Love for security, translated into a desire not to be disturbed and unsettled, leads to dogmatism, to acceptance of beliefs upon authority, to intolerance and fanaticism on one side and to irresponsible dependence and sloth on the other.

Here is where ordinary thinking and thinking that is scrupulous diverge from each other. The natural man is impatient with doubt and suspense: he impatiently hurries to be shut of it. A disciplined mind takes delight in the problematic, and cherishes it until a way out is found that approves itself upon examination. The questionable becomes an active questioning, a search; desire for the emotion of certitude gives place to quest for the objects by which the obscure and unsettled may be developed into the stable and clear. The scientific attitude may almost be defined as that which is capable of enjoying the doubtful; scientific method is, in one aspect, a technique for making a productive use of doubt by converting it into operations of definite inquiry. No one gets far intellectually who does not "love to think," and no one loves to think who does not have an interest in problems as such. Being on the alert for problems signifies that mere organic curiosity, the restless disposition to meddle and reach out, has become a truly intellectual curiosity, one that protects a person from hurrying to a conclusion and that induces him to undertake active search for new facts and ideas. Skepticism that is not such a search is as much a personal emotional indulgence as is dogmatism. Attainment of the relatively secure and settled takes place, however, only with respect to *specified* problematic situations; quest for certainty that is universal, applying to everything, is a compensatory perversion. One question is disposed of; another offers itself and thought is kept alive.

When we compare the theory of mind and its organs which develops from analysis of what takes place when precarious situations are translated into statement and resolution of problems, with other theories, the outstanding difference is that the first type of theory introduces no elements save such as are public, observable, and verifiable. In general, when there is discourse about the mental organs and processes of knowing we are told about sensations, mental images, consciousness and its various states, as if these were capable of identification in and of themselves. These mental organs having had meaning assigned to them in isolation from the operations of resolving a problematic situation, are then used to give an account of the actual operations of knowing. The more evident and observable is thus "explained" in terms of the obscure, the obscurity being hidden from view because of habits that have the weight of tradition behind them.

We do not need to repeat the results of the previous discussion. They are all connected with the theory that inquiry is a set of operations in which problematic situations are disposed of or settled. Theories which have been criticized all rest upon a different supposition; namely, that the properties of the states and acts of mind involved in knowing are capable of isolated determination – of description apart from overt acts that resolve indeterminate and ambiguous situations. The fundamental advantage of framing our account of the organs and processes of knowing on the pattern of what occurs in experimental inquiry is that nothing is introduced save what is objective and is accessible to examination and report. If it is objected that such an examination itself involves mind and its organs, the rejoinder is that the theory we have advanced is self-applying. Its only "assumption" is that something is done, done in the ordinary external sense of that word, and that this doing has consequences. We define mind and its organs in terms of this doing and its results, just as we define or frame ideas of stars, acids, and digestive tissues in terms of *their* behavior. If it be urged that we do not know whether the results of the directed operations are really knowledge or not, the answer is the objection assumes that we have some kind of advance intimation of what sort of a thing knowledge must be, and hence can use this conception as a standard for judging particular conclusions. The theory in question makes no such assumption. It asserts that by some operations conclusions emerge in which objects once uncertain and confused are rendered clear and stable. Alter names as much as you please; refuse to call one set of consequences knowledge and another error, or reverse the appellations, and these consequences remain just what they are. They present the difference between resolved and clarified situations and disordered and obscure ones. A rose by another name would smell as sweet; the gist of the theory advanced is to point to operations performed and to the consequences which issue from them.

Another point of difference is that traditional theories of mind and its organs of knowledge isolate them from continuity with the natural world. They are, in the literal sense of the word, supernatural or extra-natural. The problem of mind and body, of how it happens that bodily structures are involved in observing and thinking, is then unavoidable. When little was known about organic structures, one reason for looking down upon perception was that its connection with bodily organs, the eye and ear and hand, could not escape notice, while thought could be regarded as a purely spir-

itual act. But now we are aware that the exercise of thought bears the same relation to the brain that perception bears to sense organs, and that there is no separation, structural or functional, between the eye and ear and the central organs. Consequently it is impossible to think of sense as quasi-physical and thought as purely mental, as if the mental meant just the non-material. Yet we retain theories about the mental formed before we had this knowledge. Consequently, since those theories isolate knowing from doing, the dependence of knowing upon bodily organs becomes a mystery – a "problem."

But if knowing is one mode of doing, then it, as well as other modes of doing, properly involves bodily instruments. The metaphysical problem of the relation of mind and body is converted into a question, to be solved by observation of facts, of a differentiation of actions into those on a strictly physiological level, and those which, because of directed quality and distinctive consequences, are mental.

While traditional theories regard mind as an intruder from without into the natural development, or evolution, of organic structures, or else in the interest of natural continuity feel compelled to deny that mental behavior has any differential features, the theory that organic responses have mental quality in the degree in which they deal with the uncertain recognizes both continuity and difference. It can, in principle if not as yet in detail, give a genetic account of the development of mental and intellectual processes. There is neither a sudden jump from the merely organic to the intellectual, nor is there complete assimilation of the latter to primitive modes of the former.

On the objective side, the great difference between the conception proposed and that of traditional theory consists in recognition of the objective character of indeterminateness: it is a real property of some natural existences. Greek thought at least acknowledged the presence of contingency in natural existence, although it used this property of uncertainty to assign to natural existence a lower status than that which belongs to necessary Being. Modern thought, largely under the influence of a Newtonian philosophy of nature, tended to treat all existence as wholly determinate. The inherently incomplete was eliminated from nature along with qualities and ends. In consequence, the mental was sharply marked off from the physically natural; for the mental was obviously characterized by doubt and uncertainty.

Mind was placed outside of nature; its relation to nature in knowing the latter became a dark mystery; the uncertain and indeterminate were said to be merely subjective. The contrast between the doubtful and the determinate became one of the chief marks by which objective and subjective were demarcated from each other and placed in opposition.

According to this doctrine, *we* are doubtful, puzzled, confused, undecided; *objects* are complete, assured, fixed. It is not easy to reconcile this notion with the fact that in order to relieve our doubt, to "make up" our minds, we have to modify in some way, in imaginative or overt experimentation, the situation in which uncertainty is experienced. Moreover, the procedure of science is conclusive. If doubt and indeterminateness were wholly within the mind – whatever that may signify – purely mental processes ought to get rid of them. But experimental procedure signifies that actual alteration of an external situation is necessary to effect the conversion. A *situation* undergoes, through operations directed by thought, transition from problematic to settled, from internal discontinuity to coherency and organization.

If we define "mental" through exclusion of overt acts that terminate in a changed environment, nothing merely mental can actually resolve doubt or clarify confusion. At most it can produce only a *feeling* of certainty – something best obtained by withdrawing from the real world and cultivating fantasies. The idea that doubt and assurance are merely subjective is contradicted by the coincidence of the progress of physical inquiry with invention and use of physical instruments. In principle, the correspondence of what we do when a situation is *practically* unsatisfactory with what happens in the case of intellectual doubt is complete. If a man finds himself in a situation which is practically annoying and troublesome, he has just two courses open to him. He can make a change in himself either by running away from trouble or by steeling himself to Stoic endurance; or he can set to work to do something so as to change the conditions of which unsatisfactoriness is a quality. When the latter course is impossible, nothing remains but the former.

Some change of personal attitude is the part of wisdom in any case, for there are few if any cases of trouble into which a personal factor of desire or aversion does not enter as a productive cause. But the idea that this causal factor can be changed by purely direct means, by an exercise of "will" or

"thought" is illusory. A change of desire and purpose can itself be effected only indirectly, by a change in one's actual relation to environment. This change implies definite acts. The technological appliances and agencies that man has constructed to make these acts effective correspond to the development of instruments of scientific inquiry by which outer conditions are intentionally varied.

The relegation of the problematic to the "subjective" is a product of the habit of isolating man and experience from nature. Curiously enough, modern science has joined with traditional theology in perpetuating this isolation. If the physical terms by which natural science deals with the world are supposed to constitute that world, it follows as a matter of course that qualities we experience and which are the distinctive things in human life, fall outside of nature. Since some of these qualities are the traits that give life purpose and value, it is not surprising that many thinkers are dissatisfied with thinking of them as *merely* subjective; nor that they have found in traditional religious beliefs and in some elements of the classic philosophic tradition means by which these traits can be used to substantiate the being of a reality higher than nature, one qualified by the purpose and value that are extruded from natural existence. Modern idealism cannot be understood apart from the conditions that have generated it. Fundamentally, these conditions are the fusion of the positive results of the older metaphysics with the negative conclusions of modern science: negative, that is to say, when, because of the persistence of earlier notions about mind and the office of knowledge, science is taken to disclose an antecedent natural world.

The organism is a part of the natural world; its interactions with it are genuine additive phenomena. When, with the development of symbols, also a natural occurrence, these interactions are directed towards anticipated consequences, they gain the quality of intelligence, and knowledge accrues. Problematic situations when they are resolved then gain the meaning of all the relations which the operations of thought have defined. Things that were causally effective in producing experienced results became means to consequences; these consequences incorporate in themselves all the meanings found in the causes which *intentionally* produce them. The supposed grounds for opposing human experience to the reality of nature disappear. Situations have problematic and resolved characters in and through the actual inter-actions of the organism and the environment. To refuse to treat these qualities as characteristic of nature itself is due to an arbitrary refusal to ascribe to some modes of interaction the existential char-acter which is assigned as a matter of course to others.

We have seen that situations are precarious and perilous because the persistence of life-activity depends upon the influence which present acts have upon future acts. The continuity of a life-process is secured only as acts performed render the environment favorable to subsequent organic acts. The formal generalized statement of this fact is as follows: The occurrence of problematic and unsettled situations is due to the *characteristic union of the discrete or individual and the continuous or relational.* All perceived objects are individual-ized. They are, as such, wholes complete in themselves. Everything directly experienced is qualitatively unique; it has its own focus about which subject-matter is arranged, and this focus never exactly recurs. While every such situation shades off indefinitely, or is not sharply marked off from others, yet the pattern of arrangement of content is never exactly twice alike.

If the interactions involved in having such an individualized situation in experience were wholly final or consummatory, there would be no such thing as a situation which is problematic. In being individual and complete in itself, just what it is and nothing else, it would be discrete in the sense in which discreteness signifies complete isolation. Obscurity, for example, would be a final quality, like any other quality and as good as any other – just as the dusk of twilight is enjoyed instead of being troublesome until we need to see something the dusk interferes with seeing. Every situation has vagueness attending it, as it shades off from a sharper focus into what is indefinite; for vagueness is added quality and not something objectionable except as it obstructs gaining an eventual object.

There are situations in which self-enclosed, dis-crete, individualized characters dominate. They constitute the subject-matter of esthetic experi-ence; and every experience is esthetic in as far as it is final or arouses no search for some other experience. When this complete quality is con-spicuous the experience is denominated esthetic. The fine arts have as their purpose the construc-tion of objects of just such experiences; and under some conditions the completeness of the object enjoyed gives the experience a quality so intense

that it is justly termed religious. Peace and har-mony suffuse the entire universe gathered up into the situation having a particular focus and pattern. These qualities mark any experience in as far as its final character dominates; in so far a mystic experi-ence is simply an accentuated intensification of a quality of experience repeatedly had in the rhythm of experiences.

Interactions, however, are not isolated. No experienced situation can retain indefinitely its character of finality, for the inter-relations that constitute it are, because they are interactions, themselves changing. They produce a change in what is experienced. The effort to maintain dir-ectly a consummatory experience or to repeat it exactly is the source of unreal sentimentality and of insincerity. In the continuous ongoing of life, objects part with something of their final character and become conditions of subsequent experiences. There is regulation of the change in the degree in which a causal character is rendered preparatory and instrumental.

In other words, all experienced objects have a double status. They are individualized, consum-matory, whether in the way of enjoyment or of suffering. They are also involved in a continuity of interactions and changes, and hence are causes and potential means of later experiences. Because of this dual capacity, they become problematic. Im-mediately and directly they are just what they are; but as transitions to and possibilities of later ex-periences they are uncertain. There is a divided response; part of the organic activity is directed to them for what they immediately are, and part to them as transitive means of other experienced objects. We react to them both as finalities and in preparatory ways, and the two reactions do not harmonize.

This two-fold character of experienced objects is the source of their problematic character. Each of us can recall many occasions when he has been perplexed by disagreement between things directly present and their potential value as signs and means; when he has been torn between absorption in what is now enjoyed and the need of altering it so as to prepare for something likely to come. If we state the point in a formal way, it is signified that there is an incompatibility between the traits of an object in its direct individual and unique nature and those traits that belong to it in its relations or continuities. This incompatibility can be removed only by actions which temporally reconstruct what is given and constitute a new object having both individuality and the internal coherence of continuity in a series.

Previous discussion has been a statement of the chief factors that operate in bringing about this reconstruction – of resolving a problematic situation: Acts of analytic reduction of the gross total situation to determine data – qualities that locate the nature of the problem; formation of ideas or hypotheses to direct further operations that reveal new material; deductions and calculations that organize the new and old subject-matter together; operations that finally determine the existence of a new integrated situation with added meaning, and in so doing test or prove the ideas that have been employed.

Without retraversing that discussion, I wish to add a few words on one point involved in it. Nothing is more familiar than the standardized objects of reference designated by common nouns. Their distinction from proper names shows that they are not singular or individual, not existing things. Yet *"the* table" is both more familiar and seemingly more substantial than *this* table, the individual. "This" undergoes change all the time. It is interacting with other things and with me, who am not exactly the same person as when I last wrote upon it. "This" is an indefinitely multiple and varied series of "thises."

But save in extreme cases, these changes are indifferent, negligible, from the standpoint of means for consequences. *The* table is precisely the constancy among the serial "thises" of whatever serves as an instrument for a single end. *Knowledge* is concerned wholly with this constant, this standardized and averaged set of properties and relations: just as esthetic perception is occupied with "this" in its individuality, irrespective of value in use. In the degree in which reactions are inchoate and unformed, "this" tends to be the buzzing, blooming confusion of which James wrote. As habits form, action is stereotyped into a fairly constant series of acts having a common end in view; *the* table serves a single use, in spite of individual variations. A group of properties is set aside, corresponding to the abiding end and single mode of use which form *the* object, in distinction from "this" of unique experiences. *The* object is an abstraction, but unless it is hypostatized it is not a vicious abstraction. It designates selected relations of things which, with respect to their mode of operation, are constant within the limits practically important. Moreover, the abstracted object has a consequence *in* the individualized experiences, one

that is immediate and not merely instrumental to them. It marks an ordering and organizing of responses in a single focused way in virtue of which the original blur is definitized and rendered significant. Without habits dealing with recurrent and constant uses of things for abiding purposes, immediate esthetic perception would have neither rich nor clear meanings immanent within it.

The scientific or physical object marks an extension of the same sort of operation. *The* table, as *not* a table but as a swarm of molecules in motions of specified velocities and accelerations, corresponds to a liberated generalization of the purposes which *the* object may serve. "Table" signifies a definite but restricted set of uses; stated in the physical terms of science it is thought of in a wider environment and free from any specified set of uses; out of relation to any particular individualized experience. The abstraction is as legitimate as is that which gives rise to the idea of *the* table, for it consists of standardized relations or interactions. It is even more useful or more widely instrumental. For it has connection with an indefinite variety of unspecified but possible consummatory individual observations and enjoyments. It waits like a servant, idle for a time, but ready to be called upon as special occasion arises. When this standardized constant, the result of series of operations and expressing an indefinite multitude of possible relations among concrete things, is treated as the reality of nature, an instrument made for a purpose is hypostatized into a substance complete and self-sufficient in isolation. Then the fullness of qualities present in individual situations have to be treated as subjective impressions mysteriously produced in mind by the real object or else as products of a mysterious creative faculty of consciousness.

The bearing of the conclusion upon the qualitative values of experienced objects is evident. Interactions of things with the organism eventuate in objects perceived to be colored and sonorous. They also result in qualities that make the object hateful or delightful. All these qualities, taken as directly perceived or enjoyed, are terminal effects of natural interactions. They are individualized culminations that give static quality to a network of changes. Thus "tertiary" qualities (as they have been happily termed by Mr. Santayana), those which, in psychological analysis, we call affectional and emotional, are as much products of the doings of nature as are color, sound, pressure, perceived size and distance. But their very consummatory quality stands in the way of using the things they qualify as signs of other things. Intellectually they are even more in the way than are "secondary" qualities. With respect to preparatory acts they are useless; when they are treated as signs and means they work injury to thought and discovery. When not experienced, they are projected in thought as ends to be reached and in that dependence upon thought they are felt to be peculiarly mental. But only if *the* object, the physical object, instrumental in character, is supposed to define "the real" in an exhaustive way, do they cease to be for the philosopher what they are for the common man: real qualities of natural objects. This view forms the only complete and unadulterated realism.

The problem which is supposed to exist between two tables, one that of direct perception and use and the other that of physics (to take the favorite illustration of recent discussion) is thus illusory. The perceived and used table is the only table, for it alone has both individuality of form – without which nothing can exist or be perceived – and also includes within itself a continuum of relations or interactions brought to a focus. We may perhaps employ more instructively an illustration derived from the supposed contrast between an object experienced in perception as it is rendered by a poet and the same object described by a physicist. There is the instance of a body of water where the movement of the wind over its surface is reflected in sunlight. As an object of science, it is reported as follows: "Aethereal vibrations of various wave-lengths, reflected at different angles from the disturbed interface between air and water, reached our eyes and by photoelectric action caused appropriate stimuli to travel along optic nerves to a brain-centre." Such a statement, however, includes ordinary objects of individual perceptions; water, air, brain and nerves. Consequently, it must be reduced still further; when so reduced it consists of mathematical functions between certain physical constants having no counterpart in ordinary perception.[1]

It is worth while at this point to recur to the metric character of the physical object. Defining metric traits are reached by a series of operations of which they express the statistically constant outcome; they are not the result of a single act. Hence the physical object cannot be taken to be a single or individual thing in existence. Metric definitions are also, in large measure, reached by indirect measurements, by calculation. In other words, the conception of the physical object is, in considerable degree, the outcome of complex operations of comparison and translation. In consequence, while the physical object is *not* any one of the things compared, it enables things qualitatively unlike and individual to be treated as if they were members of a comprehensive, homogeneous, or non-qualitative system. The possibility of control of the *occurrence* of individualized objects is thereby increased. At the same time, the latter gain added meaning, for the import of the scheme of continuity of relationships with other things is incorporated within them. The procedure of physics itself, not any metaphysical or epistemological theory, discloses that physical objects cannot be individual existential objects. In consequence, it is absurd to put them in opposition to the qualitatively individual objects of concrete experience.

The vogue of the philosophy that identifies the object of knowledge as such with the reality of the subject-matter of experience makes it advisable to carry the discussion further. Physical science submits the things of ordinary experience to specifiable operations. The result is objects of thought stated in numbers, where the numbers in question permit inclusion within complex systems of equations and other mathematical functions. In the physical object everything is ignored but the relations expressed by these numbers. It is safe to assert that no physicist *while at work* ever thought of denying the full reality of the things of ordinary, coarse experience. He pays no attention to their qualities except as they are signs of operations to be performed and of inference to relations to be drawn. But in these capacities he has to admit their full reality on pain of having, logically, to deny reality to the conclusions of his operative inferences. He takes the instruments he employs, including his own sensory-motor organs and measuring instruments, to be real in the ordinary sense of the word. If he denied the reality of these things as they are had in ordinary non-cognitive perceptual experience, the conclusions reached by them would be equally discredited. Moreover, the numbers which define his metric object are themselves results of noting interactions or connections among perceived things. It would be the height of absurdity to assert the reality of these relations while denying the reality of the things between which they hold. If the latter are "subjective" what becomes of the former? Finally, observation is resorted to for verification. It is a strange world in which the conception of the real has to be corroborated by reference to that the reality of which is made dubious by the conception. To common sense these comments may seem wholly superfluous. But since common sense may also hold the doctrine from which flow the conclusions to which the critical comments are apposite, common sense should first ask whether it holds that knowledge is a disclosure of the antecedently real? If it entertains this belief, then the dismissal by science of the experienced object to a limbo of unreality, or subjectivity or the phenomenal – whatever terms be used – results logically from his own position.

Our discussion involves a summary as well as some repetition of points previously made. Its significance lies in the liberation which comes when knowing, in all its phases, conditions and organs, is understood after the pattern provided by experimental inquiry, instead of upon the groundwork of ideas framed before such knowing had a systematic career opened to it. For according to the pattern set by the practice of knowing, knowledge is the fruit of the undertakings that transform a problematic situation into a resolved one. Its procedure is public, a part and partner of the Nature in which all interactions exist. But experienced situations come about in two ways and are of two distinct types. Some take place with only a minimum of regulation, with little foresight, preparation and intent. Others occur because, in part, of the prior occurrence of intelligent action. Both kinds are *had*; they are undergone, enjoyed or suffered. The first are not known; they are not understood; they are dispensations of fortune or providence. The second have, as they are experienced, meanings that present the funded outcome of operations that substitute definite continuity for experienced discontinuity and for the fragmentary quality due to isolation. Dream, insanity and fantasy are natural products, as "real" as anything else in the world. The acts of intentional regulation which constitute thinking are also natural developments, and so are the experienced things in which they eventuate. But the latter are resolutions of the problems set by objects experienced without intent and purpose; hence they have a security and fullness of meaning the first lack. Nothing happens, as Aristotle and the scholastics said, without an end – without a terminal effectuation. *Every* experienced object is, in some sense, such a closing and consummatory closing episode: alike the doubtful and secure, the trivial and significant, the true and mistaken, the confused and ordered. Only when the ends are closing termini of

intelligent operations of thinking are they ends in the honorific sense. We always experience individual objects, but only the individual things which are fruits of intelligent action have in them intrinsic order and fullness of qualities.

The conditions and processes of nature generate uncertainty and its risks as truly as nature affords security and means of insurance against perils. Nature is characterized by a constant mixture of the precarious and the stable. This mixture gives poignancy to existence. If existence were either completely necessary or completely contingent, there would be neither comedy nor tragedy in life, nor need of the will to live. The significance of morals and politics, of the arts both technical and fine, of religion and of science itself as inquiry and discovery, all have their source and meaning in the union in Nature of the settled and the unsettled, the stable and the hazardous. Apart from this union, there are no such things as "ends," either as consummations or as those ends-in-view we call purposes. There is only a block universe, either something ended and admitting of no change, or else a predestined march of events. There is no such thing as fulfillment where there is no risk of failure, and no defeat where there is no promise of possible achievement.

Any philosophy that in its quest for certainty ignores the reality of the uncertain in the ongoing processes of nature denies the conditions out of which it arises. The attempt to include all that is doubtful within the fixed grasp of that which is theoretically certain is committed to insincerity and evasion, and in consequence will have the stigmata of internal contradiction. Every such philosophy is marked at some point by a division of its subject-matter into the truly real and the merely apparent, a subject and an object, a physical and a mental, an ideal and an actual, that have nothing to do with one another, save in some mode which is so mysterious as to create an insoluble problem.

Action is the means by which a problematic situation is resolved. Such is the net outcome of the method of science. There is nothing extraordinary about this conclusion. Interaction is a universal trait of natural existence. "Action" is the name given to one mode of this interaction, namely, that named from the standpoint of an organism. When interaction has for its consequence the settling of future conditions under which a life-process goes on, it is an "act." If it be admitted that knowing is something which occurs within nature, then it follows as a truism that knowing is an existential overt act. Only if the one who engages in knowing be outside of nature and behold it from some external locus can it be denied that knowing is an act which modifies what previously existed, and that its worth consists in the consequences of the modification. The spectator theory of knowing may, humanly speaking, have been inevitable when thought was viewed as an exercise of a "reason" independent of the body, which by means of purely logical operations attained truth. It is an anachronism now that we have the model of experimental procedure before us and are aware of the role of organic acts in all mental processes.

Our discussion has for the most part turned upon an analysis of knowledge. The theme, however, is the relation of knowledge and action; the final import of the conclusions as to knowledge resides in the changed idea it enforces as to action. The distinction once made between theory and practice has meaning as a distinction between two kinds of action: blind and intelligent. Intelligence is a quality of some acts, those which are directed; and directed action is an achievement not an original endowment. The history of human progress is the story of the transformation of acts which, like the interactions of inanimate things, take place unknowingly to actions qualified by understanding of what they are about; from actions controlled by external conditions to actions having guidance through their intent: their insight into their own consequences. Instruction, information, knowledge, is the only way in which this property of intelligence comes to qualify acts originally blind.

This conclusion is decisive for the significance of purpose and mechanism in nature. The doctrine that knowledge is ideally or in its office a disclosure of antecedent reality resulted, under the impact of the results of natural science, in relegating purpose to the purely subjective, to states of consciousness. An unsolved problem then developed out of the question as to how purpose could be efficacious in the world. Now intelligent action is purposive action; if it is a natural occurrence, coming into being under complex but specifiable conditions of organic and social interaction, then purpose like intelligence is within nature; it is a "category" having objective standing and validity. It has this status in a direct way through the place and operation of human art within the natural scene; for distinctively human conduct can be interpreted and understood only in

terms of purpose. Purpose is the dominant category of anything truly denominated history, whether in its enacting or in the writing of it, since action which is *distinctively* human is marked by intent.

Indirectly, purpose is a legitimate and necessary idea in describing Nature itself in the large. For man is continuous with nature. As far as natural events culminate in the intelligent arts of mankind, nature itself has a history, a movement toward consequences. When for convenience of study, nature is broken up into disconnected bits the parts of which are taken to have a relation to one another in isolation from other parts, the concept of purpose has no application. It is excluded by the very method of intellectual approach. Science is full of abstractions of this sort. For example, water is a combination of hydrogen and oxygen in definite proportions. This is a statement about "water" in general, not about the occurrence of any particular portion which takes place under conditions in which more than hydrogen and oxygen exist. Any individualized water is a phase of an indefinitely varied and extensive course of things. Generically, however, "water" is treated in relation to its defining constituents as if it were a complete universe in itself. As a statement of a relation that is stable amid a multitude of varying changes, each having its own individualized history, it is an instrument of control. When it is treated as if it provided a model for framing a general theory of nature, the result converts an instrument of control into a view of the world in which there is neither history nor purpose.

Generalized facts, when they are taken to be individual events complete in themselves, lead to a picture of the universe in which occurrences are exactly like one another. There is repetition but no development; mechanical production but no cumulative movement toward an integrated consequence. We take out of our logical package what we have put into it, and then convert what we draw out to be a literal description of the actual world. Things lose their individuality and are "instances" of a general law. When, however, events are viewed in their connections, as it is surely the province of philosophy to view them, nature is seen to be marked by histories, some of which terminate in the existence of human beings and finally in their intelligent activities. This issue, as the consequence of a cumulative integration of complex interactions, is such as to give anterior processes a purposive meaning. Everything depends whether we take short-sections of the course of nature in isolation, or whether we take the course of events over a span of time sufficiently long to disclose the integration of a multitude of processes toward a single outcome.[2]

A machine is a striking instance of mechanism. It is an equally striking instance of something to be understood in terms of purpose, use or function. Nature *has* mechanism. This mechanism forms the content of the objects of physical science for it fulfills the instrumental office to be performed by knowledge. If the interactions and connections involved in natural occurrences were not sufficiently like one another, sufficiently constant and uniform, so that inference and prediction from one to another were possible, control and purpose would be non-existent. Since constant relations among changes are the subject-matter of scientific thought, that subject-matter is the mechanism of events. The net effect of modern inquiry makes it clear that these constancies, whether the larger ones termed laws or the lesser ones termed facts, are statistical in nature. They are the products of averaging large numbers of observed frequencies by means of a series of operations. They are not descriptions of the exact structure and behavior of any *individual* thing, any more than the actuarial "law" of the frequency of deaths of persons having a certain age is an account of the life of one of the persons included in the calculation. Nature *has* a mechanism sufficiently constant to permit of calculation, inference and foresight. But only a philosophy which hypostatizes isolated results and results obtained for a purpose, only a substantiation of the function of being a tool, concludes that nature *is* a mechanism and only a mechanism.

It has long been recognized that some physical laws are statistical, instead of being reports of behavior of individuals as such. Heisenberg's principle, together with the discovery that mass varies with velocity, mark the generalized conclusion that all physical laws are of this character. They are, as we have noted, predictions of the *probability* of an observable event. They mark the culmination of a qualified prediction of Maxwell's so remarkable as to be worth quoting in full.

The theory of atoms and void leads us to attach more importance to the doctrines of integral numbers and definite proportions; but, in applying dynamic principles to the motion of immense numbers of atoms, the limitation of our faculties forces us to abandon the attempt to express the exact history of each atom and to be content with estimating the average condition of a group of atoms large enough to be visible. This method of dealing with groups of atoms, which I might call the statistical method, and which in the present state of our knowledge, is the only available method of studying the properties of real bodies, involves an abandonment of strict dynamical principles, and an adoption of the mathematical methods belonging to the theory of probability. It is probable that important results will be obtained by the application of this method, which is, as yet, little known and is not familiar to our minds. If the actual history of Science had been different, and if the scientific doctrines most familiar to us had been those which must be expressed in this way, it is probable that we might have considered the existence of a certain kind of contingency as a self-evident truth and treated the doctrine of philosophical necessity as a mere sophism.[3]

That which Maxwell felt that he must look upon as a trait due to the "limitation of our faculties" turns out to be a trait of natural events themselves. No mechanically exact science of an individual is possible. An individual is a history unique in character. But constituents of an individual are known when they are regarded not as qualitative, but as statistical constants derived from a series of operations.

This fact has an obvious bearing on freedom in action. Contingency is a necessary although not, in mathematical phrase, a sufficient condition of freedom. In a world which was completely tight and exact in all its constituents, there would be no room for freedom. Contingency while it gives room for freedom does not fill that room. Freedom is an actuality when the recognition of relations, the stable element, is combined with the uncertain element, in the knowledge which makes foresight possible and secures intentional preparation for probable consequences. We are free in the degree in which we act knowing what we are about. The identification of freedom with "freedom of will" locates contingency in the wrong place. Contingency of will would mean that uncertainty was uncertainly dealt with; it would be a resort to chance for a decision. The business of "will" is to be resolute; that is, to resolve, under the guidance of thought, the indeterminateness of uncertain *situations*. Choice wavers and is brought to a head arbitrarily only when circumstances compel action and yet we have no intelligent clew as to how to act.

The doctrine of "free-will" is a desperate attempt to escape from the consequences of the doctrine of fixed and immutable objective Being. With dissipation of that dogma, the need for such a measure of desperation vanishes. Preferential activities characterize every individual as individual or unique. In themselves these are differential in a *de facto* sense. They become true choices under the direction of insight. Knowledge, instead of revealing a world in which preference is an illusion and does not count or make a difference, puts in our possession the instrumentality by means of which preference may be an intelligent or intentional factor in constructing a future by wary and prepared action. Knowledge of special conditions and relations is instrumental to the action which is in turn an instrument of production of situations having qualities of added significance and order. To be capable of such action is to be free.

Physical inquiry has been taken as typical of the nature of knowing. The selection is justified because the operations of physical knowledge are so perfected and its scheme of symbols so well devised. But it would be misinterpreted if it were taken to mean that science is the only valid kind of knowledge; it is just an intensified form of knowing in which are written large the essential characters of any knowing. It is in addition the most powerful tool we possess for developing other modes of knowledge. But we know with respect to any subject-matter whatsoever in the degree in which we are able deliberately to transform doubtful situations into resolved ones. Physical knowledge has the advantage of its specialized character, its whole-hearted devotion to a single purpose. The attitude involved in it, its method, has not as yet gone far beyond its own precincts. Beliefs current in morals, politics and religion, are marked by dread of change and by the feeling that order and regulative authority can be had only through reference to fixed standards accepted as finalities, because referring to fixed antecedent realities. Outside of physical inquiry, we shy from problems; we dislike uncovering serious difficulties in their full depth and reach; we prefer to accept what is and muddle along. Hence our social and moral "sciences" consist largely in putting facts as they are into conceptual systems framed at large. Our logic in social and humane subjects is still largely that of definition and classification as until the

seventeenth century it was in natural science. For the most part the lesson of experimental inquiry has still to be learned in the things of chief concern.

We are, socially, in a condition of division and confusion because our best authenticated knowledge is obtained by directed practice, while this method is still limited to things aloof from man or concerning him only in the technologies of industries. The rest of our practice in matters that come home to us most closely and deeply is regulated not by intelligent operations, but by tradition, self-interest and accidental circumstance. The most significant phase of physical science, that which concerns its method, is unapplied in social practice, while its technical results are utilized by those in positions of privileged advantage to serve their own private or class ends. Of the many consequences that result, the state of education is perhaps the most significant. As the means of the general institution of intelligent action, it holds the key to orderly social reconstruction. But inculcation of fixed conclusions rather than development of intelligence as a method of action still dominates its processes. Devotion to training in technical and mechanical skills on one hand and to laying in a store of abstract information on the other is to one who has the power to read the scene an almost perfect illustration of the significance of the historic separation of knowledge and action, theory and practice. As long as the isolation of knowledge and practice holds sway, this division of aims and dissipation of energy, of which the state of education is typical, will persist. The effective condition of the integration of all divided purposes and conflicts of belief is the realization that intelligent action is the sole ultimate resource of mankind in every field whatsoever.

It is not claimed, therefore, that there is *no* philosophical problem of the relation of physical science to the things of ordinary experience. It is asserted that the problem *in the form* in which it has chiefly occupied modern philosophy is an artificial one, due to the continued assumption of premises formed in an earlier period of history and now having no relevancy to the state of physical inquiry. Clearing the ground of this unreal problem, however, only imposes upon philosophy the consideration of a problem which is urgently practical, growing out of the conditions of contemporary life. What revisions and surrenders of current beliefs about authoritative ends and values are demanded by the method and conclusions of natural science? What possibilities of controlled transformation of the content of present belief and practice in human institutions and associations are indicated by the control of natural energies which natural science has effected? These questions are as genuine and imperative as the traditional problem is artificial and futile.

Notes

1 The illustration is borrowed from Arthur S. Eddington, *The Nature of the Physical World* (New York: Macmillan, 1928); see pp. 316–19. It is indicative of the hold which the older tradition of knowledge as the exclusive revelation of reality has obtained, that Eddington finds no way to combine this account with the poetic account, save to suppose that while the scientific statement describes reality as it is "in itself," the creative activity of mind adds to this skeleton the qualities characterizing an object in direct experience.

2 *Purposive Evolution* (New York, 1926), by Edmund Noble, contains by far the best statement known to me of considerations of which a brief summary is given in this paragraph.

3 J. C. Maxwell, *Scientific Papers*, vol. II, p. 253. I am indebted to Dr. Charles Hartshorne for this reference.

18

The Practice of Philosophy

Susanne K. Langer

Introduction

Susanne K. Langer (1895–1985) was born in New York City and educated at Radcliffe College. She taught at Columbia University until 1950 and then at Connecticut College. Her work brings together the pragmatist commitments of Dewey and James and joins them with the concerns raised by the positivism of the Vienna Circle and philosophers such as Bertrand Russell and A. J. Ayer. This selection is from Langer's earliest work and sets the ground for her reconstruction of American philosophy in light of critiques of pragmatism and in anticipation of her own later work in aesthetics and philosophy of language.

Philosophical Technique

Many people, especially those who confuse philosophy with religion, feel an inward distress at the thought of discussing philosophical technique. This technophobia may be found among professional philosophers as well as among laymen, and arises from several causes.

Laymen usually approach philosophy as they would approach religion, hoping to find certainty for their somewhat questionable beliefs; not wishing to change their beliefs, but to have them corroborated. They naturally desire a restatement in

Taken from *The Practice of Philosophy* (New York: Henry Holt, 1930). Reprinted with permission from the publisher.

terms which they can accept or reject, not in terms which require dry protracted study in order to convey anything at all; they are looking for immediate connotations, not definitions. They want to be told that God is infinite – not that infinity involves certain mathematical properties. A definition of "infinite" serves only to destroy the romantic glamor of the word.

Professional philosophers sometimes share this love for the indefinite and occult, for high-sounding words, but usually their dislike of technique is based on more defensible considerations. It is not the fear of intellectual labor, but a haunting distrust of all its results, a fear of error, that turns them from systematic thought to a mystical resignation. Their reason has been found wanting, has played them false, led them into absurdity; then either they become bravely agnostic and renounce all hope of knowledge, or they seek some other means to this end. This other means is commonly supposed to be *intuition*.

Reason is untrustworthy because it is always indirect. Somewhere, between the object and the knower, a gap must be bridged, and this gap is the seat of all *error*. From the discouraging frequency of error has sprung the notion that reason always contains some ingredient of error, some essential *principle of falsification*, which intuition avoids – and that consequently philosophy, which seeks the fundamental truth about things, would do best to discard reason, to forego analysis and deduction and all the rest of its technique, and avail itself of the intuitive method instead.

Unfortunately, intuition is not a method, but a natural phenomenon. It occurs; it cannot be invoked or taught. Moreover, its result is not knowledge, but that fundamental experience which knowledge is *about*. If it is not liable to error, neither can it convey truth. Only propositions can be true or false; intuition never yields a proposition, but presents us with the subjects of propositions. It is our source of direct contact with the world. Contact, however, is not understanding. Understanding, like vision, requires perspective; it is at its best when a certain distance intervenes between the eye and the object. We cannot see a painting better by flattening our noses against the canvas, nor can we usually see the significance of events in the world by being in the very midst of them. But distance, of course, always allows a medium to come between, which partly determines the appearance of what we see; in understanding, too, we must be content with mediate knowledge, more or less colored by intervening factors in the knowledge-relation.

Intuition is the sense – or faculty – or function – which supplies us with the *given* in experience. In all knowledge there is an element which is simply *given*, the datum about which our knowledge is. This is the "hard datum" of Russell's metaphysics, the "Gegenstand" of Meinong's epistemology. It is this *given* which we owe to our intuition. But if we do not go beyond simple acceptance of the *given*, can we really claim to understand anything? Intuition may be direct, and never productive of error; but also, its product is not knowledge. Reason, on the other hand, is always indirect, and often erroneous; but at least, if our reasoning about a given experience is correct, then its product *is* knowledge.

Now what is the medium which is essential to all reason, but at the same time is viewed as the prime source of error? What is the ingredient that must color our knowledge in order to make it apparent at all? This factor which is always operative in reason, and perhaps never in intuition,[1] is *abstraction*.

Many renowned thinkers, such as William James and Henri Bergson, hate the very idea of dealing with abstractions, and harbor an almost superstitious fear of "the spectral dance of bloodless categories" which they suspect the pure reason will foist upon them. Abstraction, it is generally thought, is falsification. There is a grain of truth in this assertion, but no more. Abstraction involves certain dangers of falsification, against which it

behooves us to guard, and I shall call attention to these in their turn; but the fact that this greatest of intellectual assets must be carefully treated, does not vitiate its proper uses nor in any way detract from its profound importance.

It is a curious fact that the same people who decry abstraction, who demand concreteness in philosophic thought, are apt to be the ones to whom *any* generalization, such as: "All joys are transient," "All things are ordained," "No man can escape his fate," is a philosophical statement. Now, the most striking feature of such a statement is its utter lack of any concrete terms. Take the first example; there is no mention of any particular person's particular joy, but of joys in general; nor is there any specific degree or mode of transience given, but only the bare, abstract idea of transience – of passing away sometime, somehow, for some reason. A relatively concrete statement such as: "The pleasure of tasting this apple will last just until the apple is eaten," has not the philosophical character of "All joys are transient." The same is true of the assertion: "No man can escape his fate." If a doctor announces that John Smith cannot escape the effects of a cancer in his body, or a gossip is sure that he will marry Miss Jones, the doctor or the old lady is not supposed to be talking philosophy. But "No man can escape his fate," whether true or false, certainly will pass with most people for a philosophical proposition, whereof John Smith's death or marriage or other eventuality is a mere instance.

The property which distinguishes philosophical from every-day thought seems, thus, to be *generality*. This is what philosophers have in mind when they claim to talk in cosmic terms, to make statements about "the nature of things," to impart eternal truths rather than disjointed facts. The eternal truth, of which all individual cases are instances, is the *general* condition which certain particular examples illustrate. "All pleasures are transient" is the general statement which covers any number of cases, from the end of our gustatory thrill, as the apple dwindles, to the sort of transience that belongs even to love's bright moments or religious ecstasy.

By what "alchemy of thought" can one statement apply to so many, often very diverse, affairs? By dealing only with those properties which the several cases have in common. "Transience," for example, is one of those very general properties of a large class of things, such as, for instance, pleasures – a property we recognize in every member of that class, however different the members may be. In fact, the particular cases of transience may vary; there may be sudden passings or slow fadings, definite breaks or imperceptible changes; transience is that bare common element which is embodied in every instance. But the process by which we can single out this minimum of agreement, and talk about it regardless of its variegated actual forms, is the process called "abstraction." Abstraction means simply "taking away," i.e. treating separately, some *integral aspect* of the whole situation. If we do not confuse this sort of "taking away," this narrowing of interest down to a single aspect, with the sort of "taking away" that applies to physical *parts* of a thing, then we shall not be ridden by the silly question, whether an abstracted thing can "exist outside" the concrete instance; as one might question whether a clam can exist outside its shell. "Existence" which belongs to abstract elements, such as "transience," has an entirely different meaning from physical existence. There is nothing inherently false about the objects of abstraction; if they did not exist in the world, we could not honor them with our special and restricted attention. If we do, as some philosophers claim, *produce* abstract entities by an act of postulation or fancy, it is certainly strange that some things are ready instances of our abstract concepts, and others, quite brutally and objectively, are not.

It is easy enough to see how, in making a general statement, we are talking about all its specific cases at once; as when we say: "All Germans are barbarians," a great many persons will feel individually insulted. Generalization is the only art by which we could ever hope to make any statement about *everything*. The philosophers who desire to "see things together," to check up all the huge inventory of human experiences, certainly cannot – even in their fondest dreams – hope to exhaust "all-that-there-is" by enumeration. Only in generalization is there a promise of such cosmic insight as they desire. Generalization, far from being a hindrance to true thought, is the source of all thought-economy. Without it our mental life could never extend beyond the aesthetic experience of the moment; beyond the apple we are eating, the colors we are viewing, the temperature of our skin and the present medley of sounds in our ears. In fact, without generalization – and that is to say, without abstraction – there could be no language or thought, properly speaking; no knowledge, only sense.

But the concentration of many actual conditions into one blanket-assertion, such as the wise utterances of popular philosophy or the "laws" of statistical science, is not the only intellectual asset we owe to the power of abstraction. Those elements which we single out from the great flux of reality, those abstracted ingredients, are our *concepts*. And concepts as such – regardless of their origin, their application, their metaphysical status – concepts stand in definite relations to each other; they include or exclude or overlap or complement each other, they are always either compatible or incompatible. The realm of incompatible concepts is the realm of the *impossible*, and that of compatible ones is the sphere of the *possible*. But it so happens that concepts can enter into vastly more relations with each other, than the relations of actual things in the world; so the realm of possibility is greater, perhaps infinitely greater, than that of existence. Thus the art of abstraction, by giving us the pure concept, liberates the human mind from the finitude of actuality and opens to it the endless reaches of *potentiality*.

To fathom the possibilities in the world: surely that is the deepest insight that either science or philosophy can desire. Scientists have regular systems descriptive of potential situations, such as the infinite divisibility of space, the "potential energy" of a resting body. It stands to reason that space cannot, by any physical configuration, be simultaneously divided everywhere, and that a body is not expending kinetic energy when it is at rest; but the realm of possibility always *includes* the actual case, as the total system we call "a language" always includes the words we actually are using; and it is this field of possibilities which we must explore in order to understand the specific case. Without the notion of the unrealized potential, we could entertain no doubts, and ask no questions of fact. For a question always presupposes alternatives, and of these only one can be exemplified in fact. The others must lie either in the realm of mere possibility, or in the limbo of the impossible.

[...]

Understanding and Truth

The fundamental problem of meaning is not so much the interpretation of individual signs as of symbolic forms. If man (at his best) has really a reasoning faculty which is different from that of the highest non-human animals, this faculty is his ability to *find* meanings deliberately, rather than to acquire them with passive unconsciousness. Signs may teach us causal connections, may even lead us to correct predictions and proper expectations; the power to interpret signs is the intelligence which grows with experience and association. It is rudimentary in animals, highly developed in the human mind. But it is the foundation only of *learning*, not of *understanding*.

Science is supposed to begin with the recognition of physical laws, i.e. with the first generalizations of experience. This involves the apprehension of a thing (or event) as a member of a class of similar things (or events). But in fact, generalization is not the whole basis of scientific thinking; generalization and, therewith, classification, are very primitive instruments of thought, manifested wherever there is memory or association. A dog who fears all men because he has been kicked by his master, or the proverbial burned child who shuns the fire, is performing an act of generalization, not consciously, but physiologically, through his conditioned reflexes. He is using the language of signs. This language may be developed to such a degree that psychologists may hope to express in its terms a great many so-called "higher" functions – prediction, technological performance, the development of an ordered society.

But all these phenomena are possible without real science, in the sense that I wish to give to the word. Technology and prediction may arise from the familiarity of an organism with its environment, i.e. from a purely behaviouristic knowledge of things; but science, as its greatest devotees conceive it, springs from *understanding*. Its foundations are philosophical.

The culture of ancient Egypt illustrates the possibility of very complicated social and technological achievements, that involve little if any understanding. The Egyptians measured their land, but evolved no pure mathematics; they built the pyramids, but left us no theoretical physics. Their world was small, very definite in character, and of great antiquity; their lives were closely adjusted to a perfectly familiar universe. If any behaviourist or mechanist would really undertake to trace his avowed principles through the complex behaviour of a civilized human society, he would do well to choose for his example the classic civilization of the Nile valley.

But science of a theoretical sort requires a further principle, namely *abstraction*. This is not the same thing as generalization, although it entails the latter. Abstraction is the explicit recognition of a *form* which may be variously exemplified. Such a form is conceivable in purely symbolic terms, even where no other concrete example of it is known to exist. The step from generalization to abstraction, from the classification of entities or events to the appreciation of forms, is the step from inductive beliefs to logical insight, from a codification of actualities to a survey of possibilities. And therewith begins theoretical science.

Natural laws, as understood by the masters of inductive science (numbering at present most of our physicians, sociologists, technicians, and other practical educated men) are general rules which may have exceptions. They hold in *almost all cases* of events belonging to a certain class. This is the stage to which knowledge can advance by the process of classifying things according to certain traits which are more or less tacitly recognized – perhaps, in a refined way, recognized "physiologically." But once in a while these traits will deceive us, the general rule for the class will fail for one of its members. Therefore the "natural laws" may occasionally have exceptions.

But the science of forms obviates this possibility. It deals not directly with classes, but with the *defining functions* of classes; its interest is much less with predictions concerning the members of some class than with the formal conditions for membership, i.e. the *class-concept*. This, of course, allows of no exceptions. Whether it is satisfied or not, determines whether the class has members, or not.

A class-concept is a form, according to which certain entities may be conceived. They do not "have" the form over and above their individual identity; they could not be "the same" and yet fail to express this structure. I think the disagreement of philosophers concerning the internality of relations hinges upon an unrecognized confusion of the two kinds of thinking – that which begins with assumed groups of entities and infers general rules of their behaviour, and that which begins with *possible classes*, or defining functions, and interprets experience by their means, as groups of behaving entities. In the former, of course, relations appear external; in the latter, they must be thought constitutive, or internal.

But all this is merely by the way. The important point of the matter is that theoretical science is based not only upon generalized observation, but upon *principles of interpretation*, which are purely formal, and determine our recognition of events and entities. We recognize a conceived form where it is expressed in nature; where we cannot recognize any form, we cannot clearly identify things and events. But this process of recognizing a thing as a possible form with a definite experiential content rests on further principles than integration of reflexes or cumulative association – it involves a new primitive notion, which the Germans have called "Gestalt."

The recognition of structure gives the mind its ability to *find meanings*. Instead of depending upon chance associations to make a sign out of a sensory stimulus, we are able to apprehend the stimulus as a form, and make of it a *symbol* for experiences which follow the same pattern. The inestimable value of this proceeding is, of course, that very trivial symbols, little sounds or ink-marks, which are easy to manipulate in the most complex manner, may represent universes which otherwise would simply not be accessible to our experience; for the relational analogy may be established at only a few points, the implications, i.e. the details of structure, worked out entirely through the symbols, and the theorems checked up wherever the other system is given to our senses. This is the nature of scientific calculation and experiment. Our number-system is an abstract form involving relatively few primitive terms, and powerful relations. It can be symbolized by a mere handful of notational elements in elaborate but perfectly definite arrangements, a sort of visual syntax. And in turn it is exemplified by the most unwieldy, vast, heterogeneous system, so individual and inexhaustible that only the most skilful abstraction can reveal it to us as a system at all – the physical world.

Obviously, a pattern may be repeated in more than one natural instance; for example, certain functions of the number-system are applicable to the process of burning fuel, the metabolic processes in a living body, the oxidation of a piece of iron, etc. Often exactly the same formula will fit various meanings. There is, in fact, no such thing as a symbol which by its nature can have one and only one interpretation, and yet be accessible to our knowledge; for various symbolic expressions could always be invented, and for any one of these the others would be "interpretations." That is why there is no such thing as "the" meaning of a symbol; there are its possible meanings, which may be legion, of which some particular one is singled out by its relation to the interpretant. Since the interpretant may vary, the meaning of a symbol may vary, through the whole gamut of its possibilities.

All this is obvious enough as soon as the logical character of meaning relations is understood; a more interesting and less obvious consideration, however, comes to the fore when we reverse the order of the symbolic triad and ask how the *object* functions in relation to symbol and interpretant. Can this object be symbolized by only one kind of structure? Must all possible symbols which can represent the object be of the same pattern – i.e. has the object only one pattern? This question is of the utmost philosophical importance; its answer entails a whole metaphysics of truth and of reality.

A logical structure is always expressed in terms of certain primitive entities, the relata among which its basic relations are conceived to be operative. The natural prejudice of commonsense is to confuse these with possible interpretations, to think of the relata in a symbolic structure as *existent things*. The fact that they are primitive, unanalyzable *in the system*, is often confused with the notion that they are unanalyzable concrete objects. But this gratuitous inference is false. For instance, we may construct a formal geometry in terms of points and their interrelations, and this geometry may apply to the physical world; but that does not mean that points are in any sense physical things; points are *conceptual elements*, lines and planes are (in a geometry of points) *conceptual structures*.

Now, the formulæ which compose a logical system may vary, of course, with the nature of the assumed primitive entities. If we take points as our basic terms we will have other postulates and theorems than if we started with volumes, or still more, if we started with notions such as "space-time event" or with Leibnitzian "monads." Yet our various systems of geometry, of physics, and of metaphysics are all designed to describe the actual world, that is to say, they are all supposed to present a pattern which is to be found in the actual world. Geometries which have not a single proposition in common can, supposedly, be applied to the same actual space. Their respective axioms, and the properties of their respective elements, are incommensurable. They are utterly distinct forms. How, then, can a symbolic pattern be said to present the form of any real thing or event?

The answer is, that there is no such things as *the form* of a real thing, or of an event. There is no such thing as pure experience. Just as all thought must have some logical constants, though these may be variously chosen, so all experience must have some specific pattern, wherein it may be sensed, though there are many patterns possible within the same reality. All experience, of sense or thought or feeling, is selective; it must formulate its material in some way, and in just one way at a time. All concrete reality has a multiplicity of possible forms, and when it is known to us it has one actual form, with an amorphous "content."

The relation between form and content is an elusive affair; there is, in fact, nothing in nature that answers ontologically to this distinction.[2] All we can find is an indeterminate "this," which, with reference to one set of basic concepts, has one shape, and with reference to another set, takes on another perspective. This raises the baffling question: What must be the nature of an absolutely true description of a real thing?

Philosophers generally suppose that an "absolute" description would be one which included all perspectives. But here we are led astray by a deceptive analogy. The notion of "perspective" is borrowed from the domain of visual relations; it is perfectly possible to conceive a thing with reference to more than one perspective, because perspectives have points in common, and are parts of one logical system, namely visual space. (A physical object has been defined as the conjunct of all its possible appearances, from all points of view.)[3] But logical perspectives exclude each other; they cannot be ideally put together. We cannot use the measurements of a map in Mercator projection to draw on the surface of a globe. Yet, when the peculiar functions involved in the former kind of measurement are accepted, the map which results from them is exactly as true a replica of the world as the globe. The reason why it looks less perfect to the average mind is merely that we are usually thinking in other and simpler terms than those of the projection. If now we would describe the location of any place, we must use one geometry or the other; we can never assert a proposition *about the earth*,[4] which employs them both. A visual perspective really reveals an object "partially," and it is possible to supply the other parts ideally with perfect definiteness; but a logical perspective is not partial in the sense that it leaves out certain portions of the object. It is abstract, not sectional. It is not even necessarily selective in the sense of leaving out something it might include; it applies to the *whole* reality, and, if it is exhaustive, reflects the way every single bit is related to every other bit; its abstractness lies in the fact that the whole thing might be described, in different terms, to

have entirely different inner relations, whereby we would not even make the same distinction of the "given," the (ideally) amorphous "reality," into just *this* form and content, but might determine these two factors very differently. Consequently we can never speak of "*the*" form of anything in Nature, but only of *a* form; yet in such a form the entire thing may be given to us.

A concrete experience, then, may be quite legitimately "meant" by several logically diverse symbols. It is capable of exemplifying various forms, though it can display only one form at a time. Any system which fits the real experience exactly, and leaves none of its structural properties indeterminate, is an adequate description. From this it follows that there can be *several adequate descriptions* of reality.

But descriptions need not even be adequate in order to be correct. An incomplete statement, for instance, may be perfectly faithful although it leaves much of the structural detail undetermined. An outline map of the world is just as correct as one which indicates mountains, cities and rivers; it is merely less complete. A descriptive symbol must be judged by what it asserts, rather than by what it omits; only it should merely omit, never *preclude*, any detail. The preclusion of anything is another assertion.

And now the analysis of meaning brings us to the question, "What is truth?"

Truth is the relation which holds between a symbolic structure and any one of its possible objects. Truth is *always* a relation; it is meaningless to say that a symbol such as a proposition is "true" without reference to something in the world, *to* which the symbol is true. This something may be a particular state of affairs, and then the truth of the proposition (or other symbol) is empirical; or it may be a *general* condition, as in logic or mathematics, and then the proposition is *necessarily* true. Truth differs from mere meaning in that it applies only to *descriptions*, not to denotations. If we say, "This is a chair," we use the word "chair" not as a proper name, but as an abbreviation of a descriptive symbol – we are asserting that a class, whose defining functions are known to us, includes this member. Any one who uses "chair" in the same way could accept or deny our statement. Had we said, "This is an andam," the statement would be neither true nor false for any English hearer. It could not be believed or disputed.

At this point there probably arises in most philosophical minds the consideration that truth as here defined can be merely relative, not absolute. Here, as in many other cases, the *existence* of absolute truth is not so important philosophically as the *notion* as such. Few people realize that the term "absolute truth" has significance only in a certain type of philosophical system, i.e. on the basis of certain metaphysical assumptions.[5] As soon as it is used apart from these it becomes meaningless, and only bespeaks a confusion of some other terms, such as the misuse of "true" for "real."

Truth, as it figures in ordinary intellectual life, is always a relation. A proposition or other symbol which is "true," is true *to* something. We can symbolize certain situations in the world by abstracting some of their logical features and finding other specific structures exhibiting these same abstractable characteristics; by virtue of this sameness the thing which we choose to treat as a symbol is "true" to the other, which we take for the object. This may be called a "correspondence" theory, but "correspondence" in that case must be taken in a very special sense – for it is not the symbol *in toto* which corresponds to an object, and which is known, whereas the object is unknown; the correspondence is only between certain logical aspects of both entities, so that *both may be known in the same way*, i.e. through the same conceptual schema, and whichever one is more convenient to handle may be taken to represent – not duplicate – the other. This is not the "correspondence" of idea and object, which is supposed to duplicate in experience a thing essentially outside experience. A symbol is not a reproduction of its object, but an *expression* – an exhibition of certain relevant moments, whose relevance is determined by the purpose in hand.

All expression is based upon abstract features wherein symbol and object coincide; but as an object may have various and variously expressible aspects, all symbolization is necessarily selective. This means, in the end, that *all understanding is selective*, and the great work of science is to find out those ways of conceiving an object which shall be most appropriate to certain purposes. This is a point which is rarely appreciated by people who talk about "scientific truth." Originality and genius in science consist mainly in the ability to recognize the configurations which are important for a given purpose, in other words, to make *valuable* rather than merely permissible interpretations.

[...]

All knowledge is an interpretation, and we must choose such perspectives as will yield meanings of the universe which interest us. This does not imply that there could not be others. It is not the possibilities, but the particular choice we make among these, that is prompted by human interest. If we restrict "humanism" to this choice, I think we are using the word in a good sense; but it is very easy to fall into a metaphysical trap, to suppose that reality "has" only the forms we have provocation to see, or even into a slip-shod relativism, assuming that the "real" form of Nature depends on someone's point of view.

To sum up this somewhat abstruse epistemological chapter: The potential ways of understanding, the forms actually contained in the world, are many, and our choice must be made according to our intellectual purposes; but we cannot formulate reality otherwise than by the pattern it actually has from the points of reference we have chosen. Any entity which expresses such a pattern is a symbol: it is "true" to experience in so far as the analogy holds. But as there might be many formulations of experience, there is probably no eminently true proposition (or other expression), hence no such thing as *the* truth.

"Facts" are the basic formulations of any system of apperception. They are not arbitrary logical constructions, neither are they "absolute" and stark in their own form – indeed, by pure sense-experience or intuition, if there could be such a thing, facts would not even be apparent. Definite experience is possible only where impression is met with understanding. But understanding does not consist merely of appropriate reaction to a given, pre-formed universe – understanding is *systematic* interpretation, the discovery of syntactical meanings in the world. It is the recognition of truth-forms, of symbolic relationships, of which there may be many – even as it grows more and more general, and we come nearer and nearer to the ideal of philosophy, the appreciation of all-connecting orders in the world.

Insight

To self-respecting, hard-headed logicians, the title of this [section] will probably suggest a decline and fall of the author's Pure Reason, and the advent of some Practical Unreason. But I am not at all minded to show how, in sentimental and ethical matters, logic fails us, and certain very desirable propositions are sanctioned by a higher faculty than the understanding – by a special "sixth sense," called Insight. Quite to the contrary, my thesis is that insight is understanding by the five orthodox senses, is non-discursive reasoning, different from verbal expression only by peculiar characteristics of its symbolism. It is a constituent in ordinary intelligence, and, like all knowledge, involves the appreciation of symbolic structures *qua* symbolic.

A theory of meaning which either must ignore such phenomena as the significance of Art, the functioning of what has (oddly and gratuitously) been styled "unconscious" symbolism, and the existence of incommunicable knowledge, or else must refer these to an indescribable "higher" sense, commits exactly the sins of narrowness which logical philosophy is supposed to avert: it explains all the indisputable phenomena, but cannot throw any light upon those which are problematic and therefore interesting. The possibility of dealing precisely and intelligibly with the highest rather than the lowest forms of meaning is to me the crucible, the fire-test of such a theory. If we cannot account for the sort of knowledge that is called "insight," but must leave this to a special undiscovered faculty, then our theory is not an expression of universal equations.

First let us see what sort of experience may be said to come to us through insight. Essentially, one may say, emotional and æsthetic experience: the recognition of intrinsic values. It is a characteristic of these subjects that they cannot be expressed with any precision and clarity of detail, by our usual – discursive – types of symbolization. They cannot be framed in words (except in poetry, where their expression is not literal) nor clothed in even the compactest scientific formula. There is something about emotions and feelings that eludes description. Yet they are not altogether incommunicable, and certainly not unknowable. The same is true about such elements as the humor of a situation, or the "atmosphere" of a place. No one can define these things; yet we say of some artists that they render just these elements with sure insight and adequate skill – with a few strokes, perhaps. Thus the object of insight is at least sometimes expressible, though not verbally definable.

There are certain extremely complicated forms in nature, whose structure is so unlike our strung-out, i.e. "discursive" syntactical languages – speech, writing, etc. – that their translation into verbal forms becomes too abstract to exhibit any obvious symbolic relation. Forms of such different kinds are, for the plodding human mind, incommensurable, inexchangeable. Sentences which could give expression to such complexities would be monstrous labyrinths of grammar, exceeding the vastest Latin or German projects. Every word would be the name of some intricately membered concept; our positional symbols would make a mere Chinese puzzle look almost indecently obvious. We have a very tame example of this condition in mathematics: single symbols have to act as counters for previously defined complexities, and their successive order in turn is so elaborate that common speech is inadequate to express the patterns of many elements in close logical proximity to each other. And certainly those aspects of nature which lend themselves to mathematical expression are not the most complicated ones – in fact, scientists and philosophers have been struck by the simplicity of some cosmic orders, such as the law of gravitation, or the laws of gases. If they were really complex, our symbolic powers would break down. It would be impossible to see meanings in more than a selective, fragmentary way, to read even a few items of real significance at a time, and we would constantly be ignoring an inevitable fringe of uninterpreted symbolic material. In using such a transcendent construction, undoubtedly different interpreters would see different logical pictures, and give the symbol different meanings. Thus when the complexity of an object defies our apperception, the symbolic possibilities of that object *even from one point of reference* become confused for us; realized meanings become partial in the sense that we select a few features arbitrarily, because we are not mentally (though we should be logically) able to see all the given structure. Thus, for the same symbol with the same orientation, there will be your meaning, and my meaning; that is the sense of calling meanings "subjective."

Some interpretations are easily and naturally made, others require an elaborate key. The natural ones are made by our senses; this makes us say the symbol is "like" the object. Visually, for instance, a tangerine orange is "like" the earth; logically, it is not as much like the earth as a well-constructed flat map. By virtue of some conceptual key, i.e. some principle of translation, symbols may not "look" at all like their objects. Therefore a symbolic entity may have two or more meanings at once, even for the same interpreter – one with the natural key of sense-discrimination, or of unconscious association, another in some more sophisticated language. This is the principle of allegory: there we have a literal meaning – the key to this being the accepted meanings of the words and sentence-forms – and a secondary meaning, which employs some features *of the primary* meaning, as a symbol to express another structure.

But allegory is a direct and obvious form of interpretation. For the secondary meaning could really be literally expressed, being simply another story. It is verbally communicable, and does not really need the literal story for its expression. But there are ideas which no definition can render, and these are necessarily revealed only as secondary meanings. There are ideas that haunt the human mind, yet are never satisfactorily stated in words. The feeling of Fate which runs through Greek tragedy, German Epic poetry, and the novel literature of the Russians, which makes persons of all persuasions, mystic and positivist, optimist and pessimist, shudder at the seriousness and grandeur of a vague, but world-old, elusive conception – this ingredient of our emotional and intellectual life can never be fully stated in literal discourse. Philosophers themselves have tried to render it in a dozen different ways: as a doctrine of determinism, physical or psycho-physical; as superhuman will; as instinct, or law, or cosmic urge; as bio-chemical disposition; as predestination, or evolution, or self-realization. All these theories are inspired by the desire to express that principle which makes suffering significant and renunciation holy. Each formulation is made in different literal terms, and not one of them has taken the world by storm as a revelation of true propositions; but if we look beyond the statement of fact to the basic conception which it seeks to express, we cannot treat even a fantastic metaphysic lightly. Each of these systems really is a myth, not a description – a myth, which embodies the concept in an instance. The concept itself is too universal, hence too abstract, to be rendered without any irrelevancies; our common words do not refer directly to high abstractions. Yet in its most diverse incarnations we recognize a thing which, in itself, is not the subject-matter of the propositions before us – for they describe an assumed or imagined state of affairs, that is the myth – but the thing which is meant by the myth. And the only way we can extricate it from a particular myth is to express it in another one. For its elements have no names, and of its structure we have no previous concept; it is more general than any of the mythical accounts.

This sort of expression often lets us apprehend a concept before we comprehend it. For the same intelligence which allows us to see in discursive symbolism a "picture" of a fact, lets us see in any sort of fact a "picture" of a general condition. Now very frequently, the language of propositions is less easily used to picture certain facts than the language of myth. But to treat a myth as an allegory in the strict sense is useless – for *all myths expressing the same fundamental idea are allegories of each other*, but they are formulations, exemplifications, not allegories of the *concept* they embody. Therefore to treat a religious symbol, for instance, as an allegory of natural events, is merely substituting one language for another. The kernel of a myth is a remote idea, which is *shown*, not stated, in the myth. It is only the myth that is stated in words. Ernst Cassirer has made this point excellently clear in his "*Philosophie der symbolischen Formen*," and perhaps his own words are the most fit to convey it.

"It is not through accident that the Greek thinker in whom the peculiar formative power of myth is still alive and active, was the keenest opponent of this view [the allegorical], which leads inevitably to the utter defeat of the mythical image-world. Plato assumes an ironic aloofness from all the attempts at myth-interpretation, which were practiced by the Sophists and Rhetoricians of his day – all such efforts appear to him as a vain exercise of wits, and a clumsy as well as tedious sort of knowledge (ἄγροιχος σοφια Phaedrus 229D). If Goethe once extolled the 'simplicity' of Plato's natural philosophy, and contrasted it with the boundless multiplicity, heterogeneity and complexity of modern science, Plato's attitude toward myth may be taken to exemplify the same principle. For likewise in the realm of mythology his eye does not rest upon the profusion of particular motives, but to him this world appears as a self-contained whole, which he sets up against the cosmos of pure knowledge in order to measure them with one another. Thus the philosophical 'rescue' of Myth, which is at once its philosophical dissolution, consists in conceiving it as a form and a stage of actual cognition – and, in fact, as a form of cognition which is peculiar and appropriate to a definite subject-matter, to which it gives adequate expression. Plato assigned a certain conceptual content to the mythical sphere: for he regards it as the only symbolic form wherein the world of Becoming can be expressed. That which never is, but always 'becomes,' that which does not remain, like the

(219)

constructions of logical and mathematical thought, in self-identical rigidity, but appears from moment to moment as something other – that can never lend itself to any but mythical representation. . . . Herewith the language of Myth outgrows all its purely material meanings; here it is conceived as a definite, and – in its proper place – necessary *function* for our conception of the world."[6]

The Greek ideas of motion and becoming, frustrated by a mathematics that was incapable of expressing vector properties, were a complete enigma to scientific thought. But where all literal statement was impossible, and natural philosophy utterly false and inadequate, the healthy human mind *saw* the true form of all dynamic process, in the less fixed and therefore more eloquent symbolism of Myth.

All representative art is a myth. Its significance is not in its object, but in that which its particular formulation of the object is capable of expressing. But the formulation is inexhaustibly individual; the object itself is almost irrelevant, the conception of it all-important; the balance of values, line and color and light, and I know not what other elements, is so highly adjusted that no verbal proposition could hope to embody its pattern. Yet the totality is an indescribably perfected *rhythm* (which is "pattern" in a more developed sense), for which we find equally indescribable meanings in our world of experience.

Music is the purest of symbolic media. Schopenhauer has rightly given it a special place among the arts, because in not employing any mythical "literal meaning" it can represent its actual object with less obstruction than the arts which must work through a distracting specific subject. Could it be that the final object of musical expression is the endlessly intricate yet universal pattern of emotional life?

Such speculations crowd in upon the mind, as soon as it realizes the *presentative* rather than the *representative* function of a non-verbal symbolism. Perhaps they are hopelessly unscientific; yet I suspect that the concept which gives rise to them is fertile. It enables us, for instance, to understand more precisely the relation between reason and what is usually called intuition, two principles which have played so large a rôle in epistemology that men have actually taken sides as "intuitionists" and "rationalists."

Reason is apprehension through discursive language. Anything that can be *said*, in speech or writing, is rationally construed. Ideally, everything could be said – but only ideally, for such a possibility would involve an infinite vocabulary and an infinite syntax. Actually, words are our most definite and certain means of communication, but the paucity of language is astounding. Perhaps that is why rationalists, whose verbal-mindedness makes them neglect if not actually deny the symbolic possibilities of all structures which words cannot imitate, are apt to lack intuition – which I have called "insight." Other natures, living through the eye, the musical hearing, the bodily senses, see more *meaning* in artistic wholes, i.e. in things, situations, feelings, etc., than they can ever find in propositions; they feel the peculiar poverty of the conventional language. The things they appreciate are simply *non-discursive symbols*. Their knowledge, being intensive, is much harder to communicate than propositional knowledge, especially where it is humanly impossible to express it in words; but it is knowledge none the less, and the process of apperceiving such meanings is the same as that of understanding a sentence. The symbolic quality of empirical things is just the same as what Russell has called the "transparency" of an asserted proposition. But since the symbolic *possibilities* of a concrete experience are probably infinite, and no abstract meaning is fixed by convention, as in language, insight into rhythms and forms which elude words is apt to be incommunicable. This is the source of Bergson's aphorism:

"There are things that intelligence alone is able to seek, but which, by itself, it will never find. These things instinct alone could find; but it will never seek them."[7]

For Bergson, reason rests only on discursive symbolism, which is false to the form of reality – for to him, as to Plato,[8] the mystery of reality is *Becoming*, and like Plato he considers this element as essentially indescribable, knowable only by intuition.

Strange philosophies have arisen upon the supposition that everything which is known to us figures in thought as a discursive communicable proposition. In psychology, for instance, where we have to deal all the time with faculties of cognition and have in practice run across the non-discursive forms, fantastic metaphysical dogmas have been created to force the facts into the accepted limitations of what is to be called "knowledge." Consider the elaborate constructions made by the psychoanalysts, in support of a procedure which really is based upon a recognition of the importance and profusion of intensive symbolism in our psychical life! In order to explain the existence of such symbolic structures as dreams, fantasies, etc., they assume a whole "unconscious system," a mind within the mind, which "knows" the propositions corresponding to the symbols which enter our consciousness spontaneously. They must assume such a hidden mind, cut off from consciousness, because they take for granted that anything which is symbolized must previously be "known," i.e. be formulated as a proposition of some sort. The proposition which is stored away in the sub-conscious mind is a reflection of some past event, or some personal need; it is reflected in its turn through the symbol, the image or act which appears in consciousness.

But if we realize the possibility of direct intensive symbolization, then we need not assume that any proposition, "known" to the mind, is expressed in the overt symptom; it may be a state of affairs, a past event or some individual need, that is itself expressed in the symbol, and does not enter the mind in any other way. The whole structure of "unconscious mind" is really gratuitous in establishing the Freudian psychology; it is metaphysical lumber. The symptom is the *direct* expression of the fact, and stands for it exactly as a discursive proposition about it would stand for it. Through the symbolic act or image, an important past event plays into the later history of the organism, without being discursively known. But I maintain that such formulation of an idea is knowledge in a wider sense – it acts as a stimulus, puts us into *rapport* with a past event, is our present experience of that event just as a proposition might be.

The two types of symbolism which I call respectively "discursive" and "intensive," are so different that they are supposed to be apprehended by different faculties. But as a matter of fact they are both present in almost every act of cognition. Just as it is futile to divide the mental life into sense, emotion, reason, and other separately functioning motives, so it is bootless to dichotomize knowledge into intellect and intuition, one of which excludes the other. There is no knowledge without form; and probably no form is unique; therefore all knowledge can find symbolic expression. But it is the types of expression rather than the organ of recognition that determines the difference between insight and inference. In general, each type of expression is appropriate to a certain type of subject-matter which the other cannot adequately render, yet there are some conceptions that fall as easily into the one form as into the other. For instance, one person can understand through a graph what another can only grasp through an algebraic formula, and *vice versa*.

A scientist of genius is a person who can apprehend a new concept through some natural medium, for whom there are unprobed patterns in nature, which catch his mind's eye so that he can *see* the general form of a system which becomes lucid for others (and even for him) only as he gives it literal expression. This is the logical process which in popular parlance is called "having a hunch." The artist also, if he can lay claim to genius, must find symbolisms in nature; but his expression is intensive, and only clarifies the material to the point of making the hunch vaguely contagious. Of course, he need not use the same material; he may indulge in "symphonies of color," in "tonal poems" or "dynamic designs." But the scientist must have insight to convey intellectual knowledge, and the artist must have insight to inspire insight.

This power which is called insight or intuition, is based upon our perception of patterns, which some enlightened psychologists have recognized as the principle of "Gestalt," and which is "form" in a really general sense. It is the process of generalizing an apprehended configuration, be it verbal, visual, or even emotional; finding for it possible meanings in our further experience. I do not see why, in the case of intensive symbolisms, where the meaning is sometimes incommunicable, the process of understanding should be classed as "alogical"; rather it seems to me that the recognition of patterns without the help of conventional associations, the personal discovery of meanings through myth, ritual, and art, highly individual, and awe-inspiring by its subtlety, is the very acme of logical procedure, and the refinement of intelligence.

Notes

1 I do not know whether intuition ever involves abstraction. The subject has never, to my knowledge, been conclusively treated.

2 See my article, "Form and Content: A Study in Paradox," in *The Journal of Philosophy*, vol. XXIII, no. 16, Aug. 5, 1926.

3 B. Russell, "The World of Physics and the World of Sense," in *Our Knowledge of the External World*, p. 110: "Things are those series of aspects which obey the laws of physics."

4 We could, of course, assert propositions *about the systems* and *involve* propositions from both of them, but we could not *use* them.

5 Of Reality as a whole we might say that it is absolute, depending on nothing else for its character, appearance, etc., since there is nothing else. Whether we can talk significantly about Reality as a whole, is a question which has lately been raised by Wittgenstein and other philosophical logicians – the only class of people who ever question the *terms* of discourse; but, be that as it may, if there is anything we can describe as Reality *in toto*, this must presumably be absolute, since there is nothing to which it could be relative.

When we ask for absolute *truth*, however, the matter is somewhat different. Here we are asking for an *expression* of Reality which shall be perfectly exhaustive, and unique. Truth – if we do not use words loosely – belongs only to symbols; so absolute truth could belong only to a symbol which fits Reality to the minutest detail, and which includes as parts of itself all other symbols. But a symbol, be it a proposition, picture, or idea (a "mental copy," as the several varieties of dualists say) is itself a part of Reality; hence it would have to meet the further difficulty of symbolizing itself. If it is to have absolute truth, it must so thoroughly express itself and its relation to the world that nothing can be said about itself or beyond itself. That is really asking a great deal of one symbol. In fact, such a state of affairs is conceivable only if the symbol is identical with its object. This is exactly the supposed case of Hegel's "Concrete Universal" wherein symbol and object are one, and consequently truth is not a relation, but a property. Then truth means the same thing as reality. Therefore Hegel or any of his disciples has a right to distinguish between "absolute" and "relative" truth, since to say that truth is "absolute" means to him that it is no longer to be treated as a relation; it is a *property*, inferred from the behaviour of truth-relations. For the Hegelian there are two senses of the word truth – the second distinguished by the adjective "absolute." But the opposition of "absolute" and "relative" truth has been taken over by philosophers in whose vocabulary truth has only one meaning, and is not the same as reality; and that is how the vain and verbose pursuit of indefinable Somethings usually begins. Thus it is not the Hegelian, asserting that truth is absolute, who is talking nonsense, but only the non-Hegelian who denies it – even if the Hegelian is wrong.

6 The English rendering is mine. The book has not, to my knowledge, been translated.

7 *Creative Evolution* (trans. Arthur Mitchell), p. 151.

8 According to Cassirer. Cf. *Philosophie der symbolischen Formen*, vol. II, p. 5.

19

An American Urphilosophie

Robert Bunge

Introduction

Robert Bunge (1930–89), philosopher, was a graduate of DePaul University and, later, professor at
the University of South Dakota. He was fluent
in Lakota and an advocate of native American
rights. Bunge expanded language programs and encouraged appreciation of the many uses of native
culture.

Sioux Epistemology

This [section] is epistemological only in the broad
sense of the word. Traditional Lakota did not
possess any philosophical techniques for establishing the limits of knowledge or the possibility of
genuine knowledge, such as Descartes' techniques
of methodical doubt or Hegel's dialectic. Nor did
they concern themselves with "proofs" or worry
about the problem of *a priori* knowledge. Nevertheless, six distinct types of knowledge are discern-
ible among the Lakota. These six, in European
thought, fall roughly into two categories – mundane knowledge and supernatural knowledge. This
division is purely formal and *in actual fact no such
division really exists*. The division is made here to
make Lakota philosophical assumptions intelligible
to minds accustomed to thinking in the categories

Taken from *An American Urphilosophie: An American
Philosophy BP (Before Pragmatism)* (Maryland: University Press of America, 1984). Reprinted with permission from University Press of America.

of traditional European philosophy. The natural
and supernatural worlds impinge and interpenetrate each other to a degree such that no real
separation can be made. Every ordinary act is,
in some sense, religious, i.e., spiritual, and every
spiritual act has mundane manifestations and
effects. All knowledge has its source ultimately
with and in the Wakántanka and is transmitted to
man in various ways. Therefore, strictly speaking,
there is no really profane knowledge in Lakota
thought. What is designated as profane knowledge
in European thought will be called ordinary (work-
a–day) knowledge for the purposes of this paper.

Ordinary knowledge

Under this rubric is included all knowledge designated in English as profane, secular, mundane,
work–a–day knowledge of the most practical order
– knowledge needed for and acquired in what
might be called the economics of life – knowledge
sustaining material life.

This is a body of folk knowledge acquired over
the centuries as a result of trial and error. A
woman grinds corn in a certain way because this
is the way she was taught by her mother and
grandmother. A man fletches arrows in a certain
way because this is the way he was taught by his
father and grandfather. It is a knowledge of the
mechanics of things. It is "how-to" knowledge,
i.e., how to erect a tipi, how to make a travois or
pony drag, how to track and hunt. Every people
and every nation has developed knowledge of this
kind over the centuries. But in few peoples has

spiritual "how-to" knowledge fused with practical knowledge to the degree where one cannot be distinguished from the other. For every act there is a blessing. Every material action has a corresponding spiritual action. Again the preceding distinction is purely formal, not actual. To a Lakota, they are not merely complementary or supplemental parts of the same action. *They are the same action.* They are a single unity, all of a piece, metaphysically understood – a logical simple, irreducible to any more fundamental concept. According to the Indian view, it is a quibble to argue which is most important; being a unity, they cannot be separated. Neither is more important, both are all important.

A hunter may pray over the tracks of a deer, a prayer enabling him to get close enough to shoot the deer. From the Indian point of view, this is *one, single act*, not two acts – not a spiritual act (the prayer) nor a physical one (the shooting of the deer). It is not even a single act having two complementary parts – the physical and the spiritual. It is a single act.

In the Anglo-American world, the tendency is to give priority to the physical act. The prayer is "tacked on." A member of the dominant society, if pressed, would probably say that the physical act, i.e., the tracking and shooting of the deer, was the really important part of the unity known as the hunt. Although, if at all religious, he might believe the prayer might help and, in any case, would certainly do no harm, even if it could not help. But the fact remains that for the white man in today's society the prayer is a frill – "something nice tacked onto, maybe even aiding, the real business of hunting." For the Indian, even though the hunt is a unified action, if any importance were attached to a single part of the hunt, it would certainly be a bias for the spiritual aspect of the hunt. The underlying supposition, stated above, is: "Man can do nothing without power [spiritual power], but with power almost anything is possible." In other words, a man may or may not bag a deer with the ceremony, but without it he will surely fail.

This writer remembers an incident illustrating this point, when he was faculty advisor to the Tiyóšpaye Council at the University of South Dakota. An Indian student club, the Council is composed not only of Sioux but of students from many different United States tribes. It was the winter of 1979–80 and the South Dakota Legislature was considering abolishing the State Indian Scholarship Fund and the students chartered a bus and a van in order to go to Pierre (state capital) to lobby in favor of the bill, to present their side of the case to the legislators. First, however, most importantly, a pipe must be sent to a powerful medicine man on the Rosebud Sioux Reservation, a distance of about 200 miles from the University. It was mid-winter and snow drifts blocked the roads to and on the reservation. The students, many, perhaps even most of them, quite acculturated to the Anglo world, waited anxiously. For a while, the weather defied delivery of the all-important pipe to the medicine man. The students knew that unless the pipe was delivered, all attempts at lobbying were futile. Finally, a runner broached the drifts and a blinding plains blizzard and hand-carried the pipe to the medicine man. Everyone was jubilant. The pipe had been delivered in the prescribed manner; even now the medicine chief was praying for the success of their venture. All was well. Armed and fortified with the knowledge that now they had the necessary power, they boarded the vehicles for the trip to Pierre. Incidentally, the scholarship fund was saved that year.

This year, 1980–1, the scholarship fund was lost. Notified only one day in advance of the meeting on this issue, the Indian students could reach the state capital only by driving all night. There was no time for a ceremony, and the mood was apprehensive. The gesture was made, of course. A few Indian students made the all-night trip in a van to present their case before the legislative committee early the next morning. But without the pipe ceremony, there was no power in the trip. The funding was lost. And the students felt it would be so in advance. They had not had the power.

The Lakota, thus, are at once mystics and pragmatists. Any Indian, Sioux or otherwise, would agree with James's summation of the characteristics of a religious life with some modification:

1 That the visible world is part of a more spiritual universe from which it draws its chief significance.
2 That union or harmonious relation with that higher universe is our true end.
3 That prayer or inner communion with the spirit thereof – be that spirit "God" or "Law" – is a process wherein work is really done and spiritual energy flows in and produces effects, psychological or material, within the phenomenal world.[1]

James goes on to add the following two psychological characteristics:

4 A new zest which adds itself like a gift to life, and takes the form of either lyrical enchantment or of appeal to earnestness and heroism.
5 An assurance of safety and a temper of peace, and in relation to others, a preponderance of loving affections.[2]

First of all, a traditional Lakota believes not that the visible world is part of a greater spiritual world but that the spiritual world and visible world are one reality. They interpenetrate to such a degree that the line between them is but vaguely drawn, if at all. As to the second part of this proposition, the chief significance of the world (visible and invisible) is that it exists and the Wakántanka may be invoked in its maintenance and continuance.

As to the second proposition by "union of harmonious relation with the higher universe," an Indian would understand "universe" to mean all of nature.

As to the third characteristic, the traditional Lakota would agree with this without reservation or modification of any kind. Real work is accomplished in the medicine rites. The rites are not merely symbolic in nature but genuine "effects" are produced in the mundane world thereby. And herein lies one aspect of Indian pragmatic thought. His religion *works* for him. Besides a revitalizing psychological effect, genuine observable "effects" are wrought in the phenomenal world.

The fourth characteristic most often takes the form of a call to "earnestness and heroism" among the Lakota. It often takes the form of a "vow to Sun Dance or Hanbléčeya" (Cry for a Vision), i.e., fast four days on a hilltop during which the faster receives a vision or a message from the Wakántanka.

"The temper of peace and the assurance of safety" are certainly present, at least temporarily, as well as a humility and fellow feeling for all that is. Every act is a combination of the spiritual and physical.

Indian empiricism and pragmatism

Paul Radin makes much of Indian "tough-mindedness" and sets out to explode some older and, in his opinion, unwarranted theories held by ethnographers and anthropologists of an earlier generation. In particular, he attacks Lévi-Strauss,

Henri Frankfort, Walker and a host of others. Lévi-Strauss is accused of stigmatizing primitive peoples with a pre-logical or alogical, mythopaeic mentality; Radin attempts to prove that primitive man was as tough-minded, in the Jamesian sense, and as clearsighted and unsentimental in assessing a "fact" as a fact as was the toughest-minded, most unsentimental nineteenth-century Anglo-American pragmatist. He states:

He [primitive man] is pre-eminently a man of practical common sense just as is the average peasant. Now this does not merely mean manual dexterity or an exclusive interest in the purely material side of life. It has much deeper implications. This tough-mindedness leads to a recognition of all types of realities, realities which primitive man sees in all their directness and ruggedness, stripped of all that false and sentimental haze so universal among civilized peoples. . . . It is true that the facts of everyday life, in every primitive community, are clothed in a magical and ritualistic dress, yet it is not unfair to say that it is not the average native who is beguiled into an erroneous interpretation of this dress but the ethnologist.[3]

This writer feels that Radin errs too far in the opposite direction. The other ethnologists and philosophic anthropologists were wrong, he claims, in stating or implying that primitive man was so different from the modern Western European. Radin would re-cast primitive man in the *same* mold as Western European man, dividing them neatly into European schools of men who are basically empiricists and men who are basically rationalists or idealists. No such neat distinction exists in actuality. Radin himself has the typically European idea that there is a world of the spirit and ideas and then there is the "real" world, and that primitive man makes a careful distinction between them. As a European, Radin automatically differentiates between the spiritual world and the world of "facts," disregarding completely the fact that no such distinction exists. The world of fact for American aboriginal peoples does *not* exclude the spiritual. Radin is guilty of imposing his classificatory categories on aboriginal thought, the very crime of which he accuses the others mentioned above, and divides a community into men of action roughly corresponding to pragmatists and men of thought roughly corresponding to clerics, scholars, etc.

Radin offers the following story in support of his thesis:

An American Indian pursued by the enemy took refuge in a cave where he could easily defend himself against direct attack but where escape was apparently completely cut off. This particular individual was not religious. He had during his lifetime had so little interest in getting into the proper rapport with the deities of his tribe that he knew the conventional methods of addressing them but little else. In his dilemma, with death staring him in the face, he mechanically offers tobacco to the spirits. That much he knew, but he did not know what to say nor whom to address. So he prayed – if we are inclined to call this a prayer – "To you, O spirits, whoever you are, wherever you are, here is tobacco. May I be saved!" Through an almost miraculous piece of good luck, the enemy fled and he was saved. "By the Will of God," a devout Christian would have ejaculated; in Indian phraseology, "the spirits heard me." *Here, if anywhere, we might have expected an almost mystical feeling of heavenly intervention and a well-nigh complete obliteration of the mere workaday world.* Yet nothing of the kind occurred to this very hard-minded individual. *He sought to explain nothing.* I can picture him saying to himself in his humorous way – for he was the professional humorist in the tribe – "Let the medicine-man explain; they like such things. All I know is that I was pursued by the enemy; I took refuge in a cave; my attackers withdrew and here I am." The ritualistic paraphernalia were all there but they did not obscure his vision of a true fact. . . . This intense realism, this refusal to be deluded by the traditional phraseology employed, is a salient feature of most primitive communities.[4] (Writer's emphasis.)

Radin errs. To focus on this, certain sections of the tale above have been underlined. What Radin fails to realize is that a "mystical feeling of heavenly intervention" *in no wise obliterates* the mere workaday world since it is part and parcel *of* the workaday world. Radin imposes, both in thought and phraseology, Western European Christian thought. Even though he imagines the words he puts into the Indian's mouth, it is difficult to imagine any Indian, even a semi-acculturated one, being so flippant toward the spirits after a miraculous escape. Finally, he errs in making a

distinction between "ritualistic paraphernalia" and a "fact." Ritualistic paraphernalia is *one* with the fact.

In his zeal to press down the crown of European "tough-mindedness" on the aboriginal brow, Radin winds up with an argument that is internally implausible. Apparently he forgets that if someone, white or Indian, felt driven to appeal to a mystical force, as did Radin's fictional pragmatist, one would react in awe no matter what one's cultural background; otherwise the person would not have felt so compelled in the first place.

The chances are very slim that any such village skeptic or heretic would arise in the Lakota, Winnebago or any other Native American society due to the basic spiritual and metaphysical/ontological structure of those societies which persists to this day, even among Native Americans who are otherwise quite acculturated. In addition to this, the impulse to conform is much greater in Native American societies where peer-pressure is all-pervasive, thoughts of the group as a whole and cooperation rather than competition are stressed; departing from what is traditional is perceived as a voluntary severance of an individual from the roots of his being. Interestingly enough, no persecutions of heretics ever occurred in the Indian nations as they did and do very frequently in Europe and white America. Possibly this was and is so because no band of heretics ever arose for the reasons mentioned above, but more probably because of the Native American respect for individual freedom of thought. The individual skeptic would certainly be entitled to his opinion even though it might subject him to ridicule, that most effective of all social weapons.

Although he does not say it, Radin attempts to force Native American, in this case Winnebago, thought into a peculiarly western thought structure – namely, that there are so-called "men-of-action" and so-called "men of thought." The error here is quite pronounced. He assumes these two categories are mutually exclusive, which is certainly not the case in Indian societies where both are frequently embodied in one person, i.e., Crazy Horse was both thinker and war chief. So was Sitting Bull. Radin then assumes or implies that he knows what the white cultural perspective is, which is a spurious presumption at best. It is a moot point whether these two types are separable even in European culture.

Radin seems to divide people into two "natural" categories, i.e., that a person is by temperament and inclination predominantly one or the other. He makes the general assumption that the ratio of thinkers to men of action is roughly the same in primitive societies as in advanced cultures, offering only his own observations in support of this thesis.[5] The ratio of thinkers to the general population has never been large in the so-called advanced countries so Radin fixes the ratio of thinkers to men-of-action in primitive societies at 1:99, or 1 percent of the population. Accordingly, then, 99 percent of the population are men of action. Radin describes, from an ethnologist's viewpoint, the primitive penchant for spending long periods of time "doing apparently nothing."[6] Such activity – "doing apparently nothing" – is difficult for an intellectual to comprehend and is equally difficult for a man of action to understand; he then goes on to state that "ethnologists are definitely the one or the other." The question at this point is, then, based on the Radin dichotomy, into what category do these aborigines fall who spend "long periods of time in doing apparently nothing?" Are they incomprehensible to intellectual and man-of-action alike? How can this be since in primitive societies 1 percent of the population are thinkers and 99 percent men-of-action? Apparently Radin does not include himself among those observers who are deluded by the meaning-ladenness of their theories and observations; hence he occupies a Wittgensteinian "angelic" position from whence he correctly assesses the conditions that obtain in all types of primitive communities.

It is true that the Indian had an unsentimental view of the awesome natural forces surrounding him. He knew that at any moment he might have to fight for his life and the lives of his loved ones. He knew that the conditions of his life made it not only possible but very probable that he would be called upon at any time to make the grimmest sacrifice.

Samuel Johnson once said that the knowledge that one was to be hanged in the morning really cleared one's head. When a person lives constantly in an atmosphere of impending doom, his priorities quickly fall into place. When one lives knowing that each day, even each hour, may very likely be one's last, the whole of lived experience assumes a heightened and intensified aspect. To arrive at old age was no mean achievement. It had overtones and undertones of the miraculous. Under these conditions, any attempt to guide one's life by other than the light of the sternest pragmatism and practicality was not merely folly, it was suicidal. The failure to properly assess any confrontational situation by letting sentiment blind one to one's true capabilities and strength, leading the individual to overestimate his own strength and underestimate that of an enemy meant instant annihilation. But, from all this, it does not follow that the American aborigine regarded "facts" as something apart from spiritual power, or that he ever made such a distinction. In fact, an Indian would ask, "Why would anyone want to make such a distinction?"

He always slept with his weapons within easy reach and in times of good weather when raids from enemy tribes were likely everyone slept with their moccasins on, ready to run instantly. Babies were taught early not to cry because crying attracted enemies and wild animals. Old timers have told this writer that it was only in the wintertime and only during a time of very severe weather such as a blizzard, very heavy snowfall, or 50° below zero weather that the camp enjoyed a measure of security and could sleep without moccasins, knowing that no war party would be mad enough to venture forth in such weather. It was only then that weapons could be laid aside temporarily and visiting and story-telling around the campfire could be done in relative safety.

Wičówoyake (true stories)

The whole epistemological enterprise, the whole question of what the limits of knowledge are, or what we can know for certain, is closely connected with what we regard as true. The reference to story-telling in the above section leads naturally to what the Lakota regarded as another source of knowledge. The word wičówoyake includes knowledge that Anglo-Americans or Europeans would regard as "historical knowledge," i.e., stories about the Lakota's recent past such as the Indian wars and accounts of various battles – Fetterman Battle, known in the Sioux Winter Count as "the Year of the Hundred Slain;" or the Custer battle on the Little Big Horn in 1876. These accounts are told from the Indian point of view but are accepted by white people as genuine or factual accounts of actual historical events and so corroborated in white history books.

What is different about this classification of knowledge is that the wičówoyake or "true story" category also includes many tales which Anglo-Americans would regard as myth or fable such as the Lakota Creation Stories [discussed elsewhere by Bunge]. These also are regarded as true, just as the Creation Story in Genesis is regarded by many whites as true, factual history. The Creation Story in Genesis is considered by many white fundamentalist Protestants as literally true and is, in their eyes, in no sense a myth or merely a symbolical representation on the part of an anonymous ancient author to account for the fact that there is anything at all. Thus it is that these true stories constitute a major transmission belt of knowledge extending across the generations. These stories are usually told in the daytime, but there is no prohibition against the telling of them at night.

Ohúnkankan stories

These oral narratives are another source of knowledge, but not the same kind of knowledge as is transmitted by the *wówičake wičówoyake* (true stories-history). Told only in the evening, these oral narratives deal with legendary and/or fabulous beings or monsters such as Iya the Cannibal Giant, and a great many stories about Iktomi the Trickster. The majority of Lakotas consider these tales as untrue or "just for fun" stories. By "not true" is meant not true in the sense that they never really occurred. Other Lakotas, while agreeing that these beings never existed, still hesitate to label the narratives "untrue" because they regard them as psychologically true, or regard the moral illustrated by the tale as true. In *Buckskin Tokens*, which are *Ohúnkankan* tales told by contemporary Lakotas, the editor states:

> They do not moralize as is the case in the closing lines of a large number of non-Indian fables. The Ohunkankan are made up to a considerable degree of the deeds and antics of a negative behavioral model Iktomi, the trickster.[7]

The *Ohúnkankan* tales are somewhat like the biblical parables such as those found in St. Luke 6: 39–49, i.e., the parable of the blind leading the blind, the parable of the mote and the beam, the parable of the good tree and the corrupt tree, and the parable of the man who laid the foundations of his house on rock and the unwise man who laid his foundation on earth alone. The Indian tales and the biblical parables are similar in that they both teach a moral but are dissimilar as to the method of teaching – namely, the parables are explicit; non-biblical parables usually restate the moral at the end. In the *Ohúnkankan* tales the moral is implicit, i.e., unspoken, and the lis-

tener comes to see via the negative role model what behavior is to be avoided and, by contrast, what the socially correct behavior should have been.

These Lakota tales cannot be judged by European literary criteria. In tenor they are terse and uncomplicated and repetition is frequent. Character development is neglected and the characters are subsequently one-dimensional. Action is paramount, plots and settings are simple and at a minimum. The characters frequently assume animal form and have other supernatural powers. No attempt is made to be "logical" with regard to time or details.

The central figure in many of the *Ohúnkankan* stories is Iktómi whose name literally means "spider" but is most often portrayed in human form or in the guise of an animal. Originally, he was a combination of divinity and amoral deceiver. Through the years his amoral deceiver aspect has gained ascendency and he has become the embodiment of anti-social behavior. Most stories begin *Iktómi wanná ú* (Iktómi was coming along now), or "Iktómi was going along," thus indicating his socially-useless activity and he is "always up to no good." He represents man's irrational, uncontrolled side. Always deceiving people, he often deceives himself in the process. He violates all taboos, commits incest, cannibalism, cowardice, sacrilege – all the Lakota cardinal sins. He serves to remind the listener of man's dual aspect, the good and bad sides of his nature, and reminds him also that Iktómi lurks in everyman just below what can be seen and must constantly be constrained by that highest of all virtues – self control.

Wakán knowledge

Unlike the Europeans, the Lakota never concerned themselves with fixing the boundaries of the knowable. They frankly acknowledged that there were limits but, in an equally frank manner, acknowledged that they did not know these limits. The Lakota believed and still believe that there is much in the universe which is inaccessible to ordinary man or things that can only be known in a special way by special people. If the Lakota make any division in knowledge at all, it is between what is *understandable* and what is *not* understandable. A traditional full-blood has told this writer, "*What is not understandable is wakán.*" By understandable is meant understandable to the ordinary man, or things or actions falling within the normal scope of experience of the ordinary individual. If it is something requiring a medicine man then it is *wakán*, i.e., some experience outside the ken of ordinary man requiring interpretation or action by a seer or medicine man. A person becomes a medicine man by revelation, that is, a certain person may be instructed in a dream or vision during *hanblééeya* that he is to devote his life to sacred things and healing. During the vision he is usually given minute instructions as to how he is to proceed, what animal or spirit will be his guide and mentor and what he is to do and say to the elders of the tribe upon his return. Sometimes the language of the Spirits is Lakota, sometimes it is a sacred language known only by medicine men requiring interpretation by them.

This writer has personal knowledge of the ordeal of one such medicine "candidate." He made his *hanblééeya* on a high bluff some 30 miles southwest of Winner, South Dakota. He fasted the required four days and four nights. One night it rained, lightning crashed around the bluff upon which he kept his vigil. Suddenly a giant spider appeared to him and spread himself out over the vision-seeker to shelter him from the rain. "Fear not," said the spider. "No harm will come to you." Then the spider instructed the Indian to return to camp, ride naked around the camp circle four times, proclaiming that a vision had informed him that he was to be a medicine man of herbal variety (*pejúta wičáša*). As a helper, the spider presented the candidate with a stuffed owl; this was to be placed in the room of a patient over night. Should the patient grow worse during the night, the owl would inform the herb doctor. This man was the only doctor the Indians of the Winner area had for many years.

Many traditional people spoke to this writer of how the doctor went out on the hillsides at night to gather herbs; the herbs would glow in the dark so he could see and pick them. These same people said that many times the herbal doctor would appear at a house in the Winner area at 3.00 in the morning when all were asleep, saying the patient had taken a turn for the worse. This was unknown even to the family sleeping in the house. When asked how he knew his patient was failing, the doctor replied, "The owl told me."

Healing and curing, the function of the medical doctor in European society, falls within the purview of *wakán* or sacred knowledge. In fact, the Lakota word for a doctor trained in the scientific method is *Wašíču wakán*, "holy or sacred white man."

Basically, there were three types of medicine men. First, there was the *pejúta wičáša* – a literal translation of the word "medicine" (*pejúta*) and "man" (*wičáša*); from this name the English term is derived. However, among the Lakota, this term is used only for the herbal doctor who actually makes medicine from herbs and who has a knowledge of native herbs probably exceeding that of a modern registered pharmacist. Second and third were medicine men who used solely spiritual means to cure: the *wapíya wičáša* (man who renews or rejuvenates) and the *yuwípi* man. *Yuwípi* means "they wrap or roll him up;" he performs his spiritual healing tied in a star quilt from which he escapes with the aid of his spirits during the ceremony. Many excellent descriptions of the actions of all three of these healers have been set forth in a number of books so it would be redundant to comment in detail on these ceremonies here.

Among certain tribes there were holy women as well as men and among the Lakota the *win-kte* or berdache has special *wakán* powers of their own, particularly in the naming of children. The insane, among the Lakota, were *wakán*, considered as having been "divinely touched;" they could speak to the dead and had the powers of seers at times.

The word *wakán* needs a word of explanation. *Wakán* often is translated as "sacred" or "holy" and this is misleading to the English-speaker who invariably identifies the "holy" or "sacred" with the good. *Wakán* can also be evil, as the word for "devil" – *Wakánšíča* (holy evil) – indicates. Perhaps the word is better translated as "power," a power so great as to be supernatural. The word for "gun" in Lakota is *mazáwakán* (holy iron); an English speaker would have difficulty considering a destructive weapon as something "holy." The idea in Lakota language is that a gun has extraordinary powers; once used, once fired, something important and irrevocable happens. The universe is forever changed and cannot be the same again. All this is contained in the concept of *wakán*.

Revelation

Among the so-called advanced, literate nations, revelation usually comes in the form of the written word: a book such as the Bible for Christians, the Torah for the Jews, the Koran for Muslims, etc. Herein the Will of God is revealed. Revelation is a special kind of knowledge given in a special kind of way.

Among a pre-literate people, revelation cannot come through the written word; it comes through the spoken word via dreams and visions, sometimes induced, as in Crying for a Vision, where one actively seeks revelation, or in an uninduced vision or dream. This writer knows several people who claim this latter kind of vision. It simply came uninvited and, in several cases, unwanted. In one instance, the person involved, like Jonah, resisted the vision and argued against being the instrument of the *wakán* being, urging the Spirit to select someone younger, more intelligent, a better speaker, in short, more promising. When the person was informed that it was precisely because of his many faults that he was chosen, all resistance ended. This man, unlike Jonah, did not flee the judgment but, from that moment on, his life changed radically for the better – a complete 180 degree turn after thirty years of debauchery and dissipation. It matters not whether one considers this power as coming from without – heaven – or whether one considers it an inner psychological process; the fact is it *works*, and the pragmatic effects of such power received are remarkable beyond the ordinary and hence are *wakán*. This writer is acquainted with a dozen individuals who received power in this fashion.

Knowledge acquired intuitively or in a dream or vision is the highest form of knowledge for the Lakota and is unquestioned by everyone. This is the most sacred kind of knowledge.

On the other hand, power acquired in this way is definitely finite and must be renewed periodically. This renewal usually takes the form of sweat lodge, fasting or *hanbléčeya* at least once a year. Medicine men visualize their power as coming from various spirits, usually in animal form; these are bear curers, eagle curers, spider curers, etc. The more spirits, the more power. They also visualize their power as a sort of spiritual "stuff" or "substance" that flows from them to the patient. Naturally the more of this "substance" that flows to the patient, the less the medicine man has for himself. This power must be replenished by fasting or crying for a vision. The more often this is done, the more power the medicine man is considered to have.

Summary

Epistemologically speaking, the questions which concerned the European philosophers never arise among the Lakota. The Lakota accepted as fact

that men were capable of knowledge by the fact that they "knew." True, the word knowledge is used as a category here in a much broader and looser way than is customary among European philosophers. Knowledge among the Lakota also includes what Europeans would consider "feeling" or "emotion;" yet this was all part of knowing. Any appearance or anything that could be perceived or apprehended by any or all of the faculties, critical or uncritical, was "knowledge." Some of this knowledge was immediately intelligible and was obtained in various ways, i.e., through direct daily observation, or through the various kinds of oral narratives. Through these stories different kinds of knowledge could be obtained, historical, psychological, sociological, moral, etc. Other kinds of knowledge were not immediately intelligible; they were *wakán* and required the interpretation of specialists in this kind of knowledge. The Sioux frankly admitted there was much man did not and perhaps could not understand.

Sioux Metaphysics and Ontology

Questions which occupied European philosophers such as "What is being?" "What is reality?" never arose among the Lakota as questions. Theirs was not a conscious philosophy, i.e., thought about thought, but an unconscious or rather a sub-conscious philosophy. That means that for the most part the whole of the Lakota life-style and world view were conditioned by assumptions that remained unspoken but that were taken for granted as "given." Nevertheless these assumptions were present and were "philosophic."

The first premise in Lakota metaphysics was that "Being cannot come from non-being." This is evident in that in the Creation mythology of the Lakota and all other Native American peoples, the notion of *creatio ex-nihilo* was unknown based on the albeit unspoken assumption stated above. Therefore, in the mythology the world had to be made of some already existing "stuff" or substance (in the Aristotleian sense of secondary matter). What this "stuff" was varied from tribe to tribe. In some tribes, this stuff was the body of a primordial giant, a supernatural egg, or the body or bodies of the Wakántanka themselves, or as a sexual union of a god and goddess, but it could not be *ex-nihilo*. One is reminded here of philosophers from Heraclitus and Parmenides to Lucretius who comment that "being cannot come from non-being."

"Whatever can be apprehended in any way is," and corollary to this is "whatever is, lives." To be is to live. The Lakota language reinforces this belief. One cannot say the English sentence "He is dead" in Lakota. This is a logical contradiction for the Lakota and is meaningless for it encapsulates two mutually exclusive concepts, namely, the concept of being expressed by "is" and the concept of non-being expressed by "dead." One either "is," i.e., "lives," or one is "dead." One cannot be both at the same time. To translate the English "He is dead" into the Lakota language, one says simply *T'a* or *T'e* (he died).

This principle of "Whatever is, lives" can and is extended thus: "Whatever is, lives, and whatever lives is real." Ontologically, then, since "Reality cannot come from unreality," reality can only stem from reality. Therefore, if I am, I live, therefore I am real. Therefore, what I produce is real, i.e., children or thoughts. Therefore, since I am real and can only produce reality and I produce thoughts, therefore my thoughts are real, or as Radin says, "I think, therefore that which I think exists."[8] There are no linguistic distinctions between "being" and "living." All are expressed by *un* and conjugations thereof; to live is to be, and to be is to be real.

Intentional and real being

Thomistic metaphysics distinguishes between intentional being, that is, being-in-the-mind, and real being, that is, being outside the mind, and further states that to consider intentional being as equivalent to real being is to fall prey to the error of idealism. In the traditional Lakota view, however, all thought is, in some sense, from the outside, and this notion seems to be supported linguistically by the large number of stative verbs mentioned before.

Radin distinguishes three orders of reality emerging from the tribes with which he is familiar – the main North American tribe being the Winnebago, a Siouan-speaking people now living in Wisconsin and Nebraska.[9] Two of these orders of reality are as well known to the white world as they are to the Indian world. Proceeding from the most general to the most subjective and from the well known to the little known, the orders are as follows:

Phenomenal reality Known to white people as the "real world," is as objectively given to Indians as to the white man. Physiologically speaking, the Indian "sees" in the same way the white man "sees." The various external light stimuli produce the same images in the eye in the same way. An Indian standing beside a white man gazing out over the rolling hills of South Dakota sees the same grass, trees, birds and rocks the white man sees. The stimuli strike both pairs of eyes in the same way barring color blindness or some other physical defect. Why then do not they see the same things? Or, rather, why do they at once see the same things and yet do not see the same things?

There was and is an old myth still prevalent in these parts that "Indians (pronounced In-dins) have better eyes than the white man." Physiologically speaking, the Indian never had "better eyes" and, judging from the number of Indians wearing spectacles today, they may even have poorer eyes. It is not that Indians have better eyes but that they see things differently. Land is not simply ground. It is a person with every attribute of personhood, every ounce of quiddity any other person has. Moreover, it is a special kind of person. It is the breathing source of all life as humans know it. A rock is not just a rock; it is a spirit as well. It is the principle of firmness in the universe. In the Indian world some rocks talk and move. Even though the stimuli are the same, it is a different order of reality from the white world and is in no way imaginary in the white sense of the word. To the traditional Indian, these phenomena are in no wise fanciful or the products of imagination. They simply are.

Ringing Shield (*Waháčanka Hotún*), an old shaman, told Walker in 1897:

> There are a great many spirits. They control everything; and they know everything. They can make a man do anything they wish. They can make animals and trees and grasses do as they wish. They can talk with animals and they can make animals talk with men. The spirits go about in the world all the time and they make everything do as they please. Some spirits may want things done one way and others may want them done differently. Then the strongest spirits will overcome the weaker. Some spirits are very powerful and others are not so powerful. Any spirit is more powerful than a man.[10]

Another unidentified shaman is reported by Walker as telling him:

Everything has a spirit. A war club has a spirit. A bow has a spirit. A drum has a spirit. A prairie dog has two spirits: one spirit like the tree and one spirit like the breath of life. The breath of life is given by Wakan-skanskan (What Moves in a Holy Way) [writer's translation]. Wicasa Wakan (Holy Man) can talk to these spirits. The Wakan (holy) plumes of birds have a spirit. The Wakan plumes of a medicine bag are very powerful.[11]

The reason the white man and Indian see two different orders of reality while gazing out over the same piece of land stems from a theory of knowledge about land which, in turn, rests on certain metaphysical presuppositions as to what land is and in what way it is. These different orders of perceived reality, in turn, give rise to two different experiences. The white man would say, "There is nothing here." The Indian would say, "Everything is here." It seems there is absolutely no agreement on what is "here" even though both see the same phenomena.

To the white man untilled land, an absence of towns or houses, is "empty." As nature abhors a vacuum, the white man abhors what he perceives as an empty void and hastens to "fill it up" with fields, houses, barns, towns and people. The vast emptiness of what was called the "great American Desert" was strangely unsettling to the white pioneers. It was unbroken, rolling grassland stretching to the Rockies, and over this endless expanse blew a constant wind, at times softly but more often a shrieking wind, howling about the solitary cabins and farmhouses on the prairie. Stories are legion here about settlers' wives going insane from a combination of space-drunkenness and howling winds. The architecture of the Dakotas is revealing in this regard; the early settlers and farmers built very small houses. Now this could be explained away as a tribute to practicality. The settlers simply wanted shelter quickly and a small house is easier to build than a large one. But, oddly enough, the practice continued on into the present century and continues to be the case today. The houses here are tiny by eastern standards.

This raises an interesting question: "Why, when people had room to spare and presumably the leisure, did they build such small houses?" Perhaps it is an attempt to combat the void facing them, an attempt to cut space down to manageable size. Perhaps, in the void of the plains, they perceive a reflection of their own emptiness. This is a question that deserves more study. Few white men with the exception of the trappers and the mountain men felt comfortable in empty space.

The Indian, on the other hand, perceives the land as a bountiful mother who provides everything he needs. The prairie is not an empty void between the Mississippi and the Rockies but is "full" with every variety of living being, plants, animals and people. Everything is there for the taking, it does not have to be tilled or worked or coaxed to provide for its children.

Both men have meaning-laden theories about the land and land usage. In the concluding chapter more will be said about the meaning-ladenness of observation. Perhaps the Indian projects a "fullness" onto the land in the same way the white man projects an "emptiness."

This viewpoint of the phenomenal world being "full" has to be different from that of a white rancher who sees merely feathers, stones, trees and grass. This different view is the same today as it was in Walker's day (1896–1914) when he was agency physician on the Oglala Reservation in South Dakota; his sources of information were Indians who were grown men in the traditional buffalo-hunting days. Some of his informants had fought in the Custer Battle on the Little Big Horn in 1876.

To illustrate how this view has been transmitted undiluted, this is how a contemporary medicine man, John Fire, known to this writer, sees the everyday world; in an essay by a white writer, John Fire Lame Deer says:

What do you see here, my friend? Just an ordinary old cooking pot, black with soot and full of dents.

It is standing on the fire on top of that old wood stove, and the water bubbles and moves the lid as the white steam rises to the ceiling. Inside the pot is boiling water, chunks of meat with bone and fat, plenty of potatoes.

It doesn't seem to have a message, that old pot, and I guess you don't give it a thought. Except the soup smells good and reminds you that you are hungry. Maybe you are worried that this is dog stew. Well, don't worry. It's just beef – no fat puppy for a special ceremony. It's just an ordinary, everyday meal.[12]

John Fire goes on talking about the pot. Since he is an Indian, he says, he thinks about ordinary, common things. And one thing leads to another.

The pot makes him think of bubbling water which comes from the rain cloud, representing the sky. Fire reminds him of the sun "which warms us all" – meat reminds him of his animal brothers "who gave of themselves so that we should live."

> The steam is living breath. It was water; now it goes up to the sky, becomes a cloud again. These things are sacred. Looking at that pot full of good soup, I am thinking how, in this simple manner, Wakan Tanka takes care of me. We Sioux spend a lot of time thinking about everyday things which in our minds are mixed up with the spiritual. We see in the world around us many symbols that teach us the meaning of life. We have a saying that the white man sees so little, he must see with only one eye. We see a lot that you no longer notice. You could notice if you wanted to, but you are usually too busy. We Indians live in a world of symbols and images where the spiritual and commonplace are one. To you symbols are just words, spoken or written in a book. To us they are part of nature, part of ourselves – the earth, the sun, the wind and the rain, stones, trees, animals, even little insects like ants and grasshoppers. We try to understand them not with the head but with the heart, and we need no more than a hint to give us the meaning.
>
> What to you seems commonplace to us appears wondrous through symbolism. This is funny, because we don't even have a word for symbolism, yet we are all wrapped up in it. You have the word, but that is all.[13]

John Fire's view reminds one slightly of Leibnitz's monadic view of the universe wherein each thing reflects the universe to some degree.

John Fire was quoted at some length here because, first, he is a contemporary Indian having some knowledge of white culture, which Walker's informants did not; second, because it illustrates how unattenuated is the sense of the "wondrous in the commonplace" among Native Americans in this last quarter of the twentieth century.

According to existentialist thinkers such as Sartre and Heidegger, part of man's sense of alienation is a consequence of his *Geworfenheit*, as Heidegger calls it, his "thrownness" into the world. In their view, man is "thrown" into the world from someplace *outside* it. He was not asked if he wanted to be born. He is involuntarily "cast up" onto the world much as a ship-wrecked seaman is cast up on an island. In the traditional Plains Indian view, man is not "thrown" or "cast up" onto the world of lived experience from elsewhere, he is *of* the earth itself. Man is no stranger to the world; on the contrary, he has come *out* of the world. This is true both in a literal and figurative sense. Many tribes posit an underground place as the original dwelling of man: the Kiowa, Navajo and Sioux do this. Man is autochthonous in the literal Greek sense of "autokhthon," sprung from the land itself. But beyond this, man is somehow also the finished product of the world of lived experience. He is the sum, end or consequence of the "molding" done by the phenomenal world. Man, whether collective or individual, not only springs from the world but is continually shaped by the world. One of this writer's students, a 60-year-old, full-blood Sioux, first language Lakota speaker, stated in class one day that: "The Indian is so messed up today because there is so little nature to get in touch with anymore." After he spoke these words, he thought for a while and then said, "I take those words back. I've been thinking about it and I see now that what is wrong with Indians, especially the younger ones today, is that they are messed up because nature is messed up and the Indian reflects nature exactly."

According to the view of this traditional Indian, the Indian is an accurate ecological barometer. The Indian lived in perfect ecological balance with nature in the old days. Now nature has been polluted and exploited and the Indian reflects this in his own life proportionately. Paraphrasing Confucious, one could say: "Would you know how an area is faring ecologically speaking, look then at the Indian population, for they reflect the ecological balance or lack of it in an exact manner."

Social reality This next order of reality is what Radin describes as the "reality *with* which he [primitive man] is born" (writer's emphasis) which, of course, is the phenomenal world. These two orders of reality are objectively given. As Radin says, the order of social reality no more emanates from an individual than does the phenomenal world.[14] Radin notwithstanding, ancient man did not know an inanimate world which he attempted to animate by anthropomorphic projections; he simply did not know and does not know today an inanimate world. His relationship with the world is not an I–It relationship but rather an I–Thou one. His immediate world, however, was the social reality into which he was born and this reality affected him even more urgently than the objective world outside the hoop of life. True, the forest and plains beyond the circle of tipis were alive. The animals and birds all spoke the Lakota language and each animal from the cricket to the buffalo had its own power and had its own lesson to teach the people, yet the human life of the camp was the milieu in which he ate, drank, danced, sang, loved and sorrowed. It was from this world of social reality that projections were made onto the world of phenomena.

Subjective thought and individual reality In addition to the two abovementioned orders of reality, known to both Indian and white peoples, exists the realm of subjective thought and reality. White people know this order of reality. Indeed, Descartes made it the cornerstone of all knowledge whatever. However, these two peoples, Native American and white, understand this order of reality in vastly different ways. The Cartesian "cogito:" "I think, therefore I am" was arrived at via methodical doubt and, once arrived at, was "proven" by logical inference, namely, that thought presupposes a thinker both logically and actually; since "I think, I must exist to do the thinking."

The Indian cogito expressed earlier is, "I think, therefore I am, and therefore that which I think, is," and this cogito, in turn, rests on two prior metaphysical assumptions mentioned earlier – namely, "That creation *ex-nihilo* is impossible; being cannot stem from non-being," or stated more positively, "being (real being) can only produce being (real being)." Therefore, if to say "I am" is to be genuinely real, then what I produce when I say "I think" is also genuinely real.

The other assumption is pragmatic. The famous statement of Jamesian pragmatism: "If it works, it is true," or rather "what works is true," would be recast in Indian thought in a more passive manner. The Indian maxim would be: "What happens is true (real)." And since thought obviously occurs or "happens" then it is true and is therefore real.

At this point the significance or rather the use of thought in both societies needs a word of explanation. In European society in general and in Anglo-American society in particular, with the possible exception of philosophers and artists, thought is primarily envisioned as instrumental and pragmatic. Thought, real thought, is regarded primarily as a problem solving apparatus or process and does not include other kinds of mental activity, such as daydreaming, wool-gathering, fantasizing, hoping, wishing, etc. Man uses thought in the larger society to move from point A to point B. In other words, thought is the rational tool man uses to accomplish certain ends. For example, if a man wants a certain type of job, he then sets about thinking and planning (a type of thinking) the steps necessary to take in order to secure the job he has in mind. Once the goal is attained, thought about it ends and the man goes on to the next problem. Indians use thought in the same and yet a different way. In pursuit of purely practical aims, the Native American uses thought in much the same way a white man does. For example, in traditional times, he then envisioned the hunt and then set about taking all the steps necessary to reach this goal. The only difference between the Indian hunter and the white hunter might be participation in religious ceremonies needed to insure success in the chase.

Where white thought and Indian thought basically differ is that in Indian life, thought is "proof." That is, thought is considered as validating or "proving" subjective reality, and is a felt or intuited proof, as is the Cartesian cogito. Now it is true that intuited proof and logical proof may ultimately merge. Logic must in some sense be "felt" or intuited and what is intuited might ultimately prove to be in some sense "logical." If not, it is a moot point that if what is intuited is not also in some vastly stretched sense of the word "logical," that it could be taken into the ken of consciousness at all.

Now to say, as Radin says, "It gives validity to one special kind of reality, the reality of their subjective life,"[15] is only to agree with the Cartesian cogito. It too establishes the validity of the subjective reality of the individual. What is interesting and different is the manner in which this is accomplished. Descartes was not so much interested in the content of thought as in the fact that it arose at all. Moreover, Descartes knew that thought was subjective in the sense that it arose from within the individual. Therefore, put a slightly different way, the cogito becomes: This thought arises; thought is subjective inasmuch as it must arise in an individual. This thought is arising in me, therefore I exist as an individual. It is all an interior process. Suppose, however, that Descartes had assumed that thought did not arise from within an individual but was imposed from without. This was his argument in proving the existence of God, but all other thought was generated internally. The traditional Indian assumption is exactly that – that thoughts were imposed from without. Dreams, visions, thoughts were all messages from the Wakántanka and were delivered in dreams, visions or reverie by the spirits. The Indian proof then is no less logical than Descartes and it can be stated thus: A message from the Wakántanka must be sent to *someone* and delivered *to* someone *by* someone. An animal messenger delivered this message to me; since a delivery presupposes a receiver, and I have received delivery of the message, I must exist. The Indian cogito could then be worded: "I have received the message; since reception presupposes a receiver and I have received; therefore I am."

No Indian would actually say anything like this because his philosophy or *Weltansschauung* is largely subconscious and unspoken. This is admittedly an artificial construction assembled from Indian metaphysical notions and expressed in propositional form for the benefit of persons accustomed to thinking in the categories of European philosophy to enable them to better appreciate the Indian view of reality unobscured by religious trapping.

Granted, this is a rather deterministic view, but then the Indian world is largely determined by the belief that man is given a nature at birth and this nature is of a certain kind and therefore his thinking will be in accord with his nature; couple this with the belief that no man or group of men can ever be stronger than nature and one has a very definite deterministic tenor of thought. White society is not wholly liberated from this idea of thoughts coming from "without," and the English language still retains certain stock phrases supporting this belief, such as "I don't know what *got into him*," or "Whatever *possessed* you to do such a thing?" or "It hit me like a bolt from the blue;" all convey the idea of some kind of mental ingress into the individual psyche. This is not to say that when an Indian says, "I'm going to the store," that he regards this as a message from the spirit world. In the Indian view, man has limited freedom to decide and to act. However, in *important* undertakings or decisions, the spirits are always invoked and answers and thoughts on the answers almost invariably come from without. This, in turn, leads into the next and highest order of reality, not unknown to the white world, but genuine cases are so rare in the larger society that anyone claiming knowledge of this order of reality is automatically suspect.

Non-dimensional soteriological reality As mentioned previously, Native American philosophy is strongly pragmatic. It must make a difference in lived experience. It must attain to a practical result. Philosophizing for the sake of philosophizing is unknown and is considered an empty exercise or game. In the Lakota view, man and message must coincide. The Lakota will not listen to a man they consider "bad" no matter how good his message is. Among the Lakota, as in the East, the tendency is to look askance at well-dressed, well-fed "holy" men living in episcopal palaces who go around preaching self-denial and renunciation. As Hassrick says:

> The Sioux accepted Christianity without serious reluctance, even though the missionaries were instrumental in the abolition of the Sun Dance. But Christian teachings could hold little inspiration for men who themselves had actively participated in self-sacrifice in a manner far more real than had the clergy. Christianity was too mild to have much meaning for the Sioux.[16]

Soteriological reality results in a dramatic and radical change in the character of the individual – a 180° turnabout in orientation. Such reality is not unknown in the non-Indian world, but merely extremely rare. For example, the case of a confirmed alcoholic reversing his life and becoming an evangelist such as Billy Sunday. An R. J. Haldeman suddenly "finding God" in a prison cell and being released as a "born again" Christian. A smile may creep over the face of the non-Indian reader, in the case of the last example. Immediately, a host of rationalizations arise such as "What else could he do?" or "It was his way of turning defeat and disgrace into victory." His sincerity is suspect, perhaps justifiably so. Non-Indian society is suspicious of the fox who suddenly begins preaching to the chickens.

In the Lakota world such changes are taken at face value and they are quite common. This writer is personally acquainted with a score of people in whom such a change occurred. In two instances, the vision causing the change was uninduced and even unwanted; in one instance, it was resisted. Usually, however, this level of reality in vision form is sought by an individual. Usually the quest takes the form of *hanbléčeya* (Crying for a

Vision). A description of this level of conscious reality is provided by Frank Fools Crow, known to this writer personally and a medicine chief of great reputation among all the Sioux as well as his own tribe, the Oglala. Frank never went to white man's school and speaks but little English. This description of his vision quest on Bear Butte was told by him to Thomas E. Mails, the writer, through an interpreter.

First he speaks of Bear Butte which has always been neutral ground for Indians, a place where many came to make their camps and sweat lodges in preparation for the vision quest. Medicine men came here from as far away as Canada.

> When my vision came I was standing up in the seeking place. First I heard thunder booming and then a rich pleasant voice said, "My friend, my friend, look up. Your friends have come to visit you."

Frank saw four riders on four running horses coming from the west. Black, red sorrel, palomino, and white. Each Indian rider was the same color as his horse, including his clothing. The riders wore breechclouts, were barefoot. While their hair flew loose as they rode, some of the hair was tied in a knot at the back of their heads, where the coup braid might have been.

> They swept over me with booming thunder and flashing lightning following behind them, going on until they disappeared in the distance.

Then the voice told me to look up again, and the same four horsemen came from the north and swept over me once more with the sound of thunder and the flashes of lightning trailing behind them like the howling that follows a jet plane through the sky. Then the same four riders came over me in the same way from the east, and after that from the south.

When they were gone, the rich voice explained that the riders represented the four winds and the four storms. So they were the powers of the four directions. The reason the riders were shown to me was to tell me that I would be as strong with my medicine as they were, and that after that their colors would be my trademark when I did my ceremonies to heal the sick. That is why I should set out the black, red, yellow and white flags whenever possible when I did a healing ceremony.[17]

Since Frank was already living the ideal of the Teton Lakota way of life, these visions merely confirmed him in that way.

In *Black Elk Speaks*, an excellent account is given of the vision a Sioux holy man, Black Elk, passed on to John Neihardt, poet laureate of Nebraska, so there is no need to record these visions here. The point, however, is that in no sense are these visions considered as having a purely psychological origin by these men. They are definitely messages from the unseen sector of reality becoming manifest to the sincere and devoted seeker. This is the highest form of knowledge and the highest level of reality known to the Teton Sioux.

Notes

1 William James, *Varieties of Religious Experience* (New Jersey: Mentor Books, 1958), p. 367.
2 Ibid.
3 Paul Radin, *Primitive Man as Philosopher* (New York: Dover Publications, 1957), p. 19.
4 Ibid.
5 Ibid., p. 5.
6 Ibid.
7 R. D. Theisz (ed.), *Buckskin Tokens* (Aberdeen, South Dakota: North Plains Press, 1975), p. 7.
8 Radin, *Primitive Man*, p. 58.
9 Ibid.
10 James Walker, *Lakota Belief and Ritual*, edited by Raymond J. De Mallie and Elaine A. Jahner, by permission of University of Nebraska Press, p.

113. Copyright © 1980 by the University of Nebraska Press.
11 Ibid., p. 118.
12 Richard Erdoes, "The Arch and the Square," in *Literature of the American Indians*, edited by Abraham Chapman (New York: Meridian Books, 1975), pp. 77–8.
13 Ibid.
14 Radin, *Primitive Man*, p. 60.
15 Ibid., p. 58.
16 Royal B. Hassrick, *The Sioux: Life and Customs of a Warrior Society* (Norman, Oklahoma: University of Oklahoma Press, 1964), p. 343.
17 Thomas E. Mails, *Fools Crow* (New York: Avon Books, 1979), pp. 154–5.

PART IV

Community and Power

Origins and contacts, steeped in conflict and co-operation, created the basis, willingly or not, for new communities. Conceptions of appropriate forms of loyalty, group rights, and entitlements, considered in the context of power – its appropriate use and possible abuse presaged on notions of personhood – substantively shape ideas about community.

This section of the book includes accounts of the beginnings of American communities and the story of the founding of the Iroquois Confederacy, and continues with a consideration of forms of American governance.

By the end of the eighteenth century new peoples, or at least new conceptions of human difference and coexistence, began to emerge in North America. Benjamin Franklin expresses a self-concept, which includes a concept of moral perfection and virtue. His "Continuation of the Account of my Life" is an argument for individualism in the context of a view of community.

The Federalist Papers, by Alexander Hamilton, James Madison, and John Jay, were published in New York newspapers in 1787 and 1788 to help make a case for the ratification of the United States Constitution. The selections here raise the issue of how a strong centralized government will respond to forms of diversity in the European American political union.

Mercy Otis Warren strongly opposed the idea of a strong federal government in terms that recall the issues at work in the founding of the Haudenosaunee Confederacy. Warren raises numerous issues associated with life in any community of persons.

20

Traditional History of the Confederacy of the Six Nations

Committee of the Chiefs

Introduction

In response to a variety of versions of the story of the founding of the Haudenosaunee Confederacy, a council of leaders at the Six Nations Reserve in Ontario, Canada, prepared a written version of the narrative in 1911, with the assistance of Duncan Scott. This version became one of the most widely known of the founding stories when Arthur C. Parker combined it with an alternative version by Seth Newhouse, an Onondaga, into what Parker called "The Constitution of the Five Nations." While both versions focus on the original union of five nations – the Seneca, Onondaga, Mohawk, Oneida, and Cayuga – the title of the Chiefs' version reflects the name of the Confederacy after the Tuscarora nation joined in 1722. Many have argued that the Haudenosaunee form of society (that is, the union of five independent nations under a confederation of limited power) served as an important model for the union of European American colonies under the Articles of Confederation and, later, the Constitution of the United States.

The traditional narrative of the formation of the Confederation of the Five Nations, commonly known as the Iroquois, together with an account of the ancient customs, usages and ceremonies in use by these Nations in the choice and installation into office of their Ro-de-ya-ner-sonh (Lords or

Taken from *Transactions of the Royal Society of Canada*, section II (1911): 198–237.

Chiefs), including traditions relating to the lives and characters of De-ka-nah-wi-deh, the framer of the League, Hah-yonh-wa-tha (Hiawatha), Tha-do-dah-ho (and other leaders.)

The beginning of the Great Peace, or the formation of the Great League of the Confederacy of the Five Nations:

The place mentioned as the birth-place of De-ka-nah-wi-deh, was called Ka-ha-nah-yenh, somewhere in the neighbourhood of the Bay of Quinte.

According to tradition a woman was living in that neighbourhood who had one daughter, who had a stainless character and who did not travel away from home but remained with her mother constantly, and when she had attained the age of womanhood she held no manner of intercourse with man, but in course of time she showed signs of conception, and her mother was very much aggrieved and in course of time the mother spoke to her daughter and said, I am going to ask you a question and I want you to tell me the truth. What has happened to you, and how is it that you are going to bear a child?

Then the daughter replied and said, Mother I will tell you the truth, I do not know how I got the child.

Then the mother said, The reply you give me is not sufficient to remove my grief, I am sure that you did not tell me the truth concerning what I asked you. Then the daughter said, I have told you the truth concerning what you asked me. Then the mother said, Of a truth you have no love for me.

Then she began to ill-treat her daughter, and the daughter also began to feel grieved because of the ill-treatment she got from her mother, and it so happened that as the time approached when the daughter would deliver the child, the mother dreamed that she saw a man whom she did not know, and he said that he appeared as a Messenger to her on account of her troubled mind, caused by the condition of her daughter, who had in so mysterious a manner conceived a child. I am here to deliver to you a message and now I will ask you to cease your grieving and trouble of mind, and ill-treatment of your daughter from day to day as it is a fact that your daughter does not know how she got that child which she is going to deliver. I will tell you what has happened.

It is the wish of the Great Spirit that she should bear a child and when you will see the male child you shall call him De-ka-nah-wi-deh.

The reason you shall give him that name is because this child will reveal the good tidings of Peace and Power from Heaven, and shall rule and govern on earth, and I will further inform you that you and your daughter should be kind to him because he has an important office to perform in the world, and when he grows up to be a man do not prevent him from leaving home. And then the old woman asked the Messenger, What office is the child going to hold? The Messenger answered and said, His office is for peace and life to the people both on earth and in Heaven. And when the old woman woke up the next morning she then spoke to her daughter and said, My daughter I ask you to pardon me for all the ill-treatment I have given you, because I have now been satisfied that you told me the truth, when you told me that you did not know how you got the child which you are going to deliver. Then the daughter also was made glad, and when she was delivered of the child it was as had been predicted, the child was a male child, and the grandmother called him De-ka-nah-wi-deh, and the child grew up rapidly, and when he was become a young man he said, The time has come when I should begin to perform my duty in this world. I will therefore begin to build my canoe, and by to-morrow I must have it done because there is something for me to do to-morrow, when I will go away and go Eastward.

Then he began to build his canoe out of a white rock, and when he had completed it De-ka-nah-wi-deh said, I am ready now to go away from home and I will tell you that there is a tree on top of the hill and you shall have that for a sign whenever you want to find out whether I shall be living or dead. You will take an axe and chop the tree and if the

tree flows blood from the cut, you will thereby know that I am beheaded and killed, but if you find no blood running from this tree after you have chopped a chip from it, then you may know that my mission was successful.

The reason that this will happen is because I came to stop the shedding of blood among human beings.

Then De-ka-nah-wi-deh said, You come to the edge of the lake and see me start off.

Then his mother and grandmother went together with him and helped to pull the boat to the lake and when they came to the lake, then De-ka-nah-wi-deh said, Good bye for I am going to leave you for I am gone for good, when I come back I will not come this way. Then the grandmother said, How are you going to travel, because your canoe is made out of stone. It will not float.

Then De-ka-nah-wi-deh said, This will be the first sign of wonder that man will behold. That canoe made out of stone or rock will float.

Then he bade them good bye and put his canoe in the lake and got in. Then he paddled away and went Eastward, and the grandmother and his mother beheld him and saw that his canoe was going swiftly, and in a few moments he disappeared out of their sight. And it happened at that time that a party of hunters had a camp on the South side of the lake now known as Ontario and one of them went towards the lake and stood on the bank of the said lake, and beheld some object coming towards him at a distance, and the man could not understand what it was that was approaching him. Shortly afterwards he understood that it was a canoe, and saw a man in it, and the moving object was coming directly towards where he stood, and when the man (it was De-ka-nah-wi-deh) reached the shore he came out of his boat and climbed up the bank. Then De-ka-nah-wi-deh asked the man what had caused them to be where they were, and the man answered and said, We are here for a double object.

First, We are here hunting the game for our living.

Second, Because there is a great strife in our settlement.

Then De-ka-nah-wi-deh said, You will now go back to where you came from. The reason that this will occur is, because the good tidings of Peace and Friendship has come to the people, and you will find that all strife is removed from your settlement when you go back to your home. And I want you to tell your Chief and say that the Ka-rih-wi-yoh (good tidings of Peace and Power) has come and if he asks you where the good tidings of Peace and Power came from, you will say, that the good tidings of Peace and Power will come here in a few days. Then the man said, Who are you who is now speaking to me?

Then De-ka-nah-wi-deh said, It is I who came from the West and am going Eastward and I am called De-ka-nah-wi-deh in the world. Then the man wondered and beheld his canoe and saw that his canoe was made out of white stone.

Then De-ka-nah-wi-deh said, I will go and visit Tyo-den-he-deh first. Then De-ka-nah-wi-deh went down the bank and got into his boat, and passed on. Then the man also turned away, and when he came back to the camp he said, I saw a strange man coming from the lake with a canoe, his canoe is made out of white stone, and when he landed he came up the bank and I had a conversation with him. First, he asked me where I came from and when I had told him and he had understood every thing, he said, You will all go home, where you came from, there is now peace and all strife has been removed from the settlement.

Then the party went home and as soon as they reached home, they went and told the Ro-ya-ner (Lord) and said that the good tidings of Peace and Power had come. Then the Lord asked who told him the message and he said that he saw a man who was called De-ka-nah-wi-deh in the world. Then the Lord asked again where the good tidings of Peace and Power was coming from.

Then the man said again, It is coming and will come here soon.

Then the Lord said, Where did you see the man? And he said, I saw him in the lake with his canoe. He came from the West and he is going Eastward. Then the Lord began to wonder and said, he thought that the settlement should remain in silence for all will be glad and satisfied.

Then De-ka-nah-wi-deh had gone on his journey and had come to his destination where the great wizard Tha-do-dah-ho lived. This man was possessed with great power as a wizard and no man could come to him without endangering his life and even the fowls of the air whenever they flew directly over his place of abode would die and fall down on his premises, and if he saw a man approaching him he was sure to destroy him or kill him. This man was a cannibal, and had left the settlement he belonged to for a long time, and lived by himself in an isolated place. De-ka-nah-wi-deh came and approached the abode of the cannibal and saw him coming home and he was carrying a human body. He went into his house and shortly he came out again and went down to the river and drew some water. Then De-ka-nah-wi-deh went closer and when he had come to the house he went up onto the roof of the house, and from the chimney he looked in and saw the owner of the house come back with a pail of water, and put up a kettle on the fire place to cook his meal, and after it was done or cooked he took the kettle from the fire and placed it by the end of the fireplace or hearth, and said to himself, I suppose it is time for me to have my meal, and after I am through, then I will go where I am required on business.

Then De-ka-nah-wi-deh moved still closer and looked straight into the kettle. The man Tha-do-dah-ho was then moving around the house, and when he came back to take some of the meat from the kettle he looked into it and saw that a man was looking at him out of the kettle, this was the reflection of De-ka-nah-wi-deh. Then the man Tha-do-dah-ho moved back and sat down near the corner of the house and began to think seriously and he thought that it was a most wonderful thing which had happened. He said, Such a thing has never occurred before as long as I have been living in this house; I did not know that I am a great man, therefore my mode of living must be wrong. Then he said, Let me look again and be sure that what I have seen is true. Then he got up again and went to the kettle and looked into it again, and he saw the same object, that is, the face of a great man and it was looking at him. Then he took the kettle and went out and went towards the hillside and he emptied it there.

Then De-ka-nah-wi-deh came down from the roof and made great haste towards the hillside, and when Tha-do-dah-ho came up the hill he met De-ka-nah-wi-deh.

Then De-ka-nah-wi-deh asked Tha-do-dah-ho where he came from and he said, I had cooked my meal and when I took the kettle from the fire and placed it on the floor and when I thought that I would take some of the meat out of the kettle, I saw the reflection of a man's face in the kettle looking at me. I do not know what has happened. I know such a thing never occurred to me before as long as I have been living in this house, and now I have come to the conclusion that I must be wrong in the way I am and have been living, and that is why I carried the kettle out of my house and emptied it over there by the stump, and from whence I was returning when I met you. Then he said, Where did you come from?

Then De-ka-nah-wi-deh said, I came from the West and am going Eastward and then the man said, Who are you that is thus speaking to me? Then De-ka-nah-wi-deh said, It is I who is called De-ka-nah-wi-deh in this world, and then De-ka-nah-wi-deh said, Where have you come from? The man then said, There is a settlement to which I belong but I left that settlement a long time ago.

Then De-ka-nah-wi-deh said, You will now go back, for Peace and Friendship have now come to you and your settlement, and also you have now repented of the course of wrong doing which you used to pursue in times past. It shall now also occur that when you return to your settlement that you shall promote Peace and Friendship for it is a fact that Peace is now ruling in your settlement and I want you to arrange and settle all matters. I shall arrive there early tomorrow morning. I shall visit the West, first I shall visit there the house of the woman, Ji-kon-sah-seh. The reason why I shall do this (go and visit this woman first) is because the path passes there which runs from the East to the West. Then after saying these words De-ka-nah-wi-deh went on his way and arrived at the house of Ji-kon-sah-seh and said to her, that he had come on this path which passed her home and which led from the East to the West, and on which travelled the men of blood-thirsty and destructive nature.

Then he said unto her, It is your custom to feed these men when they are travelling on this path on their war expeditions.

He then told her that she must desist from practising this custom. He then told her that the reason she was to stop this custom was that the Ki-rih-wi-yoh or good tidings of Peace had come. He then said, I shall therefore now change your disposition and practice. I now charge you that you shall be the custodian of the good tidings of Peace and Power, so that the human race may live in Peace in the future.

Then De-ka-nah-wi-deh said, You shall therefore now go East where I shall meet you at the place of danger, where all matters shall be finally settled, and you must not fail to be there on the third day.

Then De-ka-nah-wi-deh said, I shall now pass on in my journey. Then he passed on and went to another settlement (or Village) and when he arrived at the settlement, he enquired who was their Ro-ya-ner (Lord or ruler or head Chief) and after

he ascertained his abode he went to his home and found him and when they met, De-ka-nah-wi-deh said, Have you heard that the good tidings of Peace and Power is coming? The Lord or head Chief then said, I have heard of it.

Then he (De-ka-nah-wi-deh) asked him what he thought about it. Then the Lord said, Since I have heard of the good news I have been thinking about it and I have not slept. Then De-ka-nah-wi-deh said, It is now at hand, that which has been the cause of your sleeplessness.

Then De-ka-nah-wi-deh said, You shall hereafter be called Hah-yonh-wa-tha (Hiawatha). Then the Lord said, To whom am I speaking? And then De-ka-nah-wi-deh answered and said, I am the man who is called on earth by the name of De-ka-nah-wi-deh, and I have come from the West and am going East for the purpose of propagating Peace, so that the shedding of human blood may cease among you.

Then the Lord (Hah-yonh-wa-tha) said, Will you wait until I go and announce the news to my colleagues. De-ka-nah-wi-deh then said that he could wait as he was on this good mission. Then the Lord, Hah-yonh-wa-tha, announced to his colleagues and people that they assemble to hear De-ka-nah-wi-deh, and when they were assembled Hah-yonh-wa-tha then said to De-ka-nah-wi-deh, Now what news have you got for the people? Then De-ka-nah-wi-deh said that the good tidings of Peace and Power had arrived and that he had come on the mission to proclaim the good news of Peace and Power, and that bloodshed might cease in the land, as the Great Spirit never intended that such should be practised by human beings.

Then the Lord Hah-yonh-wa-tha said, We have now heard the good news of Peace and Power from this man (De-ka-nah-wi-deh). He then asked his colleagues and people what answer they should give. Then one of the Chief Warriors said, What shall we do with regard to the powerful tribes on the East and West of our Village who are always hostile to us?

Then De-ka-nah-wi-deh answered and said that the hostile nations referred to had already accepted the good news of Peace and Power.

Then the Chief Warrior answered and said, I am still in doubt and would propose that this man (De-ka-nah-wi-deh) climb up a big tree by the edge of a high cliff and that then we cut the tree down and let it fall over the cliff, and then if he does not die, I shall believe the message which he has brought us. Then the Deputy Chief Warrior said, I am of the same opinion, and I approve of the suggestion of the Chief Warrior.

Then De-ka-nah-wi-deh said, I am ready and willingly accede to your request, because the good news of Peace and Power has come unto us, I now therefore place myself in your hands.

Then the Lord, Hah-yonh-wa-tha, said, It is now decided, we will now therefore all go to where the tree stands. They then started to go there and when they arrived where the tree stood, then the Lord (Hah-yonh-wa-tha) said, We have now arrived where the tree stands that we have decided upon. Then the Chief Warrior said to De-ka-nah-wi-deh, I made this proposal and you will now climb this tree so that it will be a proof, and so that the people may see your power. If you live to see tomorrow's sunrise, then I will accept your message.

Then De-ka-nah-wi-deh said, This shall be done. And he then climbed the tree and when he had reached the top of the tree he sat down on the branch, after which the tree was cut down and it fell over the cliff with him. Then the people kept vigilant watch so that they might see him, but they failed to see any signs of him. Then the Chief Warrior said that now his proposition had been carried out and that De-ka-nah-wi-deh had disappeared and now they would vigilantly watch at sunrise tomorrow morning. Then the Lord (Hah-yonh-wa-tha) said, We shall now return home. And when day dawned one of the Warriors arose before sunrise, and at once went to the place where the tree had been cut and when he arrived there he saw at a short distance a field of corn, and near it a smoke from a fire towards which the Warrior went, and when he arrived there he saw a man sitting by the fire, and after seeing the man he at once returned to the Lord (Hah-yonh-wa-tha) and when he had arrived there he said that he had seen the man sitting by the fire, and that it was the man who was on the tree which they had cut last evening.

Then Hah-yonh-wa-tha charged him to convey these tidings to his colleagues and all the people, and to summon them all to come to him. Then the Warrior went at once and informed his colleagues and all the people and in a short time all the people had assembled. Then the Lord (Hah-yonh-wa-tha) said they would now call De-ka-nah-wi-deh, and he then commissioned the Chief Warrior and the Deputy Chief Warrior to go after him, and they then went to where De-ka-nah-wi-deh had his fire

and when they arrived they told him that the Lord (Hah-yonh-wa-tha) had sent them to bring him and they would escort him to the home of Hah-yonh-wa-tha.

Then De-ka-nah-wi-deh said, It is all right, I shall go with you. They then returned and when they arrived at the abode of Hah-yonh-wa-tha the Chief Warrior spoke and said, We have returned with De-ka-nah-wi-deh and he is now in your charge and the Lord (Hah-yonh-wa-tha) then said, I am now ready to accept the good news of Peace and Power, and it now rests with you as to your opinion in this matter.

The Chief Warrior then said, I was in great doubt, but have now concluded to accept the good news of Peace and Power. Then Ro-ya-ner Hah-yonh-wa-tha said, Now see these matters are settled and finished.

Then he said, You De-ka-nah-wi-deh can now listen to the answer we have concluded to give to you. In the first place then, we have adopted the message which you brought us, and we have jointly concluded to accept the message of the good news of Peace and Power and we have now concluded all we have to say, and the matter shall now rest with you.

De-ka-nah-wi-deh then said, This day is early and young, and so is the new mind also tender and young, so also is the good tidings of Peace and Power and as the new sun of good tidings of Peace and Power arose it will proceed on its course and prosper, so also the young mind and the good tidings of Peace and Power shall also prevail and prosper. Therefore now in the future your grandchildren shall live in peace.

Then De-ka-nah-wi-deh said, You, the Chief Warrior, you have the power in warfare, but now this is all changed, and I now proclaim that since you had your doubts, you shall be now and hereafter known in the land by the name of Tha-ha-rih-ho-ken (De-ka-ri-ho-ken) which means doubting or hesitating over two things which course to adopt.

Then De-ka-nah-wi-deh said, You, the Deputy Chief Warrior, I charge you that you shall be called and known in the land by the name of Sa-de-ka-rih-wa-deh (one who respects all matters as important equally) because you have concurred in and confirmed all that you have heard.

Then De-ka-nah-wi-deh said, I have now concluded and finished and I now leave this matter in your charge and care, and you can now proceed and proclaim the good tidings of Peace and Power.

De-ka-nah-wi-deh then said, I shall now pass on and go East, and we shall meet again tomorrow to add to what we have already accomplished.

Then De-ka-nah-wi-deh passed on in his journey.

Then in the Lord (Ro-ya-ner) Hah-yonh-wa-tha's family, composed of three daughters, was the eldest taken ill and in a little time she died. Then the mind of Hah-yonh-wa-tha was troubled, then his colleagues and the people assembled at his home and condoled with him and admonished him to forget his sorrow, and he acceded to their desire.

Shortly afterwards the second daughter took sick and in a short time died. Then the sorrow and trouble of the Lord Hah-yonh-wa-tha was greatly increased, then again his colleagues and people assembled at his abode and they again tried to induce him to forget his sorrow and trouble, but he could not answer them. Then De-ka-ri-ho-ken said, I will now tell you my mind. I think that we should look for something which would console the mind of our Lord in his trouble and bereavement. Then he said, I would lay before you Warriors, for your consideration first, that you cheer him by playing a game of Lacrosse.

Then Sa-de-ka-rih-wa-deh said, I will now tell you my mind, first that the people all assemble, this shall be done as our Lord has now only one daughter left alive.

Then De-ka-ri-ho-ken confirmed all that Sa-de-ka-rih-wa-deh had said.

Then all the people assembled at the home of the Lord (Ro-ya-ner) Hah-yonh-wa-tha and they then spoke unto him words of condolence so that he might forget his grief and bereavement.

The Lord did not answer them. Then the Warriors decided that they would play a game of Lacrosse in order to cheer him up, and during the time that they were playing, the daughter of Hah-yonh-wa-tha came out of the family abode and went after some water and after she had gone half way to the spring she saw flying high up in the air above a beautiful bird, she stopped in her journey and the bird flew downwards towards her, she then cried out aloud and said, See this bird, after which she ran away.

Then the Warriors saw it, and as it was then flying low, the Warriors followed it, and as they were looking at the bird they did not notice the daughter of Hah-yonh-wa-tha before them and in their haste they ran over and trampled her to

death, and it transpired that the daughter of Hah-yonh-wa-tha was with child.

Then Sa-de-ka-rih-wa-deh went and told Hah-yonh-wa-tha that a strange bird called Teh-yoh-ronh-yoh-ron (a high-flying bird which pierces the skies) had come amongst them and that it was due to the visit of this bird that his daughter was killed.

Then Hah-yonh-wa-tha answered and said, I have now lost all my daughters and in the death of this last daughter you have accidentally and unwittingly killed two.

Then Hah-yonh-wa-tha further said, I shall now go away to the East, and he started on his way. He met De-ka-nah-wi-deh, and he (De-ka-nah-wi-deh) warned him of the danger on his way, with reference to a man who was watching as follows: There is danger in front of you, there is a man watching on your way in front of you, and it is necessary for you to go up near to him without him becoming aware of your approach until you get to him. If you can get up to him while he is unaware of your approach, then we shall prosper in our mission. You will then speak to him and ask him what he is watching for. He will answer you and say that he is watching to protect the fields of corn as the people of other Nations, and also animals take the crops and he is watching so that the crops would be protected, so that their children might live on this crop.

Then he (Hah-yonh-wa-tha) went on his journey and when he arrived where the man was sitting beside a fire near a big tree and watching the fields of corn, he asked him what he was watching, and the man answered and said, I am watching the fields of corn to protect them from other nations and from animals so that our children may live on the crop. Hah-yonh-wa-tha then said to the man, You go and tell your Lord that the good news of Peace and Power has come, and he returned and told his Lord the message given to him by Hah-yonh-wa-tha. Then the Lord said, Who told you this news? Then the man who had been watching said, A man came to me when I was watching the fields of corn and he told me the news.

Then Hah-yonh-wa-tha went to the other end of the corn field and met De-ka-nah-wi-deh. Then De-ka-nah-wi-deh said, We have now completed the (Ki-rih-wi-yoh) good tidings of Peace and Power, you shall therefore now stay in this shanty near these corn fields, which you will leave when you receive an invitation from the people. You must not go unless the invitation is official. A woman shall first come to you early tomorrow morning, who will be the first to see you, then you shall cut and prepare some elder berry twigs as follows: You shall cut them into pieces and remove the heart pulp and then you shall string them up.

Then the Lord (Ro-ya-ner) shall send a messenger to you to invite you. You must not accept the invitation until he shall send to you a string of twigs similar to your own.

Then Hah-yonh-wa-tha went on his journey and arrived at the shanty beside the cornfield and built a fire and in the morning a woman came to the cornfield and saw the smoke from the fire at the end of the cornfield, and when she arrived there she saw a man sitting there with his head hanging down.

Then the woman hurried home and went straightway to where the Lord (Ro-ya-ner) lived and when she arrived she told him that she had seen a man sitting beside a fire in the cornfield whom she had never seen before.

Then the Lord asked her, What was this man doing there?

Then the woman answered and said that the man was sitting there quietly looking on the ground.

Then the Lord said, This must be the man who sent the message that the good tidings of Peace and Power had come, I shall therefore now send a messenger to bring him here.

He then summoned the Chief Warrior and the Deputy Chief Warrior to come to him and when the two had come, the Lord said to them, You shall go after the man who is by the fire beside the cornfield and bring him to me. The Lord then said to the Deputy Chief Warrior, I send you to go after him, and then the Deputy Chief Warrior went to bring this man, and when he arrived at the place where the man had built the fire, he saw a man sitting there and he was looking at a string of elder berry twigs which was hanging on a pole horizontally placed in front of him.

Then the Deputy Chief Warrior said, I am sent after you by the Lord (Ro-ya-ner).

The man did not answer, and then the Deputy Chief Warrior repeated the message of the Lord, three times, but the man did not give any reply. Then the Deputy Chief Warrior returned to the Lord, and when he arrived back he said to the Lord, He did not reply.

The Lord then asked him, What did you see? Then the Deputy Chief Warrior answered and said, I saw a string of elder berry twigs hanging on a pole in front of him and he was looking at it.

Then the Lord answered and said, I now understand, I shall therefore make a similar string of quills, which will cause him to come. The Lord then made two strings of quills and put them on a string.

The Lord then said, I have now completed the strings and you shall both go after him and bring him here. You shall therefore take these strings of quills with you to him, and they shall become words and that will induce him to come. They then went on their journey and when they had arrived at the fire where the man was the Chief Warrior said, The Lord has sent us after you, and this string of quills are his words which are to bring you to him.

Then Hah-yonh-wa-tha answered and said, This is what should be done. He then took the string of quills and said, After I get through smoking I shall go to the Lord. They then returned to the Lord and when they had arrived they said to him, that the man had now answered and that when he had finished smoking his pipe he would come to him.

The Lord then told them to tell the people so that they would all assemble when the man would arrive.

The Chief Warrior and the Deputy Chief Warrior then went to tell the people to assemble as soon as possible at the abode of the Lord.

The people had therefore all assembled when Hah-yonh-wa-tha arrived. Then the Lord said to him, You have come amongst us and doubtless you have some important matter to convey to us. The people have already assembled and are prepared to listen to the matter which you may have to communicate to us.

Then Hah-yonh-wa-tha said, I have come here to deliver to you the message of good tidings of Peace and Power, so that our children in the future may live in peace.

Then the Lord said, We shall defer answering you until the return of a certain man whom we are waiting for, but in the meantime we desire that you shall remain in our village with us.

Then Hah-yonh-wa-tha answered and said, This can be done as I came to you on the message of good tidings of Peace and Power. Then the Lord said, I will therefore entertain you myself. This will be done because the man we are expecting will come here first, you will therefore meet him first. This will be done because the message which you have brought to us may be the same as the other man's tidings for which we are waiting, and he has sent word that he is coming. Then Hah-yonh-wa-tha said, I will approve of all this.

The people then dispersed, and when night came the Lord told Hah-yonh-wa-tha that he could sleep in the other room, then he (Hah-yonh-wa-tha) went in and retired. Shortly after he had retired he heard a voice outside which said, Are you stopping here? and Hah-yonh-wa-tha said, Yes. Then the voice from the outside said that it was now urgent for him to come out.

Then Hah-yonh-wa-tha went out and saw De-ka-nah-wi-deh standing outside. De-ka-nah-wi-deh then said, It is now urgent that we proceed on our journey. You have now accomplished all that it is necessary to be done here at present, we can go to another settlement now and return, and the man you are now waiting for will likely have returned by that time.

There is one settlement left to be visited, although I have been there before and had conversation with the man. I have promised him that I will visit him again, and for that reason when you left home you heard a loud-toned voice in front of you saying, A-soh-kek-ne—eh.

Then De-ka-nah-wi-deh said, We will now proceed on our journey. They then went and while they were on their way, De-ka-nah-wi-deh said, Let us stop here and wait a while, and you will look towards the South East. And they then stood still, then Hah-yonh-wa-tha looked towards the South East and saw the smoke arising and reaching to the sky.

Then De-ka-nah-wi-deh said, What do you see? and Hah-yonh-wa-tha said, I see smoke piercing the sky.

Then De-ka-nah-wi-deh said, That smoke which you saw is where the abode of Dyon-you-ko is. The reason you see the smoke piercing the sky is because the good tidings of Peace and Power has come to the people of that settlement but unfortunately owing to the selfishness and lack of energy of these people the good tidings of Peace and Power has not prospered and has not extended to other settlements. It is thus good that these people have received the good tidings of Peace and Power. We shall therefore take power from them which will enable us to complete the work we have undertaken to accomplish.

They then heard the loud-toned voice saying, A-soh-kek-ne—eh (It is not yet; which means impatiently waiting). Then De-ka-nah-wi-deh said, It is now very urgent for us to proceed on

our journey to where this voice comes from. They then went and they had not gone very far when they came to a lake. Then De-ka-nah-wi-deh said, It is now left with you what we shall do, you have seen the lake and it is beside this lake where the man lives whose loud voice you have heard saying, A-soh-kek-ne—eh.

De-ka-nah-wi-deh then said, There are two ways which we can pursue to get across the lake, and you can have your choice, we can take the boat which you see lying flat on the ground and paddle over or we can pass above the lake, and so get over it. De-ka-nah-wi-deh then said, That man whom you heard calling out in a loud voice is able to cause the boat to upset if he sees it, and the people to be drowned, he has ended the lives of many people in this way in the lake.

Then Hah-yonh-wa-tha said, My choice is that we pass over above the lake. Then De-ka-nah-wi-deh said, It is best to approach this man from behind; the reason we should do this is that he has been so long impatiently waiting that it would not be wise to approach him from the front and it might cause trouble. Then De-ka-nah-wi-deh said, We shall therefore now proceed on our journey. They then went on their journey and arrived at the other side of the lake. They had not gone far when Hah-yonh-wa-tha saw the man sitting on a high knoll, where it was his custom to sit. When they arrived where he was sitting De-ka-nah-wi-deh stood on the right side and Hah-yonh-wa-tha on the left. The man had not yet seen them when he called again A-soh-kek-ne—eh.

Then Hah-yonh-wa-tha saw what this man was doing and as soon as the man called out in the loud voice the lake became very rough and troubled and great billows formed on its surface. Then De-ka-nah-wi-deh spoke and said, I have now returned and according to my promise, I promised to bring some one with me, and I have now fulfilled this promise. Then the man who was sitting down turned around and saw De-ka-nah-wi-deh and said, Who is the man that has come with you? De-ka-nah-wi-deh then said, Look to your left and you will see. Then he looked to his left and saw the man standing there, then he said to the man, What are you doing here? Then Hah-yonh-wa-tha answered and said, I am standing here beside you, because all our minds are with you, and are turned toward you, for the good tidings of Peace and Power has now arrived. You will therefore now see as you turn around in every direction the smoke arising. Then the man raised his head and looked around. Then he asked, Who will do this, that the good tidings of Peace and Power will be propagated? Then De-ka-nah-wi-deh answered and said, This is now complete.

Then De-ka-nah-wi-deh said, Tomorrow (right in the daytime) the delegates will come and approach you, then all things will be completed. Then the man said, I shall wait until they shall have all arrived (that is the full quorum of delegates). Then De-ka-nah-wi-deh said, We must now return, but we must all meet again tomorrow. Then De-ka-nah-wi-deh and Hah-yonh-wa-tha went away and returned again to the abode of the Lord where he, Hah-yonh-wa-tha, had been lodging when De-ka-nah-wi-deh called him out, and when they had arrived there the Lord found out that Hah-yonh-wa-tha had returned. Then the Lord called him in and told him that the man they had been waiting for had returned and said, We are now ready to answer your message. Then Hah-yonh-wa-tha said, I am now ready, and I am accompanied by my colleague or co-worker. Then the Lord answered and said, You will now bring him in. Then Hah-yonh-wa-tha called De-ka-nah-wi-deh and he came in. Then the Lord said, The man whom we have been waiting for has now returned and he has delivered his message fully and according to our understanding, it is the same as your message, we now understand, and we now therefore have decided to accept your message. Then De-ka-nah-wi-deh said, We shall now conclude the object of this message. He then asked the question: To whom did this message of the good tidings of Peace and Power first come? The Lord answered and said, It is to the man who was guarding the cornfield. Then De-ka-nah-wi-deh said, Where is that man? You shall now therefore bring him here. Then the Lord called him in and when he had come, then the Lord said, This is the man who guarded the fields of corn so that our children might live on the crops. Then De-ka-nah-wi-deh said, I will now ask you, if you are the man who guards the cornfields and what is your power when you are so guarding the cornfields. Then the man answered and said, I rely on my bow and arrows and when I go to the cornfields I take all my arrows with me.

Then De-ka-nah-wi-deh asked the question, How or in what manner do you carry your power (meaning bow and arrows). The man then answered and said, I place them in a quiver and place it on my back. Then De-ka-nah-wi-deh said, You shall now therefore be called Oh-dah-tshe-deh (meaning the quiver bearer) as your duty as a guardian of the cornfields is now changed because the good news of Peace and Power has now come. Your duty hereafter shall now be to see that your children shall live in peace. Then De-ka-nah-wi-deh again asked the Lord and said, In the past during the long time that this man has been guarding the cornfields what did you used to do with reference to that part of the crops which was damaged?

Then the Lord answered and said, I used to send the warrior to gather the damaged crops and they brought them to me, and I would divide the corn in equal shares amongst the people.

Then De-ka-nah-wi-deh said, You shall now therefore be called Ka-non-kwe-yon-dah. It shall therefore now be your duty to propagate the good tidings of Peace and Power so that your children may live in peace.

Then De-ka-nah-wi-deh said, Where is the man whom you have been waiting for to return? The Lord then called this man and when he had arrived, De-ka-nah-wi-deh said, Are you the man for whom this people have been waiting so long to return? And the man answered, I am the man. Then De-ka-nah-wi-deh said, What was the cause of your long delay in coming? And the man answered and said, I was waiting for that other man who passed there, and who promised to return but who did not return there and while I was vigilantly watching and waiting for him, I could not see him and he failed to return as promised, and when I was on the point of returning I tore down my shanty which I had built, then I looked back to my home for the path by which I had come was plainly open before me and on each side of the path was the forest. I then left and arrived home here, when I found that the people had all heard of the good news of the message which I have brought for them, so I simply confirm what they have already heard (from Hah-yonh-wa-tha).

Then De-ka-nah-wi-deh said, Everything is now completed, and as you have torn down your shanty your duty is now all changed, and as you looked back, you saw plainly the path through the forest. You shall therefore be known in the land by the name of De-you-hah-kwe-deh. Your duty shall therefore be to propagate the good tidings of Peace and Power so that your children may live in peace in future. Then De-ka-nah-wi-deh said, I will now tell you that the people whose settlements I have passed have all accepted the good tidings of Peace and Power.

Hah-yonh-wa-tha shall therefore now go after his colleagues. Then De-ka-nah-wi-deh said, I shall now visit another place or settlement at the big mountain and see what is going on there.

I have already been there, but I have not yet received an answer or reply, and what I think now is that we shall all join together in this work, for it is now urgent that it should be done, for our time is limited and we only have until to-morrow (to complete the whole thing). Then he (De-ka-nah-wi-deh) said, It would be best to appoint two delegates to go and find the smoke. Then Hah-yonh-wa-tha said, Where shall we meet again?

Then De-ka-nah-wi-deh answered and said, We shall meet again by the lake shore where my boat is. Then Oh-dah-tshe-deh spoke and said, I shall lie across the pathway like a log and when you come to me you will come in contact with the said log and I shall then go with you; meaning that he Oh-dah-tshe-deh would be lying in wait for them and when they would come to the log (which means his settlement) he would accompany them. Then Oh-dah-tshe-deh further said that he would agree to appoint two delegates to go and look for smoke (smoke means settlements).

Then Oh-dah-tshe-deh said, It is now left with you Warriors as to which of you may volunteer to go. Then the Chief Warrior said, I shall be one of those who volunteer to go. Then Oh-dah-tshe-deh said, There is one more required to go, who will therefore volunteer? For a long time no one gave answer. Then Oh-dah-tshe-deh asked the question again, and still again no one answered. Then Oh-dah-tshe-deh said, I shall ask the question once again for the last time, and if any one desires to volunteer, let him speak at once; and from the outside of the meeting a man spoke out and said that he would be one of the volunteers.

Then De-ka-nah-wi-deh said, Go and call that man who is speaking from the outside. Then the man was called in, and he was asked to stand by the Chief Warrior in the meeting. Then De-ka-nah-wi-deh said to the Chief Warrior, You are the first to accede to the request of the Lord to volunteer, therefore your place shall be that whenever the Lord has any duties to give you you shall perform them. Then De-ka-nah-wi-deh said to the Warrior who was the second to volunteer, You came from the outside of the meeting, you shall therefore in future be an assistant to the Chief Warrior in his duties, and whenever the Chief Warrior assigns his duties to you you shall perform his duties and carry out his instructions. Then De-

ka-nah-wi-deh said, It is now completed, you have been assigned your duties. You will now go and search for the smoke and wherever you see smoke you shall go there and when you arrive there you will see the Lord of the settlement; then you shall tell him your message, you will say, We were sent here by the Lords (Ro-de-ya-ner-sonh) who will take you by the hand and invite you to the place of meeting. You will say to the Lord, You will send delegates, and on their way to the conference they will pass where the Lord lives at the big mountain and they shall invite him to accompany them. Then, if the Lord asks you the place of meeting, you shall say, By the lake where the Great wizard lives who calls out in the loud-toned voice. They then separated, the Chief Warrior and his assistant going on their mission, and De-ka-nah-wi-deh and Hah-yonh-wa-tha going to their respective settlements. And when Hah-yonh-wa-tha had arrived home he said, Everything is now completed and we shall (all colleagues) now all go to the conference. You shall therefore now all get ready.

The people watched the two delegates start on their mission and saw them become transformed into the High-flyer (a species of hawk) and they arose high in the air and soared southward and when they had arrived where the smoke piercing the sky was, then they descended and alighted near the settlement and were retransformed and proceeded to the village. They enquired the abode of the Lord, and they were conducted to him and when they had arrived they saw a man, then the Chief Warrior said, Are you the Lord? And he answered and said, I am. Are you seeking for me? The Chief Warrior then said, Yes; we are looking for you. Then the Lord said, I will now ask you upon what errand you have come here. Then the Chief Warrior said, We are sent by the Lords (Ro-de-ya-ner-sonh) who invite you to go to the place of meeting of the Conference, and you are to take your power with you (meaning peace). You shall therefore invite the Lord who lives on the Great Mountain to accompany you. Then the Lord spoke and said, Where shall we meet in conference? And the Chief Warrior answered and said, By the lake. Then the Lord said, I have known this for a long time. I shall therefore now accept your message. Then he got his pipe and said, When I get through smoking I shall then go to the conference. And the Chief Warrior and his assistant saw the pipe which was an exceedingly large one and larger than any pipe which they had ever seen before. They then returned to their own settlement and when they had returned there, Oh-dah-tshe-deh asked, Did you discover the smoke? Then the Chief Warrior answered and said, Everything is all right, all is well, and we have discovered the object which you desired, when we saw the smoke we went there and when we arrived we found the Lord and we repeated to him fully all our message, and when he had heard all, he answered and said, I had known this for a long time that I am required to attend the said conference and I now accept and approve the message.

He promised to pass, on his way to the conference, the settlement at the Great Mountain, and the people there were to accompany him to the conference. Then Oh-dah-tshe-deh said, It is now time that Hah-yonh-wa-tha should return, and as soon as he returns we shall at once go to the conference.

De-ka-nah-wi-deh had also gone to the settlement of the Great Mountain. And when he had arrived at the abode of the Lord of the settlement then he (De-ka-nah-wi-deh) said, It is now very urgent that you should reply to the message which I have left here before. Then the Lord answered and said, The Chief Warrior and his Deputy have failed to unanimously agree with me to accept the message of good tidings of Peace and Power, but I am now totally at sea, and at a loss to discover any course which might lead me to overcome this difficulty. The reason why we are thus placed in this difficulty is that the Chief Warrior and his Deputy who have the power and control of the people have disagreed with us to accept the message.

Then De-ka-nah-wi-deh said, That which has occurred with you will not make any difference. The reason why it will not make any difference is, that you (the Lord) have accepted the message. You are not alone, for they are many who have now accepted the message who will assist you to consider the difficulty in which you are now placed.

Then De-ka-nah-wi-deh said, You will now notify the Lord whose abode is on the other side of the river, that it is now urgent for him to come over the river, so that we might meet together here. Then the Lord sent a messenger to notify the Lord whose abode was on the other side of the river, and shortly after the Lord arrived at the appointed place. Then De-ka-nah-wi-deh said, We have now all met together. I will now therefore ask your mind on the matter in question.

Then the Lord who had come from over the river spoke first and said, We Lords on either side

of the river have decided to accept your message which you left. The only difficulty we have now to contend with is that the Chief Warrior and his Deputy have failed to agree with us to accept the message, and they have the power and control of the people, and we Lords on either side of the river are totally at sea and fail to see a way out of the difficulty. Then De-ka-nah-wi-deh said, I now fully understand everything and I will now tell you with reference to this matter which has occurred with you, for you are not alone who have accepted the message of good tidings of Peace and Power. Therefore, owing to that which occurred to you, you (the Lord) whose abode is on this side of the river and to whom the message first came shall be known in the land by the name of Ska-nya-dah-ri-yoh. Then he said, And you the Lord who came from over the river who has agreed in mind with your colleague on this side of the river shall be called in the land by the name of Sa-deh-ka-ronh-yes. Then De-ka-nah-wi-deh said, This is now all completed. The only thing now is for you to get ready, in a little while a man will come whom you will accompany to the conference. They then heard the man call A-soh-kek-ne—eh (It is not yet).

Then Hah-yonh-wa-tha distinctly heard where he was. Then he (Hah-yonh-wa-tha) said to his colleagues, The time is now come that we should go to the conference. They then started to go to the place appointed for the conference and when they had arrived at the place where the log (the Lord Oh-dah-tshe-deh) was lying across the path, Oh-dah-tshe-deh said, We have been impatiently waiting, for we heard the man calling with a loud voice now for a long time at the place appointed for the meeting of the conference.

Then Hah-yonh-wa-tha said, Let us now proceed to the conference. They then went to the conference. Then De-ka-nah-wi-deh said, from where he was, I shall now return to my abode, and we shall all meet at the place appointed for the conference. Then the Lords – Deh-ka-eh-yonh, Ji-non-dah-weh-hon and Dyon-yonh-keh – came from their settlement and when they arrived at the abode of Ska-nya-dah-ri-yoh they then said that the Lord had decided and arranged that they should call there on their way to the conference and that they were to invite him to accompany them.

Then Ska-nya-dah-ri-yoh said, We are ready and we have been waiting for a long time. They then went on their way to the conference.

De-ka-nah-wi-deh had arrived at the place of meeting first, and after him arrived Hah-yonh-wa-tha, Oh-dah-tshe-deh and their colleagues and shortly afterwards Ska-nya-dah-ri-yoh, Deh-ka-eh-yonh and their colleagues arrived; and after they had all assembled in conference De-ka-nah-wi-deh stood up and said, This conference met here composed of our Nations being now all assembled, you will therefore now first consider what we shall do with reference to this certain woman, our mother, who has not yet arrived. They then considered the matter and they decided that they would proceed with the business on hand and the matter would be in progress when she arrived.

Then De-ka-nah-wi-deh said, The first thing we shall do will be to cross over the lake and it shall be Hah-yonh-wa-tha and Oh-dah-tshe-deh and Deh-ka-eh-yonh and Ska-nya-dah-ri-yoh and Sa-deh-ka-ronh-yes who are the rulers with power, who shall cross first. If these Lords can safely get across the lake and make Peace, then you, the whole delegation can cross. Therefore you shall now watch and you shall see a display of power, when they leave the shore in their boat. I shall therefore appoint Hah-yonh-wa-tha to guide the boat. They then got into the boat and he (De-ka-nah-wi-deh) stood in front of the boat and Hah-yonh-wa-tha sat in the stern and the rest of the Lords then noticed that the boat was made of white marble. They then embarked in this boat from the shore and they had not proceeded far on their journey when they heard a voice calling out, A-soh-kek-ne—eh, and as soon as this voice had called out a strong wind arose and caused the lake to become very rough and troubled and great billows formed upon its surface and more especially around the boat. Then those in the boat became frightened and said, We are now going to die.

Then De-ka-nah-wi-deh spoke and said, There is no danger because Peace has prevailed. Then De-ka-nah-wi-deh further said to the wind and lake, Be quiet and rest. Then the wind and the roughness of the lake ceased. They had not gone much further when the man across the lake (Tha-do-dah-ho) again called out, A-soh-kek-ne—eh, and then the wind and roughness of the lake became still more violent. Then again De-ka-nah-wi-deh said, You, the wind and the lake, be still, for we have not crossed over the lake yet.

Then again the lake became calm. Then Hah-yonh-wa-tha began to paddle hard and the boat went so swift that when they reached the shore, it plowed deeply into the dry land on the shore bank.

Then De-ka-nah-wi-deh said, We will now get out of the boat for we have now arrived at the place we anticipated. Then he got out and the other Lords followed him and they continued on their journey; and they had only gone a short distance when they beheld a man sitting on a high round knoll and when they arrived where he was sitting they stood all around him, and De-ka-nah-wi-deh stood directly in front of him. Then he spoke and said, We have now arrived, we representing the four Nations. You will therefore now answer the message which we have left here with you. These Lords who now stand all around you have now accepted the good tidings of Peace and Power, which signifies that now hereafter the shedding of human blood shall cease, for our Creator, the Great Spirit, never intended that man should engage in any such work of destruction of human life. There are many who have perished in the direction you are now facing, and these Lords have come to induce you to join them, so that the shedding of human blood might cease, and the good tidings of Peace and Power might prevail.

Then the man (Tha-do-dah-ho) looked around and saw these men (the Lords) standing all around him, but he did not answer but kept silent. Then these Lords looked at his head while he was sitting on the ground and they saw his hair moving as if it were all alive and they saw that the movements of the hair greatly resembled serpents, and they looked at his hands and saw that his fingers were twisting and contorting continually in all directions and in all manner of shapes. And when they had become impatient because he would not answer the message, De-ka-nah-wi-deh told Hah-yonh-wa-tha, You shall now recross the lake and the Chief Warrior and De-ka-nah-wi-deh and Dyon-yonh-koh and our mother Ji-kon-sah-seh, shall accompany you back in the boat (when you return here.)

Then the man who was sitting on the ground smiled a little. Then Hah-yonh-wa-tha hurriedly went back and re-embarked in the boat and re-crossed the lake and when he had come to shore on the other side of the lake, they asked what had occurred. Then Hah-yonh-wa-tha answered and said, It is not yet complete, I have therefore come after the Chief Warrior, De-ha-rih-ho-ken and Dyon-yonh-koh and our mother Ji-kon-sah-seh. And they answered him and said, She has now arrived.

Then all those whom he had named got into the boat. Then Hah-yonh-wa-tha said, You will take as a sign that if we can get across the lake in safety and the lake remains calm all the way across that our message of Peace will be accepted.

They then embarked on the lake and the boat was rapidly propelled, and as they looked at the lake they saw that it was calm all the way across and they arrived at the shore in safety, and when they had arrived where the man was sitting Hah-yonh-wa-tha said, Now everything is completed, we are now all assembled here.

Then De-ka-nah-wi-deh said, We shall now first give thanks to the Great Spirit, we will do this because our power is now completed. He then said, It shall be that each Nation shall now have a voice in the thanksgiving and I shall therefore be the first to lead and he said, Yo—hen.

Then Oh-dah-tshe-deh also repeated, Yo—hen, and after him followed Deh-ka-eh-yonh who also repeated Yo—hen, and next in order was Ska-nya-dah-ri-yoh who also repeated Yo—hen, and after him Hah-yonh-wa-tha repeated Yo—hen. And it came to pass that when De-ka-nah-wi-deh started to address this man that the man became troubled and after all the Lords got through addressing the man he was affected and shed tears. Then De-ka-nah-wi-deh said, We the delegates of all the Nations who have accepted the good tidings of Peace and Power are now all assembled here, the course therefore that we shall now adopt is that the representatives of each Nation shall now give utterance to their opinion upon this matter.

Then Oh-dah-tshe-deh was the first to address the assembly and said, I shall be the first to give utterance to my opinion upon this matter. He then said, In my opinion this man may approve of our mission if we all lay our heads before him (this means that the Nations here represented would be submissive to this man Tha-do-dah-ho.)

Then De-ka-nah-wi-deh and Ska-nya-dah-ri-yoh spoke and said, We acquiesce in all that Oh-dah-tshe-deh has said.

Then De-ka-nah-wi-deh said to Tha-do-dah-ho, Now you will answer and say if you are satisfied with the submission of these Lords, who have now laid their heads before you. But even then Tha-do-dah-ho did not answer. Then De-ka-nah-wi-deh said, You Dyon-yonh-koh will now give utterance and express your opinion on this matter, as you now have the power. Then Dyon-yonh-koh spoke and said to Tha-do-dah-ho, The Creator, the Great Spirit, created this day, which is now

shedding its light and He also created man, and He also created the earth and the fulness thereof, now you will therefore look and see the delegates of the Four Nations sitting all around you, and you will also see the Chief Warrior and this woman, our mother (Ji-kon-sah-seh) standing before you, all of whom have approved of this message. The Lords and all the Chief Warriors and this woman, our mother, have all agreed to submit the good tidings of Peace and Power to you, and thus if you approve and confirm the message, you will have the power to be the Fire-Keeper of our Confederate Council, and the smoke from it will arise and pierce the sky, and all the Nations shall be subject to you. Then the twisting and contortionate movements of the fingers, and the snake-like movements of the hair of Tha-do-dah-ho ceased. Then he spoke and said, I will now answer the object of your mission. I now confirm and accept your message.

Then De-ka-nah-wi-deh said, We have now accomplished and completed everything that was required, with the exception of shaping and transforming him (by rubbing him down and taking the snake-like hair off him and circumcising him). The Lords therefore all took a hand in doing this and Oh-dah-tshe-deh was the first to rub down Tha-do-dah-ho and the others followed his example, so that the appearance of Tha-do-dah-ho might be like that of other men. When this had been done then De-ka-nah-wi-deh again said, You, the Chief Warrior, and you, our mother, you have the control of the Power, and we will now put upon him a sign, by placing upon his head the horns of a buck deer. The reason why we shall do this is because all people live upon the flesh of the deer, and the reason that we take the emblem of the deer's horns is that this institution will be the means of protecting our children hereafter.

Then De-ka-nah-wi-deh said, We shall now adopt these signs (or emblems) deer's horns by placing them upon the head of each other. It shall be thus then, that these horns shall be placed upon the head of every man who shall be called a "Lord" by his people and he shall have the power to rule his people. Then De-ka-nah-wi-deh further said, And now you, the Chief Warrior, and our mother, shall place these horns upon the head of him (Tha-do-dah-ho).

Then they looked and saw the horns lying on the ground in the midst of them, and then De-ka-nah-wi-deh said, Pick these horns up and put them on him. Then the woman went forward and picked them up. Then the Chief Warrior and the woman each took hold of the horns and placed them on his head. Then De-ka-nah-wi-deh said to the man who was still sitting on the ground, You will now stand up. Then the man stood up. Then De-ka-nah-wi-deh said, You, the Nations who are assembled here, see now this man, who has stood up before us. We have now completed placing the sign of the deer's horns upon his head, which signifies the emblem of authority. The people shall now therefore call him Lord Tha-do-dah-ho, in the land.

Then De-ka-nah-wi-deh said, It shall now in the future amongst us, the united Nations, be our custom whenever a Lord is to be created we shall all unite and take part in the ceremony.

Then De-ka-nah-wi-deh said, And Ska-nya-dah-ri-yoh and Sa-deh-ka-ronh-yes shall be the uncles of Deh-ka-eh-yonh.

We have now formed the Confederacy, and we shall now have two sets of Lords one on each side of the Council Fire.

Then also Hah-yonh-wa-tha and Oh-dah-tshe-deh, father and son, shall sit and face each other one on each side of the Council Fire.

Then Ska-nya-deh-ri-yoh and Sa-deh-ka-ronh-yes shall sit on one side of the Council Fire and their nephew Deh-ka-eh-yonh shall sit on the opposite side.

On one side of the Council fire shall then be seated Hah-yonh-wa-tha, Ska-nya-dah-ri-yoh and Sa-deh-ka-ronh-yes and on the opposite side shall sit Oh-dah-tshe-deh and Deh-ka-eh-yonh. And then he (De-ka-nah-wi-deh) said, And it shall be that we shall place Tha-do-dah-ho in the centre between the two sets of Lords in the Council. Then De-ka-nah-wi-deh said, We shall establish this relationship as follows: You Tha-do-dah-ho shall be the father of Oh-dah-tshe-deh and Deh-ka-eh-yonh and Hah-yonh-wa-tha, Ska-nya-dah-ri-yoh and Sa-deh-ka-ronh-yes shall be your brethren and you shall be the principals of the Confederation which we have just made and completed. The first matter which I shall lay before you for your consideration is, that, as clans are already established amongst the people, the several clans form a relationship as brothers and cousins. And it came to pass that the Lords answered and said, We have now decided to adopt your suggestion.

Then he (De-ka-nah-wi-deh) said, You Hah-yonh-wa-tha, shall be the first to name and appoint your colleagues, you are of the Turtle Clan and shall therefore appoint your colleagues of the same

Clan. Then Hah-yonh-wa-tha said, This is now all ready, they have accepted and they are as follows: De-ka-ri-ho-ken, Sa-de-ka-rih-wa-deh. Then De-ka-nah-wi-deh said, These shall therefore be your brother Colleagues, you of the Turtle Clan. And your brethren of the Wolf Clan shall be, Sa-renh-ho-wa-neh, De-yon-heh-kon and Oh-renh-reh-ko-wah.

Then De-ka-nah-wi-deh said, Your Cousins of the Bear Clan shall be De-hen-nah-ka-re-neh, Ah-stah-weh-seh-ron-tha and Soh-sko-ha-roh-wa-neh.

Then De-ka-nah-wi-deh said, You (Hah-yonh-wa-tha) have now completed appointing your Colleagues of your Nation, as the good tidings of Peace and Power first originated at Kan-yen-geh, you shall be called Ka-nyen-geh-ha-kah (Mohawk).

Then De-ka-nah-wi-deh said to Hah-yonh-wa-tha, Now it shall fall upon your son Oh-dah-tshe-deh who sits upon the opposite side of the Council fire to appoint his brother Colleagues. Then Oh-dah-tshe-deh appointed his brother Colleagues of the Turtle Clan as follows: So-non-sehs, Tho-nah-onh-ken-ah, and A-tya-donh-nenh-tha. And then he (Oh-dah-tshe-deh) appointed his cousins of the Bear Clan as follows: Deh-ha-da-weh-de-yons, Deh-ha-nyen-da-sah-deh and Roh-wa-tsha-deh-hon. These being the second Nation who accepted the message of Peace and Power and as their settlement (from whence they came) was where the historic stone was situated (O-neh-yoht) it was named O-neh-yo-deh-ha-ka (Oneidas).

Then De-ka-nah-wi-deh said, It shall now rest with you the Uncles, Ska-nya-dah-ri-yoh and Sa-deh-ka-ronh-yes to appoint your Colleagues. Then Ska-nya-dah-ri-yoh said, I (myself) shall appoint two of my brethren and my Cousin Sa-deh-ka-ronh-yes shall appoint two of his brethren. Then Ska-nya-dah-ri-yoh of the Turtle Clan said, I therefore now appoint Ka-no-kye of the Turtle Clan and Sa-tye-na-wat of the Bear Clan as my Colleagues.

Then Sa-deh-ka-ronh-yes of the Snipe Clan said, I now appoint Sa-ken-jo-wah-neh of the Pigeon Hawk Clan and Nis-ha-yeh-nehs of the Plover Clan as my Colleagues.

Then De-ka-nah-wi-deh said, You have now all appointed your Colleagues and Ka-no-kye and Sa-ken-jo-wah-neh shall be Cousins and Nis-ha-yeh-nehs and Sa-tye-na-wat shall be Cousins. He then said, You Ska-nya-dah-ri-yoh and Sa-deh-ka-ronh-yes of the Seneca Nation have now completed appointing your Colleagues. Your settlement is at the big Mountain, you shall therefore be called O-nen-do-wah-ka (people of the big Mountain) Senecas.

Then De-ka-nah-wi-deh said, And now your son Deh-ka-eh-yonh who sits on the opposite side of the Council Fire shall name and appoint his Colleagues. Then Deh-ka-eh-yonh of the big Bear Clan appointed his Colleagues as follows: I shall now appoint my son Ji-non-dah-weh-onh of the Ball Clan and my brother Ka-da-gwa-seh of the Bear Clan and my brother Sho-yonh-wehs of the young Bear Clan and Ha-tya-troh-neh of the Turtle Clan. And he (Deh-ka-eh-yonh) continued appointing as follows: Dyon-yonh-koh of the Heron Clan, and Deh-yoh-doh-weh-kon of the Wolf Clan and Dyon-weh-thoh of the Snipe Clan. These are the brother Colleagues of the above.

Then Deh-ka-eh-yonh appointed the Cousins of the above as follows: Hah-don-dah-heh-ha of the Plover Clan and Des-ka-heh of the young Bear Clan.

Then De-ka-nah-wi-deh said, You Deh-ka-eh-yonh of the Cayuga Nation have now finished appointing your Colleagues, you shall therefore be called (Queh-you-gwe-hah-ka) Cayuga, from your custom of portaging your canoe at a certain point in your settlement.

Then De-ka-nah-wi-deh said, I shall now leave it to you, Tha-do-dah-ho, to appoint your Colleagues.

Then Tha-do-dah-ho of the Bear Clan said, The first I shall appoint will be Onh-neh-sah-heh, my cousin of the Beaver Clan, and Ska-nya-da-ge-wak of the Snipe Clan and Ah-weh-ken-yath of the Ball Clan and Deh-ha-yat-kwa-eh of the Turtle Clan, and these are all brothers, and then Tha-do-dah-ho appointed their son, Ho-noh-we-yeh-deh of the Wolf Clan and then Tha-do-dah-ho appointed his (Ho-noh-we-yeh-dehs) uncles as follows: Kon-weh-neh-senh-don of the Deer Clan and Ha-he-honk also of the Deer Clan and then their brothers as follows: Ho-yonh-hye-neh of the Eel Clan and So-deh-kwa-seh also of the Eel Clan and Sa-ko-ken-heh of the Pigeon Hawk Clan, and then he (Tha-do-dah-ho) appointed the sons of the latter as follows: Ho-sah-ha-we of the Deer Clan and Ska-nah-wa-de of the small Turtle Clan.

Then De-ka-nah-wi-deh spoke and said, We have now completed appointing the Lords of the Five Nations hereby represented. These Lords have now all been crowned with deer's horns in conformity and in similar manner as Tha-do-dah-ho who was first crowned. Therefore we have now accomplished and completed the work of laying the foundation of this Confederation.

Then De-ka-nah-wi-deh spoke again and said, I will now lay before your Confederate Council for your consideration one matter and that is with reference to the conduct of the Chief Warriors of O-non-do-wa-ka (Senecas) who have refused to act in conjunction (or accord) with their Lords in accepting the message (of good tidings of Peace and Power.)

Then the Lords sent messengers for these two Chief Warriors of the O-non-do-wa-ka (Senecas) to appear. And when they had come to the Council Lord Hah-yonh-wa-tha then addressed these two Chief Warriors and said, This Confederate Council now in session together with their Warriors have unanimously accepted the message of Peace and Power and only you two (Chief Warriors) have not yet done so and you have not expressed yourselves on this matter. Then Hah-yonh-wa-tha further said, This Confederate Council and their Chief Warriors have unanimously decided to leave all the power and control of the people in your hands if you accept the message so that in case of war with other Nations you shall be the leaders of the people of the Confederate Nations in defence of their Confederacy. Then one of these two Chief Warriors spoke and said, We will now agree to accept the message.

Then De-ka-nah-wi-deh continued his address and said, Now our power is full and complete, as the two Chief Warriors of the O-non-do-wa-ka (Senecas) have agreed to accept the message of good tidings; therefore we shall now add to the number of the Lords of the Confederacy (Eh-ji-twa-nah-stah-soh-de-renh, we shall call it Ka-na-stah-ge-ko-wah) and these two Chief Warriors shall represent the door of the Confederacy (Ka-noh-hah-ge-ko-wah) meaning the great black door, through which all good and evil messages must come to reach the Confederate House of Lords or Council, and if any person or Nation has any news, message or business matter to lay before the Confederate Council he or they must come through this door.

Then De-ka-nah-wi-deh again further said, We shall now crown these two Chief Warriors with deer's horns and make them Lords also. We shall now first crown with deer's horn De-yoh-ne-oh-ka-weh of the Wolf Clan and then we shall also crown Ka-non-ke-dah-we of the Snipe Clan and these two shall be cousins and they shall guard the door of the Confederacy. And we shall now floor the doorway with slippery elm bark, and it shall be that whenever we have visitors from other nations who will have any message or any business to lay before the Confederate Council, these two door keepers shall escort and convey them before the Council, but whenever the visitor or visitors have come for evil purposes then Ka-non-ke-dah-we shall take them by the hand and lead them in and they shall slip on the slippery elm bark and fall down and they shall be reduced to a skeleton or heap of bones (Eh-yoh-so-jo-de-hah, in Onondaga language, Eh-yoh-doh-yoh-da-neh in Mohawk) that the bones of the enemy will fall into a heap before the Lords of the Confederacy. (A heap of bones here signifies a conquered Nation to be dealt with by the Lords of the Confederacy who shall decide as to what manner they will be allowed to exist in the future.)

Then De-ka-nah-wi-deh again said, We have completed the Confederation of the Five Nations. Now therefore it shall be that hereafter the Lords who shall be appointed in the future to fill vacancies caused by death or removals shall be appointed from the same families and Clans from which the first Lords were created, and from which families the hereditary title of Lordships shall descend.

Then De-ka-nah-wi-deh further said, I now transfer and set over to the women the Lordship titles vested in them, and they shall in the future have the power to appoint the successors from time to time to fill vacancies caused by death or removals from whatever cause.

Then De-ka-nah-wi-deh continued and said, We shall now build a Confederate Council fire from which the smoke shall arise and pierce the skies and all nations and peoples shall see this smoke. And now to you Tha-do-dah-ho your brother and cousin Colleagues shall be left the care and protection of the Confederate Council fire, by the Confederate Nations.

Then De-ka-nah-wi-deh further said, The Lords have unanimously decided to spread before you on the ground this great white Wampum Belt (Ska-no-dah-ken-rah-ko-wah) and (Ka-yah-ne-renh-ko-wah) which signifies purity and great peace, and the Lords have also laid before you this great Wing (Ska-weh-yeh-seh-ko-wah) and whenever any dust or stain of any description falls upon the great Belt of white Wampum, then

you shall take this great wing and sweep it clean (dust or stain means evil of any description which has a tendency to cause trouble in the Confederate Council).

Then De-ka-nah-wi-deh said, The Lords of this Confederacy have unanimously decided to lay by you this rod (Ska-nah-ka-res) and whenever you see any creeping thing which has a tendency to harm our grandchildren or creeping towards the great white Wampum Belt, then you take this rod and pry it away with it, and if you and your Colleagues fail to pry the creeping evil thing out, you shall then call out loudly so that all the Confederate Nations may hear and they will come to your assistance.

Then De-ka-nah-wi-deh said, Now you Lords of the several Confederate Nations shall now divide yourselves and sit on the opposite sides of the Council fire as follows: You and your brother Colleagues shall sit on one side of the Council fire (this was said to the Mohawks and the Senecas) and your sons the Oneidas and Cayugas shall sit directly opposite of the Council fire, and then you will begin to work and carry out the principles of the great peace (Ka-yah-ne-renh-ko-wah) you will be guided in this by the great white Wampum Belt (Ska-no-dah-ke-rah-ko-wah) which signifies great peace. Then De-ka-nah-wi-deh said, You Tha-do-dah-ho shall be the Fire-Keepers, and your duty shall be to open the Confederate Council with praise and thanksgiving to the Great Spirit and close the same. Then he (De-ka-nah-wi-deh) said, When the Council is opened Hah-yonh-wa-tha and his Colleagues shall be the first to consider and give their opinion upon all subjects which come before the Council for consideration, and when they have arrived at a decision, then they shall transfer the matter to their brethren the Senecas for their consideration, and when they (the Senecas) shall have arrived at a decision on the matter, then they shall refer it back to Hah-yonh-wa-tha and his Colleagues. Then Hah-yonh-wa-tha will announce the decision to the opposite side of the Council fire. Then Oh-dah-tshe-deh and his Colleagues will consider the matter in question and when they have arrived at a decision they will refer the matter to their brethren the Cayugas for their consideration and after they have arrived at a decision they will refer the matter back to Oh-dah-tshe-deh and his Colleagues. Then Oh-dah-tshe-deh will announce their decision to the opposite side of the Council fire. Then Hah-yonh-wa-tha will refer the matter to Tha-do-dah-ho and his Colleagues for their careful consideration and opinion of the matter in question, and if Tha-do-dah-ho and his Colleagues find that the matter has not been well considered or decided then they shall refer the matter back again to the two sides of the Council fire and they shall point out where in their estimation the decision was faulty, and the question not fully considered, and then the two sides of the Council will take up the question again and reconsider the matter, and after the two sides of the Council have fully reconsidered the question, then Hah-yonh-wa-tha will again refer it to Tha-do-dah-ho and his Colleagues, then they will again consider the matter and if they see that the decision of the two sides of the Council is correct, then Tha-do-dah-ho and his Colleagues will confirm the decision.

Then De-ka-nah-wi-deh further said, If the brethren of the Mohawks and the Senecas are divided in their opinion and cannot agree on any matter which they may have for their consideration, then Hah-yonh-wa-tha shall announce the two decisions to the opposite side of the Council fire. Then Oh-dah-tshe-deh and his brother Colleagues after they have considered the matter and if they also are divided in their decision but the divided factions each agree with the decision announced from the opposite side of the Council, then Oh-dah-tshe-deh shall also announce their two decisions to the other side of the Council fire, then Hah-yonh-wa-tha shall refer the matter to Tha-do-dah-ho and his colleagues who are the Fire Keepers. Then they will fully consider the matter and whichever decision they consider correct they will confirm. Then De-ka-nah-wi-deh said, If it should so happen that the Lords of the Mohawks and the Lords of the Senecas disagree on any matter and also on the opposite side of the Council fire, the Lords of the Oneidas and the Lords of the Cayugas disagree amongst themselves and did not agree with either of the two decisions of the opposite side of the Council fire, but they themselves give two decisions which are diverse from each other, then Hah-yonh-wa-tha shall refer the four decisions to Tha-do-dah-ho and his Colleagues who shall consider and give their decision in the matter and their decision shall be final.

Then De-ka-nah-wi-deh further said, We have now completed the system of our Great Confederate Council.

Then De-ka-nah-wi-deh further said, We now each Nation shall adopt all the rules and regulations governing the Confederate Council which we have made and we shall apply them to all our respective settlements and thereby we shall carry out the principles set forth in the message of good tidings of Peace and Power, and in dealing with the affairs of our people of the various Provinces, thus we shall secure to them contentment and happiness.

Then he (De-ka-nah-wi-deh) said, You Ka-nyen-ke-ha-ka (Mohawk) you De-ka-ri-ho-ken, Hah-yonh-wa-tha and Sa-de-ka-rih-wa-deh, you shall sit in the middle between your brother Lords of the Mohawks, and your cousin Lords of the Mohawks, and all matters under discussion shall be referred to you by your brother Lords and your cousin Lords for your approval or disapproval.

Then De-ka-nah-wi-deh said, You O-nen-do-wa-ka (Senecas), you Ska-nya-dah-ri-yoh and Sa-deh-ka-ronh-yes, you shall sit in the middle or between your brother Lords and your cousin Lords of the Senecas and all matters under discussion shall be referred to you by them for your approval or disapproval.

Then De-ka-nah-wi-deh said, You Oh-nen-yoh-de-ha-ka (Oneidas), you Oh-dah-tshe-deh, Ka-non-kwe-you-doh and De-you-hah-kwe-deh, you shall sit in the middle between your brother Lords and your cousin Lords of the Oneidas and all matters under discussion shall be referred to you by them for your approval or disapproval.

Then De-ka-nah-wi-deh said, You the Que-yonh-kwe-ha-ka (Cayugas) you Deh-ka-eh-yonh and Ji-non-da-hwe-honh, you shall sit in the middle between your brother Lords and your cousin Lords of the Cayugas, and all matters under discussion shall be referred to you by them for your approval or disapproval.

Then De-ka-nah-wi-deh said, We have now completed arranging the system of our local Councils and we shall hold our Annual Confederate Council at the settlement of Tha-do-dah-ho, the Capital or seat of Government of the Five Nations Confederacy.

Constitution of the Five Nations Confederacy

Then De-ka-nah-wi-deh said, Now I and you Lords of the Confederate Nations shall plant a tree Ska-renh-heh-se-go-wah (meaning a great tall and mighty tree) and we shall call it Jo-ne-rah-deh-seh-ko-wah (the tree of the great long leaves).

Now this tree which we have planted shall shoot forth four great long white roots (Jo-deh-ra-ken-rah-ko-wah). These great long white roots shall shoot forth one to the North and one to the South and one to the East and one to the West, and we shall place on the top of it Oh-don-yonh (an eagle) which has a great power of long vision, and we shall transact all our business under the shade of this great tree. The meaning of planting this great tree Ska-renh-heh-se-go-wah is Ka-yah-ne-renh-ko-wa (which means Great Peace), and Jo-deh-ra-ken-rah-ko-wah (meaning good tidings of Peace and Power), and the Nations of the earth shall see it and shall accept and follow the root and shall arrive here at this tree and when they arrive here you shall receive them and shall seat them in the midst of your Confederacy, and the meaning of placing an Eagle on the top of the Great tall tree is to watch the Roots which extend to the North and to the South and to the East and to the West, and the Eagle will discover if any evil is approaching your Confederacy, and will scream and give the alarm and all the Nations of the Confederacy at once shall hear the alarm and come to the front.

Then De-ka-nah-wi-deh again said, We shall now combine our power into one great power which is this Confederacy, and we shall now therefore symbolize the union of these powers by each Nation contributing one arrow (each) which we shall tie up together in a bundle, which when it is made and completely tied together no one can bend or break it.

Then De-ka-nah-wi-deh further said, We have now completed this union in securing one arrow from each Nation, it is not good that one should be lacking or taken from the bundle, for it would weaken our power and it would be still worse if two arrows were taken from the bundle. And if three arrows were taken, then any one could break the remaining arrows in the bundle.

Then De-ka-nah-wi-deh continued his address and said, We shall now therefore tie this bundle of arrows together with deer's sinews which is strong, durable and lasting and then this Institution will be strong and unchangeable. This bundle of arrows signifies that all Lords and all the Warriors and all the women of the Confederacy have become united as one person.

Then De-ka-nah-wi-deh again said, We have now completed binding this bundle of arrows and we shall leave it beside the Great tree (Ska-renh-heh-se-go-wah) beside the Confederate Council fire of Tha-do-dah-ho.

Then De-ka-nah-wi-deh said, We have now completed our power so that we, the Five Nations Confederacy, shall in the future only have one body, one head and one heart.

Then he (De-ka-nah-wi-deh) further said, If any evil should befall us in the future we shall stand or fall unitedly as one man.

Then De-ka-nah-wi-deh said, You Lords shall be symbolized as trees of the Five Confederate Nations. We therefore bind ourselves together by taking hold of each other's hands so firmly and forming a circle so strong that if a tree should fall upon it, it could not shake nor break it, so that our people and grandchildren shall remain in the circle in security, peace and happiness. And if any Lord who is crowned with the emblem of deer's horns shall break through this circle of unity, his horns shall become fastened in the circle, and if he persists after warning from the Chief Matron &c. he shall go through it without his horns and the horns shall remain in the circle, and after he has passed through the circle he shall no longer be a Lord, but shall be as an ordinary warrior and shall not be qualified to fill any office.

Then De-ka-nah-wi-deh further said, We have now completed everything in connection with the matter of Peace and Power, and it only remains for us to consider and adopt some measure as to what we shall do with reference to the disposal of the weapons of war which we have taken from our people.

Then the Lords considered the matter and decided that the best way which they could adopt with reference to the disposal of the weapons would be to uproot the Great tall tree which they have planted, and in uprooting the tree it would form a chasm so deep that it would come or reach to the swift current of the waters under it, into which the weapons of war would be thrown, and they would be borne or swept away forever by the current so that their grandchildren would never see them. And they then uprooted the Great tree and they then cast into the chasm all manner of weapons of war which their people had been in the custom of using, and they then replaced the tree in its original position.

Then De-ka-nah-wi-deh further continued and said, We have completed clearing away all manner of weapons in the way of our people.

Then he (De-ka-nah-wi-deh) continued and said, We have still one matter left to be considered and that is with reference to the hunting grounds of our people from which they derive their living.

Then the Lords said with reference to this matter, We shall now do this. We shall only have one dish (or bowl) in which will be placed one beaver's tail and we shall all have a co-equal right to it, and there shall be no knife in it, for if there be a knife in it there will be danger that it might cut some one and blood would thereby be shed. (This one dish or bowl signifies that they will place their hunting grounds in one common and all have a co-equal right to hunt within its precincts; and the knife being prohibited from being placed into the dish or bowl signifies that all danger would be removed from shedding of blood by the people of these different Nations of the Confederacy caused by differences of the right of the hunting grounds, etc.)

Then De-ka-nah-wi-deh continued and said, We have now accomplished and completed forming this great Confederacy of the Five Nations together with adopting rules and regulations in connection therewith.

Then he (De-ka-nah-wi-deh) continued and said, I will now leave all matters in the hands of you Lords and you are to work and carry out the principles of all that I have just laid before you for the welfare of your people and others, and I now place the power in your hands to add to the rules and regulations whenever necessary and I now charge you each of you Lords that you must never seriously disagree among yourselves. You are all of equal standing and of equal power, and if you seriously disagree the consequences will be most serious and this disagreement will cause you to disregard each other, and while you are quarrelling with each other, the White Lion (The Fire dragon of discord) will come and take your rights and privileges away, then your grandchildren will suffer and be reduced to poverty and disgrace.

Then he (De-ka-nah-wi-deh) continued and said, If this should ever occur, then some one, whoever can, will climb a Great tree (Ska-renh-heh-se-go-wah) and ascend to the top and will look around over the landscape, and will see if there is any way or place to escape to from the calamity of the threatening poverty and disgrace, so that our children may have a home where they may have peace and happiness in their day. And if it so occurs that he cannot see any way or place to escape the calamity he will then descend the tree. You will then look for a great swamp-elm tree (A-ka-rah-ji-ko-wah) and when you have found one with great large roots extending outwards and bracing outwards from the trunk there you will gather your heads together.

Then De-ka-nah-wi-deh continued and said, It will be hard, and your grandchildren will suffer hardship. And if it should so occur that the heads of the people of the Confederacy should roll and wander away Westward, whenever such thing will come to pass, other Nations shall see your heads rolling and wandering away, and they shall say to them, You belong to the Confederacy, you were a proud and haughty people once, and then they shall kick the heads with scorn, and they will go on their way and before they shall have gone far they shall vomit up blood (meaning that the Confederacy shall still have power enough to avenge and will avenge the injury done to its members).

Then De-ka-nah-wi-deh further said, There shall be another serious trouble, that is, whenever a person or persons of other Nations shall cut or hack any of these four great roots which grow from the Great tree which we have planted and one of the roots of which shoots to the North and one to the South and one to the East and one to the West. Whenever such thing happens then shall great trouble come into the seat of your Lords of the Confederacy.

Then De-ka-nah-wi-deh said, I shall now therefore charge each of you Lords, that your skin must be of the thickness of seven spreads of the hands (from end of thumb to the end of great finger) so that no matter how sharp a cutting instrument may be used it will not penetrate through the thickness of your skin. The meaning of the great thickness of your skins is patience and forbearance, that no matter what nature of question or business may come before you, no matter how sharp or aggravating it may be it will not penetrate your skins, but you will forbear with great patience and good will in all your deliberations and never disgrace yourselves by becoming angry. You Lords shall always be guided in all your councils and deliberations by the good tidings of Peace and Power.

Then De-ka-nah-wi-deh said, Now you Lords of the different Nations of the Confederacy I charge you to cultivate the good feeling of friendship, love and honour amongst yourselves, and I have now fulfilled my duty in assisting you in the establishment and organization of this Great Confederacy, and this Confederation if carefully guarded shall continue and last from generation to generation and as long as the sun will continue to shine, the grass grow and waters run. I shall now therefore go home, conceal, and cover myself with bark, and there shall be no successor to my title and no man in the future shall be called by my name.

Then De-ka-nah-wi-deh further continued and said, If at any time through the negligence and carelessness of the Lords, they fail to carry out the principles of the good tidings of Peace and Power and the rules and regulations of the Confederacy and the people are reduced to poverty and great suffering, then I will return.

Then De-ka-nah-wi-deh said, And it shall so happen that when you hear my name mentioned disrespectfully without reason or just cause, but spoken in levity, you shall then know that you are on the verge of trouble and sorrow.

Then he (De-ka-nah-wi-deh) said, And it shall be that the only time that it shall be proper that my name shall be mentioned is when the Condolence Ceremonies are being performed or when the good tidings of Peace and Power which I have established and organized are being discussed or rehearsed.

Then the Lords (Ro-de-ya-ner-sonh) said, We shall begin to work and carry out the instructions which he (De-ka-nah-wi-deh) has laid before us.

Then they said, We shall therefore begin first with the Confederate Council of the Five Nations; and other Nations who shall accept and come under the Constitution of the Confederacy will become as props in support of the said Confederacy, and they then said, The pure white Wampum Strings shall be the token or emblem of the Council fire, and it shall be that when the Fire Keepers shall open the Council he shall pick up this string of Wampum and hold it in his hand while he is offering thanksgiving to the Great Spirit and opening the Council. And they then also said, While the Council is in session the strings of the White Wampum shall be placed conspicuously in their midst and when they shall adjourn then the Fire Keepers shall pick up these strings of Wampum again, and again offer thanksgiving and close the Council, and all business in connection with the Council shall then be adjourned.

Then they said, We shall now establish that our custom shall be that when our Annual Confederate Council shall meet we shall then smoke the pipe of Peace.

And they, the Lords, then said, We shall now proceed to define the obligations and position of the Lords of the Confederacy as follows:

1 If a Lord is found guilty of wilful murder he shall be deposed without the warning (as shall be provided for later on) by the Lords of the Confederacy, and his horns (emblem of power) shall be handed back to the Chief Matron of his family and Clan.

2 Then the Lords said, If a Lord is guilty of rape he shall be deposed without the usual warning by the Lords of the Confederacy, and his horns (as the emblem of power) shall be handed back to the Chief Matron of his family and Clan.

3 Then the Lords said, If a Lord is found guilty of theft he shall be deposed without the usual warning by the Lords of the Confederacy and his horns (the emblem of power) shall be handed back to the Chief Matron of his family and Clan.

4 Then the Lords continued to define the obligations and position of the Lords of the Confederacy as follows:

(a) If a Lord is guilty of unwarrantably opposing the object of decisions of the Council and in that way showing disrespect for his brother Lords by urging that his own erroneous will in these matters be carried out, he shall be approached and admonished by the Chief Matron of his family and Clan to desist from such evil practices and urged to come back and act in harmony with his brother Lords.

(b) If the Lord refuses to comply with the request of the Chief Matron of his family and Clan and still persists in his evil practices of unwarrantably opposing his brother Lords, then a Warrior of his family and Clan will also approach him and admonish him to desist from pursuing his evil course.

(c) If the Lord still refuses to listen and obey, then the Chief Matron and Warrior shall go together to the Chief Warrior and they inform him that they have admonished their Lord and he refused to obey. Then the Chief Warrior will arise and go there to the Lord and will say to him, Your nephew and niece have admonished you to desist from your evil course, and you have refused to obey. Then the Chief Warrior will say, I will now admonish you for the last time and if you continue to resist to accede to and obey this request, then your duties as Lord of our family and Clan will cease, and I shall take the deer's horns from off your head, and with a broad-edged stone axe I shall cut the tree down (meaning that he shall be deposed from his position as Lord or Chief of the Confederacy). Then the Chief Warrior shall hand back the deer's horns (the emblem of power) of the deposed Lord to the Chief Matron of his family or Clan.

(d) Whenever it occurs that a Lord is thus deposed then the Chief Matron will select and appoint another Warrior of her family or Clan and crown him with the deer's horns and thus a new Lord shall be created in the place of the one deposed.

(e) Then the Lords said, That the Lords of each of the Confederate Nations shall have one Chief Warrior and his duty shall be to carry messages through the dense forests between our settlements, and also in the absence of the Lord through illness or any other impediment or cause he shall be deputed by him (his Lord) to act in his place in Council.

The Chief Warriors of the Five Nations Confederacy are as follows: Mohawks, Senecas, Onondagas, Oneidas and Cayugas.

The Lords then said, We have now completed defining the obligations and position of a Lord (Ro-ya-ner).

In accordance therefore with the custom which we now have established, it shall be that when a Lord is deposed and the deer's horns (emblem of power) is taken from him, that he shall not be allowed to sit in council or even hold office again.

(f) Then the Lords continued and said, What shall we do in case some of us Lords in whom so much dependence is placed are removed by sudden death?

In such case (this shall be done) the Chief Matron and the Warriors of the family and Clan of the deceased Lord, shall nominate another Lord from the Warriors of the family and Clan of the dead Lord to succeed him, then the matter will be submitted to their brother Lords and if they (the brother Lords) confirm the nomination then the matter will be further submitted to their cousin Lords and if they also confirm the nomination, then the candidate shall be qualified to go through the Condolence ceremony.

(g) Then the Lords continued and said, In case the family and Clan in which a Lordship title is vested shall become extinct this shall be done. It shall then be transferred and vested in the hands of the Confederate Lords, and they will consider the matter and nominate and appoint a successor from any family of the brother Lords of the deceased Lord, and the Lords may in their discretion vest the said Lordship title in same family, and such title will remain in that family so long as the Lords are satisfied.

(h) Then the Lords further continued and said, If ever it should occur that the Chief Matron in a family or Clan in which a Lordship title is vested should be removed by death and leave female infants who owing to their tender age cannot nom-

inate a candidate to bear their Lordship title, then the Lords (of the same Nation) during their pleasure and whenever the infant or heirs to the title shall come before the Lords and request that the Lordship title be restored to them, then the Lords will obtain the title and restore it accordingly.

(i) Then the Lords continued and said, We now have completed laying the foundation of our rules and regulations (Ka-ya-neh-ren-ko-wa) and we will now proceed to follow and carry out the working of these rules and regulations of the Confederacy, and the local affairs of our respective settlements; and whenever we discover a Warrior who is wise and trustworthy and who will render his services for the benefit of the people, and thus aid the Lords of the Confederacy, we will claim him into our midst and confer upon him the title of self-made (or Second) Chief (Eh-ka-neh-do-deh) and his title shall only last during his life-time and shall not be hereditary, and at his death it shall die with him.

Then the Lords (Ro-de-ya-ner-sonh) again considered and said, We have now completed the appointment of our Lords. It may so occur that before we may be quietly reseated in our respective places, we may sustain another loss by death (of a Lord). In that case we shall do this, while yet the dying Lord is suffering the agonies of death the Lords (his brother Lords) will come and take his deer's horns from off his head and place them beside the wall so that if by the will of the Great Spirit he recovers from his illness, he will resume his crown of deer's horns and resume the duties of a Lord. And they further considered this matter and said, While the Lord is ill we will place a string of black Wampum at the head of his bed, and if he dies, any one belonging to his Clan will take this string of black Wampum and announce his death to the whole circle of the Confederacy as follows:

If a Lord among the three brothers of the Mohawks, Senecas and Onondagas dies, the Chief Warrior or Warriors will convey the string of black Wampum to their son, Oh-dah-tshe-deh or De-ka-eh-yonh or their Colleagues, and he will leave it there, and while on his way from the home of the dead Lord he will repeat at regular intervals the mourning cry three times thus: Kwa—ah; Kwa—ah; Kwa—ah.

Then Oh-dah-tshe-deh or Deh-ka-eh-yonh or their Colleagues will convey the string of black Wampum to their four brothers, and so on until the whole circle of the Confederacy will become aware of the death of the Lord. And if a Lord among the four brothers of the Oneidas and Cayugas dies (since Tuscaroras and other Nations were admitted) then the Chief Warrior or any Warrior deputed, will carry and convey the string of black Wampum to De-ka-ri-ho-ken or Ska-nya-dah-ri-yoh or Tha-do-dah-ho, or their brother Colleagues, and the Chief Warrior or any Warrior so deputed will while on his way repeat the mourning cry three times at regular intervals as follows: Kwa—ah; Kwa—ah; Kwa—ah. And if a Chief Warrior on either side of the Council dies, or if a Chief of Tuscarora, Delaware, Nanticoke or Tuteloes member of the Council dies, then the mourning messenger will while on his way to announce the death of either of these repeat the mourning cry twice only as follows: Kwa—ah; Kwa—ah. In case of the sudden death of a Lord then his Colleagues will remove his crown of deer's horns and will put it to one side where the Chief Matron of the family or Clan to which he belonged will find and take it up again.

If from whatever cause the crown of deer's horns is not removed from the head of the Lord at the time of his death, then his Colleagues will remove the same at the time of his burial and will place it beside the grave where the Chief Matron will find and pick it up again.

Then the Lords said, If a Lord dies, we will do this, we will put up a pole horizontally, and we will hang a pouch upon it, and we will put into the pouch a short string of Wampum and whichever side of the Council fire sustains a loss by death then the side which has not sustained the loss will depute one of their Lords to take the pouch off the pole, then he shall follow the path and go to the opposite side of the Council fire where the loss has been sustained by the Lords, and when he arrives there (at the house where the Lord died) he will stand at one end of the hearth and he will speak consoling words to the bereaved, and he will cheer them up, and this will be our mode of condolence, and these shall consist of thirteen passages to be expressed in this Condolence (Ka-ne-kon-kets-kwa-se-rah) and thirteen Wampum strings shall be used in this ceremony as follows:

The beginning of the Condolence Ceremony used immediately after the death of a Chief (or Lord) and which is subsequently followed by the thirteen Ceremony called, "At the Wood's edge" and which is hereto attached.

1 Now hear us our Uncles, we have come to condole with you in your great bereavement.

We have now met in dark sorrow to lament together over the death of our brother Lord. For such has been your loss. We will sit together in our grief and mingle our tears together, and we four brothers will wipe off the tears from your eyes, so that for a day period you might have peace of mind. This we say and do, we four brothers.

2 Now hear us again, for when a person is in great grief caused by death, his ears are closed up and he cannot hear, and such is your condition now.

We will therefore remove the obstruction (grief) from your ears, so that for a day period you may have perfect hearing again. This we say and do, we four brothers.

3 Continue to hear the expression of us four brothers, for when a person is in great sorrow his throat is stopped with grief and such is your case now. We will therefore remove the obstruction (grief) so that for a day period you may enjoy perfect breathing and speech. This we say and do, we four brothers.

The foregoing part of the Condolence Ceremony is to be performed outside of the place of meeting.

Then the bereaved will appoint two of their Chief Warriors to conduct the four brothers into the place of meeting.

4 Continue to hear the expression of us four brothers, for when a person is in great grief caused by death, he appears to be deformed, so that our forefathers have made a form which their children may use in condoling with each other (Ja-weh-ka-ho-denh) which is that they will treat him a dose of soft drink (medicine) and which when it is taken and settled down in the stomach it will pervade the whole body and strengthen him and restore him to a perfect form of man. This we say and do, we four brothers.

5 Continue to hear the expression of us four brothers.

Now when a person is brought to grief by death, such person's seat or bed seems stained with human blood, such is now your case. We therefore wipe off those stains with soft linen, so that your seat and bed may be clean and so that you may enjoy peace for a day, for we may scarcely have taken our seats before we shall be surprised to hear of another death. This we say and do, we four brothers.

6 Continue to hear the expression of us four brothers. When a person is brought to grief through death, he is confined in the darkness of

deep sorrow, and such is now the case of you three brothers. This we say and do, we four brothers.

7 When a person is brought to grief by death, he seems to lose sight of the sky (blinded with grief) and he is crushed with sorrow. We therefore remove the mist from your eyes, so that the sky may be clear to you. This we say and do, we four brothers.

8 When a person is brought to grief by death, he seems to lose the light of the sun, this is now your case. We therefore remove the mist so that you may see the sun rising over the trees or forest in the East, and watch its course and when it arrives in mid-sky it will shed forth its rays around you, and you shall begin to see your duties and perform the same as usual. This we say and do, we four brothers.

9 Now when the remains are laid and cause the mound of clay (grave) we till the ground and place some nice grass over it and place a nice slab over it, so that his body (that of the dead Lord) may quietly lie in his resting place, and be protected from the heavy wind and great rain storms. This we say and do, we four brothers.

10 Now continue to listen, for when a person is brought to grief, and such is your condition, the sticks of wood from your fire are scattered, caused by death, so we, the four brothers, will gather up the sticks of wood and rekindle the fire, and the smoke shall rise and pierce the sky, so that all the Nations of the Confederacy may see the smoke, and when a person is in great grief caused by the death of some of our rulers the head is bowed down in deep sorrow. We therefore cause you to stand up again, our uncles, and surround the Council fire again and resume your duties. This we say and do, we four brothers.

11 Continue to listen, for when the Great Spirit created us he created a woman as the help-mate of man, and when she is called away by death it is grievously hard, for had she been allowed to live she might have raised a family to inhabit the earth, and so we four brothers raise the woman again (to encourage and cheer up their down-cast spirits) so that you may cheerfully enjoy peace and happiness for a day. This we say and do, we four brothers.

12 Now my uncle Lords you have two relations, a nephew and a niece. They are watching your course. Your niece may see that you are making a mis-step and taking a course whereby your children may suffer ruin or a calamity, or it may be your nephew who will see your evil course and never bear to listen when the woman or Warrior will approach you and remind you of your duties, and ask you to come back and carry out your obligations as a Royaner (or Lord) of the Band. This we say and do, we four brothers.

13 They say that it is hard for any one to allow his mind to be troubled too greatly with sorrow. Never allow yourself to be led to think of destroying yourself by committing suicide, for all things in this world are only vanity. Now we place in your midst a torch. We all have an equal share in the said light, and we would now call all the Ro-de-ya-ner-sonh (Lords) to their places and each perform the duties conferred upon each of them. This we say and do, we four brothers.

Now we return to you the Wampum which we received from you when you suffered the loss by death. We will therefore now conclude our discourse. Now point out to me the man whom I am to proclaim as Chief in place of the deceased.

21

Account of my Life

Benjamin Franklin

Introduction

Benjamin Franklin (1706–90) was a well-known printer, writer, and diplomat who was instrumental in the English colonies' rebellion against British authority. Franklin was a co-author of the Declaration of Independence and the Articles of Confederation. The short article on his life, of which this is an extract, was started in Passy in 1784, while he was ambassador to France. *The Autobiography*, written in the form of several letters, was published posthumously.

It is some time since I receiv'd the above Letters [letters received from Benjamin Vaughan, not included here], but I have been too busy till now to think of complying with the Request they contain. It might too be much better done if I were at home among my Papers, which would aid my Memory, & help to ascertain Dates. But my Return being uncertain, and having just now a little Leisure, I will endeavour to recollect & write what I can; If I live to get home, it may there be corrected and improv'd.

Not having any Copy here of what is already written, I know not whether an Account is given of the means I used to establish the Philadelphia publick Library, which from a small Beginning is now become so considerable, though I remember to have come down to near the Time of that Transaction, 1730. I will therefore begin here, with an Account of it, which may be struck out if found to have been already given.

Taken from *The Autobiography, Writings* (New York: The Library of America, 1987).

At the time I establish'd my self in Pennsylvania, there was not a good Bookseller's Shop in any of the Colonies to the Southward of Boston. In New-York & Philad'a the Printers were indeed Stationers, they sold only Paper, &c. Almanacks, Ballads, and a few common School Books. Those who lov'd Reading were oblig'd to send for their Books from England. The Members of the Junto had each a few. We had left the Alehouse where we first met, and hired a Room to hold our Club in. I propos'd that we should all of us bring our Books to that Room, where they would not only be ready to consult in our Conferences, but become a common Benefit, each of us being at Liberty to borrow such as he wish'd to read at home. This was accordingly done, and for some time contented us. Finding the Advantage of this little Collection, I propos'd to render the Benefit from Books more common by commencing a Public Subscription Library. I drew a Sketch of the Plan and Rules that would be necessary, and got a skilful Conveyancer Mr Charles Brockden to put the whole in Form of Articles of Agreement to be subscribed, by which each Subscriber engag'd to pay a certain Sum down for the first Purchase of Books and an annual Contribution for encreasing them. So few were the Readers at that time in Philadelphia, and the Majority of us so poor, that I was not able with great Industry to find more than Fifty Persons, mostly young Tradesmen, willing to pay down for this purpose Forty shillings each, & Ten Shillings per Annum. On this little Fund we began. The Books were imported. The Library was open one Day in the Week for lending them to the Subscribers, on their Promisory Notes to pay Double the Value if not duly returned. The Institution soon manifested its Utility, was imitated by other Towns and in other Provinces, the Librarys were augmented by Donations, Reading became fashionable, and our People having no publick Amusements to divert their Attention from Study became better acquainted with Books, and in a few Years were observ'd by Strangers to be better instructed & more intelligent than People of the same Rank generally are in other Countries.

When we were about to sign the above-mentioned Articles, which were to be binding on us, our Heirs, &c for fifty Years, Mr Brockden, the Scrivener, said to us, "You are young Men, but it is scarce probable that any of you will live to see the Expiration of the Term fix'd in this Instrument." A Number of us, however, are yet living: But the Instrument was after a few Years rendred null by a Charter that incorporated & gave Perpetuity to the Company.

The Objections, & Reluctances I met with in Soliciting the Subscriptions, made me soon feel the Impropriety of presenting one's self as the Proposer of any useful Project that might be suppos'd to raise one's Reputation in the smallest degree above that of one's Neighbours, when one has need of their Assistance to accomplish that Project. I therefore put my self as much as I could out of sight, and stated it as a Scheme of *a Number of Friends*, who had requested me to go about and propose it to such as they thought Lovers of Reading. In this way my Affair went on more smoothly, and I ever after practis'd it on such Occasions; and from my frequent Successes, can heartily recommend it. The present little Sacrifice of your Vanity will afterwards be amply repaid. If it remains a while uncertain to whom the Merit belongs, some one more vain than yourself will be encourag'd to claim it, and then even Envy will be dispos'd to do you Justice, by plucking those assum'd Feathers, & restoring them to their right Owner.

This Library afforded me the Means of Improvement by constant Study, for which I set apart an Hour or two each Day; and thus repair'd in some Degree the Loss of the Learned Education my Father once intended for me. Reading was the only Amusement I allow'd my self. I spent no time in Taverns, Games, or Frolicks of any kind. And my Industry in my Business continu'd as indefatigable as it was necessary. I was in debt for my

Printing-house, I had a young Family coming on to be educated, and I had to contend with for Business two Printers who were establish'd in the Place before me. My Circumstances however grew daily easier: my original Habits of Frugality continuing. And My Father having among his Instructions to me when a Boy, frequently repeated a Proverb of Solomon, "*Seest thou a Man diligent in his Calling, he shall stand before Kings, he shall not stand before mean Men.*" I from thence consider'd Industry as a Means of obtaining Wealth and Distinction, which encourag'd me; tho' I did not think that I should ever literally stand before Kings, which however has since happened; for I have stood before five, & even had the honour of sitting down with one, the King of Denmark, to Dinner.

We have an English Proverb that says,

  He that would thrive
  Must ask his Wife;

it was lucky for me that I had one as much dispos'd to Industry & Frugality as myself. She assisted me chearfully in my Business, folding & stitching Pamphlets, tending Shop, purchasing old Linen Rags for the Paper-makers, &c &c. We kept no idle Servants, our Table was plain & simple, our Furniture of the cheapest. For instance my Breakfast was a long time Bread & Milk (no Tea) and I ate it out of a twopenny earthen Porringer with a Pewter Spoon. But mark how Luxury will enter Families, and make a Progress, in Spite of Principle. Being Call'd one Morning to Breakfast, I found it in a China Bowl with a Spoon of Silver. They had been bought for me without my Knowledge by my Wife, and had cost her the enormous Sum of three and twenty Shillings, for which she had no other Excuse or Apology to make, but that she thought *her* Husband deserv'd a Silver Spoon & China Bowl as well as any of his Neighbours. This was the first Appearance of Plate & China in our House, which afterwards in a Course of Years as our Wealth encreas'd, augmented gradually to several Hundred Pounds in Value.

I had been religiously educated as a Presbyterian; and tho' some of the Dogmas of that Persuasion, such as the Eternal Decrees of God, Election, Reprobation, &c. appear'd to me unintelligible, others doubtful, & I early absented myself from the Public Assemblies of the Sect, Sunday being my Studying-Day, I never was without some religious Principles; I never doubted, for instance, the Existance of the Deity, that he made the World, &

govern'd it by his Providence; that the most acceptable Service of God was the doing Good to Man; that our Souls are immortal; and that all Crime will be punished & Virtue rewarded either here or hereafter; these I esteem'd the Essentials of every Religion, and being to be found in all the Religions we had in our Country I respected them all, tho' with different degrees of Respect as I found them more or less mix'd with other Articles which without any Tendency to inspire, promote or confirm Morality, serv'd principally to divide us & make us unfriendly to one another. This Respect to all, with an Opinion that the worst had some good Effects, induc'd me to avoid all Discourse that might tend to lessen the good Opinion another might have of his own Religion; and as our Province increas'd in People and new Places of worship were continually wanted, & generally erected by voluntary Contribution, my Mite for such purpose, whatever might be the Sect, was never refused.

Tho' I seldom attended any Public Worship, I had still an Opinion of its Propriety, and of its Utility when rightly conducted, and I regularly paid my annual Subscription for the Support of the only Presbyterian Minister or Meeting we had in Philadelphia. He us'd to visit me sometimes as a Friend, and admonish me to attend his Administrations, and I was now and then prevail'd on to do so, once for five Sundays successively. Had he been, *in my Opinion*, a good Preacher perhaps I might have continued, notwithstanding the occasion I had for the Sunday's Leisure in my Course of Study: But his Discourses were chiefly either polemic Arguments, or Explications of the peculiar Doctrines of our Sect, and were all to me very dry, uninteresting and unedifying, since not a single moral Principle was inculcated or enforc'd, their Aim seeming to be rather to make us Presbyterians than good Citizens. At length he took for his Text that Verse of the 4th Chapter of Philippians, *Finally, Brethren, Whatsoever Things are true, honest, just, pure, lovely, or of good report, if there be any virtue, or any praise, think on these Things*; & I imagin'd in a Sermon on such a Text, we could not miss of having some Morality. But he confin'd himself to five Points only as meant by the Apostle, viz. 1. Keeping holy the Sabbath Day. 2. Being diligent in Reading the Holy Scriptures. 3. Attending duly the Publick Worship. 4. Partaking of the Sacrament. 5. Paying a due Respect to God's Ministers. These might be all good Things, but as they were not the kind of good Things that I expected from that Text, I

despaired of ever meeting with them from any other, was disgusted, and attended his Preaching no more. I had some Years before compos'd a little Liturgy or Form of Prayer for my own private Use, viz. in 1728, entitled, *Articles of Belief & Acts of Religion*. I return'd to the Use of this, and went no more to the public Assemblies. My Conduct might be blameable, but I leave it without attempting farther to excuse it, my present purpose being to relate Facts, and not to make Apologies for them.

It was about this time that I conceiv'd the bold and arduous Project of arriving at moral Perfection. I wish'd to live without committing any Fault at any time; I would conquer all that either Natural Inclination, Custom, or Company might lead me into. As I knew, or thought I knew, what was right and wrong, I did not see why I might not *always* do the one and avoid the other. But I soon found I had undertaken a Task of more Difficulty than I had imagined. While my Care was employ'd in guarding against one Fault, I was often surpriz'd by another. Habit took the Advantage of Inattention. Inclination was sometimes too strong for Reason. I concluded at length that the mere speculative Conviction that it was our Interest to be completely virtuous was not sufficient to prevent our Slipping, and that the contrary Habits must be broken and good ones acquir'd and establish'd before we can have any Dependance on a steady, uniform Rectitude of Conduct. For this purpose I therefore contriv'd the following method.

In the various Enumerations of the moral Virtues I had met with in my Reading, I found the Catalogue more or less numerous, as different Writers included more or fewer ideas under the same Name. Temperance, for Example, was by some confin'd to eating and drinking, while by others it was extended to mean the moderating every other Pleasure, Appetite, Inclination, or Passion – bodily or mental, even to our Avarice and Ambition. I propos'd to myself, for the sake of Clearness, to use rather more Names with fewer Ideas annex'd to each than a few Names with more Ideas; and I included under Thirteen Names of Virtues all that at that time occurr'd to me as necessary or desirable, and annex'd to each a short Precept which fully express'd the Extent I gave to its Meaning.

These Names of Virtues with their Precepts were:

1 *Temperance*. Eat not to Dulness. Drink not to Elevation.

2 *Silence*. Speak not but what may benefit others or yourself. Avoid trifling Conversation.

3 *Order*. Let all your Things have their Places. Let each Part of your Business have its Time.

4 *Resolution*. Resolve to perform what you ought. Perform without fail what you resolve.

5 *Frugality*. Make no Expence but to do good to others or yourself; i.e., waste nothing.

6 *Industry*. Lose no Time. Be always employ'd in something useful. Cut off all unnecessary Actions.

7 *Sincerity*. Use no hurtful Deceit. Think innocently and justly; and, if you speak, speak accordingly.

8 *Justice*. Wrong none by doing Injuries or omitting the Benefits that are your Duty.

9 *Moderation*. Avoid Extreams. Forbear resenting Injuries so much as you think they deserve.

10 *Cleanliness*. Tolerate no Uncleanness in Body, Cloaths or Habitation.

11 *Tranquillity*. Be not disturbed at Trifles, or at Accidents common or unavoidable.

12 *Chastity*. Rarely use Venery but for Health or Offspring – never to Dulness, Weakness, or the Injury of your own or another's Peace or Reputation.

13 *Humility*. Imitate Jesus and Socrates.

My intention being to acquire the *Habitude* of all these Virtues, I judg'd it would be well not to distract my Attention by attempting the whole at once, but to fix it on one of them at a time, and when I should be Master of that, then to proceed to another, and so on till I should have gone thro' the thirteen. And as the previous Acquisition of some might facilitate the Acquisition of certain others, I arrang'd them with that View as they stand above. *Temperance* first, as it tends to procure that Coolness & Clearness of Head which is so necessary where constant Vigilance was to be kept up, and Guard maintained, against the unremitting Attraction of ancient Habits, and the Force of perpetual Temptations. This being acquir'd & establish'd, *Silence* would be more easy, and my Desire being to gain Knowledge at the same time that I improv'd in Virtue, and considering that in Conversation it was obtain'd rather by the Use of the Ears than of the Tongue, & therefore wishing to break a Habit I was getting into of Prattling, Punning & Joking, which only made me acceptable to trifling Company, I gave *Silence* the second Place. This, and the next, *Order*, I expected would allow me more Time for attending to my Project and my Studies; *Resolution* once become habitual, would keep me firm in my Endeavours to obtain all the subsequent Virtues; *Frugality* & *Industry*, by freeing me from my remaining Debt, & producing Affluence & Independance would make more easy the Practice of *Sincerity* and *Justice*, &c. &c. Conceiving then that agreeable to the Advice of Pythagoras in his Golden Verses,[1] daily Examination would be necessary, I contriv'd the following Method for conducting that Examination.

I made a little Book in which I allotted a Page for each of the Virtues. I rul'd each Page with red Ink so as to have seven Columns, one for each Day of the Week, marking each Column with a Letter for the Day. I cross'd these Columns with thirteen red Lines, marking the Beginning of each Line with the first Letter of one of the Virtues, on which Line & in its proper Column I might mark by a little black Spot every Fault I found upon Examination, to have been committed respecting that Virtue upon that Day [see figure 21.1].

I determined to give a Week's strict Attention to each of the Virtues successively. Thus in the first Week my great Guard was to avoid every the least Offence against Temperance, leaving the other Virtues to their ordinary Chance, only marking every Evening the Faults of the Day. Thus if in the first Week I could keep my first Line marked T clear of Spots, I suppos'd the Habit of that Virtue so much strengthen'd and its opposite

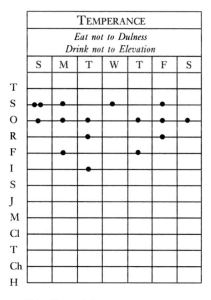

TEMPERANCE						
Eat not to Dulness *Drink not to Elevation*						
S	M	T	W	T	F	S
T						
S ●●	●		●		●	
O ●	●	●		●	●	●
R		●			●	
F	●				●	
I ●						
S						
J						
M						
Cl						
T						
Ch						
H						

Figure 21.1 Form of the pages

weaken'd, that I might venture extending my Attention to include the next, and for the following Week keep both Lines clear of Spots. Proceeding thus to the last, I could go thro' a Course compleat in Thirteen Weeks, and four Courses in a Year. And like him who having a Garden to weed, does not attempt to eradicate all the bad Herbs at once, which would exceed his Reach and his Strength, but works on one of the Beds at a time, & having accomplish'd the first proceeds to a second; so I should have (I hoped) the encouraging Pleasure of seeing on my Pages the Progress I made in Virtue, by clearing successively my Lines of their Spots, till in the End by a Number of Courses, I should be happy in viewing a clean Book after a thirteen Weeks daily Examination.

This my little Book had for its Motto these Lines from *Addison's Cato*:

Here will I hold: If there is a Pow'r above us,
(And that there is, all Nature cries aloud
Thro' all her Works) he must delight in Virtue,
And that which he delights in must be happy.

Another from *Cicero*:

O Vitae Philosophia Dux! O Virtutum indagatrix, expultrixque vitiorum! Unus dies bene, & ex preceptis tuis actus, peccanti immortalitati est anteponendus.

Another from the Proverbs of Solomon speaking of Wisdom or Virtue:

Length of Days is in her right hand, and in her Left Hand Riches and Honours; Her Ways are Ways of Pleasantness, and all her Paths are Peace. (III, 16, 17)

And conceiving God to be the Fountain of Wisdom, I thought it right and necessary to solicit his Assistance for obtaining it; to this End I form'd the following little Prayer, which was prefix'd to my Tables of Examination; for daily Use:

O Powerful Goodness! bountiful Father! merciful Guide! Increase in me that Wisdom which discovers my truest Interests; Strengthen my Resolutions to perform what that Wisdom dictates. Accept my kind Offices to thy other Children, as the only Return in my Power for thy continual Favours to me.

I us'd also sometimes a little Prayer which I took from *Thomson's* Poems. viz.:

Father of Light and Life, thou Good supreme,
O teach me what is good, teach me thy self!
Save me from Folly, Vanity and Vice,
From every low Pursuit, and fill my Soul
With Knowledge, conscious Peace,
   & Virtue pure,
Sacred, substantial, neverfading Bliss!

The Precept of *Order* requiring that *every Part of my Business should have its allotted Time*, one Page in my little Book contain'd the following Scheme of Employment for the Twenty-four Hours of a natural Day [see figure 21.2].

I enter'd upon the Execution of this Plan for Self Examination, and continu'd it with occasional Intermissions for some time. I was surpriz'd to find myself so much fuller of Faults than I had imagined, but I had the Satisfaction of seeing them diminish. To avoid the Trouble of renewing now & then my little Book, which by scraping out the Marks on the Paper of old Faults to make room for new Ones in a new Course, became full of Holes: I transferr'd my Tables & Precepts to the Ivory Leaves of a Memorandum Book, on which the Lines were drawn with red Ink that made a durable Stain, and on those Lines I mark'd my Faults with a black Lead Pencil, which Marks I could easily wipe out with a wet Sponge. After a while I went thro' one Course only in a Year, and afterwards only one in several Years; till at length I omitted them entirely, being employ'd in Voyages & Business abroad with a Multiplicity of Affairs, that interfered. But I always carried my little Book with me. My Scheme of ORDER, gave me the most Trouble, and I found, that tho' it might be practicable where a Man's Business was such as to leave him the Disposition of his Time, that of a Journey-man Printer for instance, it was not possible to be exactly observ'd by a Master, who must mix with the World, and often receive People of Business at their own Hours. *Order* too, with regard to Places for Things, Papers, &c. I found extreamly difficult to acquire. I had not been early accustomed to it, & having an exceeding good Memory, I was not so sensible of the Inconvenience attending Want of Method. This Article therefore cost me so much painful Attention & my Faults in it vex'd me so much, and I made so little Progress in Amendment, & had such frequent Relapses, that I was almost ready to give

The Morning Question:	5	Rise, wash, and address *Powerful Goodness*; contrive
What Good shall I do	6	Day's Business and take the Resolution of the Day;
this Day?	7	prosecute the present Study; and breakfast
	8	
	9	Work
	10	
	11	
	12	Read, or overlook my Accounts,
	1	and dine
	2	
	3	Work
	4	
	5	
	6	Put Things in their Places, Supper,
	7	Musick, or Diversion, or Conversation
Evening Question:	8	
What Good have I	9	Examination of the Day
done to day?	10	
	11	
	12	
	1	Sleep
	2	
	3	
	4	

Figure 21.2 Scheme of employment

up the Attempt, and content my self with a faulty Character in that respect. Like the Man who in buying an Ax of a Smith my Neighbour, desired to have the whole of its Surface as bright as the Edge; the Smith consented to grind it bright for him if he would turn the Wheel. He turn'd while the Smith press'd the broad Face of the Ax hard & heavily on the Stone, which made the Turning of it very fatiguing. The Man came every now & then from the Wheel to see how the Work went on; and at length would take his Ax as it was without farther Grinding. No, says the Smith, Turn on, turn on; we shall have it bright by and by; as yet 'tis only speckled. Yes, says the Man; but – *I think I like a speckled Ax best*. And I believe this may have been the Case with many who having for want of some such Means as I employ'd found the Difficulty of obtaining good, & breaking bad Habits, in other Points of Vice & Virtue, have given up the Struggle, & concluded that *a speckled Ax was best*. For something that pretended to be Reason was every now and then suggesting to me, that such extream Nicety as I exacted of my self might be a kind of Foppery in Morals, which if it were known would make me ridiculous; that a perfect Character might be attended with the Inconvenience of being envied and hated; and that a benevolent Man

should allow a few Faults in himself, to keep his Friends in Countenance. In Truth I found myself incorrigible with respect to *Order*; and now I am grown old, and my Memory bad, I feel very sensibly the want of it. But on the whole, tho' I never arrived at the Perfection I had been so ambitious of obtaining, but fell far short of it, yet I was by the Endeavour made a better and a happier Man than I otherwise should have been, if I had not attempted it; As those who aim at perfect Writing by imitating the engraved Copies, tho' they never reach the wish'd for Excellence of those Copies, their Hand is mended by the Endeavour, and is tolerable while it continues fair & legible.

And it may be well my Posterity should be informed, that to this little Artifice, with the Blessing of God, their Ancestor ow'd the constant Felicity of his Life down to his 79th Year in which this is written. What Reverses may attend the Remainder is in the Hand of Providence: But if they arrive the Reflection on past Happiness enjoy'd ought to help his Bearing them with more Resignation. To *Temperance* he ascribes his long-continu'd Health, & what is still left to him of a good Constitution. To *Industry* and *Frugality* the early Easiness of his Circumstances, & Acquisition of his Fortune, with all that Knowledge which enabled him to be an useful Citizen, and obtain'd for him some Degree of Reputation among the Learned. To *Sincerity* & *Justice* the Confidence of his Country, and the honourable Employs it conferr'd upon him. And to the joint Influence of the whole Mass of the Virtues, even in their imperfect State he was able to acquire them, all that Evenness of Temper, & that Chearfulness in Conversation which makes his Company still sought for, & agreable even to his younger Acquaintance. I hope therefore that some of my Descendants may follow the Example & reap the Benefit.

It will be remark'd that, tho' my Scheme was not wholly without Religion there was in it no Mark of any of the distinguishing Tenets of any particular Sect. I had purposely avoided them; for being fully persuaded of the Utility and Excellency of my Method, and that it might be serviceable to People in all Religions, and intending some time or other to publish it, I would not have any thing in it that should prejudice any one of any Sect against it. I purposed writing a little Comment on each Virtue, in which I would have shown the Advantages of possessing it, & the Mischiefs attending its opposite Vice; and I should have called my Book the ART *of Virtue*, because it would have shown the *Means & Manner* of obtaining Virtue; which would have distinguish'd it from the mere Exhortation to be good, that does not instruct & indicate the Means; but is like the Apostle's Man of verbal Charity, who only, without showing to the Naked & the Hungry *how* or where they might get Cloaths or Victuals, exhorted them to be fed & clothed: *James* II, 15, 16.

But it so happened that my Intention of writing & publishing this Comment was never fulfilled. I did indeed, from time to time put down short Hints of the Sentiments, Reasonings, &c. to be made use of in it; some of which I have still by me: But the necessary close Attention to private Business in the earlier part of Life, and public Business since, have occasioned my postponing it. For it being connected in my Mind with a *great and extensive Project* that required the whole Man to execute, and which an unforeseen Succession of Employs prevented my attending to, it has hitherto remain'd unfinish'd.

In this Piece it was my Design to explain and enforce this Doctrine, that vicious Actions are not hurtful because they are forbidden, but forbidden because they are hurtful, the Nature of Man alone consider'd: That it was therefore every one's Inter-est to be virtuous, who wish'd to be happy even in this World. And I should from this Circumstance, there being always in the World a Number of rich Merchants, Nobility, States and Princes, who have need of honest Instruments for the Management of their Affairs, and such being so rare, have endeavoured to convince young Persons, that no Qualities were so likely to make a poor Man's Fortune as those of Probity & Integrity.

My List of Virtues contain'd at first but twelve: But a Quaker Friend having kindly inform'd me that I was generally thought proud; that my Pride show'd itself frequently in Conversation; that I was not content with being in the right when discussing any Point, but was overbearing & rather insolent; of which he convinc'd me by mentioning several Instances; I determined endeavouring to cure myself if I could of this Vice or Folly among the rest, and I added *Humility* to my List, giving an extensive Meaning to the Word. I cannot boast of much Success in acquiring the *Reality* of this Virtue; but I had a good deal with regard to the *Appearance* of it. I made it a Rule to forbear all direct Contradiction to the Sentiments of others, and all positive Assertion of my own. I even forbid myself agreable to the old Laws of our Junto, the Use of every Word or Expression in the Language that imported a fix'd Opinion; such as *certainly, undoubtedly*, &c. and I adopted instead of them, *I conceive, I apprehend*, or *I imagine* a thing to be so or so, or it so appears to me at present. When another asserted something that I thought an Error, I deny'd my self the Pleasure of contradicting him abruptly, and of showing immediately some Absurdity in his Proposition; and in answering I began by observing that in certain Cases or Circumstances his Opinion would be right, but that in the present case there *appear'd* or *seem'd* to me some Difference, &c. I soon found the Advantage of this Change in my Manners. The Conversations I engag'd in went on more pleasantly. The modest way in which I propos'd my Opinions, procur'd them a readier Reception and less Contradiction; I had less Mortification when I was found to be in the wrong, and I more easily prevail'd with others to give up their Mistakes & join with me when I happen'd to be in the right. And this Mode, which I at first put on, with some violence to natural Inclination, became at length so easy & so habitual to me, that perhaps for these Fifty Years past no one has ever heard a dogmatical Expression escape me. And to this Habit (after my Character of Integrity) I think it principally owing, that I had early so much Weight with my Fellow Citizens, when I proposed new Institutions, or Alterations in the old; and so much Influence in public Councils when I became a Member. For I was but a bad Speaker, never eloquent, subject to much Hesitation in my choice of Words, hardly correct in Language, and yet I generally carried my Points.

In reality there is perhaps no one of our natural Passions so hard to subdue as *Pride*. Disguise it, struggle with it, beat it down, stifle it, mortify it as much as one pleases, it is still alive, and will every now and then peep out and show itself. You will see it perhaps often in this History. For even if I could conceive that I had compleatly overcome it, I should probably be proud of my Humility.

Note

1 Let not the stealing God of Sleep surprize,
Nor creep in Slumbers on thy weary Eyes,
Ere ev'ry Action of the former Day,
Strictly thou dost, and *righteously* survey.
With Rev'rence at thy own Tribunal stand,
And answer justly to thy own Demand.
Where have I been? In what have I transgrest?
What Good or Ill has this Day's Life exprest?
Where have I fail'd in what I ought to do?

In what to GOD, to Man, or to myself I owe?
Inquire severe whate'er from first to last,
From Morning's Dawn till Ev'nings Gloom has past.
If Evil were thy Deeds, repenting mourn,
And let thy Soul with strong Remorse be torn:
If Good, the Good with Peace of Mind repay,
And to thy secret Self with Pleasure say,
Rejoice, my Heart, for all went well to Day.

22

The Federalist Papers

Alexander Hamilton, James Madison, John Jay

Introduction

The Federalist Papers were published in New York newspapers in 1787 and 1788 to help make a case for the ratification of the United States Constitution. Although published as letters from "Publius," the papers were written by Alexander Hamilton, James Madison (the author of letters 10 and 51), and John Jay (who wrote letter 2). The selections here raise the issue of how a strong centralized government will respond to forms of diversity in the European American political union.

No. 2: Jay

When the people of America reflect that they are now called upon to decide a question, which in its consequences must prove one of the most important that ever engaged their attention, the propriety of their taking a very comprehensive, as well as a very serious, view of it will be evident.

Nothing is more certain than the indispensable necessity of government; and it is equally undeniable that whenever and however it is instituted, the people must cede to it some of their natural rights, in order to vest it with requisite powers. It is well worthy of consideration, therefore, whether it would conduce more to the interest of the people of America that they should, to all general pur-

Taken from *Federalist Papers*, 2, 10, 51 (New York: New American Library, Mentor Books, 1961), pp. 37–9, 77–84, 320–5.

poses, be one nation, under one federal government, than that they should divide themselves into separate confederacies and give to the head of each the same kind of powers which they are advised to place in one national government.

It has until lately been a received and uncontradicted opinion that the prosperity of the people of America depended on their continuing firmly united, and the wishes, prayers, and efforts of our best and wisest citizens have been constantly directed to that object. But politicians now appear who insist that this opinion is erroneous, and that instead of looking for safety and happiness in union, we ought to seek it in a division of the States into distinct confederacies or sovereignties. However extraordinary this new doctrine may appear, it nevertheless has its advocates; and certain characters who were much opposed to it formerly are at present of the number. Whatever may be the arguments or inducements which have wrought this change in the sentiments and declarations of these gentlemen, it certainly would not be wise in the people at large to adopt these new political tenets without being fully convinced that they are founded in truth and sound policy.

It has often given me pleasure to observe that independent America was not composed of detached and distant territories, but that one connected, fertile, wide-spreading country was the portion of our western sons of liberty. Providence has in a particular manner blessed it with a variety of soils and productions and watered it with innumerable streams for the delight and accommodation of its inhabitants. A succession of navigable waters forms a kind of chain round its borders, as if to bind it together; while the most noble rivers in the world, running at convenient distances, present them with highways for the easy communication of friendly aids and the mutual transportation and exchange of their various commodities.

With equal pleasure I have as often taken notice that Providence has been pleased to give this one connected country to one united people – a people descended from the same ancestors, speaking the same language, professing the same religion, attached to the same principles of government, very similar in their manners and customs, and who, by their joint counsels, arms, and efforts, fighting side by side throughout a long and bloody war, have nobly established their general liberty and independence.

This country and this people seem to have been made for each other, and it appears as if it was the design of Providence that an inheritance so proper and convenient for a band of brethren, united to each other by the strongest ties, should never be split into a number of unsocial, jealous, and alien sovereignties.

Similar sentiments have hitherto prevailed among all orders and denominations of men among us. To all general purposes we have uniformly been one people; each individual citizen everywhere enjoying the same national rights, privileges, and protection. As a nation we have made peace and war; as a nation we have vanquished our common enemies; as a nation we have formed alliances, and made treaties, and entered into various compacts and conventions with foreign states.
[...]

No. 10: Madison

Among the numerous advantages promised by a well-constructed Union, none deserves to be more accurately developed than its tendency to break and control the violence of faction. The friend of popular governments never finds himself so much alarmed for their character and fate as when he contemplates their propensity to this dangerous vice. He will not fail, therefore, to set a due value on any plan which, without violating the principles to which he is attached, provides a proper cure for it. The instability, injustice, and confusion introduced into the public councils have, in truth, been the mortal diseases under which popular governments have everywhere perished, as they continue

to be the favorite and fruitful topics from which the adversaries to liberty derive their most specious declamations. The valuable improvements made by the American constitutions on the popular models, both ancient and modern, cannot certainly be too much admired; but it would be an unwarrantable partiality to contend that they have as effectually obviated the danger on this side, as was wished and expected. Complaints are everywhere heard from our most considerate and virtuous citizens, equally the friends of public and private faith and of public and personal liberty, that our governments are too unstable, that the public good is disregarded in the conflicts of rival parties, and that measures are too often decided, not according to the rules of justice and the rights of the minor party, but by the superior force of an interested and overbearing majority. However anxiously we may wish that these complaints had no foundation, the evidence of known facts will not permit us to deny that they are in some degree true. It will be found, indeed, on a candid review of our situation, that some of the distresses under which we labor have been erroneously charged on the operation of our governments; but it will be found, at the same time, that other causes will not alone account for many of our heaviest misfortunes; and, particularly, for that prevailing and increasing distrust of public engagements and alarm for private rights which are echoed from one end of the continent to the other. These must be chiefly, if not wholly, effects of the unsteadiness and injustice with which a factious spirit has tainted our public administration.

By a faction I understand a number of citizens, whether amounting to a majority or minority of the whole, who are united and actuated by some common impulse of passion, or of interest, adverse to the rights of other citizens, or to the permanent and aggregate interests of the community.

There are two methods of curing the mischiefs of faction: the one, by removing its causes; the other, by controlling its effects.

There are again two methods of removing the causes of faction: the one, by destroying the liberty which is essential to its existence; the other, by giving to every citizen the same opinions, the same passions, and the same interests.

It could never be more truly said than of the first remedy that it was worse than the disease. Liberty is to faction what air is to fire, an aliment without which it instantly expires. But it could not be a less folly to abolish liberty, which is essential to political life, because it nourishes faction than it would be to wish the annihilation of air, which is essential to animal life, because it imparts to fire its destructive agency.

The second expedient is as impracticable as the first would be unwise. As long as the reason of man continues fallible, and he is at liberty to exercise it, different opinions will be formed. As long as the connection subsists between his reason and his self-love, his opinions and his passions will have a reciprocal influence on each other; and the former will be objects to which the latter will attach themselves. The diversity in the faculties of men, from which the rights of property originate, is not less an insuperable obstacle to a uniformity of interests. The protection of these faculties is the first object of government. From the protection of different and unequal faculties of acquiring property, the possession of different degrees and kinds of property immediately results; and from the influence of these on the sentiments and views of the respective proprietors ensues a division of the society into different interests and parties.

The latent causes of faction are thus sown in the nature of man; and we see them everywhere brought into different degrees of activity, according to the different circumstances of civil society. A zeal for different opinions concerning religion, concerning government, and many other points, as well of speculation as of practice; an attachment to different leaders ambitiously contending for preeminence and power; or to persons of other descriptions whose fortunes have been interesting to the human passions, have, in turn, divided mankind into parties, inflamed them with mutual animosity, and rendered them much more disposed to vex and oppress each other than to co-operate for their common good. So strong is this propensity of mankind to fall into mutual animosities that where no substantial occasion presents itself the most frivolous and fanciful distinctions have been sufficient to kindle their unfriendly passions and excite their most violent conflicts. But the most common and durable source of factions has been the various and unequal distribution of property. Those who hold and those who are without property have ever formed distinct interests in society. Those who are creditors, and those who are debtors, fall under a like discrimination. A landed interest, a manufacturing interest, a mercantile interest, a moneyed interest, with many lesser interests, grow up of necessity in civilized nations, and divide them into different classes, actuated by different sentiments and views. The regulation of these various and interfering interests forms the principal task of modern legislation and involves the spirit of party and faction in the necessary and ordinary operations of government.

No man is allowed to be a judge in his own cause, because his interest would certainly bias his judgment, and, not improbably, corrupt his integrity. With equal, nay with greater reason, a body of men are unfit to be both judges and parties at the same time; yet what are many of the most important acts of legislation but so many judicial determinations, not indeed concerning the rights of single persons, but concerning the rights of large bodies of citizens? And what are the different classes of legislators but advocates and parties to the causes which they determine? Is a law proposed concerning private debts? It is a question to which the creditors are parties on one side and the debtors on the other. Justice ought to hold the balance between them. Yet the parties are, and must be, themselves the judges; and the most numerous party, or in other words, the most powerful faction must be expected to prevail. Shall domestic manufacturers be encouraged, and in what degree, by restrictions on foreign manufacturers? are questions which would be differently decided by the landed and the manufacturing classes, and probably by neither with a sole regard to justice and the public good. The apportionment of taxes on the various descriptions of property is an act which seems to require the most exact impartiality; yet there is, perhaps, no legislative act in which greater opportunity and temptation are given to a predominant party to trample on the rules of justice. Every shilling with which they overburden the inferior number is a shilling saved to their own pockets.

It is in vain to say that enlightened statesmen will be able to adjust these clashing interests and render them all subservient to the public good. Enlightened statesmen will not always be at the helm. Nor, in many cases, can such an adjustment be made at all without taking into view indirect and remote considerations, which will rarely prevail over the immediate interest which one party may find in disregarding the rights of another or the good of the whole.

The inference to which we are brought is that the *causes* of faction cannot be removed and that relief is only to be sought in the means of controlling its *effects*.

If a faction consists of less than a majority, relief is supplied by the republican principle, which enables the majority to defeat its sinister views by regular vote. It may clog the administration, it may convulse the society; but it will be unable to execute and mask its violence under the forms of the Constitution. When a majority is included in a faction, the form of popular government, on the other hand, enables it to sacrifice to its ruling passion or interest both the public good and the rights of other citizens. To secure the public good and private rights against the danger of such a faction, and at the same time to preserve the spirit and the form of popular government, is then the great object to which our inquiries are directed. Let me add that it is the great desideratum by which alone this form of government can be rescued from the opprobrium under which it has so long labored and be recommended to the esteem and adoption of mankind.

By what means is this object attainable? Evidently by one of two only. Either the existence of the same passion or interest in a majority at the same time must be prevented, or the majority, having such coexistent passion or interest, must be rendered, by their number and local situation, unable to concert and carry into effect schemes of oppression. If the impulse and the opportunity be suffered to coincide, we well know that neither moral nor religious motives can be relied on as an adequate control. They are not found to be such on the injustice and violence of individuals, and lose their efficacy in proportion to the number combined together, that is, in proportion as their efficacy becomes needful.

From this view of the subject it may be concluded that a pure democracy, by which I mean a society consisting of a small number of citizens, who assemble and administer the government in person, can admit of no cure for the mischiefs of faction. A common passion or interest will, in almost every case, be felt by a majority of the whole; a communication and concert results from the form of government itself; and there is nothing to check the inducements to sacrifice the weaker party or an obnoxious individual. Hence it is that such democracies have ever been spectacles of turbulence and contention; have ever been found incompatible with personal security or the rights of property; and have in general been as short in their lives as they have been violent in their deaths. Theoretic politicians, who have patronized this species of government, have erroneously supposed that by reducing mankind to a perfect equality in their political rights, they would at the same time be perfectly equalized and assimilated in their possessions, their opinions, and their passions.

A republic, by which I mean a government in which the scheme of representation takes place, opens a different prospect and promises the cure for which we are seeking. Let us examine the points in which it varies from pure democracy, and we shall comprehend both the nature of the cure and the efficacy which it must derive from the Union.

The two great points of difference between a democracy and a republic are: first, the delegation of the government, in the latter, to a small number of citizens elected by the rest; secondly, the greater number of citizens and greater sphere of country over which the latter may be extended.

The effect of the first difference is, on the one hand, to refine and enlarge the public views by passing them through the medium of a chosen body of citizens, whose wisdom may best discern the true interest of their country and whose patriotism and love of justice will be least likely to sacrifice it to temporary or partial considerations. Under such a regulation it may well happen that the public voice, pronounced by the representatives of the people, will be more consonant to the public good than if pronounced by the people themselves, convened for the purpose. On the other hand, the effect may be inverted. Men of factious tempers, of local prejudices, or of sinister designs, may, by intrigue, by corruption, or by other means, first obtain the suffrages, and then betray the interests of the people. The question resulting is, whether small or extensive republics are most favorable to the election of proper guardians of the public weal; and it is clearly decided in favor of the latter by two obvious considerations.

In the first place it is to be remarked that however small the republic may be the representatives must be raised to a certain number in order to guard against the cabals of a few; and that however large it may be they must be limited to a certain number in order to guard against the confusion of a multitude. Hence, the number of representatives in the two cases not being in proportion to that of the constituents, and being proportionally greatest in the small republic, it follows that if the proportion of fit characters be not less in the large than in the small republic, the former will present a greater option, and consequently a greater probability of a fit choice.

In the next place, as each representative will be chosen by a greater number of citizens in the large than in the small republic, it will be more difficult for unworthy candidates to practise with success the vicious arts by which elections are too often carried; and the suffrages of the people being more free, will be more likely to center on men who possess the most attractive merit and the most diffusive and established characters.

It must be confessed that in this, as in most other cases, there is a mean, on both sides of which inconveniences will be found to lie. By enlarging too much the number of electors, you render the representative too little acquainted with all their local circumstances and lesser interests; as by reducing it too much, you render him unduly attached to these, and too little fit to comprehend and pursue great and national objects. The federal Constitution forms a happy combination in this respect; the great and aggregate interests being referred to the national, the local and particular to the State legislatures.

The other point of difference is the greater number of citizens and extent of territory which may be brought within the compass of republican than of democratic government; and it is this circumstance principally which renders factious combinations less to be dreaded in the former than in the latter. The smaller the society, the fewer probably will be the distinct parties and interests composing it; the fewer the distinct parties and interests, the more frequently will a majority be found of the same party; and the smaller the number of individuals composing a majority, and the smaller the compass within which they are placed, the more easily will they concert and execute their plans of oppression. Extend the sphere and you take in a greater variety of parties and interests; you make it less probable that a majority of the whole will have a common motive to invade the rights of other citizens; or if such a common motive exists, it will be more difficult for all who feel it to discover their own strength and to act in unison with each other. Besides other impediments, it may be remarked that, where there is a consciousness of unjust or dishonorable purposes, communication is always checked by distrust in proportion to the number whose concurrence is necessary.

Hence, it clearly appears that the same advantage which a republic has over a democracy in controlling the effects of faction is enjoyed by a large over a small republic – is enjoyed by the Union over the States composing it. Does this advantage consist in the substitution of representatives whose enlightened views and virtuous sentiments render them superior to local prejudices and to schemes of injustice? It will not be denied that the representation of the Union will be most likely to possess these requisite endowments. Does it consist in the greater security afforded by a greater variety of parties, against the event of any one party being able to outnumber and oppress the rest? In an equal degree does the increased variety of parties comprised within the Union increase this security? Does it, in fine, consist in the greater obstacles opposed to the concert and accomplishment of the secret wishes of an unjust and interested majority? Here again the extent of the Union gives it the most palpable advantage.

The influence of factious leaders may kindle a flame within their particular States but will be unable to spread a general conflagration through the other States. A religious sect may degenerate into a political faction in a part of the Confederacy; but the variety of sects dispersed over the entire face of it must secure the national councils against any danger from that source. A rage for paper money, for an abolition of debts, for an equal division of property, or for any other improper or wicked project, will be less apt to pervade the whole body of the Union than a particular member of it, in the same proportion as such a malady is more likely to taint a particular county or district than an entire State.

In the extent and proper structure of the Union, therefore, we behold a republican remedy for the diseases most incident to republican government. And according to the degree of pleasure and pride we feel in being republicans ought to be our zeal in cherishing the spirit and supporting the character of federalists.

No. 51: Madison

To what expedient, then, shall we finally resort, for maintaining in practice the necessary partition of power among the several departments as laid down in the Constitution? The only answer that can be given is that as all these exterior provisions are found to be inadequate the defect must be supplied, by so contriving the interior structure of the government as that its several constituent parts may, by their mutual relations, be the means of keeping each other in their proper places. Without presuming to undertake a full development of this important idea I will hazard a few general observations which may perhaps place it in a clearer light, and enable us to form a more correct judgment of the principles and structure of the government planned by the convention.

In order to lay a due foundation for that separate and distinct exercise of the different powers of government, which to a certain extent is admitted on all hands to be essential to the preservation of liberty, it is evident that each department should have a will of its own; and consequently should be so constituted that the members of each should have as little agency as possible in the appointment of the members of the others. Were this principle rigorously adhered to, it would require that all the appointments for the supreme executive, legislative, and judiciary magistracies should be drawn from the same fountain of authority, the people, through channels having no communication whatever with one another. Perhaps such a plan of constructing the several departments would be less difficult in practice than it may in contemplation appear. Some difficulties, however, and some additional expense would attend the execution of it. Some deviations, therefore, from the principle must be admitted. In the constitution of the judiciary department in particular, it might be inexpedient to insist rigorously on the principle: first, because peculiar qualifications being essential in the members, the primary consideration ought to be to select that mode of choice which best secures these qualifications; second, because the permanent tenure by which the appointments are held in that department must soon destroy all sense of dependence on the authority conferring them.

It is equally evident that the members of each department should be as little dependent as possible on those of the others for the emoluments annexed to their offices. Were the executive magistrate, or the judges, not independent of the legislature in this particular, their independence in every other would be merely nominal.

But the great security against a gradual concentration of the several powers in the same department consists in giving to those who administer each department the necessary constitutional means and personal motives to resist encroachments of the others. The provision for defense must in this, as in all other cases, be made commensurate to the danger of attack. Ambition must be made to counteract ambition. The interest of the man must be connected with the constitutional rights of the place. It may be a reflection on human nature that such devices should be necessary to control the abuses of government. But what is government itself but the greatest of all reflections on human nature? If men were angels, no government would be necessary. If angels were to govern men, neither external nor internal controls on government would be necessary. In framing a government which is to be administered by men over men, the great difficulty lies in this: you must first enable the government to control the governed; and in the next place oblige it to control itself. A dependence on the people is, no doubt, the primary control on the government; but experience has taught mankind the necessity of auxiliary precautions.

This policy of supplying, by opposite and rival interests, the defect of better motives, might be traced through the whole system of human affairs, private as well as public. We see it particularly displayed in all the subordinate distributions of power, where the constant aim is to divide and arrange the several offices in such a manner as that each may be a check on the other – that the private interest of every individual may be a sentinel over the public rights. These inventions of prudence cannot be less requisite in the distribution of the supreme powers of the State.

But it is not possible to give to each department an equal power of self-defense. In republican government, the legislative authority necessarily predominates. The remedy for this inconveniency is to divide the legislature into different branches; and to render them, by different modes of election and different principles of action, as little connected with each other as the nature of their common functions and their common dependence on the society will admit. It may even be necessary to guard against dangerous encroachments by still further precautions. As the weight of the legislative authority requires that it should be thus divided, the weakness of the executive may require, on the other hand, that it should be fortified. An absolute negative on the legislature appears, at first view, to be the natural defense with which the executive magistrate should be armed. But perhaps it would be neither altogether safe nor alone sufficient. On ordinary occasions it might not be exerted with the requisite firmness, and on extraordinary occasions it might be perfidiously abused. May not this defect of an absolute negative be supplied by some qualified connection between this weaker department and the weaker branch of the stronger department, by which the latter may be led to support the constitutional rights of the former, without being too much detached from the rights of its own department?

If the principles on which these observations are founded be just, as I persuade myself they are, and they be applied as a criterion to the several State constitutions, and to the federal Constitution, it will be found that if the latter does not perfectly correspond with them, the former are infinitely less able to bear such a test.

There are, moreover, two considerations particularly applicable to the federal system of America, which place that system in a very interesting point of view.

First. In a single republic, all the power surrendered by the people is submitted to the administration of a single government; and the usurpations are guarded against by a division of the government into distinct and separate departments. In the compound republic of America, the power surrendered by the people is first divided between two distinct governments, and then the portion allotted to each subdivided among distinct and separate departments. Hence a double security arises to the rights of the people. The different governments will control each other, at the same time that each will be controlled by itself.

Second. It is of great importance in a republic not only to guard the society against the oppression of its rulers, but to guard one part of the society against the injustice of the other part. Different interests necessarily exist in different classes of citizens. If a majority be united by a common interest, the rights of the minority will be insecure. There are but two methods of providing against this evil: the one by creating a will in the community independent of the majority – that is, of the society itself; the other, by comprehending in the society so many separate descriptions of citizens as will render an unjust combination of a majority of the whole very improbable, if not impracticable. The first method prevails in all governments possessing an hereditary or self-appointed authority. This, at best, is but a precarious security; because a power independent of the society may as well espouse the unjust views of the major as the rightful interests of the minor party, and may possibly be turned against both parties. The second method will be exemplified in the federal republic of the United States. Whilst all authority in it will be derived from and dependent on the society, the

society itself will be broken into so many parts, interests and classes of citizens, that the rights of individuals, or of the minority, will be in little danger from interested combinations of the majority. In a free government the security for civil rights must be the same as that for religious rights. It consists in the one case in the multiplicity of interests, and in the other in the multiplicity of sects. The degree of security in both cases will depend on the number of interests and sects; and this may be presumed to depend on the extent of country and number of people comprehended under the same government. This view of the subject must particularly recommend a proper federal system to all the sincere and considerate friends of republican government, since it shows that in exact proportion as the territory of the Union may be formed into more circumscribed Confederacies, or States, oppressive combinations of a majority will be facilitated; the best security, under the republican forms, for the rights of every class of citizen, will be diminished; and consequently the stability and independence of some member of the government, the only other security, must be proportionally increased. Justice is the end of government. It is the end of civil society. It ever has been and ever will be pursued until it be obtained, or until liberty be lost in the pursuit. In a society under the forms of which the stronger faction can readily unite and oppress the weaker, anarchy may as truly be said to reign as in a state of nature, where the weaker individual is not secured against the violence of the stronger; and as, in the latter state, even the stronger individuals are prompted, by the uncertainty of their condition, to submit to a government which may protect the weak as well as themselves; so, in the former state, will the more powerful factions or parties be gradually induced, by a like motive, to wish for a government which will protect all parties, the weaker as well as the more powerful. It can be little doubted that if the State of Rhode Island was separated from the Confederacy and left to itself, the insecurity of rights under the popular form of government within such narrow limits would be displayed by such reiterated oppressions of factious majorities that some power altogether independent of the people would soon be called for by the voice of the very factions whose misrule had proved the necessity of it. In the extended republic of the United States, and among the great variety of interests, parties, and sects which it embraces, a coalition of a majority of the whole society could seldom take place on any other principles than those of justice and the general good; whilst there being thus less danger to a minor from the will of a major party, there must be less pretext, also, to provide for the security of the former, by introducing into the government a will not dependent on the latter, or, in other words, a will independent of the society itself. It is no less certain than it is important, notwithstanding the contrary opinions which have been entertained, that the larger the society, provided it lie within a practicable sphere, the more duly capable it will be of self-government. And happily for the *republican cause*, the practicable sphere may be carried to a very great extent by a judicious modification and mixture of the *federal principle*.

Observations on the New Constitution

Mercy Otis Warren

Introduction

Mercy Otis Warren (1728–1814) opposed the idea of a strong federal government in terms that recall the issues at work in the founding of the Haudenosaunee Confederacy. Warren published this pamphlet anonymously in response to the *Federalist Papers*. Warren was also the author of numerous plays and works of poetry and, in 1805, she published an influential study of the founding of the United States, *The History of the Rise, Progress, and Termination of the American Revolution*.

All writers on government agree, and the feelings of the human mind witness the truth of these political axioms, that man is born free and possessed of certain unalienable rights – that government is instituted for the protection, safety and happiness of the people, and not for the profit, honour, or private interest of any man, family, or class of men – That the origin of all power is in the people, and that they have an incontestible right to check the creatures of their own creation, vested with certain powers to guard the life, liberty and property of the community: And if certain selected bodies of men, deputed on these principles, determine contrary to the wishes and expectations of their constituents, the people have an undoubted right to reject their decisions, to call for a revision of their conduct, to depute others in their room, or if they think proper, to demand further time for deliberation on matters of the greatest moment: it

Taken from *Old South Leaflets*, no. 226 (Boston: Old South Association, 1955), pp. 5–8, 13–15.

therefore is an unwarrantable stretch of authority or influence, if any methods are taken to preclude this reasonable and peaceful mode of enquiry and decision. And it is with inexpressible anxiety, that many of the best friends of the Union of the States – to the peaceable and equal participation of the rights of nature, and to the glory and dignity of this country, behold the insidious arts, and the strenuous efforts of the partisans of arbitrary power, by their vague definitions of the best established truths, endeavoring to envelope the mind in darkness the concomitant of slavery, and to lock the strong chains of domestic despotism on a country, which by the most glorious and successful struggles is but newly emancipated from the spectre of foreign dominion. But there are certain seasons in the course of human affairs, when Genius, Virtue, and Patriotism, seems [*sic*] to nod over the vices of the times, and perhaps never more remarkably, than at the present period; or we should not see such a passive disposition prevail in some, who we must candidly suppose, have liberal and enlarged sentiments; while a supple multitude are paying a blind and idolatrous homage to the opinions of those who by the most precipitate steps are treading down their dear bought privileges; and who are endeavouring by all the arts of insinuation, and influence, to betray the people of the United States, into an acceptance of a most complicated system of government; marked on the one side with the *dark*, *secret* and *profound intrigues*, of the statesman, long practised in the purlieus of despotism; and on the other, with the ideal projects of *young ambition*, with its wings just expanded to soar to a summit, which imagination has painted in such gawdy colours as to intoxicate the *inexperienced votary*, and to send *him* rambling from State to State, to collect materials to construct the ladder of preferment.

But as a variety of objections to the *heterogeneous phantom*, have been repeatedly laid before the public, by men of the best abilities and intentions; I will not expatiate long on a Republican *form* of government, founded on the principles of monarchy – a democratick branch with the features of aristocracy – and the extravagance of nobility pervading the minds of many of the candidates for office, with the poverty of peasantry hanging heavily on them, and insurmountable, from their taste for expence, unless a general provision should be made in the arrangement of the civil list, which may enable them with the champions of their cause to *"sail down the new pactolean channel."* Some gentlemen, with laboured zeal, have spent much time in urging the necessity of government, from the embarrassments of trade – the want of respectability abroad and confidence of the public engagements at home: These are obvious truths which no one denies; and there are few who do not unite in the general wish for the restoration of public faith, the revival of commerce, arts, agriculture, and industry, under a lenient, peaceable and energetick government: But the most sagacious advocates for the party have not by fair discussion, and rational argumentation, evinced the necessity of adopting this many headed monster; of such motley mixture, that its enemies cannot trace a feature of Democratick or Republican extract; nor have its friends the courage to denominate a Monarchy, an Aristocracy, or an Oligarchy, and the favoured bantling must have passed through the short period of its existence without a name, had not Mr. *Wilson*, in the fertility of his genius, suggested the happy epithet of a *Federal Republic*. But I leave the field of general censure on the secrecy of its birth, the rapidity of its growth, and the fatal consequences of suffering it to live to the age of maturity, and will particularize some of the most weighty objections to its passing through this continent in a gigantic size. It will be allowed by every one that the fundamental principle of a free government, is the equal representation of a free people – And I will *first* observe with a justly celebrated writer, "That the principal aim of society is to protect individuals in the absolute rights which were vested in them by the immediate laws of nature, but which could not be preserved in peace, without the mutual intercourse which is gained by the institution of friendly and social communities." And when society has thus deputed a certain number of their equals to take care of their personal rights, and the interest of the whole community, it must be considered that responsibility is the great security of integrity and honour; and that annual election is the basis of responsibility – Man is not immediately corrupted, but power without limitation, or amenability, may endanger the brightest virtue – whereas a frequent return to the bar of their Constituents is the strongest check against the corruptions to which men are liable, either from the intrigues of others of more subtle genius, or the propensities of their own hearts – and the gentlemen who have so warmly advocated in the late Convention of the Massachusetts, the change from annual to biennial elections; may have been in the same predicament, and perhaps with the same views that Mr. *Hutchinson* once acknowledged himself, when in a letter to *Lord Hillsborough*, he observed, "that the grand difficulty of making a change in government against the general bent of the people had caused him to turn his thoughts to a variety of plans, in order to find one that might be executed in spite of opposition," and the first he proposed was that, "instead of annual, the elections should be only once in three years:" but the Minister had not the hardiness to attempt such an innovation, even in the revision of colonial charters: nor has any one ever defended Biennial, Triennial, or Septennial, Elections, either in the British House of Commons, or in the debates of Provincial assemblies, on general and free principles: but it is unnecessary to dwell long on this article, as the best political writers have supported the principles of annual elections with a precision, that cannot be confuted, though they may be darkned, by the sophistical arguments that have been thrown out with design, to undermine all the barriers of freedom.

2 There is no security in the profered [*sic*] system, either for the rights of conscience or the liberty of the Press: Despotism usually while it is gaining ground, will suffer men to think, say, or write what they please; but when once established, if it is thought necessary to subserve the purposes, of arbitrary power, the most unjust restrictions may take place in the first instance, and an *imprimator* on the Press in the next, may silence the complaints, and forbid the most decent remonstrances of an injured and oppressed people.

3 There are no well defined limits of the Judiciary Powers, they seem to be left as a boundless ocean, that has broken over the chart of the Supreme Lawgiver, "*thus far shalt thou go and no further*," and as they cannot be comprehended by the clearest capacity, or the most sagacious mind, it would be an Herculean labour to attempt to describe the dangers with which they are replete.

4 The Executive and the Legislative are so dangerously blended as to give just cause of alarm, and every thing relative thereto, is couched in such ambiguous terms – in such vague and indefinite expression, as is a sufficient ground without any objection, for the reprobation of a system, that the authors dare not hazard to a clear investigation.

5 The abolition of trial by jury in civil causes. This mode of trial the learned Judge Blackstone observes, "has been coeval with the first rudiments of civil government, that property, liberty and life, depend on maintaining in its legal force the constitutional trial by jury." He bids his readers pauze, and with Sir Matthew Hale observes, how admirably this mode is adapted to the investigation of truth beyond any other the world can produce. Even the party who have been disposed to swallow, without examination, the proposals of the *secret conclave*, have started on a discovery that this essential right was curtailed; and shall a privilege, the origin of which may be traced to our Saxon ancestors – that has been a part of the law of nations, even in the fewdatory systems of France, Germany and Italy – and from the earliest records has been held so sacred, both in ancient and modern Britain, that it could never be shaken by the introduction of Norman customs, or any other conquests or change of government – shall this inestimable privilege be relinquished in America – either thro' the fear of inquisition for unaccounted thousands of public monies in the hands of some who have been officious in the fabrication of the *consolidated system*, or from the apprehension that some future delinquent possessed of more power than integrity, may be called to a trial by his peers in the hour of investigation.

6 Though it has been said by Mr. *Wilson* and many others, that a Standing-Army is necessary for the dignity and safety of America, yet freedom revolts at the idea, when the Divan, or the Despot, may draw out his dragoons to suppress the murmurs of a few, who may yet cherish those sublime principles which call forth the exertions, and lead to the best improvement of the human mind. It is hoped this country may yet be governed by milder methods than are usually displayed beneath the bannerets of military law. Standing armies have been the nursery of vice and the bane of liberty from the Roman legions to the establishment of the artful Ximenes, and from the ruin of the Cortes of Spain, to the planting of the British cohorts in the capitals of America: By the edicts of an authority vested in the sovereign power by the proposed constitution, the militia of the country, the bulwark of defence, and the security of national liberty is no longer under the controul of civil authority; but at the rescript of the Monarch, or the aristocracy, they may either be employed to extort the enormous sums that will be necessary to support the civil list – to maintain the regalia of power – and the splendour of the most useless part of the community, or they may be sent into foreign countries for the fulfilment of treaties, stipulated by the President and two thirds of the Senate.

7 Notwithstanding the delusory promise to guarantee a Republican form of government to every State in the Union – If the most discerning eye could discover any meaning at all in the engagement, there are no resources left for the support of internal government, or the liquidation of the debts of the State. Every source of revenue is in the monopoly of Congress, and if the several legislatures in their enfeebled state, should against their own feelings be necessitated to attempt a dry tax for the payment of their debts, and the support of internal police, even this may be required for the purposes of the general government.

8 As the new Congress are empowered to determine their own salaries, the requisitions for this purpose may not be very moderate, and the drain for public moneys will probably rise past all calculation: and it is to be feared when America has consolidated its despotism, the world will witness the truth of the assertion – "that the pomp of an eastern monarch may impose on the vulgar who may estimate the force of a nation by the magnificence of its palaces; but the wise man judges differently, it is by that very magnificence he estimates its weakness. He sees nothing more in the midst of this imposing pomp, where the tyrant sets enthroned, than a sumptuous and mournful decoration of the dead; the apparatus of a fastuous funeral, in the centre of which is a cold and lifeless lump of unanimated earth, a phantom of power ready to disappear before the enemy, by whom it is despised!"

9 There is no provision for a rotation, nor anything to prevent the perpetuity of office in the same hands for life; which by a little well timed bribery, will probably be done, to the exclusion of men of the best abilities from their share in the offices of government. By this neglect we lose the advantages of that check to the overbearing insolence of office, which by rendering him ineligible at certain periods, keeps the mind of man in equilibrio, and teaches him the feelings of the governed, and better qualifies him to govern in his turn.

10 The inhabitants of the United States, are liable to be draged [sic] from the vicinity of their own country, or state, to answer the litigious or unjust suit of an adversary, on the most distant borders of the Continent: in short the appelate jurisdiction of the Supreme Federal Court, includes an unwarrantable stretch of power over the liberty, life, and property of the subject, through the wide Continent of America.

11 One Representative to thirty thousand inhabitants is a very inadequate representation; and every man who is not lost to all sense of freedom to his country, must reprobate the idea of Congress altering by law, or on any pretence whatever, interfering with any regulations for time, places, and manner of choosing our own Representatives.

12 If the sovereignty of America is designed to be elective, the circumscribing the votes to only ten electors in this State, and the same proportion in all the others, is nearly tantamount to the exclusion of the voice of the people in the choice of their first magistrate. It is vesting the choice solely in an aristocratic junto, who may easily combine in each State to place at the head of the Union the most convenient instrument for despotic sway.

13 A Senate chosen for six years will, in most instances, be an appointment for life, as the influence of such a body over the minds of the people will be coequal to the extensive powers with which they are vested, and they will not only forget, but be forgotten by their constituents – a branch of the Supreme Legislature thus set beyond all responsibility is totally repugnant to every principle of a free government.

14 There is no provision by a bill of rights to guard against the dangerous encroachments of power in too many instances to be named: but I cannot pass over in silence the insecurity in which we are left with regard to warrants unsupported by evidence – the daring experiment of granting *writs of assistance* in a former arbitrary administration is not yet forgotten in the Massachusetts; nor can we be so ungrateful to the memory of the patriots who counteracted their operation, as so soon after their manly exertions to save us from such a detestable instrument of arbitrary power, to subject ourselves to the insolence of any petty revenue officer to enter our houses, search, insult, and seize at pleasure. We are told by a gentleman of too much virtue and real probity to suspect he has a design to deceive – "that the whole constitution is a declaration of rights" – but mankind must think for themselves, and to many very judicious and discerning characters, the whole constitution with very few exceptions appears a perversion of the rights of particular states, and of private citizens. But the gentleman goes on to tell us, "that the primary object is the general government, and that the rights of individuals are only incidentally mentioned, and that there was a clear impropriety in being very particular about them." But, asking pardon for dissenting from such respectable authority, who has been led into several mistakes, more from his predilection in favour of certain modes of government, than from a want of understanding or veracity. The rights of individuals ought to be the primary object of all government, and cannot be too securely guarded by the most explicit declarations in their favor. This has been the opinion of the Hampdens, the Pyms, and many other illustrious names, that have stood forth in defence of English liberties; and even the Italian master in politicks, the subtle and renouned Machiavel acknowledges, that no republic ever yet stood on a stable foundation without satisfying the common people.

15 The difficulty, if not impracticability, of exercising the equal and equitable powers of government by a single legislature over an extent of territory that reaches from the Mississippi to the Western lakes, and from them to the Atlantic Ocean, is an insuperable objection to the adoption of the new system. Mr. *Hutchinson*, the great champion for arbitrary power, in the multitude of his machinations to subvert the liberties of this country, was obliged to acknowledge in one of his letters, that, "from the extent of country from north to south, the scheme of one government was impracticable." But if the authors of the present visionary project, can by the arts of deception, precipitation and address, obtain a majority of suffrages in the conventions of the states to try the hazardous experiment, they may then make the same inglorious boast with this insidious politician,

who may perhaps be their model, that "the union of the colonies was pretty well broken, and that he hoped to never see it re[n]ewed."

16 It is an undisputed fact that not one legislature in the United States had the most distant idea when they first appointed members for a convention, entirely commercial, or when they afterwards authorized them to consider on some amendments of the Federal union, that they would without any warrant from their constituents, presume on so bold and daring a stride, as ultimately to destroy the state governments, and offer a *consolidated system*, irreversible but on conditions that the smallest degree of penetration must discover to be impracticable.

17 The first appearance of the article which declares the ratification of nine states sufficient for the establishment of the new system, wears the face of dissension, is a subversion of the union of Confederated States, and tends to the introduction of anarchy and civil convulsions, and may be a means of involving the whole country in blood.

18 The mode in which this constitution is recommended to the people to judge without either the advice of Congress, or the legislatures of the several states is very reprehensible – it is an attempt to force it upon them before it could be thoroughly understood, and may leave us in that situation, that in the first moments of slavery in the minds of the people agitated by the remembrance of their lost liberties, will be like the sea in a tempest, that sweeps down every mound of security.

But it is needless to enumerate other instances, in which the proposed constitution appears contradictory to the first principles which ought to govern mankind; and it is equally so to enquire into the motives that induced to so bold a step as the annihilation of the independence and sovereignty of the thirteen distinct states. They are but too obvious through the whole progress of the business, from the first shutting up the doors of the federal convention and resolving that no member should correspond with gentlemen in the different states on the subject under discussion; till the trivial proposition of *recommending* a few amendments was artfully ushered into the convention of the Massachusetts. The questions that were then before that honorable assembly were profound and important, they were of such magnitude and extent, that the consequences may run parallel with the existence of the country; and

to see them waved and hastily terminated by a measure too absurd to require a serious refutation, raises the honest indignation of every true lover of his country. Nor are they less grieved that the ill policy and arbitrary disposition of some of the sons of America has thus precipitated to the contemplation and discussion of questions that no one could rationally suppose would have been agitated among us till time had blotted out the principles on which the late revolution was grounded; or till the last traits of the many political tracts, which defended the separation from Britain, and the rights of men were consigned to everlasting oblivion. After the severe conflicts this country has suffered, it is presumed that they are disposed to make every reasonable sacrifice before the altar of peace. But when we contemplate the nature of men and consider them originally on an equal footing, subject to the same feelings, stimulated by the same passions, and recollecting the struggles they have recently made, for the security of their civil rights; it cannot be expected that the inhabitants of the Massachusetts, can be easily lulled into a fatal security, by the declamatory effusions of gentlemen, who, contrary to the experience of all ages would perswade them there is no danger to be apprehended, from vesting discretionary powers in the hands of man, which he may, or may not abuse. The very suggestion, that we ought to trust to the precarious hope of amendments and redress, after we have voluntarily fixed the shackles on our own necks should have awakened to a double degree of caution. This people have not forgotten the artful insinuations of a former Governor, when pleading the unlimited authority of parliament before the legislature of the Massachusetts; nor that his arguments were very similar to some lately urged by gentlemen who boast of opposing his measures, "*with halters about their necks.*"

We were then told by him, in all the soft language of insinuation, that no form of government, of human construction can be perfect – that we had nothing to fear – that we had no reason to complain – that we had only to acquiesce in their illegal claims, and to submit to the requisition of parliament, and doubtless the lenient hand of government would redress all grievances, and remove the oppressions of the people: Yet we soon saw armies of mercenaries encamped on our plains – our commerce ruined – our harbours blockaded – and our cities burnt. It may be replied that this was in consequence of an obstinate defence of our privileges; this may be true; and when the "*ultima ratio*" is called to aid, the weakest must fall. But let the best informed historian produce an instance when bodies of men were entrusted with power, and the proper checks relinquished, if they were ever found destitute of ingenuity sufficient to furnish pretences to abuse it. And the people at large are already sensible, that the liberties which America has claimed, which reason has justified, and which have been so gloriously defended by the sword of the brave; are not about to fall before the tyranny of foreign conquest: it is native usurpation that is shaking the foundations of peace, and spreading the sable curtain of despotism over the United States. The banners of freedom were erected in the wilds of America by our ancestors, while the wolf prowled for his prey on the one hand, and more savage man on the other; they have been since rescued from the invading hand of foreign power, by the valor and blood of their posterity; and there was reason to hope they would continue for ages to illumine a quarter of the globe, by nature kindly separated from the proud monarchies of Europe, and the infernal darkness of Asiatic slavery. And it is to be feared we shall soon see this country rushing into the extremes of confusion and violence, in consequence of the proceedings of a set of gentlemen, who disregarding the purposes of their appointment, have assumed powers unauthorized by any commission, have unnecessarily rejected the confederation of the United States, and annihilated the sovereignty and independence of the individual governments. The causes which have inspired a few men to assemble for very different purposes with such a degree of temerity [a]s to break with a single stroke the union of America, and disseminate the seeds of discord through the land may be easily investigated, when we survey the partizans of monarchy in the state conventions, urging the adoption of a mode of government that militates with the former professions and exertions of this country, and with all ideas of republicanism, and the equal rights of men.

Passion, prejudice, and error, are characteristics of human nature; and as it cannot be accounted for on any principles of philosophy, religion, or good policy; to these shades in the human character must be attributed the mad zeal of some, to precipitate to a blind adoption of the measures of the late federal convention, without giving opportunity for better information to those who are misled by influence or ignorance into erroneous opinions. Literary talents may be prostituted, and the powers of genius debased to subserve the purposes of ambition, or avarice; but the feelings of the heart will dictate the language of truth, and the simplicity of her accents will proclaim the infamy of those, who betray the rights of the people, under the specious, and popular pretence of *justice, consolidation,* and *dignity.*

It is presumed the great body of the people unite in sentiment with the writer of these observations, who most devoutly prays that public credit may rear her declining head, and remunerative justice pervade the land; nor is there a doubt if a free government is continued, that time and industry will enable both the public and private debtor to liquidate their arrearages in the most equitable manner. They wish to see the Confederated States bound together by the most indissoluble union, but without renouncing their separate sovereignties and independence, and becoming tributaries to a consolidated fabrick of aristocratick tyranny. They wish to see government established, and peaceably holding the reins with honour, energy, and dignity; but they wish for no *federal city* whose *"cloud cap't towers"* may screen the state culprit from the hand of justice; while its exclusive jurisdiction may protect the riot of armies encamped within its limits. They deprecate discord and civil convulsions, but they are not yet generally prepared with the ungrateful Israelites to ask a King, nor are their spirits sufficiently broken to yield the best of their olive grounds to his servants, and to see their sons appointed to run before his chariots – It has been observed by a zealous advocate for the new system, that most governments are the result of fraud or violence, and this with design to recommend its acceptance – but has not almost every step towards its fabrication been fraudulent in the extreme? Did not the prohibition strictly enjoined by the general Convention, that no member should make any communication to his Constituents, or to gentlemen of consideration and abilities in the other States, bear evident marks of fraudulent designs? – This circumstance is regretted in strong terms by Mr. Martin, a member from Maryland, who acknowledges "He had no idea that all the wisdom, integrity, and virtue of the States was contained in that Convention, and that he wished to have corresponded with gentlemen of eminent political characters abroad, and to give their sentiments due weight" – he adds, "so extremely solicitous were they, that their proceedings should not transpire, that the members were prohibited from taking copies of their resolutions, or extracts from the Journals, without express permission, by vote." And the hurry with which it has been urged to the acceptance of the people, without giving time, by adjournments, for better information, and more unanimity has a deceptive appearance; and if finally driven to resistance, as the only alternative between that and servitude, till in the confusion of discord, the reins should be seized by the violence of some enterprizing genius, that may sweep down the last barrier of liberty, it must be added to the score of criminality with which the fraudulent usurpation at Philadelphia, may be chargeable. Heaven avert such a tremendous . . . [scene] and let us still hope a more happy termination of the present ferment: – may the people be calm and wait a legal redress; may the mad transport of some of our infatuated capitals subside; and every influential character through the States, make the most prudent exertions for a new general Convention, who may vest adequate powers in Congress, for all national purposes, without annihilating the individual governments, and drawing blood from every pore by taxes, impositions and illegal restrictions. This step might again re-establish the Union, restore tranquility to the ruffled mind of the inhabitants, and save America from the distresses, dreadful even in contemplation. "The great art of governing is to lay aside all prejudices and attachments to particular opinions, classes or individual characters to consult the spirit of the people; to give way to it; and in so doing, to give it a turn capable of inspiring those sentiments, which may induce them to relish a change, which an alteration of circumstances may hereafter make necessary." The education of the advocates for monarchy should have taught them, and their memory should have suggested that "monarchy is a species of government fit only for a people too much corrupted by luxury, avarice, and a passion for pleasure, to have any love for their country, and whose vices the fear of punishment alone is able to restrain; but by no means calculated for a nation that is poor, and at the same time tenacious of their liberty – animated with a disgust to tyranny – and inspired with the generous feeling of patriotism and liberty, and at the same time, like the ancient Spartans have been hardened by temperance and manly exertions, and equally despising the fatigues of the field, and the fear of enemies" – and while they change their ground they should recollect, that Aristocracy is a still more formidable foe to public virtue, and the prosperity of a nation – that under such a govern-

ment her patriots become mercenaries – her soldiers, cowards, and the people slaves. Though several State Conventions have assented to, and ratified, yet the voice of the people appears at present strong against the adoption of the Constitution. By the chicanery, intrigue, and false colouring of those who plume themselves, more on their education and abilities, than their political, patriotic, or private virtues – by the imbecility of some, and the duplicity of others, a majority of the Convention of Massachusetts have been flattered with the ideas of amendments, when it will be too late to complain – While several very worthy characters, too timid for their situation, magnified the hopeless alternative, between the dissolution of the bands of all government, and receiving the proferred system *in toto*, after long endeavouring to reconcile it to their consciences, swallowed the indigestible panacea, and in a kind of sudden desperation lent their signature to the dereliction of the honourable station they held in the Union, and have broken over the solemn compact, by which they were bound to support their own excellent constitution till the period of revision. Yet Virginia, equally large and respectable, and who have done honour to themselves, by their vigorous exertions from the first dawn of independence, have not yet acted upon the question; they have wisely taken time to consider before they introduce innovations of a most dangerous nature: – her inhabitants are brave, her burgesses are free, and they have a Governor who dares to think for himself, and to speak his opinion (without first pouring libations on the altar of popularity) though it should militate with some of the most accomplished and illustrious characters.

Maryland, who has no local interest to lead her to adopt, will doubtless reject the system – I hope the same characters still live, and that same spirit which dictated to them a wise and cautious care, against sudden revolutions in government, and made them the last State that acceded to the independence of America, will lead them to support what they so deliberately claimed. Georgia apprehensive of a war with the Savages, has acceded in order to insure protection. Pennsylvania has struggled through much in the same manner, as the Massachusetts, against the manly feelings, and the masterly reasonings of a very respectable part of the Convention: They have adopted the system, and seen some of its authors burnt in effigy – their towns thrown into riot and confusion, and the minds of the people agitated by apprehension and discord.

New-Jersey and Delaware have united in the measure, from the locality of their situation, and the selfish motives which too generally govern mankind; the Federal City, and the seat of government, will naturally attract the intercourse of strangers – the youth of enterprize, and the wealth of the nation to the central States.

Connecticut has pushed it through with the precipitation of her neighbour, with few dissentient voices; – but more from irritation and resentment to a sister State, perhaps partiality to herself in her commercial regulations, than from a comprehensive view of the system, as a regard to the welfare of all. But New-York has motives, that will undoubtedly lead her to rejection, without being afraid to appeal to the understanding of mankind, to justify the grounds of their refusal to adopt a Constitution, that even the framers dare not to risque to the hazard of revision, amendment, or reconsideration, least the whole superstructure should be demolished by more skilful and discreet architects. I know not what part the Carolinas will take; but I hope their determinations will comport with the dignity and freedom of this country – their decisions will have great weight in the scale. But equally important are the small States of New-Hampshire and Rhode-Island: New-York, the Carolinas, Virginia, Maryland, and these two lesser States may yet support the liberties of the Continent; if they refuse a ratification or postpone their proceedings till the spirits of the community have time to cool, there is little doubt but the wise measure of another federal convention will be adopted, when the members would have the advantage of viewing, at large, through the medium of truth, the objections that have been made from various quarters; such a measure might be attended with the most salutary effects, and prevent the dread consequences of civil feuds. But even if some of those large states should hastily accede, yet we have frequently seen in the story of revolution, relief spring from a quarter least expected.

Though the virtues of a Cato could not save Rome, nor the abilities of a Padilla defend the citizens of Castile from falling under the yoke of Charles; yet a *Tell* once suddenly rose from a little obscure city, and boldly rescued the liberties of his country. Every age has its Bruti and its Decii, as well as its Caesars and Sejani: The happiness of mankind depends much on the modes of government, and the virtues of the governors; and America may yet produce characters who have genius and capacity sufficient to form the manners and correct the morals of the people, and virtue enough to lead their country to freedom. Since their dismemberment from the British empire, America has, in many instances, resembled the conduct of a restless, vigorous, luxurious youth, prematurely emancipated from the authority of a parent, but without the experience necessary to direct him to act with dignity or discretion. Thus we have seen her break the shackles of foreign dominion, and all the blessings of peace restored on the most honourable terms: She acquired the liberty of framing her own laws, choosing her own magistrates, and adopting manners and modes of government the most favourable to the freedom and happiness of society. But how little have we availed ourselves of these superior advantages: The glorious fabric of liberty successfully reared with so much labor and assiduity totters to the foundation, and may be blown away as the bubble of fancy by the rude breath of military combinations, and politicians of yesterday.

It is true this country lately armed in opposition to regal despotism – impoverished by the expences of a long war, and unable immediately to fulfil their public or private engagements that appeared in some instances, with a boldness of spirit that seemed to set at defiance all authority, government, or order, on the one hand; while on the other, there has been, not only a secret wish, but an open avowal of the necessity of drawing the reins of government much too taut, not only for a republicanism, but for a wise and limited monarchy. But the character of this people is not averse to a degree of subordination, the truth of this appears from the easy restoration of tranquility, after a dangerous insurrection in one of the states; this also evinces a little necessity of a complete revolution of government throughout the union. But it is a republican principle that the majority should rule; and if a spirit of moderation should be cultivated on both sides, till the voice of the people at large could be fairly heard it should be held sacred. And if, on such a scrutiny, the proposed constitution should appear repugnant to their character and wishes; if they, in the language of a late elegant pen, should acknowledge that "no confusion in my mind, is more terrible to them than the stern disciplined regularity and vaunted police of arbitrary governments, where every heart is depraved by fear, where mankind dare not assume their natural characters, where the free spirit must crouch to the slave in office, where genius must repress her effusions, or like the Egyptian worshippers, offer them in sacrifice to the calves in power, and where the human mind, always in shackles, shrinks from every generous effort." Who would then have the effrontery to say, it ought not to be thrown out with indignation, however some respectable names have appeared to support it. But if after all, on a dispassionate and fair discussion, the people generally give their voice for a voluntary dereliction of their privileges, let every individual who chooses the active scenes of life, strive to support the peace and unanimity of his country, though every other blessing may expire. And while the statesman is plodding for power, and the courtier practising the arts of dissimulation without check – while the rapacious are growing rich by oppression, and fortune throwing her gifts into the lap of fools, let the sublimer characters, the philosophic lovers of freedom who have wept over her exit, retire to the calm shades of contemplation, there they may look down with pity on the inconsistency of human nature, the revolutions of states, the rise of kingdoms, and the fall of empires.

PART V

Slavery and Freedom

An enduring theme in American philosophy is the moral terror that was inflicted by ethnic genocide and racial slavery, systems based on usurping the labor and wealth of a population, stereotyped as an ethnic other or an inferior race. Unlike slavery by conquest, warfare, or voluntary servitude in underdeveloped societies, American slavery continued to exist well into the industrial era. The Fourth of July, celebrated as the birth of a new nation, elicits a response other than celebration in representatives of either defeated ethnic native populations or enslaved Americans. Freedom is thus considered in relationship to forms of servitude and is, thereby, a function of resistance traditions.

Resistance traditions present controversial conceptions of what counts as misery and what counts as appropriate responses. They also reflect the narrow forms of nationalist self-interest encoded in representatives of kinds, African American or otherwise, and, at the same time, conceptions of freedom that recommend themselves across lines of ethnicity or race.

"The Pueblo Revolt (1680)," which depicts military conflict, and the 1854 "Fourth of July Address at Reidsville, New York," encourage consideration of moral issues under radically different contexts: the first, a successful defeat by native Americans of Spanish military forces; the second a consideration of the meaning of the Fourth of July by a subjugated people.

David Walker, a moral insurrectionist, argued that there is a moral duty to engage in slave insurrections; Lydia Child, suffragette and abolitionist, takes account of the moral duties of whites, given that whites have an interest in perpetuating prejudice. Henry D. Thoreau asks what count as universal principles of democracy and humanity and what sort of process is needed to end slavery. Frederick Douglass's famous Fourth of July speech queries what freedom could mean to those persons excluded from its benefits. Anna J. Cooper confronts the disparate interests and ideals of competing communities of resistance populations.

Contrary to the kind of freedom promoted earlier by Americans such as Benjamin Franklin, slavery confronts the ideals of democracy within its own context.

24

The Pueblo Revolt, 1680

Don Antonio de Otermin

Introduction

The following letter, written by Don Antonio de Otermin, an officer in the Spanish army, in September 1680, testifies to a conflict in which native populations, who would come to be known as Pueblo Indians, both Christians and traditionalist, successfully fought Spanish military forces. The letter provides a perspective on accounts of pan-Indian military cooperation and Spanish conceptions of harm and also a sense of the existence of both Christianity and Spanish authority as necessary conditions for a worthy life. The self-regard and military acumen evidenced by native populations eventually helped shape what became in 1912 the USA's 47th state: New Mexico.

My Very Reverend Father, Sir, and friend, most beloved Fray Francisco de Ayeta: The time has come when, with tears in my eyes and deep sorrow in my heart, I commence to give an account of the lamentable tragedy, such as has never before happened in the world, which has occurred in this miserable kingdom and holy custodia, His divine Majesty having thus permitted it because of my grievous sins. Before beginning my narration, I desire, as one obligated and grateful, to give your reverence the thanks due for the demonstrations of affection and kindness which you have given in your solicitude in ascertaining and inquiring for definite notices about both my life and those of the rest in this miserable kingdom, in the midst of persistent reports which had been

Taken from C. W. Hackett (ed.), *Historical Documents Relating to New Mexico, Nueva Vizcaya, and Approaches Thereto, to 1773*, vol. III (Washington: Carnegie Institution of Washington, 1937).

circulated of the deaths of myself and the others, and for sparing neither any kind of effort nor large expenditures. For this, only Heaven can reward your reverence, though I do not doubt that his Majesty (may God keep him) will do so.

After I sent my last letter to your reverence by the maese de campo, Pedro de Leiva, while the necessary things were being made ready alike for the escort and in the way of provisions, for the most expeditious dispatch of the returning wagons and their guards, as your reverence had enjoined me, I received information that a plot for a general uprising of the Christian Indians was being formed and was spreading rapidly. This was wholly contrary to the existing peace and tranquility in this miserable kingdom, not only among the Spaniards and natives, but even on the part of the heathen enemy, for it had been a long time since they had done us any considerable damage. It was my misfortune that I learned of it on the eve of the day set for the beginning of the said uprising, and though I immediately, at that instant, notified the lieutenant general on the lower river and all the other alcaldes mayors – so that they could take every care and precaution against whatever might occur, and so that they could make every effort to guard and protect the religious ministers and the temples – the cunning and cleverness of the rebels were such, and so great, that my efforts were of little avail. To this was added a certain degree of negligence by reason of the report of the uprising not having been given entire credence, as is apparent from the ease with which they captured and killed both those who were escorting some of the religious, as well as some citizens in their houses, and, particularly, in the efforts that they made to prevent my orders to the lieutenant general passing through. This was the place where most of the forces of the kingdom were, and from which I could expect some help, but of three orders which I sent to the said lieutenant general, not one reached his hands. The first messenger was killed and the others did not pass beyond Santo Domingo, because of their having encountered on the road the certain notice of the deaths of the religious who were in that convent, and of the alcalde mayor, some other guards, and six more Spaniards whom they captured on that road. Added to this is the situation of this kingdom which, as your reverence is aware, makes it so easy for the said [Indian] rebels to carry out their evil designs, for it is entirely composed of estancias, quite distant from one another.

On the eve of the day of the glorious San Lorenzo, having received notice of the said rebellion from the governors of Pecos and Tanos, who said that two Indians had left the Teguas, and particularly the pueblos of Tesuque, to which they belonged, to notify them to come and join the revolt, and that they [the governors] came to tell me of it and of how they were unwilling to participate in such wickedness and treason, saying that they now regarded the Spaniards as their brothers, I thanked them for their kindness in giving the notice and told them to go to their pueblos and remain quiet. I busied myself immediately in giving the said orders, which I mentioned to your reverence, and on the following morning as I was about to go to mass there arrived Pedro Hidalgo, who had gone to the pueblo of Tesuque, accompanying Father Fray Juan Pio, who went there to say mass. He told me that the Indians of the said pueblo had killed the said Father Fray Pio and that he himself had escaped miraculously. He told me also that the said Indians had retreated to the sierra with all the cattle and horses belonging to the convent, and with their own.

The receipt of this news left us all in the state that may be imagined. I immediately and instantly sent the maese de campo, Francisco Gomez, with a squadron of soldiers sufficient to investigate this case and also to attempt to extinguish the flame of the ruin already begun. He returned here on the same day, telling me that the report of the death of the said Fray Juan Pio was true. He said also that there had been killed that same morning Father Fray Tomas de Torres, guardian of Nambe, and his brother, with the latter's wife and a child, and another resident of Taos, and also Father Fray Luis de Morales, guardian of San Ildefonso, and

the family of Francisco de Ximenez, his wife and family, and Dona Petronila de Salas with ten sons and daughters; and that they had robbed and profaned the convents and had robbed all the haciendas of those murdered and also all the horses and cattle of that jurisdiction and La Canada.

Upon receiving this news I immediately notified the alcalde mayor of that district to assemble all the people in his house in a body, and told him to advise at once the alcalde mayor of Los Taos to do the same. On this same day I received notice that two members of a convoy had been killed in the pueblo of Santa Clara, six others having escaped by flight. Also at the same time the sergeant mayor, Bernabe Marquez, sent to ask me for assistance, saying that he was surrounded and hard pressed by the Indians of the Queres and Tanos nations. Having sent the aid for which he asked me, and an order for those families of Los Cerrillos to come to the villa, I instantly arranged for all the people in it and its environs to retire to the casas reales. Believing that the uprising of the Tanos and Pecos might endanger the person of the reverend father custodian, I wrote to him to set out at once for the villa, not feeling reassured even with the escort which the lieutenant took, at my orders, but when they arrived with the letter they found that the Indians had already killed the said father custodian; Father Fray Domingo de Vera; Father Fray Manuel Tinoco, the minister guardian of San Marcos, who was there; and Father Fray Fernando de Velasco, guardian of Los Pecos, near the pueblo of Galisteo, he having escaped that far from the fury of the Pecos. The latter killed in that pueblo Fray Juan de la Pedrosa, two Spanish women, and three children. There died also at the hands of the said enemies in Galisteo Joseph Nieto, two sons of Maestre de Campo Leiva, Francisco de Anaya, the younger, who was with the escort, and the wives of Maestre de Campo Leiva and Joseph Nieto, with all their daughters and families. I also learned definitely on this day that there had died, in the pueblo of Santo Domingo, Fathers Fray Juan de Talaban, Fray Francisco Antonio Lorenzana, and Fray Joseph de Montesdoca, and the alcalde mayor, Andres de Peralta, together with the rest of the men who went as escort.

Seeing myself with notices of so many and such untimely deaths, and that not having received any word from the lieutenant general was probably due to the fact that he was in the same exigency and confusion, or that the Indians had killed most of those on the lower river, and considering also that in the pueblo of Los Taos the father guardians of that place and of the pueblo of Pecuries might be in danger, as well as the alcalde mayor and the residents of that valley, and that at all events it was the only place from which I could obtain any horses and cattle – for all these reasons I endeavored to send a relief of soldiers. Marching out for that purpose, they learned that in La Canada, as in Los Taos and Pecuries, the Indians had risen in rebellion, joining the Apaches of the Achos nation. In Pecuries they had killed Francisco Blanco de la Vega; a mulatta belonging to the maese de campo, Francisco Xavier; and a son of the said mulatta. Shortly thereafter I learned that they also killed in the pueblo of Taos the father guardian, Fray Francisco de Mora; and Father Fray Mathias Rendon, the guardian of Pecuries; and Fray Antonio de Pro; and the alcalde mayor, as well as another fourteen or fifteen soldiers, along with all the families of the inhabitants of that valley, all of whom were together in the convent. Thereupon I sent an order to the alcalde mayor, Luis de Quintana, to come at once to the villa with all the people whom he had assembled in his house, so that, joined with those of us who were in the casas reales, we might endeavor to defend ourselves against the enemy's invasions. It was necessarily supposed that they would join all their forces to take our lives, as was seen later by experience. On Tuesday, the 13th of the said month, at about nine o'clock in the morning, there came in sight of us in the suburb of Analco, in the cultivated field of the hermitage of San Miguel, and on the other side of the river from the villa, all the Indians of the Tanos and Pecos nations and the Queres of San Marcos, armed and giving war whoops. As I learned that one of the Indians who was leading them was from the villa and had gone to join them shortly before, I sent some soldiers to summon him and tell him on my behalf that he could come to see me in entire safety, so that I might ascertain from him the purpose for which they were coming. Upon receiving this message he came to where I was, and, since he was known, as I say, I asked him how it was that he had gone crazy too – being an Indian who spoke our language, was so intelligent, and had lived all his life in the villa among the Spaniards, where I had placed such confidence in him – and was now coming as a leader of the Indian rebels. He replied to me that they had elected him as their captain, and that they were carrying two banners, one white and the other red, and that the

white one signified peace and the red one war. Thus if we wished to choose the white it must be upon our agreeing to leave the country, and if we chose the red, we must perish, because the rebels were numerous and we were very few; there was no alternative, inasmuch as they had killed so many religious and Spaniards.

On hearing this reply, I spoke to him very persuasively, to the effect that he and the rest of his followers were Catholic Christians, asking how they expected to live without the religious; and said that even though they had committed so many atrocities, still there was a remedy, for if they would return to obedience to his Majesty they would be pardoned; and that thus he should go back to this people and tell them in my name all that had been said to him, and persuade them to agree to it and to withdraw from where they were; and that he was to advise me of what they might reply. He came back from there after a short time, saying that his people asked that all classes of Indians who were in our power be given up to them, both those in the service of the Spaniards and those of the Mexican nation of that suburb of Analco. He demanded also that his wife and children be given up to him, and likewise that all the Apache men and women whom the Spaniards had captured in war be turned over to them, inasmuch as some Apaches who were among them were asking for them. If these things were not done they would declare war immediately, and they were unwilling to leave the place where they were because they were awaiting the Taos, Percuries, and Teguas nations, with whose aid they would destroy us.

Seeing his determination, and what they demanded of us, and especially the fact that it was untrue that there were any Apaches among them, because they were at war with all of them, and that these parleys were intended solely to obtain his wife and children and to gain time for the arrival of the other rebellious nations to join them and besiege us, and that during this time they were robbing and sacking what was in the said hermitage and the houses of the Mexicans, I told him (having given him all the preceding admonitions as a Christian and a Catholic) to return to his people and say to them that unless they immediately desisted from sacking the houses and dispersed, I would send to drive them away from there. Whereupon he went back, and his people received him with peals of bells and trumpets, giving loud shouts in sign of war.

With this, seeing after a short time that they not only did not cease the pillage but were advancing toward the villa with shamelessness and mockery, I ordered all the soldiers to go out and attack them until they succeeded in dislodging them from that place. Advancing for this purpose, they joined battle, killing some at the first encounter. Finding themselves repulsed, they took shelter and fortified themselves in the said hermitage and houses of the Mexicans, from which they defended themselves a part of the day with the firearms that they had and with arrows. We having set fire to some of the houses in which they were, thus having them surrounded and at the point of perishing, there appeared on the road from Tesuque a band of the people whom they were awaiting, who were all the Teguas. Thus it was necessary to go to prevent these latter from passing on to the villa, because the casas reales were poorly defended; whereupon the said Tanos and Pecos fled to the mountains and the two parties joined together, sleeping that night in the sierra of the villa. Many of the rebels remained dead and wounded, and our men retired to the casas reales with one soldier killed and the maese de campo, Francisco Gomez, and some fourteen or fifteen soldiers wounded, to attend them and entrench and fortify ourselves as best we could.

On the morning of the following day, Wednesday, I saw the enemy come down all together from the sierra where they had slept, toward the villa. Mounting my horse, I went out with the few forces that I had to meet them, above the convent. The enemy saw me and halted, making ready to resist the attack. They took up a better position, gaining the eminence of some ravines and thick timber, and began to give war whoops, as if daring me to attack them. I paused thus for a short time, in battle formation, and the enemy turned aside from the eminence and went nearer the sierras, to gain the one which comes down behind the house of the maese de campo, Francisco Gomez. There they took up their position, and this day passed without our having any further engagements or skirmishes than had already occurred, we taking care that they should not throw themselves upon us and burn the church and the houses of the villa.

The next day, Thursday, the enemy obliged us to take the same step as on the day before of mounting on horseback in fighting formation. There were only some light skirmishes to prevent their burning and sacking some of the houses which were at a distance from the main part of the villa. I knew well enough that these dilatory tactics were to give time for the people of the other nations who were missing to join them in order to besiege and attempt to destroy us, but the height of the places in which they were, so favorable to them and on the contrary so unfavorable to us, made it impossible for us to go and drive them out before they should all be joined together.

On the next day, Friday, the nations of the Taos, Pecuries, Jemez, and Queres having assembled during the past night, when dawn came more than 2,500 Indians fell upon us in the villa, fortifying and entrenching themselves in all its houses and at the entrances of all the streets, and cutting off our water, which comes through the arroyo and the irrigation canal in front of the casas reales. They burned the holy temple and many houses in the villa. We had several skirmishes over possession of the water, but, seeing that it was impossible to hold even this against them, and almost all the soldiers of the post being already wounded, I endeavored to fortify myself in the casas reales and to make a defense without leaving their walls. The Indians were so dexterous and so bold that they came to set fire to the doors of the fortified tower of Nuestra Senora de las Casas Reales, and, seeing such audacity and the manifest risk that we ran of having the casas reales set on fire, I resolved to make a sally into the plaza of the said casas reales with all my available force of soldiers, without any protection, to attempt to prevent the fire which the enemy was trying to set. With this endeavor we fought the whole afternoon, and, since the enemy, as I said above, had fortified themselves and made embrasures in all the houses, and had plenty of harquebuses, powder, and balls, they did us much damage. Night overtook us and God was pleased that they should desist somewhat from shooting us with harquebuses and arrows. We passed this night, like the rest, with much care and watchfulness, and suffered greatly from thirst because of the scarcity of water.

On the next day, Saturday, they began at dawn to press us harder and more closely with gunshots, arrows, and stones, saying to us that now we should not escape them, and that, besides their own numbers, they were expecting help from the Apaches whom they had already summoned. They fatigued us greatly on this day, because all was fighting, and above all we suffered from thirst, as we were already oppressed by it. At nightfall, because of the evident peril in which we found ourselves by their gaining the two stations where the cannon were mounted, which we had at the doors of the casas reales, aimed at the entrances of the streets, in order to bring them inside it was necessary to assemble all the forces that I had with me, because we realized that this was their [the Indians'] intention. Instantly all the said Indian rebels began a chant of victory and raised war whoops, burning all the houses of the villa, and they kept us in this position the entire night, which I assure your reverence was the most horrible that could be thought of or imagined, because the whole villa was a torch and everywhere were war chants and shouts. What grieved us most were the dreadful flames from the church and the scoffing and ridicule which the wretched and miserable Indian rebels made of the sacred things, intoning the alabado and the other prayers of the church with jeers.

Finding myself in this state, with the church and the villa burned, and with the few horses, sheep, goats, and cattle which we had without feed or water for so long that many had already died, and the rest were about to do so, and with such a multitude of people, most of them children and women, so that our numbers in all came to about a thousand persons, perishing with thirst – for we had nothing to drink during these two days except what had been kept in some jars and pitchers that were in the casas reales – surrounded by such a wailing of women and children, with confusion everywhere, I determined to take the resolution of going out in the morning to fight with the enemy until dying or conquering. Considering that the best strength and armor were prayers to appease the divine wrath, though on the preceding days the poor women had made them with such fervor, that night I charged them to do so increasingly, and told the father guardian and the other two religious to say mass for us at dawn, and exhort all alike to repentance for their sins and to conformance with the divine will, and to absolve us from guilt and punishment. These things being done, all of us who could mounted our horses, and the rest went on foot with their harquebuses, and some Indians who were in our service with their bows and arrows, and in the best order possible we directed our course toward the house of the maese de campo, Francisco Xavier, which was the place where (apparently) there were the most people and where they had been most active and boldest. On coming out of the entrance to the street it was seen that there was a great number of Indians. They were attacked in force,

and though they resisted the first charge bravely, finally they were put to flight, many of them being overtaken and killed. Then turning at once upon those who were in the streets leading to the convent, they also were put to flight with little resistance. The houses in the direction of the house of the said maese de campo, Francisco Xavier, being still full of Indians who had taken refuge in them, and seeing that the enemy with the punishment and deaths that we had inflicted upon them in the first and second assaults were withdrawing toward the hills, giving us a little room, we laid siege to those who remained fortified in the said houses. Though they endeavored to defend themselves, and did so, seeing that they were being set afire and that they would be burned to death, those who remained alive surrendered and much was made of them. The deaths of both parties in this and the other encounters exceeded three hundred Indians.

Finding myself a little relieved by this miraculous event, although I had lost much blood from two arrow wounds which I had received in the face and from a remarkable gunshot wound in the chest on the day before, I immediately had water given to the cattle, the horses, and the people. Because we now found ourselves with very few provisions for so many people, and without hope of human aid, considering that our not having heard in so many days from the people on the lower river would be because of their all having been killed, like the others in the kingdom, or at least of their being or having been in dire straits, with the view of aiding them and joining with them into one body, so as to make the decisions most conducive to his Majesty's service, on the morning of the next day, Monday, I set out for La Isleta, where I judged the said comrades on the lower river would be. I trusted in divine providence, for I left without a crust of bread or a grain of wheat or maize, and with no other provision for the convoy of so many people except four hundred animals and two carts belonging to private persons, and, for food, a few sheep, goats, and cows.

In this manner, and with this fine provision, besides a few small ears of maize that we found in the fields, we went as far as the pueblo of La Alameda, where we learned from an old Indian whom we found in a maizefield that the lieutenant general with all the residents of his jurisdictions had left some fourteen or fifteen days before to return to El Paso to meet the wagons. This news made me very uneasy, alike because I could not be persuaded that he would have left without having news of me as well as of all the others in the kingdom, and because I feared that from his absence there would necessarily follow the abandonment of this kingdom. On hearing this news I acted at once, sending four soldiers to overtake the said lieutenant general and the others who were following him, with orders that they were to halt wherever they should come up with them. Going in pursuit of them, they overtook them at the place of Fray Cristobal. The lieutenant general, Alonso Garcia, overtook me at the place of Las Nutrias, and a few days' march thereafter I encountered the maese de campo, Pedro de Leiva, with all the people under his command, who were escorting these wagons and who came to ascertain whether or not we were dead, as your reverence had charged him to do, and to find me, ahead of the supply train. I was so short of provisions and of everything else that at best I should have had a little maize for six days or so.

Thus, after God, the only succor and relief that we have rests with your reverence and in your diligence. Wherefore, and in order that your reverence may come immediately, because of the great importance to God and the king of your reverence's presence here, I am sending the said maese de campo, Pedro de Leiva, with the rest of the men whom he brought so that he may come as escort for your reverence and the wagons or mule-train in which we hope you will bring us some assistance of provisions. Because of the haste which the case demands I do not write at more length, and for the same reason I cannot make a report at present concerning the above to the senor viceroy, because the autos are not verified and there has been no opportunity to conclude them. I shall leave it until your reverence's arrival here. For the rest I refer to the account which will be given to your reverence by the father secretary, Fray Buenaventura de Verganza. I am slowly overtaking the other party, which is sixteen leagues from here, with the view of joining them and discussing whether or not this miserable kingdom can be recovered. For this purpose I shall not spare any means in the service of God and of his Majesty, losing a thousand lives if I had them, as I have lost my estate and part of my health, and shedding my blood for God. May he protect me and permit me to see your reverence in this place at the head of the relief. September 8, 1680. Your servant, countryman, and friend kiss your reverence's hand.

Don Antonio de Otermin

25

Fourth of July Address at Reidsville, New York, 1854

John Wannuaucon Quinney

Introduction

John Wannuaucon Quinney (1797–1855) was a Mahican, a population of the Algonquian family, native to the Hudson River Valley, Connecticut, who lived at different times in Norwich, Connecticut; Stockbridge, Massachusetts; and Oneida, Wisconsin. He was a promoter of native rights and integration into modernity, and he argued from the standpoint of a small northern native population.

It may appear to those whom I have the honor to address a singular taste for me, an Indian, to take an interest in the triumphal days of a people who occupy, by conquest or have usurped, the possessions of my fathers and have laid and carefully preserved a train of terrible miseries to end when my race ceased to exist.

But thanks to the fortunate circumstances of my life I have been taught in the schools and been able to read your histories and accounts of Europeans, yourselves and the Red Man; which instruct me that while your rejoicings today are commemorative of the free birth of this giant nation, they simply convey to my mind the recollection of a transfer of the miserable weakness and dependence of my race from one great power to another.

My friends, I am getting old and have witnessed for many years your increase in wealth and power while the steady consuming decline of my tribe

Taken from Wayne Moquin and C. van Doren (eds), *Great Documents of American Indian History* (New York: Prager, 1973).

admonishes me that their extinction is inevitable. They know it themselves and the reflection teaches them humility and resignation, directing their attention to the existence of those happy hunting grounds which the Great Father has prepared for all his red children.

In this spirit, my friends, as a Muh-he-con-new, and now standing upon the soil which once was and now ought to be the property of this tribe, I have thought for once and certainly the last time I would shake you by the hand and ask you to listen for a little while to what I have to say.

About the year 1645, when King Ben the last of the hereditary chiefs of the Muh-he-con-new nation was in his prime, grand council was convened of the Muh-he-con-new tribe for the purpose of conveying from the old to the young men a knowledge of the past.

Councils for this object especially had been held. Here for the space of two moons, the stores of memory were dispensed; corrections and comparisons made and the results committed to faithful breasts to be transmitted again to succeeding posterity.

Many years after, another and last council of this kind was held; and the traditions reduced to writing, by two of our young men who had been taught to read and write in the school of the Rev. John Sargent of Stockbridge, Mass. They were obtained in some way by a white man for publication, who soon after dying, all trace of them became lost. The traditions of the tribe, however, have mainly been preserved, of which I give you substantially, the following:

A great people from the northwest crossed over the salt water, and after long and weary pilgrimage, planting many colonies on their track, took possession of and built their fires upon the Atlantic coast, extending from the Delaware on the south to the Penobscott on the north. They became in process of time different tribes and interests; all, however, speaking one common dialect.

This great confederacy, Pequots, Penobscotts, and many others (Delawares, Mohegans, Munsees, Narragansetts) held its council fires once a year to deliberate on the general welfare.

Patriarchal delegates from each tribe attended, assisted by the priests and the wise men, who communicated the will and invoked the blessing of the Great and Good Spirit. The policies and decisions of this council were everywhere respected, and inviolably observed. Thus contentment smiled upon their existence and they were happy.

Their religion communicated by priest and prophet, was simple and true. The manner of worship is imperfectly transmitted; but their reverence for a Great Spirit, the observance of feasts each year, the offering of beasts in thanksgiving and atonement is clearly expressed.

They believed the soul to be immortal – in the existence of a happy land beyond the view, inhabited by those whose lives had been blameless. While for the wicked had been reserved a region of misery covered with thorns and thistles, where comfort and pleasure were unknown. Time was divided into years and seasons; twelve moons for a year, a number of years by so many winters.

The tribe to which your speaker belongs and of which there were many bands, occupied and possessed the country from the seashore at Manhattan to Lake Champlain. Having found the ebb and flow of the tide, they said: "This is Muh-he-con-new," "Like our waters which are never still." From this expression and by this name they were afterwards known, until their removal to Stockbridge in the year 1630.

Housatonic river Indians, Mohegans, Manhattans, were all names of bands in different localities, but bound together as one family by blood and descent.

At a remote period, before the advent of the European their wise men foretold the coming of a strange race from the sunrise, as numerous as the leaves upon the trees, who would eventually crowd them from their fair land possessions. But apprehension was mitigated by the knowledge and belief at that time entertained, that they originally were

not there, and after a period of years they would return to the west from which they had come. And they moreover said all Red Men are sprung from a common ancestor, made by the Great Spirit from red clay, who will unite their strength to avert a common calamity. This tradition is confirmed by the common belief, which prevails in our day with all the Indian tribes; for they recognize one another by their color, as brothers and acknowledge one Great Creator.

Two hundred and fifty winters ago, this prophecy was verified and the Muh-he-con-new for the first time beheld the paleface. Their number was small, but their canoes were big.

In the select and exclusive circles of your rich men of the present day I should encounter the gaze of curiosity, but not such as overwhelmed the senses of the Aborigines, my ancestors. Our visitors were white and must be sick. They asked for rest and kindness; we gave them both. They were strangers, and we took them in; naked and we clothed them.

The first impression of astonishment and pity was succeeded by awe and admiration of superior intelligence and address.

A passion for information and improvement possessed the Indians. A residence was given – territory offered – and covenants of friendship exchanged.

Your written accounts of events at this period are familiar to you, my friends. Your children read them every day in their school books; but they do not read – no mind at this time can conceive, and no pen record, the terrible story of recompense for kindness, which for two hundred years has been paid the simple, guileless Muh-he-con-new.

I have seen much myself – I have been connected with more – and I tell you I know all. The tradition of the wise men is figuratively true – that our home at last will be found in the west; for another tradition informs us that far beyond the setting sun, upon the smiling happy lands, we shall be gathered with our fathers, and be at rest.

Promises and professions were freely given and ruthlessly and intentionally broken. To kindle your fires was sought as a privilege; and yet at that moment you were transmitting to your kings intelligence of our possessions, "by right of discovery," and demanding assistance to assert your hold.

Where are the 25,000 in number, and the 4,000 warriors, who constituted the power and population of the great Muh-he-con-new nation in 1604?

They have been victims to vice and disease, which the white men imported. Smallpox, measles and firewater have done the work of annihilation. Divisions and feuds were insidiously promoted between the several bands. They were induced to thin each other's ranks without just cause; and subsequently were defeated and disorganized in detail.

It is curious, the history of my tribe, in its decline, in the last two centuries and a half. Nothing that deserved the name of purchase was made. From various causes, they were induced to abandon their territory at intervals and retire farther inland. Deeds were given indifferently to the government by individuals, for which little or no compensation was paid.

The Indians were informed, in many instances, that they were selling one piece of land when they were conveying another and much larger limits. Should a particular band, for purposes of hunting or fishing, for a time leave its usual place of residence, the land was said to be abandoned, and the Indian claim extinguished. To legalize and confirm titles thus acquired, laws and edicts were subsequently passed, and these laws were said then to be, and are now called, justice.

Oh, what mockery to confound justice with law! Will you look steadily at the intrigues, bargains, corruptions and log rollings of your present legislatures, and see any trace of justice? And by what test shall be tried the acts of the colonial courts and councils?

Let it not surprise you, my friends, when I say that the spot upon which I stand has never been rightly purchased or obtained. And by justice, human and Divine, is the property of the remnant of the great people from whom I am descended. They left it in the tortures of starvation and to improve their miserable existence; but a cession was never made, and their title was never extinguished.

The Indian is said to be the ward of the white man, and the negro his slave. Has it ever occurred to you, my friend, that while the negro is increasing and increased by every appliance, the Indian is left to rot and die before the inhumanities of this model republic?

You have your tears and groans and mobs and riots for the individuals of the former, while your indifference of purpose and vacillation of policy is hurrying to extinction whole communities of the latter.

What are the treaties of the general government? How often and when has its plighted faith been kept? Indian occupation is forever next year, or one removal follows another; or by the next commissioner, more wise than his predecessor, repurchased, and thus your sympathies and justice are evinced in speedily fulfilling the terrible destinies of our race.

My friends, your Holy Book, the Bible, teaches us that individual offenses are punished in an existence – when time shall be no more – and the annals of the earth are equally instructive that national wrongs are avenged, and national crimes atoned for in this world to which alone the conformation of existence adapts them.

These events are above our comprehension, and for a wise purpose; for myself and for my tribe I ask for justice – I believe it will sooner or later occur, and may the Great Spirit enable me to die in hope.

26

Appeal to the Coloured Citizens of the World, 1829

David Walker

Introduction

David Walker (1785–1830), was born in North Carolina. He published *An Appeal to the Coloured Citizens of the World* in September 1829 and distributed it with the aid of sailors in both free and slave communities. He had a second-hand clothing shop near Brattle Street, Boston. Walker was the Boston agent for the distribution of the *Freedom's Journal,* a New York-based weekly abolitionist newspaper. Walker's *Appeal* provided a secular and a theological basis for insurrection. Both the man and his work were banned in several states, although both were also instrumental in initiating slave escapes and insurrections. On June 28, 1830, Walker was found dead near his shop, almost certainly assassinated by pro-slavery forces. Walker was America's most influential insurrectionist.

Preamble

My dearly beloved Brethren and Fellow Citizens. Having travelled over a considerable portion of these United States, and having, in the course of my travels, taken the most accurate observations of things as they exist – the result of my observations has warranted the full and unshaken conviction, that we (coloured people of these United States) are the most degraded, wretched, and abject set of beings that ever lived since the

Taken from *Appeal to the Coloured Citizens of the World,* 1829 (Maryland: Black Classic Press, 1993).

world began; and I pray God that none like us ever may live again until time shall be no more. They tell us of the Israelites in Egypt, the Helots in Sparta, and of the Roman Slaves, which last were made up from almost every nation under heaven, whose sufferings under those ancient and heathen nations, were, in comparison with ours, under this enlightened and Christian nation, no more than a cypher – or, in other words, those heathen nations of antiquity, had but little more among them than the name and form of slavery; while wretchedness and endless miseries were reserved, apparently in a phial, to be poured out upon our fathers, ourselves and our children, by *Christian* Americans!

These positions I shall endeavour, by the help of the Lord, to demonstrate in the course of this *Appeal,* to the satisfaction of the most incredulous mind – and may God Almighty, who is the Father of our Lord Jesus Christ, open your hearts to understand and believe the truth.

The *causes,* my brethren, which produce our wretchedness and miseries, are so very numerous and aggravating, that I believe the pen only of a Josephus or a Plutarch, can well enumerate and explain them. Upon subjects, then, of such incomprehensible magnitude, so impenetrable, and so notorious, I shall be obliged to omit a large class of, and content myself with giving you an exposition of a few of those, which do indeed rage to such an alarming pitch, that they cannot but be a perpetual source of terror and dismay to every reflecting mind.

I am fully aware, in making this appeal to my much afflicted and suffering brethren, that I shall not only be assailed by those whose greatest earthly desires are, to keep us in abject ignorance and wretchedness, and who are of the firm conviction that Heaven has designed us and our children to be slaves and *beasts of burden* to them and their children. I say, I do not only expect to be held up to the public as an ignorant, impudent and restless disturber of the public peace, by such avaricious creatures, as well as a mover of insubordination – and perhaps put in prison or to death, for giving a superficial exposition of our miseries, and exposing tyrants. But I am persuaded, that many of my brethren, particularly those who are ignorantly in league with slave-holders or tyrants, who acquire their daily bread by the blood and sweat of their more ignorant brethren – and not a few of those too, who are too ignorant to see an inch beyond their noses, will rise up and call me cursed – Yea, the jealous ones among us will perhaps use more abject subtlety, by affirming that this work is not worth perusing, that we are well situated, and there is no use in trying to better our condition, for we cannot. I will ask one question here. Can our condition be any worse? – Can it be more mean and abject? If there are any changes, will they not be for the better, though they may appear for the worst at first? Can they get us any lower? Where can they get us? They are afraid to treat us worse, for they know well, the day they do it they are gone. But against all accusations which may or can be preferred against me, I appeal to Heaven for my motive in writing – who knows that my object is, if possible, to awaken in the breasts of my afflicted, degraded and slumbering brethren, a spirit of inquiry and investigation respecting our miseries and wretchedness in this *Republican Land of Liberty!!!!!!*

The sources from which our miseries are derived, and on which I shall comment, I shall not combine in one, but shall put them under distinct heads and expose them in their turn; in doing which, keeping truth on my side, and not departing from the strictest rules of morality, I shall endeavour to penetrate, search out, and lay them open for your inspection. If you cannot or will not profit by them, I shall have done *my* duty to you, my country and my God.

And as the inhuman system of *slavery*, is the *source* from which most of our miseries proceed, I shall begin with that *curse to nations*, which has spread terror and devastation through so many nations of antiquity, and which is raging to such a pitch at the present day in Spain and in Portugal.

It had one tug in England, in France, and in the United States of America; yet the inhabitants thereof, do not learn wisdom, and erase it entirely from their dwellings and from all with whom they have to do. The fact is, the labour of slaves comes so cheap to the avaricious usurpers, and is (as they think) of such great utility to the country where it exists, that those who are actuated by sordid avarice only, overlook the evils, which will as sure as the Lord lives, follow after the good. In fact, they are so happy to keep in ignorance and degradation, and to receive the homage and the labour of the slaves, they forget that God rules in the armies of heaven and among the inhabitants of the earth, having his ears continually open to the cries, tears and groans of his oppressed people; and being a just and holy Being will at one day appear fully in behalf of the oppressed, and arrest the progress of the avaricious oppressors; for although the destruction of the oppressors God may not effect by the oppressed, yet the Lord our God will bring other destructions upon them – for not unfrequently will he cause them to rise up one against another, to be split and divided, and to oppress each other, and sometimes to open hostilities with sword in hand. Some may ask, what is the matter with this united and happy people? – Some say it is the cause of political usurpers, tyrants, oppressors, &c. But has not the Lord an oppressed and suffering people among them? Does the Lord condescend to hear their cries and see their tears in consequence of oppression? Will he let the oppressors rest comfortably and happy always? Will he not cause the very children of the oppressors to rise up against them, and oftimes put them to death? "God works in many ways his wonders to perform."

I will not here speak of the destructions which the Lord brought upon Egypt, in consequence of the oppression and consequent groans of the oppressed – of the hundreds and thousands of Egyptians whom God hurled into the Red Sea for afflicting his people in their land – of the Lord's suffering people in Sparta or Lacedaemon, the land of the truly famous Lycurgus – nor have I time to comment upon the cause which produced the fierceness with which Sylla usurped the title, and absolutely acted as dictator of the Roman people – the conspiracy of Cataline – the conspiracy against, and murder of Caesar in the Senate house – the spirit with which Marc Antony made himself master of the commonwealth – his associating Octavius and Lipidus with himself in power

– their dividing the provinces of Rome among themselves – their attack and defeat, on the plains of Phillippi, of the last defenders of their liberty (Brutus and Cassius) – the tyranny of Tiberius, and from him to the final overthrow of Constantinople by the Turkish Sultan, Mahomed II. AD 1453. I say, I shall not take up time to speak of the *causes* which produced so much wretchedness and massacre among those heathen nations, for I am aware that you know too well, that God is just, as well as merciful! – I shall call your attention a few moments to that *Christian* nation, the Spaniards – while I shall leave almost unnoticed, that avaricious and cruel people, the Portuguese, among whom all true hearted Christians and lovers of Jesus Christ, must evidently see the judgments of God displayed. To show the judgments of God upon the Spaniards, I shall occupy but a little time, leaving a plenty of room for the candid and unprejudiced to reflect.

All persons who are acquainted with history, and particularly the Bible, who are not blinded by the God of this world, and are not actuated solely by avarice – who are able to lay aside prejudice long enough to view candidly and impartially, things as they were, are, and probably will be – who are willing to admit that God made man to serve Him *alone*, and that man should have no other Lord or Lords but Himself – that God Almighty is the *sole proprietor* or *master* of the WHOLE human family, and will not on any consideration admit of a colleague, being unwilling to divide his glory with another – and who can dispense with prejudice long enough to admit that we are *men*, notwithstanding our *improminent noses* and *woolly heads*, and believe that we feel for our fathers, mothers, wives and children, as well as the whites do for theirs. I say, all who are permitted to see and believe these things, can easily recognize the judgments of God among the Spaniards. Though others may lay the cause of the fierceness with which they cut each other's throats, to some other circumstance, yet they who believe that God is a God of justice, will believe that SLAVERY *is the principal cause.*

While the Spaniards are running about upon the field of battle cutting each other's throats, has not the Lord an afflicted and suffering people in the midst of them, whose cries and groans in consequence of oppression are continually pouring into the ears of the God of justice? Would they not cease to cut each other's throats, if they could? But how can they? The very support which they draw from government to aid them in perpetrating such enormities, does it not arise in a great degree from the wretched victims of oppression among them? And yet they are calling for *Peace! – Peace!!* Will any peace be given unto them? Their destruction may indeed be procrastinated awhile, but can it continue long, while they are oppressing the Lord's people? Has he not the hearts of all men in His hand? Will he suffer one part of his creatures to go on oppressing another like brutes always, with impunity? And yet, those avaricious wretches are calling for *Peace!!!!* I declare, it does appear to me, as though some nations think God is asleep, or that he made the Africans for nothing else but to dig their mines and work their farms, or they cannot believe history, sacred or profane. I ask every man who has a heart, and is blessed with the privilege of believing – Is not God a God of justice to *all* his creatures? Do you say he is? Then if he gives peace and tranquillity to tyrants, and permits them to keep our fathers, our mothers, ourselves and our children in eternal ignorance and wretchedness, to support them and their families, would he be to us a God of *justice?* I ask, O ye *Christians!!!* who hold us and our children in the most abject ignorance and degradation, that ever a people were afflicted with since the world began – I say, if God gives you peace and tranquillity, and suffers you thus to go on afflicting us, and our children, who have never given you the least provocation would he be to us *a God of justice?* If you will allow that we are MEN, who feel for each other, does not the blood of our fathers and of us their children, cry aloud to the Lord of Sabaoth against you, for the cruelties and murders with which you have, and do continue to afflict us. But it is time for me to close my remarks on the suburbs, just to enter more fully into the interior of this system of cruelty and oppression.

Our Wretchedness in Consequence of Slavery

My beloved brethren: The Indians of North and of South America – the Greeks – the Irish, subjected under the king of Great Britain – the Jews, that ancient people of the Lord – the inhabitants of the islands of the sea – in fine, all the inhabitants of the earth (except however, the sons of Africa) are called *men*, and of course are, and ought to be free. But we (coloured people) and our children are *brutes!!* and of course are, and *ought to be*

SLAVES to the American people and their children forever!! to dig their mines and work their farms; and thus go on enriching them, from one generation to another with our *blood* and our *tears!!!!*

I promised in a preceding page to demonstrate to the satisfaction of the most incredulous, that we (coloured people of these United States of America) are the *most wretched, degraded* and *abject* set of beings that *ever lived* since the world began, and that the white Americans having reduced us to the wretched state of *slavery*, treat us in that condition *more cruel* (they being an enlightened and Christian people) than any heathen nation did any people whom it had reduced to our condition. These affirmations are so well confirmed in the minds of all unprejudiced men, who have taken the trouble to read histories, that they need no elucidation from me. But to put them beyond all doubt, I refer you in the first place to the children of Jacob, or of Israel in Egypt, under Pharaoh and his people. Some of my brethren do not know who Pharaoh and the Egyptians were – I know it to be a fact, that some of them take the Egyptians to have been a gang of *devils*, not knowing any better, and that they (Egyptians) having got possession of the Lord's people, treated them *nearly* as cruel as *Christian Americans* do us, at the present day. For the information of such, I would only mention that the Egyptians, were Africans or coloured people, such as we are – some of them yellow and others dark – a mixture of Ethiopians and the natives of Egypt – about the same as you see the coloured people of the United States at the present day. I say, I call your attention then, to the children of Jacob, while I point out particularly to you his son Joseph, among the rest, in Egypt.

"And Pharaoh, said unto Joseph . . . thou shalt be over my house, and according unto thy word shall all my people be ruled: only in the throne will I be greater than thou."[1]

"And Pharaoh said unto Joseph, see, I have set thee over all the land of Egypt."[2]

"And Pharaoh said unto Joseph, I am Pharaoh, and without thee shall no man lift up his hand or foot in all the land of Egypt."[3]

Now I appeal to heaven and to earth, and particularly to the American people themselves, who cease not to declare that our condition is not *hard*, and that we are comparatively satisfied to rest in wretchedness and misery, under them and their children. Not, indeed, to show me a coloured President, a Governor, a Legislator, a Senator, a Mayor, or an Attorney at the Bar. But to show me a man of colour, who holds the low office of a Constable, or one who sits in a Juror Box, even on a case of one of his wretched brethren, throughout this great Republic!! – But let us pass Joseph the son of Israel a little farther in review, as he existed with that heathen nation.

"And Pharaoh called Joseph's name Zaphnath-paaneah; and he gave him to wife Asenath the daughter of Potipherah priest of On. And Joseph went out over all the land of Egypt."[4]

Compare the above, with the American institutions. Do they not institute laws to prohibit us from marrying among the whites? I would wish, candidly, however, before the Lord, to be understood, that I would not give a *pinch of snuff* to be married to any white person I ever saw in all the days of my life. And I do say it, that the black man, or man of colour, who will have his own colour (provided he can get one, who is good for any thing) and marry a white woman, to be a double slave to her, just because she is *white*, ought to be treated by her as he surely will be, viz: as a NIGGER!!!! It is not, indeed, what I care about intermarriages with the whites, which induced me to pass this subject in review; for the Lord knows, that there is a day coming when they will be glad enough to get into the company of the blacks, notwithstanding, we are, in this generation, levelled by them, almost on a level with the brute creation: and some of us they treat even worse than they do the brutes that perish. I only made this extract to show how much lower we are held, and how much more cruel we are treated by the Americans, than were the children of Jacob, by the Egyptians. We will notice the sufferings of Israel some further, under *heathen Pharaoh*, compared with ours under the *enlightened Christians of America*.

"And Pharaoh spoke unto Joseph, saying, thy father and thy brethren are come unto thee:

"The land of Egypt is before thee: in the best of the land make thy father and brethren to dwell; in the land of Goshen let them dwell: and if thou knowest any men of activity among them, then make them rulers over my cattle."[5]

I ask those people who treat us so *well*, Oh! I ask them, where is the most barren spot of land which they have given unto us? Israel had the most fertile land in all Egypt. Need I mention the very notorious fact, that I have known a poor man of colour, who laboured night and day, to acquire a little money, and having acquired it, he vested it in a small piece of land, and got him a house erected thereon, and having paid for the whole, he moved his family into it, where he was suffered to remain but nine months, when he was cheated out of his property by a white man, and driven out of door! And is not this the case generally? Can a man of colour buy a piece of land and keep it peaceably? Will not some white man try to get it from him, even if it is in a *mud hole*? I need not comment any farther on a subject, which all, both black and white, will readily admit. But I must, really, observe that in this very city, when a man of colour dies, if he owned any real estate it most generally falls into the hands of some white person. The wife and children of the deceased may weep and lament if they please, but the estate will be kept snug enough by its white possessor.

But to prove farther that the condition of the Israelites was better under the Egyptians than ours is under the whites. I call upon the professing Christians, I call upon the philanthropist, I call upon the very tyrant himself, to show me a page of history, either sacred or profane, on which a verse can be found, which maintains, that the Egyptians heaped the *insupportable insult* upon the children of Israel, by telling them that they were not of the *human family*. Can the whites deny this charge? Have they not, after having reduced us to the deplorable condition of slaves under their feet, held us up as descending originally from the tribes of *Monkeys* or *Orang-Outangs*? O! my God! I appeal to every man of feeling – is not this insupportable? Is it not heaping the most gross insult upon our miseries, because they have got us under their feet and we cannot help ourselves? Oh! pity us we pray thee, Lord Jesus, Master. Has Mr. Jefferson declared to the world, that we are inferior to the whites, both in the endowments of our bodies and our minds?[6] It is indeed surprising, that a man of such great learning, combined with such excellent natural parts, should speak so of a set of men in chains. I do not know what to compare it to, unless, like putting one wild deer in an iron cage, where it will be secured, and hold another by the side of the same, then let it go, and expect the one in the cage to run as fast as the one at liberty. So far, my brethren, were the Egyptians from heaping these insults upon their slaves, that Pharaoh's daughter took Moses, a son of Israel for her own, as will appear by the following.

"And Pharaoh's daughter said unto her, [Moses' mother] take this child away, and nurse it for me, and I will pay thee thy wages. And the woman took the child [Moses] and nursed it.

"And the child grew, and she brought him unto Pharaoh's daughter and he became her son. And she called his name Moses: and she said because I drew him out of the water."[7]

In all probability, Moses would have become Prince Regent to the throne, and no doubt, in process of time but he would have been seated on the throne of Egypt. But he had rather suffer shame, with the people of God, than to enjoy pleasures with that wicked people for a season. O! that the coloured people were long since of Moses' excellent disposition, instead of courting favour with, and telling news and lies to our *natural enemies*, against each other – aiding them to keep their hellish chains of slavery upon us. Would we not long before this time, have been respectable men, instead of such wretched victims of oppression as we are? Would they be able to drag our mothers, our fathers, our wives, our children and ourselves, around the world in chains and handcuffs as they do, to dig up gold and silver for them and theirs? This question, my brethren, I leave for you to digest; and may God Almighty force it home to your hearts. Remember that unless you are united, keeping your tongues within your teeth, you will be afraid to trust your secrets to each other, and thus perpetuate our miseries under the *Christians!!!!* – Remember, also to lay humble at the feet of our Lord and Master Jesus Christ, with prayers and fastings. Let our enemies go on with their butcheries, and at once fill up their cup. Never make an attempt to gain our freedom or *natural right*, from under our cruel oppressors and murderers, until you see your way clear[8] – when that hour arrives and you move, be not afraid or dismayed; for be you assured that Jesus Christ the King of heaven and of earth who is the God of justice and of armies, will surely go before you. And those enemies who have for hundreds of years stolen our *rights*, and kept us ignorant of Him and His divine worship, he will remove. Millions of whom, are this day, so ignorant and avaricious, that they cannot conceive how God can have an attribute of justice, and show mercy to us because it pleased Him to make us black – which colour, Mr. Jefferson calls unfortunate!!!!! As though we are not as thankful to our God, for having made us as it pleased himself, as they (the whites) are for having made them white. They think because they hold us in their infernal chains of slavery, that we wish to be white, or of their color – but they are dreadfully deceived – we wish to be just as it pleased our Creator to have made us, and no avaricious and unmerciful wretches, have any business to make slaves of, or hold us in slavery. How would they like for us to make slaves of, and hold them in cruel slavery, and murder them as they do us? – But is Mr. Jefferson's assertion true? viz. "that it is unfortunate for us that our Creator has been pleased to make us *black*." We will not take his say so, for the fact. The world will have an opportunity to see whether it is unfortunate for us, that our Creator *has made us darker* than the *whites*.

Fear not the number and education of our en-*emies*, against whom we shall have to contend for our lawful right; guaranteed to us by our Maker; for why should we be afraid, when God is, and will continue (if we continue humble) to be on our side?

The man who would not fight under our Lord and Master Jesus Christ, in the glorious and heav-enly cause of freedom and of God – to be delivered from the most wretched, abject and servile slavery, that ever a people was afflicted with since the foundation of the world, to the present day – ought to be kept with all of his children or family, in slavery, or in chains, to be butchered by his *cruel enemies*.

I saw a paragraph, a few years since, in a South Carolina paper, which, speaking of the barbarity of the Turks, it said: "The Turks are the most bar-barous people in the world – they treat the Greeks more like *brutes* than human beings." And in the same paper was an advertisement, which said: "Eight well built Virginia and Maryland *Negro fellows* and four *wenches* will positively be *sold* this day, *to the highest bidder!*" And what astonished me still more was, to see in this same *humane* paper!! the cuts of three men, with clubs and budgets on their backs, and an advertisement offering a con-siderable sum of money for their apprehension and delivery. I declare, it is really so amusing to hear the Southerners and Westerners of this country talk about *barbarity*, that it is positively, enough to make a man *smile*.

The sufferings of the Helots among the Spar-tans, were somewhat severe, it is true, but to say that theirs, were as severe as ours among the Americans, I do most strenuously deny – for in-stance, can any man show me an article on a page of ancient history which specifies, that, the Spar-tans chained, and handcuffed the Helots, and dragged them from their wives and children, chil-dren from their parents, mothers from their suck-ling babes, wives from their husbands, driving them from one end of the country to the other?

Notice the Spartans were heathens, who lived long before our Divine Master made his appearance in the flesh. Can Christian Americans deny these barbarous cruelties? Have you not, Americans, having subjected us under you, added to these miseries, by insulting us in telling us to our face, because we are helpless, that we are not of the human family? I ask you, O! Americans, I ask you, in the name of the Lord, can you deny these charges? Some perhaps may deny, by saying, that they never thought or said that we were not men. But do not actions speak louder than words? – have they not made provisions for the Greeks, and Irish? Nations who have never done the least thing for them, while *we*, who have enriched their country with our blood and tears – have dug up gold and silver for them and their children, from generation to generation, and are in more miseries than any other people under heaven, are not seen, but by comparatively, a handful of the American people? There are indeed, more ways to kill a dog, besides choking it to death with butter. Further – The Spartans or Lacedaemonians, had some frivo-lous pretext, for enslaving the Helots, for they (Helots) while being free inhabitants of Sparta, stirred up an intestine commotion, and were, by the Spartans subdued, and made prisoners of war. Consequently they and their children were con-demned to perpetual slavery.[9]

I have been for years troubling the pages of historians, to find out what our fathers have done to the *white Christians of America*, to merit such condign punishment as they have inflicted on them, and do continue to inflict on us their chil-dren. But I must aver, that my researches have hitherto been to no effect. I have therefore, come to the immoveable conclusion, that they (Ameri-cans) have, and do continue to punish us for noth-ing else, but for enriching them and their country. For I cannot conceive of anything else. Nor will I ever believe otherwise, until the Lord shall con-vince me.

The world knows, that slavery as it existed among the Romans (which was the primary cause of their destruction) was, comparatively speaking, no more than a *cypher*, when compared with ours under the Americans. Indeed I should not have noticed the Roman slaves, had not the very learned and penetrating Mr. Jefferson said, "when a master was murdered, all his slaves in the same house, or within hearing, were condemned to death."[10] – Here let me ask Mr. Jefferson (but he is gone to answer at the bar of God, for the deeds done in his body while living) I therefore ask the whole American people, had I not rather die, or be put to death, than to be a slave to any tyrant, who takes not only my own, but my wife and children's lives by the inches? Yea, would I meet death with avidity far! far!! in preference to such *servile submission* to the murderous hands of tyrants. Mr. Jefferson's very severe remarks on us have been so extensively argued upon by men whose attainments in literature, I shall never be able to reach, that I would not have meddled with it, were it not to solicit each of my brethren, who has the spirit of a man, to buy a copy of Mr. Jefferson's "Notes on Virginia," and put it in the hand of his son. For let no one of us suppose that the refutations which have been written by our white friends are enough – they are *whites* – we are *blacks*. We, and the world wish to see the charges of Mr. Jefferson refuted by the blacks *themselves*, according to their chance; for we must remember that what the whites have written respecting this subject, is other men's labours, and did not emanate from the blacks. I know well, that there are some talents and learning among the coloured people of this country, which we have not a chance to develop, in consequence of oppression; but our oppression ought not to hinder us from acquiring all we can. For we will have a chance to develop them by and by. God will not suffer us, always to be oppressed. Our sufferings will come to an *end*, in spite of all the Americans this side of *eternity*. Then we will want all the learning and talents among ourselves, and perhaps more, to govern ourselves. "Every dog must have its day," the American's is coming to an end.

But let us review Mr. Jefferson's remarks respecting us some further. Comparing our miserable fathers, with the learned philosophers of Greece, he says: "Yet notwithstanding these and other discouraging circumstances among the Romans, their slaves were often their rarest artists. They excelled too, in science, insomuch as to be usually employed as tutors to their master's children; Epictetus, Terence and Phædrus, were slaves – but they were of the race of whites. It is not their *condition* then, but *nature*, which has produced the distinction."[11] See this, my brethren!! Do you believe that this assertion is swallowed by millions of the whites? Do you know that Mr. Jefferson was one of as great characters as ever lived among the whites? See his writings for the world, and public labours for the United States of America. Do you believe that the assertions of such a man, will pass away into oblivion unob-

served by this people and the world? If you do you are much mistaken – See how the American people treat us – have we souls in our bodies? Are we men who have any spirits at all? I know that there are many *swell-bellied* fellows among us, whose greatest object is to fill their stomachs. Such I do not mean – I am after those who know and feel, that we are MEN, as well as other people; to them, I say, that unless we try to refute Mr. Jefferson's arguments respecting us, we will only establish them.

But the slaves among the Romans. Every body who has read history, knows, that as soon as a slave among the Romans obtained his freedom, he could rise to the greatest eminence in the State, and there was no law instituted to hinder a slave from buying his freedom. Have not the Americans instituted laws to hinder us from obtaining our freedom? Do any deny this charge? Read the laws of Virginia, North Carolina, &c. Further: have not the Americans instituted laws to prohibit a man of colour from obtaining and holding any office whatever, under the government of the United States of America? Now, Mr. Jefferson tells us, that our condition is not so hard, as the slaves were under the Romans!!!!!!

It is time for me to bring this article to a close. But before I close it, I must observe to my brethren that at the close of the first Revolution in this country, with Great Britain, there were but thirteen States in the Union, now there are twenty-four, most of which are slave-holding States, and the whites are dragging us around in chains and in handcuffs, to their new States and Territories to work their mines and farms, to enrich them and their children – and millions of them believing firmly that we being a little darker than they, were made by our Creator to be an inheritance to them and their children for ever – the same as a parcel of *brutes*.

Are we MEN!! – I ask you, O my brethren! are we MEN? Did our Creator make us to be slaves to dust and ashes like ourselves? Are they not dying worms as well as we? Have they not to make their appearance before the tribunal of Heaven, to answer for the deeds done in the body, as well as we? Have we any other Master but Jesus Christ alone? Is he not their Master as well as ours? – What right then, have we to obey and call any other Master, but Himself? How we could be so submissive to a gang of men, whom we cannot tell whether they are as good as ourselves or not, I never could conceive. However, this is shut up with the Lord, and we cannot precisely tell – but I declare, we judge men by their works.

The whites have always been an unjust, jealous, unmerciful, avaricious and blood-thirsty set of beings, always seeking after power and authority. We view them all over the confederacy of Greece, where they were first known to be any thing (in consequence of education) we see them there, cutting each other's throats – trying to subject each other to wretchedness and misery – to effect which, they used all kinds of deceitful, unfair, and unmerciful means. We view them next in Rome, where, the spirit of tyranny and deceit raged still higher. We view them in Gaul, Spain, and in Britain. In fine, we view them all over Europe, together with what were scattered about in Asia and Africa, as heathens, and we see them acting more like devils than accountable men. But some may ask, did not the blacks of Africa, and the mulattoes of Asia, go on in the same way as did the whites of Europe. I answer, no – they never were half so avaricious, deceitful and unmerciful as the whites, according to their knowledge.

But we will leave the whites or Europeans as heathens, and take a view of them as Christians, in which capacity we see them as cruel, if not more so than ever. In fact, take them as a body, they are ten times more cruel, avaricious and unmerciful than ever they were; for while they were heathens, they were bad enough it is true, but it is positively a fact that they were not quite so audacious as to go and take vessel loads of men, women and children, and in cold blood, and through devilishness, throw them into the sea, and murder them in all kind of ways. While they were heathens, they were too ignorant for such barbarity. But being Christians, enlightened and sensible, they are completely prepared for such hellish cruelties. Now suppose God were to give them more sense, what would they do? If it were possible, would they not *dethrone* Jehovah and seat themselves upon his throne? I therefore, in the name and fear of the Lord God of Heaven and of earth, divested of prejudice either on the side of my colour or that of the whites, advance my suspicion of them, whether they are as good by nature as we are or not. Their actions, since they were known as a people, have been the reverse, I do indeed suspect them, but this, as I before observed, is shut up with the Lord, we cannot exactly tell, it will be proved in succeeding generations. The whites have had the essence of the gospel as it was preached by my master and his apostles – the Ethiopians have not, who are to have

it in its meridian splendor – the Lord will give it to them to their satisfaction. I hope and pray my God, that they will make good use of it, that it may be well with them.[12]

Our Wretchedness in Consequence of Ignorance

Ignorance, my brethren, is a mist, low down into the very dark and almost impenetrable abyss in which, our fathers for many centuries have been plunged. The Christians, and enlightened of Europe, and some of Asia, seeing the ignorance and consequent degradation of our fathers, instead of trying to enlighten them, by teaching them that religion and light with which God had blessed them, they have plunged them into wretchedness ten thousand times more intolerable, than if they had left them entirely to the Lord, and to add to their miseries, deep down into which they have plunged them tell them, that they are an *inferior* and *distinct race* of beings, which they will be glad enough to recall and swallow by and by. Fortune and misfortune, two inseparable companions, lay rolled up in the wheel of events, which have from the creation of the world, and will continue to take place among men until God shall dash worlds together.

When we take a retrospective view of the arts and sciences – the wise legislators – the Pyramids, and other magnificent buildings – the turning of the channel of the river Nile, by the sons of Africa or of Ham, among whom learning originated, and was carried thence into Greece, where it was improved upon and refined. Thence among the Romans, and all over the then enlightened parts of the world, and it has been enlightening the dark and benighted minds of men from then, down to this day. I say, when I view retrospectively, the renown of that once mighty people, the children of our great progenitor I am indeed cheered. Yea further, when I view that mighty son of Africa, HANNIBAL, one of the greatest generals of antiquity, who defeated and cut off so many thousands of the white Romans or murderers, and who carried his victorious arms, to the very gate of Rome, and I give it as my candid opinion, that had Carthage been well united and had given him good support, he would have carried that cruel and barbarous city by storm. But they were disunited, as the coloured people are now, in the United States of America, the reason our natural enemies are enabled to keep their feet on our throats.

Beloved brethren – here let me tell you, and believe it, that the Lord our God, as true as he sits on his throne in heaven, and as true as our Saviour died to redeem the world, will give you a Hannibal, and when the Lord shall have raised him up, and given him to you for your possession, O my suffering brethren! remember the divisions and consequent sufferings of *Carthage* and of *Hayti*. Read the history particularly of Hayti, and see how they were butchered by the whites, and do you take warning. The person whom God shall give you, give him your support and let him go his length, and behold in him the salvation of your God. God will indeed, deliver you through him from your deplorable and wretched condition under the Christians of America. I charge you this day before my God to lay no obstacle in his way, but let him go.

The whites want slaves, and want us for their slaves, but some of them will curse the day they ever saw us. As true as the sun ever shone in its meridian splendor, my colour will root some of them out of the very face of the earth. They shall have enough of making slaves of, and butchering, and murdering us in the manner which they have. No doubt some may say that I write with a bad spirit, and that I being a black, wish these things to occur. Whether I write with a bad or a good spirit, I say if these things do not occur in their proper time, it is because the world in which we live does not exist, and we are deceived with regard to its existence. It is immaterial however to me, who believe, or who refuse – though I should like to see the whites repent peradventure God may have mercy on them, some however, have gone so far that their cup must be filled.

But what need have I to refer to antiquity, when Hayti, the glory of the blacks and terror of tyrants, is enough to convince the most avaricious and stupid of wretches – which is at this time, and I am sorry to say it, plagued with that scourge of nations, the Catholic religion; but I hope and pray God that she may yet rid herself of it, and adopt in its stead the Protestant faith; also, I hope that she may keep peace within her borders and be united, keeping a strict look out for tyrants, for if they get the least chance to injure her, they will avail themselves of it, as true as the Lord lives in heaven. But one thing which gives me joy is, that they are men who would be cut off to a man, before they would

yield to the combined forces of the whole world – in fact, if the whole world was combined against them, it could not do any thing with them, unless the Lord delivers them up.

Ignorance and treachery one against the other – a grovelling servile and abject submission to the lash of tyrants, we see plainly, my brethren, are not the natural elements of the blacks, as the Americans try to make us believe; but these are misfortunes which God has suffered our fathers to be enveloped in for many ages, no doubt in consequence of their disobedience to their Maker, and which do, indeed, reign at this time among us, almost to the destruction of all other principles: for I must truly say, that ignorance, the mother of treachery and deceit, gnaws into our very vitals. Ignorance, as it now exists among us, produces a state of things, Oh my Lord! too horrible to present to the world. Any man who is curious to see the full force of ignorance developed among the coloured people of the United States of America, has only to go into the southern and western states of this confederacy, where, if he is not a tyrant, but has the feelings of a human being, who can feel for a fellow creature, he may see enough to make his very heart bleed! He may see there, a son take his mother, who bore almost the pains of death to give him birth, and by the command of a tyrant, strip her as naked as she came into the world, and apply the cow-hide to her, until she falls a victim to death in the road! He may see a husband take his dear wife, not unfrequently in a pregnant state, and perhaps far advanced, and beat her for an unmerciful wretch, until his infant falls a lifeless lump at her feet! Can the Americans escape God Almighty? If they do, can he be to us a God of justice? God is just, and I know it – for he has convinced me to my satisfaction – I cannot doubt him. My observer may see fathers beating their sons, mothers their daughters, and children their parents, all to pacify the passions of unrelenting tyrants. He may also, see them telling news and lies, making mischief one upon another. These are some of the productions of ignorance, which he will see practised among my dear brethren, who are held in unjust slavery and wretchedness, by avaricious and unmerciful tyrants, to whom, and their hellish deeds, I would suffer my life to be taken before I would submit. And when my curious observer comes to take notice of those who are said to be free (which assertion I deny) and who are making some frivolous pretentions to common sense, he will see that branch of ignorance among the slaves assuming a more cunning and deceitful course of procedure. He may see some of my brethren in league with tyrants, selling their own brethren into *hell upon earth*, not dissimilar to the exhibitions in Africa, but in a more secret, servile and abject manner. Oh Heaven! I am full!!! I can hardly move my pen!!!! and as I expect some will try to put me to death, to strike terror into others, and to obliterate from their minds the notion of freedom, so as to keep my brethren the more secure in wretchedness, where they will be permitted to stay but a short time (whether tyrants believe it or not) – I shall give the world a development of facts, which are already witnessed in the courts of heaven. My observer may see some of those ignorant and treacherous creatures (coloured people) sneaking about in the large cities, endeavouring to find out all strange coloured people, where they work and where they reside, asking them questions, and trying to ascertain whether they are runaways or not, telling them, at the same time, that they always have been, are, and always will be, friends to their brethren; and, perhaps, that they themselves are absconders, and a thousand such treacherous lies to get the better information of the more ignorant! There have been and are at this day in Boston, New York, Philadelphia, and Baltimore, coloured men, who are in league with tyrants, and who receive a great portion of their daily bread, of the moneys which they acquire from the blood and tears of their more miserable brethren, whom they scandalously delivered into the bands of our *natural enemies!!!!!!*

To show the force of degraded ignorance and deceit among us some farther, I will give here an extract from a paragraph, which may be found in the Columbian Centinel of this city, for September 9, 1829, on the first page of which, the curious may find an article, headed:

"Affray and Murder"
Portsmouth (Ohio)
Aug. 22, 1829

"A most shocking outrage was committed in Kentucky, about eight miles from this place, on 14th inst. A negro driver, by the name of Gordon, who had purchased in Maryland about sixty negroes, was taking them, assisted by an associate named Allen, and the wagoner who conveyed the baggage, to the Mississippi. The men were handcuffed and chained together, in the usual manner for driving those poor wretches, while the women and children were suffered to proceed without encumbrance. It appears that, by means of a file the negroes, unobserved, had succeeded in separating the iron which bound their hands, in such a way as to be able to throw them off at any moment. About 8 o'clock in the morning, while proceeding on the state road leading from Greenup to Vanceburg, two of them dropped their shackles and commenced a fight, when the wagoner (Petit) rushed in with his whip to compel them to desist. At this moment, every negro was found to be perfectly at liberty; and one of them seizing a club, gave Petit a violent blow on the head, and laid him dead at his feet; and Allen, who came to his assistance, met a similar fate, from the contents of a pistol fired by another of the gang. Gordon was then attacked, seized and held by one of the negroes, whilst another fired twice at him with a pistol, the ball of which each time grazed his head, but not proving effectual, he was beaten with clubs, and left for dead. They then commenced pillaging the wagon, and with an axe split open the trunk of Gordon, and rifled it of the money, about $2,400. Sixteen of the negroes then took to the woods; Gordon, in the mean time, not being materially injured, was enabled, by the assistance of one of the women, to mount his horse and flee; pursued, however, by one of the gang on another horse, with a drawn pistol; fortunately he escaped with his life barely, arriving at a plantation, as the negro came in sight; who then turned about and retreated.

"The neighbourhood was immediately rallied, and a hot pursuit given – which, we understand, has resulted in the capture of the whole gang and the recovery of the greatest part of the money. Seven of the negro men and one woman, it is said were engaged in the murders, and will be brought to trial at the next court in Greenupsburg."

Here my brethren, I want you to notice particularly in the above article, the *ignorant* and *deceitful actions* of this coloured woman. I beg you to view it candidly, as for ETERNITY! Here a *notorious wretch*, with two other confederates had SIXTY of them in a gang, driving them like brutes – the men all in chains and handcuffs, and by the help of God they got their chains and hand-cuffs thrown off, and caught two of the wretches and put them to death, and beat the other until they thought he was dead, and left him for dead; however, he deceived them, and rising from the ground, this *servile woman* helped him upon his horse, and he made his escape. Brethren, what do you think of this? Was it the natural *fine feelings* of this woman, to save such a wretch alive? I know that the blacks, take them half enlightened and ignorant, are more humane and merciful than the most enlightened and refined European that can be found in all the earth. Let no one say that I assert this because I am prejudiced on the side of my colour, and against the whites or Europeans. For what I write, I do it candidly, for my God and the good of both parties: Natural observations have taught me these things; there is a solemn awe in the hearts of the blacks, as it respects *murdering* men:[13] whereas the whites (though they are great cowards) where they have the advantage, or think that there are any prospects of getting it, they murder all before them, in order to subject men to wretchedness and degradation under them. This is the natural result of pride and avarice. But I declare, the actions of this black woman are really insupportable. For my own part, I cannot think it was any thing but servile deceit, combined with the most gross ignorance: for we must remember that *humanity, kindness* and the *fear of the Lord*, does not consist in protecting *devils*. Here is a set of wretches, who had SIXTY of them in a gang, driving them around the country like *brutes*, to dig up gold and silver for them (which they will get enough of yet.) Should the lives of such creatures be spared? Are God and Mammon in league? What has the Lord to do with a gang of desperate wretches, who go sneaking about the country like robbers – light upon his people wherever they can get a chance, binding them with chains and hand-cuffs, beat and murder them as they would *rattle-snakes?* Are they not the Lord's enemies? Ought they not to be destroyed? Any person who will save such wretches from destruction, is fighting against the Lord, and will receive his just recompense. The black men acted like *blockheads*. Why did they not make sure of the wretch? He would have made sure of them, if he could. It is just the way with black men – eight white men can frighten fifty of them: whereas, if you can only get courage into the blacks, I do declare it, that one good black man can put to death six white men; and I give it as a fact, let twelve black men get well armed for battle, and they will kill and put to flight fifty whites. The reason is, the blacks, once you get them started, they glory in death. The whites have had us under them for more than three centuries, murdering, and treating us like brutes; and, as Mr. Jefferson wisely said, they have never *found us out* – they do

not know, indeed, that there is an unconquerable disposition in the breasts of the blacks, which, when it is fully awakened and put in motion, will be subdued, only with the destruction of the animal existence. Get the blacks started, and if you do not have a gang of tigers and lions to deal with, I am a deceiver of the blacks and of the whites. How sixty of them could let that wretch escape unkilled, I cannot conceive – they will have to suffer as much for the two whom, they secured, as if they had put one hundred to death: if you commence, make sure work – do not trifle, for they will not trifle with you – they want us for their slaves, and think nothing of murdering us in order to subject us to that wretched condition – therefore, if there is an *attempt* made by us, kill or be killed. Now, I ask you, had you not rather be killed than to be a slave to a tyrant, who takes the life of your mother, wife, and dear little children? Look upon your mother, wife and children, and answer God Almighty; and believe this, that it is no more harm for you to kill a man, who is trying to kill you, than it is for you to take a drink of water when thirsty; in fact, the man who will stand still and let another murder him, is worse than an infidel, and, if he has common sense, ought not to be pitied. The actions of this deceitful and ignorant coloured woman, in saving the life of a desperate wretch, whose avaricious and cruel object was to drive her, and her companions in miseries, through the country like cattle, to make his fortune on their carcasses, are but too much like that of thousands of our brethren in these states: if any thing is whispered by one, which has any allusion to the melioration of their dreadful condition, they run and tell tyrants, that they may be enabled to keep them the longer in wretchedness and miseries. Oh! coloured people of these United States, I ask you, in the name of that God who made us, have we, in consequence of oppression, nearly lost the spirit of man, and, in no very trifling degree, adopted that of brutes? Do you answer, no? – I ask you, then, what set of men can you point me to, in all the world, who are so abjectly employed by their oppressors, as we are by our *natural enemies?* How can, Oh! how can those enemies but say that we and our children are not of the HUMAN FAMILY, but were made by our Creator to be an inheritance to them and theirs for ever? How can the slaveholders but say that they can bribe the best coloured person in the country, to sell his brethren for a trifling sum of money, and take that atrocity to confirm them in their avaricious opinion, that we were made to be slaves to them and their children? How could Mr. Jefferson but say,[14] "I advance it therefore as a suspicion only, that the blacks, whether originally a distinct race, or made distinct by time and circumstances, are *inferior* to the whites in the endowments both of body and mind?" – "It," says he, "is not against experience to suppose, that different species of the same genius, or varieties of the same species, may possess different qualifications." [Here, my brethren, listen to him.] "Will not a lover of natural history, then, one who views the gradations in all the races of *animals* with the eye of philosophy, excuse an effort to keep those in the department of M AN as *distinct* as nature has formed them?" – I hope you will try to find out the meaning of this verse – its widest sense and all its bearings: whether you do or not, remember the whites do. This very verse, brethren, having emanated from Mr. Jefferson, a much greater philosopher the world never afforded, has in truth injured us more, and has been as great a barrier to our emancipation as any thing that has ever been advanced against us. I hope you will not let it pass unnoticed. He goes on further, and says: "This *unfortunate* difference of colour, and *perhaps* of *faculty*, is a powerful obstacle to the emancipation of these people. Many of their advocates, while they wish to vindicate the liberty of human nature are anxious also to preserve its *dignity* and *beauty*. Some of these, embarrassed by the question, 'What further is to be done with them?' join themselves in opposition with those who are actuated by sordid avarice only." Now I ask you candidly, my suffering brethren in time, who are candidates for the eternal worlds, how could Mr. Jefferson but have given the world these remarks respecting us, when we are so submissive to them, and so much servile deceit prevail among ourselves – when we so meanly submit to their murderous lashes, to which neither the Indians nor any other people under Heaven would submit? No, they would die to a man, before they would suffer such things from men who are no better than themselves, and *perhaps not so good*. Yes, how can our friends but be embarrassed, as Mr. Jefferson says, by the question, "What further is to be done with these people?" For while they are working for our emancipation, we are, by our treachery, wickedness and deceit, working against ourselves and our children – helping ours, and the enemies of God, to keep us and our dear little children in their infernal chains of slavery!!! Indeed, our friends cannot but relapse and join themselves "with

those who are actuated by *sordid avarice only!!!!*" For my own part, I am glad Mr. Jefferson has advanced his positions for your sake; for you will either have to contradict or confirm him by your own actions, and not by what our friends have said or done for us; for those things are other men's labours, and do not satisfy the Americans, who are waiting for us to prove to them ourselves, that we are M EN, before they will be willing to admit the fact; for I pledge you my sacred word of honour, that Mr. Jefferson's remarks respecting us, have sunk deep into the hearts of millions of the whites, and never will be removed this side of eternity. For how can they, when we are confirming him every day, by our *groveling submissions* and *treachery*? I aver, that when I look over these United States of America, and the world, and see the ignorant deceptions and consequent wretchedness of my brethren, I am brought oftimes solemnly to a stand, and in the midst of my reflections I exclaim to my God, "Lord didst thou make us to be slaves to our brethren, the whites?" But when I reflect that God is just, and that millions of my wretched brethren would meet death with glory – yea, more, would plunge into the very mouths of cannons and be torn into particles as minute as the atoms which compose the elements of the earth, in preference to a mean submission to the lash of tyrants, I am with streaming eyes, compelled to shrink back into nothingness before my Maker, and exclaim again, thy will be done, O Lord God Almighty.

Men of colour, who are also of sense, for you particularly is my APPEAL designed. Our more ignorant brethren are not able to penetrate its value. I call upon you therefore to cast your eyes upon the wretchedness of your brethren, and to do your utmost to enlighten them – *go to work and enlighten your brethren!* – Let the Lord see you doing what you can to rescue them and yourselves from degradation. Do any of you say that you and your family are free and happy, and what have you to do with the wretched slaves and other people? So can I say, for I enjoy as much freedom as any of you, if I am not quite as well off as the best of you. Look into our freedom and happiness, and see of what kind they are composed!! They are of the very lowest kind – they are the very *dregs!* – they are the most servile and abject kind, that ever a people was in possession of! If any of you wish to know how FREE you are, let one of you start and go through the southern and western States of this country, and unless you travel as a slave to a white man (a servant is a *slave* to the man whom he serves) or have your free papers (which if you are not careful they will get from you) if they do not take you up and put you in jail, and if you cannot give good evidence of your freedom, sell you into eternal slavery, I am not a living man: or any man of colour, immaterial who he is, or where he came from, if he is not *the fourth from the negro race!!* (as we are called) the white Christians of America will serve him the same they will sink him into wretchedness and degradation for ever while he lives. And yet some of you have the hardihood to say that you are free and happy! May God have mercy on your freedom and happiness!! I met a coloured man in the street a short time since, with a string of boots on his shoulders; we fell into conversation, and in course of which, I said to him, what a miserable set of people we are! He asked, why? – Said I, we are so subjected under the whites, that we cannot obtain the comforts of life, but by cleaning their boots and shoes, old clothes, waiting on them, shaving them &c. Said he (with the boots on his shoulders), "I am completely happy!!! I never want to live any better or happier than when I can get a plenty of boots and shoes to clean!" Oh! how can those who are actuated by avarice only, but think, that our Creator made us to be an inheritance to them for ever, when they see that our greatest glory is centered in such mean and low objects? Understand me, brethren, I do not mean to speak against the occupations by which we acquire enough and sometimes scarcely that, to render ourselves and families comfortable through life. I am subjected to the same inconvenience, as you all. My objections are, to our *glorying* and being *happy* in such low employments; for if we are men, we ought to be thankful to the Lord for the past, and for the future. Be looking forward with thankful hearts to higher attainments than *wielding the razor* and *cleaning boots and shoes.* The man whose aspirations are not *above,* and even *below* these, is indeed, ignorant and wretched enough. I advanced it therefore to you, not as a *problematical,* but as an unshaken and for ever immovable *fact,* that your full glory and happiness, as well as all other coloured people under Heaven, shall never be fully consummated, but with the *entire emancipation of your enslaved brethren all over the world.* You may therefore, go to work and do what you can to rescue, or join in with tyrants to oppress them and yourselves, until the Lord shall come upon you all like a thief in the night. For I believe it is the will of the Lord that our greatest happiness shall consist in working for

the salvation of our whole body. When this is accomplished a burst of glory will shine upon you, which will indeed astonish you and the world. Do any of you say this never will be done? I assure you that God will accomplish it – if nothing else will answer, he will hurl tyrants and devils into *atoms* and make way for his people. But O my brethren! I say unto you again, you must go to work and prepare the way of the Lord.

There is a great work for you to do, as trifling as some of you may think of it. You have to prove to the Americans and the world, that we are MEN, and not *brutes,* as we have been represented, and by millions treated. Remember, to let the aim of your labours, among your brethren, and particularly the youths, be the dissemination of education and religion.[15] It is lamentable, that many of our children go to school, from four until they are eight or ten, and sometimes fifteen years of age, and leave school knowing but a little more about the grammar of their language than a horse does about handling a musket – and not a few of them are really so ignorant, that they are unable to answer a person correctly, general questions in geography, and to hear them read, would only be to disgust a man who has a taste for reading; which, to do well, as trifling as it may appear to some (to the ignorant in particular) is a great part of learning. Some few of them, may make out to scribble tolerably well, over a half sheet of paper, which I believe has hitherto been a powerful obstacle in our way, to keep us from acquiring knowledge. An ignorant father, who knows no more than what nature has taught him, together with what little he acquires by the senses of hearing and seeing, finding his son able to write a neat hand, sets it down for granted that he has as good learning as any body; the young, ignorant gump, hearing his father or mother, who perhaps may be ten times more ignorant, in point of literature, than himself, extolling his learning, struts about, in the full assurance, that his attainments in literature are sufficient to take him through the world, when, in fact, he has scarcely any learning at all!!!!

I promiscuously fell in conversation once, with an elderly coloured man on the topics of education, and of the great prevalency of ignorance among us: Said he, "I know that our people are very ignorant but my son has a good education: I spent a great deal of money on his education: he can write as well as any white man, and I assure you that no one can fool him," &c. Said I, what else can your son do, besides writing a good hand? Can he post a set of books in a mercantile manner? Can he write a neat piece of composition in prose or in verse? To these interrogations he answered in the negative. Said I, did your son learn, while he was at school, the width and depth of English Grammar? To which he also replied in the negative, telling me his son did not learn those things. Your son, said I, then, has hardly any learning at all – he is almost as ignorant, and more so, than many of those who never went to school one day in all their lives. My friend got a little put out, and so walking off, said that his son could write as well as any white man. Most of the coloured people, when they speak of the education of one among us who can write a neat hand, and who perhaps knows nothing but to scribble and puff pretty fair on a small scrap of paper, immaterial whether his words are grammatical, or spelt correctly, or not; if it only looks beautiful, they say he has as good an education as any white man – he can write as well as any white man, &c. The poor, ignorant creature, hearing this, he is ashamed, forever after, to let any person see him humbling himself to another for knowledge but going about trying to deceive those who are more ignorant than himself, he at last falls an ignorant victim to death in wretchedness. I pray that the Lord may undeceive my ignorant brethren, and permit them to throw away pretensions, and seek after the substance of learning. I would crawl on my hands and knees through mud and mire, to the feet of a learned man, where I would sit and humbly supplicate him to instil into me, that which neither devils nor tyrants could remove, only with my life – for coloured people to acquire learning in this country, makes tyrants quake and tremble on their sandy foundation. Why, what is the matter? Why, they know that their infernal deeds of cruelty will be made known to the world. Do you suppose one man of good sense and learning would submit himself, his father, mother, wife and children, to be slaves to a wretched man like himself, who, instead of compensating him for his labours, chains, hand-cuffs and beats him and family almost to death, leaving life enough in them, however, to work for, and call him master? No! no! he would cut his devilish throat from ear to ear, and well do slave-holders know it. The bare name of educating the coloured people, scares our cruel oppressors almost to death. But if they do not have enough to be frightened for yet, it will be, because they can always keep us ignorant, and because God approbates their cruelties, with which they have been for

centuries murdering us. The whites shall have enough of the blacks, yet, as true as God sits on his throne in Heaven.

Some of our brethren are so very full of learning, that you cannot mention any thing to them which they do not know better than yourself!! – nothing is strange to them!! – they knew every thing years ago! – if any thing should be mentioned in company where they are, immaterial how important it is respecting us or the world, if they had not divulged it; they make light of it, and affect to have known it long before it was mentioned and try to make all in the room, or wherever you may be, believe that your conversation is nothing!! – not worth hearing! All this is the result of ignorance and ill-breeding; for a man of good-breeding, sense and penetration, if he had heard a subject told twenty times over, and should happen to be in company where one should commence telling it again, he would wait with patience on its narrator, and see if he would tell it as it was told in his presence before – paying the most strict attention to what is said, to see if any more light will be thrown on the subject: for all men are not gifted alike in telling, or even hearing the most simple narration. These ignorant, vicious, and wretched men, contribute almost as much injury to our body as tyrants themselves, by doing so much for the promotion of ignorance amongst us; for they, making such pretensions to knowledge, such of our youth as are seeking after knowledge, and can get access to them, take them as criterions to go by, who will lead them into a channel, where, unless the Lord blesses them with the privilege of seeing their folly, they will be irretrievably lost forever, while in time!!!

I must close this article by relating the very heart-rending fact, that I have examined school-boys and young men of colour in different parts of the country, in the most simple parts of Murray's English Grammar, and not more than one in thirty was able to give a correct answer to my interrogations. If any one contradicts me, let him step out of his door into the streets of Boston, New-York, Philadelphia, or Baltimore (no use to mention any other, for the Christians are too charitable further south or west!) – I say, let him who disputes me, step out of his door into the streets of either of those four cities, and promiscuously collect one hundred school-boys, or young men of colour, *who have been to school*, and who are considered by the coloured people to have received an excellent education, because, perhaps, some of them can write a good hand, but who, notwithstanding their neat writing, may be almost as ignorant, in comparison, as a horse. And, I say it, he will hardly find (in this enlightened day, and in the midst of this *charitable* people) five in one hundred, who are able to correct the false grammar of their language. The cause of this almost universal ignorance among us, I appeal to our schoolmasters to declare. Here is a fact, which I this very minute take from the mouth of a young coloured man, who has been to school in this state (Massachusetts) nearly nine years, and who knows grammar this day, *nearly* as well as he did the day he first entered the schoolhouse, under a white master. This young man says: "My master would never allow me to study grammar." I asked him, why? "The school committee," said he "forbid the coloured children learning grammar – they would not allow any but the white children to study grammar." It is a notorious fact, that the major part of the white Americans, have, ever since we have been among them, tried to keep us ignorant, and make us believe that God made us and our children to be slaves to them and theirs. *Oh! my God, have mercy on Christian Americans!!!*

Notes

1 See Genesis, ch. xli: 39–40.
2 Ibid. 41.
3 Ibid. 44.
4 Ibid. 45.
5 Genesis, ch. xlvii: 5, 6.
6 [The reference is to Jefferson's *Notes on Virginia*, Query XIV. All of Walker's references to Jefferson are to this section of the *Notes*. Ed.]
7 See Exodus, ch. ii: 9, 10.
8 It is not to be understood here, that I mean for us to wait until God shall take us by the hair of our heads and drag us out of abject wretchedness and slavery, nor do I mean to convey the idea for us to wait until our enemies shall make preparations, and call us to seize those preparations, take it away from them, and put every thing before us to death, in order to gain our freedom which God has given us. For you must remember that we are men as well as they. God has been pleased to give us two eyes, two hands, two feet, and some sense in our heads as well as they. They have no more right to hold us in slavery than we have to hold them, we have just as much right, in the sight of God, to hold them and their children in slavery and wretchedness, as they have to hold us, and no more.
9 See Dr. Goldsmith's *History of Greece*, p. 9. See also, *Plutarch's Lives*. The Helots subdued by Agis, king of Sparta. [Walker's citation is to Oliver Goldsmith, *A History of Greece from the Earliest State to the Death of Alexander the Great*. Fifth American edition, 2 vols in 1 (Philadelphia, 1817). Ed.]
10 See his *Notes on Virginia*, p. 210.
11 See his *Notes on Virginia*, p. 211.
12 It is my solemn belief, that if ever the world becomes Christianized (which must certainly take place before long) it will be through the means, under God of the *Blacks*, who are now held in wretchedness, and degradation, by the white *Christians* of the world, who before they learn to do justice to us before our Maker – and be reconciled to us, and reconcile us to them, and by that means have clear consciences before God and man – Send out Missionaries to convert the Heathens, many of whom after they cease to worship gods, which neither see nor hear, become ten times more the children of Hell, than ever they were, why what is the reason? Why the reason is obvious, they must learn to do justice at home, before they go into distant lands, to display their charity, Christianity, and benevolence; when they learn to do justice, God will accept their offering (no man may think that I am against Missionaries for I am not, my object is to see justice done at home, before we go to convert the Heathens).
13 Which is the reason the whites take the advantage of us.
14 See his *Notes on Virginia*, p. 213.
15 Never mind what the ignorant ones among us may say, many of whom when you speak to them for their good, and try to enlighten their minds, laugh at you, and perhaps tell you plump to your face, that they want no instruction from you or any other Nigger, and all such aggravating language. Now if you are a man of understanding and sound sense, I conjure you in the name of the Lord, and of all that is good, to impute their actions to ignorance, and wink at their follies, and do your very best to get around them some way or other, for remember they are your brethren; and I declare to you that it is for your interests to teach and enlighten them.

27

Prejudices Against People of Color, and our Duties in Relation to this Subject

Lydia Maria Francis Child

Introduction

Lydia Maria Francis Child (1802–80) was born in Medford, Massachusetts. Her literary career began with the publication of *Hobomok, A Tale of Early Times* in 1821 and closed with *Aspirations of the World* in 1878. In 1833 she sacrificed much of her popularity by her *Appeal on Behalf of that Class of Americans Called Africans*, which argued for the abolition of slavery and for intermarriage between races for the purpose of eventually ending racial differences. From 1825 to 1828 she ran a private school in Watertown, MA. After her marriage in 1828, she and her husband David became ardent abolitionists. However, as a result of their activities as insurrectionist, which included using their home as a station in the Underground Railroad, the Childs were ostracized and *Juvenile Miscellany*, the first monthly magazine for children in the United States, which Lydia had started in 1826, failed.

"A negro has a soul, an' please your honor," said the Corporal (doubtingly.)

"I am not much versed, Corporal," quoth my Uncle Toby, "in things of that kind; but I suppose God would not leave him without one, any more than thee or me."

"It would be putting one sadly over the head of the other," quoth the Corporal.

"It would so," said my Uncle Toby.

Taken from *An Appeal on Behalf of that Class of Americans Called Africans* (Boston: Allen and Ticknor, 1833), pp. 208–32.

"Why then, an' please your honor, is a black man to be used worse than a white one?"

"I can give no reason," said my Uncle Toby.

"Only," cried the Corporal, shaking his head, "because he has no one to stand up for him."

"It is that very thing, Trim," quoth my Uncle Toby, "which recommends him to protection."

While we bestow our earnest disapprobation on the system of slavery, let us not flatter ourselves that we are in reality any better than our brethren of the South. Thanks to our soil and climate, and the early exertions of the Quakers, the *form* of slavery does not exist among us; but the very *spirit* of the hateful and mischievous thing is here in all its strength. The manner in which we use what power we have, gives us ample reason to be grateful that the nature of our institutions does not intrust us with more. Our prejudice against colored people is even more inveterate than it is at the South. The planter is often attached to his negroes, and lavishes caresses and kind words upon them, as he would on a favorite hound: but our cold-hearted, ignoble prejudice admits of no exception – no intermission.

The Southerners have long continued habit, apparent interest and dreaded danger, to palliate the wrong they do; but we stand without excuse. They tell us that Northern ships and Northern capital have been engaged in this wicked business; and the reproach is true. Several fortunes in this city have been made by the sale of negro blood. If these criminal transactions are still carried on, they are done in silence and secrecy, because public opinion has made them disgraceful. But if the free States wished to cherish the system of slavery forever, they could not take a more direct course than they now do. Those who are kind and liberal on all other subjects, unite with the selfish and the proud in their unrelenting efforts to keep the colored population in the lowest state of degradation; and the influence they unconsciously exert over children early infuses into their innocent minds the same strong feelings of contempt.

The intelligent and well informed have the least share of this prejudice; and when their minds can be brought to reflect upon it, I have generally observed that they soon cease to have any at all. But such a general apathy prevails and the subject is so seldom brought into view, that few are really aware how oppressively the influence of society is made to bear upon this injured class of the community. When I have related facts, that came under my own observation, I have often been listened to with surprise, which gradually increased to indignation. In order that my readers may not be ignorant of the extent of this tyrannical prejudice, I will as briefly as possible state the evidence, and leave them to judge of it, as their hearts and consciences may dictate.

In the first place, an unjust law exists in this Commonwealth, by which marriages between persons of different color is pronounced illegal. I am perfectly aware of the gross ridicule to which I may subject myself by alluding to this particular; but I have lived too long, and observed too much, to be disturbed by the world's mockery. In the first place, the government ought not to be invested with power to control the affections, any more than the consciences of citizens. A man has at least as good a right to choose his wife, as he has to choose his religion. His taste may not suit his neighbors; but so long as his deportment is correct, they have no right to interfere with his concerns. In the second place, this law is a *useless* disgrace to Massachusetts. Under existing circumstances, none but those whose condition in life is too low to be much affected by public opinion, will form such alliances; and they, when they choose to do so, *will* make such marriages, in spite of the law. I know two or three instances where women of the laboring class have been united to reputable, industrious colored men. These husbands regularly bring home their wages, and are kind to their families. If by some of the odd chances, which not unfrequently occur in the world, their wives should become heirs to any property, the children

may be wronged out of it, because the law pronounces them illegitimate. And while this injustice exists with regard to *honest*, industrious individuals, who are merely guilty of differing from us in a matter of taste, neither the legislation nor customs of slave-holding States exert their influence against *immoral* connexions.

In one portion of our country this fact is shown in a very peculiar and striking manner. There is a numerous class at New Orleans, called Quateroons, or Quadroons, because their colored blood has for several successive generations been intermingled with the white. The women are much distinguished for personal beauty and gracefulness of motion; and their parents frequently send them to France for the advantages of an elegant education. White gentlemen of the first rank are desirous of being invited to their parties, and often become seriously in love with these fascinating but unfortunate beings. Prejudice forbids matrimony, but universal custom sanctions temporary connexions, to which a certain degree of respectability is allowed, on account of the peculiar situation of the parties. These attachments often continue for years – sometimes for life – and instances are not unfrequent of exemplary constancy and great propriety of deportment.

What eloquent vituperations we should pour forth, if the contending claims of nature and pride produced such a tissue of contradictions in some other country, and not in our own!

There is another Massachusetts law, which an enlightened community would not probably suffer to be carried into execution under any circumstances; but it still remains to disgrace the statutes of this Commonwealth. It is as follows:

"No African or Negro, other than a subject of the Emperor of Morocco, or a citizen of the United States (proved so by a certificate of the Secretary of the State of which he is a citizen) shall tarry within this Commonwealth longer than two months; and on complaint a justice shall order him to depart in ten days; and if he do not then, the justice may commit such African or Negro to the House of Correction, there to be kept at hard labor; and at the next term of the Court of C. P., he shall be tried, and if convicted of remaining as aforesaid, shall be whipped not exceeding ten lashes; and if he or she shall not *then* depart such process shall be repeated and punishment inflicted *tolies quoties*." Stat. 1788, Ch. 54.

An honorable Haytian or Brazilian, who visited this country for business or information, might come under this law, unless public opinion rendered it a mere dead letter.

There is among the colored people an increasing desire for information, and a laudable ambition to be respectable in manners and appearance. Are we not foolish as well as sinful, in trying to repress a tendency so salutary to themselves, and so beneficial to the community? Several individuals of this class are very desirous to have persons of their own color qualified to teach something more than mere reading and writing. But in the public schools, colored children are subject to many discouragements and difficulties; and into the private schools they cannot gain admission. A very sensible and well-informed colored woman in a neighboring town, whose family have been brought up in a manner that excited universal remark and approbation, has been extremely desirous to obtain for her eldest daughter the advantages of a private school; but she has been resolutely repulsed, on account of her complexion. The girl is a very light mulatto, with great modesty and propriety of manners; perhaps no young person in the Commonwealth was less likely to have a bad influence on her associates. The clergyman respected the family, and he remonstrated with the instructer; but while the latter admitted the injustice of the thing, he excused himself by saying such a step would occasion the loss of all his white scholars.

In a town adjoining Boston, a well-behaved colored boy was kept out of the public school more than a year, by vote of the trustees. His mother, having some information herself, knew the importance of knowledge, and was anxious to obtain it for her family. She wrote repeatedly and urgently; and the school-master himself told me that the correctness of her spelling, and the neatness of her hand-writing formed a curious contrast with the notes he received from many white parents. At last, this spirited woman appeared before the committee, and reminded them that her husband, having for many years paid taxes as a citizen, had a right to the privileges of a citizen; and if her claim were refused, or longer postponed, she declared her determination to seek justice from a higher source. The trustees were, of course, obliged to yield to the equality of the laws, with the best grace they could. The boy was admitted, and made good progress in his studies. Had his mother been too ignorant to know her rights, or too abject to demand them, the lad would have had a fair chance to get a living out

of the State as the occupant of a workhouse, or penitentiary.

The attempt to establish a school for African girls at Canterbury, Connecticut, has made too much noise to need a detailed account in this volume. I do not know the lady who first formed the project, but I am told that she is a benevolent and religious woman. It certainly is difficult to imagine any other motives than good ones, for an undertaking so arduous and unpopular. Yet had the Pope himself attempted to establish his supremacy over that commonwealth, he could hardly have been repelled with more determined and angry resistance. Town meetings were held, the records of which are not highly creditable to the parties concerned. Petitions were sent to the Legislature, beseeching that no African school might be allowed to admit individuals not residing in the town where said school was established; and strange to relate, this law, which makes it impossible to collect a sufficient number of pupils, was sanctioned by the State. A colored girl, who availed herself of this opportunity to gain instruction, was warned out of town, and fined for not complying; and the instructress was imprisoned for persevering in her benevolent plan.

It is said, in excuse, that Canterbury will be inundated with vicious characters, who will corrupt the morals of the young men; that such a school will break down the distinctions between black and white; and that marriages between people of different colors will be the probable result. Yet they seem to assume the ground that colored people *must* always be an inferior and degraded class – that the prejudice against them *must* be eternal; being deeply founded in the laws of God and nature. Finally, they endeavored to represent the school as one of the *incendiary* proceedings of the Anti-Slavery Society; and they appeal to the Colonization Society, as an aggrieved child is wont to appeal to its parent.

The objection with regard to the introduction of vicious characters into a village, certainly has some force; but are such persons likely to leave cities for a quiet country town, in search of moral and intellectual improvement? Is it not obvious that the *best* portion of the colored class are the very ones to prize such an opportunity for instruction? Grant that a large proportion of these unfortunate people *are* vicious – is it not our duty, and of course our wisest policy, to try to make them otherwise? And what will so effectually elevate their character and condition, as knowledge? I beseech you, my countrymen, think of these things wisely, and in season.

As for intermarriages, if there be such a repugnance between the two races, founded in the laws of *nature*, methinks there is small reason to dread their frequency.

The breaking down of distinctions in society, by means of extended information, is an objection which appropriately belongs to the Emperor of Austria, or the Sultan of Egypt.

I do not know how the affair at Canterbury is *generally* considered; but I have heard individuals of all parties and all opinions speak of it – and never without merriment or indignation. Fifty years hence, the *black* laws of Connecticut will be a greater source of amusement to the antiquarian, than her famous *blue* laws.

A similar, though less violent opposition arose in consequence of the attempt to establish a college for colored people at New Haven. A young colored man, who tried to obtain education at the Wesleyan college in Middleton, was obliged to relinquish the attempt on account of the persecution of his fellow students. Some collegians from the South objected to a colored associate in their recitations; and those from New England promptly and zealously joined in the hue and cry. A small but firm party were in favor of giving the colored man a chance to pursue his studies without insult or interruption; and I am told that this manly and disinterested band were all Southerners. As for those individuals, who exerted their influence to exclude an unoffending fellow-citizen from privileges which ought to be equally open to all, it is to be hoped that age will make them wiser – and that they will learn, before they die, to be ashamed of a step attended with more important results than usually belong to youthful follies.

It happens that these experiments have all been made in Connecticut; but it is no more than justice to that State to remark that a similar spirit would probably have been manifested in Massachusetts, under like circumstances. At our debating clubs and other places of public discussion, the demon of prejudice girds himself for the battle, the moment negro colleges and high schools are alluded to. Alas, while we carry on our lips that religion which teaches us to "love our neighbor as ourselves," how little do we cherish its blessed influence within our hearts! How much republicanism we have to *speak* of, and how little do we practise!

Let us seriously consider what injury a negro college could possibly do us. It is certainly a fair presumption that the scholars would be from the better portion of the colored population; and it is an equally fair presumption that knowledge would improve their characters. There are already many hundreds of colored people in the city of Boston. In the street they generally appear neat and respectable; and in our houses they do not "come between the wind and our nobility." Would the addition of one or two hundred more even be perceived? As for giving offence to the Southerners by allowing such establishments – they have no right to interfere with our internal concerns, any more than we have with theirs. Why should they not give up slavery to please us, by the same rule that we must refrain from educating the negroes to please them? If they are at liberty to do wrong, we certainly ought to be at liberty to do right. They may talk and publish as much about us as they please; and we ask for no other influence over them.

It is a fact not generally known that the brave Kosciusko left a fund for the establishment of a negro college in the United States. Little did he think he had been fighting for a people, who would not grant one rood of their vast territory for the benevolent purpose!

According to present appearances, a college for colored persons will be established in Canada; and thus, by means of our foolish and wicked pride, the credit of this philanthropic enterprise will be transferred to our mother country.

The preceding chapters show that it has been no uncommon thing for colored men to be educated at English, German, Portuguese and Spanish Universities.

In Boston there is an Infant School, three Primary Schools, and a Grammar School. The two last, are I believe supported by the public; and this fact is highly creditable. A building for the colored Grammar School is not supplied by the city, though such provision is àlways made for similar institutions for white boys. The apartment is close and uncomfortable, and many pupils stay away, who would gladly attend under more convenient circumstances. There ought likewise to be a colored teacher instead of a white one. Under the dominion of existing prejudices, it is difficult to find a white man, well qualified to teach such a school, who feels the interest he ought to feel, in these Pariahs[1] of our republic. The parents would repose more confidence in a colored instructer; and he, both from sympathy and pride, would be better fitted for his task.

It is peculiarly incumbent on the city authorities to supply a commodious building for the colored grammar school, because public prejudice excludes these oppressed people from all lucrative employments, and they cannot therefore be supposed to have ample funds of their own.

I was much pleased with the late resolution awarding Franklin medals to the colored pupils of the grammar school; and I was still more pleased with the laudable project, originated by Josiah Holbrook, Esq. for the establishment of a colored Lyceum. Surely a better spirit *is* beginning to work in this cause; and when once begun, the good sense and good feeling of the community will bid it go on and prosper. How much this spirit will have to contend with is illustrated by the following fact. When President Jackson entered this city, the white children of all the schools were sent out in uniform, to do him honor. A member of the Committee proposed that the pupils of the African schools should be invited likewise; but he was the only one who voted for it. He then proposed that the yeas and nays should be recorded; upon which, most of the gentlemen walked off, to prevent the question from being taken. Perhaps they felt an awkward consciousness of the incongeniality of such proceedings with our republican institutions. By order of the Committee the vacation of the African schools did not commence until the day after the procession of the white pupils; and a note to the instructer intimated that the pupils were not expected to appear on the Common. The reason given was because "their numbers were so few;" but in private conversation, fears were expressed lest their sable faces should give offence to our slave-holding President. In all probability the sight of the colored children would have been agreeable to General Jackson, and seemed more like home, than anything he witnessed.

In the theatre, it is not possible for respectable colored people to obtain a decent seat. They must either be excluded, or herd with the vicious.

A fierce excitement prevailed, not long since, because a colored man had bought a pew in one of our churches. I heard a very kind-hearted and zealous democrat declare his opinion that "the fellow ought to be turned out by constables, if he dared to occupy the pew he had purchased." Even at the communion-table, the mockery of human pride is mingled with the worship of Jehovah. Again and again have I seen a solitary negro come up to the altar, meekly and timidly, after all the white communicants had retired. One Epis-copal clergyman of this city, forms an honorable exception to this remark. When there is room at the altar, Mr —— often makes a signal to the colored members of his church to kneel beside their white brethren; and once, when two white infants and one colored one were to be baptized, and the parents of the latter bashfully lingered far behind the others, he silently rebuked the unchristian spirit of pride, by first administering the holy ordinance to the little dark-skinned child of God.

An instance of prejudice lately occurred, which I should find it hard to believe, did I not positively know it to be a fact. A gallery pew was purchased in one of our churches for two hundred dollars. A few Sabbaths after, an address was delivered at that church, in favor of the Africans. Some colored people, who very naturally wished to hear the discourse, went into the gallery; probably because they thought they should be deemed less intrusive there than elsewhere. The man who had recently bought a pew, found it occupied by colored people, and indignantly retired with his family. The next day, he purchased a pew in another meeting-house, protesting that nothing would tempt him again to make use of seats, that had been occupied by negroes.

A well known country representative, who makes a very loud noise about his democracy, once attended the Catholic church. A pious negro requested him to take off his hat, while he stood in the presence of the Virgin Mary. The white man rudely shoved him aside, saying, "You son of an Ethiopian, do you dare to speak to me!" I more than once heard the hero repeat this story; and he seemed to take peculiar satisfaction in telling it. Had he been less ignorant, he would not have chosen "son of an *Ethiopian*" as an *ignoble* epithet; to have called the African his own equal would have been abundantly more sarcastic. The same republican dismissed a strong, industrious colored man, who had been employed on the farm during his absence. "I am too great a democrat," quoth he, "to have any body in my house, who don't sit at my table; and I'll be hanged, if I ever eat with the son of an Ethiopian."

Men whose education leaves them less excuse for such illiberality, are yet vulgar enough to join in this ridiculous prejudice. The colored woman, whose daughter has been mentioned as excluded from a private school, was once smuggled into a stage, upon the supposition that she was a white woman, with a sallow complexion. Her manners were modest and prepossessing, and the gentlemen were very polite to her. But when she stopped at her own door, and was handed out by her curly-headed husband, they were at once surprised and angry to find they had been riding with a mulatto – and had, in their ignorance, been really civil to her!

A worthy colored woman, belonging to an adjoining town, wished to come into Boston to attend upon a son, who was ill. She had a trunk with her, and was too feeble to walk. She begged permission to ride in the stage. But the passengers with *noble* indignation, declared they would get out, if she were allowed to get in. After much entreaty, the driver suffered her to sit by him upon the box. When he entered the city, his comrades began to point and sneer. Not having sufficient moral courage to endure this, he left the poor woman, with her trunk, in the middle of the street, far from the place of her destination; telling her, with an oath, that he would not carry her a step further.

A friend of mine, lately wished to have a colored girl admitted into the stage with her, to take care of her babe. The girl was very lightly tinged with the sable hue, had handsome Indian features, and very pleasing manners. It was, however, evident that she was not white; and therefore the passengers objected to her company. This of course, produced a good deal of inconvenience on one side, and mortification on the other. My friend repeated the circumstance to a lady, who, as the daughter and wife of a clergyman, might be supposed to have imbibed some liberality. The lady seemed to think the experiment was very preposterous; but when my friend alluded to the mixed parentage of the girl, she exclaimed, with generous enthusiasm, "Oh, that alters the case, *Indians* certainly *have* their rights."

Every year a colored gentleman and scholar is becoming less and less of a rarity – thanks to the existence of the Haytian Republic, and the increasing liberality of the world! Yet if a person of refinement from Hayti, Brazil, or other countries, which we deem less enlightened than our own, should visit us, the very boys of this republic would dog his footsteps with the vulgar outcry of "Nigger! Nigger!" I have known this to be done, from no other provocation than the sight of a colored man with the dress and deportment of a gentleman. Were it not that republicanism, like Christianity, is often perverted from its true spirit by the bad passions of mankind, such things as these would make every honest mind disgusted with the very name of republics.

I am acquainted with a gentleman from Brazil who is shrewd, enterprising, noble-spirited, and highly respectable in character and manners; yet he has experienced almost every species of indignity on account of his color. Not long since, it became necessary for him to visit the southern shores of Massachusetts, to settle certain accounts connected with his business. His wife was in a feeble state of health, and the physicians had recommended a voyage. For this reason, he took passage for her with himself in the steam-boat; and the captain, as it appears, made no objection to a colored gentleman's money. After remaining on deck some time, Mrs —— attempted to pass into the cabin; but the captain prevented her; saying, "You must go down forward." The Brazilian urged that he had paid the customary price, and therefore his wife and infant had a right to a place in the ladies' cabin. The captain answered, "Your wife a'n't a lady; she is a nigger." The forward cabin was occupied by sailors; was entirely without accommodations for women, and admitted the seawater, so that a person could not sit in it comfortably without keeping the feet raised in a chair. The husband stated that his wife's health would not admit of such exposure; to which the captain still replied, "I don't allow any niggers in my cabin." With natural and honest indignation, the Brazilian exclaimed, "You Americans talk about the Poles! You are a great deal more Russian than the Russians." The affair was concluded by placing the colored gentleman and his invalid wife on the shore, and leaving them to provide for themselves as they could. Had the cabin been full, there would have been some excuse; but it was occupied only by two sailors' wives. The same individual sent for a relative in a distant town on account of illness in his family. After staying several weeks, it became necessary for her to return; and he procured a seat for her in the stage. The same ridiculous scene occurred; the passengers were afraid of losing their dignity by riding with a neat, respectable person, whose face was darker than their own. No public vehicle could be obtained, by which a colored citizen could be conveyed to her home; it therefore became absolutely necessary for the gentleman to leave his business and hire a chaise at great expense. Such proceedings are really inexcusable. No authority can be found for them in religion, reason, or the laws.

The Bible informs us that "a man of Ethiopia, an eunuch of great authority under Candace,

Queen of the Ethiopians, who had charge of all her treasure, came to Jerusalem to worship." Returning in his chariot, he read Esaias, the Prophet; and at his request Phillip went up into the chariot and sat with him, explaining the Scriptures. Where should we now find an apostle, who would ride in the same chariot with an Ethiopian!

Will any candid person tell me why respectable colored people should not be allowed to make use of public conveyances, open to all who are able and willing to pay for the privilege? Those who enter a vessel, or a stage-coach, cannot expect to select their companions. If they can afford to take a carriage or boat for themselves, then, and then only, they have a right to be exclusive. I was lately talking with a young gentleman on this subject, who professed to have no prejudice against colored people, except so far as they were ignorant and vulgar; but still he could not tolerate the idea of allowing them to enter stages and steam-boats. "Yet, you allow the same privilege to vulgar and ignorant white men, without a murmur," I replied; "Pray give a good republican reason why a respectable colored citizen should be less favored." For want of a better argument, he said – (pardon me, fastidious reader) – he implied that the presence of colored persons was less agreeable than Otto of Rose, or Eau de Cologne; and this distinction, he urged was made by God himself. I answered, "Whoever takes his chance in a public vehicle, is liable to meet with uncleanly white passengers, whose breath may be redolent with the fumes of American cigars, or American gin. Neither of these articles have a fragrance peculiarly agreeable to nerves of delicate organization. Allowing your argument double the weight it deserves, it is utter nonsense to pretend that the inconvenience in the case I have supposed is not infinitely greater. But what is more to the point, do you dine in a fashionable hotel, do you sail in a fashionable steam-boat, do you sup at a fashionable house, without having negro servants behind your chair. Would they be any more disagreeable, as *passengers* seated in the corner of a stage, or a steam-boat, than as *waiters* in such immediate attendance upon your person?"

Stage-drivers are very much perplexed when they attempt to vindicate the present tyrannical customs; and they usually give up the point, by saying they themselves have no prejudice against colored people – they are merely afraid of the public. But stage-drivers should remember that in a popular government, they, in common with every other citizen, form a part and portion of the dreaded public.

The gold was never coined for which I would barter my individual freedom of acting and thinking upon any subject, or knowingly interfere with the rights of the meanest human being. The only true courage is that which impels us to do right without regard to consequences. To fear a populace is as servile as to fear an emperor. The only salutary restraint is the fear of doing wrong.

Our representatives to Congress have repeatedly rode in a stage with colored servants at the request of their masters. Whether this is because New Englanders are willing to do out of courtesy to a Southern gentleman, what they object to doing from justice to a colored citizen – or whether those representatives, being educated men, were more than usually divested of this absurd prejudice – I will not pretend to say.

The state of public feeling not only makes it difficult for the Africans to obtain information, but it prevents them from making profitable use of what knowledge they have. A colored man, however intelligent, is not allowed to pursue any business more lucrative than that of a barber, a shoe-black, or a waiter. These, and all other employments, are truly respectable, whenever the duties connected with them are faithfully performed; but it is unjust that a man should, on account of his complexion, be prevented from performing more elevated uses in society. Every citizen ought to have a fair chance to try his fortune in any line of business, which he thinks he has ability to transact. Why should not colored men be employed in the manufactories of various kinds? If their ignorance is an objection, let them be enlightened, as speedily as possible. If their moral character is not sufficiently pure, remove the pressure of public scorn, and thus supply them with motives for being respectable. All this can be done. It merely requires an earnest wish to overcome a prejudice, which has "grown with our growth and strengthened with our strength," but which is in fact opposed to the spirit of our religion, and contrary to the instinctive good feelings of our nature. When examined by the clear light of reason, it disappears. Prejudices of all kinds have their strongest holds in the minds of the vulgar and the ignorant. In a community so enlightened as our own, they must gradually melt away under the influence of public discussion. There is no want of kind feelings and liberal sentiments in the

American people; the simple fact is, they have not *thought* upon this subject. An active and enterprising community are not apt to concern themselves about laws and customs, which do not obviously interfere with their interests or convenience; and various political and prudential motives have combined to fetter free inquiry in this direction. Thus we have gone on, year after year, thoughtlessly sanctioning, by our silence and indifference, evils which our hearts and consciences are far enough from approving.

It has been shown that no other people on earth indulge so strong a prejudice with regard to color, as we do. It is urged that negroes are civilly treated in England, because their numbers are so few. I could never discover any great force in this argument. Colored people are certainly not sufficiently rare in that country to be regarded as a great show, like a giraffe, or a Sandwich Island king; and on the other hand, it would seem natural that those who were more accustomed to the sight of dark faces would find their aversion diminished, rather than increased.

The absence of prejudice in the Portuguese and Spanish settlements is accounted for, by saying that the white people are very little superior to the negroes in knowledge and refinement. But Doctor Walsh's book certainly gives us no reason to think meanly of the Brazilians; and it has been my good fortune to be acquainted with many highly intelligent South Americans, who were divested of this prejudice, and much surprised at its existence here.

If the South Americans are really in such a low state as the argument implies, it is a still greater disgrace to us to be outdone in liberality and consistent republicanism by men so much less enlightened than ourselves.

Pride will doubtless hold out with strength and adroitness against the besiegers of its fortress; but it is an obvious truth that the condition of the world is rapidly improving, and that our laws and customs must change with it.

Neither ancient nor modern history furnishes a page more glorious than the last twenty years in England; for at every step, free principles, after a long and arduous struggle, have conquered selfishness and tyranny. Almost all great evils are resisted by individuals who directly suffer injustice or inconvenience from them; but it is a peculiar beauty of the abolition cause that its defenders enter the lists against wealth, and power, and talent, not to defend their own rights, but to protect weak and injured neighbors, who are not allowed to speak for themselves.

Those, who become interested in a cause laboring so heavily under the pressure of present unpopularity, must expect to be assailed by every form of bitterness and sophistry. At times, discouraged and heart-sick, they will perhaps begin to doubt whether there are in reality any unalterable principles of right and wrong. But let them cast aside the fear of man, and keep their minds fixed on a few of the simple, unchangeable laws of God, and they will certainly receive strength to contend with the adversary.

Paragraphs in the Southern papers already begin to imply that the United States will not look tamely on, while England emancipates her slaves; and they inform us that the inspection of the naval stations has become a subject of great importance since the recent measures of the British Parliament. A republic declaring war with a monarchy, because she gave freedom to her slaves, would indeed form a beautiful moral picture for the admiration of the world!

Mr Garrison was the first person who dared to edit a newspaper, in which slavery was spoken of as altogether wicked and inexcusable. For this crime the Legislature of Georgia have offered five thousand dollars to any one who will "arrest and prosecute him to conviction *under the laws of that State*." An association of gentlemen in South Carolina have likewise offered a large reward for the same object. It is, to say the least, a very remarkable step for one State in this Union to promulgate such a law concerning a citizen of another State, merely for publishing his opinions boldly. The disciples of Fanny Wright promulgate the most zealous and virulent attacks upon Christianity, without any hindrance from the civil authorities; and this is done upon the truly rational ground that individual freedom of opinion ought to be respected – that what is false cannot stand, and what is true cannot be overthrown. We leave Christianity to take care of itself; but slavery is a "delicate subject" – and whoever attacks that must be punished. Mr Garrison is a disinterested, intelligent, and remarkably pure-minded man, whose only fault is that he cannot be moderate on a subject which it is exceedingly difficult for an honest mind to examine with calmness. Many, who highly respect his character, and motives, regret his tendency to use wholesale and unqualified expressions; but it is something to have the truth told, even if it be not in the most judicious way. Where an evil is powerfully supported by the self-interest and prejudice of the community, none but an ardent individual will venture to meddle with it. Luther was deemed indiscreet even by those who liked him best; yet a more prudent man would never have given an impetus sufficiently powerful to heave the great mass of corruption under which the church was buried. Mr Garrison has certainly the merit of having first called public attention to a neglected and very important subject. I believe whoever fairly and dispassionately examines the question, will be more than disposed to forgive the occasional faults of an ardent temperament, in consideration of the difficulty of the undertaking, and the violence with which it has been opposed.

The palliator of slavery assures the abolitionists that their benevolence is perfectly quixotic – that the negroes are happy and contented, and have no desire to change their lot. An answer to this may, as I have already said, be found in the Judicial Reports of slave-holding States, in the vigilance of their laws, in advertisements for runaway slaves, and in the details of their own newspapers. The West India planters make the same protestations concerning the happiness of their slaves; yet the cruelties proved by undoubted and unanswerable testimony are enough to break a compassionate heart. It is said that slavery is a great deal worse in the West Indies than in the United States; but I believe precisely the reverse of this proposition has been true within late years; for the English government have been earnestly trying to atone for their guilt, by the introduction of laws expressly framed to guard the weak and defenceless. A gentleman who has been a great deal among the planters of both countries, and who is by no means favorable to anti-slavery, gives it as his decided opinion that the slaves are better off in the West Indies, than they are in the United States. It is true we *hear* a great deal more about West Indian cruelty than we do about our own. English books and periodicals are continually full of the subject; and even in the colonies, newspapers openly denounce the hateful system, and take every opportunity to prove the amount of wretchedness it produces. In this country, we have not, until very recently, dared to publish anything upon the subject. Our books, our reviews, our newspapers, our almanacs, have all been silent, or exerted their influence on the wrong side. The negro's crimes are repeated, but his sufferings are never told. Even in our geographies it is taught that the colored race *must* always be degraded. Now and then anecdotes of cruelties committed in the slave-holding States are told by individuals who witnessed them; but they are almost always afraid to give their names to the public, because the Southerners will call them "a disgrace to the soil," and the Northerners will echo the sentiment. The promptitude and earnestness with which New England has aided the slave-holders in repressing all discussions which they were desirous to avoid, has called forth many expressions of gratitude in their public speeches, and private conversation; and truly we have well earned Randolph's favorite appellation, "the white slaves of the North," by our tameness and servility with regard to a subject where good feeling and good principle alike demanded a firm and independent spirit.

We are told that the Southerners will of themselves do away slavery, and they alone understand how to do it. But it is an obvious fact that all their measures have tended to perpetuate the system; and even if we have the fullest faith that they mean to do their duty, the belief by no means absolves us from doing ours. The evil is gigantic; and its removal requires every heart and head in the community.

It is said that our sympathies ought to be given to the masters, who are abundantly more to be pitied than the slaves. If this be the case, the planters are singularly disinterested not to change places with their bondmen. Our sympathies *have* been given to the masters – and to those masters who seemed most desirous to remain forever in their pitiable condition. There are hearts at the South sincerely desirous of doing right in this cause; but their generous impulses are checked by the laws of their respective States, and the strong disapprobation of their neighbors. I know a lady in Georgia, who would, I believe, make any personal sacrifice to instruct her slaves, and give them freedom; but if she were found guilty of teaching the alphabet, or manumitting her slaves, fines and imprisonment would be the consequence; if she sold them, they would be likely to fall into hands less merciful than her own. Of such slave-owners we cannot speak with too much respect and tenderness. They are comparatively few in number, and stand in a most perplexing situation; it is a duty to give all our sympathy to *them*. It is mere mockery to say, what is so often said, that the Southerners, as a body, really wish to abolish slavery. If they wished it, they certainly would make the attempt. When the majority

321

heartily desire a change, it is effected, be the difficulties what they may. The Americans are peculiarly responsible for the example they give; for in no other country does the unchecked voice of the people constitute the whole of government.

We must not be induced to excuse slavery by the plausible argument that England introduced it among us. The wickedness of beginning such a work unquestionably belongs to her; the sin of continuing it is certainly our own. It is true that Virginia, while a province, did petition the British government to check the introduction of slaves into the colonies; and their refusal to do so was afterward enumerated among the public reasons for separating from the mother country: but it is equally true that when we became independent, the Southern States stipulated that the slave trade should not be abolished by law until 1808.

The strongest and best reason that can be given for our supineness on the subject of slavery, is the fear of dissolving the Union. The Constitution of the United States demands our highest reverence. Those who approve, and those who disapprove of particular portions, are equally bound to yield implicit obedience to its authority. But we must not forget that the Constitution provides for any change that may be required for the general good. The great machine is constructed with a safety valve, by which any rapidly increasing evil may be expelled whenever the people desire it.

If the Southern politicians are determined to make a Siamese question of this also – if they insist that the Union shall not exist without slavery – it can only be said that they join two things, which have no affinity with each other, and which cannot permanently exist together. They chain the living and vigorous to the diseased and dying; and the former will assuredly perish in the infected neighborhood.

The universal introduction of free labor is the surest way to consolidate the Union, and enable us to live together in harmony and peace. If a history is ever written entitled "The Decay and Dissolution of the North American Republic," its author will distinctly trace our downfall to the existence of slavery among us.

There is hardly anything bad, in politics or religion, that has not been sanctioned or tolerated by a suffering community, because certain powerful individuals were able to identify the evil with some other principle long consecrated to the hearts and consciences of men.

Under all circumstances, there is but one honest course; and that is to do right, and trust the consequences to Divine Providence. "Duties are ours; events are God's." Policy, with all her cunning, can devise no rule so safe, salutary, and effective, as this simple maxim.

We cannot too cautiously examine arguments and excuses brought forward by those whose interest or convenience is connected with keeping their fellow creatures in a state of ignorance and brutality; and such we shall find in abundance, at the North as well as the South. I have heard the abolition of slavery condemned on the ground that New England vessels would not be employed to export the produce of the South, if they had free laborers of their own. This objection is so utterly bad in its spirit, that it hardly deserves an answer. Assuredly it is a righteous plan to retard the progress of liberal principles, and "keep human nature forever in the stocks" that some individuals may make a few hundred dollars more per annum! Besides, the experience of the world abundantly proves that all such forced expedients are unwise. The increased prosperity of one country, or of one section of a country, always contributes, in some form or other, to the prosperity of other states. To "love our neighbor as ourselves" is, after all, the shrewdest way of doing business.

In England, the abolition of the *traffic* was long and stoutly resisted, in the same spirit, and by the same arguments, that characterize the defence of the *system* here; but it would now be difficult to find a man so reckless, that he would not be ashamed of being called a slave dealer. Public opinion has nearly conquered one evil, and if rightly directed, it will ultimately subdue the other.

Is it asked what can be done? I answer, much, very much, can be effected, if each individual will try to deserve the commendation bestowed by our Saviour on the woman of old – "She hath done what she could."

The Quakers – always remarkable for fearless obedience to the inward light of conscience – early gave an example worthy of being followed. At their annual meeting in Pennsylvania, in 1688, many individuals urged the incompatibility of slavery, and Christianity; and their zeal continued until, in 1776, all Quakers who bought or sold a slave, or refused to emancipate those they already owned, were excluded from communion with the society. Had it not been for the early exertions of these excellent people, the fair and flourishing State of

Pennsylvania might now, perchance, be withering under the effects of slavery. To this day, the Society of Friends, both in England and America, omit no opportunity, public or private, of discountenancing this bad system; and the Methodists (at least in England) have earnestly labored in the same glorious cause.

The famous Anthony Benezet, a Quaker in Philadelphia, has left us a noble example of what may be done for conscience' sake. Being a teacher, he took effectual care that his scholars should have ample knowledge and christian impressions concerning the nature of slavery; he caused articles to be inserted in the almanacs likely to arrest public attention upon the subject; he talked about it, and wrote letters about it; he published and distributed tracts at his own expense; if any person was going a journey, his first thought was how he could make him instrumental in favor of his benevolent purposes; he addressed a petition to the Queen for the suppression of the slave-trade; and another to the good Countess of Huntingdon beseeching that the rice and indigo plantations belonging to the orphan-house, which she had endowed near Savannah, in Georgia, might not be cultivated by those who encouraged the slave trade; he took care to increase the comforts and elevate the character of the colored people within his influence; he zealously promoted the establishment of an African school, and devoted much of the two last years of his life to personal attendance upon his pupils. By fifty years of constant industry he had amassed a small fortune; and this was left, after the decease of his widow, to the support of the African school.

Similar exertions, though on a less extensive scale, were made by the late excellent John Kenrick, of Newton, Mass. For more than thirty years the constant object of his thoughts, and the chief purpose of his life, was the abolition of slavery. His earnest conversation aroused many other minds to think and act upon the subject. He wrote letters, inserted articles in the newspapers, gave liberal donations, and circulated pamphlets at his own expense.

Cowper contributed much to the cause when he wrote the "Negro's Complaint," and thus excited the compassion of his numerous readers. Wedgewood aided the work, when he caused cameos to be struck, representing a kneeling African in chains, and thus made even capricious fashion an avenue to the heart. Clarkson assisted by patient investigation of evidence; and Fox and Wilberforce by eloquent speeches. Mungo Park gave his powerful influence by the kind and liberal manner in which he always represented the Africans. The Duchess of Devonshire wrote verses and caused them to be set to music; and wherever those lines were sung, some hearts were touched in favor of the oppressed. This fascinating woman made even her far-famed beauty serve in the cause of benevolence. Fox was returned for Parliament through her influence, and she is said to have procured more than one vote, by allowing the yeomanry of England to kiss her beautiful cheek.

All are not able to do so much as Anthony Benezet and John Kenrick have done; but we can all do something. We can speak kindly and respectfully of colored people upon all occasions; we can repeat to our children such traits as are honorable in their character and history; we can avoid making odious caricatures of negroes; we can teach boys that it is unmanly and contemptible to insult an unfortunate class of people by the vulgar outcry of "Nigger! – Nigger!" – Even Mahmoud of Turkey rivals us in liberality – for he long ago ordered a fine to be levied upon those who called a Christian a dog; and in his dominions the *prejudice* is so great that a Christian must be a degraded being. A residence in Turkey might be profitable to those Christians who patronize the eternity of prejudice; it would afford an opportunity of testing the goodness of the rule, by showing how it works both ways.

If we are not able to contribute to African schools, or do not choose to do so, we can at least refrain from opposing them. If it be disagreeable to allow colored people the same rights and privileges as other citizens, we can do with our prejudice, what most of us often do with better feelings – we can conceal it.

Our almanacs and newspapers can fairly show both sides of the question; and if they lean to either party, let it not be to the strongest. Our preachers can speak of slavery, as they do of other evils. Our poets can find in this subject abundant room for sentiment and pathos. Our orators (provided they do not want office) may venture an allusion to our *in*-"glorious institutions."

The union of individual influence produces a vast amount of moral force, which is not the less powerful because it is often unperceived. A mere change in the *direction* of our efforts, without any increased exertion, would in the course of a few years, produce an entire revolution of public feeling. This slow but sure way of doing good is almost the only means by which benevolence can effect its purpose.

Sixty thousand petitions have been addressed to the English parliament on the subject of slavery, and a large number of them were signed by women. The same steps here would be, with one exception, useless and injudicious; because the general government has no control over the legislatures of individual States. But the District of Columbia forms an exception to this rule. *There* the United States have power to abolish slavery; and it is the duty of the citizens to petition year after year, until a reformation is effected. But who will present remonstrances against slavery? The Hon. John Q. Adams was intrusted with fifteen petitions for the abolition of slavery in the District of Columbia; yet, clearly as that gentleman sees and defines the pernicious effects of the system, he offered the petitions only to protest against them! Another petition to the same effect, intrusted to another Massachusetts representative, was never noticed at all. "Brutus is an honorable man: – So are they all – all honorable men." Nevertheless, there is, in this popular government, a subject on which it is *impossible* for the people to make themselves heard.

By publishing this book I have put my mite into the treasury. The expectation of displeasing all classes has not been unaccompanied with pain. But it has been strongly impressed upon my mind that it was a duty to fulfil this task; and earthly considerations should never stifle the voice of conscience.

Note

1 The Pariahs are the lowest and most degraded caste in Hindostan. The laws prevent them from ever rising in their condition, or mingling with other castes.

28

Civil Disobedience

Henry David Thoreau

Introduction

Henry David Thoreau (1817–62) was born on July 12, 1817 at Concord, Massachusetts. He received a degree from Harvard University in 1837 and, after a brief career as an educator and lecturer, retired in 1845 to a cabin on the shore of Walden Pond near Concord, where he began writing the journals later published as *Walden: or, Life in the Woods*. His early work was strongly influenced by Emerson's essay, *Nature*. Emerson eventually became a close friend of Thoreau, publishing some of Thoreau's work in his journal *The Dial* (co-edited by Emerson and Margaret Fuller), and helping Thoreau through financial difficulties by hiring him for a variety of jobs including handyman and tutor. In the 1850s, in order to support himself, Thoreau became a surveyor, even as he became an increasingly active abolitionist and participant in the Underground Railroad. In 1857, Thoreau met and became a supporter of the abolitionist John Brown, who was hanged in 1859 for leading a slave revolt at Harpers Ferry, Virginia. Thoreau became ill in 1860 and died at Concord on May 6, 1862, probably of tuberculosis. The essay printed here was written in 1849 after Thoreau had been arrested and briefly jailed for not paying his poll tax. Although he was quickly released after an unidentified friend paid the back taxes, the experience provided a focus for applying his philosophical perspective to issues of human freedom and the relation of individuals to society.

Taken from Howard E. Jones, E. E. Leisy, and R. M. Ludwig (eds), *Major American Writers*, 3rd edn (New York: Harcourt Brace and Co., 1952).

I heartily accept the motto – "That government is best which governs least;" and I should like to see it acted up to more rapidly and systematically. Carried out, it finally amounts to this, which also I believe – "That government is best which governs not at all;" and when men are prepared for it, that will be the kind of government which they will have. Government is at best but an expedient; but most governments are usually, and all governments are sometimes, inexpedient. The objections which have been brought against a standing army, and they are many and weighty, and deserve to prevail, may also at last be brought against a standing government. The standing army is only an arm of the standing government. The government itself, which is only the mode which the people have chosen to execute their will, is equally liable to be abused and perverted before the people can act through it. Witness the present Mexican war,[1] the work of comparatively a few individuals using the standing government as their tool; for, in the outset, the people would not have consented to this measure.

This American government – what is it but a tradition, though a recent one, endeavoring to transmit itself unimpaired to posterity, but each instant losing some of its integrity? It has not the vitality and force of a single living man; for a single man can bend it to his will. It is a sort of wooden gun to the people themselves. But it is not the less necessary for this; for the people must have some complicated machinery or other, and hear its din, to satisfy that idea of government which they have.

Governments show thus how successfully men can be imposed on, even impose on themselves, for their own advantage. It is excellent, we must all allow. Yet this government never of itself furthered any enterprise, but by the alacrity with which it got out of its way. *It does not keep the country free. It does not settle the West. It does not educate.* The character inherent in the American people has done all that has been accomplished; and it would have done somewhat more, if the government had not sometimes got in its way. For government is an expedient by which men would fain succeed in letting one another alone; and, as has been said, when it is most expedient, the governed are most let alone by it. Trade and commerce, if they were not made of india-rubber, would never manage to bounce over the obstacles which legislators are continually putting in their way; and, if one were to judge these men wholly by the effects of their actions and not partly by their intentions, they would deserve to be classed and punished with those mischievous persons who put obstructions on the railroads.

But, to speak practically and as a citizen, unlike those who call themselves no-government men, I ask for, not at once no government, but *at once* a better government. Let every man make known what kind of government would command his respect, and that will be one step toward obtaining it.

After all, the practical reason why, when the power is once in the hands of the people, a majority are permitted, and for a long period continue, to rule is not because they are most likely to be in the right, nor because this seems fairest to the minority, but because they are physically the strongest. But a government in which the majority rule in all cases cannot be based on justice, even as far as men understand it. Can there be a government in which majorities do not virtually decide right and wrong, but conscience? – in which majorities decide only those questions to which the rule of expediency is applicable? Must the citizen ever for a moment, or in the least degree, resign his conscience to the legislator? Why has every man a conscience, then? I think that we should be men first, and subjects afterward. It is not desirable to cultivate a respect for the law, so much as for the right. The only obligation which I have a right to assume is to do at any time what I think right. It is truly enough said that a corporation has no conscience; but a corporation of conscientious men is a corporation *with* a conscience. Law never made men a whit more just; and, by means of their respect for it, even the well-disposed are daily made the agents of injustice. A common and natural result of an undue respect for law is, that you may see a file of soldiers, colonel, captain, corporal, privates, powder-monkeys, and all, marching in admirable order over hill and dale to the wars, against their wills, ay, against their common sense and consciences, which makes it very steep marching indeed, and produces a palpitation of the heart. They have no doubt that it is a damnable business in which they are concerned; they are all peaceably inclined. Now, what are they? Men at all? or small movable forts and magazines, at the service of some unscrupulous man in power? Visit the Navy-Yard,[2] and behold a marine, such a man as an American government can make, or such as it can make a man with its black arts – a mere shadow and reminiscence of humanity, a man laid out alive and standing, and already, as one may say, buried under arms with funeral accompaniments, though it may be,

Not a drum was heard, not a funeral note,
As his corse to the rampart we hurried;
Not a soldier discharged his farewell shot
O'er the grave where our hero we buried.[3]

The mass of men serve the state thus, not as men mainly, but as machines, with their bodies. They are the standing army, and the militia, jailers, constables, *posse comitatus,*[4] etc. In most cases there is no free exercise whatever of the judgment or of the moral sense; but they put themselves on a level with wood and earth and stones; and wooden men can perhaps be manufactured that will serve the purpose as well. Such command no more respect than men of straw or a lump of dirt. They have the same sort of worth only as horses and dogs. Yet such as these even are commonly esteemed good citizens. Others – as most legislators, politicians, lawyers, ministers, and office-holders – serve the state chiefly with their heads; and, as they rarely make any moral distinctions, they are as likely to serve the devil, without *intending* it, as God. A very few – as heroes, patriots, martyrs, reformers in the great sense, and *men* – serve the state with their consciences also, and so necessarily resist it for the most part; and they are commonly treated as enemies by it. A wise man will only be useful as a man, and will not submit to be "clay," and "stop a hole to keep the wind away,"[5] but leave that office to his dust at least:

> I am too high-born to be propertied,
> To be a secondary at control,
> Or useful serving-man and instrument
> To any sovereign state throughout the world.[6]

He who gives himself entirely to his fellow-men appears to them useless and selfish; but he who gives himself partially to them is pronounced a benefactor and philanthropist.

How does it become a man to behave toward this American government to-day?[7] I answer, that he cannot without disgrace be associated with it. I cannot for an instant recognize that political organization as *my* government which is the *slave's* government also.

All men recognize the right of revolution; that is, the right to refuse allegiance to, and to resist, the government, when its tyranny or its inefficiency are great and unendurable. But almost all say that such is not the case now. But such was the case, they think, in the Revolution of '75. If one were to tell me that this was a bad government because it taxed certain foreign commodities brought to its ports, it is most probable that I should not make an ado about it, for I can do without them. All machines have their friction; and possibly this does enough good to counterbalance the evil. At any rate, it is a great evil to make a stir about it. But when the friction comes to have its machine, and oppression and robbery are organized, I say, let us not have such a machine any longer. In other words, when a sixth of the population of a nation which has undertaken to be the refuge of liberty are slaves, and a whole country[8] is unjustly overrun and conquered by a foreign army, and subjected to military law, I think that it is not too soon for honest men to rebel and revolutionize. What makes this duty the more urgent is the fact that the country so overrun is not our own, but ours is the invading army.

Paley, a common authority with many on moral questions, in his chapter on the "Duty of Submission to Civil Government," resolves all civil obligation into expediency; and he proceeds to say "that so long as the interest of the whole society requires it, that is, so long as the established government cannot be resisted or changed without public inconveniency, it is the will of God . . . that the established government be obeyed — and no longer. This principle being admitted, the justice of every particular case of resistance is reduced to a computation of the quantity of the danger and grievance on the one side, and of the probability and expense of redressing it on the other."[9] Of this, he says, every man shall judge for himself. But Paley appears never to have contemplated those cases to which the rule of expediency does not apply, in which a people, as well as an individual, must do justice, cost what it may. If I have unjustly wrested a plank from a drowning man, I must restore it to him though I drown myself. This, according to Paley, would be inconvenient. But he that would save his life, in such a case, shall lose it. This people must cease to hold slaves, and to make war on Mexico, though it cost them their existence as a people.

In their practice, nations agree with Paley; but does any one think that Massachusetts does exactly what is right at the present crisis?

> A drab of state, a cloth-o'-silver slut,
> To have her train borne up, and her soul trail in
> the dirt.

Practically speaking, the opponents to a reform in Massachusetts are not a hundred thousand politicians at the South, but a hundred thousand merchants and farmers here, who are more interested in commerce and agriculture than they are in humanity, and are not prepared to do justice to the slave and to Mexico, *cost what it may.* I quarrel not with far-off foes, but with those who, near at home, coöperate with, and do the bidding of, those far away, and without whom the latter would be harmless. We are accustomed to say, that the mass of men are unprepared; but improvement is slow, because the few are not materially wiser or better than the many. It is not so important that many should be as good as you, as that there be some absolute goodness somewhere; for that will leaven the whole lump.[10] There are thousands who are *in opinion* opposed to slavery and to the war, who yet in effect do nothing to put an end to them; who, esteeming themselves children of Washington and Franklin, sit down with their hands in their pockets, and say that they know not what to do, and do nothing; who even postpone the question of freedom to the question of free trade, and quietly read the prices-current along with the latest advices from Mexico, after dinner, and, it may be, fall asleep over them both. What is the price-current of an honest man and patriot to-day? They hesitate, and they regret, and sometimes they petition; but they do nothing in earnest and with effect. They will wait, well disposed, for others to remedy the evil, that they may no longer have it to regret. At most, they give only a cheap vote, and a feeble countenance and Godspeed, to the right, as it goes by them. There are nine hundred and ninety-nine patrons of virtue to one virtuous man. But it is easier to deal with the real possessor of a thing than with the temporary guardian of it.

All voting is a sort of gaming, like checkers or backgammon, with a slight moral tinge to it, a playing with right and wrong, with moral questions; and betting naturally accompanies it. The character of the voters is not staked. I cast my vote, perchance, as I think right; but I am not vitally concerned that that right should prevail. I am willing to leave it to the majority. Its obligation, therefore, never exceeds that of expediency. Even voting *for the right* is *doing* nothing for it. It is only expressing to men feebly your desire that it should prevail. A wise man will not leave the right to the mercy of chance, nor wish it to prevail through the power of the majority. There is but little virtue in the action of masses of men. When the majority shall at length vote for the abolition of slavery, it will be because they are indifferent to slavery, or because there is but little slavery left to be abolished by their vote. *They* will then be the only slaves. Only *his* vote can hasten the abolition of slavery who asserts his own freedom by his vote.

I hear of a convention to be held at Baltimore,[11] or elsewhere, for the selection of a candidate for the Presidency, made up chiefly of editors, and men who are politicians by profession; but I think, what is it to any independent, intelligent, and respectable man what decision they may come to? Shall we not have the advantage of his wisdom and honesty, nevertheless? Can we not count upon some independent votes? Are there not many individuals in the country who do not attend conventions? But no: I find that the respectable man, so called, has immediately drifted from his position, and despairs of his country, when his country has more reason to despair of him. He forthwith adopts one of the candidates thus selected as the only *available* one, thus proving that he is himself *available* for any purposes of the demagogue. His vote is of no more worth than that of any unprincipled foreigner or hireling native, who may have been bought. O for a man who is a *man*, and, as my neighbor says, has a bone in his back which you cannot pass your hand through! Our statistics are

at fault: the population has been returned too large. How many *men* are there to a square thousand miles in this country? Hardly one. Does not America offer any inducement for men to settle here? The American has dwindled into an Odd Fellow[12] – one who may be known by the development of his organ of gregariousness, and a manifest lack of intellect and cheerful self-reliance; whose first and chief concern, on coming into the world, is to see that the almshouses are in good repair; and, before yet he has lawfully donned the virile garb,[13] to collect a fund for the support of the widows and orphans that may be; who, in short, ventures to live only by the aid of the Mutual Insurance company, which has promised to bury him decently.

It is not a man's duty, as a matter of course, to devote himself to the eradication of any, even the most enormous, wrong; he may still properly have other concerns to engage him; but it is his duty, at least, to wash his hands of it, and, if he gives it no thought longer, not to give it practically his support. If I devote myself to other pursuits and contemplations, I must first see, at least, that I do not pursue them sitting upon another man's shoulders. I must get off him first, that he may pursue his contemplations too. See what gross inconsistency is tolerated. I have heard some of my townsmen say, "I should like to have them order me out to help put down an insurrection of the slaves, or to march to Mexico – see if I would go;" and yet these very men have each, directly by their allegiance, and so indirectly, at least, by their money, furnished a substitute. The soldier is applauded who refuses to serve in an unjust war by those who do not refuse to sustain the unjust government which makes the war; is applauded by those whose own act and authority he disregards and sets at naught; as if the state were penitent to that degree that it hired one to scourge it while it sinned, but not to that degree that it left off sinning for a moment. Thus, under the name of Order and Civil Government, we are all made at last to pay homage to and support our own meanness. After the first blush of sin comes its indifference; and from immoral it becomes, as it were, *un*moral, and not quite unnecessary to that life which we have made.

The broadest and most prevalent error requires the most disinterested virtue to sustain it. The slight reproach to which the virtue of patriotism is commonly liable, the noble are most likely to incur. Those who, while they disapprove of the character and measures of a government, yield to it their allegiance and support are undoubtedly its most conscientious supporters, and so frequently the most serious obstacles to reform. Some are petitioning the State to dissolve the Union, to disregard the requisitions of the President. Why do they not dissolve it themselves – the union between themselves and the State – and refuse to pay their quota into its treasury? Do not they stand in the same relation to the State that the State does to the Union? And have not the same reasons prevented the State from resisting the Union which have prevented them from resisting the State?

How can a man be satisfied to entertain an opinion merely, and enjoy *it*? Is there any enjoyment in it, if his opinion is that he is aggrieved? If you are cheated out of a single dollar by your neighbor, you do not rest satisfied with knowing that you are cheated, or with saying that you are cheated, or even with petitioning him to pay you your due; but you take effectual steps at once to obtain the full amount, and see that you are never cheated again. Action from principle, the perception and the performance of right, changes things and relations; it is essentially revolutionary, and does not consist wholly with anything which was. It not only divides States and churches, it divides families; ay, it divides the *individual*, separating the diabolical in him from the divine.

Unjust laws exist: shall we be content to obey them, or shall we endeavor to amend them, and obey them until we have succeeded, or shall we transgress them at once? Men generally, under such a government as this, think that they ought to wait until they have persuaded the majority to alter them. They think that, if they should resist, the remedy would be worse than the evil. But it is the fault of the government itself that the remedy *is* worse than the evil. *It* makes it worse. Why is it not more apt to anticipate and provide for reform? Why does it not cherish its wise minority? Why does it cry and resist before it is hurt? Why does it not encourage its citizens to be on the alert to point out its faults, and *do* better than it would have them? Why does it always crucify Christ, and excommunicate Copernicus and Luther,[14] and pronounce Washington and Franklin rebels?

One would think, that a deliberate and practical denial of its authority was the only offense never contemplated by government; else, why has it not assigned its definite, its suitable and proportionate penalty? If a man who has no property refuses but once to earn nine shillings for the State, he is put in prison for a period unlimited by any law that I know, and determined only by the discretion of those who placed him there; but if he should steal ninety times nine shillings from the State, he is soon permitted to go at large again.

If the injustice is part of the necessary friction of the machine of government, let it go, let it go: perchance it will wear smooth – certainly the machine will wear out. If the injustice has a spring, or a pulley, or a rope, or a crank, exclusively for itself, then perhaps you may consider whether the remedy will not be worse than the evil; but if it is of such a nature that it requires you to be the agent of injustice to another, then, I say, break the law. Let your life be a counter friction to stop the machine. What I have to do is to see, at any rate, that I do not lend myself to the wrong which I condemn.

As for adopting the ways which the State has provided for remedying the evil, I know not of such ways. They take too much time, and a man's life will be gone. I have other affairs to attend to. I came into this world, not chiefly to make this a good place to live in, but to live in it, be it good or bad. A man has not everything to do, but something; and because he cannot do *everything*, it is not necessary that he should do *something* wrong. It is not my business to be petitioning the Governor or the Legislature any more than it is theirs to petition me; and if they should not hear my petition, what should I do then? But in this case the State has provided no way: its very Constitution is the evil. This may seem to be harsh and stubborn and unconciliatory; but it is to treat with the utmost kindness and consideration the only spirit that can appreciate or deserves it. So is all change for the better, like birth and death, which convulse the body.

I do not hesitate to say, that those who call themselves Abolitionists should at once effectually withdraw their support, both in person and property, from the government of Massachusetts, and not wait till they constitute a majority of one, before they suffer the right to prevail through them. I think that it is enough if they have God on their side, without waiting for that other one. Moreover, any man more right than his neighbors constitutes a majority of one already.

I meet this American government, or its representative, the State government, directly, and face to face, once a year – no more – in the person of its tax-gatherer; this is the only mode in which a man situated as I am necessarily meets it; and it then says distinctly, Recognize me; and the simplest, the most effectual, and, in the present posture of affairs, the indispensablest mode of treating with it on this head, of expressing your little satisfaction with and love for it, is to deny it then. My civil neighbor, the tax-gatherer, is the very man I have to deal with – for it is, after all, with men and not with parchment that I quarrel – and he has voluntarily chosen to be an agent of the government. How shall he ever know well what he is and does as an officer of the government, or as a man, until he is obliged to consider whether he shall treat me, his neighbor, for whom he has respect, as a neighbor and well-disposed man, or as a maniac and disturber of the peace, and see if he can get over this obstruction to his neighborliness without a ruder and more impetuous thought or speech corresponding with his action. I know this well, that if one thousand, if one hundred, if ten men whom I could name – if ten *honest* men only – ay, if *one* HONEST man, in this State of Massachusetts, *ceasing to hold slaves*, were actually to withdraw from this copartnership, and be locked up in the county jail therefor, it would be the abolition of slavery in America. For it matters not how small the beginning may seem to be: what is once well done is done forever. But we love better to talk about it: that we say is our mission. Reform keeps many scores of newspapers in its service, but not one man. If my esteemed neighbor, the State's ambassador,[15] who will devote his days to the settlement of the question of human rights in the Council Chamber, instead of being threatened with the prisons of Carolina, were to sit down the prisoner of Massachusetts, that State which is so anxious to foist the sin of slavery upon her sister – though at present she can discover only an act of inhospitality to be the ground of a quarrel with her – the Legislature would not wholly waive the subject the following winter.

Under a government which imprisons any unjustly, the true place for a just man is also a prison. The proper place to-day, the only place which Massachusetts has provided for her freer and less desponding spirits, is in her prisons, to be put out and locked out of the State by her own act, as they have already put themselves out by their principles. It is there that the fugitive slave, and the Mexican prisoner on parole, and the Indian come to plead the wrongs of his race should find them; on that separate, but more free and honorable ground, where the State places those who are not

with her, but *against* her – the only house in a slave State in which a free man can abide with honor. If any think that their influence would be lost there, and their voices no longer afflict the ear of the State, that they would not be as an enemy within its walls, they do not know by how much truth is stronger than error, nor how much more eloquently and effectively he can combat injustice who has experienced a little in his own person. Cast your whole vote, not a strip of paper merely, but your whole influence. A minority is powerless while it conforms to the majority; it is not even a minority then; but it is irresistible when it clogs by its whole weight. If the alternative is to keep all just men in prison, or give up war and slavery, the State will not hesitate which to choose. If a thousand men were not to pay their tax-bills this year, that would not be a violent and bloody measure, as it would be to pay them, and enable the State to commit violence and shed innocent blood. This is, in fact, the definition of a peaceable revolution, if any such is possible. If the tax-gatherer, or any other public officer, asks me, as one has done, "But what shall I do?" my answer is, "If you really wish to do anything, resign your office." When the subject has refused allegiance, and the officer has resigned his office, then the revolution is accomplished. But even suppose blood should flow. Is there not a sort of blood shed when the conscience is wounded? Through this wound a man's real manhood and immortality flow out, and he bleeds to an everlasting death. I see this blood flowing now.

I have contemplated the imprisonment of the offender, rather than the seizure of his goods – though both will serve the same purpose – because they who assert the purest right, and consequently are most dangerous to a corrupt State, commonly have not spent much time in accumulating property. To such the State renders comparatively small service, and a slight tax is wont to appear exorbitant, particularly if they are obliged to earn it by special labor with their hands. If there were one who lived wholly without the use of money, the State itself would hesitate to demand it of him. But the rich man – not to make any invidious comparison – is always sold to the institution which makes him rich. Absolutely speaking, the more money, the less virtue; for money comes between a man and his objects, and obtains them for him; and it was certainly no great virtue to obtain it. It puts to rest many questions which he would otherwise be taxed to answer; while the only new question which it puts is the hard but superfluous one, how to spend it. Thus his moral ground is taken from under his feet. The opportunities of living are diminished in proportion as what are called the "means" are increased. The best thing a man can do for his culture when he is rich is to endeavor to carry out those schemes which he entertained when he was poor. Christ answered the Herodians according to their condition. "Show me the tribute-money,"[16] said he – and took one penny out of his pocket; if you use money which has the image of Caesar on it and which he has made current and valuable, that is, *if you are men of the State*, and gladly enjoy the advantages of Caesar's government, then pay him back some of his own when he demands it. "Render therefore to Caesar that which is Caesar's, and to God those things which are God's" – leaving them no wiser than before as to which was which; for they did not wish to know.

When I converse with the freest of my neighbors, I perceive that, whatever they may say about the magnitude and seriousness of the question, and their regard for the public tranquillity, the long and the short of the matter is, that they cannot spare the protection of the existing government, and they dread the consequences to their property and families of disobedience to it. For my own part, I should not like to think that I ever rely on the protection of the State. But, if I deny the authority of the State when it presents its tax-bill, it will soon take and waste all my property, and so harass me and my children without end. This is hard. This makes it impossible for a man to live honestly, and at the same time comfortably, in outward respects. It will not be worth the while to accumulate property; that would be sure to go again. You must hire or squat somewhere, and raise but a small crop, and eat that soon. You must live within yourself, and depend upon yourself always tucked up and ready for a start, and not have many affairs. A man may grow rich in Turkey even, if he will be in all respects a good subject of the Turkish government. Confucius said: "If a state is governed by the principles of reason, poverty and misery are subjects of shame; if a state is not governed by the principles of reason, riches and honors are the subjects of shame."[17] No: until I want the protection of Massachusetts to be extended to me in some distant Southern port, where my liberty is endangered, or until I am bent solely on building up an estate at home by peaceful enterprise, I can afford to refuse allegiance to Massachusetts,[18] and her right to my property and life. It costs me less in every sense to incur the penalty of disobedience to the State than it would to obey. I should feel as if I were worth less in that case.

Some years ago, the State met me in behalf of the Church, and commanded me to pay a certain sum toward the support of a clergyman whose preaching my father attended, but never I myself. "Pay," it said, "or be locked up in the jail." I declined to pay. But, unfortunately, another man saw fit to pay it. I did not see why the schoolmaster should be taxed to support the priest, and not the priest the schoolmaster; for I was not the State's schoolmaster, but I supported myself by voluntary subscription. I did not see why the lyceum should not present its tax-bill, and have the State to back its demand, as well as the Church. However, at the request of the selectmen, I condescended to make some such statement as this in writing: "Know all men by these presents, that I, Henry Thoreau, do not wish to be regarded as a member of any incorporated society which I have not joined." This I gave to the town clerk; and he has it. The State, having thus learned that I did not wish to be regarded as a member of that church, has never made a like demand on me since; though it said that it must adhere to its original presumption that time. If I had known how to name them, I should then have signed off in detail from all the societies which I never signed on to; but I did not know where to find a complete list.

I have paid no poll-tax for six years. I was put into a jail once on this account, for one night; and, as I stood considering the walls of solid stone, two or three feet thick, the door of wood and iron, a foot thick, and the iron grating which strained the light, I could not help being struck with the foolishness of that institution which treated me as if I were mere flesh and blood and bones, to be locked up. I wondered that it should have concluded at length that this was the best use it could put me to, and had never thought to avail itself of my services in some way. I saw that, if there was a wall of stone between me and my townsmen, there was a still more difficult one to climb or break through before they could get to be as free as I was. I did not for a moment feel confined, and the walls seemed a great waste of stone and mortar. I felt as if I alone of all my townsmen had paid my tax. They plainly did not know how to treat me, but behaved like persons who are underbred. In every threat and in every compliment there was a blunder; for they thought that my chief desire was to stand the other side of that stone wall. I could not but smile to see how industriously they locked the door on my meditations, which followed them out again without let or hindrance, and *they* were really all that was dangerous. As they could not reach me, they had resolved to punish my body; just as boys, if they cannot come at some person against whom they have a spite, will abuse his dog. I saw that the State was half-witted, that it was timid as a lone woman with her silver spoons, and that it did not know its friends from its foes, and I lost all my remaining respect for it, and pitied it.

Thus the State never intentionally confronts a man's sense, intellectual or moral, but only his body, his senses. It is not armed with superior wit or honesty, but with superior physical strength. I was not born to be forced. I will breathe after my own fashion. Let us see who is the strongest. What force has a multitude? They only can force me who obey a higher law than I. They force me to become like themselves. I do not hear of *men* being *forced* to live this way or that by masses of men. What sort of life were that to live? When I meet a government which says to me, "Your money or your life," why should I be in haste to give it my money? It may be in a great strait, and not know what to do: I cannot help that. It must help itself; do as I do. It is not worth the while to snivel about it. I am not responsible for the successful working of the machinery of society. I am not the son of the engineer. I perceive that, when an acorn and a chestnut fall side by side, the one does not remain inert to make way for the other, but both obey their own laws, and spring and grow and flourish as best they can, till one, perchance, overshadows and destroys the other. If a plant cannot live according to its nature, it dies; and so a man.

The night in prison was novel and interesting enough. The prisoners in their shirt-sleeves were enjoying a chat and the evening air in the doorway, when I entered. But the jailer said, "Come, boys, it is time to lock up;" and so they dispersed, and I heard the sound of their steps returning into the hollow apartments. My room-mate was introduced to me by the jailer as "a first-rate fellow and a clever man." When the door was locked, he showed me where to hang my hat, and how he managed matters there. The rooms were white-washed once a month; and this one, at least, was the whitest, most simply furnished, and probably the neatest apartment in the town. He naturally

wanted to know where I came from, and what brought me there; and, when I had told him, I asked him in my turn how he came there, presuming him to be an honest man, of course; and, as the world goes, I believe he was. "Why," said he, "they accuse me of burning a barn: but I never did it." As near as I could discover, he had probably gone to bed in a barn when drunk, and smoked his pipe there; and so a barn was burnt. He had the reputation of being a clever man, had been there some three months waiting for his trial to come on, and would have to wait as much longer; but he was quite domesticated and contented, since he got his board for nothing, and thought that he was well treated.

He occupied one window, and I the other; and I saw that if one stayed there long, his principal business would be to look out the window. I had soon read all the tracts that were left there, and examined where former prisoners had broken out, and where a grate had been sawed off, and heard the history of the various occupants of that room; for I found that even here there was a history and a gossip which never circulated beyond the walls of the jail. Probably this is the only house in the town where verses are composed, which are afterward printed in circular form, but not published. I was shown quite a long list of verses which were composed by some young men who had been detected in an attempt to escape, who avenged themselves by singing them.

I pumped my fellow-prisoner as dry as I could, for fear I should never see him again; but at length he showed me which was my bed, and left me to blow out the lamp.

It was like traveling into a far country, such as I had never expected to behold, to lie there for one night. It seemed to me that I never had heard the town clock strike before, nor the evening sounds of the village; for we slept with the windows open, which were inside the grating. It was to see my native village in the light of the Middle Ages, and our Concord was turned into a Rhine stream, and visions of knights and castles passed before me. They were the voices of old burghers that I heard in the streets. I was an involuntary spectator and auditor of whatever was done and said in the kitchen of the adjacent village-inn – a wholly new and rare experience to me. It was a closer view of my native town. I was fairly inside of it. I never had seen its institutions before. This is one of its peculiar institutions; for it is a shire town. I began to comprehend what its inhabitants were about.

In the morning, our breakfasts were put through the hole in the door, in small oblong-square tin pans, made to fit, and holding a pint of chocolate, with brown bread, and an iron spoon. When they called for the vessels again, I was green enough to return what bread I had left; but my comrade seized it, and said that I should lay that up for lunch or dinner. Soon after he was let out to work at haying in a neighboring field, whither he went every day, and would not be back till noon; so he bade me good-day, saying that he doubted if he should see me again.

When I came out of prison – for some one interfered, and paid that tax – I did not perceive that great changes had taken place on the common, such as he observed who went in a youth and emerged a tottering and gray-headed man; and yet a change had to my eyes come over the scene – the town, and State, and country – greater than any that mere time could effect. I saw yet more distinctly the State in which I lived. I saw to what extent the people among whom I lived could be trusted as good neighbors and friends; that their friendship was for summer weather only; that they did not greatly propose to do right; that they were a distinct race from me by their prejudices and superstitions, as the Chinamen and Malays are; that in their sacrifices to humanity they ran no risks, not even to their property; that after all they were not so noble but they treated the thief as he had treated them, and hoped, by a certain outward observance and a few prayers, and by walking in a particular straight though useless path from time to time, to save their souls. This may be to judge my neighbors harshly; for I believe that many of them are not aware that they-have such an institution as the jail in their village.

It was formerly the custom in our village, when a poor debtor came out of jail, for his acquaintances to salute him, looking through their fingers, which were crossed to represent the grating of a jail window, "How do ye do?" My neighbors did not thus salute me, but first looked at me, and then at one another, as if I had returned from a long journey. I was put into jail as I was going to the shoemaker's to get a shoe which was mended. When I was let out the next morning, I proceeded to finish my errand, and, having put on my mended shoe, joined a huckleberry party, who were impatient to put themselves under my conduct; and in half an hour – for the horse was soon tackled – was in the midst of a huckleberry field, on one of our highest hills, two miles off, and then the State was nowhere to be seen.

This is the whole history of "My Prisons."[19]

I have never declined paying the highway tax, because I am as desirous of being a good neighbor as I am of being a bad subject; and as for supporting schools, I am doing my part to educate my fellow-countrymen now. It is for no particular item in the tax-bill that I refuse to pay it. I simply wish to refuse allegiance to the State, to withdraw and stand aloof from it effectually. I do not care to trace the course of my dollar, if I could, till it buys a man or a musket to shoot one with – the dollar is innocent – but I am concerned to trace the effects of my allegiance. In fact, I quietly declare war with the State, after my fashion, though I will still make what use and get what advantage of her I can, as is usual in such cases.

If others pay the tax which is demanded of me, from a sympathy with the State, they do but what they have already done in their own case, or rather they abet injustice to a greater extent than the State requires. If they pay the tax from a mistaken interest in the individual taxed, to save his property, or prevent his going to jail, it is because they have not considered wisely how far they let their private feelings interfere with the public good.

This, then, is my position at present. But one cannot be too much on his guard in such a case, lest his action be biased by obstinacy or an undue regard for the opinions of men. Let him see that he does only what belongs to himself and to the hour.

I think sometimes, Why, this people mean well, they are only ignorant; they would do better if they knew how: why give your neighbors this pain to treat you as they are not inclined to? But I think again, This is no reason why I should do as they do, or permit others to suffer much greater pain of a different kind. Again, I sometimes say to myself, When many millions of men, without heat, without ill will, without personal feeling of any kind, demand of you a few shillings only, without the possibility, such is their constitution, of retracting or altering their present demand, and without the possibility, on your side, of appeal to any other millions, why expose yourself to this overwhelming brute force? You do not resist cold and hunger, the winds and the waves, thus obstinately; you quietly submit to a thousand similar necessities. You do not put your head into the fire. But just in proportion as I regard this as not wholly a brute force, but partly a human force, and consider that I have relations to those millions as to so many millions of men, and not of mere brute or inanimate things, I see that appeal is possible, first and instantaneously, from them to the Maker of them, and, secondly, from them to themselves. But if I put my head deliberately into the fire, there is no appeal to fire or to the Maker of fire, and I have only myself to blame. If I could convince myself that I have any right to be satisfied with men as they are, and to treat them accordingly, and not according, in some respects, to my requisitions and expectations of what they and I ought to be, then, like a good Mussulman and fatalist, I should endeavor to be satisfied with things as they are, and say it is the will of God. And, above all, there is this difference between resisting this and a purely brute or natural force, that I can resist this with some effect; but I cannot expect, like Orpheus, to change the nature of the rocks and trees and beasts.

I do not wish to quarrel with any man or nation. I do not wish to split hairs, to make fine distinctions, or set myself up as better than my neighbors. I seek rather, I may say, even an excuse for conforming to the laws of the land. I am but too ready to conform to them. Indeed, I have reason to suspect myself on this head; and each year, as the tax-gatherer comes round, I find myself disposed to review the acts and position of the general and State governments, and the spirit of the people, to discover a pretext for conformity.

> We must affect our country as our parents,
> And if at any time we alienate
> Our love or industry from doing it honor,
> We must respect effects and teach the soul
> Matter of conscience and religion,
> And not desire of rule or benefit.

I believe that the State will soon be able to take all my work of this sort out of my hands, and then I shall be no better a patriot than my fellow-countrymen. Seen from a lower point of view, the Constitution, with all its faults, is very good; the law and the courts are very respectable; even this State and this American government are, in many respects, very admirable, and rare things, to be thankful for, such as a great many have described them; but seen from a point of view a little higher, they are what I have described them; seen from a higher still, and the highest, who shall say what they are, or that they are worth looking at or thinking of at all?

However, the government does not concern me much, and I shall bestow the fewest possible thoughts on it. It is not many moments that I live under a government, even in this world. If a man is thought-free, fancy-free, imagination-free, that which *is not* never for a long time appearing *to be* to him, unwise rulers or reformers cannot fatally interrupt him.

I know that most men think differently from myself; but those whose lives are by profession devoted to the study of these or kindred subjects content me as little as any. Statesmen and legislators, standing so completely within the institution, never distinctly and nakedly behold it. They speak of moving society, but have no resting-place without it. They may be men of a certain experience and discrimination, and have no doubt invented ingenious and even useful systems, for which we sincerely thank them; but all their wit and usefulness lie within certain not very wide limits. They are wont to forget that the world is not governed by policy and expediency. Webster never goes behind government, and so cannot speak with authority about it. His words are wisdom to those legislators who contemplate no essential reform in the existing government; but for thinkers, and those who legislate for all time, he never once glances at the subject. I know of those whose serene and wise speculations on this theme would soon reveal the limits of his mind's range and hospitality. Yet, compared with the cheap professions of most reformers, and the still cheaper wisdom and eloquence of politicians in general, his are almost the only sensible and valuable words, and we thank Heaven for him. Comparatively, he is always strong, original, and, above all, practical. Still, his quality is not wisdom, but prudence. The lawyer's truth is not Truth, but consistency or a consistent expediency. Truth is always in harmony with herself, and is not concerned chiefly to reveal the justice that may consist with wrong-doing. He well deserves to be called, as he has been called, the Defender of the Constitution.[20] There are really no blows to be given by him but defensive ones. He is not a leader, but a follower. His leaders are the men of '87.[21] "I have never made an effort," he says, "and never propose to make an effort; I have never countenanced an effort, and never mean to countenance an effort, to disturb the arrangement as originally made, by which the various States came into the Union."[22] Still thinking of the sanction which the Constitution gives to slavery, he says, "Because it was a part of the original compact – let it stand." Notwithstanding his special acuteness and ability, he is unable to take a fact out of its merely political relations, and behold it as it lies absolutely to be disposed of by the intellect – what, for instance, it behooves a man to do here in America to-day with regard to slavery – but ventures, or is driven, to make some such desperate answer as the following, while professing to speak absolutely, and as a private man – from which what new and singular code of social duties might be inferred? "The manner," says he, "in which the governments of those States where slavery exists are to regulate it is for their own consideration, under their responsibility to their constituents, to the general laws of propriety, humanity, and justice, and to God. Associations formed elsewhere, springing from a feeling of humanity, or any other cause, have nothing whatever to do with it. They have never received any encouragement from me, and they never will."[23]

They who know of no purer sources of truth, who have traced up its stream no higher, stand, and wisely stand, by the Bible and the Constitution, and drink at it there with reverence and humility; but they who behold where it comes trickling into this lake or that pool, gird up their loins once more, and continue their pilgrimage toward its fountain-head.

No man with a genius for legislation has appeared in America. They are rare in the history of the world. There are orators, politicians, and eloquent men, by the thousand; but the speaker has not yet opened his mouth to speak who is capable of settling the much-vexed questions of the day. We love eloquence for its own sake, and not for any truth which it may utter, or any heroism it may inspire. Our legislators have not yet learned the comparative value of free trade and of freedom, of union, and of rectitude, to a nation. They have no genius or talent for comparatively humble questions of taxation and finance, commerce and manufactures and agriculture. If we were left solely to the wordy wit of legislators in

Congress for our guidance, uncorrected by the seasonable experience and the effectual complaints of the people, America would not long retain her rank among the nations. For eighteen hundred years, though perchance I have no right to say it, the New Testament has been written; yet where is the legislator who has wisdom and practical talent enough to avail himself of the light which it sheds on the science of legislation?

The authority of government, even such as I am willing to submit to – for I will cheerfully obey those who know and can do better than I, and in many things even those who neither know nor can do so well – is still an impure one: to be strictly just, it must have the sanction and consent of the governed. It can have no pure right over my person and property but what I concede to it. The progress from an absolute to a limited monarchy, from a limited monarchy to a democracy, is a progress toward a true respect for the individual. Even the Chinese philosopher was wise enough to regard the individual as the basis of the empire. Is a democracy, such as we know it, the last improvement possible in government? Is it not possible to take a step further towards recognizing and organizing the rights of man? There will never be a really free and enlightened State until the State comes to recognize the individual as a higher and independent power, from which all its own power and authority are derived, and treats him accordingly. I please myself with imagining a State at last which can afford to be just to all men, and to treat the individual with respect as a neighbor; which even would not think it inconsistent with its own repose if a few were to live aloof from it, not meddling with it, nor embraced by it, who fulfilled all the duties of neighbors and fellow-men. A State which bore this kind of fruit, and suffered it to drop off as fast as it ripened, would prepare the way for a still more perfect and glorious State, which also I have imagined, but not yet anywhere seen.

Notes

1 Begun May 11, 1846, and concluded Feb. 2, 1848. The essay was composed during the struggle.
2 At Charlestown (now a part of Boston).
3 The first stanza of "The Burial of Sir John Moore at Corunna" (1817) by Charles Wolfe (1791–1823).
4 The sheriff's posse, or body of men armed with legal authority to arrest.
5 Cf. *Hamlet*, Act v, scene I, lines 201–4.
6 From *King John*, Act v, scene 2, lines 79–82.
7 i.e., the administration of Polk.
8 Mexico.
9 William Paley (1743–1805), influential English moral philosopher, whose *Principles of Moral and Political Philosophy* appeared in 1785. The quotation here may

be found in vol. II, p. 142, of the edition of 1793 (London).

10 Cf. I Cor. 5: 6.

11 Presumably the Democratic convention of 1848.

12 The Independent Order of Odd Fellows, the first establishment of which in America seems to date from 1806, but which was officially separated from the English branch of the society in 1842–3.

13 Humorous allusion to the *toga virilis*, which the Roman boy put on when he reached man's estate.

14 Nicolaus Copernicus (1473–1543) was not excommunicated, but Martin Luther (1483–1543) was officially condemned in 1520.

15 Samuel Hoar, of Concord, officially sent by Massachusetts to protest against the unconstitutional imprisonment of colored Massachusetts seamen by South Carolina, and driven from Charleston by threats.

16 Cf. *Matt.* 22: 19–21, from which the following quotation is also taken.

17 Confucius (about 550–478 BC), Chinese philosopher. The quotation is from his *Four Books*.

18 In 1838 Thoreau refused to pay taxes for the support of the church, but he was not then put in jail. In 1845, however, on a visit from Walden Pond to Concord to get his shoes mended, Thoreau was imprisoned by Sam Staples, the Concord constable, for refusing to pay his poll tax, spent a night in jail, and was released when the tax was paid for him without his knowledge.

19 The allusion is to a famous book by Silvio Pellico (1788–1854), Italian poet and dramatist, entitled *Le mie prigioni* (1832), detailing the story of his arrest and imprisonment by the tyrannical Austrian Government.

20 The phrase particularly followed upon Webster's second speech on Foote's Resolution – the so-called Reply to Hayne (1830).

21 The fathers of the Constitution. The Constitution was completed and submitted to the several states in 1787.

22 The quotations are from a speech by Webster on the Texas question, delivered Dec. 22, 1845, and may be found in the National edition of his *Writings*, vol. IX, p. 57.

23 From a speech by Webster on the bill to exclude slavery from the territories, delivered Aug. 12, 1848. See *Writings*, vol. X, p. 38.

29

Oration, Delivered in Corinthian Hall, Rochester, July 5, 1852

Frederick Douglass

Introduction

Frederick Douglass (1817–95) was born Frederick Augustus Washington Bailey near Tuckahoe, Maryland. He was born into slavery, yet rose above its tendency to sustain self-deprecators, fought his master, and eventually escaped to freedom in 1838 to New Bedford, Massachusetts, where he assumed the name Frederick Douglass. Although he was a house servant, he had been taught to read, only later to be sent out to the fields to work. After his escape, he began lecturing in the north and in 1845 published *Narrative of the Life of Frederick Douglass, an American Slave*. He left for Europe and began lecturing there on the plight of slaves. In 1847 he returned to America, having purchased his freedom. Along with Martin Delany, he created *North Star*, an abolitionist periodical, which was later named *Frederick Douglass's Paper*. After being falsely accused of aiding John Brown's violent slave insurrection at Harper's Ferry, Virginia, he sought refuge in Canada in 1859. He urged President Lincoln to free the slaves and helped to recruit black troops to fight in the Civil War. In addition to speaking out on emancipation, he also spoke out on women's suffrage issues. During his lifetime, he held several governmental appointments, including assistant secretary to the Santo Domingo Commission, Marshal of Washington, DC, district recorder of deeds, and ambassador to Haiti. In 1881 he finalized revisions of his autobiography, *The Life and Times of Frederick Douglass*.

Taken from Leonard Harris (ed.), *Philosophy Born of Struggle* (Iowa: Dubuque, 1999).

Mr. President, Friends, and Fellow Citizens:

He who could address this audience without a quailing sensation has stronger nerves than I have. I do not remember ever to have appeared as a speaker before any assembly more shrinkingly, nor with greater distrust of my ability, than I do this day. A feeling has crept over me, quite unfavorable to the exercise of my limited powers of speech. The task before me is one which requires much previous thought and study for its proper performance. I know that apologies of this sort are generally considered flat and unmeaning. I trust, however, that mine will not be so considered. Should I seem at ease, my appearance would much misrepresent me. The little experience I have had in addressing public meetings, in country school houses, avails me nothing on the present occasion.

The papers and placards say that I am to deliver a Fourth of July oration. This certainly sounds large and out of the common way for me. It is true that I have often had the privilege to speak in this beautiful hall, and to address many who now honor me with their presence. But neither their familiar faces nor the perfect gauge I think I have of Corinthian Hall seems to free me from embarrassment.

That fact is, ladies and gentlemen, the distance between this platform and the slave plantation from which I escaped is considerable – and the difficulties to be overcome in getting from the latter to the former are by no means slight. That I am here today, is, to me, a matter of astonishment as well as of gratitude. You will not, therefore, be surprised if in what I have to say I evince no elaborate preparation, nor grace my speech with any high-sounding exordium. With little experience and with less learning, I have been able to throw my thoughts hastily and imperfectly together; and trusting to your patient and generous indulgence, I will proceed to lay them before you.

This, for the purpose of this celebration, is the Fourth of July. It is the birthday of your national independence and of your political freedom. This, to you, is what the Passover was to the emancipated people of God. It carries your minds back to the day and the act of your great deliverance, and to the signs and to the wonders associated with that act and that day. This celebration also marks the beginning of another year of your national life and reminds you that the Republic of America is now seventy-six years old. I am glad, fellow citizens, that your nation is so young. Seventy-six years, though a good old age for a man, is but a mere speck in the life of a nation. Three score years and ten is the allotted time for individual men; but nations number their years by thousands. According to this fact, you are even now only in the beginning of your national career, still lingering in the period of childhood. I repeat, I am glad this is so. There is hope in the thought, and hope is much needed, under the dark clouds which lower above the horizon. The eye of the reformer is met with angry flashes, portending disastrous times; but his heart may well beat lighter at the thought that America is young, and that she is still in the impressible stage of her existence. May he not hope that high lessons of wisdom, of justice, and of truth will yet give direction to her destiny? Were the nation older, the patriot's heart might be sadder, and the reformer's brow heavier. Its future might be shrouded in gloom, and the hope of its prophets go out in sorrow. There is consolation in the thought that America is young. Great streams are not easily turned from channels, worn deep in the course of ages. They may sometimes rise in quiet and stately majesty and inundate the land, refreshing and fertilizing the earth with their mysterious properties. They may also rise in wrath and fury, and bear away, on their angry waves, the accumulated wealth of years of toil and hardships. They, however, gradually flow back to the same old channel, and flow on as serenely as ever. But while the river may not be turned aside, it may dry up, and leave nothing behind but the withered branch and the

unsightly rock to howl in the abyss-sweeping wind the sad tale of departed glory. As with rivers, so with nations.

Fellow citizens, I shall not presume to dwell at length on the associations that cluster about this day. The simple story of it is that, seventy-six years ago, the people of this country were British subjects. The style and title of your "sovereign people" (in which you now glory) was not then born. You were under the British Crown. Your fathers esteemed the English government as the home government, and England as the fatherland. This home government, you know, although a considerable distance from your home, did, in the exercise of its parental prerogatives, impose upon its colonial children such restraints, burdens, and limitations as, in its mature judgment, it deemed wise, right, and proper.

But your fathers, who had not adopted the fashionable idea of this day of the infallibility of government and the absolute character of its acts, presumed to differ from the home government in respect to the wisdom and the justice of some of those burdens and restraints. They went so far in their excitement as to pronounce the measures of government unjust, unreasonable, and oppressive, and altogether such as ought not to be quietly submitted to. I scarcely need say, fellow citizens, that my opinion of those measures fully accords with that of your fathers. Such a declaration of agreement on my part would not be worth much to anybody. It would certainly prove nothing as to what part I might have taken, had I lived during the great controversy of 1776. To say *now* that America was right and England wrong is exceedingly easy. Everybody can say it; the dastard, not less than the noble brave, can flippantly discant of the tyranny of England towards the American colonies. It is fashionable to do so; but there was a time when to pronounce against England and in favor of the cause of the colonies tried men's souls. They who did so were accounted in their day plotters of mischief, agitators and rebels, dangerous men. To side with the right, against the wrong, with the weak against the strong, and with the oppressed against the oppressor! *here* lies the merit, and the one which, of all others, seems unfashionable in our day. The cause of liberty may be stabbed by the men who glory in the deeds of your fathers. But, to proceed.

Feeling themselves harshly and unjustly treated by the home government, your fathers, like men of honesty and men of spirit, earnestly sought redress. They petitioned and remonstrated; they did so in a decorous, respectful, and loyal manner. Their conduct was wholly unexceptionable. This, however, did not answer the purpose. They saw themselves treated with sovereign indifference, coldness and scorn. Yet they persevered. They were not the men to look back.

As the sheet anchor takes a firmer hold, when the ship is tossed by the storm, so did the cause of your fathers grow stronger as it breasted the chilling blasts of kingly displeasure. The greatest and best of British statesmen admitted its justice, and the loftiest eloquence of the British Senate came to its support. But with the blindness which seems to be the unvarying characteristic of tyrants since Pharaoh and his hosts were drowned in the Red Sea, the British government persisted in the exactions complained of.

The madness of this course, we believe, is admitted now, even by England; but we fear the lesson is wholly lost on our present rulers.

Oppression makes a wise man mad. Your fathers were wise men, and if they did not go mad, they became restive under this treatment. They felt themselves the victims of grievous wrongs, wholly incurable in their colonial capacity. With brave men there is always a remedy for oppression. Just here, the idea of a total separation of the colonies from the crown was born! It was a startling idea, much more so than we at this distance of time regard it. The timid and the prudent (as has been intimated) of that day were of course shocked and alarmed by it.

Such people lived then, had lived before, and will probably ever have a place on this planet; and their course, in respect to any great change (no matter how great the good to be attained, or the wrong to be redressed by it) may be calculated with as much precision as can be the course of the stars. They hate all changes but silver, gold, and copper change! Of this sort of change they are always strongly in favor.

These people were called tories in the days of your fathers; and the appellation probably conveyed the same idea that is meant by a more modern though a somewhat less euphonious term, which we often find in our papers applied to some of our old politicians.

Their opposition to the then-dangerous thought was earnest and powerful; but amid all their terror and affrighted vociferations against it, the alarming and revolutionary idea moved on, and the country with it.

On the second of July, 1776, the old Continental Congress, to the dismay of the lovers of ease and the worshippers of property, clothed that dreadful idea with all the authority of national sanction. They did so in the form of a resolution; and as we seldom hit upon resolutions, drawn up in our day, whose transparency is at all equal to this, it may refresh your minds and help my story if I read it: "Resolved. That these united colonies *are*, and of right, ought to be free and Independent States; that they are absolved from all allegiance to the British Crown; and that all political connection between them and the State of Great Britain *is*, and ought to be, dissolved."

Citizens, your fathers made good that resolution. They succeeded; and today you reap the fruits of their success. The freedom gained is yours; and you, therefore, may properly celebrate this anniversary. The Fourth of July is the first great fact in your nation's history – the very ring-bolt in the chain of your yet undeveloped destiny.

Pride and patriotism, not less than gratitude, prompt you to celebrate and to hold it in perpetual remembrance. I have said that the Declaration of Independence is the *ringbolt* to the chain of your nation's destiny; so indeed I regard it. The principles contained in that instrument are saving principles. Stand by those principles, be true to them on all occasions, in all places, against all foes, and at whatever cost.

From the round top of your ship of state, dark and threatening clouds may be seen. Heavy billows, like mountains in the distance, disclose to the leeward huge forms of flinty rocks! That *bolt* drawn, that *chain* broken, and all is lost. *Cling to this day – cling to it*, and to its principles, with the grasp of a storm-tossed mariner to a spar at midnight.

The coming into being of a nation in any circumstances is an interesting event. But besides general considerations, there were peculiar circumstances which make the advent of this republic an event of special attractiveness.

The whole scene, as I look back to it, was simple, dignified, and sublime.

The population of the country, at the time, stood at the insignificant number of three millions. The country was poor in the munitions of war. The population was weak and scattered, and the country a wilderness unsubdued. There were then no means of concert and combination such as exist now. Neither steam nor lightning had then been reduced to order and discipline. From the Potomac to the Delaware was a journey of many days.

Under these and innumerable other disadvantages, your fathers declared for liberty and independence and triumphed.

Fellow citizens, I am not wanting in respect for the fathers of this republic. The signers of the Declaration of Independence were brave men. They were great men, too – great enough to give fame to a great age. It does not often happen to a nation to raise, at one time, such a number of truly great men. The point from which I am compelled to view them is not certainly the most favorable; and yet I cannot contemplate their great deeds with less than admiration. They were statesmen, patriots, and heroes, and for the good they did, and the principles they contended for, I will unite with you to honor their memory.

They loved their Country better than their own private interests; and though this is not the highest form of human excellence, all will concede that it is a rare virtue, and that when it is exhibited, it ought to command respect. He who will intelligently lay down his life for his country is a man whom it is not in human nature to despise. Your fathers staked their lives, their fortunes, and their sacred honor on the cause of their country. In their admiration of liberty, they lost sight of all other interests.

They were peace men; but they preferred revolution to peaceful submission to bondage. They were quiet men; but they did not shrink from agitating against oppression. They showed forbearance; but they knew its limits. They believed in order; but not in the order of tyranny. With them, nothing was *settled* that was not right. With them, justice, liberty, and humanity were *final*; not slavery and oppression. You may well cherish the memory of such men. They were great in their day and generation. Their solid manhood stands out the more as we contrast it with these degenerate times.

How circumspect, exact, and proportionate were all their movements! How unlike the politicians of an hour! Their statesmanship looked beyond the passing moment, and stretched away in strength into the distant future. They seized upon eternal principles, and set a glorious example in their defense. Mark them!

Fully appreciating the hardships to be encountered, firmly believing in the right of their cause, honorably inviting the scrutiny of an onlooking world, reverently appealing to heaven to attest their sincerity, soundly comprehending the solemn responsibility they were about to assume, wisely measuring the terrible odds against them, your fathers, the fathers of this republic, did most de-liberately, under the inspiration of a glorious patriotism and with a sublime faith in the great principles of justice and freedom, lay deep the cornerstone of the national superstructure, which has risen and still rises in grandeur around you.

Of this fundamental work, this day is the anniversary. Our eyes are met with demonstrations of joyous enthusiasm. Banners and pennants wave exultingly on the breeze. The din of business, too, is hushed. Even mammon seems to have quitted his grasp on this day. The ear-piercing fife and the stirring drum unite their accents with the ascending peal of a thousand church bells. Prayers are made, hymns are sung, and sermons are preached in honor of this day; while the quick martial tramp of a great and multitudinous nation, echoed back by all the hills, valleys, and mountains of a vast continent, bespeak the occasion one of thrilling and universal interest – a nation's jubilee.

Friends and citizens, I need not enter further into the causes which led to this anniversary. Many of you understand them better than I do. You could instruct me in regard to them. That is a branch of knowledge in which you feel, perhaps, a much deeper interest than your speaker. The causes which led to the separation of the colonies from the British crown have never lacked for a tongue. They have all been taught in your common schools, narrated at your firesides, unfolded from your pulpits, and thundered from your legislative halls, and are as familiar to you as household words. They form the staple of Your national poetry and eloquence.

I remember also that, as a people, Americans are remarkably familiar with all facts which make in their own favor. This is esteemed by some as a national trait – perhaps a national weakness. It is a fact that whatever makes for the wealth or for the reputation of Americans and can be had *cheap!* will be found by Americans. I shall not be charged with slandering Americans if I say I think the American side of any question may be safely left in American hands.

I leave, therefore, the great deeds of your fathers to other gentlemen whose claim to have been regularly descended will be less likely to be disputed than mine!

The Present

My business, if I have any here today, is with the present. The accepted time with God and his cause is the ever-living now.

Trust no future, however pleasant.
 Let the dead past bury its dead;
Act, act in the living present,
 Heart within, and God overhead.

We have to do with the past only as we can make it useful to the present and to the future. To all inspiring motives, to noble deeds which can be gained from the past, we are welcome. But now is the time, the important time. Your fathers have lived, died, and have done their work, and have done much of it well. You live and must die, and you must do your work. You have no right to enjoy a child's share in the labor of your fathers, unless your children are to be blest by your labors. You have no right to wear out and waste the hard-earned fame of your fathers to cover your indolence. Sydney Smith tells us that men seldom eulogize the wisdom and virtues of their fathers, but to excuse some folly or wickedness of their own. This truth is not a doubtful one. There are illustrations of it near and remote, ancient and modern. It was fashionable, hundreds of years ago, for the children of Jacob to boast, we have "Abraham to our father," when they had long lost Abraham's faith and spirit. That people contented themselves under the shadow of Abraham's great name, while they repudiated the deeds which made his name great. Need I remind you that a similar thing is being done all over this country today? Need I tell you that the Jews are not the only people who built the tombs of the prophets, and garnished the sepulchres of the righteous? Washington could not die till he had broken the chains of his slaves. Yet his monument is built up by the price of human blood, and the traders in the bodies and souls of men shout – "We have Washington to '*our father.*'" – Alas! that it should be so; yet so it is.

The evil that men do, lives after them,
The good is oft' interred with their bones.

Fellow citizens, pardon me, allow me to ask, why am I called upon to speak here today? What have I, or those I represent, to do with your national independence? Are the great principles of political freedom and of natural justice, embodied in that Declaration of Independence, extended to us? and am I, therefore, called upon to bring our humble offering to the national altar, and to confess the benefits and express devout gratitude for the blessings resulting from your independence to us?

Would to God, both for your sakes and ours, that an affirmative answer could be truthfully returned to these questions! Then would my task be light, and my burden easy and delightful. For *who* is there so cold that a nation's sympathy could not warm him? Who so obdurate and dead to the claims of gratitude that would not thankfully acknowledge such priceless benefits? Who so stolid and selfish that would not give his voice to swell the hallelujahs of a nation's jubilee, when the chains of servitude had been torn from his limbs? I am not that man. In a case like that, the dumb might eloquently speak, and the "lame man leap as an hart."

But such is not the state of the case. I say it with a sad sense of the disparity between us. I am not included within the pale of this glorious anniversary! Your high independence only reveals the immeasurable distance between us. The blessings in which you, this day, rejoice, are not enjoyed in common. The rich inheritance of justice, liberty, prosperity, and independence bequeathed by your fathers is shared by you, not by me. The sunlight that brought life and healing to you has brought stripes and death to me. This Fourth of July is *yours*, not *mine*. *You* may rejoice, *I* must mourn. To drag a man in fetters into the grand illuminated temple of liberty, and call upon him to join you in joyous anthems, were inhuman mockery and sacrilegious irony. Do you mean, citizens, to mock me, by asking me to speak today? If so, there is a parallel to your conduct. And let me warn you that it is dangerous to copy the example of a nation whose crimes, towering up to heaven, were thrown down by the breath of the Almighty, burying that nation in irrecoverable ruin! I can today take up the plaintive lament of a peeled and woe-smitten people!

By the rivers of Babylon, there we sat down. Yea! we wept when we remembered Zion. We hanged our harps upon the willows in the midst thereof. For there, they that carried us away captive, required of us a song; and they who wasted us required of us mirth, saying, Sing us one of the songs of Zion. How can we sing the Lord's song in a strange land? If I forget thee, O Jerusalem, let my right hand forget her cunning. If I do not remember thee, let my tongue cleave to the roof of my mouth. (Ps. 137: 1–6)

Fellow citizens; above your national, tumultuous joy, I hear the mournful wail of millions!

whose chains, heavy and grievous yesterday, are today rendered more intolerable by the jubilee shouts that reach them. If I do forget, if I do not faithfully remember those bleeding children of sorrow this day, "may my right hand forget her cunning, and may my tongue cleave to the roof of my mouth!" To forget them, to pass lightly over their wrongs, and to chime in with the popular theme, would be treason most scandalous and shocking, and would make me a reproach before God and the world. My subject, then, fellow citizens, is AMERICAN SLAVERY. I shall see this day and its popular characteristics from the slave's point of view. Standing there, identified with the American bondman, making his wrongs mine, I do not hesitate to declare with all my soul that the character and conduct of this nation never looked blacker to me than on this Fourth of July! Whether we turn to the declarations of the past or to the professions of the present, the conduct of the nation seems equally hideous and revolting. America is false to the past, false to the present, and solemnly binds herself to be false to the future. Standing with God and the crushed and bleeding slave on this occasion, I will, in the name of humanity which is outraged, in the name of liberty which is fettered, in the name of the constitution and the Bible, which are disregarded and trampled upon, dare to call in question and to denounce, with all the emphasis I can command, everything that serves to perpetuate slavery – the great sin and shame of America! "I will not equivocate; I will not excuse"; I will use the severest language I can command; and yet not one word shall escape me that any man, whose judgment is not blinded by prejudice or who is not at heart a slaveholder, shall not confess to be right and just.

But I fancy I hear some one of my audience say, it is just in this circumstance that you and your brother abolitionists fail to make a favorable impression on the public mind. Would you argue more, and denounce less, would you persuade more, and rebuke less, your cause would be much more likely to succeed. But, I submit, where all is plain there is nothing to be argued. What point in the antislavery creed would you have me argue? on what branch of the subject do the people of this country need light? Must I undertake to prove that the slave is a man? That point is conceded already. Nobody doubts it. The slaveholders themselves acknowledge it in the enactment of laws for their government. They acknowledge it when they punish disobedience on the part of the slave. There are seventy-two crimes in the state of Virginia which if committed by a black man (no matter how ignorant he be) subject him to the punishment of death; while only two of the same crimes will subject a white man to the like punishment. What is this but the acknowledgement that the slave is a moral, intellectual, and responsible being. The manhood of the slave is conceded. It is admitted in the fact that southern statute books are covered with enactments forbidding, under severe fines and penalties, the teaching of the slave to read or to write. When you can point to any such laws, in reference to the beasts of the field, then I may consent to argue the manhood of the slave. When the dogs in your streets, when the fowls of the air, when the cattle on your hills, when the fish of the sea, and the reptiles that crawl, shall be unable to distinguish the slave from a brute, *then* will I argue with you that the slave is a man!

For the present, it is enough to affirm the equal manhood of the Negro race. Is it not astonishing that, while we are ploughing, planting, and reaping, using all kinds of mechanical tools, erecting houses, constructing bridges, building ships, working in metals or brass, iron, copper, silver, and gold; that, while we are reading, writing and ciphering, acting as clerks, merchants, and secretaries, having among us lawyers, doctors, ministers, poets, authors, editors, orators, and teachers; that, while we are engaged in all manner of enterprises common to other men, digging gold in California, capturing the whale in the Pacific, feeding sheep and cattle on the hillside, living, moving, acting, thinking, planning, living in families as husbands, wives and children, and, above all, confessing and worshipping the Christian's God, and looking hopefully for life and immortality beyond the grave, we are called upon to prove that we are men!

Would you have me argue that man is entitled to liberty? that he is the rightful owner of his own body? You have already declared it. Must I argue the wrongfulness of slavery? Is that a question for Republicans? Is it to be settled by the rules of logic and argumentation, as a matter beset with great difficulty, involving a doubtful application of the principle of justice, hard to be understood? How should I look today, in the presence of Americans, dividing and subdividing a discourse to show that men have a natural right to freedom? speaking of it relatively, and positively, negatively, and affirmatively. To do so would be to make myself ridiculous, and to offer an insult to your understanding. There is not a man beneath the canopy of heaven that does not know that slavery is wrong *for him*.

What, am I to argue that it is wrong to make men brutes, to rob them of their liberty, to work them without wages, to keep them ignorant of their relations to their fellow men, to beat them with sticks, to flay their flesh with the lash, to load their limbs with irons, to hunt them with dogs, to sell them at auction, to sunder their families, to knock out their teeth, to burn their flesh, to starve them into obedience and submission to their masters? Must I argue that a system thus marked with blood and stained with pollution is *wrong*? No! I will not. I have better employment for my time and strength than such arguments would imply.

What, then, remains to be argued? Is it that slavery is not divine; that God did not establish it; that our doctors of divinity are mistaken? There is blasphemy in the thought. That which is inhuman cannot be divine! Who can reason on such a proposition? They that can, may; I cannot. The time for such argument is past.

At a time like this, scorching irony, not convincing argument, is needed. O! had I the ability, and could I reach the nation's ear, I would today pour out a fiery stream of biting ridicule, blasting reproach, withering sarcasm, and stern rebuke. For it is not light that is needed, but fire; it is not the gentle shower, but thunder. We need the storm, the whirlwind, and the earthquake. The feeling of the nation must be quickened; the conscience of the nation must be roused; the propriety of the nation must be startled; the hypocrisy of the nation must be exposed; and its crimes against God and man must be proclaimed and denounced.

What, to the American slave, is your Fourth of July? I answer; a day that reveals to him, more than all other days in the year, the gross injustice and cruelty to which he is the constant victim. To him, your celebration is a sham; Your boasted liberty, an unholy license; your national greatness, swelling vanity; your sounds of rejoicing are empty and heartless; your denunciations of tyrants, brass-fronted impudence; your shouts of liberty and equality, hollow mockery; your prayers and hymns, your sermons and thanksgivings, with all your religious parade and solemnity, are to him mere bombast, fraud, deception, impiety, and hypocrisy – a thin veil to cover up crimes which would disgrace a nation of savages. There is not a nation on the earth guilty of practices more shocking and bloody than are the people of these United States, at this very hour.

Go where you may, search where you will, roam through all the monarchies and despotisms of the old world, travel through South America, search out every abuse, and when you have found the last, lay your facts by the side of the everyday practices of this nation, and you will say with me that, for revolting barbarity and shameless hypocrisy, America reigns without a rival....

Religious Liberty

I take this law [the Fugitive Slave Law] to be one of the grossest infringements of Christian liberty, and if the churches and ministers of our country were not stupidly blind or most wickedly indifferent, they too would so regard it.

At the very moment that they are thanking God for the enjoyment of civil and religious liberty, and for the right to worship God according to the dictates of their own consciences, they are utterly silent in respect to a law which robs religion of its chief significance, and makes it utterly worthless to a world lying in wickedness. Did this law concern the *"mint, anise* and *cummin"* – abridge the right to sing psalms, to partake of the sacrament, or to engage in any of the ceremonies of religion – it would be smitten by the thunder of a thousand pulpits. A general shout would go up from the church, demanding *repeal, repeal, instant repeal!* – And it would go hard with that politician who presumed to solicit the votes of the people without inscribing this motto on his banner. Further, if this demand were not complied with, another Scotland would be added to the history of religious liberty, and the stern old covenanters would be thrown into the shade. A John Knox would be seen at every church door, and heard from every pulpit, and Fillmore would have no more quarter than was shown by Knox to the beautiful but treacherous Queen Mary of Scotland. The fact that the church of our country (with fractional exceptions) does not esteem the Fugitive Slave Law as a declaration of war against religious liberty implies that that church regards religion simply as a form of worship, an empty ceremony, and *not* a vital principle, requiring active benevolence, justice, love and good will towards man. It esteems sacrifice above mercy; psalm-singing above right doing; solemn meetings above practical righteousness. A worship that can be conducted by persons

343

who refuse to give shelter to the houseless, to give bread to the hungry, clothing to the naked, and who enjoin obedience to a law forbidding these acts of mercy, is a curse, not a blessing to mankind. The Bible addresses all such persons as "scribes, pharisees, hypocrites, who pay tithe of *mint, anise,* and *cummin,* and have omitted the weightier matters of the law, judgment, mercy and faith" (Matt. 23: 23).

The Church Responsible

But the church of this country is not only indifferent to the wrongs of the slave, it actually takes sides with the oppressors. It has made itself the bulwark of American slavery, and the shield of American slave-hunters. Many of its most eloquent Divines, who stand as the very lights of the church, have shamelessly given the sanction of religion and the Bible to the whole slave system. They have taught that man may, properly, be a slave; that the relation of master and slave is ordained of God; that to send back an escaped bondman to his master is clearly the duty of all the followers of the Lord Jesus Christ; and this horrible blasphemy is palmed off upon the world for Christianity.

For my part, I would say, welcome infidelity! welcome atheism! welcome anything! in preference to the gospel, *as preached by those Divines!* They convert the very name of religion into an engine of tyranny and barbarous cruelty, and serve to confirm more infidels, in this age, than all the infidel writings of Thomas Paine, Voltaire, and Bolingbroke put together have done. These ministers make religion a cold and flinty-hearted thing, having neither principles of right action nor bowels of compassion. They strip the love of God of its beauty, and leave the throne of religion a huge, horrible, repulsive form. It is a religion for oppressors, tyrants, man-stealers, and *thugs.* It is not that "*pure and undefiled religion*" which is from above, and which is "*first pure, then peaceable, easy to be entreated,* full of mercy and good fruits, *without partiality, and without hypocrisy.*" But a religion which favors the rich against the poor; which exalts the proud above the humble; which divides mankind into two classes, tyrants and slaves; which says to the man in chains, stay there; and to the oppressor, oppress on; it is a religion which may be professed and enjoyed by all the robbers and enslavers of mankind; it makes God a respecter of

persons, denies his fatherhood of the race, and tramples in the dust the great truth of the brotherhood of man. All this we affirm to be true of the popular church, and the popular worship of our land and nation – a religion, a church, and a worship which, on the authority of inspired wisdom, we pronounce to be an abomination in the sight of God. In the language of Isaiah, the American church might be well addressed. "Bring no more vain oblations; incense is an abomination unto me: the new moons and Sabbaths, the calling of assemblies, I cannot away with; it is iniquity, even the solemn meeting. Your new moons, and your appointed feasts my soul hateth. They are a trouble to me; I am weary to bear them; and when ye spread forth your hands I will hide mine eyes from you. Yea! when ye make many prayers, I will not hear. YOUR HANDS ARE FULL OF BLOOD; cease to do evil, learn to do well; seek judgment; relieve the oppressed; judge for the fatherless; plead for the widow."

The American church is guilty, when viewed in connection with what it is doing to uphold slavery; but it is superlatively guilty when viewed in connection with its ability to abolish slavery.

The sin of which it is guilty is one of omission as well as of commission. Albert Barnes but uttered what the common sense of every man at all observant of the actual state or the case will receive as truth, when he declared that "there is no power out of the church that could sustain slavery an hour, if it were not sustained in it."

Let the religious press, the pulpit, the Sunday school, the conference meeting, the great ecclesiastical, missionary, bible, and tract associations of the land array their immense powers against slavery, and slaveholding; and the whole system of crime and blood would be scattered to the winds, and that they do not do this involves them in the most awful responsibility of which the mind can conceive.

In prosecuting the antislavery enterprise, we have been asked to spare the church, to spare the ministry; but *how,* we ask, could such a thing be done? We are met on the threshold of our efforts for the redemption of the slave, by the church and ministry of the Country, in battle arrayed against us; and we are compelled to fight or flee. From *what* quarter, I beg to know, has proceeded a fire so deadly upon our ranks, during the last two years, as from the northern pulpit? As the champions of oppressors, the chosen men of American theology have appeared – men, honored for their so-called piety and their real learning. The LORDS of Buffalo, the SPRINGS of New York, the LATHROPS of Auburn, the COXES and SPENCERS of Brooklyn, the GANNETS and SHARPS of Boston, the DEWEYS of Washington, and other great religious lights of the land have, in utter denial of the authority of *Him* by whom they professed to be called to the ministry, deliberately taught us, against the example of the Hebrews, and against the remonstrance of the Apostles, they teach *that we ought to obey man's law before the law of God.*

My spirit wearies of such blasphemy; and how such men can be supported as the "standing types and representative of Jesus Christ" is a mystery which I leave others to penetrate. In speaking of the American church, however, let it be distinctly understood that I mean the *great mass* of the religious organizations of our land. There are exceptions, and I thank God that there are. Noble men may be round, scattered all over these northern states, of whom Henry Ward Beecher of Brooklyn, Samuel J. May of Syracuse, and my esteemed friend on the platform [Reverend R. R. Raymond] are shining examples; and let me say further that upon these men lies the duty to inspire our ranks with high religious faith and zeal, and to cheer us on in the great mission of the slave's redemption from his chains.

Religion in England and Religion in America

One is struck with the difference between the attitude of the American church towards the antislavery movement and that occupied by the churches in England towards a similar movement in that country. There, the church, true to its mission of ameliorating, elevating, and improving the condition of mankind, came forward promptly, bound up the wounds of the West Indian slave, and restored him to his liberty. There, the question of emancipation was a high religious question. It was demanded in the name of humanity and according to the law of the living God. The Sharps, the Clarksons, the Wilberforces, the Buxtons, the Burchells, and the Knibbs were alike famous for their piety and for their philanthropy. The antislavery movement *there* was not an antichurch movement, for the reason that the church took its full share in prosecuting that movement: and the antislavery movement in this country will cease to be an antichurch movement when the church of this country shall assume a favorable instead of a hostile position towards that movement.

Americans! your republican politics, not less than Your republican religion, are flagrantly inconsistent. You boast of your love of liberty, your superior civilization, and your pure Christianity, while the whole political power of the nation (as embodied in the two great political parties) is solemnly pledged to support and perpetuate the enslavement of three millions of your countrymen. You hurl your anathemas at the crowned-headed tyrants of Russia and Austria, and pride yourselves on your democratic institutions, while you yourselves consent to be the mere *tools* and *bodyguards* of the tyrants of Virginia and Carolina. You invite to your shores fugitives of oppression from abroad, honor them with banquets, greet them with ovations, cheer them, toast them, salute them, protect them, and pour out your money to them like water; but the fugitives from your own land you advertise, hunt, arrest, shoot, and kill. You glory in your refinement, and your universal education; yet you maintain a system as barbarous and dreadful as ever stained the character of a nation – a system begun in avarice, supported in pride, and perpetuated in cruelty. You shed tears over fallen Hungary, and make the sad story of her wrongs the theme of your poets, statesmen, and orators, till your gallant soils are ready to fly to arms to vindicate her cause against her oppressors; but, in regard to the ten thousand wrongs of the American slave, you would enforce the strictest silence, and would hail him as an enemy of the nation who dares to make those wrongs the subject of public discourse! You are all on fire at the mention of liberty for France or for Ireland, but are as cold as an iceberg at the thought of liberty for the enslaved of America. You discourse eloquently on the dignity of labor; yet you sustain a system which, in its very essence, casts a stigma upon labor. You can bare your bosom to the storm of British artillery, to throw off a threepenny tax on tea; and yet wring the last hard-earned farthing from the grasp of the black laborers of your country. You profess to believe "that, of one blood, God made all nations of men to dwell on the face of all the earth," and hath commanded all men everywhere to love one another; yet you notoriously hate (and glory in your hatred) all men whose skins are not colored like your own. You declare before the world and are understood by the world to declare that you *"hold these truths to be self evident, that all men are created equal; and are endowed by their Creator with certain inalienable rights; and that, among these are, life, liberty, and the pursuit of happiness"*; and yet you hold securely, in a bondage which according to your own Thomas Jefferson *"is worse than ages of that which your fathers rose in rebellion to oppose,"* a *seventh part* of the inhabitants of your country.

Fellow citizens! I will not enlarge further on your national inconsistencies. The existence of slavery in this country brands your republicanism as a sham, your humanity as a base pretense, and your Christianity as a lie. It destroys your moral power abroad; it corrupts your politicians at home. It saps the foundation of religion; it makes your name a hissing, and a byword to a mocking earth. It is the antagonistic force in your government, the only thing that seriously disturbs and endangers your union. It fetters your progress; it is the enemy of improvement, the deadly foe of education; it fosters pride; it breeds insolence; it promotes vice; it shelters crime; it is a curse to the earth that supports it; and yet you cling to it, as if it were the sheet anchor of all your hopes. Oh! be warned! be warned! a horrible reptile is coiled up in your nation's bosom; the venomous creature is nursing at the tender breast of your youthful republic; *for the love of God, tear away*, and fling from you the hideous monster, and *let the weight of twenty millions crush and destroy it forever* ....

Allow me to say, in conclusion, notwithstanding the dark picture I have this day presented of the state of the nation, I do not despair of this country. There are forces in operation which must inevitably work the downfall of slavery. *"The arm of the Lord is not shortened"* (Isa. 59: 1), and the doom of slavery is certain. I therefore leave off where I began, with *hope*. While drawing encouragement from the Declaration of Independence, the great principles it contains, and the genius of American institutions, my spirit is also cheered by the obvious tendencies of the age. Nations do not now stand in the same relation to each other that they did ages ago. No nation can now shut itself up, from the surrounding world, and trot round in the same old path of its fathers without interference. The time *was* when such could be done. Long-established customs of hurtful character could formerly fence themselves in, and do their evil work with social impunity. Knowledge was then confined and enjoyed by the privileged few, and the multitude walked on in mental darkness. But a change has now come over the affairs of mankind. Walled cities and empires have become unfashionable. The arm of commerce has borne away the gates of the strong city. Intelligence is penetrating the darkest corners of the globe. It makes its pathway over and under the sea, as well as on the earth. Wind, steam, and lightning are its chartered agents. Oceans no longer divide, but link nations together. From Boston to London is now a holiday excursion. Space is comparatively annihilated – Thoughts expressed on one side of the Atlantic are distinctly heard on the other.

The far off and almost fabulous Pacific rolls in grandeur at our feet. The celestial empire, the mystery of ages, is being solved. The fiat of the Almighty, *Let there be Light*, has not yet spent its force. No abuse, no outrage whether in taste, sport, or avarice, can now hide itself from the all-pervading light. The iron shoe and crippled foot of China must be seen, in contrast with nature. *Africa must rise and put on her yet-unwoven garment. "Ethiopia shall stretch out her hand unto God"* (Ps. 68: 31).

30

Woman Versus the Indian

Anna J. Cooper

Introduction

Anna J. Cooper (1858–1964) was born in Raleigh, North Carolina. She received her bachelor of arts degree from Oberlin College in 1884 and an MA in mathematics from Oberlin in 1887. At the age of 67 she earned a PhD, officiated by Alain L. Locke, from the Université de Paris. In 1892 Cooper published a collection of her essays, *A Voice from the South*. Cooper was a teacher and head of M Street High School, later to become Dunbar High School, in Washington DC. In 1930 she became the president of Frelinghuysen University, Washington DC. Frelinghuysen was made up of a collection of adult education schools. Cooper wrote provocatively as a moral suasionist on issues of collective identity, duty, gender, and civilization.

In the National Woman's Council convened at Washington in February 1891, among a number of thoughtful and suggestive papers read by eminent women, was one by the Rev. Anna Shaw, bearing the above title.

That Miss Shaw is broad and just and liberal in principal is proved beyond contradiction. Her noble generosity and womanly firmness are unimpeachable. The unwavering stand taken by herself and Miss Anthony in the subsequent color ripple in Wimodaughsis ought to be sufficient to allay forever any doubts as to the pure gold of these two women.

Taken from *A Voice from the South*, 1852 (New York: Negro University Press, 1969).

Of Wimodaughsis (which, being interpreted for the uninitiated, is a woman's culture club whose name is made up of the first few letters of the four words wives, mothers, daughters, and sisters) Miss Shaw is president, and a lady from the Blue Grass State *was* secretary.

Pandora's box is opened in the ideal harmony of this modern Eden without an Adam when a colored lady, a teacher in one of our schools, applies for admission to its privileges and opportunities.

The Kentucky secretary, a lady zealous in good works and one who, I can't help imagining, belongs to that estimable class who daily thank the Lord that He made the earth that they may have the job of superintending its rotations, and who really would like to help "elevate" the colored people (in her own way of course and so long as they understand their places) is filled with grief and horror that any persons of Negro extraction should aspire to learn type-writing or languages or to enjoy any other advantages offered in the sacred halls of Wimodaughsis. Indeed, she had not calculated that there were any wives, mothers, daughters, and sisters, except white ones; and she is really convinced that *Whimodaughsis* would sound just as well, and then it need mean just *white mothers, daughters and sisters*. In fact, so far as there is anything in a name, nothing would be lost by omitting for the sake of euphony, from this unique mosaic, the letters that represent wives. *Whiwimodaughsis* might be a little startling, and on the whole wives would better yield to white; since clearly all women are not wives, while surely all wives are daughters. The daughters therefore could represent the wives and this immaculate assembly for propagating liberal and progressive ideas and disseminating a broad and humanizing culture might be spared the painful possibility of the sight of a black man coming in the future to escort from an evening class this solitary cream-colored applicant. Accordingly the Kentucky secretary took the cream-colored applicant aside, and, with emotions befitting such an epoch-making crisis, told her, "as kindly as she could," that colored people were not admitted to the classes, at the same time refunding the money which said cream-colored applicant had paid for lessons in type-writing.

When this little incident came to the knowledge of Miss Shaw, she said firmly and emphatically, NO. As a minister of the gospel and as a Christian woman, she could not lend her influence to such unreasonable and uncharitable discrimination; and she must resign the honor of president of Wimodaughsis if persons were to be proscribed solely on account of their color.

To the honor of the board of managers, be it said, they sustained Miss Shaw; and the Kentucky secretary, and those whom she succeeded in inoculating with her prejudices, resigned.

'Twas only a ripple – some bewailing of lost opportunity on the part of those who could not or would not seize God's opportunity for broadening and enlarging their own souls – and then the work flowed on as before.

Susan B. Anthony and Anna Shaw are evidently too noble to be held in thrall by the provincialisms of women who seem never to have breathed the atmosphere beyond the confines of their grandfathers' plantations. It is only from the broad plateau of light and love that one can see petty prejudice and narrow priggishness in their true perspective; and it is on this high ground, as I sincerely believe, these two grand women stand.

As leaders in the woman's movement of to-day, they have need of clearness of vision as well as firmness of soul in adjusting recalcitrant forces, and wheeling into line the thousand and one none-such, never-to-be-modified, won't-be-dictated-to banners of their somewhat mottled array.

The black woman and the southern woman, I imagine, often get them into the predicament of the befuddled man who had to take singly across a stream a bag of corn, a fox and a goose. There was no one to help, and to leave the goose with the fox was death – with the corn, destruction. To re-christen the animals, the lion could not be induced

to lie down with the lamb unless the lamb would take the inside berth.

The black woman appreciates the situation and can even sympathize with the actors in the serio-comic dilemma.

But, may it not be that, as women, the very lessons which seem hardest to master now, are possibly the ones most essential for our promotion to a higher grade of work?

We assume to be leaders of thought and guardians of society. Our country's manners and morals are under our tutoring. Our standards are law in our several little worlds. However tenaciously men may guard some prerogatives, they are our willing slaves in that sphere which they have always conceded to be woman's. Here, no one dares demur when her fiat has gone forth. The man would be mad who presumed, however inexplicable and past finding out any reason for her action might be, to attempt to open a door in her kingdom officially closed and regally sealed by her.

The American woman of to-day not only gives tone directly to her immediate world, but her tiniest pulsation ripples out and out, down and down, till the outermost circles and the deepest layers of society feel the vibrations. It is pre-eminently an age of organizations. The "leading woman," the preacher, the reformer, the organizer "enthuses" her lieutenants and captains, the literary women, the thinking women, the strong, earnest, irresistible women; these in turn touch their myriads of church clubs, social clubs, culture clubs, pleasure clubs and charitable clubs, till the same lecture has been duly administered to every married man in the land (not to speak of sons and brothers) from the President in the White House to the stone-splitter of the ditches. And so woman's lightest whisper is heard as in Dionysius' ear, by quick relays and endless reproductions, through every recess and cavern as well as on every hilltop and mountain in her vast domain. And her mandates are obeyed. When she says "thumbs up," woe to the luckless thumb that falters in its rising. They may be little things, the amenities of life, the little nothings which cost nothing and come to nothing, and yet can make a sentient being so comfortable or so miserable in this life, the oil of social machinery, which we call the courtesies of life, all are under the magic key of woman's permit.

The American woman then is responsible for American manners. Not merely the right ascension and declination of the satellites of her own drawing room; but the rising and the setting of the pestilential or life-giving orbs which seem to wander afar in space, all are governed almost wholly through her magnetic polarity. The atmosphere of street cars and parks and boulevards, of cafes and hotels and steamboats is charged and surcharged with her sentiments and restrictions. Shop girls and serving maids, cashiers and accountant clerks, scribblers and drummers, whether wage earner, salaried toiler, or proprietress, whether laboring to instruct minds, to save souls, to delight fancies, or to win bread – the working women of America in whatever station or calling they may be found, are subjects, officers, or rulers of a strong centralized government, and bound together by a system of codes and countersigns, which, though unwritten, forms a network of perfect subordination and unquestioning obedience as marvelous as that of the Jesuits. At the head and center in this regime stands the Leading Woman in the principality. The one talismanic word that plays along the wires from palace to cook-shop, from imperial Congress to the distant plain, is *Caste*. With all her vaunted independence, the American woman of to-day is as fearful of losing caste as a Brahmin in India. That is the law under which she lives, the precepts which she binds as frontlets between her eyes and writes on the doorposts of her homes, the lesson which she instils into her children with their first baby breakfasts, the injunction she lays upon husband and lover with direst penalties attached.

The queen of the drawing room is absolute ruler under this law. Her pose gives the cue. The microscopic angle at which her pencilled brows are elevated, signifies who may be recognized and who are beyond the pale. The delicate intimation is, quick as electricity, telegraphed down. Like the wonderful transformation in the House that Jack Built (or regions thereabouts) when the rat began to gnaw the rope, the rope to hang the butcher, the butcher to kill the ox, the ox to drink the water, the water to quench the fire, the fire to burn the stick, the stick to beat the dog, and the dog to worry the cat, and on, and on, and on – when miladi causes the inner arch over her matchless orbs to ascend the merest trifle, *presto*! the Miss at the notions counter grows curt and pert, the dress goods clerk becomes indifferent and taciturn, hotel waiters and ticket dispensers look the other way, the Irish street laborer snarls and scowls, conductors, policemen and park superintendents jostle and push and threaten, and society suddenly seems trans-

formed into a band of organized adders, snapping, and striking and hissing just because they like it on general principles. The tune set by the head singer, sung through all keys and registers, with all qualities of tone – the smooth, flowing, and gentle, the creaking, whizzing, grating, screeching, growling – according to ability, taste, and temperament of the singers. Another application of like master, like man. In this case, like mistress, like nation.

It was the good fortune of the Black Woman of the South to spend some weeks, not long since, in a land over which floated the Union Jack. The Stars and Stripes were not the only familiar experiences missed. A uniform, matter-of-fact courtesy, a genial kindliness, quick perception of opportunities for rendering any little manly assistance, a readiness to give information to strangers – a hospitable, thawing-out atmosphere everywhere – in shops and waiting rooms, on cars and in the streets, actually seemed to her chilled little soul to transform the commonest boor in the service of the public into one of nature's noblemen, and when the old whipped-cur feeling was taken up and analyzed she could hardly tell whether it consisted mostly of self pity for her own wounded sensibilities, or of shame for her country and mortification that her countrymen offered such an unfavorable contrast.

Some American girls, I noticed recently, in search of novelty and adventure, were taking an extended trip through our country unattended by gentleman friends; their wish was to write up for a periodical or lecture the ease and facility, the comfort and safety of American travel, even for the weak and unprotected, under our well-nigh perfect railroad systems and our gentlemanly and efficient corps of officials and public servants. I have some material I could furnish these young ladies, though possibly it might not be just on the side they wish to have illuminated. The Black Woman of the South has to do considerable travelling in this country, often unattended. She thinks she is quiet and unobtrusive in her manner, simple and inconspicuous in her dress, and can see no reason why in any chance assemblage of *ladies*, or even a promiscuous gathering of ordinarily well-bred and dignified individuals, she should be signaled out for any marked consideration. And yet she has seen these same "gentlemanly and efficient" railroad conductors, when their cars had stopped at stations having no raised platforms, making it necessary for passengers to take the long and trying leap from the car step to the ground or step on the narrow little stool placed under by the conductor, after standing at their posts and handing woman after woman from the steps to the stool, thence to the ground, or else relieving her of satchels and bags and enabling her to make the descent easily, deliberately fold their arms and turn round when the Black Woman's turn came to alight – bearing her satchel, and bearing besides another unnamable burden inside the heaving bosom and tightly compressed lips. The feeling of slighted womanhood is unlike every other emotion of the soul. Happily for the human family, it is unknown to many and indescribable to all. Its poignancy, compared with which even Juno's *spretae injuria formae* is earthly and vulgar, is holier than that of jealousy, deeper than indignation, tenderer than rage. Its first impulse of wrathful protest and proud self vindication is checked and shamed by the consciousness that self assertion would outrage still further the same delicate instinct. Were there a brutal attitude of hate or of ferocious attack, the feminine response of fear or repulsion is simple and spontaneous. But when the keen sting comes through the finer sensibilities, from a hand which, by all known traditions and ideals of propriety, should have been trained to reverence and respect them, the condemnation of man's inhumanity to woman is increased and embittered by the knowledge of personal identity with a race of beings so fallen.

I purposely forbear to mention instances of personal violence to colored women travelling in less civilized sections of our country, where women have been forcibly ejected from cars, thrown out of seats, their garments rudely torn, their person wantonly and cruelly injured. America is large and must for some time yet endure its out-of-the-way jungles of barbarism as Africa its uncultivated tracts of marsh and malaria. There are murderers and thieves and villains in both London and Paris. Humanity from the first has had its vultures and sharks, and representatives of the fraternity who prey upon mankind may be expected no less in America than elsewhere. That this virulence breaks out most readily and commonly against colored persons in this country, is due of course to the fact that they are, generally speaking, weak and can be imposed upon with impunity. Bullies are always cowards at heart and may be credited with a pretty safe instinct in scenting their prey. Besides, society, where it has not exactly said to its dogs "s-s-sik him!" has at least engaged to be looking in another direction or studying the rivers on Mars. It is not of the dogs and their doings, but of society holding the leash that I shall speak. It is those subtle exhalations of atmospheric odors for which woman is accountable, the indefinable, unplaceable aroma which seems to exude from the very pores in her finger tips like the delicate sachet so dexterously hidden and concealed in her linens; the essence of her teaching, guessed rather than read, so adroitly is the lettering and wording manipulated; it is the undertones of the picture laid finely on by woman's own practiced hand, the reflection of the lights and shadows on her own brow; it is, in a word, the reputation of our nation for general politeness and good manners and of our fellow citizens to be somewhat more than cads or snobs that shall engage our present study. There can be no true test of national courtesy without travel. Impressions and conclusions based on provincial traits and characteristics can thus be modified and generalized. Moreover, the weaker and less influential the experimenter, the more exact and scientific the deductions. Courtesy "for revenue only" is not politeness, but diplomacy. Any rough can assume civilty toward those of "his set," and does not hesitate to carry it even to servility toward those in whom he recognizes a possible patron or his master in power, wealth, rank, or influence. But, as the chemist prefers distilled H_2O in testing solutions to avoid complications and unwarranted reactions, so the Black Woman holds that her femineity linked with the impossibility of popular affinity or unexpected attraction through position and influence in her case makes her a touchstone of American courtesy exceptionally pure and singularly free from extraneous modifiers. The man who is courteous to her is so, not because of anything he hopes or fears or sees, but because *he is a gentleman.*

I would eliminate also from the discussion all uncharitable reflections upon the orderly execution of laws existing in certain states of this Union, requiring persons known to be colored to ride in one car, and persons supposed to be white in another. A good citizen may use his influence to have existing laws and statutes changed or modified, but a public servant must not be blamed for obeying orders. A railroad conductor is not asked to dictate measures, nor to make and pass laws. His bread and butter are conditioned on his managing his part of the machinery as he is told to do. If, therefore, I found myself in that compartment of a train designated by the sovereign law of the state for presumable Caucasians, and for colored persons only when traveling in the capacity of nurses and maids, should a conductor inform me, as a gentleman might, that I had made a mistake, and offer to show me the proper car for black ladies; I might wonder at the expensive arrangements of the company and of the state in providing special and separate accommodations for the transportation of the various hues of humanity, but I certainly could not take it as a want of courtesy on the conductor's part that he gave the information. It is true, public sentiment precedes and begets all laws, good or bad; and on the ground I have taken, our women are to be credited largely as teachers and moulders of public sentiment. But when a law has passed and received the sanction of the land, there is nothing for our officials to do but enforce it till repealed; and I for one, as a loyal American citizen, will give those officials cheerful support and ready sympathy in the discharge of their duty. But when a great burly six feet of masculinity with sloping shoulders and unkempt beard swaggers in, and, throwing a roll of tobacco into one corner of his jaw, growls out at me over the paper I am reading, "Here gurl," (I am past thirty) "you better git out 'n dis kyar 'f yer don't, I'll put yer out," – my mental annotation is *Here's an American citizen who has been badly trained. He is sadly lacking in both "sweetness" and "light"*; and when in the same section of our enlightened and progressive country, I see from the car window, working on private estates, convicts from the state penitentiary, among them squads of boys from fourteen to eighteen years of age in a chain-gang, their feet chained together and heavy blocks attached – not in 1850, but in 1890, '91 and '92, I make a note on the fly-leaf of my memorandum, *The women in this section should organize a Society for the Prevention of Cruelty to Human Beings, and disseminate civilizing tracts, and send throughout the region apostles of anti-barbarism for the propagation of humane and enlightened ideas.* And when farther on in the same section our train stops at a dilapidated station, rendered yet more unsightly by dozens of loafers with their hands in their pockets while a productive soil and inviting climate beckon in vain to industry; and when, looking a little more closely, I see two dingy little rooms with "FOR LADIES" swinging over one and "FOR COLORED PEOPLE" over the other; while wondering under which head I come, I notice a little way off the only hotel proprietor of the place whittling a pine stick as he sits with one leg thrown across an empty goods box; and as my eye falls on a sample room

next door which seems to be driving the only wide-awake and popular business of the commonwealth, I cannot help ejaculating under my breath, "What a field for the missionary woman." I know that if by any fatality I should be obliged to lie over at that station, and, driven by hunger, should be compelled to seek refreshments or the bare necessaries of life at the only public accommodation in the town, that same stick-whittler would coolly inform me, without looking up from his pine splinter, "We doan uccommodate no niggers hyur." And yet we are so scandalized at Russia's barbarity and cruelty to the Jews! We pay a man a thousand dollars a night just to make us weep, by a recital of such heathenish inhumanity as is practiced on Sclavonic soil.

A recent writer on Eastern nations says: "If we take through the earth's temperate zone, a belt of country whose northern and southern edges are determined by certain limiting isotherms, not more than half the width of the zone apart, we shall find that we have included in a relatively small extent of surface almost all the nations of note in the world, past or present. Now, if we examine this belt and compare the different parts of it with one another, we shall be struck by a remarkable fact. *The peoples inhabiting it grow steadily more personal as we go west.* So unmistakable is this gradation, that one is almost tempted to ascribe it to cosmical rather than to human causes. It is as marked as the change in color of the human complexion observable along any meridian, which ranges from black at the equator to blonde toward the pole. In like manner the sense of self grows more intense as we follow in the wake of the setting sun, and fades steadily as we advance into the dawn. America, Europe, the Levant, India, Japan, each is less personal than the one before. *... That politeness should be one of the most marked results of impersonality* may appear surprising, yet a slight examination will show it to be a fact. Considered *a priori*, the connection is not far to seek. Impersonality by lessening the interest in one's self, induces one to take an interest in others. Looked at *a posteriori*, we find that where the one trait exists the other is most developed, while an absence of the second seems to prevent the full growth of the first. This is true both in general and in detail. *Courtesy increases as we travel eastward round the world, coincidently with a decrease in the sense of self.* Asia is more courteous than Europe, Europe than America. Particular races show the same concomitance of characteristics. France, the most impersonal nation of Europe, is at the same time the most polite." And by inference, Americans, the most personal, are the least courteous nation on the globe.

The Black Woman had reached this same conclusion by an entirely different route; but it is gratifying to vanity, nevertheless, to find one's self sustained by both science and philosophy in a conviction, wrought in by hard experience, and yet too apparently audacious to be entertained even as a stealthy surmise. In fact the Black Woman was emboldened some time since by a well put and timely article from an Editor's Drawer on the "Mannerless Sex," to give the world the benefit of some of her experience with the "*Mannerless Race*"; but since Mr. Lowell shows so conclusively that the entire Land of the West is a *mannerless continent*, I have determined to plead with our women, the mannerless sex on this mannerless continent, to institute a reform by placing immediately in our national curricula a department for teaching GOOD MANNERS.

Now, am I right in holding the American Woman responsible? Is it true that the exponents of woman's advancement, the leaders in woman's thought, the preachers and teachers of all woman's reforms, can teach this nation to be courteous, to be pitiful, having compassion one of another, not rendering evil for inoffensiveness, and railing in proportion to the improbability of being struck back; but contrariwise, being *all* of one mind, to love as brethren?

I think so.

It may require some heroic measures, and like all revolutions will call for a determined front and a courageous, unwavering, stalwart heart on the part of the leaders of the reform.

The "*all*" will inevitably stick in the throat of the Southern woman. She must be allowed, please, to except the "darkey" from the "all"; it is too bitter a pill with black people in it. You must get the Revised Version to put it, "*love all white people as brethren.*" She really could not enter any society on earth, or in heaven above, or in – the waters under the earth, on such unpalatable conditions.

The Black Woman has tried to understand the Southern woman's difficulties; to put herself in her place, and to be as fair, as charitable, and as free from prejudice in judging her antipathies, as she would have others in regard to her own. She has honestly weighed the apparently sincere excuse, "But you must remember that these people were once our slaves"; and that other,

"But civility towards the Negroes will bring us on *social equality* with them."

These are the two bugbears; or rather, the two humbugbears: for, though each is founded on a most glaring fallacy, one would think they were words to conjure with, so potent and irresistible is their spell as an argument at the North as well as in the South.

One of the most singular facts about the unwritten history of this country is the consummate ability with which Southern influence, Southern ideas and Southern ideals, have from the very beginning even up to the present day, dictated to and domineered over the brain and sinew of this nation. Without wealth, without education, without inventions, arts, sciences, or industries, without well-nigh every one of the progressive ideas and impulses which have made this country great, prosperous and happy, personally indolent and practically stupid, poor in everything but bluster and self-esteem, the Southerner has nevertheless with Italian finesse and exquisite skill, uniformly and invariably, so manipulated Northern sentiment as to succeed sooner or later in carrying his point and shaping the policy of this government to suit his purposes. Indeed, the Southerner is a magnificent manager of men, a born educator. For two hundred and fifty years he trained to his hand a people whom he made absolutely his own, in body, mind, and sensibility. He so insinuated differences and distinctions among them, that their personal attachment for him was stronger than for their own brethren and fellow sufferers. He made it a crime for two or three of them to be gathered together in Christ's name without a white man's supervision, and a felony for one to teach them to read even the Word of Life; and yet they would defend his interest with their life blood; his smile was their happiness, a pat on the shoulder from him their reward. The slightest difference among themselves in condition, circumstances, opportunities, became barriers of jealousy and disunion. He sowed his blood broadcast among them, then pitted mulatto against black, bond against free, house slave against plantation slave, even the slave of one clan against like slave of another clan; till, wholly oblivious of their ability for mutual succor and defense, all became centers of myriad systems of repellent forces, having but one sentiment in common, and that their entire subjection to that master hand.

And he not only managed the black man, he also hoodwinked the white man, the tourist and investigator who visited his lordly estates. The slaves were doing well, in fact couldn't be happier – plenty to eat, plenty to drink, comfortably housed and clothed – they wouldn't be free if they could; in short, in his broad brimmed plantation hat and easy aristocratic smoking gown, he made you think him a veritable patriarch in the midst of a lazy, well fed, good natured, over-indulged tenantry.

Then, too, the South represented blood – not red blood, but blue blood. The difference is in the length of the stream and your distance from its source. If your own father was a pirate, a robber, a murderer, his hands are dyed in red blood, and you don't say very much about it. But if your great great great grandfather's grandfather stole and pillaged and slew, and you can prove it, your blood has become blue and you are at great pains to establish the relationship. So the South had neither silver nor gold, but she had blood; and she paraded it with so much gusto that the substantial little Puritan maidens of the North, who had been making bread and canning currants and not thinking of blood the least bit, began to hunt up the records of the Mayflower to see if some of the passengers thereon could not claim the honor of having been one of William the Conqueror's brigands, when he killed the last of the Saxon kings and, red-handed, stole his crown and his lands. Thus the ideal from out the Southland brooded over the nation and we sing less lustily than of yore

Kind hearts are more than coronets
And simple faith than Norman blood.

In politics, the two great forces, commerce and empire, which would otherwise have shaped the destiny of the country, have been made to pander and cater to Southern notions. "Cotton is King" meant the South must be allowed to dictate or there would be no fun. Every statesman from 1830 to 1860 exhausted his genius in persuasion and compromises to smooth out her ruffled temper and gratify her petulant demands. But like a sullen younger sister, the South has pouted and sulked and cried: "I won't play with you now; so there!" and the big brother at the North has coaxed and compromised and given in, and – ended by letting her have her way. Until 1860 she had as her pet an institution which it was death by the law to say anything about, except that it was divinely instituted, inaugurated by Noah, sanctioned by Abraham, approved by Paul, and just ideally perfect in

every way. And when, to preserve the autonomy of the family arrangements, in '61, '62 and '63, it became necessary for the big brother to administer a little wholesome correction and set the obstreperous Miss vigorously down in her seat again, she assumed such an air of injured innocence, and melted away so lugubriously, the big brother has done nothing since but try to sweeten and pacify and laugh her back into a companionable frame of mind.

Father Lincoln did all he could to get her to repent of her petulance and behave herself. He even promised she might keep her pet, so disagreeable to all the neighbors and hurtful even to herself, and might manage it at home to suit herself, if she would only listen to reason and be just tolerably nice. But, no – she was going to leave and set up for herself; she didn't propose to be meddled with; and so, of course, she had to be spanked. Just a little at first – didn't mean to hurt, merely to teach her who was who. But she grew so ugly, and kicked and fought and scratched so outrageously, and seemed so determined to smash up the whole business, the head of the family got red in the face, and said: "Well, now, he couldn't have any more of that foolishness. Arabella must just behave herself or take the consequences." And after the spanking, Arabella sniffed and whimpered and pouted, and the big brother bit his lip, looked half ashamed, and said: "Well, I didn't want to hurt you. You needn't feel so awfully bad about it, I only did it for your good. You know I wouldn't do anything to displease you if I could help it; but you would insist on making the row, and so I just had to. Now, there – there – let's be friends!" and he put his great strong arms about her and just dared anybody to refer to that little unpleasantness – he'd show them a thing or two. Still Arabella sulked – till the rest of the family decided she might just keep her pets, and manage her own affairs and nobody should interfere.

So now, if one intimates that some clauses of the Constitution are a dead letter at the South and that only the name and support of that pet institution are changed while the fact and essence, minus the expense and responsibility, remain, he is quickly told to mind his own business and informed that he is waving the bloody shirt.

Even twenty-five years after the fourteenth and fifteenth amendments to our Constitution, a man who has been most unequivocal in his outspoken condemnation of the wrongs regularly and systematically heaped on the oppressed race in this country, and on all even most remotely connected with them – a man whom we had thought our staunchest friend and most noble champion and defender – after a two weeks' trip in Georgia and Florida immediately gives signs of the fatal inception of the virus. Not even the chance traveller from England or Scotland escapes. The arch-manipulator takes him under his special watch-care and training, uses up his stock arguments and gives object lessons with his choicest specimens of Negro depravity and worthlessness; takes him through what, in New York, would be called "the slums," and would predicate there nothing but the duty of enlightened Christians to send out their light and emulate their Master's aggressive labors of love; but in Georgia is denominated "our terrible problem, which people of the North so little understand, yet vouchsafe so much gratuitous advice about." With an injured air he shows the stupendous and atrocious mistake of reasoning about these people as if they were just ordinary human beings, and amenable to the tenets of the Gospel; and not long after the inoculation begins to work, you hear this old-time friend of the oppressed delivering himself something after this fashion: "Ah, well, the South must be left to manage the Negro. She is most directly concerned and must understand her problem better than outsiders. We must not meddle. We must be very careful not to widen the breaches. The Negro is not worth a feud between brothers and sisters."

Lately a great national and international movement characteristic of this age and country, a movement based on the inherent right of every soul to its own highest development, I mean the movement making for Woman's full, free, and complete emancipation, has, after much courting, obtained the gracious smile of the Southern woman – I beg her pardon – the Southern *lady*.

She represents blood, and of course could not be expected to leave that out; and firstly and foremostly she must not, in any organization she may deign to grace with her presence, be asked to associate with "these people who were once her slaves."

Now the Southern woman (I may be pardoned, being one myself) was never renowned for her reasoning powers, and it is not surprising that just a little picking will make her logic fall to pieces even here.

In the first place she imagines that because her grandfather had slaves who were black, all the blacks in the world of every shade and tint were once in the position of her slaves. This is as bad as the Irishman who was about to kill a peaceable Jew in the streets of Cork – having just learned that Jews slew his Redeemer. The black race constitutes one-seventh the known population of the globe; and there are representatives of it here as elsewhere who were never in bondage at any time to any man – whose blood is as blue and lineage as noble as any, even that of the white lady of the South. That her slaves were black and she despises her slaves, should no more argue antipathy to all dark people and peoples, than that Guiteau, an assassin, was white, and I hate assassins, should make me hate all persons more or less white. The objection shows a want of clear discrimination.

The second fallacy in the objection grows out of the use of an ambiguous middle, as the logicians would call it, or assigning a double signification to the term "*Social equality.*"

Civility to the Negro implies social equality. I am opposed to *associating* with dark persons on terms of social equality. Therefore, I abrogate civility to the Negro. This is like

> Light is opposed to darkness.
> Feathers are light.
> *Ergo*, Feathers are opposed to darkness.

The "social equality" implied by civility to the Negro is a very different thing from forced association with him socially. Indeed it seems to me that the mere application of a little cold common sense would show that uncongenial social environments could by no means be forced on any one. I do not, and cannot be made to associate with all dark persons, simply on the ground that I am dark; and I presume the Southern lady can imagine some whose faces are white, with whom she would no sooner think of chatting unreservedly than, were it possible, with a veritable "darkey." Such things must and will always be left to individual election. No law, human or divine, can legislate for or against them. Like seeks like; and I am sure with the Southern lady's antipathies at their present temperature, she might enter ten thousand organizations besprinkled with colored women without being any more deflected by them than by the proximity of a stone. The social equality scare then is all humbug, conscious or unconscious, I know not which. And were it not too bitter a thought to utter here, I might add that the overtures for forced association in the past history of these two races were not made by the manacled black man, nor by *the silent and suffering black woman!*

When I seek food in a public café or apply for first-class accommodations on a railway train, I do so because my physical necessities are identical with those of other human beings of like constitution and temperament, and crave satisfaction. I go because I want food, or I want comfort – not because I want association with those who frequent these places; and I can see no more "social equality" in buying lunch at the same restaurant, or riding in a common car, than there is in paying for dry goods at the same counter or walking on the same street.

The social equality which means forced or unbidden association would be as much deprecated and as strenuously opposed by the circle in which I move as by the most hide-bound Southerner in the land. Indeed I have been more than once annoyed by the inquisitive white interviewer, who, with spectacles on nose and pencil and note-book in hand, comes to get some "points" about "*your people.*" My "people" are just like other people – indeed, too like for their own good. They hate, they love, they attract and repel, they climb or they grovel, struggle or drift, aspire or despair, endure in hope or curse in vexation, exactly like all the rest of unregenerate humanity. Their likes and dislikes are as strong; their antipathies – and prejudices too I fear, are as pronounced as you will find anywhere; and the entrance to the inner sanctuary of their homes and hearts is as jealously guarded against profane intrusion.

What the dark man wants then is merely to live his own life, in his own world, with his own chosen companions, in whatever of comfort, luxury, or emoluments his talent or his money can in an impartial market secure. Has he wealth, he does not want to be forced into inconvenient or unsanitary sections of cities to buy a home and rear his family. Has he art, he does not want to be cabined and cribbed into emulation with the few who merely happen to have his complexion. His talent aspires to study without proscription the masters of all ages and to rub against the broadest and fullest movements of his own day.

Has he religion, he does not want to be made to feel that there is a white Christ and a black Christ, a white Heaven and a black Heaven, a white Gospel and a black Gospel – but the one ideal of perfect manhood and womanhood, the one universal longing for development and growth, the one desire for being, and being better, the one great yearning, aspiring, outreaching, in all the heart-throbs of humanity in whatever race or clime.

A recent episode in the Corcoran art gallery at the American capital is to the point. A colored woman who had shown marked ability in drawing and coloring, was advised by her teacher, himself an artist of no mean rank, to apply for admission to the Corcoran school in order to study the models and to secure other advantages connected with the organization. She accordingly sent a written application accompanied by specimens of her drawings, the usual *modus operandi* in securing admission.

The drawings were examined by the best critics and pronounced excellent, and a ticket of admission was immediately issued together with a highly complimentary reference to her work.

The next day my friend, congratulating her country and herself that at least in the republic of art no caste existed, presented her ticket of admission *in propria persona.* There was a little preliminary side play in Delsarte pantomine – aghast – incredulity – wonder; then the superintendent told her in plain unartistic English that of course he had not dreamed a colored person could do such work, and had he suspected the truth he would never have issued the ticket of admission; that, to be right frank, the ticket would have to be cancelled – she could under no condition be admitted to the studio.

Can it be possible that even art in America is to be tainted by this shrivelling caste spirit? If so, what are we coming to? Can any one conceive a Shakespeare, a Michael Angelo, or a Beethoven putting away any fact of simple merit because the thought, or the suggestion, or the creation emanated from a soul with an unpleasing exterior?

What is it that makes the great English bard preeminent as the photographer of the human soul? Where did he learn the universal language, so that Parthians, Medes and Elamites, and the dwellers in Mesopotamia, in Egypt and Libya, in Crete and Arabia do hear every one in our own tongue the wonderful revelations of this myriad mind? How did he learn our language? Is it not that his own soul was infinitely receptive to Nature, the dear old nurse, in all her protean forms? Did he not catch and reveal her own secret by his sympathetic listening as she "would constantly sing a more wonderful song or tell a more marvellous tale" in the souls he met around him?

"Stand off! I am better than thou!" has never yet painted a true picture, nor written a thrilling song, nor given a pulsing, a soul-burning sermon.

'Tis only sympathy, another name for love – that one poor word which, as George Eliot says, "expresses so much of human insight" – that can interpret either man or matter.

It was Shakespeare's own all-embracing sympathy, that infinite receptivity of his, and native, all-comprehending appreciation, which proved a key to unlock and open every soul that came within his radius. And *he received as much as he gave*. His own stores were infinitely enriched thereby. For it is decreed

> Man like the vine supported lives,
> The strength he gains is from th' embrace he gives.

It is only through clearing the eyes from bias and prejudice, and becoming one with the great all pervading soul of the universe that either art or science can

> Read what is still unread
> In the manuscripts of God.

No true artist can allow himself to be narrowed and provincialized by deliberately shutting out any class of facts or subjects through prejudice against externals. And American art, American science, American literature can never be founded in truth, the universal beauty; can never learn to speak a language intelligible in all climes and for all ages, till this paralyzing grip of caste prejudice is loosened from its vitals, and the healthy sympathetic eye is taught to look out on the great universe as holding no favorites and no black beasts, but bearing in each plainest or loveliest feature the handwriting of its God.

And this is why, as it appears to me, woman in her lately acquired vantage ground for speaking an earnest helpful word, can do this country no deeper and truer and more lasting good than by bending all her energies to thus broadening, humanizing, and civilizing her native land.

"Except ye become as little children" is not a pious precept, but an inexorable law of the universe. God's kingdoms are all sealed to the seedy, moss-grown mind of self-satisfied maturity. Only the little child in spirit, the simple, receptive, educable mind can enter. Preconceived notions, blinding prejudices, and shrivelling antipathies must be wiped out, and the cultivable soul made a *tabula rasa* for whatever lesson great Nature has to teach.

This, too, is why I conceive the subject to have been unfortunately worded which was chosen by Miss Shaw at the Woman's Council and which stands at the head of this chapter.

Miss Shaw is one of the most powerful of our leaders, and we feel her voice should give no uncertain note. Woman should not, even by inference, or for the sake of argument, seem to disparage what is weak. For woman's cause is the cause of the weak; and when all the weak shall have received their due consideration, then woman will have her "rights," and the Indian will have his rights, and the Negro will have his rights, and all the strong will have learned at last to deal justly, to love mercy, and to walk humbly; and our fair land will have been taught the secret of universal courtesy which is after all nothing but the art, the science, and the religion of regarding one's neighbor as one's self, and to do for him as we would, were conditions swapped, that he do for us.

It cannot seem less than a blunder, whenever the exponents of a great reform or the harbingers of a noble advance in thought and effort allow themselves to seem distorted by a narrow view of their own aims and principles. All prejudices, whether of race, sect or sex, class pride and caste distinctions are the belittling inheritance and badge of snobs and prigs.

The philosophic mind sees that its own "rights" are the rights of humanity. That in the universe of God nothing trivial is or mean; and the recognition it seeks is not through the robber and wild beast adjustment of the survival of the bullies but through the universal application ultimately of the Golden Rule.

Not unfrequently has it happened that the impetus of a mighty thought wave has done the execution meant by its Creator in spite of the weak and distorted perception of its human embodiment. It is not strange if reformers, who, after all, but think God's thoughts after him, have often "builded more wisely than they knew;" and while fighting consciously for only a narrow gateway for themselves, have been driven forward by that irresistible "Power not ourselves which makes for righteousness" to open a high road for humanity. It was so with our sixteenth century reformers. The fathers of the Reformation had no idea that they were inciting an insurrection of the human mind against all domination. None would have been more shocked than they at our nineteenth century deductions from their sixteenth century premises. Emancipation of mind and freedom of thought would have been as appalling to them as it was distasteful to the pope. They were right, they argued, to rebel against Romish absolutism – because Romish preaching and Romish practicing were wrong. They denounced popes for hacking heretics and forthwith began themselves to roast witches: The Spanish Inquisition in the hands of Philip and Alva was an institution of the devil; wielded by the faithful, it would become quite another thing. The only "rights" they were broad enough consciously to fight for was the right to substitute the absolutism of their conceptions, their party, their "*ism*" for an authority whose teaching they conceived to be corrupt and vicious. Persecution for a belief was wrong only when the persecutors were wrong and the persecuted right. The sacred prerogative of the individual to decide on matters of belief they did not dream of maintaining. Universal tolerance and its twin, universal charity, were not conceived yet. The broad foundation stone of all human rights, the great democratic principle "A man's a man, *and his own sovereign* for a' that" they did not dare enunciate. They were incapable of drawing up a Declaration of Independence for humanity. The Reformation to the Reformers meant one bundle of authoritative opinions vs. another bundle of authoritative opinions. Justification by faith, vs. justification by ritual. Submission to Calvin vs. submission to the Pope. English and Germans vs. the Italians.

To our eye, viewed through a vista of three centuries, it was the death wrestle of the principle of thought enslavement in the throttling grasp of personal freedom; it was the great Emancipation Day of human belief, man's intellectual Independence Day, prefiguring and finally compelling the world-wide enfranchisement of his body and all its activities. Not Protestant vs. Catholic, then; not Luther vs. Leo, not Dominicans vs. Augustinians, nor Geneva vs. Rome – but humanity rationally free, vs. the clamps of tradition and superstition which had manacled and muzzled it.

The cause of freedom is not the cause of a race or a sect, a party or a class – it is the cause of human kind, the very birthright of humanity. Now unless we are greatly mistaken the Reform of our day, known as the Woman's Movement, is essentially such an embodiment, if its pioneers could only realize it, of the universal good. And specially important is it that there be no confusion of ideas among its leaders as to its scope and universality. All mists must be cleared from the eyes of woman if she is to be a teacher of morals and manners: the

former strikes its roots in the individual and its training and pruning may be accomplished by classes; but the latter is to lubricate the joints and minimize the friction of society, and it is important and fundamental that there be no chromatic or other aberration when the teacher is settling the point, "Who is my neighbor?"

It is not the intelligent woman vs. the ignorant woman; nor the white woman vs. the black, the brown, and the red – it is not even the cause of woman vs. man. Nay, 'tis woman's strongest vindication for speaking that *the world needs to hear her voice*. It would be subversive of every human interest that the cry of one-half the human family be stifled. Woman in stepping from the pedestal of statue-like inactivity in the domestic shrine, and daring to think and move and speak – to undertake to help shape, mold, and direct the thought of her age, is merely completing the circle of the world's vision. Hers is every interest that has lacked an interpreter and a defender. Her cause is linked with that of every agony that has been dumb – every wrong that needs a voice.

It is no fault of man's that he has not been able to see truth from her standpoint. It does credit both to his head and heart that no greater mistakes have been committed or even wrongs perpetrated while she sat making tatting and snipping paper flowers. Man's own innate chivalry and the mutual interdependence of their interests have insured his treating her cause, in the main at least, as his own. And he is pardonably surprised and even a little chagrined, perhaps, to find his legislation not considered "perfectly lovely" in every respect. But in any case his work is only impoverished by her remaining dumb. The world has had to limp along with the wobbling gait and one-sided hesitancy of a man with one eye. Suddenly the bandage is removed from the other eye and the whole body is filled with light. It sees a circle where before it saw a segment. The darkened eye restored, every member rejoices with it.

What a travesty of its case for this eye to become plaintiff in a suit, *Eye vs. Foot*. "There is that dull clod, the foot, allowed to roam at will, free and untrammelled; while I, the source and medium of light, brilliant and beautiful, am fettered in darkness and doomed to desuetude." The great burly black man, ignorant and gross and depraved, is allowed to vote; while the franchise is withheld from the intelligent and refined, the pure-minded and lofty souled white woman. Even the untamed and untamable Indian of the prairie, who can answer nothing but "ugh" to great economic and civic questions is thought by some worthy to wield the ballot which is still denied the Puritan maid and the first lady of Virginia.

Is not this hitching our wagon to something much lower than a star? Is not woman's cause broader, and deeper, and grander, than a blue stocking debate or an aristocratic pink tea? Why should woman become plaintiff in a suit versus the Indian, or the Negro or any other race or class who have been crushed under the iron heel of Anglo-Saxon power and selfishness? If the Indian has been wronged and cheated by the puissance of this American government, it is woman's mission to plead with her country to cease to do evil and to pay its honest debts. If the Negro has been deceitfully cajoled or inhumanly cuffed according to selfish expediency or capricious antipathy, let it be woman's mission to plead that he be met as a man and honestly given half the road. If woman's own happiness has been ignored or misunderstood in our country's legislating for bread winners, for rum sellers, for property holders, for the family relations, for any or all the interests that touch her vitally, let her rest her plea, not on Indian inferiority, nor on Negro depravity, but on the obligation of legislators to do for her as they would have others do for them were relations reversed. Let her try to teach her country that every interest in this world is entitled at least to a respectful hearing, that every sentiency is worthy of its own gratification, that a helpless cause should not be trampled down, nor a bruised reed broken; and when the right of the individual is made sacred, when the image of God in human form, whether in marble or in clay, whether in alabaster or in ebony, is consecrated and inviolable, when men have been taught to look beneath the rags and grime, the pomp and pageantry of mere circumstance and have regard unto the celestial kernel uncontaminated at the core – when race, color, sex, condition, are realized to be the accidents, not the substance of life, and consequently as not obscuring or modifying the inalienable title to life, liberty, and pursuit of happiness – then is mastered the science of politeness, the art of courteous contact, which is naught but the practical application of the principal of benevolence, the back bone and marrow of all religion; then woman's lesson is taught and woman's cause is won – not the white woman nor the black woman nor the red woman, but the cause of every man or woman who has writhed silently under a mighty wrong. The pleading of the American woman for the right and the opportunity to employ the American method of influencing the disposal to be made of herself, her property, her children in civil, economic, or domestic relations is thus seen to be based on a principle as broad as the human race and as old as human society. Her wrongs are thus indissolubly linked with all undefended woe, all helpless suffering, and the plenitude of her "rights" will mean the final triumph of all right over might, the supremacy of the moral forces of reason and justice and love in the government of the nation.

God hasten the day.

PART VI

Democracy and Utopia

Conceptions of democracy are constantly faced with questions such as "democracy for whom? and under what conditions?".

The authors in this section offer their ideal of democracy, each fully aware of the problems, and they do so while facing the existing national formation of "America." Whatever their heritage, they are all American in the limited sense that they use English as a primary language, have been influenced by Christianity, seek to manage their lives within the national state of the United States, and want the benefits of modernity (transportation, communication techniques, routinized labor) without necessarily agreeing with all the values associated with modernity.

John Humphrey Noyes, who founded the Oneida Community, reveals a utopian conception of democracy intended to promote radical egalitarianism. The unique practices of "complex marriage," male continence, stirpiculture, and mutual criticism set Oneida apart from other communities of its type. It was positively against a broad range of traditions and forms of modernity. In many ways, Oneida calls into question the merit of conceptions of democracy that appeal either to tradition (whether that means the authority of the chief or modern forms of presidential authority) as a way of creating a good society or to modern forms of routinized labor, ownership, and distribution. Although Oneida hardly lived up to its ideals, the views offered by Noyes should encourage us to rethink the meaning of democracy when it is extended to the personal.

Walt Whitman offers a post-Civil War vision of democracy that eschews the notion of a unified and undifferentiated population. He promotes the need for a democratic aesthetic that allows the inclusion of a democracy that is not simply enlivened by general principles but includes social connections not coded by law.

In rethinking democracy, Jane Addams develops a modern feminist sensibility to the misery of the least well-off, and develops a view of democracy informed by pragmatism.

Emma Goldman was an anarchist. She was deported for her views but continued to develop a way of thinking about the limitations and benefits of democracy.

The argument for socialism offered by George Washington Woodbey considers the entitlements of the least well-off as paramount. The negation of class divisions, for Woodbey, is a precondition for the possibility of democracy.

Luther Standing Bear asks "What the Indian Means to America," given that the "Indian" is positioned outside "America." He considers the Indian to be inside "America" because he thinks of the pre-United States nation as "America," despite its romantic idealization; he must, however, respond to the reality of an empowered United States.

Laura M. C. Kellogg promotes a form of democracy as a good built on revitalizing traditions and relatively separate self-determined populations.

Alain L. Locke considers the possibility of a democracy that stretches across lines of ethnic, racial, and national location – a form of cosmopolitanism given unremitting conflicts of interests and locations.

31

Male Continence

John Humphrey Noyes

Introduction

John Humphrey Noyes (1811–86), founder of the Oneida Community, was born in Brattleboro, Vermont, and educated at Dartmouth College and Yale Divinity School. In 1833 he was licensed as a Congregational minister, but he lost his license in 1884 because of his "perfectionist" doctrine, which attributed a dual sexual nature to God. He taught that no one was bound by any moral code because Jesus Christ saved the human race from sin. Noyes established the Perfectionist Community in Putney, Vermont, in the late 1830s. In 1846 public condemnation of his tenet of "complex marriage," the practice of free sexual sharing within a community, forced him to disband his community; two years later he re-established it in Oneida, New York. Faced with charges of adultery, Noyes fled to Canada in 1880. He wrote a number of religious treatises, including *Bible Communism* (1848) and *Scientific Propagation* (1873?).

The Oneida Community has long been receiving almost daily letters of inquiry respecting its method of controlling propagation. Many of these letters evidently come from intelligent and respectable persons. We will give a few recent specimens. Here is one from an English clergyman:

London, March 11, 1872.

Taken from *Male Continence* (New York: Office of Oneida Circular, 1872).

Mr. J. H. Noyes:

Dear Sir: For some time past I have wished to ask you to inform me what is the "scientific discovery" you have made relating to Male Continence, referred to by Hepworth Dixon in New America, 6th Ed., 1867. As a clergyman I think a knowledge of it would be exceedingly useful to me and to some of my brethren in pastoral work.

Hoping you will take the trouble to answer my request, I am, Dear Sir,

Yours most truly,—— ——

The following is from an American clergyman:

——, *Ohio, May* 11, 1872.

Mr. J. H. Noyes:

Dear Sir: Please send me a copy of your letter on "*Male Continence.*" My object is to get some reliable information as to how to prevent conception, without injury to either husband or wife. I am a married man; and the delicate state of my wife's health, besides having a family of seven children, renders it very desirable, if not absolutely necessary, to adopt some safe means to prevent conception in future. Any information you can give will be thankfully received.

I am a Congregational minister by profession.

Very respectfully yours,—— ——

We have on file many letters from intelligent men and women in ordinary married life, who were induced to seek information about Male Continence by seeing and suffering the miseries of involuntary propagation. Here is a specimen re-

361

markable for its details of horrors, which, according to recent disclosures, are being enacted everywhere, even in the high places of society, though seldom exposed. It is a mother who writes:

———, *May* 12, 1872.

(*Addressed to a lady in the Community*.)

I must tell you a sad story. Two years ago last September my daughter was married; the next June she had a son born; the next year in July she had a daughter born; and if nothing happens to prevent she will be confined for the third time in the coming June; that is three times in less than two years. Her children are sickly, and she is sick and discouraged. When she first found she was in the family way this last time, she acted like a crazy person; went to her family physician, and talked with him about having an operation performed. He encouraged her in it, and performed it before she left the office, but without success. She was in such distress that she thought she could not live to get home. I was frightened at her looks, and soon learned what she had done. I tried to reason with her, but found her reason had left her on that subject. She said she never would have this child if it cost her life to get rid of it. After a week she went to the doctor again. He did not accomplish his purpose, but told her to come again in three months. She went at the time appointed in spite of my tears and entreaties. I told her that I should pray that Christ would discourage her; and sure enough she had not courage to try the operation, and came home, but cannot be reconciled to her condition. She does not appear like the same person she was three years ago, and is looking forward with sorrow instead of joy to the birth of her child. I often think if the young women of the Community could have a realizing sense of the miseries of married life as it is in the world, they would ever be thankful for their home.

Your sincere friend,——— ———

It has been impossible to refuse sympathy to such inquirers, or to entirely neglect their requests for information. But considering ourselves engaged in an unfinished experiment of social science, and therefore in the stage of learners rather than teachers, we have for many years contented ourselves with very brief answers. And we have been induced to pursue this policy partly by the fear that bad men might avail themselves of our sexual theories for licentious purposes. This fear, however, has proved to be nearly groundless, at least so far as the doctrine of Male Continence is concerned; for we have found licentious persons almost uniformly opposing that doctrine with bitterness and scorn. The real self-denial which it requires cannot be adjusted to their schemes of pleasure-seeking. And in any case the actual use of it by such persons could only improve their morals and mitigate the evils of their misdoings.

Six years ago we ventured a little beyond the limits of our reticent policy on the occasion of receiving the following letter from a Medical student:

New York, July 20, 1866.

EDITOR OF THE CIRCULAR:

Dear Sir: I have taken your paper for several months, and although I do not agree with all your religious theories, I have read each paper attentively, and with special interest in your communistic ideas. I am now preparing to go to Europe to study medicine, and shall therefore no longer be able to receive your paper. But before bidding good-bye, I would like to avail myself of your invitation to those who are not satisfied with your account of the Oneida Community as published in the CIRCULAR, to ask further. As I am to be a medical man, I would like to know definitely what you mean by your principle of "Male Continence." I have just graduated from college, and after hearing considerable discussion there in the shape of lectures, some relating directly to this subject, I am ignorant of any means of legitimate Male Continence except abstinence from intercourse. Of course I am well aware of the tricks of the French voluptuaries, by which Male Continence is effectually secured on all occasions, but such barbarous means of procedure cannot possibly be employed by you. These and all other artificial methods are liable to the charge of abusing the organs, which should above all things be held sacred and kept sound. I would like to have a detailed account of your process, which could not but be interesting to any professional man.

I remain yours, &c., ——— ———

To this inquiry we returned the following answer:

New York, July 26, 1866.

MR. ——— ———:

Dear Sir: Your letter addressed to the CIRCULAR, asking for information in regard to our method of controlling propagation, has been sent to me, and as it seems to come from a well-disposed person (though unknown to me), I will endeavor to give it a faithful answer – such, at least, as will be sufficient for scientific purposes.

The first question, or rather, perhaps I should say, the *previous* question in regard to Male Continence is, whether it is desirable or proper that men and women should establish intelligent voluntary control over the propagative function. Is it not better (it may be asked), to leave "nature" to take its course (subject to the general rules of legal chastity), and let children come as chance or the unknown powers may direct, without putting any restraint on sexual intercourse after it is once licensed by marriage, or on the freedom of all to take out such license? If you assent to this latter view, or have any inclination toward it, I would recommend to you the study of *Malthus on Population*; not that I think he has pointed out anything like the true *method* of voluntary control over propagation, but because he has demonstrated beyond debate the absolute *necessity* of such control in some way, unless we consent and expect that the human race, like the lower animals, shall be forever kept down to its necessary limits, by the ghastly agencies of war, pestilence and famine.

For my part, I have no doubt that it is perfectly proper that we should endeavor to rise above "nature" and the destiny of the brutes in this matter. There is no reason why we should not seek and hope for discovery in this direction, as freely as in the development of steam power or the art of printing; and we may rationally expect that He who has promised the "good time" when vice and misery shall be abolished, will at last give us sure light on this darkest of all problems – how to subject human propagation to the control of science.

But whether study and invention in this direction are proper or not, they are actually at work in all quarters, reputable and disreputable. Let us see how many different ways have already been proposed for limiting human increase.

In the first place, the practice of child-killing, either by exposure or violence, is almost as old as the world, and as extensive as barbarism. Even Plato recommended something of this kind, as a waste-gate for vicious increase, in his scheme of a model republic.

Then we have the practice of abortion reduced in modern times to a science, and almost to a distinct profession. A large part of this business is carried on by means of medicines advertized in obscure but intelligible terms as embryo-destroyers or preventives of conception. Every large city has its professional abortionist. Many ordinary physicians destroy embryos to order; and the skill to do this terrible deed has even descended among the common people.

Then what a variety of artificial tricks there are for frustrating the natural effects of the propagative act. You allude to several of these contrivances, in terms of condemnation from which I should not dissent. The least objectionable of them (if there is any difference), seems to be that recommended many years ago by Robert Dale Owen, in a book entitled Moral Physiology; viz., the simple device of withdrawing immediately before emission.

Besides all these disreputable methods, we have several more respectable schemes for attaining the great object of limiting propagation. Malthus proposes and urges that all men, and especially the poor, shall be taught their responsibilities in the light of science, and so be put under inducements *not to marry*. This prudential check on population – the discouragement of marriage – undoubtedly operates to a considerable extent in all civilized society, and to the greatest extent on the classes most enlightened. It seems to have been favored by Saint Paul (see 1st Cor. 7); and probably would not be condemned generally by people who claim to be considerate. And yet its advocates have to confess that it increases the danger of licentiousness; and on the whole the teaching that is most popular, in spite of Malthus and Paul, is that marriage, with all its liabilities, is a moral and patriotic duty.

Finally, Shakerism, which actually prohibits marriage on religious grounds, is only the most stringent and imposing of human contrivances for avoiding the woes of undesired propagation.

All these experimenters in the art of controlling propagation may be reduced in principle to three classes, viz.:

1 Those that seek to prevent the intercourse of the sexes, such as Malthus and the Shakers.
2 Those that seek to prevent the natural effects of the propagative act, viz., the French inventors and Owen.
3 Those that seek to destroy the living results of the propagative act, viz., the abortionists and child-killers.

Now it may seem to you that any new scheme of control over propagation must inevitably fall to one of these three classes; but I assure you that we have a method that does not fairly belong to any of them. I will try to show you our fourth way.

We begin by *analyzing* the act of sexual intercourse. It has a beginning, a middle, and an end. Its beginning and most elementary form is the simple *presence* of the male organ in the female. Then usually follows a series of reciprocal *motions*. Finally this exercise brings on a nervous action or ejaculatory *crisis* which expels the seed. Now we insist that this whole process, up to the very moment of emission, is *voluntary*, entirely under the control of the moral faculty, and *can be stopped at any point*. In other words, the *presence* and the *motions* can be continued or stopped at will, and it is only the final *crisis* of emission that is automatic or uncontrollable.

Suppose, then, that a man, in lawful intercourse with woman, choosing for good reasons not to beget a child or to disable himself, should stop at the primary stage and content himself with simple *presence* continued as long as agreeable? Would there be any harm? It cannot be injurious to refrain from voluntary excitement. Would there be no *good*? I appeal to the memory of every man who has had good sexual experience to say whether, on the whole, the sweetest and noblest period of intercourse with woman is not that *first* moment of simple presence and spiritual effusion, before the muscular exercise begins.

But we may go farther. Suppose the man chooses for good reasons, as before, to enjoy not only the simple *presence*, but also the *reciprocal motion*, and yet to stop short of the final *crisis*. Again I ask, Would there be any harm? Or would it do no good? I suppose physiologists might say, and I would acknowledge, that the excitement by motion *might* be carried so far that a voluntary suppression of the commencing crisis would be injurious. But what if a man, knowing his own power and limits, should not even *approach* the crisis, and yet be able to enjoy the presence and the motion *ad libitum*? If you say that this is impossible, I answer that I *know* it is possible – nay, that it is easy.

I will admit, however, that it may be impossible to some, while it is possible to others. Paul intimates that some cannot "contain." Men of certain temperaments and conditions are afflicted with involuntary emissions on very trivial excitement and in their sleep. But I insist that these are exceptional morbid cases that should be disciplined and improved; and that, in the normal con-

dition, men are entirely competent to choose in sexual intercourse whether they will stop at any point in the voluntary stages of it, and so make it simply an act of communion, or go through to the involuntary stage, and make it an act of propagation.

The situation may be compared to a stream in the three conditions of a fall, a course of rapids above the fall, and still water above the rapids. The skillful boatman may choose whether he will remain in the still water, or venture more or less down the rapids, or run his boat over the fall. But there is a point on the verge of the fall where he has no control over his course; and just above that there is a point where he will have to struggle with the current in a way which will give his nerves a severe trial, even though he may escape the fall. If he is willing to learn, experience will teach him the wisdom of confining his excursions to the region of easy rowing, unless he has an object in view that is worth the cost of going over the falls.

You have now our whole theory of "Male Continence." It consists in analyzing sexual intercourse, recognizing in it two distinct acts, the social and the propagative, which can be separated practically, and affirming that it is best, not only with reference to remote prudential considerations, but for immediate pleasure, that a man should content himself with the social act, except when he intends procreation.

Let us see now if this scheme belongs to any of the three classes I mentioned. (1) It does not seek to prevent the intercourse of the sexes, but rather gives them more freedom by removing danger of undesired consequences. (2) It does not seek to prevent the natural *effects* of the propagative act, but to prevent the propagative act itself, except when it is intended to be effectual. (3) Of course it does not seek to destroy the living *results* of the propagative act, but provides that impregnation and child-bearing shall be voluntary, and of course desired.

And now, to speak affirmatively, the exact thing that our theory does propose, is to take that same power of moral restraint and self-control, which Paul, Malthus, the Shakers, and all considerate men use in one way or another to limit propagation, and instead of applying it, as they do, to the prevention of the intercourse of the sexes, to introduce it at another stage of the proceedings, viz., *after* the sexes have come together in social effusion, and *before* they have reached the propagative crisis; thus allowing them all and more than all the ordinary freedom of love (since the crisis always interrupts the romance), and at the same time avoiding undesired procreation and all the other evils incident to male incontinence. This is our fourth way, and we think it the better way.

The wholesale and ever ready objection to this method is that it is *unnatural, and unauthorized by the example of other animals.* I may answer in a wholesale way, that cooking, wearing clothes, living in houses, and almost everything else done by civilized man, is unnatural in the same sense, and that a close adherence to the example of the brutes would require us to forego speech and go on "all fours!" But on the other hand, if it is natural in the best sense, as I believe it is, for rational beings to forsake the example of the brutes and improve nature by invention and discovery in all directions, then truly the argument turns the other way, and we shall have to confess that until men and women find a way to elevate their sexual performances above those of the brutes, by introducing into them moral culture, they are living in *unnatural* degradation.

But I will come closer to this objection. The real meaning of it is, that Male Continence in sexual intercourse is a difficult and injurious interruption of a natural act. But every instance of self-denial is an interruption of some natural act. The man who virtuously contents himself with a look at a beautiful woman is conscious of such an interruption. The lover who stops at a kiss denies himself a natural progression. It is an easy, descending grade through all the approaches of sexual love, from the first touch of respectful friendship, to the final complete amalgamation. Must there be no interruption of this natural slide? Brutes, animal or human, tolerate none. Shall their ideas of self-denial prevail? Nay, it is the glory of man to control himself, and the Kingdom of Heaven summons him to self-control in ALL THINGS. If it is noble and beautiful for the betrothed lover to respect the law of marriage in the midst of the glories of courtship, it may be even more noble and beautiful for the wedded lover to respect the laws of health and propagation in the midst of the ecstacies of sexual union. The same moral culture that ennobles the antecedents and approaches of marriage will some time surely glorify the consummation.

Of course, you will think of many other objections and questions, and I have many answers

ready for you; but I will content myself for the present with this limited presentation.

Yours respectfully,　　J. H. NOYES

This letter soon after its date was printed in tract form, as a convenient answer to many letters of inquiry that were pouring in upon the Editors of the CIRCULAR. That little tract is all that we have offered the public directly on the subject of Male Continence since 1866; and it has been sent only where it was explicitly demanded. Four editions of it have been called for and exhausted, and the demand still continues and increases. Thus the time seems to have come for something more elaborate; and meanwhile our experience has been maturing, so that we have more to say. Instead, therefore, of issuing simply a fifth edition of the tract, it has been thought best now to make the exposition more complete by adding to the brief theory therein presented, some account of the origin, history, and practical results of that theory.

To those who regard the principle of Male Continence as a valuable addition to science, it will be interesting to learn how it was discovered; and the misrepresentations on this point which have been put in circulation by Hepworth Dixon and others make it proper and even necessary that the true story of the discovery should be put on record. I tell that story in few words thus:

I was married in 1838, and lived in the usual routine of matrimony till 1846. It was during this period of eight years that I studied the subject of sexual intercourse in connection with my matrimonial experience, and discovered the principle of Male Continence. And the discovery was occasioned and even forced upon me by very sorrowful experience. In the course of six years my wife went through the agonies of five births. Four of them were premature. Only one child lived. This experience was what directed my studies and kept me studying. After our last disappointment, I pledged my word to my wife that I would never again expose her to such fruitless suffering. I made up my mind to live apart from her, rather than break this promise. This was the situation in the summer of 1844. At that time I conceived the idea that the sexual organs have a social function which is distinct from the propagative function; and that these functions may be separated practically. I experimented on this idea, and found that the self-control which it requires is not difficult; also that my enjoyment was increased; also that my wife's experience was very satisfactory, as it had never been before; also that we had escaped the horrors and the fear of involuntary propagation. This was a great deliverance. It made a happy household. I communicated my discovery to a friend. His experience and that of his household were the same. In the course of the next two years I studied all the essential details and bearings of the discovery. In 1846 we commenced Community life at Putney, Vt. In 1848, soon after our removal to Oneida, I published the new theory in a pamphlet which passed through several editions, but is now out of print. This is the only true account of my discovery of Male Continence.

The pamphlet referred to embraced a general exhibition of the principles of the kingdom of heaven promised in the Bible, and for this reason it was entitled *The Bible Argument*; but the most important chapter of it was that which undertook to show "*How the sexual function is to be redeemed and true relations between the sexes are to be restored.*" Under this caption the doctrine of Male Continence was propounded substantially as it is in the letter to the Medical student, but more in detail and with less reserve. For the sake of showing what we believed and printed on this subject twenty-five years ago – which therefore essentially belongs to the history of Male Continence – I will now venture to reprint that notable chapter.

From the Bible Argument, printed in 1848

The amative and propagative functions of the sexual organs are distinct from each other, and may be separated practically. They are confounded in the world, both in the theories of physiologists and in universal practice. The amative function is regarded merely as a bait to the propagative, and is merged in it. The sexual organs are called "organs of reproduction," or "organs of generation," but not organs of love or organs of union. But if amativeness is the first and noblest of the social affections, and if the propagative part of the sexual relation was originally secondary, and became paramount by the subversion of order in the fall (as had previously been shown), we are bound to raise the amative office of the sexual organs into a distinct and paramount function. It is held in the world, that the sexual organs have two distinct functions, viz., the urinary and the propagative. We affirm that they have *three* – the urinary, the propagative, and the amative, i.e., they are conductors, first of the urine, secondly of the semen, and thirdly of the social magnetism. And the amative is as distinct from the propagative, as the propagative is from the urinary. In fact, strictly speaking, the organs of propagation are *physiologically* distinct from the organs of union in both sexes. The testicles are the organs of reproduction in the male, and the uterus in the female. These are distinct from the organs of union. The sexual conjunction of male and female no more necessarily involves the discharge of the semen than of the urine. The discharge of the semen, instead of being the main act of sexual intercourse, properly so called, is really the sequel and termination of it. Sexual intercourse, pure and simple, is the conjunction of the organs of union, and the interchange of magnetic influences, or conversation of spirits, through the medium of that conjunction. The communication from the seminal vessels to the uterus, which constitutes the propagative act, is distinct from, subsequent to, and not necessarily connected with, this intercourse. On the one hand, the seminal discharge can be voluntarily withheld in sexual connection; and on the other, it can be produced without sexual connection, as it is in masturbation. This latter fact demonstrates that the discharge of the semen and the pleasure connected with it, is not essentially social, since it can be produced in solitude; it is a personal and not a dual affair. This, indeed, is evident from a physiological analysis of it. The pleasure of the act is not produced by contact and interchange of life with the female, but by the action of the seminal fluid on the internal nerves of the male organ. The appetite and that which satisfies it are both within the man, and of course the pleasure is personal, and may be obtained without sexual intercourse. We insist, then, that the amative function – that which consists in a simple union of persons, making "of twain one flesh," and giving a medium of magnetic and spiritual interchange – is a distinct and independent function, as superior to the reproductive as we have shown amativeness to be to propagation.

We may strengthen the preceding argument by an analogy. The *mouth* has three distinct functions, viz., those of breathing, eating, and speaking. Two of these, breathing and eating, are purely physical; and these we have in common with the brutes. The third function, that of speaking, is social, and subservient to the intellectual and spiritual. In this we rise above the brutes. They are destitute of it except in a very inferior degree. So, the two primary functions of the sexual organs – the urinary and reproductive – are physical, and we have them in common with the brutes. The third, viz., the amative, is social, and subservient to the spiritual. In this again we rise above the brutes. They have it only as a bait to the reproductive. As speech, the distinctive glory of man, is the superior function of the mouth, so the social office of the sexual organs is their superior function, and that which gives man a position above the brutes.

The method of controlling propagation which results from our argument is natural, healthy, favorable to amativeness, and effectual.

First, it is *natural*. The useless expenditure of seed certainly is not natural. God cannot have designed that men should sow seed by the wayside, where they do not expect it to grow, or in the same field where seed has already been sown and is growing; and yet such is the practice of men in ordinary sexual intercourse. They sow seed habitually where they do not *wish* it to grow. This is wasteful of life and cannot be natural. So far the Shakers and Grahamites are right. Yet it is equally manifest that the natural instinct of our nature demands frequent congress of the sexes, not for propagative, but for social and spiritual purposes. It results from these opposite indications, that simple congress of the sexes, *without the propagative crisis*, is the order of nature for the gratification of ordinary amative instincts; and that the act of propagation should be reserved for its legitimate occasions, when conception is intended. The idea that sexual intercourse, pure and simple, is impossible or difficult, and therefore not natural, is contradicted by the experience of many. Abstinence from masturbation is impossible or difficult, where habit has made it a second nature; and yet no one will say that habitual masturbation is natural. So abstinence from the propagative part of sexual intercourse may seem impracticable to depraved natures, and yet be perfectly natural and easy to persons properly trained to chastity. Our method simply proposes the subordination of the flesh to the spirit, teaching men to seek principally the elevated spiritual pleasures of sexual connection, and to be content with them in their general intercourse with women, restricting the more sensual part to its proper occasions. This is certainly natural and easy to spiritual men, however difficult it may be to the sensual.

Secondly, this method is *healthy*. In the first place, it secures woman from the curses of involuntary and undesirable procreation; and, secondly, it stops the drain of life on the part of man. This cannot be said of Owen's method or of any other that merely prevents the *propagative effects* of the emission of the seed, and not the emission itself.

Thirdly, this method is *favorable to amativeness*. Owen can only say of his method that it does not *much diminish* the pleasure of sexual intercourse; but we can say of ours, that it *vastly increases* that pleasure. Ordinary sexual intercourse (in which the amative and propagative functions are confounded) is a momentary affair, terminating in exhaustion and disgust. If it begins in the spirit, it soon ends in the flesh; i.e., the amative, which is spiritual, is drowned in the propagative, which is sensual. The exhaustion which follows naturally breeds self-reproach and shame, and this leads to dislike and concealment of the sexual organs, which contract disagreeable associations from the fact that they are the instruments of pernicious excess. This undoubtedly is the philosophy of the origin of shame after the fall. Adam and Eve first sunk the spiritual in the sensual, in eating the forbidden fruit; and then, having lost the true balance of their natures, they sunk the spiritual in the sensual in their intercourse with each other, by pushing prematurely beyond the amative to the propagative, and so became ashamed, and began to look with an evil eye on the instruments of their folly. On the same principle we may account for the process of "cooling off" which takes place between lovers after marriage and often ends in indifference and disgust. Exhaustion and self-reproach make the eye evil not only toward the instruments of excess, but toward the person who tempts to it. In contrast with all this, lovers who use their sexual organs simply as the servants of their spiritual natures, abstaining from the propagative act, except when procreation is intended, may enjoy the highest bliss of sexual fellowship for any length of time, without satiety or exhaustion; and thus marriage life may become permanently sweeter than courtship or even the honey-moon.

Fourthly, this method of controlling propagation is *effectual*. The habit of making sexual intercourse a quiet affair, like conversation, restricting the action of the organs to such limits as are necessary to the avoidance of the sensual crisis, can easily be established, and then there is no risk of conception without intention.

Ordinary sexual intercourse, i.e., the performance of the propagative act without the intention of procreation, is properly to be classed with masturbation. The habit in the former case is less liable to become besotted and ruinous than in the latter, simply because a woman is less convenient than the ordinary means of masturbation. It must be admitted, also, that the amative affection favorably modifies the sensual act to a greater extent in sexual commerce than in masturbation. But this is perhaps counterbalanced by the cruelty of forcing or risking undesired conception, which attends sexual commerce, and does not attend masturbation.

Our theory, separating the amative from the propagative, not only relieves us of involuntary and undesirable procreation, but opens the way for *scientific* propagation. We are not opposed, after the Shaker fashion, or even after Owen's fashion, to the increase of population. We believe that the order to "multiply" attached to the race in its original integrity, and that propagation, rightly conducted and kept within such limits as life can fairly afford, is a blessing second only to sexual love. But we are opposed to *involuntary* procreation. A very large proportion of all children born under the present system are begotten contrary to the wishes of both parents, and lie nine months in their mother's womb under their mother's curse or a feeling little better than a curse. Such children cannot be well organized. We are opposed to *excessive*, and of course oppressive procreation, which is almost universal. We are opposed to *random* procreation, which is unavoidable in the marriage system. But we are in favor of *intelligent, well-ordered* procreation. The physiologists say that the race cannot be raised from ruin till propagation is made a matter of science; but they point out no way of making it so. Propagation is controlled and reduced to a science in the case of valuable domestic brutes; but marriage and fashion forbid any such system among human beings. We believe the time will come when involuntary and random propagation will cease, and when scientific combination will be applied to human generation as freely and successfully as it is to that of other animals. The way will be open for this when amativeness can have its proper gratification without drawing after it procreation, as a necessary sequence. And at all events, we believe that good sense and benevolence will *very soon* sanction and enforce the rule that women shall bear children only when they choose. They have the principal burdens of breeding to bear, and they rather than men should have their choice of time and circumstances, at least till science takes charge of the business.

The separation of the amative from the propagative, places amative sexual intercourse on the same footing with other ordinary forms of social interchange. So long as the amative and propagative are confounded, sexual intercourse carries with it physical consequences which necessarily take it out of the category of mere social acts. If a man under the cover of a mere social call upon a woman, should leave in her apartments a child for her to breed and provide for, he would do a mean wrong. The call might be made without previous negotiation or agreement, but the sequel of the call – the leaving of the child – is a matter so serious that it is to be treated as a business affair, and not be done without good reason and agreement of the parties. But the man who under the cover of social intercourse commits the propagative act, leaves his child with the woman in a more oppressive way than if he should leave it full born in her apartment; for he imposes upon her not only the task of breeding and providing for it, but the sorrows and pains of pregnancy and childbirth. It is right that law, or at least public opinion, should frown on such proceedings even more than it does, and it is not to be wondered at that women, to a considerable extent, look upon ordinary sexual intercourse with more dread than pleasure, regarding it as a stab at their life, rather than a joyful act of fellowship. But separate the amative from the propagative – let the act of fellowship stand by itself – and sexual intercourse becomes a purely social affair, the same in kind with other modes of kindly communion, differing only by its superior intensity and beauty. Thus the most popular, if not the most serious objection, to communistic love is removed. The difficulty so often urged, of knowing to whom children belong in complex-marriage, will have no place in a Community trained to keep the amative distinct from the propagative. Thus also the only plausible objection to amative intercourse between near relatives, founded on the supposed law of nature that "breeding in and in" deteriorates offspring (which law, however, was not recognized in Adam's family) is removed; since science may dictate in this case as in all others, in regard to propagation, and yet amativeness may be free.

In society trained to these principles, as propagation will become a science, so amative intercourse will have place among the "fine arts." Indeed, it will take rank above music, painting, sculpture, etc.; for it combines the charms and benefits of them all. There is as much room for cultivation of taste and skill in this department as in any.

The practice which we propose will give new speed to the advance of civilization and refinement. The self-control, retention of life, and ascent out of sensualism, which must result from making freedom of love a bounty on the chastening of physical indulgence, will raise the race to new vigor and beauty, moral and physical. And the refining effects of sexual love (which are recognized more or less in the world) will be increased a thousand-fold, when sexual intercourse becomes an honored method of innocent and useful communion, and each is married to all.

This exposition, designed, as it manifestly was, to sweep the whole theoretical area of Male Continence and glance at all its logical results, present and prospective, was nevertheless hedged about with much practical conservatism. It stood in the midst of a serious religious theory, and expressly declined all responsibility for the doings of those who should attempt to make a separate hobby of it, and carry it into practice without the fear of the Lord. The keynote of the whole Bible Argument, reiterated on every page of it, is heard in such passages as these:

> The first thing to be done in an attempt to redeem man and reörganize society is to bring about reconciliation with God; and the second thing is to bring about a true union of the sexes. In other words, religion is the first subject of interest, and sexual morality the second, in the great enterprise of establishing the kingdom of God on earth. Bible Communists are operating in this order. Their main work from 1834 to 1846 was to develop the religion of the New Covenant and establish union with God. Their second work, in which they are now specially engaged, is the laying the foundation of a new state of society by developing the true theory of sexual morality.

> Any attempt to revolutionize sexual morality before settlement with God is out of order. Holiness must go before free love. Bible Communists are not responsible for the proceedings of those who meddle with the sexual question before they have laid the foundation of true faith and union with God.

The theory thus carefully launched was not left to a chance-career. The Oneida Community in an important sense owed its existence to the discovery of Male Continence, and has evidently been the Committee of Providence to test its value in actual life. The original conservatism and other qualifications of this Committee were set forth in the introduction to the *Bible Argument* in the following specifications:

1 It is not immodest, in the present exigency, to affirm that the leading members of the Putney Association belonged to the most respectable families in Vermont, had been educated in the best schools of New England morality and refinement, and were by the ordinary standards irreproachable in their conduct, so far as sexual matters are concerned, till they deliberately commenced, in 1846, the experiment of a new state of society, on principles which they had been long maturing and were prepared to defend before the world.
2 It may also be affirmed without fear of contradiction, that the main body of those who have joined the Community at Oneida are sober, substantial men and women, of good previous character and position in society.
3 The principles discussed in the ensuing argument have never been carried into full practical embodiment, either at Putney or Oneida, but have been held by the Community as the principles of an *ultimate state*, toward which society among them is advancing slowly and carefully, with all due deference to sentiments and relations established by the old order of things.
4 The Community, in respect to practical innovations, limits itself to its own family circle, not invading society around it; and no just complaint of such invasions can be found at Putney or Oneida.

The testing Committee, thus qualified, has now been in session twenty-five years. Two hundred and fifty sober persons have lived together a quarter of a century under the rule of Male Continence in constant observation of its tendencies and effects. Their experiment has gone on through all the vicissitudes that reach from one generation to a second. Many applications of their sexual discovery which were in the far-off future when it was first published, are now matters of experience. They have tested Male Continence even in its application to Scientific Propagation. In a word, the rosy but infantile theory of 1848 has reached the manhood of robust embodiment in 1872. Has that rosy theory fulfilled its promises? It is time the Committee should report. If the experiment is still unfinished, it is far enough advanced to warrant some conclusions. We shall doubtless be able to make a more full *exposé* after another quarter of a century's experience; but we will briefly report progress up to this time.

In the first place, in regard to the *injurious* effects of Male Continence, which have been anticipated and often predicted, the Community has to report, in general, that they have not been realized. For example:

It is seriously believed by many that nature requires a periodical and somewhat frequent discharge of the seed, and that the retention of it is liable to be injurious. Even if this were true, it would be no argument against Male Continence, but rather an argument in favor of masturbation; for it is obvious that before marriage men have no lawful method of discharge but masturbation; and after marriage it is as foolish and cruel to expend one's seed on a wife merely for the sake of getting rid of it, as it would be to fire a gun at one's best friend merely for the sake of unloading it. If a blunderbuss must be emptied, and the charge cannot be drawn, it is better to fire into the air than to kill somebody with it. But it is not true that the seed is an excrement like the urine, that requires periodical and frequent discharge. Nature has provided other ways of disposing of it. In fact it has an *immanent value*, and is in its best function while retained. It is the presence of the seed, and not the discharge of it, that makes the bull superior to the ox. The Community has had no trouble from retention of seed; but, on the other hand, has nearly exterminated masturbation by the reflex influence of Male Continence. Masturbation is a disreputable branch of the same seed-wasting business that is carried on more decently in ordinary matrimonial intercourse, and is evidently destined to pass away with it.

Closely connected with this popular fallacy respecting the seed, is the suggestion of certain medical men that the practice of Male Continence would lead to seminal degeneracy and impotence. The experience of the Community has signally refuted this suggestion in the only effectual way, viz., by a great number of intentional impregnations, which have occurred, within a few years, between persons who have been longest in the practice of Male Continence.

Another apprehension suggested by medical men has been, that the avoidance of the crisis in sexual intercourse would so increase and prolong the excitement as to induce excesses, which would lead to various nervous diseases. This suggestion, it must be confessed, has some antecedent probability; but the general experience of the Community has not confirmed it. The New York *Medical Gazette* of October, 1870, in a review of our article on Scientific Propagation, published in the *Modern Thinker* of that year, took occasion to criticise our practice of Male Continence, as likely to prove injurious in the way above suggested; and expressed a wish to see the statistics of nervous diseases in the Community. Whereupon a professional examination was instituted and a report made by Theodore R. Noyes, M. D., in which it was shown, by careful comparison of our statistics with those of the U.S. census and other public documents, that the rate of nervous diseases in the Community is considerably below the average in ordinary society. This report was published by the *Medical Gazette*, and was pronounced by the editor "a model of careful observation, bearing intrinsic evidence of entire honesty and impartiality."

It was, however, admitted in that Report that there had been one or two cases of nervous disorder in the Community, which could be traced with probability to a misuse of Male Continence in the way suggested by the *Gazette*; and I will here take occasion to add that I have no doubt the greatest danger attending the practice of Male Continence is, and ever will be, the temptation to make a separate hobby of it and neglect the religious conditions out of which it originally issued and to which it belongs. Male Continence in its essence is self-control, and that is a virtue of universal importance. To cultivate self-control in respect to the seminal crisis, but neglect it in other sexual indulgences, is evidently Male Continence in a spurious and dangerous form. It is certain that this spurious self-control may be cultivated even for the purpose of gaining freedom for sensual and riotous pleasure. We may be thankful that such a counterfeit cannot escape the checks prepared for universal vice. Nothing less than heart-abandonment to the grace of God, which teaches and gives *temperance in all things*, can ever release us from the old tutelage of suffering. Our theory in its oldest form defined the sexual organs as conveyancers, not only of the seed, but of the "social magnetism." Now it is certain that the social magnetism is a vital element, as real as the seed, and as really limited in its supply; and that the loss of it in excessive quantities entails diseases as atrocious as those which follow seminal waste. And to this liability women are as much exposed as men. So much of warning the experience of the Community enables it to contribute; though it has had no actual shipwrecks on this coast of danger.

But after all it is not to be forgotten that the effects of nervous exaltation may be good as well as evil. Herein the spiritual view is perhaps a little different from the medical. A degree of excitement which would injure a sick man may be harmless and even invigorating to the healthy. And this principle must be carried upward, as our definition of health rises. We must not seek examples of nervous phenomena exclusively among the weaklings of debauchery, as writers on sexual pathology generally do. Human nature certainly does not reach its normal condition till it is the temple of the Holy Spirit, filled with all the fullness of God. A nervous system in that condition can bear a weight, not only of suffering but of glory, which would destroy ordinary health. Paul's philosophy teaches that even the Lord's Supper, received unworthily, may work damnation, thus causing physical weakness and death (see I Cor. XI: 29, 30). The ultimate way to escape nervous injury will be found, not in the direction of abstinence from excitement, but in the toning of the nervous system to the divine standard of health by fellowship with resurrection-life.

As evidence of the *good* effects of Male Continence, we mention, in the first place, the universal feeling and testimony of the Community in its favor. Allowance of course must be made for party feeling in such testimony, and it must pass only for what it is worth. But it seems incredible that so large a body of sober persons as the Oneida Community should be entirely mistaken in thinking, as they certainly do, that Male Continence, in an experience of twenty-five years, has more than fulfilled its early promises. A young member who is just closing his career at college, expresses the general feeling of men and women, not only of the first generation but of the second, in the following enthusiastic terms:

DEAR MR. NOYES:

I want to tell you how much it stirs my spirit to hear our people magnify Male Continence. It seems to me that we are just beginning to say the good things that will be said of it; and it makes me happy to think of the honor that is sooner or later certain to be poured upon it. I love the principle of Male Continence with my whole soul, for I know that it has been and is a help to my fellowship with Christ.

This Yankee nation claims to be a nation of inventors, but the discovery of Male Continence puts you, in my mind, at the head of all inventors. There has certainly been no higher conservation of force than that realized by Male Continence, and I am confident that the blessings which will flow from it cannot be measured by those which have followed the steam-engine and the electric telegraph.

Yours truly,—— ——

The general condition of the Community may properly be put in as evidence of the good effects of Male Continence. It is the principle to which the Community in some sense owes its existence, and which has been the very soul of its working constitution. Such a principle, in a trial of twenty-five years, must inevitably manifest its real character for weal or woe, in the morals and physical conditions of its adherents. In the place of any testimony from ourselves, the following picture of the Community, drawn by a gentleman well known for his intelligence and power of observation, will give the reader the best means of judging what have been the general results of Male Continence.

Sketch of the Oneida Community by T. W. Higginson in the Woman's Journal

Having lately a day's interval between two lecturing engagements in central New York, I spent that time at the Oneida Community. After a tolerably extensive acquaintance with the various types of religious enthusiasm, I can truly say that I never met with a body of men and women in whom that enthusiasm seemed a more genuine thing, or less alloyed by base motive. The very fact that some of their main principles seem to me false, and others actually repulsive, should give additional weight to this testimony.

As you approach the stately brick edifice of the Community on a winter day you hear the voices of children, while a little army of sleds outside the main entrance, shows that outdoor happiness is at hand for them. Entering, you find yourself in a sort of palace of plain comfort: admirably warmed and ventilated, with spacious corridors, halls, parlors, library and natural history museum. You are received with as much courtesy as in any private house. The men you meet are well dressed, well mannered, well educated. The women, though disfigured by the plainest of all possible bloomer dresses, look healthy and cheerful. At table and in the dining-hall, where the sexes meet, you see cordial and inoffensive manners. Your food is well cooked and served, with home-made wine, if you wish, and the delicious bread-and-butter and snowy table-cloths of the Shakers. After dinner, perhaps, they give you an improvised concert. The family assembles in the great hall. The side door of the wide stage opens, and half a dozen little children from two to three years old are let in as the advance-guard of the juvenile department. They toddle about the stage at their will – its edge being protected by a light partition for their benefit – and shout and crow to their parents, who sit below. The little ones are all rosy and healthy, all about the same size, and all neatly dressed in little frocks and fresh, white aprons. It is a pretty prelude for an afternoon's performance. Then twenty of the elder children follow, and sing songs. They also look happy and well cared for; and are neatly, though ungracefully dressed. Then you listen to a really excellent or-chestra of six or seven instruments, led by a thor-oughly trained leader – a young man brought up in the Community and musically educated at their expense – while a boy of eleven plays the second violin. They play good German music, while the little ones find their way down upon the floor, and are petted by their special parents, and watched with apparent admiration and affection by men and women generally. This, at least, was what I saw that day. Later I saw the machine-shops and the silk-factory; but these can be seen anywhere. But a family of two hundred living in apparent harmony and among the comforts which associated life secures – this is not to be seen every day, and this is what one at least convinces himself that he sees at Oneida.

Meanwhile the essential theories upon which all this rests appear to the observer – to me at least – all wrong. At Oneida they practice community of property. I disbelieve in it, and only believe in association and cooperation. At Oneida they sub-ordinate all the relation of the sexes to the old Greek theory – held by them as Christian – that the Community has a right to control parentage, and to select and combine the parents of the next generation of the human race, as in rearing domes-tic animals. Such a theory I abhor; I believe it must cause much suffering in its application, and that it will defeat its own end, by omitting from these unions all deep personal emotion. Therefore I utterly dissent from the essential theories of the Oneida Community. All the more reason for trying to do them justice. In the wonderful variety and complexity of human nature, it often happens that the theories which would be injurious and even degrading in your hands or mine, are somehow purged of the expected ill effects in the hands which hold them. There is a divine compensation that limits the demoralizing effects of bad prin-ciples, when these are honestly adopted. I found a good deal of such compensation at Oneida.

It must be remembered that the whole organiza-tion is absolutely based upon a special theology, that none who do not adopt this would in any case be admitted to membership. As a matter of fact, they have for several years admitted no new members whatever, having no room. This cuts off all floating and transient membership, and excludes all the driftwood of reform. Members must be either very sincere proselytes to a religious theory, or else very consummate hypocrites. The Community rejects the whole theory of "attractive industry" of Fourier, and accepts a theory of self-sacrifice. In the same way it rejects the whole theory of "affinities" in love and marriage. It accepts, instead, a theory of self-control, and even what seems unlawful and repulsive indul-gence must be viewed against this stern back-ground of predominant self-sacrifice.

The two things they most sternly resist in prac-tice are, first – lawlessness, or doing what is right in one's own eyes; and secondly – exclusive own-ership, whether of property, or wife and child. All must be subordinated to the supposed good of the whole. They admit that this theory would be ut-terly disastrous to the world in its present stage, if adopted without preparation. Nothing but reli-gious enthusiasm would make it practicable, even in a Community of two hundred, without its resulting either in agony or degradation.

But now, as a matter of fact, how is it? I am bound to say as an honest reporter, that I looked in vain for the visible signs of either the suffering or the sin. The Community makes an impression utterly unlike that left by the pallid joylessness of the Shakers, or the stupid sensualism which im-pressed me in the few Mormon households I have seen. I saw some uninteresting faces, and some with that look of burnt-out fire of which every radical assembly shows specimens, but I did not see a face that I should call coarse, and there were very few that I should call joyless. The fact that the children of the Community hardly ever wish to leave it; that the young men whom they send to Yale College, and the young women whom they send for musical instruction to New York, always return eagerly and devote their lives to the Community; this proves a good deal. There is no coercion to keep them, as in Mormonism, and there are no monastic vows, as in the Roman Catholic church. This invariable return, therefore, shows that there is happiness to be found in the Community, and that it is of a kind which wins the respect of the young and generous. A body must have great confidence in itself when it thus voluntarily sends its sheep into the midst of the world's wolves, and fearlessly expects their return.

I came away from the Community with increased respect for the religious sentiment which, in however distorted a form, can keep men and women from the degradation which one could expect to result from a life which seems to me so wrong. I brought away, also, increased respect for the principle of association, which will yet secure to the human race, in the good time coming, better things than competition has to give. I saw men and women there whom I felt ready to respect and love. I admire the fidelity with which they maintain the equality of the sexes. Nevertheless, I should count it a calamity for a boy or girl to be brought up at Oneida.

T. W. H.

In conclusion, I will mention one specific and very significant symptom of *moral* health which has manifestly resulted from Male Continence. The natural desire for children, which has almost died out in general society, has returned to us, with all the vigor that it had in the young and healthy ages. Instead of voluntary abortions and continual dread of child-bearing, the demand for offspring in the Community and especially among the women, though liberally provided for and enjoying ordinary success, is far ahead of the supply.

32

Democratic Vistas

Walt Whitman

Introduction

Walt Whitman (1819–1892) was born on Long Island in New York and grew up in Brooklyn, where he learned to be a printer. In his early twenties he became a journalist, editing a Brooklyn daily, until his support for the Free Soil movement led to his dismissal in 1848. He worked for a time in New Orleans and eventually returned to Brooklyn where he once again worked as a journalist and editor. In 1855, he published the first edition of his collection of poems, *Leaves of Grass*. He would continue to edit and expand *Leaves of Grass* until the final edition was published in 1892. After his brother was wounded in the Civil War battle of Fredericksburg, Whitman spent time with the Union Army, sometimes as a clerk and sometimes visiting wounded soldiers from both sides at the Union hospitals near Washington. His experiences in the war became the basis for parts of his prose work, *Specimen Days*, and for a volume of poetry, *Drum Taps*, later included in *Leaves of Grass*. The essay, "Democratic Vistas," extracts of which are reproduced here, was originally published in 1871. It presents a post-Civil War conception of democracy grounded both in the development of a unified American community and in fostering individual differences. Rather than seeing democracy established on the basis of universal principles alone, Whitman argues for the need for a democratic aesthetic that focuses on particularity, the connections between people and their places, the recognition of the role of their histories, and

Taken from *Complete Poetry and Selected Prose*, ed. James E. Miller, Jr. (Boston: Houghton Mifflin, 1959).

the importance of the future in giving meaning to the present. Whitman represents a turning point in the idea of American community that helps to set the stage for the social philosophers who followed in the late nineteenth and early twentieth centuries.

As the greatest lessons of Nature through the universe are perhaps the lessons of variety and freedom, the same present the greatest lessons also in New World politics and progress. If a man were ask'd, for instance, the distinctive points contrasting modern European and American political and other life with the old Asiatic cultus, as lingering-bequeath'd yet in China and Turkey, he might find the amount of them in John Stuart Mill's profound essay on Liberty in the future, where he demands two main constituents, or substrata, for a truly grand nationality – 1st, a large variety of character – and 2nd, full play for human nature to expand itself in numberless and even conflicting directions – (seems to be for general humanity much like the influences that make up, in their limitless field, that perennial health-action of the air we call the weather – an infinite number of currents and forces, and contributions, and temperatures, and cross purposes, whose ceaseless play of counterpart upon counterpart brings constant restoration and vitality). With this thought – and not for itself alone, but all it necessitates, and draws after it – let me begin my speculations.

America, filling the present with greatest deeds and problems, cheerfully accepting the past, including feudalism (as, indeed, the present is but the legitimate birth of the past, including feudalism), counts, as I reckon, for her justification and success (for who, as yet, dare claim success?) almost entirely on the future. Nor is that hope unwarranted. Today, ahead, though dimly yet, we see, in vistas, a copious, sane, gigantic offspring. For our New World I consider far less important for what it has done, or what it is, than for results to come. Sole among nationalities, these States have assumed the task to put in forms of lasting power and practicality, on areas of amplitude rivaling the operations of the physical kosmos, the moral political speculations of ages, long, long deferr'd, the democratic republican principle, and the theory of development and perfection by voluntary standards, and self-reliance. Who else, indeed, except the United States, in history, so far, have accepted in unwitting faith, and, as we now see, stand, act upon, and go security for, these things?

But preluding no longer, let me strike the keynote of the following strain. First premising that, though the passages of it have been written at widely different times (it is, in fact, a collection of memoranda, perhaps for future designers, comprehenders), and though it may be open to the charge of one part contradicting another – for there are opposite sides to the great question of democracy, as to every great question – I feel the parts harmoniously blended in my own realization and convictions, and present them to be read only in such oneness, each page and each claim and assertion modified and temper'd by the others. Bear in mind, too, that they are not the result of studying up in political economy, but of the ordinary sense, observing, wandering among men, these States, these stirring years of war and peace. I will not gloss over the appaling dangers of universal suffrage in the United States. In fact, it is to admit and face these dangers I am writing. To him or her within whose thought rages the battle, advancing, retreating, between democracy's convictions, aspirations, and the people's crudeness, vice, caprices, I mainly write this essay. I shall use the words America and democracy as convertible terms. Not an ordinary one is the issue. The United States are destined either to surmount the gorgeous history of feudalism, or else prove the most tremendous failure of time. Not the least doubtful am I on any prospects of their material success. The triumphant future of their business, geographic and productive departments, on larger scales and in more varieties than ever, is certain. In those respects the republic must soon (if she does not already) outstrip all examples hitherto afforded, and dominate the world.

Admitting all this, with the priceless value of our political institutions, general suffrage (and fully acknowledging the latest, widest opening of the doors), I say that, far deeper than these, what finally and only is to make of our Western world a nationality superior to any hitherto known, and outtopping the past, must be vigorous, yet unsuspected Literatures, perfect personalities and sociologies, original, transcendental, and expressing (what, in highest sense, are not yet express'd at all) democracy and the modern. With these, and out of these, I promulge new races of Teachers, and of perfect Women, indispensable to endow the birth-stock of a New World. For feudalism, caste, the ecclesiastic traditions, though palpably retreating from political institutions, still hold essentially, by their spirit, even in this country, entire possession of the more important fields, indeed the very subsoil, of education, and of social standards and literature.

I say that democracy can never prove itself beyond cavil, until it founds and luxuriantly grows its own forms of art, poems, schools, theology, displacing all that exists, or that has been produced anywhere in the past, under opposite influences. It is curious to me that while so many voices, pens, minds, in the press, lecture rooms, in our Congress, etc., are discussing intellectual topics, pecuniary dangers, legislative problems, the suffrage, tariff and labor questions, and the various business and benevolent needs of America, with propositions, remedies, often worth deep attention, there is one need, a hiatus the profoundest, that no eye seems to perceive, no voice to state. Our fundamental want today in the United States, with closest, amplest reference to present conditions, and to the future, is of a class, and the clear idea of a class, of native authors, literatuses, far different, far higher in grade, than any yet known, sacerdotal, modern, fit to cope with our occasions, lands, permeating the whole mass of American mentality, taste, belief, breathing into it a new breath of life, giving it decision, affecting politics far more than the popular superficial suffrage, with results inside and underneath the elections of Presidents or Congresses – radiating, begetting appropriate teachers, schools, manners, and, as its grandest result, accomplishing (what neither the schools nor the churches and their clergy have hitherto accomplish'd, and without which this nation will no more stand, permanently, soundly, than a house will stand without a sub-stratum), a religious and moral character beneath the political and productive and intellectual bases of the States. For know you not, dear, earnest reader, that the people of our land may all read and write, and may all possess the right to vote – and yet the main things may be entirely lacking? – (and this to suggest them).

View'd, today, from a point of view sufficiently over-arching, the problem of humanity all over the civilized world is social and religious, and is to be finally met and treated by literature. The priest departs, the divine literatus comes. Never was anything more wanted than, today, and here in the States, the poet of the modern is wanted, or the great literatus of the modern. At all times, perhaps, the central point in any nation, and that whence it is itself really sway'd the most, and whence it sways others, is its national literature, especially its archetypal poems. Above all previous lands, a great original literature is surely to become the justification and reliance (in some respects the sole reliance of American democracy).

[...]

In short, as though it may not be realized, it is strictly true, that a few first-class poets, philosophs, and authors have substantially settled and given status to the entire religion, education, law, sociology, etc., of the hitherto civilized world, by tingeing and often creating the atmospheres out of which they have arisen, such also must stamp, and more than ever stamp, the interior and real democratic construction of this American continent, today, and days to come. Remember also this fact of difference, that, while through the antique and through the mediæval ages, highest thoughts and ideals realized themselves, and their expression made its way by other arts, as much as, or even more than by, technical literature (not open to the mass of persons, or even to the majority of eminent persons), such literature in our day and for current purposes is not only more eligible than all the other arts put together, but has become the only general means of morally influencing the world. Painting, sculpture, and the dramatic theatre, it would seem, no longer play an indispensable or even important part in the workings and mediumship of intellect, utility, or even high æsthetics. Architecture remains, doubtless with capacities, and a real future. Then music, the combiner, nothing more spiritual, nothing more sensuous, a god, yet completely human, advances, prevails,

holds highest place; supplying in certain wants and quarters what nothing else could supply. Yet in the civilization of today it is undeniable that, over all the arts, literature dominates, serves beyond all – shapes the character of church and school – or, in any rate, is capable of doing so. Including the literature of science, its scope is indeed unparallel'd.

[...]

I say we had best look our times and lands searchingly in the face, like a physician diagnosing some deep disease. Never was there, perhaps, more hollowness at heart than at present, and here in the United States. Genuine belief seems to have left us. The underlying principles of the States are not honestly believ'd in (for all this hectic glow, and these melodramatic screamings), nor is humanity itself believ'd in. What penetrating eye does not everywhere see through the mask? The spectacle is appalling. We live in an atmosphere of hypocrisy throughout. The men believe not in the women, nor the women in the men. A scornful superciliousness rules in literature. The aim of all the *littérateurs* is to find something to make fun of. A lot of churches, sects, etc., the most dismal phantasms I know, usurp the name of religion. Conversation is a mass of badinage. From deceit in the spirit, the mother of all false deeds, the offspring is already incalculable. An acute and candid person, in the revenue department in Washington, who is led by the course of his employment to regularly visit the cities, north, south, and west, to investigate frauds, has talked much with me about his discoveries. The depravity of the business classes of our country is not less than has been supposed, but infinitely greater. The official services of America, national, state, and municipal, in all their branches and departments, except the judiciary, are saturated in corruption, bribery, falsehood, maladministration; and the judiciary is tainted. The great cities reek with respectable as much as non-respectable robbery and scoundrelism. In fashionable life, flippancy, tepid amours, weak infidelism, small aims, or no aims at all, only to kill time. In business (this all-devouring modern word, business), the one sole object is, by any means, pecuniary gain. The magician's serpent in the fable ate up all the other serpents; and moneymaking is our magician's serpent, remaining today sole master of the field. The best class we show, is but a mob of fashionably dress'd speculators and vulgarians. True, indeed, behind this fantastic farce, enacted on the visible stage of society, solid things and stupendous labors are to be discover'd, existing crudely and going on in the background, to advance and tell themselves in time. Yet the truths are none the less terrible. I say that our New World democracy, however great a success in uplifting the masses out of their sloughs, in materialistic development, products, and in a certain highly deceptive superficial popular intellectuality, is, so far, an almost complete failure in its social aspects, and in really grand religious, moral, literary, and æsthetic results. In vain do we march with unprecedented strides to empire so colossal, outvying the antique, beyond Alexander's, beyond the proudest sway of Rome. In vain have we annex'd Texas, California, Alaska, and reach north for Canada and south for Cuba. It is as if we were somehow being endow'd with a vast and more and more thoroughly appointed body and then left with little or no soul.

Let me illustrate further, as I write, with current observation, localities, etc. The subject is important, and will bear repetition. After an absence, I am now again (September, 1870) in New York City and Brooklyn, on a few weeks' vacation. The splendor, picturesqueness, and oceanic amplitude and rush of these great cities, the unsurpassed situation, rivers and bay, sparkling sea-tides, costly and lofty new buildings, façades of marble and iron, of original grandeur and elegance of design, with the masses of gay color, the preponderance of white and blue, the flags flying, the endless ships, the tumultuous streets, Broadway, the heavy, low, musical roar, hardly ever intermitted, even at night, the jobbers' houses, the rich shops, the wharves, the great Central Park, and the Brooklyn Park of hills (as I wander among them this beautiful fall weather, musing, watching, absorbing) – the assemblages of the citizens in their groups, conversations, trades, evening amusements, or along the by-quarters – these, I say, and the like of these, completely satisfy my senses of power, fullness, motion, etc., and give me, through such senses and appetites, and through my æsthetic conscience, a continued exaltation and absolute fulfillment. Always and more and more, as I cross the East and North rivers, the ferries, or with the pilots in their pilot-houses, or pass an hour in Wall Street, or the Gold Exchange, I realize (if we must admit such partialisms) that not Nature alone is great in her fields of freedom and the open air, in her storms, the shows of night and day, the mountains, forests, sea – but in the artificial, the work of man too is equally great – in this profusion of teeming humanity – in these ingenuities, streets, goods, houses, ships – these hurrying, feverish, electric crowds of men, their complicated business genius (not least among the geniuses), and all this mighty, many-threaded wealth and industry concentrated here.

But sternly discarding, shutting our eyes to the glow and grandeur of the general superficial effect, coming down to what is of the only real importance, Personalities, and examining minutely, we question, we ask, Are there, indeed, *men* here worthy the name? Are there athletes? Are there perfect women, to match the generous material luxuriance? Is there a pervading atmosphere of beautiful manners? Are there crops of fine youths, and majestic old persons? Are there arts worthy freedom and a rich people? Is there a great moral and religious civilization – the only justification of a great material one? Confess that to severe eyes, using the moral microscope upon humanity, a sort of dry and flat Sahara appears, these cities, crowded with petty grotesques, malformations, phantoms, playing meaningless antics. Confess that everywhere, in shop, street, church, theatre, barroom, official chair, are pervading flippancy and vulgarity, low cunning, infidelity – everywhere the youth puny, impudent, foppish, prematurely ripe – everywhere an abnormal libidinousness, unhealthy forms, male, female, painted, padded, dyed, chignon'd, muddy complexions, bad blood, the capacity for good motherhood deceasing or deceas'd, shallow notions of beauty, with a range of manners, or rather lack of manners (considering the advantages enjoy'd), probably the meanest to be seen in the world.

Of all this, and these lamentable conditions, to breathe into them the breath recuperative of sane and heroic life, I say a new-founded literature, not merely to copy and reflect existing surfaces, or pander to what is called taste – not only to amuse, pass away time, celebrate the beautiful, the refined, the past, or exhibit technical, rhythmic, or grammatical dexterity – but a literature underlying life, religious, consistent with science, handling the elements and forces with competent power, teaching and training men – and, as perhaps the most precious of its results, achieving the entire redemption of woman out of these incredible holds and webs of silliness, millinery, and every kind of dyspeptic depletion – and thus insuring to the States a strong and sweet Female Race, a race of perfect Mothers – is what is needed.

And now, in the full conception of these facts and points, and all that they infer, pro and con – with yet unshaken faith in the elements of the American masses, the composites, of both sexes, and even consider'd as individuals – and ever recognizing in them the broadest bases of the best literary and æsthetic appreciation – I proceed with my speculations, Vistas.

First, let us see what we can make out of a brief, general, sentimental consideration of political democracy, and whence it has arisen, with regard to some of its current features, as an aggregate, and as the basic structure of our future literature and authorship. We shall, it is true, quickly and continually find the origin-idea of the singleness of man, individualism, asserting itself, and cropping forth, even from the opposite ideas. But the mass, or lump character, for imperative reasons, is to be ever carefully weigh'd, borne in mind, and provided for. Only from it, and from its proper regulation and potency, comes the other, comes the chance of individualism. The two are contradictory, but our task is to reconcile them.

The political history of the past may be summ'd up as having grown out of what underlies the words, order, safety, caste, and especially out of the need of some prompt deciding authority, and of cohesion at all cost. Leaping time, we come to the period within the memory of people now living, when, as from some lair where they had slumber'd long, accumulating wrath, sprang up and are yet active (1790, and on even to the present, 1870) those noisy eructations, destructive iconoclasms, a fierce sense of wrongs, amid which moves the form, well known in modern history, in the Old World, stain'd with much blood, and mark'd by savage reactionary clamors and demands. These bear, mostly, as on one inclosing point of need.

For after the rest is said – after the many time-honor'd and really true things for subordination, experience, rights of property, etc., have been listen'd to and acquiesced in – after the valuable and well-settled statement of our duties and relations in society is thoroughly conn'd over and exhausted – it remains to bring forward and modify everything else with the idea of that Something a man is (last precious consolation of the drudging poor), standing apart from all else, divine in his own right, and a woman in hers, sole and untouchable by any canons of authority, or any rule derived from precedent, state-safety, the acts of legislatures, or even from what is called religion, modesty, or art. The radiation of this truth is the key of the most significant doings of our immediately preceding three centuries, and has been the political genesis and life of America. Advancing visibly, it still more advances invisibly. Underneath the fluctuations of the expressions of society, as well as the movements of the politics of the leading nations of the world, we see steadily pressing ahead and strengthening itself, even in the midst of immense tendencies toward aggregation, this image of completeness in separatism, of individual personal dignity, of a single person, either male or female, characterized in the main, not from extrinsic acquirements or position, but in the pride of himself or herself alone; and, as an eventual conclusion and summing up (or else the entire scheme of things is aimless, a cheat, a crash), the simple idea that the last, best dependence is to be upon humanity itself, and its own inherent, normal, full-grown qualities without any superstitious support whatever. This idea of perfect individualism it is indeed that deepest tinges and gives character to the idea of the aggregate. For it is mainly or altogether to serve independent separatism that we favor a strong generalization, consolidation. As it is to give the best vitality and freedom to the rights of the States (every bit as important as the right of nationality, the union), that we insist on the identity of the Union at all hazards.

The purpose of democracy – supplanting old belief in the necessary absoluteness of establish'd dynastic rulership, temporal, ecclesiastical, and scholastic, as furnishing the only security against chaos, crime, and ignorance – is, through many transmigrations and amid endless ridicules, arguments, and ostensible failures, to illustrate, at all hazards, this doctrine or theory that man, properly train'd in sanest, highest freedom, may and must become a law, and series of laws, unto himself, surrounding and providing for, not only his own personal control, but all his relations to other individuals, and to the State; and that, while other theories, as in the past histories of nations, have proved wise enough, and indispensable perhaps for their conditions, *this*, as matters now stand in our civilized world, is the only scheme worth working from, as warranting results like those of Nature's laws, reliable, when once establish'd, to carry on themselves.

The argument of the matter is extensive, and, we admit, by no means all on one side. What we shall offer will be far, far from sufficient. But while leaving unsaid much that should properly even prepare the way for the treatment of this many-sided question of political liberty, equality, or republicanism – leaving the whole history and consideration of the feudal plan and its products, embodying humanity, its politics and civilization, through the retrospect of past time (which plan and products, indeed, make up all of the past, and a large part of the present) – leaving unanswer'd, at least by any specific and local answer, many a well-wrought argument and instance, and many a con-scientious declamatory cry and warning – as, very lately, from an eminent and venerable person abroad – things, problems, full of doubt, dread, suspense (not new to me, but old occupiers of many an anxious hour in city's din, or night's silence), we still may give a page or so, whose drift is opportune. Time alone can finally answer these things. But as a substitute in passing, let us, even if fragmentarily, throw forth a short direct or indirect suggestion of the premises of that other plan, in the new spirit, under the new forms, started here in our America.

As to the political section of Democracy, which introduces and breaks ground for further and vaster sections, few probably are the minds, even in these republican States, that fully comprehend the aptness of that phrase, "the government of the people, by the people, for the people," which we inherit from the lips of Abraham Lincoln; a formula whose verbal shape is homely wit, but whose scope includes both the totality and all minutiæ of the lesson.

The People! Like our huge earth itself, which, to ordinary scansion, is full of vulgar contradic-tions and offence, man, viewed in the lump, dis-pleases, and is a constant puzzle and affront to the merely educated classes. The rare, cosmical, artist-mind, lit with the Infinite, alone confronts his manifold and oceanic qualities – but taste, intelli-gence and culture (so-called), have been against the masses, and remain so. There is plenty of glamour about the most damnable crimes and hog-gish meannesses, special and general, of the feudal and dynastic world over there, with its *personnel* of lords and queens and courts, so well dress'd and so handsome. But the People are ungrammatical, untidy, and their sins gaunt and ill bred.

Literature, strictly consider'd, has never recog-nized the People, and, whatever may be said, does not today. Speaking generally, the tendencies of literature, as hitherto pursued, have been to make mostly critical and querulous men. It seems as if, so far, there were some natural repugnance be-tween a literary and professional life, and the rude rank spirit of the democracies. There is, in later literature, a treatment of benevolence, a char-ity business, rife enough it is true; but I know nothing more rare, even in this country, than a fit scientific estimate and reverent appreciation of the People – of their measureless wealth of latent power and capacity, their vast, artistic contrasts of lights and shades – with, in America, their entire reliability in emergencies, and a certain breadth of historic grandeur, of peace or war, far surpassing all the vaunted samples of book-heroes, or any *haut ton* coteries, in all the records of the world.

[. . .]

I say the mission of government, henceforth, in civilized lands, is not repression alone, and not authority alone, not even of law, nor by that favor-ite standard of the eminent writer, the rule of the best men, the born heroes and captains of the race (as if such ever, or one time out of a hundred, get into the big places, elective or dynastic) – but higher than the highest arbitrary rule, to train communities through all their grades, beginning with individuals and ending there again, to rule themselves. What Christ appear'd for in the moral-spiritual field for human-kind, namely, that in respect to the absolute soul, there is in the possession of such by each single individual, some-thing so transcendent, so incapable of gradations (like life), that, to that extent, it places all beings on a common level, utterly regardless of the distinc-tions of intellect, virtue, station, or any height or lowliness whatever – is tallied in like manner, in this other field, by democracy's rule that men, the nation, as a common aggregate of living identities, affording in each a separate and complete subject for freedom, worldly thrift and happiness, and for a fair chance for growth, and for protection in citizenship, etc., must, to the political extent of the suffrage or vote, if no further, be placed, in each and in the whole, on one broad, primary, universal, common platform.

The purpose is not altogether direct; perhaps it is more indirect. For it is not that democracy is of exhaustive account in itself. Perhaps, indeed, it is (like Nature), of no account in itself. It is that, as we see, it is the best, perhaps only, fit and full means, formulater, general caller-forth, trainer, for the million, not for grand material personalities only, but for immortal souls. To be a voter with the rest is not so much; and this, like every insti-tute, will have its imperfections. But to become an enfranchised man, and now, impediments re-moved, to stand and start without humiliation, and equal with the rest; to commence, or have the road clear'd to commence, the grand experiment of development, whose end (perhaps requiring several generations), may be the forming of a full-grown man or woman – that *is* something. To ballast the State is also secured, and in our times is to be secured, in no other way.

We do not (at any rate I do not), put it either on the ground that the People, the masses, even the best of them, are, in their latent or exhibited qualities, essentially sensible and good – nor on the ground of their rights; but that good or bad, rights or no rights, the democratic formula is the only safe and preservative one for coming times. We endow the masses with the suffrage for their own sake, no doubt; then, perhaps still more, from another point of view, for community's sake. Leaving the rest to the sentimentalists, we present freedom as sufficient in its scientific aspect, cold as ice, reasoning, deductive, clear and passionless as crystal.

Democracy too is law, and of the strictest, amplest kind. Many suppose (and often in its own ranks the error), that it means a throwing aside of law, and running riot. But, briefly, it is the superior law, not alone that of physical force, the body, which, adding to, it supersedes with that of the spirit. Law is the unshakable order of the universe forever; and the law over all, and law of laws, is the law of successions; that of the superior law, in time, gradually supplanting and overwhelming the inferior one. (While, for myself, I would cheerfully agree – first covenanting that the formative tendencies shall be administered in favor, or at least not against it, and that this reservation be closely construed – that until the individual or community show due signs, or be so minor and fractional as not to endanger the State, the condition of authoritative tutelage may continue, and self-government must abide its time.) Nor is the æsthetic point, always an important one, without fascination for highest aiming souls. The common ambition strains for elevations, to become some privileged exclusive. The master sees greatness and health in being part of the mass; nothing will do as well as common ground. Would you have in yourself the divine, vast, general law? Then merge yourself in it.

And, topping democracy, this most alluring record, that it alone can bind, and ever seeks to bind, all nations, all men, of however various and distant lands, into a brotherhood, a family. It is the old, yet ever-modern dream of earth, out of her eldest and her youngest, her fond philosophers and poets. Not that half only, individualism, which isolates. There is another half, which is adhesiveness or love, that fuses, ties, and aggregates, making the races comrades, and fraternizing all. Both are to be vitalized by religion (sole worthiest elevator of man or State), breathing into the proud, material tissues, the breath of life. For I say at the core of democracy, finally, is the religious element. All the religions, old and new, are there. Nor may the scheme step forth, clothed in resplendent beauty and command, till these, bearing the best, the latest fruit, the spiritual, shall fully appear.

A portion of our pages we might indite with reference toward Europe, especially the British part of it, more than our own land, perhaps not absolutely needed for the home reader. But the whole question hangs together, and fastens and links all peoples. The liberalist of today has this advantage over antique or medieval times, that his doctrine seeks not only to individualize but to universalize. The great word Solidarity has arisen. Of all dangers to a nation, as things exist in our day, there can be no greater one than having certain portions of the people set off from the rest by a line drawn – they not privileged as others, but degraded, humiliated, made of no account. Much quackery teems, of course, even on democracy's side, yet does not really affect the orbic quality of the matter. To work in, if we may so term it, and justify God, His divine aggregate, the People (or, the veritable horned and sharp-tailed Devil, *His* aggregate, if there be who convulsively insist upon it) – this, I say, is what democracy is for; and this is what our America means, and is doing – may I not say, has done? If not, she means nothing more, and does nothing more, than any other land. And, as by virtue of its cosmical, antiseptic power, Nature's stomach is fully strong enough not only to digest the morbific matter always presented, not to be turn'd aside, and perhaps, indeed, intuitively gravitating thither – but even to change such contributions into nutriment for highest use and life – so American democracy's. That is the lesson we, these days, send over to European lands by every western breeze.

And truly, whatever may be said, in the way of abstract argument, for or against the theory of a wider democratizing of institutions in any civilized country, much trouble might well be saved to all European lands by recognizing this palpable fact (for a palpable fact it is), that some form of such democratizing is about the only resource now left. *That*, or chronic dissatisfaction continued, mutterings which grow annually louder and louder, till, in due course, and pretty swiftly in most cases, the inevitable crisis, dynastic ruin. Anything worthy to be call'd statesmanship in the Old World, I should say, among the advanced students, adepts, or men of any brains, does not debate today whether to hold on, attempting to lean back and monarchize, or to look forward and democratize – but *how*, and in what degree and part, most prudently to democratize.

The eager and often inconsiderate appeals of reformers and revolutionists are indispensable, to counterbalance the inertness and fossilism making so large a part of human institutions. The latter will always take care of themselves – the danger being that they rapidly tend to ossify us. The former is to be treated with indulgence, and even with respect. As circulation to air, so is agitation and a plentiful degree of speculative license to political and moral sanity. Indirectly, but surely, goodness, virtue, law (of the very best), follow freedom. These, to democracy, are what the keel is to the ship, or saltness to the ocean.

The true gravitation-hold of liberalism in the United States will be a more universal ownership of property, general homesteads, general comfort – a vast, intertwining reticulation of wealth. As the human frame, or, indeed, any object in this manifold universe, is best kept together by the simple miracle of its own cohesion, and the necessity, exercise, and profit thereof, so a great and varied nationality, occupying millions of square miles, were firmest held and knit by the principle of the safety and endurance of the aggregate of its middling property owners. So that, from another point of view, ungracious as it may sound, and a paradox after what we have been saying, democracy looks with suspicion, ill-satisfied eye upon the very poor, the ignorant, and on those out of business. She asks for men and women with occupations, well-off, owners of houses and acres, and with cash in the bank – and with some cravings for literature, too; and must have them, and hastens to make them. Luckily, the seed is already well sown, and has taken ineradicable root.

[...]

What, however, do we more definitely mean by New World literature? Are we not doing well enough here already? Are not the United States this day busily using, working, more printer's type, more presses, than any other country? uttering and absorbing more publications than any other? Do not our publishers fatten quicker and deeper? (helping themselves, under shelter of a delusive and sneaking law, or rather absence of law, to most of their forage, poetical, pictorial, historical, romantic, even comic, without money and without price – and fiercely resisting the timidest proposal to pay for it). Many will come under this delusion – but my purpose is to dispel it. I say that a nation may hold and circulate rivers and oceans of very readable print, journals, magazines, novels, library books, "poetry," etc. – such as the States today possess and circulate – of unquestionable aid and value – hundreds of new volumes annually composed and brought out here, respectable enough, indeed unsurpass'd in smartness and erudition – with further hundreds, or rather millions (as by free forage or theft aforementioned), also thrown into the market – and yet, all the while, the said nation, land, strictly speaking, may possess no literature at all.

Repeating our inquiry, what, then, do we mean by real literature? especially the democratic literature of the future? Hard questions to meet. The clues are inferential, and turn us to the past. At best, we can only offer suggestions, comparisons, circuits.

It must still be reiterated, as, for the purpose of these memoranda, the deep lesson of history and time, that all else in the contributions of a nation or age, through its politics, materials, heroic personalities, military *éclat*, etc., remains crude, and defers, in any close and thoroughgoing estimate, until vitalized by national, original archetypes in literature. They only put the nation in form, finally tell anything – prove, complete anything – perpetuate anything. Without doubt, some of the richest and most powerful and populous communities of the antique world, and some of the grandest personalities and events, have, to after and present times, left themselves entirely unbequeath'd. Doubtless, greater than any that have come down to us, were among those lands, heroisms, persons, that have not come down to us at all, even by name, date, or location. Others have arrived safely, as from voyages over wide, century-stretching seas. The little ships, the miracles that have buoy'd them, and by incredible chances safely convey'd them (or the best of them, their meaning and essence) over long wastes, darkness, lethargy, ignorance, etc., have been a few inscriptions – a few immortal compositions, small in size, yet compassing what measureless values of reminiscence, contemporary portraitures, manners, idioms, and beliefs, with deepest inference, hint, and thought, to tie and touch forever the old, new body, and the old, new soul! These! and still these! bearing the freight so dear – dearer than pride – dearer than love. All the best experience of humanity, folded, saved, freighted to us here. Some of these tiny ships we call Old and New Testament, Homer, Eschylus, Plato, Juvenal, etc. Precious minims! I think, if we were forced to choose, rather than have you, and the likes of you, and what belongs to, and has grown of you, blotted out and gone, we could better afford, appalling as that would be, to lose all actual ships, this day fasten'd by wharf, or floating on wave, and see them, with all their cargoes, scuttled and sent to the bottom.

Gathered by geniuses of city, race or age, and put by them in highest of art's forms, namely, the literary form, the peculiar combinations and the out-shows of that city, age, or race, its particular modes of the universal attributes and passions, its faiths, heroes, lovers and gods, wars, traditions, struggles, crimes, emotions, joys (or the subtle spirit of these), having been pass'd on to us to illumine our own selfhood, and its experiences – what they supply, indispensable and highest, if taken away, nothing else in all the world's boundless storehouses could make up to us, or ever again return.

For us, along the great highways of time, those monuments stand – those forms of majesty and beauty. For us those beacons burn through all the nights. Unknown Egyptians, graving hieroglyphs; Hindus, with hymn and apothegm and endless epic; Hebrew prophet, with spirituality, as in flashes of lightning, conscience like red-hot iron, plaintive songs and screams of vengeance for tyrannies and enslavement; Christ, with bent head, brooding love and peace, like a dove; Greek, creating eternal shapes of physical and æsthetic proportion; Roman, lord of satire, the sword, and the codex – of the figures, some far off and veil'd, others nearer and visible; Dante, stalking with lean form, nothing but fiber, not a grain of superfluous flesh; Angelo, and the great painters, architects, musicians; rich Shakspere, luxuriant as the sun, artist and singer of feudalism in its sunset, with all the gorgeous colors, owner thereof, and using them at will; and so to such as German Kant and Hegel, where they, though near us, leaping over the ages, sit again, impassive, imperturbable, like the Egyptian gods. Of these, and the like of these, is it too much, indeed, to return to our favorite figure and view them as orbs and systems of orbs, moving in free paths in the spaces of that other heaven, the kosmic intellect, the soul?

Ye powerful and resplendent ones! ye were, in your atmospheres, grown not for America, but rather for her foes, the feudal and the old – while our genius is democratic and modern. Yet could ye, indeed, but breathe your breath of life into our New World's nostrils – not to enslave us, as now, but, for our needs, to breed a spirit like your own – perhaps (dare we to say it?) to dominate, even destroy, what you yourselves have left! On your plane, and no less, but even higher and wider, must we mete and measure for today and here. I demand races of orbic bards, with unconditional, uncompromising sway. Come forth, sweet democratic despots of the west!

By points like these we, in reflection, token what we mean by any land's or people's genuine literature. And thus compared and tested, judging amid the influence of loftiest products only, what do our current copious fields of print, covering in manifold forms, the United States, better, for an analogy, present, than, as in certain regions of the sea, those spreading, undulating masses of squid, through which the whale swimming, with head half out, feeds?

Not but that doubtless our current so-called literature (like an endless supply of small coin) performs a certain service, and maybe too, the service needed for the time (the preparation-service, as children learn to spell). Everybody reads, and truly nearly everybody writes, either books, or for the magazines or journals. The matter has magnitude, too, after a sort. But is it really advancing? or, has it advanced for a long while? There is something impressive about the huge editions of the dailies and weeklies, the mountain-stacks of white paper piled in the press-vaults, and the proud, crashing, ten-cylinder presses, which I can stand and watch any time by the half hour. Then (though the States in the field of imagination present not a single first-class work, not a single great literatus), the main objects, to amuse, to titillate, to pass away time, to circulate the news, and rumors of news, to rhyme, and read rhyme, are yet attain'd, and on a scale of infinity. Today, in books, in the rivalry of writers, especially novelists, success (so-called) is for him or her who strikes the mean flat average, the sensational appetite for stimulus, incident, persiflage, etc., and depicts, to the common caliber, sensual, exterior life. To such, or the luckiest of them, as we see, the audiences are limitless and profitable; but they cease presently. While this day, or any day, to workmen portraying interior or spiritual life, the audiences were limited, and often laggard – but they last forever.

Compared with the past, our modern science soars, and our journals serve – but ideal and even ordinary romantic literature, does not, I think, substantially advance. Behold the prolific brood of the contemporary novel, magazine tale, theatre play, etc. The same endless thread of tangled and superlative love story, inherited, apparently from the Amadises and Palmerins of the 13th, 14th, and 15th centuries over there in Europe. The costumes and associations brought down to date, the seasoning hotter and more varied, the dragons and ogres left out – but the *thing*, I should say, has not advanced – is just as sensational, just as strain'd – remains about the same, nor more, nor less.

What is the reason our time, our lands, that we see no fresh local courage, sanity, of our own – the Mississippi, stalwart Western men, real mental and physical facts, Southerners, etc., in the body of our literature? especially the poetic part of it. But always, instead, a parcel of dandies and ennuyees, dapper little gentlemen from abroad, who flood us with their thin sentiment of parlors, parasols, piano songs, tinkling rhymes, the five-hundredth importation – or whimpering and crying about something, chasing one aborted conceit after another, and forever occupied in dyspeptic amours with dyspeptic women. While, current and novel, the grandest events and revolutions, and stormiest passions of history, are crossing today with unparalleled rapidity and magnificence over the stages of our own and all the continents, offering new materials, opening new vistas, with largest needs, inviting the daring launching forth of conceptions in literature, inspired by them, soaring in highest regions, serving art in its highest (which is only the other name for serving God, and serving humanity), where is the man of letters, where is the book, with any nobler aim than to follow in the old track, repeat what has been said before – and, as its utmost triumph, sell well, and be erudite or elegant?

Mark the roads, the processes, through which these States have arrived, standing easy, henceforth ever-equal, ever-compact, in their range today. European adventures? the most antique? Asiatic or African? old history – miracles – romances? Rather, our own unquestion'd facts. They hasten, incredible, blazing bright as fire. From the deeds and days of Columbus down to the present, and including the present – and especially the late Secession War – when I con them, I feel, every leaf, like stopping to see if I have not made a mistake, and fall'n on the splendid figments of some dream. But it is no dream. We stand, live, move, in the huge flow of our age's materialism – in its spirituality. We have founded for us the most positive of lands. The founders have pass'd to other spheres – but what are these terrible duties they have left us?

Their policies the United States have, in my opinion, with all their faults, already substantially establish'd, for good, on their own native, sound, long-vista'd principles, never to be overturn'd, offering a sure basis for all the rest. With that, their future religious forms, sociology, literature, teachers, schools, costumes, etc., are of course to make a compact whole, uniform, on tallying principles. For how can we remain, divided, contradicting ourselves this way? I say we can only attain harmony and stability by consulting ensemble and the ethic purports, and faithfully building upon them. For the New World, indeed, after two grand stages of preparation-strata, I perceive that now a third stage, being ready for (and without which the other two were useless), with unmistakable signs appears. The First stage was the planning and putting on record the political foundation rights of immense masses of people – indeed all people – in the organization of republican National, State, and municipal governments, all constructed with reference to each, and each to all. This is the American programme, not for classes, but for universal man, and is embodied in the compacts of the Declaration of Independence, and, as it began and has now grown, with its amendments, the Federal Constitution – and in the State governments, with all their interiors, and with general suffrage; those having the sense not only of what is in themselves, but that their certain several things started, planted, hundreds of others in the same direction duly arise and follow. The Second stage relates to material prosperity, wealth, produce, laborsaving machines, iron, cotton, local, State, and continental railways, intercommunication and trade with all lands, steamships, mining, general employment, organization of great cities, cheap appliances for comfort, numberless technical schools, books, newspapers, a currency for money circulation, etc. The Third stage, rising out of the previous ones, to make them and all illustrious, I, now, for one, promulge, announcing a native expression-spirit, getting into form, adult, and through mentality, for these

States, self-contain'd, different from others, more expansive, more rich and free, to be evidenced by original authors and poets to come, by American personalities, plenty of them, male and female, traversing the States, none excepted – and by native superber tableaux and growths of language, songs, operas, orations, lectures, architecture – and by a sublime and serious Religious Democracy sternly taking command, dissolving the old, sloughing off surfaces, and from its own interior and vital principles, reconstructing, democratizing society.

For America, type of progress, and of essential faith in man, above all his errors and wickedness – few suspect how deep, how deep it really strikes. The world evidently supposes, and we have evidently supposed so too, that the States are merely to achieve the equal franchise, an elective government – to inaugurate the respectability of labor, and become a nation of practical operatives, law-abiding, orderly, and well-off. Yes, those are indeed parts of the task of America; but they not only do not exhaust the progressive conception, but rather arise, teeming with it, as the mediums of deeper, higher progress. Daughter of a physical revolution – mother of the true revolutions, which are of the interior life, and of the arts. For so long as the spirit is not changed, any change of appearance is of no avail.

The old men, I remember as a boy, were always talking of American independence. What is independence? Freedom from all laws or bonds except those of one's own being, control'd by the universal ones. To lands, to man, to woman, what is there at last to each, but the inherent soul, nativity, idiosyncrasy, free, highest poised, soaring its own flight, following out itself?

At present, these States, in their theology and social standards (of greater importance than their political institutions) are entirely held possession of by foreign lands. We see the sons and daughters of the New World, ignorant of its genius, not yet inaugurating the native, the universal, and the near still importing the distant, the partial, and the dead. We see London, Paris, Italy – not original, superb, as where they belong – but second-hand here, where they do not belong. We see the shreds of Hebrews, Romans, Greeks; but where, on her own soil, do we see, in any faithful, highest, proud expression, America herself? I sometimes question whether she has a corner in her own house.

Not but that in one sense, and a very grand one, good theology, good art, or good literature, has certain features shared in common. The combination fraternizes, ties the races – is, in many particulars, under laws applicable indifferently to all, irrespective of climate or date, and, from whatever source, appeals to emotions, pride, love, spirituality, common to human-kind. Nevertheless, they touch a man closest (perhaps only actually touch him), even in these, in their expression through autochthonic lights and shades, flavors, fondnesses, aversions, specific incidents, illustrations, out of his own nationality, geography, surroundings, antecedents, etc. The spirit and the form are one, and depend far more on association, identity, and place, than is supposed. Subtly interwoven with the materiality and personality of a land, a race – Teuton, Turk, Californian, or what not – there is always something – I can hardly tell what it is – history but describes the results of it – it is the same as the untellable look of some human faces. Nature, too, in his stolid forms, is full of it – but to most it is there a secret. This something is rooted in the invisible roots, the profoundest meanings of that place, race, or nationality; and to absorb and again effuse it, uttering words and products as from its midst, and carrying it into highest regions, is the work, or a main part of the work, of any country's true author, poet, historian, lecturer, and perhaps even priest and philosoph. Here, and here only, are the foundations for our really valuable and permanent verse, drama, etc.

But at present (judged by any higher scale than that which finds the chief ends of existence to be to feverishly make money during one half of it, and by some "amusement," or perhaps foreign travel, flippantly kill time, the other half), and considered with reference to purposes of patriotism, health, a noble personality, religion, and the democratic adjustments, all these swarms of poems, literary magazines, dramatic plays, resultant so far from American intellect, and the formation of our best ideas, are useless and a mockery. They strengthen and nourish no one, express nothing characteristic, give decision and purpose to no one, and suffice only the lowest level of vacant minds.

Of what is called the drama, or dramatic presentation in the United States, as now put forth at the theatres, I should say it deserves to be treated with the same gravity, and on a par with the questions of ornamental confectionery at public dinners, or the arrangement of curtains and hangings in a ballroom – nor more, nor less. Of the other, I will not insult the reader's intelligence (once really entering into the atmosphere of these Vistas), by supposing it necessary to show, in detail, why the copious dribble, either of our little or well-known rhymesters, does not fulfill, in any respect, the needs and august occasions of this land. America demands a poetry that is bold, modern, and all-surrounding and kosmical, as she is herself. It must in no respect ignore science or the modern, but inspire itself with science and the modern. It must bend its vision toward the future, more than the past. Like America, it must extricate itself from even the greatest models of the past, and, while courteous to them, must have entire faith in itself, and the products of its own democratic spirit only. Like her, it must place in the van, and hold up at all hazards, the banner of the divine pride of man in himself (the radical foundation of the new religion). Long enough have the People been listening to poems in which common humanity, deferential, bends low, humiliated, acknowledging superiors. But America listens to no such poems. Erect, inflated, and fully self-esteeming be the chant; and then America will listen with pleased ears.

Nor may the genuine gold, the gems, when brought to light at last, be probably usher'd forth from any of the quarters currently counted on. Today, doubtless, the infant genius of American poetic expression (eluding those highly refined imported and gilt-edged themes, and sentimental and butterfly flights, pleasant to orthodox publishers – causing tender spasms in the coteries, and warranted not to chafe the sensitive cuticle of the most exquisitely artificial gossamer delicacy), lies sleeping far away, happily unrecognized and uninjur'd by the coteries, the art-writers, the talkers and critics of the saloons, or the lecturers in the colleges – lies sleeping, aside, unrecking itself, in some western idiom, or native Michigan or Tennessee repartee, or stump speech – or in Kentucky or Georgia, or the Carolinas – or in some slang or local song or allusion of the Manhattan, Boston, Philadelphia, or Baltimore mechanic – or up in the Maine woods – or off in the hut of the California miner, or crossing the Rocky Mountains, or along the Pacific railroad – or on the breasts of the young farmers of the north-west, or Canada, or boatmen of the lakes. Rude and coarse nursing beds, these; but only from such beginnings and stocks, indigenous here, may haply arrive, be grafted, and sprout in time, flowers of genuine American aroma, and fruits truly and fully our own.

I say it were a standing disgrace to these States – I say it were a disgrace to any nation, distinguish'd above others by the variety and vastness of its territories, its materials, its inventive activity, and the splendid practicality of its people, not to rise and soar above others, also in its original styles in literature and art, and its own supply of intellectual and æsthetic masterpieces, archetypal, and consistent with itself. I know not a land except ours that has not, to some extent, however small, made its title clear. The Scotch have their born ballads, subtly expressing their past and present, and expressing character. The Irish have theirs. England, Italy, France, Spain, theirs. What has America? With exhaustless mines of the richest ore of epic, lyric, tale, tune, picture, etc., in the Four Years' War; with, indeed, I sometimes think, the richest masses of material ever afforded a nation, more variegated, and on a larger scale – the first sign of proportionate, native, imaginative Soul, and first-class works to match, is (I cannot too often repeat), so far wanting.

Long ere the second centennial arrives, there will be some forty to fifty great States, among them Canada and Cuba. When the present century closes, our population will be sixty or seventy millions. The Pacific will be ours, and the Atlantic mainly ours. There will be daily electric communication with every part of the globe. What an age! What a land! Where, elsewhere, one so great? The individuality of one nation must then, as always, lead the world. Can there be any doubt who the leader ought to be? Bear in mind, though, that nothing less than the mightiest original non-subordinated SOUL has ever really, gloriously led, or ever can lead. (This Soul – its other name, in these Vistas, is LITERATURE.)

In fond fancy leaping those hundred years ahead let us survey America's works, poems, philosophies, fulfilling prophecies, and giving form and decision to best ideals. Much that is now undream'd of, we might then perhaps see establish'd, luxuriantly cropping forth, richness, vigor of letters and of artistic expression, in whose products character will be a main requirement, and not merely erudition or elegance.

Intense and loving comradeship, the personal and passionate attachment of man to man – which, hard to define, underlies the lessons and ideals of the profound saviors of every land and age, and which seems to promise, when thoroughly develop'd, cultivated, and recognized in manners and literature, the most substantial hope and safety of the future of these States, will then be fully express'd.

A strong-fibered joyousness and faith, and the sense of health *al fresco*, may well enter into the preparation of future noble American authorship. Part of the test of a great literatus shall be the absence in him of the idea of the covert, the lurid, the maleficent, the devil, the grim estimates inherited from the Puritans, hell, natural depravity, and the like. The great literatus will be known, among the rest, by his cheerful simplicity, his adherence to natural standards, his limitless faith in God, his reverence, and by the absence in him of doubt, ennui, burlesque, persiflage, or any strained and temporary fashion.

Nor must I fail, again and yet again, to clinch, reiterate more plainly still (O that indeed such survey as we fancy may show in time this part completed also!) the lofty aim, surely the proudest and the purest, in whose service the future literatus, of whatever field, may gladly labor. As we have intimated, offsetting the material civilization of our race, our nationality, its wealth, territories, factories, population, products, trade, and military and naval strength, and breathing breath of life into all these, and more, must be its moral civilization – the formulation, expression, aidancy whereof, is the very highest height of literature. The climax of this loftiest range of civilization, rising above all the gorgeous shows and results of wealth, intellect, power, and art, as such – above even theology and religious fervor – is to be its development, from the eternal bases, and the fit expression, of absolute Conscience, moral soundness, Justice. Even in religious fervor there is a touch of animal heat. But moral conscientiousness, crystalline, without flaw, not Godlike only, entirely human, awes and enchants forever. Great is emotional love, even in the order of the rational universe. But, if we must make gradations, I am clear there is something greater. Power, love, veneration, products, genius, æsthetics, tried by subtlest comparisons, analyses, and in serenest moods, somewhere fail, somehow become vain. Then noiseless, with flowing steps, the lord, the sun, the last ideal comes. By the names right, justice, truth, we suggest, but do not describe it. To the world of men it remains a dream, an idea as they call it. But no dream is it to the wise – but the proudest, almost only solid lasting thing of all. Its analogy in the material universe is what holds together this world, and every object upon it, and carries its dynamics on forever sure and safe. Its lack, and the persistent shirking of it, as in life, sociology, literature, politics, business, and even sermonizing these times, or any times, still leaves the abysm, the mortal flaw and smutch, mocking civilization today, with all its unquestion'd triumphs, and all the civilization so far known.

Present literature, while magnificently fulfilling certain popular demands, with plenteous knowledge and verbal smartness, is profoundly sophisticated, insane, and its very joy is morbid. It needs tally and express Nature, and the spirit of Nature, and to know and obey the standards. I say the question of Nature, largely considered, involves the questions of the æsthetic, the emotional, and the religious – and involves happiness. A fitly born and bred race, growing up in right conditions of outdoor as much as indoor harmony, activity and development, would probably, from and in those conditions, find it enough merely to *live* – and would, in their relations to the sky, air, water, trees, etc., and to the countless common shows, and in the fact of life itself, discover and achieve happiness – with Being suffused night and day by wholesome extasy, surpassing all the pleasures that wealth, amusement, and even gratified intellect, erudition, or the sense of art, can give.

In the prophetic literature of these States (the reader of my speculations will miss their principal stress unless he allows well for the point that a new Literature, perhaps a new Metaphysics, certainly a new Poetry, are to be, in my opinion, the only sure and worthy supports and expressions of the American Democracy), Nature, true Nature, and the true idea of Nature, long absent, must, above all, become fully restored, enlarged, and must furnish the pervading atmosphere to poems, and the test of all high literary and æsthetic compositions. I do not mean the smooth walks, trimm'd hedges, poseys and nightingales of the English poets, but the whole orb, with its geologic history, the kosmos, carrying fire and snow, that rolls through the illimitable areas, light as a feather, though weighing billions of tons. Furthermore, as by what we now partially call Nature is intended, at most, only what is entertainable by the physical conscience, the sense of matter, and of good animal health – on these it must be distinctly accumulated, incorporated, that man, comprehending these, has, in towering superaddition, the moral and spiritual consciences, indicating his destination beyond the ostensible, the mortal.

To the heights of such estimate of Nature indeed ascending, we proceed to make observations for our Vistas, breathing rarest air. What is I believe called Idealism seems to me to suggest (guarding against extravagance, and ever modified even by its opposite) the course of inquiry and desert of favor for our New World metaphysics, their foundation of and in literature, giving hue to all.

[...]

Our lands, embracing so much (embracing indeed the whole, rejecting none), hold in their breast that flame also, capable of consuming themselves, consuming us all. Short as the span of our national life has been, already have death and downfall crowded close upon us – and will again crowd close, no doubt, even if warded off. Ages to come may never know, but I know, how narrowly during the late Secession War – and more than once, and more than twice or thrice – our Nationality (wherein bound up, as in a ship in a storm, depended, and yet depend, all our best life, all hope, all value), just grazed, just by a hair escaped destruction. Alas! to think of them! the agony and bloody sweat of certain of those hours! those cruel, sharp, suspended crises!

Even today, amid these whirls, incredible flippancy, and blind fury of parties, infidelity, entire lack of first-class captains and leaders, added to the plentiful meanness and vulgarity of the ostensible masses – that problem, the labor question, beginning to open like a yawning gulf, rapidly widening every year – what prospect have we? We sail a dangerous sea of seething currents, cross and undercurrents, vortices – all so dark, untried – and whither shall we turn? It seems as if the Almighty had spread before this nation charts of imperial destinies, dazzling as the sun, yet with many a deep intestine difficulty, and human aggregate of cankerous imperfection – saying, lo! the roads, the only plans of development, long and varied with all terrible balks and ebullitions. You said in your soul, I will be empire of empires, overshadowing all else, past and present, putting the history of Old-World dynasties, conquests behind me, as of no account – making a new history, a history of democracy, making old history a dwarf – I alone inaugurating largeness, culminating time. If these, O lands of America, are indeed the prizes, the determination of your soul, be it so. But behold the cost, and already specimens of the cost. Thought you greatness was to ripen for you like a pear? If you would have greatness, know that you must conquer it through ages, centuries – must pay for it with a proportionate price. For you too, as for all lands, the struggle, the traitor, the wily person in office, scrofulous wealth, the surfeit of prosperity, the demonism of greed, the hell of passion, the decay of faith, the long postponement, the fossil-like lethargy, the ceaseless need of revolutions, prophets, thunderstorms, deaths, births, new projections and invigorations of ideas and men.

Yet I have dream'd, merged in that hidden-tangled problem of our fate, whose long unraveling stretches mysteriously through time – dream'd out, portray'd, hinted already – a little or a larger band – a band of brave and true, unprecedented yet – arm'd and equipt at every point – the members separated, it may be, by different dates and States, or south, or north, or east, or west – Pacific, Atlantic, Southern, Canadian – a year, a century here, and other centuries there – but always one, compact in soul, conscience-conserving, God-inculcating, inspired achievers, not only in literature, the greatest art, but achievers in all art – a new, undying order, dynasty, from age to age transmitted – a band, a class, at least as fit to cope with current years, our dangers, needs, as those who, for their times, so long, so well, in armor or in cowl, upheld and made illustrious, that far-back feudal, priestly world. To offset chivalry, indeed, those vanish'd countless knights, old altars, abbeys, priests, ages and strings of ages, a knightlier and more sacred cause today demands, and shall supply, in a New World, to larger, grander work, more than the counterpart and tally of them.

Arrived now, definitely, at an apex for these Vistas, I confess that the promulgation and belief in such a class or institution – a new and greater literatus order – its possibility (nay certainty), underlies these entire speculations – and that the rest, the other parts, as superstructures, are all founded upon it. It really seems to me the condition, not only of our future national and democratic development, but of our perpetuation. In the highly artificial and materialistic bases of modern civilization, with the corresponding arrangements and methods of living, the force-infusion of intellect alone, the depraving influences of riches just as much as poverty, the absence of all high ideals in character – with the long series of tendencies, shapings, which few are strong enough to resist, and which now seem, with steam-engine speed, to be everywhere turning out the generations of humanity like uniform iron castings – all of which, as compared with the feudal ages, we can yet do nothing better than accept, make the best of, and even welcome, upon the whole, for their oceanic practical grandeur, and their restless wholesale kneading of the masses – I say of all this tremendous and dominant play of solely materialistic bearings upon current life in the United States, with the results as already seen, accumulating, and reaching far into the future, that they must either be confronted and met by at least an equally subtle and tremendous force-infusion for purposes of spiritualization, for the pure conscience, for genuine æsthetics, and for absolute and primal manliness and womanliness – or else our modern civilization, with all its improvements, is in vain, and we are on the road to a destiny, a status, equivalent, in its real world, to that of the fabled damned.

Prospecting thus the coming unsped days, and that new order in them – marking the endless train of exercise, development, unwind, in nation as in man, which life is for – we see, fore-indicated, amid these prospects and hopes, new law-forces of spoken and written language – not merely the pedagogue-forms, correct, regular, familiar with precedents, made for matters of outside propriety, fine words, thoughts definitely told out – but a language fann'd by the breath of Nature, which leaps overhead, cares mostly for impetus and effects, and for what it plants and invigorates to grow – tallies life and character, and seldomer tells a thing than suggests or necessitates it. In fact, a new theory of literary composition for imaginative works of the very first class, and especially for highest poems, is the sole course open to these States. Books are to be call'd for, and supplied, on the assumption that the process of reading is not a half-sleep, but, in highest sense, an exercise, a gymnast's struggle; that the reader is to do something for himself, must be on the alert, must himself or herself construct indeed the poem, argument, history, metaphysical essay – the text furnishing the hints, the clue, the start or framework. Not the book needs so much to be the complete thing, but the reader of the book does. That were to make a nation of supple and athletic minds, well-train'd, intuitive, used to depend on themselves, and not on a few coteries of writers.

Investigating here, we see, not that it is a little thing we have, in having the bequeath'd libraries, countless shelves of volumes, records, etc.; yet how serious the danger, depending entirely on them, of the bloodless vein, the nerveless arm, the false application, at second or third hand. We see that the real interest of this people of ours in the theology, history, poetry, politics, and personal models of the past (the British islands, for instance, and indeed all the past), is not necessarily to mold ourselves or our literature upon them, but to attain fuller, more definite comparisons, warnings, and the insight to ourselves, our own present, and our own far grander, different, future history, religion, social customs, etc. We see that almost everything that has been written, sung, or stated, of old, with reference to humanity under the feudal and oriental institutes, religions, and for other lands, needs to be rewritten, resung, restated, in terms consistent with the institution of these States, and to come in range and obedient uniformity with them.

We see, as in the universes of the material kosmos, after meteorological, vegetable, and animal cycles, man at last arises, born through them, to prove them, concentrate them, to turn upon them with wonder and love – to command them, adorn them, and carry them upward into superior realms – so, out of the series of the preceding social and political universes, now arise these States. We see that while many were supposing things established and completed, really the grandest things always remain; and discover that the work of the New World is not ended, but only fairly begun.

We see our land, America, her literature, æsthetics, etc., as, substantially, the getting in form, or effusement and statement, of deepest basic elements and loftiest final meanings, of history and man – and the portrayal (under the eternal laws and conditions of beauty) of our own physiognomy, the subjective tie and expression of the objective, as from our own combination, continuation, and points of view – and the deposit and record of the national mentality, character, appeals, heroism, wars, and even liberties – where these, and all, culminate in native literary and artistic formulation, to be perpetuated; and not having which native, first-class formulation, she will flounder about, and her other, however imposing, eminent greatness, prove merely a passing gleam; but truly having which, she will understand herself, live nobly, nobly contribute, emanate, and, swinging, poised safely on herself, illumin'd and illuming, become a full-form'd world, and divine Mother not only of material but spiritual worlds, in ceaseless succession through time – the main thing being the average, the bodily, the concrete, the democratic, the popular, on which all the superstructures of the future are to permanently rest.

33

Newer Ideals of Peace

Jane Addams

Introduction

Jane Addams (1860–1934) was born in Cedarville, Illinois, and received a bachelor's degree from nearby Rockford College in 1882. Although well educated and interested in the problems of American society, Addams found that few opportunities existed for women to make a difference in wider society. She attended medical school for a time, but illness forced her to give up her studies. After two extended trips to Europe, in which she studied approaches used by social activists there to address issues of poverty in urban areas, Addams and Ellen Starr founded Hull House on Halsted Street in the center of Chicago's poorest immigrant neighborhood. Here, Addams established a comprehensive social service organization, including education programs, a clinic, a shelter for women and children, a library, a food shelf, and an advocacy organization that worked toward bettering living conditions for the poor. Her efforts in Chicago had an even wider impact, contributing to the passage of laws that established the 40-hour working week, restrictions on child labor, and the juvenile court system. John Dewey and Josiah Royce were regular visitors at Hull House, often giving lectures to the community and participating in classes on social theory and action. Addams's first book, *Democracy and Social Ethics* (1902), helped to establish her as an important theorist in American social philosophy. In 1910 she published her autobiography, *Twenty Years at Hull House*, which illustrated her conception of a democratic

Taken from *Newer Ideals of Peace* (New York: Macmillan, 1907).

community and the connections between theory and practice. In 1915, she became a peace activist, meeting with the European leaders involved in the beginning of the First World War, and founding the Women's International League for Peace and Freedom. For her efforts toward peace, she was co-winner of the Nobel Peace Prize in 1931. The selection included here is from her 1906 volume, *Newer Ideals of Peace*, in which Addams argues that habits of social sympathy can replace habits of violence and war as the foundation for a democratic society.

Introduction

The following pages present the claims of the newer, more aggressive ideals of peace, as over against the older dovelike ideal. These newer ideals are active and dynamic, and it is believed that if their forces were made really operative upon society, they would, in the end, quite as a natural process, do away with war. The older ideals have required fostering and recruiting, and have been held and promulgated on the basis of a creed. Their propaganda has been carried forward during the last century in nearly all civilized countries by a small body of men who have never ceased to cry out against war and its iniquities and who have preached the doctrines of peace along two great lines. The first has been the appeal to the higher imaginative pity, as it is found in the modern, moralized man. This line has been most effectively followed by two Russians, Count Tolstoy in his earlier writings and Verestchagin in his paintings. With his relentless power of reducing all life to personal experience Count Tolstoy drags us through the campaign of the common soldier in its sordidness and meanness and constant sense of perplexity. We see nothing of the glories we have associated with warfare, but learn of it as it appears to the untutored peasant who goes forth at the mandate of his superior to suffer hunger, cold, and death for issues which he does not understand, which, indeed, can have no moral significance to him. Verestchagin covers his canvas with thousands of wretched wounded and neglected dead, with the waste, cruelty, and squalor of war, until he forces us to question whether a moral issue can ever be subserved by such brutal methods.

High and searching as is the preaching of these two great Russians who hold their art of no account save as it serves moral ends, it is still the appeal of dogma, and may be reduced to a command to cease from evil. And when this same line of appeal is presented by less gifted men, it often results in mere sentimentality, totally unenforced by a call to righteousness.

The second line followed by the advocates of peace in all countries has been the appeal to the sense of prudence, and this again has found its ablest exponent in a Russian subject, the economist and banker, Jean de Bloch. He sets forth the cost of warfare with pitiless accuracy, and demonstrates that even the present armed peace is so costly that the burdens of it threaten social revolution in almost every country in Europe. Long before the reader comes to the end of de Bloch's elaborate computation he is ready to cry out on the inanity of the proposition that the only way to secure eternal peace is to waste so much valuable energy and treasure in preparing for war that war becomes impossible. Certainly no theory could be devised which is more cumbersome, more roundabout, more extravagant, than the *reductio ad absurdum* of the peace-secured-by-the-preparation-for-war theory. This appeal to prudence was constantly emphasized at the first Hague Conference and was shortly afterward demonstrated by Great Britain when she went to war in South Africa, where she was fined one hundred million pounds and lost ten thousand lives. The fact that Russia also, and the very Czar who invited the Conference, disregarded the conclusions of the Hague Tribunal makes this line of appeal at least for the moment seem impotent to influence empires which command enormous resources and which lodge the power of expenditure in officials who have nothing to do with accumulating the treasure they vote to expend.

It would, however, be the height of folly for responsible statesmen to ignore the sane methods of international discussion and concession which have been evolved largely as a result of these appeals. The Interparliamentary Union for International Arbitration and the Institute of International Law represent the untiring efforts of the advocates of peace through many years. Nevertheless universal peace, viewed from the point of the World's Sovereignty or of the Counsel of Nations, is discouraging even when stated by the most ardent promoters of the peace society. Here it is quite possible that the mistake is being repeated which the old annalists of history made when they never failed to chronicle the wars and calamities which harassed their contemporaries, although, while the few indulged in fighting, the mass of them peacefully prosecuted their daily toil and followed their own conceptions of kindliness and equity. An English writer[1] has recently bidden us to look at the actual state of affairs existing at the present moment. He says, "Universal and permanent peace may be a vision; but the gradual change whereby war, as a normal state of international relations, has given place to peace as the normal state, is no vision, but an actual process of history palpably forwarded in our own day by the development of international law and of morals, and voluntary arbitration based thereon." He insists that it is the function of international lawyers merely to give coherent expression to the best principles which the common moral sense of civilized Governments recognizes; in other words, that international law should be like primitive law within the nation, a formal expression of custom resting on the sense of a reciprocal restraint which has been found to be necessary for the common good.

Assuming that the two lines of appeal – the one to sensibility and the other to prudence – will persist, and that the international lawyers, in spite of the fact that they have no court before which to plead and no executive to enforce their findings, will continue to formulate into codes the growing moral sense of the nations, the following pages hope not only to make clear the contention that these forces within society are so dynamic and vigorous that the impulses to war seem by comparison cumbersome and mechanical, but also to point out the development of those newer social forces which it is believed will at last prove a "sovereign intervention" by extinguishing the possibility of battle at its very source.

It is difficult to formulate the newer dynamic peace, embodying the later humanism, as over against the old dogmatic peace. The word "non-resistance" is misleading, because it is much too feeble and inadequate. It suggests passivity, the goody-goody attitude of ineffectiveness. The words "overcoming," "substituting," "re-creating," "readjusting moral values," "forming new centres of spiritual energy" carry much more of the meaning implied. For it is not merely the desire for a conscience at rest, for a sense of justice no longer outraged, that would pull us into new paths where there would be no more war nor preparations for war. There are still more strenuous forces at work reaching down to impulses and experiences as primitive and profound as are those of struggle itself. That "ancient kindliness which sat beside the cradle of the race," and which is ever ready to assert itself against ambition and greed and the desire for achievement, is manifesting itself now with un-usual force, and for the first time presents inter-national aspects.

Moralists agree that it is not so much by the teaching of moral theorems that virtue is to be promoted as by the direct expression of social sentiments and by the cultivation of practical habits; that in the progress of society sentiments and opinions have come first, then habits of action and lastly moral codes and institutions. Little is gained by creating the latter prematurely, but much may be accomplished to the utilization of human interests and affections. The Advocates of Peace would find the appeal both to Pity and Prudence totally unnecessary, could they utilize the cosmopolitan interest in human affairs with the resultant social sympathy that at the present moment is developing among all the nations of the earth.

By way of illustration, I may be permitted to cite the London showman who used to exhibit two skulls of Shakespeare – one when he was a youth and went poaching, another when he was a man and wrote plays. There was such a striking differ-ence between the roystering boy indulging in illicit sport and the mature man who peopled the London stage with all the world, that the showman grew confused and considered two separate acts of

creation less improbable than that such an amazing change should have taken place. We can easily imagine the gifted youth in the little group of rustics at Stratford-on-Avon finding no adequate outlet for his powers save in a series of break-neck adventures. His only alternative was to sit by the fire with the village cronies, drinking ale so long as his shillings held out. But if we follow him up to London, through all the charm and wonder of the stage which represented his unfolding mind, if we can imagine his delight as he gradually gained the freedom, not only of that big town, but of the human city as well, we can easily see that illicit sport could no longer attract him. To have told the great dramatist the night Hamlet first stepped upon the boards that it was a wicked thing to poach, to have cautioned him that he must con-sider the cost of preserving the forest and of raising the deer, or to have made an appeal to his pity on behalf of the wounded creatures, would have been the height of folly, because totally unnecessary. All desire, almost all memory of those days, had dropped from him, through his absorption in the great and exciting drama of life. His effort to understand it, to portray it, had utilized and drained his every power. It is equally true of our contemporaries, as it was of the great play-wright, that the attainment of this all-absorbing passion for multiform life, with the desire to understand its mysteries and to free its capacities, is gradually displacing the juvenile propensities to warfare.

From this standpoint the advocates of the newer Ideals of Peace would have little to do but to insist that the social point of view be kept paramount, realizing at the same time that the social senti-ments are as blind as the egoistic sentiments and must be enlightened, disciplined and directed by the fullest knowledge. The modern students of human morality have told us that primitive man, by the very necessities of his hard struggle for life, came at last to identify his own existence with that of his tribe. Tribal life then made room within itself for the development of that compassion which is the first step towards sens-ibility and higher moral sentiment. If we accept this statement then we must assume that the new social morality, which we so sadly need, will of necessity have its origin in the social affections – we must search in the dim borderland between compassion and morality for the beginnings of that cosmopolitan affection, as it is prematurely called.

The life of the tribal man inevitably divided into two sets of actions, which appeared under two different ethical aspects: the relation within the tribe and the relation with outsiders, the double conception of morality maintaining itself until now. But the tribal law differed no more widely from inter-tribal law than our common law does from our international law. Until society manages to combine the two we shall make no headway toward the Newer Ideals of Peace.

If we would institute an intelligent search for the social conditions which make possible this combination we should naturally seek for them in the poorer quarters of a cosmopolitan city where we have, as nowhere else, the conditions for breaking into this double development; for making a fresh start, as it were, toward a synthesis upon a higher moral line which shall include both. There is every opportunity and necessity for compassion and kindliness such as the tribe itself afforded, and there is in addition, because of the many nationalities which are gathered there from all parts of the world, the opportunity and necessity for breaking through the tribal bond. Early associations and affections were not based so much on ties of blood as upon that necessity for defense against the hostile world outside which made the life of every man in a tribe valuable to every other man. The fact of blood was, so to speak, an accident. The moral code grew out of solidarity of emotion and action essential to the life of all.

In the midst of the modern city which, at moments, seems to stand only for the triumph of the strongest, the successful exploitation of the weak, the ruthlessness and hidden crime which follow in the wake of the struggle for existence on its lowest terms, there come daily – at least to American cities – accretions of simple people, who carry in their hearts a desire for mere goodness. They regularly deplete their scanty livelihood in response to a primitive pity, and, independent of the religions they have professed, of the wrongs they have suffered, and of the fixed morality they have been taught, have an unquenchable desire that charity and simple justice shall regulate men's relations. It seems sometimes, to one who knows them, as if they continually sought for an outlet for more kindliness, and that they are not only willing and eager to do a favor for a friend, but that their kindheartedness lies in ambush, as it were, for a chance to incorporate itself in our larger relations, that they persistently expect that it shall be given some form of governmental expression.

This is doubtless due partly to the fact that emotional pity and kindness are always found in greatest degree among the unsuccessful. We are told that unsuccessful struggle breeds emotion, not strength; that the hard-pressed races are the emotional races; and that wherever struggle has long prevailed emotion becomes the dominant force in fixing social relations. Is it surprising, therefore, that among this huge mass of the unsuccessful, to be found in certain quarters of the modern city, we should have the "medium," in which the first growth of the new compassion is taking place?

In addition to this compassion always found among the unsuccessful, emotional sentiment runs high among the newly arrived immigrants as a result of the emotional experiences of parting from home and kindred, to which he has been so recently subjected. An unusual mental alertness and power of perception also results from the upheaval. The multitudes of immigrants flooding the American cities have many times sundered social habits cherished through a hundred generations, and have renounced customs that may be traced to the habits of primitive man. These old habits and customs have a much more powerful hold than have mere racial or national ties. In seeking companionship in the new world, all the immigrants are reduced to the fundamental equalities and universal necessities of human life itself, and they inevitably develop the power of association which comes from daily contact with those who are unlike each other in all save the universal characteristics of man.

When looked at too closely, this nascent morality disappears, and one can count over only a thousand kindly acts and neighborly offices. But when mediated upon in the whole, there at once emerge again those vast and dominant suggestions of a new peace and holiness. It would seem as if our final help and healing were about to issue forth from broken human nature itself, out of the pathetic striving of ordinary men, who make up the common substance of life: from those who have been driven by economic pressure or governmental oppression out of a score of nations.

These various peoples who are gathered together in the immigrant quarters of a cosmopolitan city worship goodness for its own value, and do not associate it with success any more than they associate success with themselves; they literally "serve God for nought." If we would adduce evidence that we are emerging from a period of industrialism into a period of humanitarianism, it is to such quarters that we must betake ourselves. These are the places in which it is easiest to study the newer manifestations of government, in which personal welfare is considered a legitimate object; for a new history of government begins with an attempt to make life possible and human in large cities, in those crowded quarters which exhibit such an undoubted tendency to barbarism and degeneracy when the better human qualities are not nourished. Public baths and gymnasiums, parks and libraries, are provided first for those who are without the security for bare subsistence, and it does not seem strange to them that it should be so. Such a community is made up of men who will continue to dream of Utopian Governments until the democratic government about them expresses kindliness with protection. Such men will continue to rely upon neighborly friendliness until organized charity is able to identify impulsive pity with well-considered relief. They will naïvely long for an education for their children that will fit them to earn money until public education shall come to consider industrial efficiency. As their hopes and dreams are a prophecy of the future development in city government, in charity, in education, so their daily lives are a forecast of coming international relations. Our attention has lately been drawn to the fact that it is logical that the most vigorous efforts in governmental reform, as well as the most generous experiments in ministering to social needs, have come from the larger cities and that it is inevitable that they should be to-day "the centers of radicalism," as they have been traditionally the "cradles of liberty."[2]

If we once admit the human dynamic character of progress, then it is easy to understand why the crowded city quarters become focal points of that progress.

A deeper and more thorough-going unity is required in a community made up of highly differentiated peoples than in a more settled and stratified one, and it may be logical that we should find in this commingling of many peoples a certain balance and concord of opposing and contending forces; a gravitation toward the universal. Because of their difference in all external matters, in all of the non-essentials of life, the people in a cosmopolitan city are forced to found their community of interests upon the basic and essential likenesses of their common human nature; for, after all, the things that make men alike are stronger and more primitive than the things that separate them. It is natural that this synthesis of the varying nations

should be made first at the points of the greatest congestion, quite as we find that selfishness is first curbed and social feeling created at the points where the conflict of individual interests is sharpest. One dares not grow too certain as to the wells of moral healing which lie under the surface of the sullen work-driven life which the industrial quarters of the modern city present. They fascinate us by their mere size and diversity, as does the city itself; but certain it is, that these quarters continually confound us by their manifestations of altruism. It may be that we are surprised simply because we fail to comprehend that the individual, under such pressure, must shape his life with some reference to the demands of social justice, not only to avoid crushing the little folk about him, but in order to save himself from death by crushing. It is an instance of the irresistible coalescing of the altruistic and egoistic impulse which is the strength of social morality. We are often told that men under this pressure of life become calloused and cynical, whereas anyone who lives with them knows that they are sentimental and compassionate.

It is possible that we shall be saved from warfare by the "fighting rabble" itself, by the "quarrelsome mob" turned into kindly citizens of the world through the pressure of a cosmopolitan neighborhood. It is not that they are shouting for peace – on the contrary, if they shout at all, they will continue to shout for war – but that they are really attaining cosmopolitan relations through daily experience. They will probably believe for a long time that war is noble and necessary both to engender and cherish patriotism; and yet all of the time, below their shouting, they are living in the kingdom of human kindness. They are laying the simple and inevitable foundations for an international order as the foundations of tribal and national morality have already been laid. They are developing the only sort of patriotism consistent with the intermingling of the nations; for the citizens of a cosmopolitan quarter find an insuperable difficulty when they attempt to hem in their conception of patriotism either to the "old country" or to their adopted one. There arises the hope that when this newer patriotism becomes large enough, it will overcome arbitrary boundaries and soak up the notion of nationalism. We may then give up war, because we shall find it as difficult to make war upon a nation at the other side of the globe as upon our next-door neighbor.

These humble harbingers of the Newer Ideals of Peace, venturing themselves upon a larger relationship, are most touching; and while the success of their efforts can never be guaranteed or spoken of too confidently, they stir us with a strange hope, as if new vistas of life were opening before us – vistas not illuminated with the glare of war, but with a mellowed glow of their own. These paths are seen distinctly only as we ascend to a more enveloping point of view and obtain a larger and bulkier sense of the growing sentiment which rejects the old and negative bonds of discipline and coercion and insists upon vital and fraternal relationship, subordinating the lower to the higher. To make this hope valid and intelligible, is indeed the task before these humble brethren of ours and of those who would help them. They encourage us to hope for the discovery of a new vital relation – that of the individual to the race – which may lay the foundation for a new religious bond adequate to the modern situation; and we almost come to believe that such a foundation is, in fact, being laid now – not in speculation, but in action.

That which secured for the early Hebrew shepherd his health, his peace of mind, and his sense of connection with the Unseen, became the basis for the most wonderful and widespread religion the world has ever known. Perhaps, at this moment, we need to find that which will secure the health, the peace of mind, and the opportunity for normal occupation and spiritual growth to the humblest industrial worker, as the foundation for a rational conduct of life adapted to an industrial and cosmopolitan era.

Even now we only dimly comprehend the strength and irresistible power of those "universal and imperious ideals which are formed in the depths of anonymous life," and which the people insist shall come to realization, not because they have been tested by logic or history, but because the mass of men are eager that they should be tried as a living experience. According to our different methods of viewing society, we express this newer ideal which is after all so old as to have been engendered in the tribe itself. He who makes the study of society a mere corollary of biology, speaks of the "theory of the unspecialized," that the simple cell develops much more rapidly when new tissue is needed than the more highly developed one; he who views society from the economic standpoint and finds hope only in a changed industrial order, talks of the "man at the bottom of society," of the proletarian who shall eventually come into his own; he who believes that a wiser and a saner education will cure our social ill,

speaks ever and again of "the wisdom of the little child" and of the necessity to reveal and explore his capacity; while he who keeps close to the historic deductions upon which the study of society is chiefly founded, uses the old religious phrase, "the counsel of imperfection," and bids us concern ourselves with "the least of these."

The French have a phrase *l'imperieuse bonté* by which they designate those impulses towards compassionate conduct which will not be denied, because they are as imperative in their demand for expression as is the impulse to make music or to soften life by poesy and decoration. According to this definition, St. Francis was a genius in exactly the same sense as was Dante or Raphael, and he revealed quite as they did, possibilities and reaches of the human soul hitherto unsuspected. This genius for goodness has in the past largely expressed itself through individuals and groups, but it may be that we are approaching a period which shall give it collective expression, and shall unite into one all those private and parochial efforts. It would be no more strange than was that marvelous coming together of the artists and the people in the thirteenth century which resulted in the building of the Gothic cathedrals. We may be waiting for a religious enthusiasm, for a divine fire to fuse together the partial and feeble efforts at "doing good" into a transfigured whole which shall take on international proportions as naturally as the cathedrals towered into unheard-of heights. The Gothic cathedrals were glorious beyond the dreams of artists, notwithstanding that they were built by unknown men, or rather by so many men that it was a matter of indifference to record their names. Could we compare the present humanitarian efforts to the building of a spiritual cathedral, it would seem that the gargoyles had been made first, that the ground is now strewn with efforts to "do good" which have developed a diabolical capacity for doing harm. But even these may fall into place. The old cathedral-builders fearlessly portrayed all of life, its inveterate tendency to deride as well as to bless; its trickery as well as its beauty. Their art was catholic enough to portray all, and the cathedral was huge enough to mellow all they portrayed into a flowing and inspired whole.

At the present moment it requires the philosopher to unify these spiritual efforts of the common man into the internationalism of good will, as in the past it was natural that the philosophers, the men who looked at life as a whole, should have been the first to sigh for negative peace which they declared would be "eternal."

Speculative writers, such as Kant, Bentham, and Buckle, long ago pointed out that the subsidence of war was inevitable as society progressed. They contended that every stage of human progress is marked by a further curtailment of brute force, a limitation of the area in which it is permitted. At the bottom is the small savage community in a perpetual state of warfare; at the top an orderly society stimulated and controlled by recognized ideals of social justice. In proportion as the savage society comes under the dominion of a common moral consciousness, it moves up, and in proportion as the civilized society reverts to the use of brute force, it goes down. Reversion to that brute struggle may at any moment cost the destruction of the painfully acquired bonds of equity, the ties of mutual principle, which are wrought with such effort and loosed with such ease. But these earlier philosophers could not possibly have foreseen the tremendous growth of industry and commerce with their inevitable cosmopolitanism which has so recently taken place, nor without knowledge of this could they possibly have prognosticated the leap forward and the aggressive character which the concern for human welfare has latterly evinced. The speculative writers among our contemporaries are naturally the only ones who formulate this new development, or rather bid us heed its presence among us. An American philosopher[3] has lately reminded us of the need to "discover in the social realm the moral equivalent for war – something heroic that will speak to men as universally as war has done, and yet will be as compatible with their spiritual natures as war has proved itself to be incompatible." It may be true that we are even now discovering these moral substitutes, although we find it so difficult to formulate them. Perhaps our very hope that these substitutes may be discovered has become the custodian of a secret change that is going on all about us. We care less each day for the heroism connected with warfare and destruction, and constantly admire more that which pertains to labor and the nourishing of human life. The new heroism manifests itself at the present moment in a universal determination to abolish poverty and disease, a manifestation so widespread that it may justly be called international.

In illustration of this new determination one immediately thinks of the international effort to rid the face of the earth of tuberculosis, in which Germany, Italy, France, England and America are engaged with such enthusiasm. This movement has its international congresses, its discoverers and veterans, also its decorations and rewards for bravery. Its discipline is severe; it requires self-control, endurance, self-sacrifice and constant watchfulness. Its leaders devote hours to careful teaching and demonstration, they reclaim acres of bad houses, and make over the food supply of huge cities. One could instance the determination to do away with neglected old age, which finds expression in the Old Age Pension Acts of Germany and Australia, in the State Savings Banks of Belgium and France, in the enormous number of Mutual Benefit Societies in England and America. In such undertakings as these, with their spontaneous and universal manifestations, are we beginning to see the first timid forward reach of one of those instinctive movements which carry onward the progressive goodness of the race.

It is possible that this substitution of nurture for warfare is analogous to that world-wide effort to put a limit to revenge which one nation after another essayed as each reached a certain stage of development. To compel the avenger to accept blood-money in lieu of the blood of his enemy may have been but a short step in morals, but at least it destroyed the stimulus to further shedding of blood which each avenged death had afforded, and it laid the foundations for court adjudications. The newer humanitarianism is more aggressive and substitutes emotional stimuli as well as codes of conduct. We may predict that each nation quite as a natural process will reach the moment when virile good-will will be substituted for the spirit of warfare. The process of extinguishing war, however, compared to the limiting of revenge, will be amazingly accelerated. Owing to the modern conditions of intercourse, each nation will respond, not to an isolated impulse, but will be caught in the current of a world-wide process.

We are much too timid and apologetic in regard to this newer humanitarianism, and do not yet realize what it may do for us in the way of courage and endurance. We continue to defend war on the ground that it stirs the nobler blood and the higher imagination of the nation, and thus frees it from moral stagnation and the bonds of commercialism. We do not see that this is to borrow our virtues from a former age and to fail to utilize our own. We find ourselves in this plight because our modern morality has lacked fibre, because our humanitarianism has been much too soft and literary, and has given itself over to unreal and high-sounding phrases. It appears that our only hope for a genuine adjustment of our morality and courage to our present social and industrial developments, lies in a patient effort to work it out by daily experience. We must be willing to surrender ourselves to those ideals of the humble, which all religious teachers unite in declaring to be the foundations of a sincere moral life.

The following pages attempt to uncover these newer ideals as we may daily experience them in the modern city. It may be found that certain survivals of militarism in municipal government are responsible for much of the failure in the working of democratic institutions. We may discover that the survivals of warfare in the labor movement and all the other dangers of class morality rest largely upon an appeal to loyalties which are essentially a survival of the virtues of a warlike period. The more aggressive aspects of the newer humanitarianism may be traced in the movement for social amelioration and in the protective legislation which regards the weakest citizen as a valuable asset. The same spirit which protests against the social waste of child labor also demands that the traditional activity of woman shall be utilized in civic life. When the State protects its civic resources, as it formerly defended its citizens in time of war, industrialism versus militarism comes to be nurture versus conquest. In order to trace the displacement of the military ideals of patriotism by those of a rising concern for human welfare, we must take an accounting between those forms of governmental machinery and social organization which are the historic outgrowth of conquest and repression and the newer forms arising in their midst which embody the social energy instantly recognizable as contemporaneous with our sincerest moral life. To follow this newer humanitarianism even through its obvious manifestations requires at the very outset a definite abandonment of the eighteenth-century philosophy upon which so much of our present democratic theory and philanthropic activity depends. It is necessary from the very beginning to substitute the scientific method of research for the a priori method of the school men if we would deal with real people and obtain a sense of participation with our fellows. The eighteenth-century humanitarian hotly insisted upon "the rights of man," but he loved the people without really knowing them, which is by no means an impossible achievement. "The love of those whom a man does not know is quite as

elemental a sentiment as the love of those whom a man does know," but with this difference, that he shuts himself away from the opportunity of being caught and carried forward in the stream of their hopes and aspirations, a bigger and warmer current than he dreams of. The eighteenth-century humanitarian substituted his enthusiastic concept of "the natural man" for the warmth which this stream might have given him, and so long as he dealt with political concepts it answered his purpose. Mazzini made a most significant step between the eighteenth-century morality and our own by appealing beyond "the rights of man" to the "duties to humanity;" but although an impassioned democrat, he was still a moralist of the earlier type. He realized with them that the appeal to humanity would evoke a finer and deeper response than that to patriotism or to any sectional morality; but he shared the eighteenth-century tendency to idealization. It remained for the moralist of this generation to dissolve "humanity" into its component parts of men, women, and children and to serve their humblest needs with an enthusiasm which, so far from being dependent upon glamour, can be sustained only by daily knowledge and constant companionship.

It is no easy task to detect and to follow the tiny paths of progress which the unencumbered proletarian with nothing but his life and capacity for labor, is pointing out for us. These paths lead to a type of government founded upon peace and fellowship as contrasted with restraint and defence. They can never be discovered with the eyes of the doctrinaire. From the nature of the case, he who would walk these paths must walk with the poor and oppressed, and can only approach them through affection and understanding. The ideals of militarism would forever shut him out from this new fellowship.

[...]

Passing of the War Virtues

Of all the winged words which Tolstoy wrote during the war between Russia and Japan, perhaps none are more significant than these: "The great strife of our time is not that now taking place between the Japanese and the Russians, nor that which may blaze up between the white and the yellow races, nor that strife which is carried on by mines, bombs, and bullets, but that spiritual strife which, without ceasing, has gone on and is going on between the enlightened consciousness of mankind now awaiting for manifestation and that darkness and that burden which surrounds and oppresses mankind." In the curious period of accommodation in which we live, it is possible for old habits and new compunctions to be equally powerful, and it is almost a matter of pride with us that we neither break with the old nor yield to the new. We call this attitude tolerance, whereas it is often mere confusion of mind. Such mental confusion is strikingly illustrated by our tendency to substitute a statement of the historic evolution of an ideal of conduct in place of the ideal itself. This almost always occurs when the ideal no longer accords with our faithful experience of life and when its implications are not justified by our latest information. In this way we spare ourselves the necessity of pressing forward to newer ideals of conduct.

We quote the convictions and achievements of the past as an excuse for ourselves when we lack the energy either to throw off old moral codes which have become burdens or to attain a morality proportionate to our present sphere of activity.

At the present moment the war spirit attempts to justify its noisy demonstrations by quoting its great achievements in the past and by drawing attention to the courageous life which it has evoked and fostered. It is, however, perhaps significant that the adherents of war are more and more justifying it by its past record and reminding us of its ancient origin. They tell us that it is interwoven with every fibre of human growth and is at the root of all that is noble and courageous in human life, that struggle is the basis of all progress, that it is now extended from individuals and tribes to nations and races.

We may admire much that is admirable in this past life of courageous warfare, while at the same time we accord it no right to dominate the present, which has traveled out of its reach into a land of new desires. We may admit that the experiences of war have equipped the men of the present with pluck and energy, but to insist upon the selfsame expression for that pluck and energy would be as stupid a mistake as if we would relegate the full-grown citizen, responding to many claims and demands upon his powers, to the school-yard fights of his boyhood, or to the college contests of his cruder youth. The little lad who stoutly defends himself on the school-ground may be worthy of much admiration, but if we find him, a dozen years later, the bullying leader of a street-gang who bases his prestige on the fact that "no one can whip him," our admiration cools amazingly, and we say that the carrying over of those puerile instincts into manhood shows arrested development which is mainly responsible for filling our prisons.

This confusion between the contemporaneous stage of development and the historic rôle of certain qualities, is intensified by our custom of referring to social evolution as if it were a force and not a process. We assume that social ends may be obtained without the application of social energies, although we know in our hearts that the best results of civilization have come about only through human will and effort. To point to the achievement of the past as a guarantee for continuing what has since become shocking to us is stupid business; it is to forget that progress itself depends upon adaptation, upon a nice balance between continuity and change. Let us by all means acknowledge and preserve that which has been good in warfare and in the spirit of warfare; let us gather it together and incorporate it in our national fibre. Let us, however, not be guilty for a moment of shutting our eyes to that which for many centuries must have been disquieting to the moral sense, but which is gradually becoming impossible, not only because of our increasing sensibilities, but because great constructive plans and humanized interests have captured our hopes and we are finding that war is an implement too clumsy and barbaric to subserve our purpose. We have come to realize that the great task of pushing forward social justice could be enormously accelerated if primitive methods as well as primitive weapons were once for all abolished.

The past may have been involved in war and suffering in order to bring forth a new and beneficent courage, an invincible ardor for conserving and healing human life, for understanding and elaborating it. To obtain this courage is to distinguish between a social order founded upon law enforced by authority and that other social order which includes liberty of individual action and complexity of group development. The latter social order would not suppress the least germ of promise, of growth and variety, but would nurture all into a full and varied life. It is not an easy undertaking to obtain it and it cannot be carried forward without conscious and well-defined effort. The task that is really before us is first to see to it, that the old virtues bequeathed by war are not retained after they have become a social deterrent and that social progress is not checked by a certain contempt for human nature which is but the inherited result of conquest. Second, we must act upon the assumption that spontaneous and fraternal action as virile and widespread as war itself is the only method by which substitutes for the war virtues may be discovered.

It was contended in the first chapter of this book that social morality is developed through sentiment and action. In this particular age we can live the truth which has been apprehended by our contemporaries, that truth which is especially our own, only by establishing nobler and wiser social relations and by discovering social bonds better fitted to our requirements. Warfare in the past has done much to bring men together. A sense of common danger and the stirring appeal to action for a common purpose, easily open the channels of sympathy through which we partake of the life about us. But there are certainly other methods of opening those channels. A social life to be healthy must be consciously and fully adjusted to the march of social needs, and as we may easily make a mistake by forgetting that enlarged opportunities are ever demanding an enlarged morality, so we will fail in the task of substitution if we do not demand social sympathy in a larger measure and of a quality better adapted to the contemporaneous situation.

Perhaps the one point at which this undertaking is most needed is in regard to our conception of patriotism, which, although as genuine as ever before, is too much dressed in the trappings of the past and continually carries us back to its beginnings in military prowess and defence. To have been able to trace the origin and development of patriotism and then to rest content with that, and to fail to insist that it shall respond to the stimulus of a larger and more varied environment with which we are now confronted, is a confession of weakness; it exhibits lack of moral enterprise and of national vigor.

We have all seen the breakdown of village standards of morality when the conditions of a great city are encountered. To do "the good lying next at hand" may be a sufficient formula when the village idler and his needy children live but a few doors down the street, but the same dictum may be totally misleading when the villager becomes a city resident and finds his next-door neighbors prosperous and comfortable, while the poor and overburdened live many blocks away where he would never see them at all, unless he were stirred by a spirit of social enterprise to go forth and find them in the midst of their meagre living and their larger needs. The spirit of village gossip, penetrating and keen as it is, may be depended upon to bring to the notice of the kind-hearted villager all cases of suffering – that someone is needed "to sit up all night" with a sick neighbor, or that the village loafer has been drunk again and beaten his wife; but in a city divided so curiously into the regions of the well-to-do and the congested quarters of the immigrant, the conscientious person can no longer rely upon gossip. There is no intercourse, not even a scattered one, between the two, save what the daily paper brings, with its invincible propensity to report the gossip of poverty and crime, perhaps a healthier tendency than we imagine. The man who has moved from the village to the cosmopolitan city and who would continue even his former share of beneficent activity must bestir himself to keep informed as to social needs and to make new channels through which his sympathy may flow. Without some such conscious effort, his sympathy will finally become stratified along the line of his social intercourse and he will be unable really to care for any people but his "own kind." American conceptions of patriotism have moved, so to speak, from the New England village into huge cosmopolitan cities. They find themselves bewildered by the change and have not only failed to make the adjustment, but the very effort in that direction is looked upon with deep suspicion by their old village neighbors. Unless our conception of patriotism is progressive, it cannot hope to embody the real affection and the real interest of the nation. We know full well that the patriotism of common descent is the mere patriotism of the clan – the early patriotism of the tribe – and that, while the possession of a like territory is an advance upon that first conception, both of them are unworthy to be the patriotism of a great cosmopolitan nation. We shall not have made any genuine advance until we have grown impatient of a patriotism founded upon military prowess and defence, because this really gets in the way and prevents the growth of that beneficent and progressive patriotism which we need for the understanding and healing of our current national difficulties.

To seek our patriotism in some age other than our own is to accept a code that is totally inadequate to help us through the problems which current life develops. We continue to found our patriotism upon war and to contrast conquest with nurture, militarism with industrialism, calling the latter passive and inert and the former active and aggressive, without really facing the situation as it exists. We tremble before our own convictions, and are afraid to find newer manifestations of courage and daring lest we thereby lose the virtues bequeathed to us by war. It is a pitiful acknowledgment that we have lost them already and that we shall have to give up the ways of war, if for no other reason than to preserve the finer spirit of courage and detachment which it has engendered and developed.

We come at last to the practical question as to how these substitutes for the war virtues may be found. How may we, the children of an industrial and commercial age, find the courage and sacrifice which belong to our industrialism. We may begin with August Comte's assertion that man seeks to improve his position in two different ways, by the destruction of obstacles and by the construction of means, or, designated by their most obvious social results, if his contention is correct, by military action and by industrial action, and that the two must long continue side by side. Then we find ourselves asking what may be done to make more picturesque those lives which are spent in a monotonous and wearing toil, compared to which the camp is exciting and the barracks comfortable. How shall it be made to seem as magnificent patiently to correct the wrongs of industrialism as to do battle for the rights of the nation? This transition ought not to be so difficult in America, for to begin with, our national life in America has been largely founded upon our success in invention and engineering, in manufacturing and commerce. Our prosperity has rested upon constructive labor and material progress, both of them in striking contrast to warfare. There is an element of almost grim humor in the nation's reverting at last to the outworn methods of battle-ships and defended harbors. We may admit that idle men need war to keep alive their courage and endurance, but we have few idle men in a nation engaged in industrialism. We constantly see subordination of sensation to sentiment in hundreds of careers which are not military; the thousands of miners in Pennsylvania doubtless endure every year more bodily pain and peril than the same number of men in European barracks.

Industrial life affords ample opportunity for endurance, discipline, and a sense of detachment, if the struggle is really put upon the highest level of industrial efficiency. But because our industrial life is not on this level, we constantly tend to drop the newer and less developed ideals for the older ones of warfare, we ignore the fact that war so readily throws back the ideals which the young are nourishing into the mold of those which the old should be outgrowing. It lures young men not to develop, but to exploit; it turns them from the courage and toil of industry to the bravery and endurance of war, and leads them to forget that civilization is the substitution of law for war. It incites their ambitions, not to irrigate, to make fertile and sanitary, the barren plain of the savage, but to fill it with military posts and tax-gatherers, to cease from pushing forward industrial action into new fields and to fall back upon military action.

We may illustrate this by the most beneficent acts of war, when the military spirit claiming to carry forward civilization invades a country for the purpose of bringing it into the zone of the civilized world. Militarism enforces law and order and insists upon obedience and discipline, assuming that it will ultimately establish righteousness and foster progress. In order to carry out this good intention, it first of all clears the decks of impedimenta, although in the process it may extinguish the most precious beginnings of self-government and the nucleus of self-help, which the wise of the native community have long been anxiously hoarding.

It is the military idea, resting content as it does with the passive results of order and discipline, which confesses a totally inadequate conception of the value and power of human life. The charge of obtaining negative results could with great candor be brought against militarism, while the strenuous task, the vigorous and difficult undertaking, involving the use of the most highly developed human powers, can be claimed for industrialism.

It is really human constructive labor which must give the newly invaded country a sense of its place in the life of the civilized world, some idea of the effective occupations which it may perform. In order to accomplish this its energy must be freed and its resources developed. Militarism undertakes to set in order, to suppress and to govern, if necessary to destroy, while industrialism undertakes to liberate latent forces, to reconcile them to new conditions, to demonstrate that their aroused activities can no longer follow caprice, but must fit into a larger order of life. To call this latter undertaking, demanding ever new powers of insight, patience, and fortitude, less difficult, less manly, less strenuous, than the first, is on the face of it absurd. It is the soldier who is inadequate to the difficult task, who strews his ways with blunders and lost opportunities, who cannot justify his vocation by the results, and who is obliged to plead guilty to a lack of rational method.

Of British government in the Empire, an Englishman has recently written, "We are obliged in practise to make a choice between good order and justice administered autocratically in accordance with British standards on the one hand, and delicate, costly, doubtful, and disorderly experiments in self-government on British lines upon the other, and we have practically everywhere decided upon the former alternative. It is, of course, less difficult."[4] Had our American ideals of patriotism and morality in international relations kept pace with our experience, had we followed up our wide commercial relations with an adequate ethical code, we can imagine a body of young Americans, "the flower of our youth," as we like to say, proudly declining commercial advantages founded upon forced military occupation and informing their well-meaning government that they declined to accept openings on any such terms as these, that their ideals of patriotism and of genuine government demanded the play of their moral prowess and their constructive intelligence. Certainly in America we have a chance to employ something more active and virile, more inventive, more in line with our temperament and tradition, than the mere desire to increase commercial relations by armed occupation as other governments have done. A different conduct is required from a democracy than from the mere order-keeping, bridge-building, tax-gathering Roman, or from the conscientious Briton carrying the blessings of an established government and enlarged commerce to all quarters of the globe.

It has been the time-honored custom to attribute unjust wars to the selfish ambition of rulers who remorselessly sacrifice their subjects to satisfy their greed. But, as Lecky has recently pointed out, it remains to be seen whether or not democratic rule will diminish war. Immoderate and uncontrolled desires are at the root of most national as well as of most individual crimes, and a large number of persons may be moved by unworthy ambitions quite as easily as a few. If the electorate of a democracy accustom themselves to take the commercial view of life, to consider the extension of trade as the test of a national prosperity, it becomes comparatively easy for mere extension of commercial opportunity to assume a moral aspect and to receive the moral sanction. Unrestricted commercialism is an excellent preparation for governmental aggression. The nation which is accustomed to condone the questionable business methods of a rich man because of his success, will find no difficulty in obscuring the moral issues involved in any undertaking that is successful. It becomes easy to deny the moral basis of self-government and to substitute militarism. The soldier formerly looked down upon the merchant whom he now obeys, as he still looks down upon the laborer as a man who is engaged in a business inferior to his own, as someone who is dull and passive and ineffective. When our public education suceeds in freeing the creative energy and developing the skill which the advance of industry demands, this attitude must disappear, and a spectacle such as that recently seen in London among the idle men returned from service in South Africa, who refused to work through a contemptuous attitude towards the "slow life" of the laborer, will become impossible. We have as yet failed to uncover the relative difficulty and requisite training for the two methods of life.

It is difficult to illustrate on a national scale the substitution of the ideals of labor for those of warfare.

At the risk of being absurd, and with the certainty of pushing an illustration beyond its legitimate limits, I am venturing to typify this substitution by the one man whom the civilized world has most closely associated with military ideals, the present Emperor of Germany. We may certainly believe that the German Emperor is a conscientious man, who means to do his duty to all his subjects; that he regards himself, not only as general and chief of the army, but also as the fostering father of the humble people. Let us imagine the quite impossible thing that for ten years he does not review any troops, does not attend any parades, does not wear a uniform, nor hear the clang of the sword as he walks, but that during these ten years he lives with the peasants "who drive the painful plow," that he constantly converses with them, and subjects himself to their alternating hopes and fears as to the result of the harvest, at best so inadequate for supplying their wants and for paying their taxes. Let us imagine that the German Emperor during these halcyon years, in addition to the companionship of the humble, reads only the folk-lore, the minor poetry and the plaintive songs in which German literature is so rich, until he comes to see each man of the field as he daily goes forth to his toil "with a soldier tied to his back," exhausted by the double strain of his burden and his work.

Let us imagine this Emperor going through some such profound moral change as befell Count Tolstoy when he quitted his military service in the Caucasus and lived with the peasants on his estate, with this difference that, instead of feeling directly responsible for a village of humble folk, he should come to feel responsible for all the toilers of the "Fatherland" and for the international results of the German army. Let us imagine that in his self-surrender to the humblest of his people, there would gradually grow up in his subconsciousness, forces more ideal than any which had possessed him before; that his interests and thoughts would gradually shift from war and the manœuvres and extensions of the army, to the unceasing toil, the permanent patience, which lie at the bottom of all national existence; that the life of the common people, which is so infinite in its moral suggestiveness, would open up to him new moral regions, would stir new energies within him, until there would take place one of those strange alterations in personality of which hundreds of examples are recorded. Under a glow of generous indignation, magnanimity, loyalty to his people, a passion of self-surrender to his new ideals, we can imagine that the imperial temperament would waste no time in pinings and regret, but that, his energies being enlisted in an overmastering desire to free the people from the burden of the army, he would drive vigorously in the direction of his new ideals. It is impossible to imagine him "passive" under this conversion to the newer ideals of peace. He would no more be passive than St. Paul was after his conversion. He would regard the four million men in Europe shut up in barracks, fed in idleness by toiling peasants, as an actual wrong and oppression. They would all have to be freed and returned to normal life and occupation – not through the comparatively easy method of storming garrisons, in which he has had training, but through conviction on the part of rulers and people of the wrong and folly of barrack idleness and military glitter. The freeing of the Christians from the oppressions of the Turks, of the Spaniards from the Moslems, could offer no more strenuous task – always, however, with the added difficulty and complication that the change in the people must be a moral

change analogous to the one which had already taken place within himself; that he must be debarred from the use of weapons, to which his earlier life had made him familiar; that his high task, while enormous in its proportion, was still most delicate in its character, and must be undertaken without the guarantee of precedent, and without any surety of success. "Smitten with the great vision of social righteousness," as so many of his contemporaries have been, he could not permit himself to be blinded or to take refuge in glittering generalities, but, even as St. Paul arose from his vision and went on his way in a new determination never again changed, so he would have to go forth to a mission, imperial indeed in its magnitude, but "over-imperial" in the sweep of its consequences and in the difficulty of its accomplishment.

Certainly counting all the hours of the Emperor's life spent in camp and court dominated by military pomp and ambition, he has given more than ten years to military environment and much less than ten years to the bulk of his people, and it would not be impossible to imagine such a conversion due to the reaction of environment and interest. Such a change having taken place, should we hold him royal in temper or worthy of the traditions of knight-errantry, if he were held back by commercial considerations, if he hesitated because the Krupp Company could sell no more guns and would be thrown out of business? We should say to this Emperor whom our imaginations have evoked, Were your enthusiasms genuine enough, were your insights absolutely true, you would see of how little consequence these things really are, and how easily adjusted. Let the Krupp factories, with their tremendous resources in machinery and men, proceed to manufacture dredging machines for the reclaiming of the waste land in Posen; let them make new inventions to relieve the drudgery of the peasant, agricultural implements adequate to Germany's agricultural resources and possibilities. They will find need for all the power of invention which they can command, all the manufacturing and commercial ability which they now employ. It is part of your new vocation to adjust the industries now tributary to the standing armies and organization of warfare, to useful and beneficent occupations; to transform and readjust all their dependent industries, from the manufacturing of cannon and war-ships to that of gold braid and epaulets. It is your mission to revive and increase agriculture, industry, and commerce, by diverting all the energy which is now directed to the feeding, clothing, and arming of the idle, into the legitimate and normal channels of life.

It is certainly not more difficult to imagine such a change occurring to an entire people than in the mind and purpose of one man – in fact, such changes are going on all about us.

The advance of constructive labor and the subsidence and disappearance of destructive warfare is a genuine line of progression. One sees much of protection and something of construction in the office of war, as the Roman bridges survived throughout Europe long after the legions which built them and crossed them for new conquests had passed out of mind. Also, in the rising tide of labor there is a large admixture of warfare, of the purely militant spirit which is sometimes so dominant that it throws the entire movement into confusion and leads the laborer to renounce his birthright; but nevertheless the desire for battle is becoming constantly more restricted in area. It still sways in regions where men of untamed blood are dwelling, and among men who, because they regard themselves as a superior race, imagine that they are free from the ordinary moral restraints; but its territory constantly grows smaller and its manifestations more guarded. Doubtless war will exist for many generations among semi-savage tribes, and it will also break out in those nations which may be roused and dominated by the unrestricted commercial spirit; but the ordinary life of man will go on without it, as it becomes transmitted into a desire for normal human relationship.

It is difficult to predict at what moment the conviction that war is foolish or wasteful or unjustifiable may descend upon the earth, and it is also impossible to estimate among how many groups of people this conviction has already become established.

The Doukhobors are a religious sect in Russia whose creed emphasizes the teaching of non-resistance. A story is told of one of their young men who, because of his refusal to enter the Russian army, was brought for trial before a judge, who reasoned with him concerning the folly of his course and in return received a homily upon the teachings of Jesus. "Quite right you are," answered the judge, "from the point of abstract virtue, but the time has not yet come to put into practise the literal sayings of Christ." "The time may not have come for you, your Honor," was the reply, "but the time has come for us." Who can tell at what hour vast numbers of Russian peasants

upon those Russian steppes will decide that the time has come for them to renounce warfare, even as their prototype, the mujik, Count Tolstoy, has already decided that it has come for him? Conscious as the peasants are of religious motive, they will meet a cheerful martyrdom for their convictions, as so many of the Doukhobors have done. It may, however, be easy to overestimate this changed temper because of the simple yet dramatic formulation given by Tolstoy to the non-resisting spirit. How far Tolstoy is really the mouthpiece of a great moral change going on in the life of the Russian peasant and how far he speaks merely for himself, it is, of course, impossible to state. If only a few peasants are experiencing this change, his genius has certainly done much to make their position definite. The man who assumes that a new degree of virtue is possible, thereby makes it real and tangible to those who long to possess it but lack courage. Tolstoy at least is ready to predict that in the great affairs of national disarmament, it may easily be true that the Russian peasants will take the first steps.

Their armed rebellion may easily be overcome by armed troops, but what can be done with their permanent patience, their insatiable hunger for holiness? All idealism has its prudential aspects, and, as has been pointed out by Mr. Perris,[5] no other form of revolution is so fitted to an agricultural people as this continued outburst of passive resistance among whole communities, not in theory, but in practise. This peasant movement goes on in spite of persecution, perfectly spontaneous, self-reliant, colossal in the silent confidence and power of endurance. In this day of Maxim guns and high explosives, the old method of revolt would be impossible to an agricultural people, but the non-resistant strike against military service lies directly in line with the temperament and capacity of the Russian people. That "the government cannot put the whole population in prison, and, if it could, it would still be without material for an army, and without money for its support," is an almost irrefutable argument. We see here, at least, the beginnings of a sentiment that shall, if sufficiently developed, make war impossible to an entire people, a conviction of sin manifesting itself throughout a nation.

Whatever may have been true of the revolutionist of the past when his spike was on a certain level of equality with the bayonet of the regular soldier, and his enthusiasm and daring could, in large measure, overcome the difference, it is certainly true now that such simple arms as a revolutionist could command, would be utterly futile against the equipment of the regular soldier. To continue the use of armed force means, under these circumstances, that we must refer the possibilities of all social and industrial advance to the consent of the owners of the Maxim guns. We must deny to the humble the possibility of the initiation of progressive movements employing revolution or, at least, we must defer all advance until the humble many can persuade the powerful few of the righteousness of their cause, and we must throw out the working class from participation in the beginnings of social revolutions. Tolstoy would make non-resistance aggressive. He would carry over into the reservoirs of moral influence all the strength which is now spent in coercion and resistance. It is an experiment which in its fullness has never been tried in human history, and it is worthy of a genius. As moral influence has ever a larger place in individual relationship and as physical force becomes daily more restricted in area, so Tolstoy would "speed up" the process in collective relationships and reset the whole of international life upon the basis of good will and intelligent understanding. It does not matter that he has entered these new moral fields through the narrow gateway of personal experience; that he sets forth his convictions with the limitations of the Russian governmental environment; that he is regarded at this moment by the Russian revolutionists as a quietist and reactionary. He has nevertheless reached down into the moral life of the humble people and formulated for them as for us the secret of their long patience and unremitting labor. Therefore, in the teachings of Tolstoy, as in the life of the peasants, coextensive with the doctrine of non-resistance, stress is laid upon productive labor. The peasant Bandereff, from whom Tolstoy claims to have learned much, has not only proclaimed himself as against war, but has written a marvelous book entitled "Bread Labor," expressing once more the striking antithesis, the eternal contrast between war and labor, and between those who abhor the one and ever advocate the other.

War on the one hand – plain destruction, Von Moltke called it – represents the life of the garrison and the tax-gatherer, the Roman emperor and his degenerate people, living upon the fruits of their conquest. Labor, on the other hand, represents productive effort, holding carefully what has been garnered by the output of brain and muscle, guarding the harvest jealously because it is the precious bread men live by.

It is quite possible that we have committed the time-honored folly of looking for a sudden change in men's attitude toward war, even as the poor alchemists wasted their lives in searching for a magic fluid and did nothing to discover the great laws governing chemical changes and reactions, the knowledge of which would have developed untold wealth beyond their crude dreams of transmuted gold.

The final moral reaction may at last come, accompanied by deep remorse, too tardy to reclaim all the human life which has been spent and the treasure which has been wasted, or it may come with a great sense of joy that all voluntary destruction of human life, all the deliberate wasting of the fruits of labor, have become a thing of the past, and that whatever the future contains for us, it will at least be free from war. We may at last comprehend the truth of that which Ruskin has stated so many times, that we worship the soldier, not because he goes forth to slay, but to be slain.

That this world peace movement should be arising from the humblest without the sanction and in some cases with the explicit indifference, of the church founded by the Prince of Peace, is simply another example of the strange paths of moral evolution.

To some of us it seems clear that marked manifestations of this movement are found in the immigrant quarters of American cities. The previous survey of the immigrant situation would indicate that all the peoples of the world have become part of the American tribunal, and that their sense of pity, their clamor for personal kindness, their insistence upon the right to join in our progress, can no longer be disregarded. The burdens and sorrows of men have unexpectedly become intelligent and urgent to this nation, and it is only by accepting them with some magnanimity that we can develop the larger sense of justice which is becoming world-wide and is lying in ambush, as it were, to manifest itself in governmental relations. Men of all nations are determining upon the abolition of degrading poverty, disease, and intellectual weakness, with their resulting industrial inefficiency, and are making a determined effort to conserve even the feeblest citizen to the State. To join in this determined effort is to break through national bonds and to unlock the latent fellowship between man and man. In a political campaign men will go through every possible hardship in response to certain political loyalties; in a moment of national danger men will sacrifice every personal advantage. It is but necessary to make this fellowship wider, to extend its scope without lowering its intensity. Those emotions which stir the spirit to deeds of self-surrender and to high enthusiasm, are among the world's most precious assets. That this emotion has so often become associated with war, by no means proves that it cannot be used for other ends. There is something active and tangible in this new internationalism, although it is difficult to make it clear, and in our striving for a new word with which to express this new and important sentiment, we are driven to the rather absurd phrase of "cosmic patriotism." Whatever it may be called, it may yet be strong enough to move masses of men out of their narrow national considerations and cautions into new reaches of human effort and affection. Religion has long ago taught that only as the individual can establish a sense of union with a power for righteousness not himself, can he experience peace; and it may be possible that the nations will be called to a similar experience.

The International Peace Conference held in Boston in 1904 was opened by a huge meeting in which men of influence and modern thought from four continents, gave reasons for their belief in the passing of war. But none was so modern, so fundamental and so trenchant, as the address which was read from the prophet Isaiah. He founded the cause of peace upon the cause of righteousness, not only as expressed in political relations, but also in industrial relations. He contended that peace could be secured only as men abstained from the gains of oppression and responded to the cause of the poor; that swords would finally be beaten into plowshares and pruning-hooks, not because men resolved to be peaceful, but because all the metal of the earth would be turned to its proper use when the poor and their children should be abundantly fed. It was as if the ancient prophet foresaw that under an enlightened industrialism peace would no longer be an absence of war, but the unfolding of world-wide processes making for the nurture of human life. He predicted the moment which has come to us now that peace is no longer an abstract dogma but has become a rising tide of moral enthusiasm slowly engulfing all pride of conquest and making war impossible.

Notes

1 L. T. Hobhouse, *Democracy and Reaction* (London: T. F. Unwin, 1904), p. 197.

2 A. T. Weber, *The Growth of Cities in the Nineteenth Century* (Ithaca, NY: Cornell University Press, 1963), p. 432.

3 William James, Professor of Philosophy at Harvard University.

4 John A. Hobson, *Imperialism* (London: Allen and Unwin, 1938), p. 128.

5 G. H. Perris, "The Grand Mujik," in *Leo Tolstoy* (Folcroft, PA: Folcroft Library Editions, 1977).

34

Anarchism: What It Really Stands For

Emma Goldman

Introduction

Emma Goldman (1869–1940) was an influential figure in the history of American anarchism, feminism, and anti-war movements. She was an early advocate of free speech, birth control, women's equality and independence, union organization, and the 8-hour working day. Her criticism of mandatory conscription of men into the military during World War I led to a two-year prison sentence, and then her deportation in 1919 to Russia, although she had lived her life from the age of 16 as an American. For the rest of her life, until her death in 1940, she continued to participate in the social and political movements of her age, from the Russian Revolution to the Spanish Civil War. She published *Anarchism and Other Essays* (1910), *The Social Significance of the Modern Drama* (1914), *My Disillusionment in Russia* (1923), and *Living My Life* (1931).

Anarchy

Ever reviled, accursed, ne'er understood,
  Thou art the grisly terror of our age.
"Wreck of all order," cry the multitude,
  "Art thou, and war and murder's endless rage."
O, let them cry. To them that ne'er have striven

Taken from *Anarchism and Other Essays* (New York: Dover Books, 1969). Reprinted with permission from Dover Publications Inc.

The truth that lies behind a word to find,
To them the word's right meaning was not given.
  They shall continue blind among the blind.
But thou, O word, so clear, so strong, so pure,
  Thou sayest all which I for goal have taken.
I give thee to the future! Thine secure
  When each at least unto himself shall waken.
Comes it in sunshine? In the tempest's thrill?
  I cannot tell – but it the earth shall see!
I am an Anarchist! Wherefore I will
  Not rule, and also ruled I will not be!

John Henry Mackay

The history of human growth and development is at the same time the history of the terrible struggle of every new idea heralding the approach of a brighter dawn. In its tenacious hold on tradition, the Old has never hesitated to make use of the foulest and cruelest means to stay the advent of the New, in whatever form or period the latter may have asserted itself. Nor need we retrace our steps into the distant past to realize the enormity of opposition, difficulties, and hardships placed in the path of every progressive idea. The rack, the thumbscrew, and the knout are still with us; so are the convict's garb and the social wrath, all conspiring against the spirit that is serenely marching on.

Anarchism could not hope to escape the fate of all other ideas of innovation. Indeed, as the most revolutionary and uncompromising innovator, Anarchism must needs meet with the combined ignorance and venom of the world it aims to reconstruct.

To deal even remotely with all that is being said and done against Anarchism would necessitate the writing of a whole volume. I shall therefore meet only two of the principal objections. In so doing, I shall attempt to elucidate what Anarchism really stands for.

The strange phenomenon of the opposition to Anarchism is that it brings to light the relation between so-called intelligence and ignorance. And yet this is not so very strange when we consider the relativity of all things. The ignorant mass has in its favor that it makes no pretense of knowledge or tolerance. Acting, as it always does, by mere impulse, its reasons are like those of a child. "Why?" "Because." Yet the opposition of the uneducated to Anarchism deserves the same consideration as that of the intelligent man.

What, then, are the objections? First, Anarchism is impractical, though a beautiful ideal. Second, Anarchism stands for violence and destruction, hence it must be repudiated as vile and dangerous. Both the intelligent man and the ignorant mass judge not from a thorough knowledge of the subject, but either from hearsay or false interpretation.

A practical scheme, says Oscar Wilde, is either one already in existence, or a scheme that could be carried out under the existing conditions; but it is exactly the existing conditions that one objects to, and any scheme that could accept these conditions is wrong and foolish. The true criterion of the practical, therefore, is not whether the latter can keep intact the wrong or foolish; rather is it whether the scheme has vitality enough to leave the stagnant waters of the old, and build, as well as sustain, new life. In the light of this conception, Anarchism is indeed practical. More than any other idea, it is helping to do away with the wrong and foolish; more than any other idea, it is building and sustaining new life.

The emotions of the ignorant man are continuously kept at a pitch by the most blood-curdling stories about Anarchism. Not a thing too outrageous to be employed against this philosophy and its exponents. Therefore Anarchism represents to the unthinking what the proverbial bad man does to the child – a black monster bent on swallowing everything; in short, destruction and violence.

Destruction and violence! How is the ordinary man to know that the most violent element in society is ignorance; that its power of destruction is the very thing Anarchism is combating? Nor is he aware that Anarchism, whose roots, as it were, are part of nature's forces, destroys, not healthful tissue, but parasitic growths that feed on the life's essence of society. It is merely clearing the soil from weeds and sagebrush, that it may eventually bear healthy fruit.

Someone has said that it requires less mental effort to condemn than to think. The widespread mental indolence, so prevalent in society, proves this to be only too true. Rather than to go to the bottom of any given idea, to examine into its origin and meaning, most people will either condemn it altogether, or rely on some superficial or prejudicial definition of non-essentials.

Anarchism urges man to think, to investigate, to analyze every proposition; but that the brain capacity of the average reader be not taxed too much, I also shall begin with a definition, and then elaborate on the latter.

ANARCHISM: The philosophy of a new social order based on liberty unrestricted by man-made law; the theory that all forms of government rest on violence, and are therefore wrong and harmful, as well as unnecessary.

The new social order rests, of course, on the materialistic basis of life; but while all Anarchists agree that the main evil today is an economic one, they maintain that the solution of that evil can be brought about only through the consideration of *every phase* of life – individual, as well as the collective; the internal, as well as the external phases.

A thorough perusal of the history of human development will disclose two elements in bitter conflict with each other; elements that are only now beginning to be understood, not as foreign to each other, but as closely related and truly harmonious, if only placed in proper environment: the individual and social instincts. The individual and society have waged a relentless and bloody battle for ages, each striving for supremacy, because each was blind to the value and importance of the other. The individual and social instincts – the one a most potent factor for individual endeavor, for growth, aspiration, self-realization; the other an equally potent factor for mutual helpfulness and social well-being.

The explanation of the storm raging within the individual, and between him and his surroundings, is not far to seek. The primitive man, unable to understand his being, much less the unity of all life, felt himself absolutely dependent on blind, hidden forces ever ready to mock and taunt him. Out of that attitude grew the religious concepts of man as a mere speck of dust dependent on superior powers on high, who can only be appeased by complete surrender. All the early sagas rest on that idea, which continues to be the *Leitmotiv* of the biblical tales dealing with the relation of man to God, to the State, to society. Again and again the same motif, *man is nothing, the powers are everything*. Thus Jehovah would only endure man on condition of complete surrender. Man can have all the glories of the earth, but he must not become conscious of himself. The State, society, and moral laws all sing the same refrain: Man can have all the glories of the earth, but he must not become conscious of himself.

Anarchism is the only philosophy which brings to man the consciousness of himself; which maintains that God, the State, and society are non-existent, that their promises are null and void, since they can be fulfilled only through man's subordination. Anarchism is therefore the teacher of the unity of life; not merely in nature, but in man. There is no conflict between the individual and the social instincts, any more than there is between the heart and the lungs: the one the receptacle of a precious life essence, the other the repository of the element that keeps the essence pure and strong. The individual is the heart of society, conserving the essence of social life; society is the lungs which are distributing the element to keep the life essence – that is, the individual – pure and strong.

"The one thing of value in the world," says Emerson, "is the active soul; this every man contains within him. The soul active sees absolute truth and utters truth and creates." In other words, the individual instinct is the thing of value in the world. It is the true soul that sees and creates the truth alive, out of which is to come a still greater truth, the re-born social soul.

Anarchism is the great liberator of man from the phantoms that have held him captive; it is the arbiter and pacifier of the two forces for individual and social harmony. To accomplish that unity, Anarchism has declared war on the pernicious influences which have so far prevented the harmonious blending of individual and social instincts, the individual and society.

Religion, the dominion of the human mind; Property, the dominion of human needs; and Government, the dominion of human conduct, represent the stronghold of man's enslavement and all the horrors it entails. Religion! How it dominates man's mind, how it humiliates and degrades his soul. God is everything, man is nothing, says religion. But out of that nothing God has created a kingdom so despotic, so tyrannical, so cruel, so terribly exacting that naught but gloom and tears and blood have ruled the world since gods began. Anarchism rouses man to rebellion against this black monster. Break your mental fetters, says Anarchism to man, for not until you think and judge for yourself will you get rid of the dominion of darkness, the greatest obstacle to all progress.

Property, the dominion of man's needs, the denial of the right to satisfy his needs. Time was when property claimed a divine right, when it came to man with the same refrain, even as religion, "Sacrifice! Abnegate! Submit!" The spirit of Anarchism has lifted man from his prostrate position. He now stands erect, with his face toward the light. He has learned to see the insatiable, devouring, devastating nature of property, and he is preparing to strike the monster dead.

"Property is robbery," said the great French Anarchist Proudhon. Yes, but without risk and danger to the robber. Monopolizing the accumulated efforts of man, property has robbed him of his birth-right, and has turned him loose a pauper and an outcast. Property has not even the time-worn excuse that man does not create enough to satisfy all needs. The ABC student of economics knows that the productivity of labor within the last few decades far exceeds normal demand. But what are normal demands to an abnormal institution? The only demand that property recognizes is its own gluttonous appetite for greater wealth, because wealth means power; the power to subdue, to crush, to exploit, the power to enslave, to outrage, to degrade. America is particularly boastful of her great power, her enormous national wealth. Poor America, of what avail is all her wealth, if the individuals comprising the nation are wretchedly poor? If they live in squalor, in filth, in crime, with hope and joy gone, a homeless, soilless army of human prey.

It is generally conceded that unless the returns of any business venture exceed the cost, bankruptcy is inevitable. But those engaged in the business of producing wealth have not yet learned even this simple lesson. Every year the cost of production in human life is growing larger (50,000 killed, 100,000 wounded in America last year); the returns to the masses, who help to create wealth, are ever getting smaller. Yet America continues to be blind to the inevitable bankruptcy of our business of production. Nor is this the only crime of the latter. Still more fatal is the crime of turning the producer into a mere particle of a machine, with less will and decision than his master of steel and iron. Man is being robbed not merely of the products of his labor, but of the power of free initiative, of originality, and the interest in, or desire for, the things he is making.

Real wealth consists in things of utility and beauty, in things that help to create strong, beautiful bodies and surroundings inspiring to live in. But if man is doomed to wind cotton around a spool, or dig coal, or build roads for thirty years of his life, there can be no talk of wealth. What he gives to the world is only gray and hideous things, reflecting a dull and hideous existence – too weak to live, too cowardly to die. Strange to say, there are people who extol this deadening method of centralized production as the proudest achievement of our age. They fail utterly to realize that if we are to continue in machine subserviency, our slavery is more complete than was our bondage to the King. They do not want to know that centralization is not only the death-knell of liberty, but also of health and beauty, of art and science, all these being impossible in a clock-like, mechanical atmosphere.

Anarchism cannot but repudiate such a method of production: its goal is the freest possible expression of all the latent powers of the individual. Oscar Wilde defines a perfect personality as "one who develops under perfect conditions, who is not wounded, maimed, or in danger." A perfect personality, then, is only possible in a state of society where man is free to choose the mode of work, the conditions of work, and the freedom to work. One to whom the making of a table, the building of a house, or the tilling of the soil, is what the painting is to the artist and the discovery to the scientist – the result of inspiration, of intense longing, and deep interest in work as a creative force. That being the ideal of Anarchism, its economic arrangements must consist of voluntary productive and distributive associations, gradually developing into free communism, as the best means of producing with the least waste of human energy. Anarchism, however, also recognizes the right of the individual, or numbers of individuals, to arrange at all times for other forms of work, in harmony with their tastes and desires.

Such free display of human energy being possible only under complete individual and social freedom, Anarchism directs its forces against the third and greatest foe of all social equality; namely, the State, organized authority, or statutory law – the dominion of human conduct.

Just as religion has fettered the human mind, and as property, or the monopoly of things, has subdued and stifled man's needs, so has the State enslaved his spirit, dictating every phase of conduct. "All government in essence," says Emerson, "is tyranny." It matters not whether it is government by divine right or majority rule. In every instance its aim is the absolute subordination of the individual.

Referring to the American government, the greatest American Anarchist, David Thoreau, said: "Government, what is it but a tradition, though a recent one, endeavoring to transmit itself unimpaired to posterity, but each instance losing its integrity; it has not the vitality and force of a single living man. Law never made man a whit more just; and by means of their respect for it, even the well disposed are daily made agents of injustice."

Indeed, the keynote of government is injustice. With the arrogance and self-sufficiency of the King who could do no wrong, governments ordain, judge, condemn, and punish the most insignificant offenses, while maintaining themselves by the greatest of all offenses, the annihilation of individual liberty. Thus Ouida is right when she maintains that "the State only aims at instilling those qualities in its public by which its demands are obeyed, and its exchequer is filled. Its highest attainment is the reduction of mankind to clockwork. In its atmosphere all those finer and more delicate liberties, which require treatment and spacious expansion, inevitably dry up and perish. The State requires a taxpaying machine in which there is no hitch, an exchequer in which there is never a deficit, and a public, monotonous, obedient, colorless, spiritless, moving humbly like a flock of sheep along a straight high road between two walls."

Yet even a flock of sheep would resist the chicanery of the State, if it were not for the corruptive, tyrannical, and oppressive methods it employs to serve its purposes. Therefore Bakunin repudiates the State as synonymous with the surrender of the liberty of the individual or small minorities – the destruction of social relationship, the curtailment, or complete denial even, of life itself, for its own aggrandizement. The State is the altar of political freedom and, like the religious altar, it is maintained for the purpose of human sacrifice.

In fact, there is hardly a modern thinker who does not agree that government, organized authority, or the State, is necessary *only* to maintain or protect property and monopoly. It has proven efficient in that function only.

Even George Bernard Shaw, who hopes for the miraculous from the State under Fabianism, nevertheless admits that "it is at present a huge machine for robbing and slave-driving of the poor by brute force." This being the case, it is hard to see why the clever prefacer wishes to uphold the State after poverty shall have ceased to exist.

Unfortunately there are still a number of people who continue in the fatal belief that government rests on natural laws, that it maintains social order and harmony, that it diminishes crime, and that it prevents the lazy man from fleecing his fellows. I shall therefore examine these contentions.

A natural law is that factor in man which asserts itself freely and spontaneously without any external force, in harmony with the requirements of nature. For instance, the demand for nutrition, for sex gratification, for light, air, and exercise, is a natural law. But its expression needs not the machinery of government, needs not the club, the gun, the handcuff, or the prison. To obey such laws, if we may call it obedience, requires only spontaneity and free opportunity. That governments do not maintain themselves through such harmonious factors is proven by the terrible array of violence, force, and coercion all governments use in order to live. Thus Blackstone is right when he says, "Human laws are invalid, because they are contrary to the laws of nature."

Unless it be the order of Warsaw after the slaughter of thousands of people, it is difficult to ascribe to governments any capacity for order or social harmony. Order derived through submission and maintained by terror is not much of a safe guaranty; yet that is the only "order" that governments have ever maintained. True social harmony grows naturally out of solidarity of interests. In a society where those who always work never have anything, while those who never work enjoy everything, solidarity of interests is non-existent; hence social harmony is but a myth. The only way organized authority meets this grave situation is by extending still greater privileges to those who have already monopolized the earth, and by still further enslaving the disinherited masses. Thus the entire arsenal of government – laws, police, soldiers, the courts, legislatures, prisons – is strenuously engaged in "harmonizing" the most antagonistic elements in society.

The most absurd apology for authority and law is that they serve to diminish crime. Aside from the fact that the State is itself the greatest criminal, breaking every written and natural law, stealing in the form of taxes, killing in the form of war and capital punishment, it has come to an absolute standstill in coping with crime. It has failed utterly to destroy or even minimize the horrible scourge of its own creation.

Crime is naught but misdirected energy. So long as every institution of today, economic, political, social, and moral, conspires to misdirect human energy into wrong channels; so long as most people are out of place doing the things they hate to do, living a life they loathe to live, crime will be inevitable, and all the laws on the statutes can only increase, but never do away with, crime. What does society, as it exists today, know of the process of despair, the poverty, the horrors, the fearful struggle the human soul must pass on its way to crime and degradation. Who that knows this terrible process can fail to see the truth in these words of Peter Kropotkin:

> Those who will hold the balance between the benefits thus attributed to law and punishment and the degrading effect of the latter on humanity; those who will estimate the torrent of depravity poured abroad in human society by the informer, favored by the Judge even, and paid for in clinking cash by governments, under the pretext of aiding to unmask crime; those who will go within prison walls and there see what human beings become when deprived of liberty, when subjected to the care of brutal keepers, to coarse, cruel words, to a thousand stinging, piercing humiliations, will agree with us that the entire apparatus of prison and punishment is an abomination which ought to be brought to an end.

The deterrent influence of law on the lazy man is too absurd to merit consideration. If society were only relieved of the waste and expense of keeping a lazy class, and the equally great expense of the paraphernalia of protection this lazy class requires, the social tables would contain an abundance for all, including even the occasional lazy individual. Besides, it is well to consider that laziness results either from special privileges, or physical and mental abnormalities. Our present insane system of production fosters both, and the most astounding phenomenon is that people should want to work at all now. Anarchism aims to strip labor of its deadening, dulling aspect, of its gloom and compulsion. It aims to make work an instrument of joy, of strength, of color, of real harmony, so that the poorest sort of a man should find in work both recreation and hope.

To achieve such an arrangement of life, government, with its unjust, arbitrary, repressive measures, must be done away with. At best it has but imposed one single mode of life upon all, without regard to individual and social variations and needs. In destroying government and statutory laws, Anarchism proposes to rescue the self-respect and independence of the individual from all restraint and invasion by authority. Only in freedom can man grow to his full stature. Only in freedom will he learn to think and move, and give the very best in him. Only in freedom will he realize the true force of the social bonds which knit men together, and which are the true foundation of a normal social life.

But what about human nature? Can it be changed? And if not, will it endure under Anarchism?

Poor human nature, what horrible crimes have been committed in thy name! Every fool, from king to policeman, from the flatheaded parson to the visionless dabbler in science, presumes to speak authoritatively of human nature. The greater the mental charlatan, the more definite his insistence on the wickedness and weaknesses of human nature. Yet, how can any one speak of it today, with every soul in a prison, with every heart fettered, wounded, and maimed?

John Burroughs has stated that experimental study of animals in captivity is absolutely useless. Their character, their habits, their appetites undergo a complete transformation when torn from their soil in field and forest. With human nature caged in a narrow space, whipped daily into submission, how can we speak of its potentialities?

Freedom, expansion, opportunity, and, above all, peace and repose, alone can teach us the real dominant factors of human nature and all its wonderful possibilities.

Anarchism, then, really stands for the liberation of the human mind from the dominion of religion; the liberation of the human body from the dominion of property; liberation from the shackles and restraint of government. Anarchism stands for a social order based on the free grouping of individuals for the purpose of producing real social wealth; an order that will guarantee to every human being free access to the earth and full enjoyment of the necessities of life, according to individual desires, tastes, and inclinations.

This is not a wild fancy or an aberration of the mind. It is the conclusion arrived at by hosts of intellectual men and women the world over; a conclusion resulting from the close and studious observation of the tendencies of modern society: individual liberty and economic equality, the twin forces for the birth of what is fine and true in man.

As to methods. Anarchism is not, as some may suppose, a theory of the future to be realized through divine inspiration. It is a living force in the affairs of our life, constantly creating new conditions. The methods of Anarchism therefore do not comprise an iron-clad program to be carried out under all circumstances. Methods must grow out of the economic needs of each place and clime, and of the intellectual and temperamental requirements of the individual. The serene, calm character of a Tolstoy will wish different methods for social reconstruction than the intense, overflowing personality of a Michael Bakunin or a Peter Kropotkin. Equally so it must be apparent that the economic and political needs of Russia will dictate more drastic measures than would England or America. Anarchism does not stand for military drill and uniformity; it does, however, stand for the spirit of revolt, in whatever form, against everything that hinders human growth. All Anarchists agree in that, as they also agree in their opposition to the political machinery as a means of bringing about the great social change.

"All voting," says Thoreau, "is a sort of gaming, like checkers, or backgammon, a playing with right and wrong; its obligation never exceeds that of expediency. Even voting for the right thing is doing nothing for it. A wise man will not leave the right to the mercy of chance, nor wish it to prevail through the power of the majority." A close examination of the machinery of politics and its achievements will bear out the logic of Thoreau.

What does the history of parliamentarism show? Nothing but failure and defeat, not even a single reform to ameliorate the economic and social stress of the people. Laws have been passed and enactments made for the improvement and protection of labor. Thus it was proven only last year that Illinois, with the most rigid laws for mine protection, had the greatest mine disasters. In States where child labor laws prevail, child exploitation is at its highest, and though with us the workers enjoy full political opportunities, capitalism has reached the most brazen zenith.

Even were the workers able to have their own representatives, for which our good Socialist politicians are clamoring, what chances are there for their honesty and good faith? One has but to bear in mind the process of politics to realize that its path of good intentions is full of pitfalls: wire-pulling, intriguing, flattering, lying, cheating; in fact, chicanery of every description, whereby the political aspirant can achieve success. Added to that is a complete demoralization of character and conviction, until nothing is left that would make one hope for anything from such a human derelict. Time and time again the people were foolish enough to trust, believe, and support with their last farthing aspiring politicians, only to find themselves betrayed and cheated.

It may be claimed that men of integrity would not become corrupt in the political grinding mill. Perhaps not; but such men would be absolutely helpless to exert the slightest influence in behalf of labor, as indeed has been shown in numerous instances. The State is the economic master of its servants. Good men, if such there be, would either remain true to their political faith and lose their economic support, or they would cling to their economic master and be utterly unable to do the slightest good. The political arena leaves one no alternative, one must either be a dunce or a rogue.

The political superstition is still holding sway over the hearts and minds of the masses, but the true lovers of liberty will have no more to do with it. Instead, they believe with Stirner that man has as much liberty as he is willing to take. Anarchism therefore stands for direct action, the open defiance of, and resistance to, all laws and restrictions, economic, social, and moral. But defiance and resistance are illegal. Therein lies the salvation of man. Everything illegal necessitates integrity, self-reliance, and courage. In short, it calls for free, independent spirits, for "men who are men, and who have a bone in their backs which you cannot pass your hand through."

Universal suffrage itself owes its existence to direct action. If not for the spirit of rebellion, of the defiance on the part of the American revolutionary fathers, their posterity would still wear the King's coat. If not for the direct action of a John Brown and his comrades, America would still trade in the flesh of the black man. True, the trade in white flesh is still going on; but that, too, will have to be abolished by direct action. Trade-unionism, the economic arena of the modern gladiator, owes its existence to direct action. It is but recently that law and government have attempted to crush the trade-union movement, and condemned the exponents of man's right to organize to prison as conspirators. Had they sought to assert their cause through begging, pleading, and compromise, trade-unionism would today be a negligible quantity. In France, in Spain, in Italy, in Russia, nay even in England (witness the growing rebellion of English labor unions), direct, revolutionary, economic action has become so strong a force in the battle for industrial liberty as to make the world realize the tremendous importance of labor's power. The General Strike, the supreme expression of the economic consciousness of the workers, was ridiculed in America but a short time ago. Today every great strike, in order to win, must realize the importance of the solidaric general protest.

Direct action, having proven effective along economic lines, is equally potent in the environment of the individual. There a hundred forces encroach upon his being, and only persistent resistance to them will finally set him free. Direct action against the authority in the shop, direct action against the authority of the law, direct action against the invasive, meddlesome authority of our moral code, is the logical, consistent method of Anarchism.

Will it not lead to a revolution? Indeed, it will. No real social change has ever come about without a revolution. People are either not familiar with their history, or they have not yet learned that revolution is but thought carried into action.

Anarchism, the great leaven of thought, is today permeating every phase of human endeavor. Science, art, literature, the drama, the effort for economic betterment, in fact every individual and social opposition to the existing disorder of things, is illumined by the spiritual light of Anarchism. It is the philosophy of the sovereignty of the individual. It is the theory of social harmony. It is the great, surging, living truth that is reconstructing the world, and that will usher in the Dawn.

35

What to Do and How to Do It

George Washington Woodbey

Introduction

George W. Woodbey (1854–1915?) was born into slavery in Johnson County, Tennessee. He learned to read and write after the emancipation of 1865. Woodbey was ordained a Baptist minister in Emporia, Kansas in 1874; he was active in the Republican Party of Missouri, and was a leader in the Prohibition Party in Kansas, where he ran unsuccessfully for lieutenant-governor and for Congress on the Prohibition ticket. In 1902 he became the minister of Mount Zion Baptist Church in San Diego and was the leading black Christian Socialist in the first decade of the twentieth century. He was elected to the executive board of the Socialist Party and was nominated to be the vice-presidential candidate for Eugene V. Debs's presidential campaign in 1908. Woodbey authored such fiery pamphlets as *What to Do and How to Do It or Socialism vs. Capitalism* (1903) and *Why the Negro Should Vote the Socialist Ticket* (1910). He was influenced by Edward Bellamy's *Looking Backward* (1887), and authored a form of Christian Socialism in *The Bible and Socialism* (1904).

Dedication

This little book is dedicated to that class of citizens who desire to know what the Socialists want to do and how they propose to do it. By

Taken from Philip S. Foner (ed.), *Black Socialist Preacher* (California: Synthesis Publications, 1983).

one who was once a chattel slave freed by the proclamation of Lincoln and now wishes to be free from the slavery of capitalism.

Preface

Nothing original is claimed for this little book, the principal object of which has been to make the subjects treated as plain as possible to the reader. To the Socialist who may think it worth while to read it, the author would say that its object is to meet the demands of that large and increasing class of persons who have not yet accepted Socialism, but would do so if they could see any possible way of putting it into practice. No one knows better than he that any plans suggested may undergo various modifications; yet it would not be sensible to start to build a house without a plan.

The author has tried to describe the workings of the capitalistic system in a few brief words; and to make plain the impossibility of taking over the entire industrial plant except through the organization of the working class into a political party for that purpose. He has tried to show how the Socialist Party if in power might proceed to take over the industries; and also a possible plan by which the whole people might operate the land, factories, and means of transportation, as joint owners, for their own benefit.

The author's experience as a speaker has shown him that many things said, while perfectly plain to the Socialist, go over the head of the hearer who has not studied the question; and so with much that is written in some otherwise excellent books on the subject.

If this book is found to have any merit it will be seen in its attempt to make the subject treated plain, so that "the wayfaring man though a fool may not err therein." People are often confronted by attempts at explanation which they cannot understand. As to whether this book is open to the same objection, the reader must decide.

As to the needs of simple explanation in making Socialists, the author speaks largely from his own experience in becoming a Socialist, and in trying to make others understand. He has been asked many times to embody some of the things he has said to the thousands who have listened to his talks, in a written form, and this is an attempt to answer that request.

Introductory

It was at the breakfast table the first morning after my nearly seventeen years' absence from her that mother said to me: "I believe you look very much like you used to, but I never was so much astonished as when you wrote me you had gone off with the Socialists. Have you given up the Bible and the ministry and gone into politics?"

No, I replied, since studying Socialism I believe more firmly in every word of it if possible than I did before. Much of it I just now begin to understand. I know and respect your firm belief in the Bible, so let me remind you of a few things that perhaps you haven't thought of.

Well, the first thing the book tells us is that the earth was given to mankind as a home, and that he was to have dominion over it; not only over the earth, but the fish of the sea and the fowls of the air, and everything that lives on the face of the earth (Gen. 1, 26–9).

We are told that God overthrew the people of Egypt and delivered the Jews, because their masters had taken their labor for nothing. And the reason the Jews were told on leaving the country to go and borrow every one of his master, gold, silver and raiment, was because their labor had produced it all and they were entitled to it (read Ex. iii: 7–9. Ex. xi: 2).

The first thing after their delivery from slavery and oppression was to give them a government in whose constitution there were ten articles known as commandments, which were read to both the men and the women for their acceptance (Ex. xx). This government was administered by judges, appointed by the people, for five hundred years, until the people rejected God's plan, we are told in the book of Samuel, and set up a monarchy (I Sam. viii).

Under that government the jubilee law prevented the making of public debts (Lev. xxv: 8–17). The land could not be deeded away forever (Lev. xxv: 23). Interest and mortgages were unlawful (Neh. v: 1–13). The prophets spent their time largely in preaching against the corrupt governments of the world, including the Jews, when they broke the law. And one of the principal charges was that they oppressed the poor by taking the products of their labor. "For ye have eaten up the vineyard, the spoils of the poor are in your houses. What mean ye that ye beat my people to pieces and grind the face of the poor? saith the Lord of Hosts" (Isaiah iii: 14–15). Some politics in that, isn't there mother? The prophet points out here the law of surplus value which is the spoils of the poor taken by the rich, creating the class struggle.

Christ drove the bankers and profit-mongers out of the temple, and called them thieves; and if their business was stealing it would have been as bad anywhere else as in the temple (Matt. xxi: 12–13).

"But George," said my mother, "some of the men in your Socialist party don't believe in either God or the Bible, or that the world, or man, was created."

Yes, I said, and I found a still larger number of unbelievers in the Republican party before I left it some twenty years ago, and I understand that the other parties have their equal portion. While I believe in the Bible account of God, the origin of the earth and man, and that God gave the earth to man as a home, my Socialist comrade who does not accept that will agree with me that man is here, and the earth is here, and that it is the present home of the race, at least.

While I believe in the reality of life here and hereafter, I will not fail to agree with them about Socialism because we cannot agree about the hereafter. Whoever is willing to make things better here, which the Bible teaches is essential to the hereafter, I will join hands with as far as we can go. And as Socialism is a scheme for bettering things here first, and each skeptical comrade thinks he can hold his own peculiar views of God, creation, and the future and not find it necessary to give them up in order to become a good Socialist, neither am I required to give up my belief in all these things in order to be equally as good a Socialist.

Some may hold that only science teaches Socialism, but I am free to believe that both science and the Bible teach it. Some are Socialists only because they think it for their best interest here to favor it; others, like myself, are Socialists because they think that mankind is entitled to the best of everything in both this world and the next.

Some other time I will tell you more about what the Bible teaches on this subject. What you want to know at present is, what the Socialists want and how they expect to get it.

So under Socialism every person will be free to have their own religion or none, just as they please, so long as they do not interfere with others.

Capitalism

Before I try to make plain to you what the Socialists want, let us take a look at the present condition of things. If the present conditions are all right, then we do not need any change.

We all agree that the earth is the home of man; the Bible, science, and common sense all teach us that. From our very nature we must have land, air, and water in order to live. When I say we need land, I mean all the earth contains that which is necessary for our life and happiness, such as food, clothing, houses, etc. Now, you can see that if all the people allow a few of the people to in any way get possession of the earth – which is the home of all – then the majority will find themselves without a right to live on the earth unless they pay others for the privilege. You can see, mother, that is just the condition we are in at the present time. Since no man, or set of men, made the earth, no man, or set of men, have the right to attempt to divide the land among men by title deeds, or sell or rent to us the right to live on the earth. Who gave the first man the right to sell the land?

If a man has a right to any amount of land under deed, then he has a right to all he can get. If a limit is to be placed on it, where can we fix it so as to be sure not to injure future generations? The Creator said, "The land is mine and it shall not be sold forever," and philosophers like Marx, Spencer, and others, have recognized the truth of that principle, namely, that the land shall not be sold forever.

But I started to tell you why we call the system we are living under now capitalism. By capital, we mean the tools, buildings, machines, and all other things we use to work with. By capitalism, we mean the system which allows a number of the people to own the earth, the tools, buildings, machines, factories, railroads, and other means of travel, production, and transportation, and thus take from the worker what he produces.

With the land, machinery, and means of transportation privately owned, those who are not owners cannot live on the earth, work with machinery, transport anything, or travel, without paying rent for a home, giving nearly all their labor will produce to the owner of the machines and then with their wages buy back what they have produced in the shop or factory, or on the farm, with a large profit added.

If the laborer produces in a small way and undertakes to ship his produce, the owners of the railroads and steamships get it all; so it comes about that under capitalism we have rent, interest, and profits, which enables a few to live at the expense of the many.

I suppose I need not remind you that here again the Bible stands with the Socialists; when speaking of both the brother and the stranger it says: "Take thou no usury of him or increase – thou shalt not give him thy money upon usury, nor lend thy victuals, for increase" (Lev. xxv: 36–7). Mark you, all increase is here forbidden. The people doomed to destruction in the land of Canaan were the only ones the Jews might loan to on increase until Socialism is established, which will, as we proceed, be shown to be only the golden rule put into practice. Christ said: "Loan hoping to receive nothing" (Luke vi: 35).

The system under which we now live, where each man produces for himself and competes with his neighbor for a market, is sometimes called the competitive system, but as this is growing less and less so, as the trust organizes and gets the capital into the hands of the few, we prefer to call it the capitalistic system. This system of private ownership is lawful only because the capitalists, who are the owning class, make all the laws; and the things that are now owned by the people are managed by the capitalists so as to get as much out of them for this class as possible. The enormous price paid to the railroads for carrying the mail – some forty-three millions of dollars annually – shows what I mean.

Under capitalism the money of the people has been given to the capitalists, the public lands have been given to that class, valuable franchises granted, on one pretense or another, through laws of their own making.

Billions of national, state, and municipal debts have been created and held by the capitalistic class on which to draw interest out of the labor of the poor; for labor pays everything, on the universally admitted principle that all wealth is created by labor. Labor exists first and produces all capital; which is simply the tools, machines, and other things with which it works, as I have said before.

It follows, therefore, as a rule, that the capitalist, who is not a producer, furnishes nothing except as he takes it through rent, interest, and profits from the worker, by private ownership of capital, and places it in other enterprises. It is in the very nature of things impossible for all to become capitalists except through cooperative ownership of all capital.

In the past some have made their first start into capitalism by saving their earnings as wage workers; but single persons could succeed at saving only because the masses did not try the same thing; for the reason that had all, or even a majority, tried saving, the thing they were working at for wages would have stopped and thrown them out of employment; because there would, under the capitalist system, have been no market for the product of their labor. The laborers largely form the market for the sale of what they produce for the capitalist. Under the system of capitalism now in operation it is the man who spends his money who keeps things going, and not the man who saves it.

That capitalism has not been a blessing to the masses of mankind, the condition of extreme wealth on the one hand, and extreme poverty on the other, shows too plainly to need any argument. It cannot be denied, even by the opponents of Socialism, that whatever of misery, poverty, and dissatisfaction exists now, is the result of capitalism. The present system divides men into two classes, the capitalists who rule, and the poor, who, as I have said, produce the wealth. Thus men are divided into hostile, warring camps.

You may ask, if the Bible as well as science favors Socialism, why haven't we got it before now? Because the world is not yet ready for it; these teachings are to get us ready. According to the Bible we have had first the age of the patriarchs, which suited the conception of men at that time. Then followed the period of the law, which upon questions of economics, as we have shown,

stood where the Socialist stands as to land and interest, and against the exploiting of the poor. "The law was our schoolmaster to bring us unto Christ." "The law made nothing perfect," but was the training school to bring men to those higher ideals found in Christ (Gal iii: 24).

When we get to Christ we find in him and his teachings the perfect doctrine of social brotherhood. That some people who accept Christ in other things have not grown to a full understanding of his economic teachings is not strange, since he taught for all time to come. We cannot afford to denounce men who have not grown as fast as we have, but must continue to teach them, and at the same time go on learning ourselves.

Every Socialist will recollect that there was a time when these things, which now look so plain to him, were first brought to his notice, and that many of us who are now Socialists were equally as slow to accept the truth as those we are now dealing with both in and out of the church; so it is not common sense to denounce men for not seeing at once what it took us years to find out. The capitalists are not yet all united along the line of their class interest, as the many independent business concerns, not yet united by the trust, shows. The trusts are organizing the capitalists, and the Socialists are organizing the workers for the final contest at the ballot box.

Socialism

"I think I understand what you have said," mother replied. "I have to pay rent to one of the richest men in town for the right to set my house on the earth that God made. The thing I want to know now is, what you Socialists want to give us in the place of what we have? When I know that, I can begin to know what to expect when the Socialist party is elected to power."

Well, mother, the Socialist platforms, not only in the United States but in all countries where there is any, ask for the cooperative ownership of the means of production and distribution. To one who understands Socialism, that is all plain enough and easily understood, but to you, mother, it may need some explanation.

In a factory, or on a railroad, the workers all cooperate, or work together, like the wheels of a clock; but, as I have shown, the owners of the machines, or of the roads, get nearly all of the products of their labor, because the workers don't own the factories and the roads. A carpenter produces a house by means of his knowledge in using his tools on the raw material. By means of hand and brain, skilled in the use of tools, we produce wealth.

"How can we produce anything without money, George?"

Money never produces anything; it only represents things; it only entitles one to go into the markets and get so much wealth. What little money the laboring man gets is a check to the store for so much of the wealth his own labor has produced, and which the owners of the capital took from him and now sell back to him at a profit. The laborer gets thirty-two cents for producing a Stetson hat in a factory for which he would have to pay five dollars in order to buy it. If the people who do the work owned the factory, the worker would get the hat at cost, and so with all other things.

Just as old Mr. Jones and his sons who own the farm over there don't have to buy at a profit what they raise on the farm – they earned that by their labor – so if the whole nation works together like Mr. Jones and his boys and raise crops of all kinds, animals of all kinds, make furniture, build houses, run railroads, and steamboats, in fact do everything they now do, they owning the tools, and the land and roads, as the Jones' do their farm, they will not need to buy what their own labor produces.

"I have heard some Socialists talk, but when they get done I couldn't understand what they did want to do; but so far I can understand you all right," said mother.

What the Socialists want is simple enough for a child to understand. There are only four things they demand: First, they want all the people to have an equal interest in the land, like Jones and his boys in their farm, because the earth is our home and no one can live without it. It is the source from which we get everything. I have shown you how we would produce what we need by working together.

The second thing the Socialists want is to have the whole people own the tools they work with to produce wealth from the earth. Everything, from a spade to a large factory, is simply a tool which is used to work with. If the workers allow a few of the people to own all the tools they will still charge them nearly all they produce, for the use of the tools, just as they do now; yet all these tools are made by the workers and represent what they had to leave in the hands of the capitalists in order to get the work without which they would starve.

The third thing the Socialists want, is to have the workers, who are to own the earth and the tools, own also the means of taking both themselves and their goods wherever necessary or desirable. This means that the people should own all the railroads, ships, and other means for hauling their goods, or for travel. The fourth thing is the working class must have the right to make all the laws to govern the industries by direct vote.

"Then George," asked mother, "you wouldn't have anybody own anything, themselves?"

Yes, all these things when produced, and distributed to the people who produced them, would be their private property; but all the people who were capable of it would have to do their part of the work, or get nothing. No one could live, then, by charging them for the use of the land, tools, and means of hauling persons and goods.

"But," questioned mother anxiously, "I have worked awful hard for this little old shell of a house; would I have to give it up?"

I suppose you wouldn't mind having a better one, would you? With your share of the products of the nation you could have a good house, all fireproof, with the latest modern improvements in it. That house with all its belongings would be yours – your children could have the same, and the other people as well. The people can make their own houses just as well as their own postage-stamps.

"You keep on talking about wealth, and means of production and distribution; what do you mean?" asked mother, rising and beginning to clear up the table.

By the means of production, we mean, as I have said, any tools, or process by which we produce wealth. By wealth we mean anything that is necessary for human comfort or pleasure, such as the necessary food, clothing, houses, and fuel.

As man is not altogether an animal, it is necessary for him to have knowledge through the means of books and other sources; and pleasure through travel and intercourse with his fellow men.

The earth with its various things, such as coal, iron, lead, copper, zinc, and other treasures too numerous to mention, together with the things growing out of it, and roaming over it, forms the principal source of wealth. We sometimes fail to distinguish between these sources of wealth, and actual wealth, which can only be produced by the skill of man in preparing them for his various uses.

Our mental necessities, which can only be supplied to us through means of books, travel, and intercourse with others, are largely dependent on our skill in the use of the sources of wealth, in their promotion; for we can have neither knowledge, pleasure, or intercourse, in their completeness, without the use of these resources of the earth, in a greater or lesser degree, as necessity may require.

Under the head of means of production, I repeat, would come the earth, and the various machinery now in use, or to be used in the production of the necessities of life. All these the socialists want the whole people to own, instead of a few individuals, as now.

By way of illustration, just as in a joint stock company consisting of one hundred men with one share each, who are equal owners of the whole concern, so the whole people, under the cooperative system, will be equal shareholders in all the wealth of the United States.

While the post office is not conducted on a basis of equality in compensation for the services rendered, as it would be under complete Socialism, the ownership is vested in the whole people, just where the Socialists would put everything else. In this way all would be interested, all being equal shareholders in the plants of industry. There would then be no class without property. And there would be no more danger of your losing your equal share in the cooperative commonwealth than there is now of your losing your share in the post office, the public road, or the public school.

Agitation

The first step toward bringing about Socialism is agitation, which is the only means by which the public can be educated. It may be done through the press, the pulpit, the rostrum, and private conversation. Socialism is now passing through this period of agitation and thousands are anxiously listening to the glad tidings.

It has been well said that the cooperative commonwealth must first be builded in the minds of the people before it can be put into actual practice. This work of building the new commonwealth is now going on night and day in all parts of the world. Socialism when once intelligently understood is a fire in the bones of its converts, and must flash out; so when you have made one intelligent Socialist, he makes another one, and so on indefinitely.

The Socialist press throughout the world is now a great power amounting to many hundred publi-

cations, from monthly magazines to great dailies; and these in the languages of all the civilized nations. Vast book concerns are running night and day, sending out tons of literature. In all ages the agitators of new ideas, in religion, science, or government, have created a new literature adapted to their purpose, just as the Socialists are now doing.

The American Revolution was brought on by agitators. Moses and the prophets were agitators, who met with great opposition. Christ was an agitator and sent forth the twelve as such; in fact, all founders of new systems of religion, science, or politics, have, in the very nature of the case, been agitators. The delivering of speeches and the writing of books have always formed a necessary part of the work.

We are not contending that a thing is necessarily right because it has its agitators and its literature; the claims of a question at issue, to be right, rest upon a different ground.

"Then," said mother, "all that don't make the Socialists right, George."

No, of course not. All I was trying to show in this connection is, that the Socialists are proceeding in the usual way with the work before them. Among all the men of history, Paul was possibly the greatest agitator, both as speaker and writer. In the very nature of the case every true preacher is an agitator. In this country the Socialists are following in the footsteps of the abolitionists in agitating the question at issue, and in the use of press, literature, and speakers. Speakers, books, periodicals, and papers are increasing daily.

In the beginning of the movement many persons were imprisoned and otherwise maltreated, in all countries; but Socialism has steadily grown, until almost all legislative bodies of the world have their Socialist members and the question can no longer be ignored. While in some nations Socialism promises to become dominant at no distant day, the most significant thing in the Socialist movement is to be found in the substantial agreement of Socialists throughout the world.

The first thing the capitalist parties of this country have done is to ignore the movement. But that day has about passed, and when they have to meet the Socialist agitation, the growth of Socialism will be much more rapid.

The attention given Socialist speakers and the demand for literature is significant.

[...]

417

Socialist Government

"How are you going to govern your new common-wealth? And will not your representatives sell you out?" mother questioned.

When Socialism is established the representative system of government will be at an end.

"But," urged mother, "how are you going to get along without someone to make the laws? Won't you always be voting?"

No; when the land, factories, and means of transportation all belong to the people collectively, we will need but few laws. We make a large number of laws now, trying to regulate and govern all kinds of things in private hands. All that will then be done away with. We make many criminal laws now, because men are led into all kinds of wickedness in order to make a living.

The present system of privately owned industries keeps us in a state of strife with one another, even forcing the unfortunate to steal or rob in order to live. The capitalist class makes laws legalizing their methods of exploiting the people; and thus protect themselves in so doing, and the poor are imprisoned if they violate them.

Under Socialist government any general law affecting the people could be drawn up by any citizen, and when petitioned for by the requisite number of voters – for example, five per cent, as in some countries where this is already in effect as a means of making laws – a vote could be taken and if carried by a majority would become a law.

All rules and laws regulating departments, or which only related to particular departments and did not affect the interests of the general public, could be left to the workers of such departments, because they alone would best understand them. These rules of the several departments could be submitted to a vote of the workers in each department by the same method used in submitting the general laws to the whole people.

As each worker would be an equal shareholder, not only the department in which he was a worker, but also in all the other industries of the country, no bosses would be needed in any place where the workers understood their work; as we would need no boss to keep us at our own work we would have less bosses and more workers.

Thus you see that under Socialism the people would make all their own laws by voting for or against them, instead of voting for a few men to make laws by which they must abide whether they liked them or not. So the majority of the people would make the laws by which the officials would be governed, in place of the officials making the laws to govern the whole people, and the majority of the people would therefore constitute the head of the government; and the officers, who would be merely occupying clerical and executive positions instead of being lawmakers, would do what the people said, or the voters who elected them would drop them back into the ranks and put others in their places.

Under Socialism criminals would soon disappear, because the conditions which breed crime – those embraced by our present industrial system – would be gone. Men would, as now, have to abide by the laws made by the majority, or suffer whatever penalty was prescribed by the law. So long as tribunals for the enforcement of the law were needed, they would be provided by the people, and no longer. There would be no private interests to defeat the ends of justice, such as big corporation suits, wills, deeds, and so on.

A general law establishing an equal distribution of the products of industry would be inevitable, because when it came to a vote on distribution the workers – each of whom would be an equal shareholder with every other – would agree to nothing less, and if there were any who did not like it they would have to abide by it; as the majority would decide what it thought was just and right.

Under Socialism the free schools of the nation would be fitting men and women for their positions in the public industries; and with equal opportunities much of the apparent differences among individuals would disappear. The unequal distribution of wealth is an outgrowth of capitalism. The few who privately own the capital decide how the wealth of the nation shall be distributed; but under Socialism the worker would own the capital, and would decide as to the distribution of wealth by a majority vote.

The justice of economic equality can be seen in the fact that all the different workers are equally essential to the mechanism of production as are its different parts of machinery to a watch.

The people could by vote fix by law the number of hours all must work, as is often done now, except that the people do not get a vote on it. These hours could be changed with the advancement of machinery. If any would not abide by the laws passed by the majority of the workers, they would have to go without a living, as there would be no private employment, all the industries being owned and operated by the whole people.

The statistics of each department would of course be published that the workers might know just what had been produced for their use. Taxation would then be a thing of the past, as that which was formerly taxed as private property would then have become public property.

It is quite probable that under Socialism the largest number of persons would live in towns for the sake of association, but as municipal ownership would then be completely established, the government of towns and cities would doubtless be left to the direct vote of the people, just as the larger industries would be governed. It is as true of city government that few laws would be needed under Socialism, as of the government of the industries, when everything is owned and operated by the entire people.

The Socialists are doubtless now in their government through the locals gradually developing the form of government that will control the co-operative commonwealth in place of our representative form of law making.

Conclusion

It is sometimes said that it is useless to attempt to outline any possible plan of procedure for cooperative industry, and that all must be left to the future. But it has always seemed to me that certain great principles of industrial management cannot be avoided under the new commonwealth.

For instance, most of the departments which I have mentioned are already operated by the workers collectively, and must still be operated in that manner when taken over by the working class, so far as labor is concerned, the difference being one of ownership and government.

Then again, the opposition to what is known as government ownership on the part of the scientific Socialists is based on the fact that under our representative form of government large salaries would be voted by the irresponsible representatives to themselves, while a comparatively small wage would be given to the real wealth producers. This abuse being inherent in the nature of our representative form of government it would be asking too much to insist upon leaving the same power in the hands of any set of men; it should be given to the whole people to whom it rightly belongs. Hence what I have said as to a new form of government here, is as pertinent as though we were living under a monarchy. Unless the possibility of this fraud is taken away, everything would have to depend upon the continued honesty of our class conscious representatives after Socialism was established.

"I think I have heard Socialists themselves say that it was not possible to say beforehand just how things could be managed," observed mother.

What we have said is only to show that it is possible to do the things that must be done and [this plan] will not be followed out if anything better can be done. But when, as a speaker, men have questioned me as to how things could be carried out I have found it not at all convincing to tell them I could see no way and we must wait till the time came before offering a possible plan.

As things are going now everything will be organized to our hand and all we will have to do is to take the industries and go on with the work.

"Well, you have convinced me that I am about as much of a slave now as I was in the south, and I am ready to accept any way out of this drudgery," mother remarked as the conversation turned on other subjects.

36

What the Indian Means to America

Luther Standing Bear

Introduction

Luther Standing Bear (Ota Kte, Mochunozhin), (1868–1939), was Chief of the Oglala, Lakota, from 1905 until his death. He was born Ota Kte on the Pine Ridge Reservation in South Dakota. Standing Bear was raised as a traditional Sioux, growing up in Nebraska and South Dakota, and he was a hereditary chief of the Dakotas. He was one of the first students to attend the Carlisle Indian School in Pennsylvania. He held various jobs, including teacher, minister, and clerk, and in 1898 he toured with the Buffalo Bill Wild West Show, which led him to California and the world of acting. In the 1920s and 1930s he fought to improve conditions for Indians on the reservations, writing several books about Indian life and government policy. Standing Bear was a member of the National League for Justice to the American Indian, Oglala Council, the Actors' Guild of Hollywood, and the Indian Actors' Association. He called for an examination of American Indian philosophy and its relevance to education. At the time of the Wounded Knee Massacre in 1891, he was deeply moved by the injustice of American forces.

The feathered and blanketed figure of the American Indian has come to symbolize the American continent. He is the man who through centuries has been moulded and sculpted by the same hand that shaped its mountains, forests, and plains, and marked the course of its rivers.

Taken from *Land of the Spotted Eagle*, 1933 (Lincoln: University of Nebraska Press, 1978).

The American Indian is of the soil, whether it be the region of forests, plains, pueblos, or mesas. He fits into the landscape, for the hand that fashioned the continent also fashioned the man for his surroundings. He once grew as naturally as the wild sunflowers; he belongs just as the buffalo belonged.

With a physique that fitted, the man developed fitting skills – crafts which today are called American. And the body had a soul, also formed and moulded by the same master hand of harmony. Out of the Indian approach to existence there came a great freedom – an intense and absorbing love for nature; a respect for life; enriching faith in a Supreme Power; and principles of truth, honesty, generosity, equity, and brotherhood as a guide to mundane relations.

Becoming possessed of a fitting philosophy and art, it was by them that native man perpetuated his identity; stamped it into the history and soul of this country – made land and man one.

By living – struggling, losing, meditating, imbibing, aspiring, achieving – he wrote himself into ineraceable evidence – an evidence that can be and often has been ignored, but never totally destroyed. Living – and all the intangible forces that constitute that phenomenon – are brought into being by Spirit, that which no man can alter. Only the hand of the Supreme Power can transform man; only Wakan Tanka can transform the Indian. But of such deep and infinite graces finite man has little comprehension. He has, therefore, no weapons with which to slay the unassailable. He can only foolishly trample.

420

The white man does not understand the Indian for the reason that he does not understand America. He is too far removed from its formative processes. The roots of the tree of his life have not yet grasped the rock and soil. The white man is still troubled with primitive fears; he still has in his consciousness the perils of this frontier continent, some of its fastnesses not yet having yielded to his questing footsteps and inquiring eyes. He shudders still with the memory of the loss of his forefathers upon its scorching deserts and forbidding mountain-tops. The man from Europe is still a foreigner and an alien. And he still hates the man who questioned his path across the continent.

But in the Indian the spirit of the land is still vested; it will be until other men are able to divine and meet its rhythm. Men must be born and reborn to belong. Their bodies must be formed of the dust of their forefathers' bones.

The attempted transformation of the Indian by the white man and the chaos that has resulted are but the fruits of the white man's disobedience of a fundamental and spiritual law. The pressure that has been brought to bear upon the native people, since the cessation of armed conflict, in the attempt to force conformity of custom and habit has caused a reaction more destructive than war, and the injury has not only affected the Indian, but has extended to the white population as well. Tyranny, stupidity, and lack of vision have brought about the situation now alluded to as the "Indian Problem."

There is, I insist, no Indian problem as created by the Indian himself. Every problem that exists today in regard to the native population is due to the white man's cast of mind, which is unable, at least reluctant, to seek understanding and achieve adjustment in a new and a significant environment into which it has so recently come.

The white man excused his presence here by saying that he had been guided by the will of his God; and in so saying absolved himself of all responsibility for his appearance in a land occupied by other men.

Then, too, his law was a written law; his divine decalogue reposed in a book. And what better proof that his advent into this country and his subsequent acts were the result of divine will! He brought the Word! There ensued a blind worship of written history, of books, of the written word, that has denuded the spoken word of its power and sacredness. The written word became established as a criterion of the superior man – a symbol of emotional fineness. The man who could write his name on a piece of paper, whether or not he possessed the spiritual fineness to honor those words in speech, was by some miraculous formula a more highly developed and sensitized person than the one who had never had a pen in hand, but whose spoken word was inviolable and whose sense of honor and truth was paramount. With false reasoning was the quality of human character measured by man's ability to make with an implement a mark upon paper. But granting this mode of reasoning be correct and just, then where are to be placed the thousands of illiterate whites who are unable to read and write? Are they, too, "savages"? Is not humanness a matter of heart and mind, and is it not evident in the form of relationship with men? Is not kindness more powerful than arrogance; and truth more powerful than the sword?

True, the white man brought great change. But the varied fruits of his civilization, though highly colored and inviting, are sickening and deadening. And if it be the part of civilization to maim, rob, and thwart, then what is progress?

I am going to venture that the man who sat on the ground in his tipi meditating on life and its meaning, accepting the kinship of all creatures, and acknowledging unity with the universe of things was infusing into his being the true essence of civilization. And when native man left off this form of development, his humanization was retarded in growth.

Another most powerful agent that gave native man promise of developing into a true human was the responsibility accepted by parenthood. Mating among Lakotas was motivated, of course, by the same laws of attraction that motivate all beings; however, considerable thought was given by parents of both boy and girl to the choosing of mates. And a still greater advantage accrued to the race by the law of self-mastery which the young couple voluntarily placed upon themselves as soon as they discovered they were to become parents. Immediately, and for some time after, the sole thought of the parents was in preparing the child for life. And true civilization lies in the dominance of self and not in the dominance of other men.

How far this idea would have gone in carrying my people upward and toward a better plane of existence, or how much of an influence it was in the development of their spiritual being, it is not possible to say. But it had its promises. And it cannot be gainsaid that the man who is rising to a higher estate is the man who is putting into his being the essence of humanism. It is self-effort that develops, and by this token the greatest factor today in dehumanizing races is the manner in which the machine is used – the product of one man's brain doing the work for another. The hand is the tool that has built man's mind; it, too, can refine it.

37

Our Democracy and the American Indian

Laura M. C. Kellogg

Introduction

Laura M. C. Kellogg (Indian name, Wynnogene), (1880–1949), is credited with being the best Iroquois orator and manager of its syntax. She was most influential in re-establishing the League of Iroquois Confederacy (Six Nations) by reconstructing the traditional political offices at the Onondaga Reservation, the historical capital of the League. She graduated with honors from Grafton Hall, Episcopal Diocese, and attended numerous colleges. One of the original three theorists of the Society of American Indians (along with Arthur C. Parker and Dennison Wheelock), she was compared to Booker T. Washington in her call for self-help for the Indian race. She advocated communal development projects for each tribal village, and equity, self-sufficiency, and special consideration of individual tribal resources. Her Lolomi plan (a Hopi term meaning "perfect goodness be upon you") was a blueprint for restoring traditional values, the clan system, tribal sovereignty, and sustainable communal development. Democracy is to fit the traditions and self-interest of a given race.

To the American People

The idea of the League of Nations and Democracy originated on the American Continent about 600 years ago. It came from an American Indian.

Taken from *Our Democracy and the American Indian* (Missouri: Kansas City, 1920).

At a time when the jungles of wilderness in what is now the Empire State, and the region of the Great Lakes resounded with the war-wshoop of enemy tribes, and the great stock of the Iroquois were living bloody days, a son was born to the Turtle clan. He had been predicted by the seers. His parents had been selected for him by the clan and its Council leadership. In those primitive days, the greatest interest in the life of the Iroquois was the production of the physically perfect and fearless man. This time the seers said to his mother: "A leader to all the Iroquois and to all the tribes of this Great Island is to come soon. Prepare for him." And when he was born the Council sent a runner to all the tribes of the Iroquois to announce him. They watched him grow. They watched his eye, they watched his body. Physically he was of that type of man of whom Kipling has since written:

> He trod the ring like a buck in spring
> And he looked like a lance in rest.

Almost too early he excelled in the games; almost too soon he changed his voice, and the old chiefs shook their heads with grave concern over his matchless courage and ambitions, and his youth. Already the Long Trail called to him, the Long Trail, that more than severe Epictetan school of the American Indian, which said to the young man at puberty, "Go, find yourself in the Great Silence, and do not come back without achievement."

When he went away, they sent the prophet to his mother to tell her the smokes promised his return.

And when Sagoyewhatha, the Awakener of the people, had finished all his lessons, and the last fast was upon him, he put his ear close to Mother Earth, and begged for the message of the Great Spirit. It was the message of peace and love to his fellow-man. It was the message of organization, confederacy, government, order, progress.

Sagoyewhatha went home, and after many councils, the Iroquois Confederacy, the League of the Five Nations, was launched. When the organization was completed they adopted the King of Birds as the national emblem. The nations called themselves ongwe-onwe, which means real people, as distinguished from odwaganha, which means savages.

Once cohered, they marked out the territory of each separate nation, and created the policy that the home of the Nations was not to be the ground of wars. They began offensive warfare, taking in the peaceful tribes and their conquests, and of all these they exacted the learning of the Iroquois language, and tribute for their protection. They expanded westward to the Ohio Valley, they conquered and held certain strips southward as far as the Carolinas. They dreamed of finally allying themselves with the Aztecs and subduing the Great Island into a peaceful empire.

Once only they were whipped after this; that was by the French General who did not know their position. It was the first time they had met modern ammunition. Later, because of this, when the contest between the French and English arose, for the possession of this continent, the Five Nations allied themselves with the Anglo-Saxon. They constituted the balance of power which was necessary to win the continent for the English.

The great note in the Iroquois constitution was confederation upon qualification. As proof of this the Tuscaroras later came into the League as the Sixth Nation, though they were years trying to get in.

When Franklin and the other writers of the Constitution of the United States sat at Albany, they sent for a delegation of the Five Nations to come before them. And when they were asked to explain their constitution their head chief took the wampam, that sacred strand, the touch of which was necessary to give oath.

"This strand is the record of the Galiwhago," he said, "these five figures of men holding hands means that in times of peace each Nation is free unto itself like a man. But when the eagle, which scans the heights and the valleys over the home of the Nations, gives the cry, then are they, one heart, one head, one man."

Tradition says Franklin brought his hand down on the table and said: "That's the greatest wisdom I have heard among the nations of men." And so, historically, he admitted elsewhere that the idea of a separate states government within the Federal was an inspiration he received from the Five Nations. And this is the fact that makes the Constitution of the United States different from any other in history.

The great democratic principles behind the United States are freedom and equal opportunity to each nation, under the protection of a Confederate Government. Without these bases for a commonwealth, Liberty is impossible. Without the spirit which promoted the first Awakener of the People to lay the foundations of American liberty, democracy is dead.

When the Colonists were struggling for liberty, the Oneidas of the Six Nations remained true to the dream of Sagoyewhata, and they sent every fighting man they had to the front.

And so I love my country. I love her every stream and rock and tree. To me there is hope in the thundering strength of her mountains. There is solace in the sweet ways of her valleys. And I love the ideals which made her a republic. I love the ideals of her enlightenment, just as my fathers, who planted the first seed of civilization in the land – just as my fathers who first dreamed of democracy on this continent – just as my fathers who bled for the liberty of the land. In noblesse oblige I could not do less.

But what shall I say to you now, Americans of my America? Shall I make soft speeches here for the acts of a Nation which in an individual would forever have forfeited liberty? Shall I fawn upon you with nauseating flattery, because you are rich and powerful? Have we departed so far from the truths of our fathers that we cannot now face the facts? Have you so soon forgotten the spectacle you have created of my people, whose shortcomings were that they were rich and primitive – the spectacle indeed of Belgium and Russia in the United States? You, the Christian Nation of the world! Just look over the land, and count the billions that have gone to erect your temples of worship, your edifices of stone and mortar. Why the price of your stained windows alone would have settled whole tribes in comfort forever! The husks of doctrine your pulpits offer the hungry soul – there is no corn in them. The American Indian cannot understand –

Aye – have you not robbed my people of a real god for your million "golden calves" of hypocrisy?

Have you not pauperized and debauched a whole people who were not only the richest in possessions, but whose native character has inspired those of your arts and literature which contain national distinction?

Have you not overcome with your foul diseases that physical excellence in the race which even the Greek did not surpass?

Have not 98 per cent of your treaties with the Indian been "scraps of paper?"

Are you going to be guilty of these things while you preach from the housetops the self-determination of peoples and the democratization of the whole world?

Shall the American Indian who first conceived the democracy of this continent call for liberty in vain?

To the American Indian

If I did not believe there were enough left of my red clan to make it worth while to say the last word, I should not speak. If I did not believe enough of you remain staunch to our ancestral standards of truth, to stand the ugly facts that concern us now, I should not speak. If I did not think there remained in you the mettle of men who smiled at death itself, I would not speak the burning word of criticism before the world. If I did not believe the spark can still be struck out of your dormant souls, I should not act. For the drama we have been enacting is a tragedy, nearly ended.

There was a time, my Red brothers, when our racial training taught us that to endure pain was a virtue, when silence meant self-containment and the unflinching endurance of pain the better part of manhood. But that is past. Today our very tolerance of the demoralization and subservience which have been coerced upon us, has become our burning shame. To the world, our seeming complacence with the outrages upon us is a mark of our slow awakening, a reflection indeed upon our intelligence, our racial character, our national honor.

And we will take the blame upon ourselves to the extent that we have been too long dazed in the chaos which surrounds us. We have presented no respectable comprehensive measure, which is capable of solving our embarrassment.

We will take the blame upon ourselves for having been simple enough to trust our fate into the hands of incompetent and dishonest government officials too long.

In our fate, like Russia, in our appearance, like Russia, we are a motley throng; and as a throng, there are times when we seem unworthy of the trust we crave. We have no consensus of opinion, no national judgment, no collective action. We have been systematically used to defeat these things.

As individuals there are times when we seem to have nothing in common but oppression. Some of you have been willing to let our enemy tell you our place in history. Some of you have no appreciation of the heritage of noble primitive stock, which differed from every other primitive stock in the world, in its advanced philosophy of life, its depth of nature, its inherent superiority of character. You have no real knowledge of these things.

We have a class among us, who constitute the Indian Bureau's School of Sycophants, with a few notable exceptions, they have been trained to petty trickery. They are recruited from the low mixtures of race with the proverbial "little larnin" from the Government school, they are the most cock-sure of theorists that the present order is good enough. They have not reached the point where they can be factors in any organization promoting ideals, for they are still the slaves of their whims and their fancies, their jealousies and their hatreds. These are the fellows who have their hands at the throat of your opportunity. These fellows were found when Tecumseh wanted to nationalize the race, and they have been part and parcel of the policy of centralization ever since. When the Bureau wishes to create factions among the tribes, their "warehouse Indians" are its executors. Our solidarity will be threatened by them just so long as you do not wake up and refuse to allow them to represent you.

There comes a time when men must measure themselves by the things they have not done. We have reached that time, my Red brothers, when the individual attitude of this race can no longer be indifferent, any more than any self-respecting soul can be indifferent over the atrocities of Belgium or the wanton outrages of Bolshevism.

Our children have been maimed with disease, mal-practice, and a broken-limbed system of education which carries its own publicity campaign to deceive the world at our expense.

Our aged starve, while the young generation is intimidated into cowardice and vice, and we are "dubbed" a race of beggars before the world, for whom the United States Government has done everything and yet we fail. What a spectacle we are – we of this generation.

Is the verdict of the blanket Indian correct, when he says, "The mind of this generation is like a broken reed, it cannot say no – a smile, and a pat, and our cause is undone!"

There have been times when I thought all one Indian had in common with another were ignorance and oppression. There have been times when I thought there were Indians and Indians ad infinitum. I had not then broken through the fastnesses of the wilderness, I had not then found the fraternity. The fraternity whose spirit cannot be broken by a million years of persecution, the fraternity who, regardless of ethnic culture or Bureau propaganda cannot be coerced into demoralization. The fraternity whom exile and "a reign of terror" have only strengthened. The fraternity to whom death is sweet if that is the price. My heart has not ached through the mountains in vain. The heroes of my childhood are not all gone from the earth. But, they are not begging a bean of politics with which to drag out a miserable existence. They are not around fawning upon the Paleface. Long ago they analyzed the situation – "no use, we must wait for our turn to die." What is starvation to them?

And there are some of you who have gone out into the new world and without theory or bias leaped into the thing which came your way first. Some of you are Anglo–Americans, some of you are not, in either case you are not credited to the race, for you have succeeded and even "beaten the Paleface at his own game." You have been like a great wind from the mountain tops. The fraternity is still larger than I thought. But you so long have believed nothing can be done, I wonder if you are open to conviction, and when convinced have you energy and patriotism?

Or, has the blood of our clan turned to water that we can be bent and broken into paupers and puppets cringing before the insolent arrogance and arbitrary dictation of political bosses who rise to positions of absolute despots over us?

How long shall our tongues lap the vulgar adulation which can silence the most glaring outrage?

Where are the sons of the race who did not steal, who did not lie? Where the sons of the race who fell defending their homes, their children, their country?

Where are the sons of the men who bled for Liberty – I hear a cry from the fastnesses of the wilderness. I see the fires over the tops of the mountains. Bring me the buckskin robe embroidered in the art of the people I love. Bring me the eagle plume that stands for vision and valor. I want to be with the fraternity, for it is very dark before the dawn – and tomorrow emancipation.

The Lolomi Program of Self-government

Years of search brought me the Indian word which means just what I wish to bring to the race. Lolomi is a Hopi term and it means "perfect goodness be upon you."

So long has this race had Siberian exile, that the only order which can in any way atone for crushed spirits, broken hopes, plundered fortunes, wasted lives is one which can obtain, secure and maintain real independence in modern times. I emphasize the modern times. The Red man had independence once, of a kind that could not be more idyllic. He followed the beautiful water courses and shot rapids in the romantic canoe, in the solemn solitudes of the great forests pursued the chase. Aesthetic even in the greater part of getting his livelihood, he was a brother of the gods and knew little irksome routine. And he was Lord of the richest continent on the globe. The Commercial age had not yet cast her lustful eyes upon his pure simplicity. But when she did, she came, and she is here to be reckoned with.

There is not a semblance left of that independence, outside of the refinement in the real Indian. Till he is gone, there will always be a certain nobility of nature, and a fine physique. Independence and leisure, with a fine philosophy of life behind them create fine spirit and fine bones. Whenever I have reminisced upon that Homeric time and have remarked upon the type which that great life bred and nurtured, people have immediately jumped to the conclusion that, after all, I am merely a dreamer with the Lolomi program, that I am indulging my fancy to lead me into paths impossible. Not so. I am merely trying to show the contrast between the man who was an exponent of better days and the man whom modern civilization with all its fallacies and vulgarity has produced. I am merely trying to show how vast the difference between them can be in a short period of time. I am merely arguing that the highest results of an upward movement are obtained when the human equation is given consideration. Like the structures of a beautiful stone wall, some one must conceive it first in the realm of dreams.

Then how many arts and what care must be employed to lay each stone with regard to color, line, fitness, durability. A slow process, building up, but it may all be pulled down into a heap in seconds. So it is with the races of men. No, it should not be hard for one who thinks to see how vain is any attempt to reproduce all the peculiar things of beauty in our primitive life. What a sight is before us of the failure of that former independence to convince this age of its rights. How far would any order succeed which did not take this modern day into its calculations? But on the other hand, how far has any attempt at remedying the present maladies of the race gone, which has swung to the other extreme and not taken the man as its first consideration! The whole trouble has been that of all the philanthropists outside of the race, who have given themselves to the Cause, and of those of the race who have ardently longed to do something for their own, there did not happen to be one whose experience was that of the race itself. Not one has lived so close to the old days that he could honestly glory in the Red man's inheritance, and yet know its hardship. No one has tasted the sweets and the bitters of this civilization so that he could give it its true values, not hating it broadcast, not loving it broadcast. I dwell upon this point because I do not see how I could keep from giving back something to the influences and the conditions that have led me to the discovery of what I ardently believe to be the final solution, if any, to the whole Indian situation.

As a child, my aunts and my grandfather and the old people who to a soul have since departed, contributed to this find by the wonderful things they told me of the life they knew. There were Epic tales whose kindred spirits I found in the Iliad, or the Anaeid many years later. There were tales of state in the old Iroquois civilization, which were confirmed by researches long after. From my infancy I had been taught what we Oneidas had contributed to American Liberty and civilization. What did it matter then, what wrenchings I might receive after that from the Paleface. I had been preserved from the spirit-breaking Indian schools through my father's wonderful foresight.

My psychology, therefore, had not been shot to pieces by that cheap attitude of the Indian Service, whose one aim was to "civilize" the race youth, by denouncing his parents, his customs, his people wholesale, and filling the vacuum they had created with their vulgar notions of what constituted civilization. I had none of those processes of the Bur-

eaucratic mill in my tender years, to make me into a "pinch-back white man." Had it been imposed upon me, I am certain something would have happened to it then.

I have gone a long way to show that a social order which intends to rebuild a broken people must come from an experience which is big enough to realize the real facts in the situation. It must know at first hand the good things and the short-comings of the Red man, as well as the good things and the bad of the Paleface and his civilization. It must seek to avoid the evils of both, to combine their higher values, and then to weave them into the hardest-headed kind of BUSINESS. That is it, it must have business. But while its head must be high enough to have its eyes on the horizon, it must have a voice of thunder. It must be abreast with the institutions of the times that succeed. It must gather the fragments of the race, nurture them back to health and spirit, and under the kindest and best trained of guidance, promote them to be producers of the highest efficiency. The school must be carried to the gardens whence comes the maintenance. Work must be a pleasure, not servile and brow-beaten, but it must be done. The reward for effort must come in the possession of peaceful and pleasant homes in attractive surroundings, in maintenance that is stable for all times, in real education, in dividends, in leisure enough for proper recreation, in the security of these things so that the speculator and the politician cease to be our daily night-mares. The structure upon which all these things depend is the ECONOMIC one. This is the task and the preparation of the LOLOMI.

The Lolomi policy is diametrically opposed to Bureaucracy in all things. It carries an order of protected self-government by means of a Federal incorporation into industrial communities.

It is plain the Indian himself does not know what theory to advance to save himself and his possessions, but he realizes that the concrete thing he wants is to save them.

It is plain the American people do not know what to advocate, but that that element of them who save situations anywhere, would like to see the Indian protected. Many of them know the failings of the government and would like to see a new order but they fear to remove the Federal hawk-eye, lest they throw him open to their own millions of highwaymen.

There is only one combination in all the world which can avoid becoming another Bureau and at the same time secure protection. That is a Federal incorporation of a self-governing body. When I have advocated this, I have met with three classes of opinion:

One says, "why ask the Federal Government which has already made a botch of Indian affairs to again have a hand in it. Why not merely get the fee simple to all Indian lands and incorporate the Indian's assets under the laws of the various states?"

Another says, "Incorporate! – why look at the white man's corporations? Even he cannot always cope with the exploitation possible under them. Where would the Indian be?"

A third class say, "Why has this not been done before?"

The Lolomi enjoys answering these questions: As to the first, incorporation under the state laws would mean petty politics. A small population of Indians in a state would have as much chance with state legislatures as a lamb would with a hungry lion. Whole states are eternally clamoring now for Indian possessions. There is no room to speculate what would happen to Indian shareholders under laws influenced by the white constituents of a state.

What, for instance would prevent a white politician from ingratiating himself in the affections of an influential Indian to whom he could say, "you buy A and B, and C, and D, out and you sell to me. When we get the control of the organization we can advance its development and own the whole business." To go from one scoundrel to another can not be entertained. There might be found a state where public sentiment would not allow it but it behooves us hereafter to beware. The Lolomi takes no chances.

The second brings up the defects of the modern corporation as it stands. Economic authorities agree that the greatest evil in the constitution of the corporations of the United States is their form of representation.

Now then, to avoid the domination of the rich man over the smaller shareholder, the Lolomi provides "that each member of said corporation shall have only one vote irrespective of the number of shares he or she may hold."

Inasmuch as the idea of incorporating is to save and promote Indian assets, and to educate the race in the forms and responsibilities of self-government, homogeneity is necessary. By this fact the door is positively closed against the white speculator and by the following provision, "that shares of stock shall not be transferred without the consent of all the Board of Directors, and cannot be transferred to any individual but to the corporation only," we close the door on the unscrupulous Indian, for no organization with any vision can leave the latter out of the consideration. One of the pillars in the success of the Mormon communities of the West was homogeneity. All successful organization is based on likeness of kind. I believe where white communities have co-operative organizations that have failed, the fact that they were composed of all kinds of race elements has counted largely.

I wish now to show how the Lolomi settles other questions which have seemed incapable of solution. Just as soon as the assets are pooled, Indian property is of necessity turned into the fee simple title. With that stroke is done away piecemeal legislation enacted without precedent, and out of which proceeds the present exploitation of the ward by politics.

It does away with the indefiniteness of taxation. It does away with the present ban on the development of our natural resources by ourselves. It gives us something to do under direction.

It does away with the status of semi-citizenship (the status of wardship), which is at once unconstitutional and chaotic. This state has invited more evil to the race than any other one thing. Till we secure uniformity in our legal status from which we can gauge standards and check up on them, the burden of legislation for the Indian will remain unpleasant, unreliable, unjust, and everlastingly disgraceful to the statesmanship of the American Nation.

That long circuitous road from the unallotted reservation through the Trust patent to the fee simple title will be cut off and the clerical force which spends its time writing, "your matter is under consideration" will have to make an honest living by cleaning up back-yards.

I have previously mentioned the settlement of the question of taxation by incorporation. By any other method of granting the fee simple, the experience of the Red man has been a disastrous one. When the old Indian objected to allotments, he feared to trust himself with that form of property holding he did not understand and could not promote. And he was right. Nowhere else in the United States is property taxed which is denied the right of production.

In one of my sojourns into the wilderness, I came upon one of the old leaders whose eyes were faded from the years of persecution. But he was strong and he still commanded his band of followers.

After some discussion in which he pictured to me, on the sand with a stick, what he would like to see in a model village, he said, "This Lolomi law is written to a certain point but where is it written about how we shall act? What shall we do to govern ourselves?" And so while he had his Council together, we drew up the Constitution and By-laws for his particular band. This brought about the deepest inquiry.

Before we left it, I said to them, "There is one feature of the Lolomi you may not like. And that is that after the trial period of its existence it will have to pay taxes. Do you think you could take care of the Community's taxes?"

Their chief answered, "In the old days, when our people were one in action, we bore all our burdens together and did not feel them. So again, if we had peace instead of fear in our minds, my braves are anxious to do something. But what is the use, tomorrow we may have to leave our homes." And thus it is the paralysis of the reservation is but an index of the state of mind.

I need not dwell at length upon the possibilities of combination. Where for example, the individual Indian has $500 in assets, it is obvious this is no kind of a start to the ostracized, unskilled, uneducated man. The handling of $500 is not even an experience which would teach him a lesson in frugality. Removing the restrictions from it simply means the dissipation of it. But let us take 1,000 or 2,000 of them and pool them and immediately we have a capitalization big enough to promote an independent industry.

The present method of making citizens, by the Department of the Interior is by sending out a Competency Commission, composed of its subordinate officials, who decide when and how an Indian is competent, and upon whose decision this man gets his fee simple title, then his relations with the Government are forever severed. I have been told that those who "shot the last arrow" and "kissed the plow" under the special auspices of the Secretary of the Interior several years ago, have all lost their property and are shifting around. This same will happen to most of them and boiled down to the last analysis this is DISSIPATION, and carried out far enough there will be no per capita wealth to combine in a short time. When the present Secretary of the Interior came into office, we had great hope that Indian Affairs would re-

ceive his vitalizing touch, and that a new order was in store for us. I made many attempts to see him personally with regard to the Lolomi before going to Congress with it. But he was inaccessable, due, I always thought, to the fact that a now ex-private Secretary was there serving the double task of being a watch dog for the Oil Trust whom I had investigated.

I went so far as to try to get the ear of the National Committeeman from Texas, who is the present head incumbent of the Bureau. He assured me he could not possibly take me to the Secretary, but that he would be pleased to take what I had to say to the Secretary himself. In order that I might not be guilty of having left one straw unturned, in the wake of conservative measures, I thanked him and proceeded to tell him. I had not gone through my first sentence when he went on after this fashion: "I just want to show you what I receive every day from all parts of the country," and with that he piled into my hands telegrams and letters to him of a flattering kind. I tried to resume the subject of my visit but it was quite impossible.

The Indian appropriation by Congress of ten or twelve million dollars, "for the support and civilization of the Indian" has been the great argument by the Bureaucrat of what this country through the Government is doing for the race. Here again is a deceiving figure. The most the last appropriation passed by Congress prior to our declaration of War, contained of gratuity moneys was a little over seven million. There is a reimbursable fund "for encouraging industry and self-help" among the tribes which in policy is most pernicious. It authorizes this Bureau to spend so many hundreds of thousands or so many millions of the Indian funds for projects the Bureau and members of Congress may deem fit. For example, the Blackfeet Irrigation project of Montana, a $3,000,000 project, is an experiment, for which the Blackfeet fund is mortgaged. If this project fails, the Blackfeet lose the money, no one else, since the national government has protected itself.

I asked the Blackfeet, "who does the work on this project?" and the prompt answer was, "the white men, of course, the constituents of our representatives."

The expense to the government of the maladministration upon the Indian will not show till years later when the claims of the race will be forthcoming for these Acts of today which the local constituents of a state are continually bringing upon the Nation.

The aggregate wealth of the race left in the United States was said to be about $50,000,000,000 nine years ago. Most of this was undeveloped. This would make the per capita wealth about $1,600. Of course these figures are misleading, for there are tribes who have very little left, while there are those who have considerable. But even where members of a tribe have a per capita wealth of $200 there is still something to combine, but the present methods of dismembering the Indian domain and then creating individual titles out of it, piecemeal, for the Paleface, and the rate at which the fee simple is being handed out under the guise of competency, as proved by the Curtis Act, is a matter of caution. The time left for saving property by combination is not long.

The Lolomi in its program of development recognizes several necessary first steps. Among them is the race's lack of credit. No race of men under the sun who have no credit, and no environment in which to labor, and no freedom for initiative can acquire the beginnings of business. The most humble immigrant who comes to the United States with his possessions upon his back, can go out to the remotest parts of our country and go into debt for a home and the necessary equipment for a farm, all upon his racial reputation. The Indian has a reputation for indolence which discriminates him against the world of business. That reputation comes through the fact that the farms of the reservation have been allotted with a great noise about making him into a farmer, and that after so many years of this attempt, they present the most dismal aspect. No one seems to have known that the real nature and the real object of Bureaucracy is to make inefficient and dependent men and women.

Leaving out the question of deserts, for the sake of argument, what other possible way of promoting Indian property is there outside of combination? What other possible way of getting credit is there outside of creating a body by law which shall be responsible according to the business regulations of the land? What other possible way is there of preserving what the Indian has left, and still not interfering with the order in which we live. I challenge anyone to present that way.

I do not excuse all the members of the race from indolence, but knowing what timber remains, I would govern the indolent and promote the industrious.

There have come to my notice, innumerable instances of what I am about to relate: A young Omaha came to me six years ago. I had been to his reservation and I knew about him. He had built up on his inherited estate a well improved farm. This land was better than his allotment which was several miles away. He had gone into debt to a speculating white man for his equipment. This man had taken into account the young man's energy and intelligence and honesty and had taken a chance in giving him $5,000 for improvements. Looking over the implements and stock one could readily see where this money had gone. He had figured out that by selling the allotment and buying an extra piece of land adjoining his inherited estate he would be able to get out of this debt, and thereby stop the interest, and would have a fine farm in one piece. But because of the prejudice of the local agent against him he could not persuade the latter to his point of view. So he came to Washington and begged of me to take the photos of his farm and stock and to go to the Secretary of the Interior and show him just what he wanted to have done. He added, "of course if you cannot get his ear and this goes back through the same channels of the agent and his coterie, there is no hope for me." I went to the Secretary. I got together a concise statement and took the photos. The Secretary listened to me kindly, but to show how utterly impossible it is for individual matters to receive his personal attention, this went back to the very channels instituted to handle these questions and the Omaha, after being juggled further for a year had to do the things he did not want to do. I often wonder when something is credited to the head of the Interior Department whether he ever saw it or heard of it. The body of minute details which encumber the offices of the United States Government make it a physical impossibility for individual justice unless the pressure becomes so acute that there can be no indifference about it. This fact makes it impossible for us to longer put any hope in the personnel of an office. The hopelessness of going higher up for justice is known by the subordinates, and so, often too, the ambitious Indian recognizes the fact and the result is that he wants to stand in with the agent.

I have made it my business to know if there are any yearnings in the hearts of the people who are going to make the Lolomi a success or a failure. I have gone farther, I must know if all the timber is not dead. I have gone to the contractors of many large business projects who employed Indians and asked them all the same question, "Why do you hire a lot of lazy Indians to do your work?" To a man they have responded in substance this: "I know no lazy Indians. I have tried every class of labor in the United States and I'll put none ahead of the Indian. The faithfulness of the Red man to details, his honesty in labor and his quiet dignity and intelligence makes him indispensable to the world outside of the bureau."

One of the boasts of the Indian Office is that no class of household labor compares with the girls they have trained in the Indian school. I want to say here that that is because they have trained the girl who might have become an instructor or manager of some business into being the servant of the race which has oppressed her people. My objection to turning the Indian into the white man's world of labor, after he has been stripped of his assets, as the Carlisle theorists would do, is that a man who is capable of something better is coerced into the hopelessness of the landless laborer.

Having settled the question of credit, the Lolomi now takes up the matter of supplying the individuals of the Community. Again I turn to the Mormons for example.

When the Mormons arrived in the deserts of Utah, a persecuted people, the first institution they put up was a Co-operative store. They had no money with which to capitalize, however, and they had to find some other way out, so they capitalized on labor. They kept on the books of the Co-operative store the schedule of wages and balances. They gave every man credit for a year in advance and after his necessities had been deducted from his earnings, they found out much about the members of their Community. Some had a good balance left to be credited to shares of stock. Some came out even, a few fell behind. These last could not remain.

One of the most perplexing questions which confronts our populations is how to secure the necessaries of life without paying three prices for it. This co-operative store will do away with the exploitation practiced at present by the local merchants.

One other question is one which has often been asked me. "How can you take care of the equalization of burdens. There are bound to be some more efficient than others, some more frugal, some more worthy. How can your institution distribute reward according to merit? The failure to do this is one of the great draw-backs to Indian Communism or any other Communism which has not been modernized.

The system of salaries and wages is fixed for all Community work. Every man and woman fits into the place where he or she can do the most effective work. Already every one knows what each particular class of work pays. That is established and cannot be partial. Beyond this there is a community of effort and behind this is the industrial school for the adult.

The background for the Lolomi is the out-of-door pursuits. It may be agriculture, it may be horticulture, it may be herding in the main, but there must always remain the garden of the home, out of which the living for the individual family must largely come.

Large area farming is not attractive to the race. It is not attractive to any man, when he is poor. This part passes over to the burden of the corporation and where a single man struggled hitherto with poor machinery and poor horses, the corporation has the best of improved machinery. I could never see any virtue in grinding a man's energies on drudgeries which exist as a result of deficit. I would make the place where human beings earn their bread as attractive as possible, so that work would become a pleasure where each one wanted to give his best.

In choosing the business of the organization, there are other things to be taken into the reckoning besides soil. One is the natural bent of the group. Those Indians like the Navajoes for example, who are at the height of the pastoral stage should not be expected to do scientific farming in the place of herding. But these are all matters of detail.

So far as business accountability is concerned, I want this borne in mind, there is no other organ which can save the Indian. This alone can separate personal liberty from property, and while we have a legal restriction on the dissipation of his property, we have freed his energies. We have guarded him against the scheming individual, white or Indian, against Bureaucracy, against politics, against himself.

Incorporation presupposes a state of self-government in which to succeed. If the corporations of the United States which have brought a new era of development into the world, were tied to Bureaus they were obliged to consult for every next move, or if politics every four years changed their heads, the business of the greatest industrial country in the world would long ago have gone to smash, and the red-blooded men of organizing genius would have sought another flag.

The type of man it takes to run large affairs is not one bred in a state of subservience. "In a state of fixity where there are no fields of opportunities for independent and private initiative and enterprise by individuals or associations of individuals, the spirit which demands self-government is selectively bred out and kept bred out of a nation."

The time has come for the final settlement between the American and American Indian. Shall it become necessary for us to beg a Supreme Court of Justice of the League of Nations to settle the most disgraceful and low-browed state of affairs ever enacted in a Democracy?

Cultural Pluralism

Alain L. Locke

Introduction

Alain L. Locke (1885–1954) was born in Philadelphia, Pennsylvania. He earned a bachelor of arts degree from Harvard University and became a Rhodes Scholar (1907–11) at Hertford College, Oxford. He also studied at the University of Berlin in 1910–11 and graduated with a PhD in philosophy from Harvard in 1918. Locke has often been credited with initiating the Harlem Renaissance with his editorship of *The New Negro* (1925), which presented African Americans not as minstrel characters but as full persons. It included spirituals, African art, poetry, and articles by intellectuals that would shape a good deal of American intellectual life for the remainder of the twentieth century. Locke wrote and edited books for the Bronze Booklets, a series of books sponsored by the Associates in Negro Folk Education and the American Association for Adult Education. Locke also edited, with Bernard J. Stern, a major work on group conflict and association, *When Peoples Meet* (1942); he created a version of pragmatism, critical pragmatism, and fostered cultural pluralism.

Pluralism and Intellectual Democracy

When William James inaugurated his all-out campaign against intellectual absolutism, though radical empiricism and pragmatism were his shield

Taken from Leonard Harris (ed.), *The Philosophy of Alain Locke* (Philadelphia: Temple University Press, 1989).

and buckler, his trusty right-arm sword, we should remember, was pluralism. He even went so far as to hint, in a way that his generation was not prepared to understand, at a vital connection between pluralism and democracy. Today, in our present culture crisis, it is both timely to recall this, and important, for several reasons, to ponder over it.

In the first place, absolutism has come forward again in new and formidable guise, social and political forms of it, with their associated intellectual tyrannies of authoritarian dogmatism and uniformitarian universality. We are warrantably alarmed to see these vigorous, new secular absolutisms added to the older, waning metaphysical and doctrinal ones to which we had become somewhat inured and from which, through science and the scientific spirit, we acquired some degree of immunity. Though alarmed, we do not always realize the extent to which these modern Frankensteins are the spawn of the older absolutistic breeds, or the degree to which they are inherent strains, so to speak, in the germ plasm of our culture.

In the second place, in the zeal of culture defense, in the effort to bring about the rapprochement of a united front, we do not always stop to envisage the danger and inconsistency of a fresh crisis uniformitarianism of our own. There exists, fortunately, a sounder and more permanent alternative, the possibility of a type of agreement such as may stem from a pluralistic base. Agreement of this common denominator type would, accordingly, provide a flexible, more democratic nexus, a unity in diversity rather than another counter-uniformitarianism.

Third, we should realize that the cure radical empiricism proposed for intellectual absolutism was stultified when it, itself, became arbitrary and dogmatic. With its later variants – behaviorism, positivism, and what not – it fell increasingly into the hands of the empirical monists, who, in the cause of scientific objectivity, squeezed values and ideals out completely in a fanatical cult of "fact." Not all the recalcitrance, therefore, was on the side of those disciplines and doctrines, which, being concerned with the vital interests of "value" as contrasted with "fact," are after all functionally vital in our intellectual life and tradition. Today, we are more ready to recognize them and concede these value considerations a place, though not necessarily to recognize or condone them in the arbitrary and authoritarian guise they still too often assume.

In this connection, it is encouraging to see empiricism abdicating some of its former arbitrary hardness and toning down its intransigent attitudes toward the more traditional value disciplines. This is a wise and potentially profitable concession on the part of science to the elder sisters, philosophy and religion, especially if it can be made the *quid pro quo* of their renunciation, in turn, of their dogmatic absolutisms. The admirable paper of Professor Morris, prepared for this conference, does just this, I think, by redefining a more liberal and humane empiricism, which not only recognizes "values," but provides, on the basis of sound reservations as to the basic primacy of factual knowledge, for reconcilable supplementations of our knowledge of fact by value interpretations and even by value systems and creeds. This reverses the previous tactic of empiricists to deny any validity to values and so to create a hopeless divide between the sciences of fact and the value disciplines. Here again, in this more liberal empiricism, pluralism, and particularly value pluralism, has a sound and broadly acceptable basis of rapprochement to offer. Such rapprochement being one of the main objectives as well as one of the crucial problems of this conference, it is perhaps relevant to propose the consideration of pluralism as a working base and solution for this problem. This would be all the more justified if it could be shown that pluralism was a proper and congenial rationale for intellectual democracy.

James, pluralistically tempered, did not take the position, it is interesting to note, which many of his followers have taken. He did propose giving up for good and all the "game of metaphysics" and the "false" and categorical rationalizing of values, but he did not advocate sterilizing the "will to believe" or abandoning the search for pragmatic sanctions for our values. As Horace Kallen aptly states it,

James insisted that each event of experience must be acknowledged for what it appears to be, and heard for its own claims. To neither doubt nor belief, datum nor preference, term nor relation, value nor fact, did he concede superiority over the others.... He pointed out to the rationalist the coordinate presence in experience of so much more than reason; he called the monist's attention to the world's diversity; the pluralist's to its unity. He said to the materialist: You shall not shut your eyes to the immaterial; to the spiritualist: You shall take cognizance also of the nonspiritual. He was a rationalist without unreason; an empiricist without prejudice. His empiricism was radical, preferring correctness to consistency, truth to logic.[1]

I do not quote for complete agreement, because I think we have come to the point where we can and must go beyond this somewhat anarchic pluralism and relativism to a more systematic relativism. This becomes possible as we are able to discover through objective comparison of basic human values certain basic equivalences among them, which we may warrantably call "functional constants" to take scientifically the place of our outmoded categoricals and our banned arbitrary "universals." However, the present point is that James did not intend to invalidate values in his attack on absolutes and categoricals or to abolish creeds in assailing dogma. Nor was he intent on deepening the divide between science, philosophy and religion: on the contrary, he was hoping for a new rapprochement and unity among them, once philosophy and religion had renounced absolutist metaphysics and its dogmatisms.

Is such rapprochement possible? As we have already seen, only if empiricists and rationalists both make concessions. Further, these concessions must be comparable, and provide, in addition, a workable base of contact. From either side this is difficult. And lest the concession proposed for the value disciplines seem unequal or unduly great, let us make note of the fact that it is a very considerable concession, from the point of view of orthodox empiricism, to concede the scientific monism of mechanism, determinism and materialism. The scientific point of view, by making a place for values, makes obviously the concession of pluralism. In a complementary concession, the value disciplines, it seems to me, should make the concession of relativism. Frankly, this asks that they dethrone their absolutes, not as values or even as preferred values, but nonetheless as arbitrary universals, whether they be "sole ways of salvation," "perfect forms of the state or society," or self evident intellectual systems of interpretation. Difficult as this may be for our various traditional value systems, once they do so, they thereby not only make peace with one another, but make also an honorable peace with science. For, automatically in so doing, they cease to be rival interpretations of that objective reality which it is the function of science to analyze, measure and explain, or monopolistic versions of human nature and experience, which it is, similarly, the business of social science to record and describe.

Such value pluralism, with its corollary of relativity, admittedly entails initial losses for the traditional claims and prestige of our value systems. But it also holds out to them an effective *pax romana* of values, with greater and more permanent eventual gains. It calls, in the first place, for a resolving or at least an abatement of the chronic internecine conflict of competing absolutes, now so hopelessly snared in mutual contradictoriness. Not that there must be, in consequence of this relativistic view, an anarchy or a complete downfall of values, but rather that there should be only relative and functional rightness, with no throne or absolute sovereignty in dispute. To intelligent partisans, especially those who can come within hailing distance of Royce's principle of "loyalty to loyalty," such value reciprocity might be acceptable and welcome. As we shall see later, this principle has vital relevance to the whole question of a democracy of values, which basically entails value tolerance.

There would also be as a further possibility of such value relativism a more objective confirmation of many basic human values, and on a basis of proof approximating scientific validity. For if once this broader relativistic approach could discover beneath the expected culture differentials of time and place such functional "universals" as actually may be there, these common-denominator values would stand out as pragmatically confirmed

by common human experience. Either their observable generality or their comparatively established equivalence would give them status far beyond any "universals" merely asserted by orthodox dogmatisms. And the standard of value justification would then not be so very different from the accepted scientific criterion of proof – confirmable invariability in concrete human experience. After an apparent downfall and temporary banishment, many of our most prized "universals" would reappear, clothed with a newly acquired vitality and a pragmatic validity of general concurrence. So confirmed, they would be more widely acceptable and more objectively justified than would ever be possible either by the arbitrary fiat of belief or the brittle criterion of logical consistency. Paradoxically enough, then, the pluralistic approach to values opens the way to a universality and objectivity for them quite beyond the reach of the *a priori* assertions and dogmatic demands which characterize their rational and orthodox promulgations.

More important, however, than what this view contributes toward a realistic understanding of values, are the clues it offers for a more practical and consistent way of holding and advocating them. It is here that a basic connection between pluralism and intellectual democracy becomes evident. In the pluralistic frame of reference value dogmatism is outlawed. A consistent application of this invalidation would sever the trunk nerves of bigotry or arbitrary orthodoxy all along the line, applying to religious, ideological and cultural as well as to political and social values. Value profession or adherence on that basis would need to be critical and selective and tentative (in the sense that science is tentative) and revisionist in procedure rather than dogmatic, final and *en bloc*. One can visualize the difference by saying that with any articles of faith, each article would need independent scrutiny and justification and would stand, fall or be revised, be accepted, rejected or qualified accordingly. Fundamentalism of the "all or none" or "this goes with it" varieties could neither be demanded, expected nor tolerated. Value assertion would thus be a tolerant assertion of preference, not an intolerant insistence on agreement or finality. Value disciplines would take on the tentative and revisionist procedure of natural science.

Now such a rationale is needed for the effective implementation of the practical corollaries of value pluralism – tolerance and value reciprocity, and one might add, as a sturdier intellectual base for

435

democracy. We know, of course, that we cannot get tolerance from a fanatic or reciprocity from a fundamentalist of any stripe, religious, philosophical, cultural, political or ideological. But what is often overlooked is that we cannot, soundly and safely at least, preach liberalism and at the same time abet and condone bigotry, condemn uniformitarianism and placate orthodoxy, promote tolerance and harbor the seeds of intolerance. I suggest that our duty to democracy on the plane of ideas, especially in time of crisis, is the analysis of just this problem and some consideration of its possible solution.

In this connection it is necessary to recall an earlier statement that we are for the most part unaware of the latent absolutism at the core of many of our traditional loyalties, and of the fact that this may very well condition current concepts and sanctions of democracy. The fundamentalist lineage of "hundred per-centism," for all its ancient and sacrosanct derivation, is only too obvious. It is a heritage and carry-over from religious dogmatism and extends its blind sectarian loyalties to the secular order. So hoary and traditional is it that one marvels that it could still be a typical and acceptable norm of patriotism, political or cultural. Equally obvious is the absolutist loyalty of the secular dogma of "my country, right or wrong." Such instances confront us with the paradox of democratic loyalties absolutistically conceived, dogmatically sanctioned and undemocratically practiced. Far too much of our present democratic creed and practice is cast in the mold of such blind loyalty and *en bloc* rationalization, with too many of our citizens the best of democrats for the worst of reasons – mere conformity. Apart from the theoretical absolutistic taint, it should be disconcerting to ponder that by the same token, if transported, these citizens would be "perfect" Nazis and the best of totalitarians.

But to come to less obvious instances – our democratic tolerance – of whose uniqueness and quantity we can boast with some warrant, seems on close scrutiny qualitatively weak and unstable. It is uncritical because propagated on too emotional and too abstract a basis. Not being anchored in any definite intellectual base, it is too easily set aside in time of stress and challenge. [So it] is tolerance only in name, [or] it is simply indifference and *laissez faire* rationalized. We are all sadly acquainted with how it may blow away in time of crisis or break when challenged by self-interest, and how under stress we find ourselves, after all, unreasonably biased in favor of "our own," whether it be the mores, ideas, faiths or merely "our crowd." This is a sure sign that value bigotry is somehow still deep-rooted there. Under the surface of such frail tolerance some unreconstructed dogmatisms lie, the latent source of the emerging intolerance. This is apt to happen to any attitude lacking the stamina of deep intellectual conviction, that has been nurtured on abstract sentiment, and that has not been buttressed by an objective conception of one's own values and loyalties.

Democratic professions to the contrary, there is a reason for all this shallow tolerance, this grudging and fickle reciprocity, this blind and fanatical loyalty persisting in our social behavior. Democracy has promulgated these virtues and ideals zealously, but as attitudes and habits of thought has not implemented them successfully. First, they have been based on moral abstractions, with vague sentimental sanctions as "virtues" and "ideals," since, on the whole, idealistic liberalism and good-will humanitarianism have nursed our democratic tradition. Rarely have these attitudes been connected sensibly with self-interest or realistically bound up with a perspective turned toward one's own position and its values. Had this been the case, a sturdier tolerance and a readier reciprocity would have ensued, and with them a more enlightened type of social loyalty.

But a more enlightened loyalty involves of necessity a less bigoted national and cultural tradition. Democratic liberalism, limited both by the viewpoint of its generation and by its close affiliation with doctrinal religious and philosophical traditions, modeled its rationale of democracy too closely to authoritarian patterns, and made a creed of democratic principles. For wide acceptance or easy assent it condoned or compromised with too much dogmatism and orthodoxy. Outmoded scientifically and ideologically today, this dogmatism is the refuge of too much provincialism, intolerance and prejudice to be a healthy, expanding contemporary base for democracy. Our democratic values require an equally liberal but also a more scientific and realistic rationale today. This is why we presume to suggest pluralism as a more appropriate and effective democratic rationale.

We must live in terms of our own particular institutions and mores, assert and cherish our own specific values, and we could not, even if it were desirable, uproot our own traditions and loyalties. But that is no justification for identifying them *en bloc* with an ideal like democracy, as though they were a perfect set of architectural specifications for the concept itself. So the only way of freeing our minds from such hypostasizing, from its provincial limitations and dogmatic bias, is by way of a relativism which reveals our values in proper objective perspective with other sets of values. Through this we may arrive at some clearer recognition of the basic unity or correspondence of our values with those of other men, however dissimilar they may appear on the surface or however differently they may be systematized and sanctioned. Discriminating objective comparison of this sort, using the same yardstick, can alone give us proper social and cultural scale and perspective. Toward this end, value pluralism has a point of view able to lift us out of the egocentric and ethnocentric predicaments which are without exception involved. This should temper our loyalties with intelligence and tolerance and scotch the potential fanaticism and bigotry which otherwise lurk under blind loyalty and dogmatic faith in our values. We can then take on our particular value systems with temperate and enlightened attachment, and can be sectarian without provincialism and loyal without intolerance.

Since the relativist point of view focuses in an immediately transformed relationship and attitude toward one's own group values, it is no rare and distant principle, but has, once instated, practical progressive applicability to everyday life. It has more chances thus of becoming habitual. Most importantly perhaps, it breaks down the worship of the form – that dangerous identification of the symbol with the value, which is the prime psychological root of the fallacies and errors we have been discussing. We might pose it as the acid test for an enlightened value loyalty that it is able to distinguish between the symbol and form of its loyalty and the essence and objective of that loyalty. Such critical insight, for example, would recognize a real basic similarity or functional equivalence in other values, even when cloaked in considerable superficial difference. Nor, on the other hand, would it credit any merely superficial conformity with real loyalty. And so, the viewpoint equips us not only to tolerate difference but enables us to bridge divergence by recognizing commonality wherever present. In social practice this is no scholastic virtue; it has high practical consequences for democratic living, since it puts the premium upon equivalence not upon identity, calls for cooperation rather than for conformity and promotes reciprocity instead of factional antagonism. Au-

thoritarianism, dogmatism and bigotry just cannot take root and grow in such intellectual soil.

Finally, we may assess the possible gains under this more pragmatic and progressive rationale for democratic thought and action briefly under two heads: what these fresh and stimulating sanctions promise internally for democracy on the national front and what they require externally on the international front in terms of what is vaguely – all too vaguely – styled world democracy.

For democracy in its internal aspects, much of pluralism's gains would consist in a more practical implementation of the traditional democratic values, but there would also be some new sanctions and emphases. So far, of course, as these things can be intellectually implemented, new support would unquestionably be given to the enlargement of the democratic life, and quite as importantly, some concern taken for the correction of its aberrations and abuses. On the corrective side, particular impetus needs to be given toward the liberalizing of democracy's tradition of tolerance, to more effective protection and integration of minority and non-conformist groups, for the protection of the majority itself against illiberalism, bigotry and cultural conceit, and toward the tempering of the quality of patriotism and sub-group loyalties. As to new sanctions, the campaign for the re-vamping of democracy has already put special emphasis on what is currently styled "cultural pluralism" as a proposed liberal rationale for our national democracy. This indeed is but a corollary of the larger relativism and pluralism under discussion. Under it, much can be done toward the more effective bridging of the divergencies of institutional life and traditions which, though sometimes conceived as peculiarly characteristic of American society, are rapidly becoming typical of all cosmopolitan modern society. These principles call for promoting respect for difference, for safeguarding respect for the individual, thus preventing the submergence of the individual in enforced conformity, and for the promotion of commonality over and above such differences. Finally, more on the intellectual side, additional motivation is generated for the reinforcement of all the traditional democratic freedoms, but most particularly for the freedom of the mind. For it is in the field of social thinking that freedom of the mind can be most practically established, and no more direct path to that exists than through the promotion of an unbiased scientific conception of the place of the national culture in the world.

For democracy in its external aspects both the situation and the prospects are less clear. However, the world crisis poses the issues clearly enough. Democracy has encountered a fighting antithesis, and has awakened from considerable lethargy and decadence to a sharpened realization of its own basic values. This should lead ultimately to a clarified view of its ultimate objectives. The crisis holds also the potential gain of more realistic understanding on the part of democracy of its own shortcomings, since if totalitarianism is its moral antithesis as well as its political enemy, it must fight internally to purge its own culture of the totalitarian qualities of dogmatism, absolutism and tyranny, latent and actual.

Yet as a nation we are vague about world democracy and none too well equipped for its prosecution. It was our intellectual unpreparedness as a nation for thinking consistently in any such terms which stultified our initiative in the peace of 1918 and our participation in the germinal efforts of a democratic world order under the League of Nations plan, or should we say concept, since the plan minimized it so seriously? Today again, we stand aghast before a self-created dilemma of an impracticable national provinciality of isolationism and a vague idea of a world order made over presumably on an enlarged pattern of our own. There is danger, if we insist on identifying such a cause arbitrarily with our own institutional forms and culture values of its becoming a presumptuous, even though well-intentioned idealistic uniformitarianism. Should this be the case, then only a force crusade for democratic uniformitarianism is in prospect, for that could never come about by force of persuasion.

It is here that the defective perspective of our patriotism and our culture values reveals its seriously limiting character. This is intellectually the greatest single obstacle to any extension of the democratic way of life on an international scale. Surely here the need for the insight and practical sanity of the pluralistic viewpoint is clear. There is a reasonable chance of success to the extent we can disengage the objectives of democracy from the particular institutional forms by which we practice it, and can pierce through to common denominators of equivalent objectives.

The intellectual core of the problems of the peace, should it lie in our control and leadership, will be the discovery of the necessary common denominators and the basic equivalences involved in a democratic world order or democracy on a world scale. I do not hazard to guess at them; but certain specifications may be stated which I believe they will have to meet, if they are to be successful. A reasonable democratic peace (like no other peace before it) must integrate victors and vanquished alike, and justly. With no shadow of cultural superiority, it must respectfully protect the cultural values and institutional forms and traditions of a vast congeries of peoples and races – European, Asiatic, African, American, Australasian. Somehow cultural pluralism may yield a touchstone for such thinking. Direct participational representation of all considerable groups must be provided for, although how imperialism is to concede this is almost beyond immediate imagining. That most absolutistic of all our secular concepts, the autonomous, sacrosanct character of national sovereignty, must surely be modified and voluntarily abridged. Daring reciprocities will have to be worked out if the basic traditional democratic freedoms are ever to be transposed to world practice, not to mention the complicated reconstruction of economic life which consistent reciprocity will demand in this field. One suspects that the practical exigencies of world reconstruction will force many of these issues to solution from the practical side, leaving us intellectuals to rationalize the changes *ex post facto*. Out of the crisis may yet come the forced extension of democratic values and mechanisms in ways that we have not had courage to think of since the days of democracy's early eighteenth century conception, when it was naively, but perhaps very correctly assumed that to have validity at all democracy must have world vogue.

What intellectuals can do for the extension of the democratic way of life is to discipline our thinking critically into some sort of realistic world-mindedness. Broadening our cultural values and tempering our orthodoxies is of infinitely more service to enlarged democracy than direct praise and advocacy of democracy itself. For until broadened by relativism and reconstructed accordingly, our current democratic traditions and practice are not ready for world-wide application. Considerable political and cultural dogmatism, in the form of culture bias, nation worship, and racism, still stands in the way and must first be invalidated and abandoned. In sum, if we refuse to orient ourselves courageously and intelligently to a universe of peoples and cultures, and continue to base our prime values on fractional segments of nation, race, sect, or particular types of institutional culture, there is indeed little or no hope for a stable world order of any kind – democratic or otherwise. Even when the segment is itself a democratic order, its expansion to world proportions will not necessarily create a world democracy. The democratic mind needs clarifying for the better guidance of the democratic will.

But fortunately, the same correctives needed for the sound maintenance of democracy are also the most promising basis for its expansion. The hostile forces both within and without are of the same type, and stem from absolutism of one sort or another. The initial suggestion of a vital connection between democracy and pluralism arose from the rather more apparent connection between absolutism and monism. But so destructive has pluralism been of the closed system thinking on which absolutist values and authoritarian dogmatisms thrive that it has proved itself no mere logical antithesis but their specific intellectual antidote. In the present crisis democracy needs the support of the most effective rationale available for the justification and defense of its characteristic values. While we should not be stampeded into pluralism merely by the present emergency, it is nonetheless our handiest intellectual weapon against the totalitarian challenge, but if, as we have seen, it can also make a constructive contribution to the internal fortification of democracy, then it is even more permanently justified and should on that score be doubly welcomed.

Appendix

Lyman Bryson: I am heartily in accord with this paper, on all of its chief points, and I admire the conciseness and clarity with which it states so much that is *à propos* of the deliberations of this Conference. My comments are only notes added in the hope that they are what Professor Locke himself might have said in a longer discussion.

More could be made, I believe, of the dangers of the overweening desire for personal integration that fails to take into account the fact that the personality, also, is in some ways better off for the practice of a judicious pluralism. By this I mean that we have a natural tendency toward an agglutination of values. If we are loyal to one set of institutions, such as what we call "democracy," we are uncomfortable unless we assert that the other values, to which we may also be loyal, such as what we call "Christianity," are necessary to democracy. At our Conference meetings we have heard many assertions that democracy can exist only in a Christian state, in spite of history and all contemporary facts to the contrary. We are not content to say that democracy and the Christian-Judaic tradition are highly sympathetic with each other, or useful to each other. They must be, each to the other, *sine qua non*. Professor Locke might have pointed out that within each single pattern of loyalties an organic diversity may make not for weakness but for flexibility and strength.

The author might also have pointed out, as was perhaps implied in some of the things he did have space for, that unity becomes the more desirable as the issues rise in the levels of generality. Thus, roughly, we need not agree on how freedom should be used but we would still agree that it was a value to be supremely prized. We might agree on the importance of exercising political suffrage but disagree in our use of it. And still above this, we might argue about freedom but agree that values, to be desirable, must contribute to the strength and dignity of men. The value that has been repeatedly called the chief good of democratic peoples, the supreme worth of the individual, is just such a value of the highest possible generality and we are dogmatic in our assertion of it. Diversity does not have the same utility on all levels but, one must add, an authoritarian determination of the levels on which diversity can be permitted is a very effective enslavement. I would have enjoyed a discussion of this point in the paper.

I could wish, also, that there had been more space to consider the importance of diversity, or plural systems of values, in relation to social change. It is when a culture is undergoing transformation, when diversity is most difficult to maintain, that it is of greatest importance. It is true, I think, that pluralistic groups change with less cost and more efficiency, whenever environment makes change rationally desirable, than do any other kinds of groups. This is one of the strongest arguments in favor of democratic procedures in all forms of social decision.

Erwin R. Goodenough: The Conference was originally called together to see what scientists, philosophers, and theologians could do to unite the more abstract thought and thinkers of the present in defending democracy. We were alarmed at what we had seen happen to our ideas (and our kind) in Russia, Italy and Germany, and we met to defend our way of life and thought and to strengthen the organization of society which makes such life and thought possible.

This paper is one of the few which seemed to me presented in the original spirit of our meeting. That philosophy which recognizes the conflict of various suggested ultimates and axioms and the complete inadequacy of our data to select between them (as witnessed by the inability of reasoning philosophers of different schools to convince each other by reasoning); that philosophy which tries to take the very conflict as its starting point and develop a *modus vivendi* out of it, is called pluralism. It is satisfactory to no one, or to very few, as an ultimate philosophy. Certainly Professor Locke is peering behind and beyond it as steadily, as wistfully, as any idealist. He proposes it, and I enthusiastically support it, precisely for what it is – a way of uniting for action in a world of conflict and ignorance. It is a typically American philosophy, or at least Anglo-Saxon, and it is not coincidence that it is best understood in the countries most bitterly opposed to totalitarianism. Over and again the various absolutist philosophies suggested in the Conference have shown that once in power they would be dangerously like the closed systems (at least in being closed), which we want to oppress. Here is genuinely the philosophy of democracy – not a very brilliant philosophy, as democracy itself is not a very brilliant form of organizing society, but still the philosophy which made democratic arguments, from those in the village store to those in the Senate, possible. I am sure that if we go on to discuss more practical problems at next year's meeting, our discussion will be based, tacitly if not otherwise, upon the wise principles Professor Locke has set forth. I am still more sure that if our discussion of practical problems is not thus based, it will get nowhere.

Lawrence K. Frank: In emphasizing the need for pluralistic understanding, this paper has pointed to an exceedingly important problem that will face the post-World War. If we look forward to the construction of some sort of world order in which the peoples of different cultures and religions can participate, we will need a pluralistic understanding and a broader, more sympathetic approach to many of the exigent questions of human welfare and social order; otherwise a parochial devotion to our own metaphysics and religious convictions, however precious to us, will inevitably hamper us in any attempt to achieve world order and peace in concert with peoples whose cultural traditions and beliefs are so radically different from our own.

In pleading for a relativistic approach to our own values and to those of other peoples and in calling for a recognition of equivalents in cultures rather than demanding identity, Dr. Locke has contributed something that merits the careful consideration of all those participating in this conference. Without such understanding, we are more than liable to continue the same dogmatic intolerance that has so long blighted Western European culture and blinded us to the values and virtues which other peoples, often with longer and richer historical pasts than we, cherish as their way of life.

[…]

Cultural Relativism and Ideological Peace

Now that a considerable body of opinion within the Conference has crystallized around the position of value pluralism and relativism, with special emphasis this year, it seems, on the principle and concept of "cultural relativity," it seems opportune to turn from the initial task of establishing and vindicating this point of view to the next logical step – and the more practical one, of discussing its possible implementation. Already several papers[2] in this year's symposium have addressed themselves to one or more aspects of this practical side of the problem, and it is a pleasant duty to acknowledge general indebtedness to them at the outset of this further attempt to discuss some of the practical implications of the concept of cultural relativism. Three such principles of practical application seem to derive so directly and logically from the core principle in question that they may warrantably be regarded as three *basic corollaries of cultural relativity*.

In proceeding to discuss them, extended argument for the general position offered earlier by papers presented to this and previous Conferences, including one of my own written for the Second Conference,[3] may be taken to justify the assumption that there is little need or obligation to retrace in detail the argument for the main position itself. Here it should suffice to point out, for immediate perspective particularly, the practical and important relevance of cultural relativity to the main issue of this year's discussion topic – the prospects and techniques of "an enduring peace."

There seems to be, in fact, a twofold bearing of the culture-relativity principle upon our chosen

Conference problem. One can readily recognize, in the first place, without needing to assume any direct logical connection between cultural relativity and pacifism or any demonstrable correlation between attitudes of tolerance and a predisposition to peace, that the relativistic philosophy nips in the psychological bud the passion for arbitrary unity and conformity. This mind-set, we know only too well and sorrowfully, constitutes the intellectual base and ideological root of all those absolutistic dogmatisms that rationalize orthodoxy. In so doing, they fortify with convictions of finality and self-righteousness the countless crusades for conformity which provide the moral and intellectual sanctions, not only for war but for most of our other irreconcilable culture conflicts. In this indirect but effective way, cultural relativism, as its influence spreads, may become an important force for ideological peace through disavowing and discouraging the chief intellectual sanctions for belligerent partisanship.

Relativism, it should be noted, contradicts value dogmatism and counteracts value bigotry without destroying the sense of active value loyalty. For scientific relativism, some interpretations notwithstanding, does not propagate indifference, scepticism, or cynicism about values. Thus, through remaining hospitable and receptive to values except as they are dogmatic and too arbitrarily held, relativism retains a usefulness which, if followed through consistently, enables it to become at the very least a scientifically impartial interpreter of human values, and sometimes even a referee and mediator among conflicting values. There is, then, this second and more positive role for relativism to exercise in the issues of ideological competition and conflict – one which can lead to an even more constructive usefulness in the interests of peace, so far as peace can be safeguarded intellectually. Cultural relativism, of course more fully and positively developed than at present, can become a very constructive philosophy by way of integrating values and value systems that might otherwise never react to one another, or, if they did, would do so only in opposition, rivalry, and conflict. We can very profitably examine, therefore, at this juncture of human affairs the constructive potentialities of the relativistic position as a possible ideological peacemaker, particularly in the relationships of group cultures and their otherwise antagonistic or incommensurable values.

Paradoxically enough, absolutism in all its varieties – religious, philosophical, political, and cultural – despite the insistent linking together of unity *and* universality, seems able, so far as historical evidence shows, to promote unity only at the cost of universality. For absolutism's way to unity is the way of orthodoxy, which involves authoritarian conformity and subordination. From such premises, dogmatism develops sooner or later, and thereafter, history shows us, come those inevitable schisms which disrupt the parent dogmatism and try to deny it in the name of a new orthodoxy. Relativism, with no arbitrary specifications of unity, no imperious demand for universality, nevertheless enjoins a beneficent neutrality between divergent positions, and, in the case of the contacts of cultures, would in due course promote, step by step, from an initial stage of cultural tolerance, mutual respect, reciprocal exchange, some specific communities of agreement and, finally, with sufficient mutual understanding and confidence, commonality of purpose and action. If in its practical manifestations cultural relativism could promote such results or even attitudes conducive to them, it would be a most fruitful source of such progressive integrations as are so crucially needed in the world today.

Once we fully realize the divisive general effect of fundamentalist ideas and all their institutional incorporations, and understand that orthodox conformity inevitably breeds its opposite – *sectarian disunity* – we reach a position where we can recognize relativism as a safer and saner approach to the objectives of practical unity. What is achieved through relativistic rapprochement is, of course, somewhat different from the goal of the absolutists. It is a fluid and functional unity rather than a fixed and irrevocable one, and its vital norms are equivalence and reciprocity rather than identity or complete agreement. But when we consider the odds against a complete community of culture for mankind, and the unlikelihood of any all-inclusive orthodoxy of human values, one is prepared to accept or even to prefer an attainable concord of understanding and cooperation as over against an unattainable unanimity of institutional beliefs.

Ironically, the very social attribute which man has most in common – his loyalty to his culture and, one might just as well say his inevitable commitment to various culture groups – is the basis of his deepest misunderstandings and a source of his most tragic conflict with his fellow men. When we consider this, we can appreciate the deep-seated desire and the ever-recurrent but Utopian dream of the idealist that somehow a single faith, a common culture, an all-embracing institutional life and its confraternity should some day unite man by merging all these loyalties and culture values. But the day still seems distant, even with almost complete intercommunication within the world's practical grasp. What seems more attainable, realistically, is some reconstruction of the attitudes and rationalizations responsible for this conflict over our separate loyalties.

It is at this point that relativism has its great chance. It may be destined to have its day in the channeling of human progress – not, however, as a mere philosophy or abstract theory of values, though it began as such, but as a new base and technique for our study and understanding of human cultures and as a new way of controlling through education our attitudes toward our various group cultures. Only, then, through having some objective and factual base in the sciences of man and society can cultural relativism implement itself for this task of reconstructing our basic social and cultural loyalties or of lifting them, through some basically new perspective, to a plane of enlarged mutual understanding. For such a task anthropology in the broadest sense must be the guide and adjutant, and the trend toward this new alliance of disciplines, so inevitable in view of the nature of the problem, is already becoming apparent in scholarship generally. As a concrete example we have an increasing segment of it in the deliberations of this Conference.

There never has been a new age without a new scholarship or, to put it more accurately, without a profound realignment of scholarship. And if our times are as cataclysmal as they seem to be, we should reasonably expect today fundamental changes of this sort in ideas and points of view. Through the aid of anthropology, whose aim is to see man objectively and impartially in all his variety, cultural relativism seems capable of opening doors to such new understandings and perspectives as are necessary for the new relationships of a world order and its difficult juxtapositions of many divergent cultures. Only on such a basis can scholarship hope to serve the social situations of the present time. To do so, however, it will be necessary for scholarship to free itself from the provincialisms and partisanships of many of its past traditions. Culture outlooks and philosophies rooted in fanatical religious orthodoxy, or in inflated cultural bias and partisanship, or in overweening national and racial chauvinism, have been outmoded and outflanked by the developments of the age, not to mention their basic theor-

etical invalidation, which is because they are all subjective and unscientific. All these provincialisms survive considerably, however, but more and more precariously as time goes on. Accordingly, there is crucial importance and scope for well-grounded, rigorously objective relativism.

On such a background, one can more readily see and state the possible uses of cultural relativism as a realistic instrument of social reorientation and cultural enlightenment. As corollaries of its main view of culture, three working principles seem to be derivable for a more objective and scientific understanding of human cultures and for the more reasonable control of their interrelationships. They are:

1   The principle of *cultural equivalence*, under which we would more wisely press the search for functional similarities in our analyses and comparisons of human cultures; thus offsetting our traditional and excessive emphasis upon cultural difference. Such functional equivalences, which we might term "*culture-cognates*" or "*culture-correlates*," discovered underneath deceptive but superficial institutional divergence, would provide objective but soundly neutral common denominators for intercultural understanding and cooperation;

2   The principle of *cultural reciprocity*, which, by a general recognition of the reciprocal character of all contacts between cultures and of the fact that all modern cultures are highly composite ones, would invalidate the lump estimating of cultures in terms of generalized, *en bloc* assumptions of superiority and inferiority, substituting scientific, point-by-point comparisons with their correspondingly limited, specific, and objectively verifiable superiorities or inferiorities;

3   The principle of *limited cultural convertibility*, that, since culture elements, though widely interchangeable, are so separable, the institutional forms from their values and the values from their institutional forms, the organic selectivity and assimilative capacity of a borrowing culture becomes a limiting criterion for cultural exchange. Conversely, pressure acculturation and the mass transplanting of culture, the stock procedure of groups with traditions of culture "superiority" and dominance, are counterindicated as against both the

interests of cultural efficiency and the natural trends of cultural selectivity.

Here, then, we seem to have three objectively grounded principles of culture relations that, if generally carried through, might correct some of our basic culture dogmatism and progressively cure many of our most intolerant and prejudicial culture attitudes and practices.

If they could come into general acceptance, cultural absolutism and its still prevalent presumptions would be basically discredited and perhaps effectively countered. Cultural difference, surely, would be purged of most of its invidiousness, and much cultural divergence would on deeper inspection turn out to be functionally similar. We would be more prone to recognize the legitimate jurisdictions of other cultures as well as to respect the organic integrity of the weaker cultures. Moreover, tolerance and the reciprocities of cultural pluralism within the larger, more complex bodies of culture would become much more matters of course than they are at present, and to the extent we were really influenced by the relativistic point of view, we would all wear our group labels and avow our culture loyalties less provocatively, not to mention the important factor of regarding our culture symbols with less irrationality. Particularly, and most important of all, the proprietary doctrine of culture would be outmoded, as both unreasonable and contrary to fact. Claims of cultural superiority or counter-judgments of cultural inferiority would be specific and carefully circumscribed and would be significant and allowable if substantiated by fair, objective comparison. For I take it, we would not disallow such judgmental valuations as might stem from an objectively scientific criterion of more effective or less effective adaptation. It was only in its initial form that the relativist viewpoint, in disestablishing dogmatic absolutism in cultural valuations, had to be iconoclastic almost to the point of value anarchism. Through functional comparison a much more constructive phase of cultural relativism seems to be developing, promising the discovery of some less arbitrary and more objective norms. Upon them, perhaps we can build sounder intercultural understanding and promote a more equitable collaboration between cultures. The primary fact to be noted is that, however speculative and uncertain a relativistic ethic of culture may be, cultural relativism itself stands on the very firm base of a now rather formidable body of established scientific facts,

with the support of an increasing consensus of scientific opinion among the students of human culture.

Nevertheless, there is certainly no warrant for expecting rapid or revolutionary change in traditional human attitudes and viewpoints merely because of the preponderant weight of evidence back of a scientific theory or point of view. Relativism, like any other way of thinking, will have to make headway slowly against intrenched opposition, and gather considerably more reinforcements than it can now muster. We may expect no sudden recanting of our traditional cultural absolutisms and orthodoxies, no more than in the case of similar absolutist doctrines. The one practical hope in this regard seems to be the emergency character of the present world crisis, which may well be more coercive in effect than the logic of reason or the force of scientific facts. It is in the context of the grave practical issues of the present world conflict that the more realistic and wider-horizoned views of human cultures which we have been discussing have their best prospects for a speedier than normal adoption and a more than academic vindication.

Certainly, without having the formal concepts to hand, hundreds of thousands to millions are today acutely aware, as they have never previously been, of the facts of cultural diversity, of the need for less cultural antagonism and conflict, of the desirability of some working agreements between differing creeds and cultures based on reciprocity, and of the probable futility of any world plan cut to the pattern of the old values and principles. Here, it seems, is the challenge and the chance. It is for that reason that one can so heartily concur in the suggestions of Professor Northrop's paper that a value analysis of our basic cultures in broadscale comparison is the philosophical, or rather the scholarly, task of the hour.

Specifically[4] Dr. Northrop calls for this as "philosophy's task with respect to the peace" and proposes:

(1) An analysis of the major cultures of the Western and Eastern worlds designating the basic theoretical assumptions from which the social institutions and practices that they value proceed. (2) The specification of a common single set of assumptions possessed of the greater generality which permits the largest possible number of the resultant

diverse, traditional assumptions logically compatible to be retained and acted upon without conflict. (3) The reconstruction of all the traditional assumptions to the extent that this is necessary, in order to bring them more in accord with the nature of things as revealed by contemporary as well as traditional philosophical and scientific knowledge.

A cultural relativist will likely have some doubts and reservations over the practicability of such a synthesis as Professor Northrop's third point proposes, especially if a main objective is a unity and agreement based on an extensive "reconstruction of traditional cultural assumptions." In looking for cultural agreements on a world scale, we shall probably have to content ourselves with agreement of the common-denominator type and with "unity in diversity" discovered in the search for unities of a functional rather than a content character, and therefore of a pragmatic rather than an ideological sort. Indeed, cultural relativism and its approach suggest that mankind is not so much at odds over basic end values as over divergent institutional means and symbols irrationally identified with these basic ends. Although thus uncertain that our basic culture values would reduce so easily or submit as readily to ideological reconstructions as Professor Northrop considers requisite, indeed not regarding such value-content unity as vitally necessary, the relativist position would be in substantial agreement on the need for an objective comparative analysis on a world scale of our major culture values.

In this undertaking cultural relativism would have two important suggestions to make. First, that considerable clarification, with an attendant cultural sanity and harmony, would result from any wide-scale comparison set to discover whatever pragmatic similarities already pertain underneath a variety of divergent value symbols and their traditional rationalizations merely through making manifest such common denominators and basic equivalences. Second, it should be equally obvious that the chances for discovering vital agreements of this sort are infinitely greater on the basis of a functional analysis of our major culture values than through an analytical, merely descriptive one. The main question, however, is neither methodology nor anticipation of the result, but an immediate and collaborative undertaking of what is becoming obvious as one of the most urgent and promiseful tasks yet confronted by the scholarship of our generation in the field of human relations.

One can, of course, foresee, even in advance of such a search for value correlations, one inevitably oncoming content unity among our various cultures, a base denominator of modern science and technology. We can hardly conceive our modern world dispensing with this, whatever its other factionalisms. But even if destined to become the common possession of humanity, science and technology are relatively value neutral, and, since they can be fitted in to such different systems of end values, cannot be relied upon to become deeply influential as unifiers. Indeed, linked to present-day culture feuds and value intolerances, they can quite more easily serve to intensify the conflict as the geographical distance between cultures is shortened and their technological disparities are leveled off. It is, after all, our values and value systems that have divided us, apart from and in many cases over and above our material issues of rivalry and conflict. If we are ever to have less conflict and more unity, it must come about in considerable part from some deep change in our value attitudes and our cultural allegiances. The increasing proximity of cultures in the modern world makes all the more necessary some corrective adjustment of their "psychological distance."

No single factor could serve this end more acceptably and effectively than a relativistic concept of culture, which, by first disestablishing the use of one's own culture as a contrast norm for other cultures, leads through the appreciation of the functional significance of other values in their respective cultures to the eventual discovery and recognition of certain functional common denominators. These culture constants or "culture cognates," as the case might be, would then furnish a base not only for mutual cultural tolerance and appreciation but eventually for effective cultural integration. If discoverable in any large number, they might well constitute a new base for a direct educational development of world-mindedness, a realistic scientific induction into world citizenship. Surely it would be a great gain if we could shift or even supplement our sentimental and moralistic efforts for world-mindedness to an objective educational and scientific basis. As stated by the writer in a previous Conference paper:[5]

For if once this broader relativistic approach could discover beneath the culture differentials of time and place such functional "universals" as actually may be there, these common-denominator values will stand out as pragmatically confirmed by common human experience. Either this observable generality or their comparatively established equivalence would give them status far beyond any "universals" merely asserted by orthodox dogmatisms.

Indeed by some such new and indirect substantiation, we may even be able to reestablish, on a less arbitrary foundation, some of the disestablished certainties among our culture values.

Notes

1 Horace Kallen, "William James and Henri Bergson," pp. 10–11 (Complete reference unknown – Ed.).
2 The papers by F. S. C. Northrop, Charles W. Morris, Bingham Dai, Krishnalal Shridharani, and Clyde Kluckhohn. See *Approaches to World Peace*, ed. Lyman Bryson, L. Finfelstein, R. M. MacIver (New York: Harper and Brothers, 1944).
3 "Pluralism and Intellectual Democracy," *Science, Philosophy and Religion*, Second Symposium (1942), pp. 196–209.
4 "Philosophy and World Peace," in *Approaches to World Peace*, ed. Bryson et al., p. 651f.
5 "Pluralism and Intellectual Democracy," p. 200.

Index

CPSIA information can be obtained at www.ICGtesting.com
Printed in the USA
LVOW052046070312

271907LV00004B/2/P